EARNING MY DEGREE

MEMOIRS OF AN AMERICAN UNIVERSITY PRESIDENT

DAVID PIERPONT GARDNER

WITH A FOREWORD BY VARTAN GREGORIAN

UNIVERSITY OF CALIFORNIA PRESS
BERKELEY   LOS ANGELES   LONDON

University of California Press
Berkeley and Los Angeles, California

University of California Press, Ltd.
London, England

© 2005 by The Regents of the University of California

Library of Congress Cataloging-in-Publication Data

Gardner, David Pierpont, 1933–.
     Earning my degree : memoirs of an American university
  president / David Pierpont Gardner ; with a foreword by
  Vartan Gregorian.
        p.   cm.
     Includes bibliographical references and index.
     ISBN 0-520-24183-5 (alk. paper).
     1. Gardner, David Pierpont, 1933–.   2. College presidents—
  United States—Biography.   3. University of California,
  Berkeley—Presidents—Biography.   I. Title.

  LA2317.G25A3   2005
  378.1'11—dc22   2004008787

Manufactured in the United States of America

13   12   11   10   09   08   07   06   05
11   10   9   8   7   6   5   4   3   2   1

The paper used in this publication meets the minimum requirements of ANSI/NISO Z39.48–1992 (R 1997) (*Permanence of Paper*).

TO MY WIFE, SHEILA, whose encouragement and constant support during the writing of these memoirs made them possible and whose love underpins my life and so enhances its meaning and purpose.

TO MY LATE WIFE, LIBBY, whose steady and selfless love made the difference in my life and that of our family's, and who shared so much of what these memoirs recall.

TO MY CHILDREN AND GRANDCHILDREN, AND TO MY PARENTS: my mother, whom I hardly knew but whose life and example endures; my stepmother, who helped raise me from age eight with wisdom and love; and my father, whose quiet, steady, and gentle nature guided me over the years.

CONTENTS

Plates follow pages 140 and 300

FOREWORD

As I read Gardner's memoirs—which are also a deep, heartfelt, and loving appreciation of the University of California, which he presided over as president for almost a decade—I was reminded of what a complex, exhausting, exasperating, and yet exhilarating life one leads when one chooses to spend a good part of one's career in the field of higher education.

While at Brown University, I came to appreciate the former Brown president (1937–55) Henry Wriston's description of the president's job: the president, he said, is "expected to be an educator, to have been at some time a scholar, to have judgment about finance, to know something about construction, maintenance, and labor policy, to speak virtually continuously in words that charm and never offend, to take bold positions with which no one will disagree, to consult everyone, and to follow all proffered advice, and do everything through committees, but with great speed and without error" (Wriston, *The Structure of Brown University*, 1946).

Recently I once again came across Clark Kerr's somewhat expanded but equally evocative description of the job in his Godkin lectures, which he delivered in 1963 at Harvard University. He said, "The American university president is expected to be a friend of the students, a colleague of the faculty, a good fellow with the alumni, a sound administrator with the trustees, a good speaker with the public, an astute bargainer with the foundations and the federal agencies, a politician with the state legislature, a friend of industry, labor and agriculture, a persuasive diplomat with donors, a champion of education generally[,] . . . a spokesman to the press, a scholar in his own right, a public servant at the state and national levels, a devotee of opera and football equally, a decent human being, a good husband and father, an active member of a church. . . . He should be firm, yet gentle; sensitive to others, insensitive to himself; look to the past and the future, yet be firmly planted in the present; he should be both visionary and sound; affable, yet reflective; know the value of a dollar and realize that ideas cannot be bought[;] . . . a good American but ready to criticize the status quo fearlessly; a seeker of truth where the truth may not hurt too much; a source of public-policy pronouncements when they do not reflect on his own institution." David Gardner is the embodiment of that multifaceted, multitalented, and apparently tireless human being.

It has been a great honor for me to have known David Gardner for some thirty years in his capacity as president of the University of Utah, chairman of the National Commission on Excellence in Education, president of the University of California, president of the William and Flora Hewlett Foundation, chairman of the Salt Lake City–based Eccles Foundation, and as a member and later chairman of the board of trustees of the J. Paul Getty Trust. And knowing him for as long as I have, I believe that I am more than qualified to say that the title of his book, *Earning My Degree,* is too modest, for Gardner has earned *many* degrees, not only in education but also in civic life, in philanthropy, and as a distinguished citizen who has served our nation with dedication, energy, and utter commitment. Many people would have considered themselves lucky—and have been proud, I'm sure—to have headed just one university, or just chaired a famous national commission that literally changed the course of public education in the United States, or presided over just one philanthropic foundation. But Gardner, a native of Berkeley, California—that restless, energetic, intellectual, challenging, and sometimes quixotic place—has played not one or even two but many leadership roles and has had a major influence on the history of higher education in general and that of California in particular. This book, which is judicious in its analysis, meticulous in its research, well written, and, unlike some others, shares due credit with many colleagues past and present, constitutes a comprehensive history of the university and of higher education in California. It is also a veritable ode to the University of California, one of the great public universities, and to its impact on the national, intellectual, social, economic, and political life of the state and of the country.

As David Gardner writes, the aim of these memoirs is to help "illuminate California's recent past, inform the present, and anticipate the future by recalling the verve, boldness, confidence, and risk taking that characterized those who went before us and on whose shoulders we now stand." It is also written in the hope that it will help "those now responsible for its present and foreseeable future to remember what made the University of California the world's greatest public university and one of the most remarkable and renowned centers of learning ever known." These are critical lessons to bear in mind because, as we note in reading the memoirs, to forget the past and to neglect its lesson risks UC's future; for while it is remarkably resilient and adaptive, it is, like most large, complex, and multilayered institutions, vulnerable as well.

In his memoirs Gardner has done justice to the history of this magnificent, democratic, pluralistic, and public institution, writing from a deep knowledge that comes from having served the institution as vice-chancellor, vice president, and then president. The book is also a fitting tribute to his parents, his family, and his Mormon upbringing and to the beliefs he was raised with, which hinge on the idea that hard work is the one true way to find life's rewards. Not only have his upbringing and faith served Gardner well and informed every step of his personal life and career, but his book also acquaints us with the values that shaped his early life and that he has drawn on every day since then: the moral and ethical traditions of rural America, family-centeredness, honoring one's parents, thrift, honesty, education, responsible conduct, self-reliance, self-discipline, and respect for the sensibilities and needs of other members of one's family and one's community.

David Gardner, the man and the professional, has been molded by the above virtues and by his intense curiosity about life, coupled with a dedication to the notion of duty and service. His memoirs draw on a deep well of knowledge and a keen eye for both subtext and wider meaning to provide us with detailed, engaging, and often revealing insights into the history of the University of California as he writes candidly about the personality conflicts, political upheavals, and major controversies that convulsed the institution, including issues involving minority students, affirmative action, and, earlier, the university's loyalty oath (his dissertation, written more than thirty years ago and published as *The California Oath Controversy*, is still considered a definitive analysis of the 1949–52 oath controversy, which nearly tore the institution apart).

In reading Gardner's book, we are also provided with lessons of courage, tact, trust, diplomacy, patience, hard work, the ability to navigate political and personality conflicts, and above all, about the calm, steady, and thoughtful stewardship—backed, I will add, by a powerful and incisive intellect—that were required of him when he served as chairman of the National Commission on Excellence in Education, which in 1983 issued the landmark report *A Nation at Risk: The Imperative for Educational Reform*. The report famously warned that "the educational foundations of our society are presently being eroded by a rising tide of mediocrity that threatens our very future as a Nation and a people." At a recent symposium celebrating the twentieth anniversary of the release of the report, Gardner remarked that during that period in American education, "We were expecting less from our students and they were giving it to us."

The report's metaphorical call to arms—"If an unfriendly power had attempted to impose on America the mediocre educational performance that exists today we might well have viewed it as an act of war"—was shocking to the American public and a bombshell dropped in the lap of both state and federal governments; even today, its impact is almost immeasurable. It made thoughtful, intelligent, and urgent recommendations about curriculum content, standards, expectations, the efficient use of students' and schools' time, teacher preparation, educational leadership, and much more. It was disseminated widely, received focused and ongoing attention from the press, the public, and policymakers, and was referred to as the seminal document for the many efforts to improve education that followed in its wake. Almost every reform in recent educational history stems, in some manner or another, from the effects of that report.

Gardner rightly observes that thanks to the timing and impact of *A Nation at Risk,* one particular and intriguing result of the report was that during his first term as president of the United States, Ronald Reagan abandoned the Republican Party's educational platform and his campaign pledge to abolish the U.S. Department of Education—as well as to return prayer to the schools and to enact tuition tax credit and a school voucher system. Gardner credits then–U.S. Secretary of Education Terrel H. Bell with playing a crucial role in the president's decision to postpone those mandates, in part through the support he provided to Gardner and the other members of the commission as they did their work. And ironically, by issuing its *Nation at Risk* report, the commission Bell appointed to help find alternatives to the Department of Education helped undo rather than advance the Republican Party's education agenda.

Clearly, when David Gardner put his mind to effecting change, change happened. One memorable example: on becoming president of the University of Utah, he told the institution's faculty and administrators that one of his continuing goals would be to remind the state of its obligation to the university system, and he made good on his pledge under a Democratic governor—and then some. Later, under a Republican governor, George Deukmejian (1983–91), Gardner was able in his first year in office to persuade the legislature and the governor to increase the budget of the University of California by one-third. To quote the late president of the University of California Clark Kerr in his memoir *The Gold and the Blue,* "Under President David Gardner (1983–92), a wonderful combination of circumstances literally saved the university from academic decline. . . . Gardner saw the possibilities of the situation, took the risk of proposing, and then securing, the passage of an almost one-third increase in state funds for the university in a single year. His triumph equalized faculty salaries (that had fallen 18.5 percent below those of comparable institutions) and made possible many other gains." According to Kerr, "Gardner also restored the effectiveness of the university presidency, which had deteriorated over the past twenty years."

In addition to his contributions to higher education, including his stewardship of the universities of Utah and California, Gardner also played a major role in multiple areas ranging from science to population issues to higher education, thus contributing to improving the life of Californians and of Americans nationwide. He also worked tirelessly to advance the nation's philanthropic sector by helping shape the programs and history of the Hewlett and Eccles foundations and of the Getty Trust, providing visionary leadership to these vital and influential organizations.

All of these accomplishments, however, do not address the fact of David Gardner's basic decency, his moral and intellectual integrity, his humanity, his generosity, and his humility. We all owe Gardner a debt of gratitude for writing so movingly about his early life, his long and fruitful career, his dedication to improving education, and the institutions and organizations he so clearly and deeply loved.

Vartan Gregorian

PREFACE

The title of these memoirs, *Earning My Degree,* carries multiple meanings and, therefore, warrants an explanation. The significance of any degree is in the earning of it; and, by way of a rough simile, this is true of life experiences in general. For example, applicants "enroll" on accepting a job offer. There are "grades" for performance as they "advance" from one assignment to another, one position to another, each stage and new position denoting heightened levels of difficulty and complexity. "Degrees" are awarded or withheld at certain milestones in any career, reflecting judgments of performance from persons possessing authority, experience, and competence. A degree is required to seek another more advanced one, just as a new position assumes mastery of the previously held ones.

This complex simile was driven home to me one afternoon in early 1984 when I addressed the Berkeley division of the University of California's Academic Senate. It was my first official visit since being appointed as the university's new president in August 1983. As I looked out at the assemblage, I noticed several professors under whom I had studied as a graduate student twenty-five years earlier, members of the faculty who were friends of many years, and other famous scientists and scholars, some of whom I knew but most of whom I only recognized. I also noted the presence in the front rows of several Nobel laureates.

I thought to myself as I began my remarks, it made no difference that I came to my post with two graduate degrees from Berkeley, that I had been a member of the faculty and vice-chancellor at UC Santa Barbara, that I had served as a vice president of the university and held a full professorship on the Berkeley campus, that I had served as president of the University of Utah for ten years, or that I had just concluded my work as chairman of the National Commission on Excellence in Education and that our report, *A Nation at Risk,* was internationally famous. None of this mattered.

I was standing alone in front of the Berkeley faculty as the university's new president; and I knew right there that I was going to have to "earn my degree all over again."

Here in the auditorium was the core of the Berkeley faculty. On them, together with their colleagues at the other eight campuses, rested the university's reputation in the world of higher education; these professors, waiting for me to begin my remarks, had led to Berkeley being ranked as the "best balanced distinguished university in the country."[1] Here were colleagues worth serving, worth knowing, worth supporting. I had much to learn from them and much to do on their behalf. They were now preparing to "grade" me as president. *Earning My Degree* from them, once again, was an opportunity unsurpassed.

ACKNOWLEDGMENTS

Not long after my retirement as president of the University of California in 1992, Ann Lage of the Regional Oral History Project at UC Berkeley's Bancroft Library asked if I would be willing to be interviewed for my oral history. I agreed but asked that the interviews be scheduled after two or three years had lapsed. The resulting interviews were conducted in 1995 and 1996 and published by the Regional Oral History Office in 1997.

When Jim Clark, then the long-serving director of the University of California Press, read the oral history, he asked if I would be willing to redo the history in book form, as he believed the UC Press would wish to publish it. This would, he added, be the first such oral history by a former UC president to be reborn in book form and published by the press. I agreed to do so and undertook the work in 1997. Nearly six years have passed in the preparation of these memoirs, and another one will be required by the press to ready them for publication.

While I did almost all of my own research and all of the writing for these memoirs, I remain forever indebted to those who helped me in this endeavor. Their encouragement, criticism, advice, and personal and professional help have been indispensable. The memoirs are more accurate, more sensitive, more inclusive, more salient, and more interestingly written than they would otherwise have been without the aid I so much needed and was so generously and helpfully offered.

My research relied on the official records of the University of Utah and the University of California; documents in my possession or in the hands of friends and colleagues, such as those involved in the work of the National Commission on Excellence in Education; the oral history of several regents, university officers, faculty, staff, and students conducted by Berkeley's Regional Oral History Office (see appendix 4); the archives at the University of California and the University of Utah; accounts in newspapers and journals in both California and Utah, as well as national publications; published and unpublished documents of many kinds available from private and institutional sources, including my own files; and my own memory, when documents did not exist and I could not check my version of events with that of others who had been involved.

In all of this, I received every consideration and possible assistance from the archivists at Utah and UC Santa Barbara; from William Roberts, Berkeley's just retired and long-serving archivist, and from David Farrell, his acting successor; from the secretary of the regents, Leigh Trivette, and her very helpful and able staff, especially Anne Shaw and Erica Nietfeld; from Connie Williams of the Office of Executive Records; from others in the Office of the President, especially Pat Pelfrey and Cecile Cuttitta; and, of course, from the university's immediate past president, Richard Atkinson, who not only encouraged me in this effort but helped in innumerable ways throughout.

In addition, I received the unqualified support of the staff at UC Berkeley's Center for Studies in Higher Education, especially from its late director, Professor Arnold Leiman, and from several colleagues there, including John Douglass and Marian Gade. The staff of the main libraries at Utah, Berkeley, and Santa Barbara were similarly helpful, as were several friends and colleagues who fleshed out or corrected my recollection of events included in these memoirs. Ann Hinckley, my research assistant at Utah, and friends Professors Tony Morgan and R. J. Snow, also of Utah, were helpful and encouraging throughout my research.

The manuscript in its early, middle, and even later drafts was read variously and critically by President Emeritus Clark Kerr, UC's president from 1958 to 1967 and Berkeley's first chancellor from 1952 to 1958; President Emeritus Jack Peltason, UC's president from 1992 to 1995 and former chancellor at UC Irvine from 1984 to 1992; Marian Gade, Kerr's very capable associate of many years and a sometime Kerr coauthor; and Professor Emeritus Burton Clark of UCLA. The critical assistance of University Professor of Sociology Emeritus Neil Smelser and of Professor of Public Policy Emeritus Martin Trow, both of Berkeley, was simply indispensable. Their multiple readings of my several drafts of the manuscript were telling and deeply appreciated, and their straightforward criticisms were not noticeably influenced by our many years of friendship. I am forever in their debt, both for their help with this manuscript and their support and counsel during my nearly ten years as UC's president, 1983–92.

Sections or chapters of the memoirs were also helped with respect to their treatment of fiscal and budgetary matters when reviewed by UC Vice President Larry Hershman, and the discussion of *A Nation at Risk* (chapter 4) when read by Dr. Milton Goldberg, former executive director of the National Commission on Excellence in Education.

In the text of my memoirs, I sought also to acknowledge the enduring appreciation I have for my many colleagues over the years. Obviously, I could not mention everyone; but without their hard work, dedication, intelligence, wisdom, and sound judgment, most of what we were able to accomplish would have been unattainable.

So too it has been in the writing of these memoirs, although I take full responsibility for and ascribe to none other what I have chosen to include or to omit and the language I have employed to write them. For whatever errors or offense or slight or oversight that may be discovered, I should be held solely to account; in the end, it is my work and my memoirs, written as fairly and as accurately as I could but also as straightforwardly as needed to make my points or to recall the essence of issues or events. And I tried to take responsibility for my own shortcomings. Readers of these memoirs may have different views of what I have written, of course, as persons judge issues and events differently by virtue of their individual points of departure, assumptions, experience, and motives.

I apologize to those who feel their role in the memoirs was not sufficiently noted or was even misrepresented. No such distortion was knowing or intended, and no malice or absence of respect or regard was implied. I did my best and will have to leave it at that.

I also know that I have not sufficiently allowed for the role and contributions of countless colleagues and friends who over the years have meant so much to me, who have strengthened, helped, and encouraged me beyond reason, who have themselves been so much responsible for all of the good we were together able to do in serving our universities. But I remember and remain grateful beyond what mere words can convey.

I wish also to thank Dawn Regan and Liz Littlefield of ALTA Business Services, San Mateo, California, for their very competent and timely secretarial services throughout the preparation of this manuscript.

So too for the highly professional and always helpful efforts of colleagues at the University of California Press, especially Sheila Levine, Suzanne Knott, Alice Falk, and Edith Gladstone, who so ably and honestly offered suggestions, advice, and criticism that markedly improved the manuscript, and not to slight others who helped in the book's design, marketing, and publicizing.

I wish also to express my gratitude to Maureen Kawaoka, who was willing to take on the burdens of preparing the manuscript in proper form, identifying errors and problems everyone else, including me, had missed, and working with UC Press to assure an easy and effective flow of work among and between all interested parties.

And finally, I wish to take appreciative note of the study and research grant provided by the Hewlett Foundation at the urging of its chairman, Walter Hewlett, to assist me in meeting the out-of-pocket costs of my research and in the writing of these memoirs. I am similarly grateful to Richard Atkinson, UC's seventeenth president, for the material support his office also helpfully provided in this effort.

INTRODUCTION

FIAT LUX

In 1933, the year I was born, Berkeley's population was some 83,000. Most of California's approximately 6 million residents were clustered around the San Francisco Bay Area, the Sacramento and San Joaquin valleys, Greater Los Angeles, and San Diego.

Berkeley was still recovering from the effects of the Great Fire of 1923, which burned most of the area north of the University of California campus; the flames were stopped or turned when they reached Hearst Avenue, then the university's northern boundary. Berkeley's public schools were excellent: well-educated and trained teachers, small classes, excellent facilities, and a rich curriculum. The streets were safe; the city's commercial center and neighborhood shops and stores were well kept and for the most part financially viable. Crime was low and the police were respected.

The city prospered but in a more steady than erratic fashion. There was an active civic life both within and across neighborhoods, complemented by the university's intellectual and cultural presence. My family lived in north Berkeley, and most of our neighbors were university professors, staff, and administrators or professionals and entrepreneurs of one kind or another. My parents thought of themselves as middle-class; the wealth concentrated in Piedmont to Berkeley's south and across the bay in San Francisco and down its southern peninsula.

Franklin Delano Roosevelt was inaugurated as president of the United States in the midst of the Great Depression, indeed very nearly at its nadir.

The bank holiday he declared in March 1933, together with the outpouring of New Deal legislation enacted by Congress in the early to mid-1930s, forever changed the character of American life and the relationship of government to the governed. These policies were the object of intense and bitter controversy within the country, as were widespread disputes between labor and management against a backdrop of unprecedented levels of unemployment and a profound sense of despair both about the nation itself and the economic and philosophical underpinnings of capitalism.

California's fortunes had blown hot and cold ever since the discovery of gold in the Sierra foothills east of Sacramento in 1849. Immigration, however, had been a near constant: pioneers seeking land and a new start; fortune hunters and opportunists from throughout the world; military deserters; Chinese laborers who mostly built the railroad through the Sierra Nevada and on to Promontory Point in Utah, connecting by rail the country's two coasts in the mid-1860s; Mexicans, whose land this had been until recently; and Native Americans, who had lived here for thousands of years.

Energy and entrepreneurship abounded (as they do today). The state grew and prospered, a function of its favored geographic position, its social mobility, its ethnic and economic diversity, its remoteness from the centers of governmental and political power, and its congenial climate both for people and for the growing of a vast variety of crops in its rich and expansive Central Valley and along the length of its golden coast.

California also possessed great virgin forests including the redwoods of the north coast and some central and midcoastal regions, abundant water and mineral wealth in the Sierra Nevada that formed its eastern boundary, snow-fed rivers on the Sierra's western flank where gold lay almost for the taking, and natural harbors in San Francisco, Monterey, Santa Barbara, Los Angeles, and San Diego visited by ships from throughout the world, but mostly those sailing the Pacific sea lanes between Asia and North America's west coast.

During the Great Depression of the 1930s, large numbers of dispossessed and poverty-stricken midwesterners moved to California, mostly from the failed agricultural lands and dust bowls of the Great Plains, as John Steinbeck's novel *The Grapes of Wrath* poignantly recalled. And in the next decade millions of soldiers, sailors, and airmen moved in and out of California on their way to, or on their return from, the war with Japan in the Pacific. Millions of them stayed in California. Large numbers of African Americans also came to California in wartime to work in the state's defense industry, especially in northern California's Richmond shipyards across the bay from San Francisco. So too did the Mexicans who worked the crops and moved with the seasons, migrating the length and breadth of California as the state's orchards, row crops, vineyards, and other agricultural lands ripened and were ready for the harvest.

California's postwar economy boomed, driven by population growth, international trade, the defense industry, high-tech businesses, the entertainment industry, and the vast and diverse character of its agriculture—then, as now, one of the state's and nation's most important industries. The University of California contributed much to the state's overall development as well. It attained remarkably high levels of academic excellence and intellectual capability in a relatively brief period of time and garnered talent and ideas for the state, thus helping to fuel California's prosperity and spread its fame. The state's modern infrastructure—its freeway and water systems, seaports, airports, bridges, and telecommunications systems—was set in place mostly in the 1950s and 1960s. Its schools grew with the state, as did its colleges and universities both in scale and significance.

These were golden times for California from the close of World War II until the late 1980s and early 1990s. These years, of course, were not free of problems, indeed challenges abounded: social dislocations at the war's end; large-scale migration into the state; civil rights, civil liberties, and anti–Vietnam War protests throughout the state and on its campus; the Watts riots in Los Angeles; the OPEC-induced crisis in oil prices; labor conflicts in the Central Valley and on the docks. There were also fires, mudslides, droughts, earthquakes, and more. But on balance life was good and the future looked even better.

Most parties end, however, and at least for a time California's did, beginning in the early 1990s, as the state's economy slipped slowly downward into recession, the depth of which had not been seen in California since the Great Depression sixty years earlier. The state had been living on the momentum of its earlier investments in water systems, roads, freeways, bridges, universities, and schools. It had been overly content with its economic success, overly focused on the present, overly congratulatory of its accomplishments. California had undervalued the basic forces and institutions that had given impetus to its success. It had relied unreasonably on its famous defense industry to secure California's favored economic position, especially when the fall of the Berlin wall and the Soviet Union in the early 1990s brought an abrupt end to the cold war and a recession in the defense industry. There were also marked reductions in the state's military installations on which both California and the United States had come so heavily to depend during and after World War II.

As the new millennium began, however, California had more than recovered from the economic downturn of the early 1990s. Unemployment rates were down dramatically, crime had declined, and governmental revenues were at record high levels. Domestic and international demand for the products of California's entertainment industry and its ranches, farms, vineyards and orchards, Silicon Valley, and other centers of high-tech and "new economy" companies clustered around the state's leading public and private universities drove the state's economy. Yet the bursting of the high-tech bubble and a precipitous drop in the stock markets of 2000–2003 with their corresponding and negative effects on the state's revenue and business climate put these favorable economic trends at risk.

Who could have predicted in 1933 that California would change almost beyond recognition, as its population grew nearly sixfold, from six million then to thirty-five million in 2002? But to have lived through most of it and to have participated in much of it, and to compare and contrast today's California with what it was helps inform my perspective and humbles my sense of confidence about what it all means for the future; and this is true not only for the state but for its famed University of California as well.

I hope these memoirs, using my own life as surrogate, will among other things help illuminate California's recent past, inform the present, and anticipate the future by recalling the verve, boldness, confidence, and risk taking that characterized those who went before us and on whose shoulders we now stand.

For the University of California, it is my desire to help those responsible for its present and foreseeable future to remember what made the University of California the world's greatest public university and one of the most remarkable and renowned centers of learning ever known. To forget the past or to neglect its lessons risks UC's future, for it is an institution that is at once vulnerable and fragile and yet remarkably resilient and adaptive. It is also at the very center of California's educational, economic, civic, social, and cultural aspirations and, therefore, uncommonly susceptible to political and sectarian pressures, threats, promises, and enticements of one kind or another.

The academic and intellectual principles on which UC's strength rests, and which I seek in these memoirs to explicate and defend, are those on which all the free universities of our civilization have depended for nine centuries. They need to be recalled, to be refreshed, to be remembered, to be honored, to be sustained. They are not to be surrendered or relinquished point by point, incident by incident, or bartered away for short-term gains or because they are inconvenient to defend or because of fiscal exigencies, donor pressures, political threats, or promises. No. They are to be advanced, defended, explained, and employed in the university's service, costs and penalties aside.

And we should be reminded that our predecessors in the Western world, from the twelfth century on, somehow managed in the face of complacency, indifference, ignorance, hostility, or despair to raise the university's lamp high enough to illuminate not only the university's sense of its own purpose and future, but also its link to a more broadly civilized and cultured society. *Fiat lux.*

These memoirs also recall the momentous events of 1968–71 at UC Santa

Barbara where the cultural wars, ethnic divisions, and anti–Vietnam War protests were as persistent and profound as to their effect on the University of California and the course of higher education as elsewhere. This story, while told well by some observers, has not been recounted by anyone from the inside (I was centrally involved at the time in the UCSB administration), where the weight of both responsibility and accountability came to rest and where the key decisions were made, amid efforts to take account of the contending parties' irreconcilable but legitimate claims (chapter 2).

Chapter 3 of these memoirs accounts for the ten years I served as the tenth president of the University of Utah, 1973–83. This decade deserves a full chapter not only because of the improvement in academic quality and range of programs, the ability of entering students, and the growth of the university's research, but also because I drew on my experience there as I met my responsibilities during the more than nine years I served as the fifteenth president of the University of California, 1983–92.

The memoirs also recount the work of the National Commission on Excellence in Education whose report of 1983, entitled *A Nation at Risk*, proved to be a seminal event in the history of American public education: the commission's origin and effect on President Ronald Reagan and the Republican Party's education platform, its influence on the K–12 school reforms subsequently undertaken, and its impact on the public's awareness of these matters. As the chairman of the commission, I am able to describe the commission's work from the inside (chapter 4).

The remainder of these memoirs, except for chapter 1 and the epilogue, deals with my years as president of UC, 1983–92: the governance, management, structure, financing, culture, politics, and formulation of academic and administrative policies of the university itself; the interplay between UC and its many external constituencies—governors, legislators, alumni, donors, and other interested parties—and the dynamic within the UC community itself, among regents, chancellors, vice presidents, and the Academic Senate, unions, staff, students, and faculty; along with the bumps, barriers, and crises that helped define my administration and its achievements, failures, false starts, and unexpected triumphs (chapters 5 through 10).

I also explain my actions, decisions, viewpoints, and biases within the context of my own upbringing and the values and beliefs that influenced me from childhood to young adulthood on the one hand (chapter 1), and on the other the principles, values, and obligations that formed my decision making as president of two of the nation's major research universities during my more mature years, 1973–92.

The final chapter (the epilogue) accounts for the more than ten years since my retirement from UC in 1992. At the end I include a small section in which I share my personal reflections, at age seventy, of what I have come to value and what I regard as of less consequence in life. Perhaps these thoughts will be helpful to young and old alike who in the thundering crosscurrents of personal aspirations and societal and familial expectations find that the preferences or power of others or a confused sense of their own perceived options too often drive their choices or decisions. But polls or others cannot drive our lives; only we do. I have always tried to remember this, and while I have not always been successful, I am the better for having at least tried, and I believe the institutions I served have been as well.

ONE

YOUTH AND LESSONS LEARNED

EARLY LIFE

Centered on the spine of America's western coastline, the city of San Francisco is a fabled place of surpassing beauty and wealth, intellectual and cultural riches, accommodating nearly every taste and lifestyle and welcoming the world's trade, commerce, peoples, cultures, and ideas through its Golden Gate. Since the gold rush of 1849, San Francisco has dominated the great bay that carries its name and one of the world's most spectacular and visited natural harbors.

Berkeley

One of the cities on the bay's eastern shore is Berkeley. Berkeley's flatlands, site of its commercial and industrial sectors and most of its schools, interspersed with diverse and colorful neighborhoods, front the bay. The more favored residences and neighborhoods nestle eastward in the Berkeley hills flanking one of the world's most famous centers of learning: the Berkeley campus of the University of California.

The city bears the name of George Berkeley, bishop of Cloyne, and his line "Westward the course of empire takes its way" conveyed a special meaning to the leaders of the university movement in 1868, as they gave substance and expression to the bishop's sense of empire while fixing the university's locale in this distant township, then harboring mostly farms, orchards, and open space.

Fogs rising from the cool waters of the northern Pacific course over the hills of San Francisco and through its valleys, then slip like slender fingers through the Golden Gate and across the bay clearing the Berkeley flatlands and crowding into the eastern lying hills of the city, to envelop the uplands of Berkeley for much of the morning and evening hours, especially during the months of spring and summer.

Along with the Pacific's winds and misty fogs, a disproportionate share of the new talent and diverse peoples then flowing into California also found shelter in the Bay Area. These immigrants to California arrived mostly by ship in San Francisco Bay's protected waters and later by transcontinental rail with its terminus in neighboring Oakland. These newcomers enriched Berkeley, infused it with a sense of future and vibrancy, and provided the nascent university with a stream of scholars and teachers willing to leave positions in the eastern universities to try their hand at something as new and promising as the University of California appeared to be.

It was in this city that I was born, and in its foggy hills that my parents built our family home, and in its public schools that I studied, and in its civic and cultural life that I grew up and lived for the first eighteen years of my life.

Family and Utah Heritage

Two such immigrants to California were my parents, who moved to Berkeley from Utah in 1925. My father, Reed Snow Gardner, and my mother, Margaret Pierpont, had been high school sweethearts in Provo, Utah, and found little opportunity in their native state, but much of it in golden California.

After his graduation from Brigham Young University (BYU) and my mother's from the University of Utah, my father in 1925 accepted a position in Berkeley first in banking and later as a federal civil servant holding responsible positions with the Farm Credit Administration and the Federal Land Banks until his retirement in 1966.

My older brother, Reed, was born in 1929, just as the economic good times were ending. I was born four years later as the Great Depression was either bottoming out or gathering momentum; and my parents had no way to tell which it was to be when I was born in Berkeley's Alta Bates Hospital on March 24, 1933.

As my father was employed and held a steady position with the government, he and my mother decided to build the family home at the very end of Spruce Street, one-half block from the city's northern boundary. We lived across the street from one of the city's main reservoirs, then uncovered and resembling a wooded lake. Around the corner was Wildcat Canyon and the western entrance to Tilden Park, a large regional park encompassing much of the Oakland and Berkeley hills that served as a playground for those of us who lived there.

Vacant lots were as common as houses in our neighborhood. Our home was a two-story Dutch colonial facing west with uninterrupted views of the bay, Alcatraz Island (then a federal penitentiary), San Francisco, the Golden Gate Bridge, and beyond. On crystal clear days, we could see the Farallon Islands lying just west of the Marin headlands. The home cost $6,700 to build in the mid-1930s, and my father's annual salary was about $2,500.

In the depth of the Great Depression our family never wanted, although we traveled hardly at all (except to Utah in the summers), owned one car, and lived comfortably but frugally. My father's offices were on Fulton Street in the building later housing University Extension, and then on Milvia Street in what is now the Berkeley City Hall.

Dad was born in 1900 and grew up in the small (100–125 population) cattle and lumber town of Pine Valley, Utah. Pine Valley is in the extreme southwestern part of Utah, near its borders with Nevada and Arizona at an elevation of 6,700 feet, a paradise in the summer but a less hospitable place in the winter, with the deep dry powder snows of Utah piling high in the narrow valley that cradles this old mountain pioneer settlement.

His father, Hyrum Osro, was born in 1862. He was a cattleman, and my father, his three older brothers, and other cowboys worked the family's extended herds of cattle throughout the vast territory bordering Utah, Arizona, and Nevada—wild, unfenced, majestic, red rock country, peopled mostly by Indians, Mormon pioneers and their descendants, farmers, stockmen, drifters, outlaws, and zealots of one kind or another. Dad's mother, Maryetta Snow, had also grown up in Pine Valley.

During his childhood and youth well into the twentieth century, Dad lived a nineteenth-century life on the ranch. Travel was by horseback, wagon, carriage, sleigh, or on foot; the valley had no paved or reliable road. There was no electricity, no indoor plumbing, no professional medical or dental care or pharmaceuticals, and almost no contact with the outside world. He attended grades one through eight in a one-room schoolhouse, on the ground floor of a small two-story New England–like church. The upper floor provided a place of worship for Pine Valley's small and close-knit religious community.

Dad's paternal grandfather and grandmother (and his maternal grandparents) had been among the first Mormon pioneers to enter the Salt Lake Valley in 1847. My great-grandfather Robert Gardner was an accomplished lumberman serving first the building needs of Salt Lake City and environs and later those of the small pioneer settlements of southern Utah, eastern and southern Nevada, and the Arizona strip. He was asked to cut and haul the wood for the great organ in the Mormon Tabernacle at Salt Lake City, and he did, freighting the lumber for 325 miles from St. George by ox teams and wagons in the mid-1800s.

My father's heritage, which he impressed upon me, featured hard work, family-centeredness, honor to one's parents, thrift, honesty, education, responsible conduct, self-reliance, self-discipline, and respect for the sensibilities and needs of others. These were the values I have sought to live by, and they are derived at least as much from nineteenth-century rural American life as from the tenets of my Mormon faith, although for the most part these were interactive and mutually reinforcing influences.

My mother, Margaret Pierpont, was born in 1903 and grew up in Provo, Utah, some 45 miles south of Salt Lake City at the foot of the Wasatch Range in the Rocky Mountains. Her mother was Vilate Smoot, the daughter of A. O. Smoot, a prominent and early Utah pioneer. One of her half brothers was Reed Smoot, a powerful United States senator for over three decades who is remembered today mostly for the Smoot-Hawley Tariff, which when enacted by the United States Congress in 1930 helped deepen the country's Great Depression.

My mother's father was Thomas F. Pierpont, an entirely self-made man with an eighth-grade education who was born in the mid-1870s about the time of General Custer's defeat at the battle of the Little Bighorn in Montana's grasslands. He became a very successful businessman, owned his own foundry (as had his father), and made and lost three fortunes, the last loss just before his death in the mid-1950s.

My mother, one of eight children, was a gifted orator and widely recognized for her debating skills at a young age, and especially as a student on the debate team at the University of Utah. None of her siblings shared her religious commitment but instead beat a hasty and unrelenting retreat from their indigenous Mormon faith. But all eight children were very bright, personable, irascible, unconventional, and variously successful. They possessed high energy levels, were passionate about everything, and loved to disagree; their behavior was wholly unpredictable. Family reunions resembled brawls more than a shared kinship; and I stood amazed during most of them wondering if I had inherited any genes from the Pierpont side of the family.

What a contrast between my father's side of the family: sober, steady, hardworking, responsible, conscientious, religious people and my mother's side: volatile, passionate, unpredictable, imbibing with only nominal restraint, confrontative, erratic, and with occasional spontaneous outbursts of what only they would have regarded as responsible conduct.

I loved them all, thirteen aunts and uncles, and my sixty-five first cousins. Sometimes I and my siblings found ourselves challenged by a mix of these conflicting genes. By and large I come down more on the Gardner than on the Pierpont side, but the Pierpont genes occasionally express themselves, startling me as well as my family and friends and often when least expected.

My Early and Teenage Years

The amazing confluence of peoples, cultures, and ideas that defines Berkeley made growing up there more than a memorable experience. My extended neighborhood and those on either side of the Berkeley campus were home to world-famous scientists and scholars, entrepreneurs, businessmen and businesswomen, professionals, teachers, musicians, artists, and other extraordinary people, mostly middle-class in economic terms but talented people whose interests and accomplishments proved to be contagious when shared within our common and then mostly cohesive community. The city's one high school enrolled students from throughout the city, and students came from the four corners of the globe to attend its world-famous university.

To walk down our city streets in those days was to see people from throughout the world, many wearing their native dress. To visit the campus was to observe and to hear political radicals of one stripe or another including communists, socialists, anarchists, and assorted others as they held forth just outside Sather Gate (but not on the campus proper, which in those days was not accessible for such purposes).

The university's spacious and beautiful grounds were another playground for my friends and me when I was a boy. Its lawns were our football and baseball fields. Its stadium was an annual source of pleasure as we watched Cal's Golden Bears during the fall football season each year, accompanied by my father or admitted free as junior traffic boys at Cragmont Grammar School; occasionally we got access by means as unconventional as they were unofficial.

No small part of my childhood was compromised, however, by my mother's death at age thirty-six on August 30, 1939, after a prolonged and determined fight against cancer. She died the day before Nazi Germany's invasion of Poland, the effective beginning of World War II. My sister, Vilate, born in 1938, was then one, Reed was ten, and I was six. Mom's death had a profound and lasting affect on us all, and I believe none of us ever fully recovered from it.

A series of housekeepers for about two years did what they could to help Dad and the family with the daily essentials of life, but we did not warm to the arrangement, however unavoidable. The result was that from the age of six I had a level of discretion and independence in my life that my mother would not have permitted and Dad could not control: long walks alone through Tilden Park and Wildcat Canyon, frequent visits to the Berkeley campus for play, athletics, or public ceremonies (such as Charter Day), and later for artistic events both visual and performing that were open to the public or lectures that interested me, and regular visits to a World War II rest camp in nearby Tilden Park for soldiers recovering from combat in the Pacific. Or I would go alone, sometimes with a friend, to the Berkeley pier jutting well into the bay and fish for bass, smelt, crabs, and other bay fish (most then edible), either taking a bus to the pier or walking the four or five miles to or from home as required.

Because of this freedom, I developed an unusual level of self-confidence, self-reliance, and curiosity about life that persists to this day. I learned to grieve in constructive rather than destructive ways. I learned how to make my own way and to seek my own interests and to be quite independent of pressure—either encouragement or disapproval—from peers and others. All and all, I managed to cope with my mother's early death by growing stronger and looking mostly inward for my sense of direction, meaning, and purpose in my young life.

During the summer months of my childhood, Dad would drive me to Utah to work on my uncles' farms and ranches, especially in Delta, Utah, on Highway 50 just east of Fallon, Nevada, in an arid western desert where the temperatures moved in a narrow band between the high 90s and low 100s during the summer months. From age seven or eight until my middle teens I worked on the farm all summer, thinning sugar beets with a short-handled hoe alongside the Indians and Mexicans, who moved from one job to another with the maturing and cycling of crops. I helped clean irrigation ditches, plowed and harrowed the fields with my uncle's tractor or his brace of horses, tromped hay, swam in the irrigation canals, and enjoyed my relatives and their farms or their ranches, where I worked with both sheep and cattle, helping in the late spring drive from their winter range in the western Utah desert to their summer feed in the high alpine meadows of Utah's Wasatch Range to the east.

During these summers, my appreciation for physical labor and a healthy body, early rising, hard work, self-reliance, dependability, and like values and lifestyle preferences grew. None of this was burdensome, nor oppressive, nor exploitive. It was good for me, and I am very grateful to have been nurtured in such a loving but demanding and expectant environment.

My father had remarried about two years after my mother's death. My stepmother was Allie Dixon of Provo, Utah, a second cousin of my mother's, an accomplished and experienced nurse and courageous woman to take on three children. Within a couple of years she added one of her own, my second brother, Jim, who was born in 1943. She had her hands full at home as all of us adjusted, not to another housekeeper, but to a stepmom. She met her responsibilities with love, patience, helpful and purposeful intent, always encouraging, always considerate, and made sure that Dad and the kids remained the focus of her interest and attention. It could not have been easy, however, living some distance from her close-knit and very large family and entering ours, which had been so disrupted by Mother's death. She and Dad remained happily married until their deaths ten days apart in 1983.

World War II began on December 7, 1941, for the United States of America. I was eight years old and still remember it clearly as church was let out early on that Sunday morning when reports of the Japanese bombing of Pearl Harbor came in by radio. I was a third-grade student at Cragmont in the Berkeley hills, and to this day I recall being taken into the cafeteria to hear President Franklin D. Roosevelt's radio address asking Congress to declare war on Japan. Life changed for everyone: parents of my friends, young men in the neighborhood, many drafted into and others volunteering for military service; mock air raid drills, black curtains pulled at night over the windows at home, eating dinner in the basement; parts of the Pacific fleet blackening San Francisco Bay when we went to bed and gone when we awoke; planes flying from Europe to the Pacific after Germany's defeat in 1945, shaking the ground as they flew over the Bay Area on their way to Hawaii; and soldiers, sailors, and airmen everywhere. Nearly a ship a day was being launched from Kaiser's Richmond shipyards, and there were ration cards for gasoline, meat, and other scarce commodities, air raid drills at school, and name bracelets or necklaces to be worn by children at all times.

But the war itself was far away. And being much too young to participate, I experienced it as a great adventure with everyone working together to win it and as quickly as possible, as the atomic bombs surely did when dropped in August 1945 on Hiroshima and Nagasaki, about which I heard while delivering newspapers on my route in north Berkeley. I vividly remember spring 1942 when General James Doolittle led his air raid, later made famous by the movie *Thirty Seconds Over Tokyo*, over that city and on to China, our Asian ally. What a morale booster it was for the country and for the adults, but for the children, it was a source of great excitement.

One of many jobs I had beginning at age eight was a newspaper route. My route took in the apartment area just north of the Berkeley campus, where tenants proved to be more willing to receive the paper than to pay for it, a not inconsequential consideration as the *Berkeley Daily Gazette* required me to pay so much per paper. I had to collect that amount from the person to whom the paper had been delivered and, usually, a small additional amount for my profit. When one month I discovered that it had cost me $20 to deliver the paper to unreliable customers, mostly students, I gave up delivering the *Gazette*.

My next paper route was in my neighborhood and included Admiral Chester Nimitz, former commander of United States Naval Forces in the Pacific during the war but by then living in retirement on Santa Barbara Avenue in Berkeley. He would always stop his gardening when I came by to deliver the paper and would walk over to say hello and visit for a few minutes. I could hardly believe it. He was one of my heroes.

During the war I had also collected and sold old newspapers; later I washed cars, did yard work for neighbors, sold clothes at Smith's in Oakland (since I am color-blind, this was an unusual challenge for me and for my customers too), stocked shelves at local stores, packed merchandise at local warehouses, and changed tires at a garage in Oakland—the usual things young people did to meet their financial needs—since I got a weekly allowance of 25¢ and was expected to pay for everything myself after age thirteen except food and lodging.

In my mid- to late teens, summer work came at the City of Berkeley's family camp at Echo Lake, near the top of the mountains rimming the western boundary of the Tahoe basin and south of that magnificent lake nestled in the eastern portion of California's high Sierra. Some of my fondest memories and experiences are of the three summers I and close high school friends worked at Echo Lake.

Emery Curtice and his wife, Minerva, managed the camp. Emery later became principal of Burbank Junior High School in Berkeley and then of Berkeley High School. He taught me to know and love the mountains: their peaks and valleys, rivers and lakes, their flora and fauna. And he taught me how to fly-fish. He taught me to respect authority, if wisely and carefully exercised. He taught me important things about respect for others, how to help and not to ridicule, how to work and derive pleasure and satisfaction from a job done well. Other than my father, more than any other adult male Emery Curtice had an enduring impact on my value system, sense of self, and self-confidence. I shall always be in his debt. He passed away in 2000 at his home in Calistoga, at the most northern reach of California's famed Napa Valley, still young at age ninety-two.

Music was also very much part of my early years. I studied piano for four years and pipe organ for five. Early morning was for piano practice at home and even earlier at our church on Vine and Virginia streets in north Berkeley, where I first learned to play the pipe organ.

Not only did I play both the piano and the pipe organ, I gave recitals in each during the war and afterward, including a private piano recital at the Keith home just north of the Berkeley campus for delegates attending the founding of the United Nations in San Francisco in 1945. I still recall the Russian officers in their high and highly polished boots who, of all those attending the recital, seemed to be the most appreciative and encouraging. As one of the youngest members of the American Guild of Organists, I later gave recitals in various Bay Area churches and even considered making the pipe organ my profession of preference. When I turned seventeen, I was offered the summer organist position at one of Oakland's largest Protestant churches, which had a splendid five manual (keyboard) pipe organ. The position paid $10 for weddings and funerals and $35 for Sunday services, a princely sum in those days for a teenager.

But Emery Curtice also asked me to wash dishes and pots and pans that same summer at Echo Lake where his daughter Lou, in whom I was much interested, was to be waiting tables. And as any reasonable seventeen-year-old would guess, I happily accepted the Echo Lake position; and as any reasonable father would understand, mine reacted. Nevertheless he did not interfere with my choice. And while I came to appreciate the unattractiveness of daily dish washing, I failed to sustain my interest in the pipe organ and that was that.

I should note, however, that I had come to love music, respect musicians, and in studying the pipe organ learned what real concentration meant: singular attention to the task, intellectual engagement, interplay of mind and body. I also came to appreciate in music the obviousness of error and the deep sense of accomplishment, almost exhilaration, in giving a beautiful score powerful expression by the correct and sensitive interplay of two hands on a pipe organ with five manual keyboards (and over threescore stops), of both feet on a sixth manual (controlling the stops for that keyboard as well as for the organ's overall volume) and all the while seeking to read and interpret creatively a three-staffed sheet of music. It was wonderful.

The School Years

I was very fortunate to be enrolled in Berkeley's public schools, first Cragmont Grammar School, then Garfield Junior High School (now Martin Luther King Junior High School), and Berkeley High School. School was something I always welcomed, never dreaded. I started school in midterm (in late January, not in September) and ours was a small class—never more than 20 students except once or twice during my grammar school years with only 220–250 in my high school class out of a total school enrollment approximating 2,000.

I enjoyed my studies although my performance was uneven. I owe a great deal to the teachers under whom I studied. And I enjoyed every other aspect of school: the sports, social life, and student activities. In my final year at Garfield I was student body president, as I was at Berkeley High during my senior year. I felt at ease speaking in front of a live audience of any size, thanks in part to student body activities and to practice at my church, which regularly called young people from age five on to give a $2\frac{1}{2}$ minute talk to the congregation once or twice a year. It helps that I can think on my feet, having chosen never to memorize my speeches or remarks, just remembering the key points instead.

Some of this ability must be genetic, through my mother, and some of it is simply experience. In any event, it was of great help to me throughout my professional life in appearing before congressional and legislative committees, in chairing or conducting meetings of the regents of two universities as well as national commissions, academic and administrative meetings, and on other occasions as required.

In short, I was blessed to be born in Berkeley, to have been raised by loving parents, to have been educated in the Berkeley public schools, to have sampled urban and rural life, to be moved and inspired by the work of the University of California at a very young age, to have experienced the rough beautiful outdoors of the high Sierra and the Rocky Mountains and the beauty of music and the arts, to have had a range of friends from every racial, social, and economic strata of the community, to have worked, to have been challenged, to have carried responsibility, to have developed and matured with a comfortable set of values and priorities, to have had a spiritual as well as a secular upbringing, and to have had good health and a sound body. How very fortunate I was, the tragedy of my young mother's death excepted.

THE COLLEGE YEARS

I graduated from Berkeley High in January 1951, entered Cal as a freshman, found its environment overly familiar at a time when I was seeking something new and different, and enrolled at Brigham Young the following fall, much to my father's dismay: one of his reasons for settling in Berkeley was anticipation of his children's enrolling at Cal, which only my younger brother chose to do. In addition to living away from home, which was a good thing for any eighteen-year-old college student to do, I also wanted to sample Mormon culture, in contrast to Berkeley's.

The transition from Berkeley to Provo, Utah, and from Cal to BYU was not easy. The campus was small, with some 4,000 students enrolled. The climate was dramatically different, the intellectual demands were modest, and whereas I had many friends in Berkeley and at Cal, I knew almost no one at BYU. The students were mostly from Utah, and I found them somewhat insular, both in their thinking and social skills. But I came to love the university and the area, and within a year or so I had my own circle of friends. I studied hard, not because it was required, but because I wanted to learn. I enjoyed the more intimate campus environment and welcomed the proximity of the high Rocky Mountains with their rivers, lakes, forests, snows, glaciers, and alpine meadows.

Graduating in 1955 with majors in political science, history, and geography (I liked them all and thus majored in three subjects), I applied and was admitted to Boalt Hall at Berkeley for the study of law. The Korean War had ended in 1953, but the draft remained in force. One of my cousins from Berkeley had been drafted into the army during his Mormon mission, and the Berkeley draft board at that time was known for its decidedly unfriendly attitude toward members of my religious faith. Thus, when I inquired of the "powers that were" if I could rely on my student deferment to see me through Boalt Hall, I was informed that no such assurance could be made.

Hence I decided not to enroll at Boalt Hall only to face the prospect of being drafted midway through my studies. Instead, I enlisted in the army for a two-year period of service on September 12, 1955, both to get my military service over with and to have access to the GI bill, which would be a great help in meeting the costs of my further education when I returned to civilian life. This proved to be a sound decision except that Congress had unexpectedly terminated the GI bill just before my enlistment. My experiences in the army were both maturing and memorable. And after my discharge I also had a much more assured sense of my interests and desires.

THE ARMY YEARS

Basic training took place at Fort Ord on the California coast just north of Monterey. On balance, it was a valuable learning experience for me although I readily acknowledge that eight weeks of basic training were decidedly preferable to any other number of additional weeks. Near the end of my basic training it appeared that infantry, artillery, or armor were to be part of my future, the first with its seasonal rigors and not wholly congenial set of killing instruments, the second with its cannons, noise, and ear-deafening protocols, and the third with tanks, armored carriers, and other such claustrophobia-inducing machines. In my mind, these were all markedly unattractive options.

The army's counterintelligence unit and its training center at Fort Holabird, Baltimore, Maryland, held greater appeal for me, and I arranged a visit with the unit's representative at Fort Ord. The conversation proved to be brief. The sergeant in charge responded to my inquiry by telling me that the new class for counterintelligence training at Fort Holabird, which would coincide with the end of my basic training, was filled. He was a very nice person, though, and we visited briefly as I was leaving his office. Almost as an aside as I reached the door he asked, "By the way, where did you go to college?" I said I had recently graduated from BYU.

"Are you a Mormon?" he asked.

I said, "Yes."

He said, "You're in!"

"But I understood a minute ago the class was full!"

"Not for you," he answered.

He then went on to explain that the nation's intelligence services welcomed members of my faith because they were honest and dependable, did not drink, use drugs, or womanize, and thus were good security risks. I observed that while there were both notable and not infrequent exceptions to his generalization, if he wanted me I was ready, visions of long marches, ear-numbing cannons, and rumbling tanks fading from my future as I spoke.

On the way back to my barracks, the Berkeley draft board's hostility toward me because of my religion and the army's enthusiasm for persons of my faith struck me as being quite odd, indeed astonishing, and in each instance quite wrong because I believed then, as I do now, that persons should be judged as individuals on their own merits and for their own lives and not because of any one or any combination of reasons based on their associations, ethnicity, or religion. My research and book on the University of California's loyalty oath controversy of 1949–52, accomplished several years later, helped me better understand and strengthen my commitment to this principle.

The program at Fort Holabird lasted six months from November 1955 through April 1956. This was a program for enlisted personnel, not for officers. It was, however, a wonderful learning experience, especially as my class included bright people from throughout the country. At its close I had been slotted to a unit in Europe but at the last minute was reassigned to Japan/Korea. I learned only later that covert actions in East Asia had resulted in several casualties within the unit to which I was being assigned and had made my reassignment necessary. We were in "peacetime" now. On arrival in Japan, the five of us ordered to this region of the world were transferred out of counterintelligence and into a unit that was not countering espionage and sabotage against the United States by others but instead was one engaging in such activities in East Asia, especially on the western and northern coastlines of the Korean Peninsula, in Manchuria, and in China north of the Yellow River. All at once the long infantry marches, ear-numbing cannons, and rumbling tanks seemed to be not so bad after all. But the die was cast.

Following several weeks of additional training near Tokyo, I was assigned to a small field unit in Korea. My first post was at Wolmi Do, a small island just west of Inchon on the Yellow Sea but connected by a long causeway to the city itself, and one later was at Yong Dong Po, then just outside Seoul on its western edge. Whereas even today I am not free to recount these nearly two years of service in any substantive detail, perhaps it's enough to say that at age twenty-three I only thought I was grown up. The work we engaged in was necessary, hard, ruthless, dangerous, and unevenly successful. The operations were entirely covert and my name, rank, and unit were mere conveniences arranged on the one hand to mask our real work and on the other required to provide the army deniability of my unit's members and our covert endeavors.

Our sampans, junks, crash boats, and other watercraft used in our duties were equipped with muffled, powerful diesel engines. They were armed and manned by tough, seasoned, and capable Korean crews. On moonless nights we plied the waters of the Yellow Sea, its principal ports and the more remote coastal regions of China, Manchuria, and North Korea, and the Han River, which in the far western part of the Korean Peninsula delineates the demilitarized zone dividing North and South Korea, a smugglers' haven. I knew almost nothing about this world and, indeed, found it difficult to contemplate even while doing my job. I never knew the real names of the men with whom I worked but I remember them with appreciation and affection. They were brave men doing a job for their country just as I was striving to do.

Inchon, the famous port of entry for General Douglas MacArthur's bold and wholly unexpected invasion in September 1950 early in the Korean War, was a place of mystery and intrigue, as well as the main port for smuggling along the eastern coast of the Yellow Sea. The port had one of the largest tides in the world (30 to 32 feet), where the harbor's deep and expansive mud banks served to anchor the ships that were left high and mostly dry at the tide's twice-daily changing.

I would rendezvous with our agents in the early morning hours in sections of Inchon that were decidedly unsafe to enter even in broad daylight. These contained our "safe houses," and I was well armed with a .45 pistol on my hip, a .38 pistol under my left arm, a sleeve knife on my right lower arm, and a blackjack in my pocket; and I knew how to use them. Each of us also carried a cyanide capsule in the event of being kidnapped within the country or captured outside it; rewards in rubles had been placed on our heads. There were no streetlights but many scurrying rats and cut glass or bamboo chimes outside the homes and shops sounding in the cool or chilling winds blowing off the Yellow Sea. These conditions combined to assure me of full alertness even though it was usually 2:00–4:00 A.M. Oddly, I felt less at ease in the safe houses than I did on the realistically riskier assignments on and around the Yellow Sea.

In any event, my time in Korea went fast, as did our rest and rehabilitation at special hotels in the Japanese Alps where we recovered our bearings and equilibrium after a series of difficult missions (the possibility of our being kidnapped by hostile parties precluded travel elsewhere).

South Korea in those days was a wreck. Buildings were pockmarked by bullet holes, cannon fire, and shrapnel from bombs. Others were still in ruins. There was a thriving black market back of the Chosen Hotel in downtown Seoul, where we bartered packs or cartons of Marlboro filter-tip cigarettes for the parts we needed for our jeep but could not get from army supply, as such parts were routinely stolen between their arrival by freighter at Inchon Harbor and delivery to the inland army supply depots. Orphans and thieves were everywhere, as were poverty and violent crimes; a cardboard box containing two to three dozen cartons of Marlboro filter-tips was the going street price for contracted murder.

I was once sent to purchase some North Korean currency from a Catholic priest responsible for a large orphanage near Seoul who quoted me an outrageous price for the money. We needed it for one of our upcoming missions. When I protested the price, he swept his arm around the orphanage, told me the number of children he was caring for, what it cost, and the problems he was having. I paid. His source(s) for this currency went unmentioned.

In June 1957 my commanding officer entered my room, informed me that one of our agents had been captured, that my cover name was being broadcast over Radio Pyongyang and Radio Peking, that I had two hours to pack, and that a plane was waiting for me at Kimpo Airbase just outside Seoul for a flight to Tokyo. On arrival in Tokyo, I was to be flown immediately to the Oakland army base in California, where I would be discharged within two days, and I was, just in time for summer session at the Berkeley campus of the University of California.

I would not have missed my army experience for anything. Asia, with its myriad languages, diverse cultures, teeming population, then mostly poverty-stricken and still partially war-destroyed cities and infrastructure, its foods, lifestyles, and ancient religions, captured my imagination and upended many of my world's realities. Danger proved to be both unnerving and strengthening, and I developed an even more pronounced sense of self-confidence and independence in doing a difficult job under adverse circumstances.

This experience helped me deal with protesting students in the late 1960s, early 1970s, and mid- to late 1980s. In important and enduring ways, the army was basic training for my life.

BACK TO BERKELEY

Summer session at Berkeley in 1957 was a difficult one, not because of the academic work or my studies, but simply because of the jarring shift from periodic violence and always stressful conditions of my work in East Asia to the comfort and leisurely life of a Berkeley student. In some respects, I was unhinged when I returned to Berkeley after my military service. I was more worldly, somewhat more cynical, more knowledgeable of the world's ways, stressed, and troubled. It took time to get over it all, and applicable military laws forbade me to say anything about the true nature of my work. Thus I internalized much of my inner turmoil, as I had when my mother died, and fought it through by myself.

My major adviser in fall 1957 at Berkeley was Professor Eugene Lee. He was young, an inspiring teacher, and a fine person (he was later to serve as one of Clark Kerr's vice presidents for the UC system). He helped with my course of study, encouraged me, helped to secure my internship with the city manager's office in Berkeley, and made the earning of my master's degree in political science a productive learning experience.

My choice of political science rather than law corresponded to my interest in becoming a city manager some day and grew out of an important decision I had made in Korea. It seemed right for me, until I served in 1958 as an intern under John Phillips, Berkeley's city manager. Not that he was to blame, indeed he and his colleagues were quite wonderful to me, but I had misunderstood the politics of the job and, therefore, chose not to pursue this line of work however much I had benefited from my internship, the drafting of new dog leash ordinances and the like excepted.

On completion of my master's degree in 1958, I went to work as an assistant to Richard Owens, then the administrative head of the California Farm Bureau Federation, a powerful Berkeley-based voice for California agriculture and a real influence on the California State Legislature and governor. In that capacity, I traveled throughout California learning about agriculture in its many forms, its diversity, troubles, and opportunities. And something also about how real politics then worked in California.

But it was also clear that there was no future to be had in working for a farm organization, and when the California Alumni Association on the Berkeley campus advertised for a director of their alumni scholarship and field programs to work with their alumni clubs and scholarship committees throughout California and in the major cities of the United States and abroad, I was encouraged to apply for it by Emery Curtice, and by my father. I did and was appointed to this position, effective January 1, 1960.

The association's executive director was Richard Erickson, a famous quarterback for the Golden Bears during their great years in the late 1940s when Cal often represented the PAC-8 at the Rose Bowl. Dick was a wonderful leader of the association, a fine boss, and a good friend. He spent countless hours, often with his wife, Jan, traveling the state, promoting the university, and strengthening alumni ties to Cal. He later granted me time off during certain hours and days to work toward my Ph.D. in higher education at Berkeley.

Dick Erickson and Gene Lee were only the first of many Berkeley personalities with whom I came to be acquainted and to whom I am indebted for all they did to help me along, first with my studies and then with my career. The alumni association staff and those on its governing council were also hardworking and committed people, kind and always helpful to me, including but not in any way limited to Mike Koll, who ran the alumni's summer programs in the high Sierra, a fine outdoorsman and athlete; Viola Birchland, the person who really ran the place and who was a friend to thousands of students and alumni during her several decades of service at Alumni House as the director's chief assistant; Verne Stadtman, who was editor of the *California Monthly* and later author of the principal publications concerned with the university's history during its centennial year in 1968; and John Mage, Norris Nash, William Hudson, Wake Taylor, Margaret "Sis" Collins, and others who led the alumni association during my four years there.

My work with the association acquainted me with an array of university citizens, many of whom were to be meaningful figures in my later career. For example, Professors Gerald Marsh and Garff Wilson of speech, Armin Rappaport of history, and Robert Scalapino of political science were all alumni favorites among the faculty; and in the administration, the chancellor of

Berkeley; Glenn Seaborg, a Nobel laureate in chemistry; Clark Kerr, Berkeley's first chancellor and then president of the university; Robert Gordon Sproul, for twenty-eight years the university's president, then emeritus; James Corley, one of Sproul's key vice presidents and the university's representative in Sacramento (when I was young, his wife, Marcellene, was my Cub Scout den mother); Frank Kidner and Elmo Morgan, both vice presidents under Clark Kerr; Edward Strong, chancellor at Berkeley; a well-known and highly respected professor of philosophy on the Berkeley faculty; several Cal coaches; and many others. In those days the Berkeley campus seemed to me to be an extended family, and I still cherish those memories and the friendships I have with those who are still living.

In 1962, during the last two years of my work at the alumni association, Erickson asked me to serve as the founding director of the California Alumni Foundation, Cal's first organized and comprehensive initiative to seek funds for the Berkeley campus from private sources and the precursor of the Berkeley Foundation, now administered by the university directly. Our success was measured in the hundreds of thousands of dollars in those days while today it is in the millions. Nevertheless, we got it started and successfully so, with a twenty-six-member foundation board of trustees comprised of well-known alumni. The board was chaired by Ralph Edwards, a Berkeley alumnus, Hollywood notable, producer, and creative talent whose efforts and loyalty to the university proved to be crucial.[1]

These were heady times for the University of California under Clark Kerr's leadership: the size of the university's student body doubled in the 1960s, and the number of campuses expanded from six to nine (Santa Cruz, Irvine, and San Diego), with three other campuses being designated as general rather than as specialized campuses (Riverside, Davis, and Santa Barbara). The contacts I made while serving with the alumni association from 1960 to 1964 gave me a unique opportunity to meet and travel with many of the university's leading faculty members and top administrators from throughout the UC system, including the chancellors of the university's established six campuses and those leading the three new ones.

I also enjoyed the cosmopolitan nature of the university's student body and faculty and the enriching range and reach of its programs: the study of knowledge and ideas in all their dimensions and manifestations and at the highest levels of sophistication and complexity. I welcomed the presence of bright young people, mostly eager to learn, and the established and younger scholars and scientists committed to their teaching and research. I was awed by the museums, laboratories, clinics, libraries, lecture halls, athletic fields and facilities, and the grounds and buildings in general, but mostly by the wondrous things accomplished in or on them.

UC's wondrous and expansive riches, together with the supportive Governor Edmund G. "Pat" Brown and a friendly legislature, offered unlimited opportunities for a young person properly prepared and eager to work. These thoughts were in my mind as I reenrolled in Berkeley's graduate school and prepared myself to succeed in a university that had high academic standards and a no-nonsense approach to intellectual work. The faculty, assembled from throughout the world, was as talented as could be found in any other public university anywhere. The university was a tough and demanding environment for academic administrators, and its student body was as unpredictable then as it is today.

Graduate Studies at Berkeley

I had been urged along this course to a doctorate by then-Chancellor Seaborg, President Kerr, friends on the faculty and staff, and alumni with whom I worked. Dick Erickson really made it possible by agreeing to adjust my work schedule to accommodate this arrangement if I decided to proceed in fall 1962. I would, of course, be obliged to do my job at the association while taking on average two graduate courses a term and learning to read French and Spanish at university levels.

Frank Kidner, then one of Kerr's vice presidents, was especially helpful as I made up my mind. In the course of a visit one day he asked, "Dave, what is it that you wish to do in the university: teach, write, administer, or what?" I answered by saying, "I wasn't really certain because I had an interest in doing all three."

"Do you wish to be a chancellor someday?" he asked. The question surprised me because such a prospect for someone in his late twenties in my position seemed not only remote but quite unattainable. Kidner took the lack of clarity in my answer to this question as unresponsive and asked me the same question once again. This time I said, "Having observed the lives led by chancellors and presidents, informed by my acquaintance with Kerr, Sproul, and Chancellors Seaborg and Strong at Berkeley, Mrak at Davis, McHenry at Santa Cruz, and Aldrich at Irvine, and the demands made of them both professionally and personally, I wasn't at all certain I wished to seek such a position."

He finally asked, and with some impatience, "Dave, would you like to have the satisfaction of at least being offered a chancellorship even if you turned it down?"

"Yes," I said, "I think I might."

Kidner then proceeded to tell me what I needed to do: first, to earn my doctorate, and he urged me to study higher education under Berkeley Professor T. R. McConnell, a national leader in the field, "if he would take you"; second, to seek a responsible position, at the appropriate time, with one of the chancellors; third, "to gain some experience in the Office of the President so as to become acquainted with the university as a whole"; and fourth, to do enough teaching, research, and intellectual work, coincident with my administrative duties, to earn faculty promotions in competition with other faculty members though I, he suggested, "would be on a dual track, not a single one." Kidner's observations and advice proved to be uncannily correct, but as I listened to him at the time these possibilities all seemed to me to be wildly improbable.

In any event, the first steps mark out a path. Mine were to seek admission to the graduate school at Berkeley—I was admitted—and to persuade Professor McConnell to take me as one of his graduate students. After a series of conversations with me, he agreed to accept me as a candidate for the Graduate School of Education's Ph.D. program in higher education in the fall term of 1962. This field of study focused on the American university and sought to acquaint the student with every aspect of its work, not only in modern American life, but within its historical context as well. Such a course of study encompassed a wide-ranging set of disciplines as the degree was to be, by definition, more cross-disciplinary in its scope than other more specialized doctorate programs.

My course work extended over two years and covered the history of universities in the Western world, the history of ideas, and the differential development in Western civilization of freedom of speech on the one hand and academic freedom on the other, these being quite different concepts, albeit often used interchangeably in today's parlance, thus confusing the meaning of each. We also studied how universities had organized themselves from the Middle Ages on, how they interacted with religious institutions, other patrons, and governments, both tyrannical and benevolent, how they arranged their financial affairs, and sought to support the efforts of the students and faculty, who in the most elemental sense are the university. I also learned to read French and Spanish at the university level, which I studied at lunchtime and while waiting for the bus to and from work.

I enjoyed my studies, colleagues, and professors: T. R. McConnell, Martin Trow, Burton Clark, Leland Medsker, Lyman Glenny, and Paul Heist in higher education; Albert Lepawsky, Joseph Harris, and Gene Lee in public administration and political science; and Frederick Lilge in educational philosophy, among many others.

When my written and oral examinations were completed in 1964, I began my dissertation, pursuing my research on the University of California's loyalty oath controversy that ravaged the university during the years 1949–52.

My dissertation committee consisted of three distinguished senior Berkeley professors—McConnell, Lepawsky, and Lilge. None had encouraged me to study the loyalty oath controversy, doubting that I could gain access to primary sources so soon after the events (roughly ten years) or, even if I did, that I could do so without offending important members of the faculty and other influential individuals and interests regardless of how scholarly and fair the finished product. They knew of the long-standing animosities and resentments set off during the controversy but even in 1964 still evident in relationships among and between faculty members and administrators across and within departments of the Berkeley campus and the president's office.

Nevertheless, I thought the story of this great controversy should be told since I believed that what had been written was transparently polemical and mostly conceived in the heat of battle, lacked balance, and could not be relied on by interested parties and historians over the years to reflect fairly on the contending parties or to illuminate the principles, subtleties, and nuances of this traumatic episode. If I had really understood what my advisers were telling me or how hard it was going to be or how right they really were as to its consequences for me, I might never have started my research or chosen this topic. But naïveté and ignorance triumphed over judiciousness and prudence and I started my research with this element of risk hovering over the entire endeavor.

My research was a challenge. Primary source materials did not exist in abundance, were hard to come by, were not complete, and were much dispersed. I had been a student at Berkeley High School during this controversy, had played no role in it whatsoever, had known people on both sides of the issue, and had no real views about who was right and who was wrong or what had really happened. But I believed that if I worked hard enough and conscientiously enough to produce an impartial, complete, and judicious account of the events that the benefits to history, to scholarship, and to me would more than offset the risks.

I prepared a matrix of persons holding primary source materials. I listed individuals in descending order from the most likely to cooperate to the least likely and started at the top. The research went well but not without hard-slogging work and a little luck. For example, when it came time to invite President Emeritus Sproul's help and seek access to his private papers on the loyalty oath (he was UC's president during the controversy and a central figure in it), he was very generous with his time, memorabilia, and records on this subject. But his confidential memos to the file were in the possession of the Office of the President at the university's statewide headquarters in Berkeley. Sproul said it would take him two weeks to obtain his confidential memoranda and I should return then. When I did, Sproul informed me that he had hit a snag but would have them for me within ten days.

When I returned a week and a half later, Sproul asked me into his office and showed me a stack of binders containing his confidential memos to the file on the loyalty oath controversy. He then read from the letter that had accompanied these papers. The letter stated, in essence, that these papers were being delivered to Sproul at his expressed behest, that they were to be returned when he had finished with them, that they were for "his eyes only," and that care should be taken to secure them while they were in his possession.

With a smile Sproul turned to me, pushed the binders my way, indicated that his eyes weren't what they use to be, and asked if I would be willing to read them as a help to him so that he in turn could better answer my questions. I hardly knew what to say except "yes." I read them at Sproul's office over a period of days, excerpting what I needed and taking whatever time I needed, seeking clarification from him or his long-serving and quite remarkable executive secretary, Agnes Robb, one of the university's true characters who helped me a great deal with my research needs.

The successful completion of my research depended very much on having access to these papers. For example, Sproul would dictate a memo to the file each time he had a telephone or personal conversation about the oath with another party or parties, recalling the essence of the call and thus making my cross-checking with the opposite party's records even more meaningful.

These documents later served another and comparably useful purpose, in helping me gain access to the private papers of the late regent John Francis Neylan, longtime attorney for the William Randolph Hearst interests and a powerful senior regent on the university's governing board at the time of the controversy. During its course, he and Sproul came bitterly to be on opposite sides, although they had previously been close friends.

Neylan's papers were at the Bancroft Library on the Berkeley campus, and the library's director was Professor George Hammond, a highly regarded member of the Berkeley faculty whom I had come to know while working on campus. Hammond said he would be pleased to arrange for my use of the Neylan papers (twelve to fifteen boxes of them, as I recall) but could not, as they had been sealed for many years and would not be available for scholarly purposes until well into the 1970s. I asked on whose authority they had been sealed and on whose advice. Hammond said that Mrs. Neylan, who was still living, had ordered them sealed on the advice of her lawyer, Herman Phelger, of the then-famed San Francisco law firm Brobeck, Phelger & Harrison, and a very prominent Berkeley alumnus. Fortunately, Phelger and I knew each other in connection with the activities of the California Alumni Association and the California Alumni Foundation.

We met at his office in San Francisco to discuss access to the Neylan papers. I told him about my research, the faculty members overseeing it, my reasons for wanting to do it, and how essential it was to report and characterize Regent Neylan's role in a fair and proper fashion. He asked only two questions. The first was, "Dave, whose papers are you seeking?" I showed him my research matrix of sources. "And do you have President Sproul's papers?" he asked. I said I did, had read and could use them, and hoped he would encourage Mrs. Neylan to make her late husband's papers comparably accessible. His answer was immediate, "Well, if you have Sproul's, you have to have Neylan's." He indicated that he would contact Mrs. Neylan promptly and invite her cooperation, which he did, and which she gave.

My dissertation was completed in 1966, signed by all three professors comprising my dissertation committee. My degree was granted that June, and the dissertation published by UC Press in 1967. It was widely noticed and reviewed, quite favorably, except for two or three nonsigners or those sympathetic to them who believed that I had failed to accord their views either comparably sympathetic and/or adequate attention.

While many people helped me with this effort, I wish to single out Professor Lilge, well known to be quite demanding of his students (to put it mildly). I had taken an independent study course from him, half of the reading being in French, and knew I needed to be prepared to discuss these readings, and I mean prepared, for our weekly tutorial. I learned from Professor Lilge and came to appreciate his standards and the demands he made of me.

When I had completed three chapters of my dissertation in draft form in summer 1965, I asked my dissertation committee for early comments. The comments I received from McConnell and Lepawsky were helpful and constructive, but when I read Lilge's comments, I was not only dumbfounded by his criticism but angry as well. After all, I rationalized, I knew more about this controversy than he did and he might have allowed for some positive comments as well as negative, hurtful ones. I was so angry that I put the letter aside for about a week and then read it again slowly and carefully. I concluded much to my dismay that he was essentially correct in his criticisms and on nearly all counts. I threw out most of my summer's work, set aside most of the three draft chapters, and started over again.

When Professor Lilge had signed my completed dissertation in 1966, he invited me for lunch at his Berkeley home. As I was leaving, and after he had once again commended me on my work, I worked up the courage to inquire about the purpose of his earlier letter, the tone as well as the substance. He laughed and said only that he thought I had more in me than I had evidenced in the first drafts—that this story should be told as well as possible, that he thought I could do it, and that he wanted a publishable work to emerge. I remain very much in his debt.

Meeting Libby and Marriage

In mid-1954 Elizabeth Fuhriman and I met at the Skaggs-Stone Warehouse on the Oakland waterfront where we both worked for the summer months. She was eighteen and I was twenty-one. Our mothers had served together on missions in the early 1920s for the Mormon Church in Boston and New York. Libby and I had never met, however. She had attended Piedmont High School and then Stanford University for her freshman year.

But when we met, she was heading off to BYU for the fall term of 1954, unable to stay at Stanford as there was no real financial aid then available to students. We dated some that summer and occasionally throughout the 1954–55 academic year at BYU. By summer 1955, when we were again back at the warehouse in Oakland, we saw each other every day at work and dated every weekend. But all this came to an abrupt end when I enlisted in the army on September 12, 1955.

While I was away serving our country, she was enjoying her life at BYU, being a vivacious, intelligent, and beautiful young woman. We wrote about once a week. At the close of her junior year at BYU, she enrolled in the dental school at the University of California's San Francisco campus, seeking a degree in dental hygiene.

When I returned from Korea in June 1957, she was living at home in Oakland, and we found ourselves working once again at the warehouse. It was clear to me that I had formidable competition for her affection from the future doctors studying at UC San Francisco. But my unexpected return from Korea in the early summer of 1957 gave me a marked advantage over those med students who were away from the Bay Area during the summer months. As the fall term began, both for Libby and for me, I traveled twice weekly from Berkeley to San Francisco to see her. I drove over in the first car I ever owned, a 1955 two-door Ford, black, with an engine as mundane as its overall appearance. I paid $1,000 for the car, which should have told me something.

Parking was never easy around the San Francisco campus, as is true today. Libby lived halfway up Third Avenue, just off Parnassus. My car's engine was incapable of carrying me past her apartment and usually died just short of it, Third Avenue being one of the steepest streets in San Francisco. And if I ever made it to Parnassus, the somewhat erratic performance of my brakes meant I didn't dare turn down Third. So when I picked her up, I was obliged with some hazard and embarrassment to her and myself to back down Third Avenue, a maneuver nearly as unnerving as my service in Korea. But Libby was worth it all, and by Thanksgiving of 1957 I had triumphed over her stable of suitors, and we became engaged to be married the following June.

On June 27, 1958, we were married in the Mormon Temple in Salt Lake City. Following the ceremony and a wedding breakfast, we flew directly to Oakland arriving just in time for our wedding reception at Alumni House on the Berkeley campus. It was a wonderful and memorable celebration, marking the beginning of our lives together surrounded with the good wishes and love of our large and extended families and nearly four hundred friends.

Our oldest daughter, Karen, was born in 1960, and our second daughter, Shari, in 1962. We were living in Orinda, just over and east of the Berkeley hills (our home cost $23,700). I was working for the alumni association, busing to and from the campus as we had only one car and Libby needed it more than I. She kept us financially solvent while we were living in Orinda, working in Berkeley as a dental hygienist three days a week, with either her mother or mine taking the children.

Life was good. Libby supported me then as she did throughout thirty-two years of married life: always encouraging but never pushing, always supportive but never for her sake alone, always willing to do more than her share at home, looking after the girls and me as the family grew. She was my anchor and my source of love, encouragement, support, and motivation.

We enjoyed the alumni association activities together and developed a pattern of common involvement and participation in the life of the university, as we also did in our church. We were family-oriented, not only because this priority comported with our common values, but also because we had no money, often ending the month with $10 to $15 in the bank. We had no complaints, however, loving each other and being together with our daughters, all of us healthy, a modest home we called our own, friends, family, and a set of shared, not separate, professional activities from which we derived much personal happiness and enduring memories.

I returned to graduate school in September 1962, the month Shari, our second daughter, was born. This was not easy. In addition to my full-time work schedule at the alumni association, taking two graduate courses, and learning two foreign languages, I had my hands full at home, wanting to help Libby as much as possible, and wanting to know and experience our daughters' young lives. We managed, thanks to Libby's evenhandedness, organizational skills, and tenaciousness.

These were wonderful years, and in 1964 when my work at the alumni association came to an end and hers in dental hygiene stopped because I accepted a position as assistant to the chancellor for university relations at the university's Santa Barbara campus (the position included community, alumni, and press relations, among others), we looked back happily on our days together in Berkeley and Orinda and set off for our new home in Santa Barbara with Karen and Shari, ages four and two respectively.

On the way down the coast, we heard radio accounts of Mario Savio and scores of others holding a police car captive on Sproul Plaza at the Berkeley campus. This marked the start of the now famous Free Speech Movement. We were not thinking about all of this, however, as we headed down California's beautiful coast with our two young children on our way to a new home in Santa Barbara and a growing campus full of promise. We were excited about being "really on our own," leaving farther behind with each passing mile family and friends in the Bay Area while having neither family nor friends awaiting us in Santa Barbara. It was a big move for us, and it proved to be the right one in every way.

TWO

THE APPRENTICESHIP YEARS

THE SANTA BARBARA YEARS

Our family arrived in Santa Barbara on October 1, 1964, ready for a change, excited about the city and its strikingly beautiful environs, and prepared for a new and promising professional opportunity. We bought a small but pleasant home in the Goleta Valley up the coast from Santa Barbara, in a neighborhood with safe streets and younger children with whom our own could easily play and conveniently make friends. We were only minutes away from the beach, shopping, and Santa Barbara's exceptionally attractive downtown, with its Spanish-style architecture and historical buildings. And the campus was six minutes away, also by car.

The city was blessed with a theater for stage productions, a small but respected Museum of Art, a well regarded symphony orchestra, and cultural institutions, such as the Music Academy of the West and the Museum of Natural History. Together with adjoining Montecito, Santa Barbara had some of the most attractive homes and gardens that could be found anywhere, many with sweeping vistas of the coastline. The Channel Islands and Pacific Ocean were to the south and the Santa Ynez Mountains to the north, and all of this with an annual mean temperature of 72 degrees. The local newspaper possessed high journalistic standards and helped foster a sense of pride and community in this remarkable place tucked away on the southern California coast just 90 miles north of Los Angeles. Had we died and gone to heaven?

The Santa Barbara campus of the University of California where I was to work for nearly seven years held an important place in our family's life and memories. It was not in the city but in the Goleta Valley 9 miles up the coast and on the coastline, in an unincorporated section of the county of Santa Barbara. The valley was a less elegant residential enclave than Santa Barbara or Montecito, but pleasant enough and growing with the nearby campus, providing housing and a commercial center for students, faculty, and staff.

Origins of the University of California–Santa Barbara

The university's Santa Barbara campus had its origins as a state teachers' college. Founded in 1909, it was sited within the City of Santa Barbara and served the higher education needs of a small number of students from this part of California and did so admirably. Episodic efforts were made over several years to encourage the University of California's acquisition of the college but to no avail, as the university was looking not to compete with the state's growing number of colleges but to settle on and carve out its own distinctive role and mission.

In 1943 the state enacted legislation proposing the transfer of all college properties and personnel to the University of California should the university's constitutionally independent Board of Regents find favor with the proposed arrangements. The board initially divided on the issue but finally agreed in 1944 to accept the legislature's offer.

Following World War II, the campus was closed, and this newest of the university's campuses was moved to an old Marine Corps base in Goleta. It was a spectacular site but one seemingly defined more by the wooden barracks it inherited than by the beautiful coastline on which it was located. Its views were of the Pacific to the east, south, and west and the mountains to the north; the area in between was blanketed with citrus, walnut, and avocado groves and fruit orchards interspersed with small tracts of housing.

The Santa Barbara campus, like the Davis and Riverside campuses but unlike those at Berkeley or Los Angeles, was at the outset to have a more limited academic role within the university: its student body was to be confined to undergraduate students with an enrollment ceiling of 2,500. Its emphasis was to be on the liberal arts, "the Williams College of the West" as some came to think of it. Professional schools were not contemplated nor was promotion of the faculty—many teachers had transferred to UC along with the college's properties—beyond the first of six steps on the university's professorial scale, because the college's academic standards for appointment and promotion were not judged to fit the University of California's. These were expedient rather than strategic decisions as UC was sorting out how its future and that of California's growing community college and state college systems were to relate, especially as to standards for admission, enrollment levels, academic mission, and governance.

With Clark Kerr's appointment as president of the university in 1958, and in the face of a projected enrollment surge expected to double the university's student body in the 1960s, the Board of Regents designated Santa Barbara College, the College of Agriculture at Davis, and the Citrus Experiment Station at Riverside as general rather than specialized UC campuses and shortly thereafter authorized the building of three new general campuses at Santa Cruz, Irvine, and San Diego. A general campus was to offer a full range of undergraduate programs and courses of study and a rich mix of graduate and professional schools with their corresponding and inseparable obligations of teaching, research, and public service. Dramatic increases in enrollment were also planned for all of the university's now nine campuses.

These transforming decisions put UC Santa Barbara on a new and challenging trajectory, solidified the multicampus nature of the University of California, helped give definition and staying power to the 1960 Master Plan for Higher Education in California, and gave impetus to the one-university, nine-campus concept that laid the groundwork for a public university that in size, scale, depth, breadth, and, above all, intellectual capability came to be without peer in the world.

UCSB: 1964–1967

It was into this most exciting and stimulating of endeavors that I moved as an assistant to the chancellor at UCSB on October 1, 1964. I was determined to complete the writing of my dissertation on the UC loyalty oath controversy. I also needed to learn about my administrative assignment and what I could about managing a UC campus. My portfolio included alumni, press, community relations, fund-raising, and a position on the chancellor's cabinet, which met weekly. The cabinet included the chancellor, four vice-chancellors, the assistant to the chancellor for budget, and myself. These seven comprised UCSB's senior administration in 1964.

I had been invited to serve at UCSB by Chancellor Vernon I. Cheadle, former head of the American Botanical Society. He became the second chancellor of UCSB in 1962, succeeding Samuel Gould who had served briefly before accepting the chancellorship of the State University of New York, a new and just forming system of higher education on the nation's opposite coast. Just before his appointment as chancellor, Cheadle had been vice-chancellor at Davis, where he was a close and longtime friend of Daniel Aldrich, Jr., a soils and plant nutritionist, then universitywide dean of agricultural sciences.

I had known Aldrich when working with the alumni association at Berkeley. He and his wife, Jean, also lived just down the street from where Libby and I had been living the first months of our marriage. Aldrich was one of my references for the UCSB position, and I have no doubt that his judgment and advice helped settle in Cheadle's mind the offer he made to me to serve as an assistant to the chancellor. (In 1963 Aldrich arrived at Irvine as its chancellor and served in that capacity until he retired in 1984 during my second year as UC's president. He was one of UC's great leaders. He later served at my invitation as acting chancellor at UC Riverside and as acting chancellor at UC Santa Barbara—we called him UC's "utility chancellor"—and was loved and effective wherever he served. The positive influence he had on my professional development would be hard to overstate, especially with respect to understanding UC's more nuanced and subtle workings.)

Chancellor Cheadle and his wife, Mary, were both gems to work with. They took Libby and me under their experienced and caring "wings," introduced us to key figures both on and off campus, and included us in most of their social events, usually held on campus at their official residence. They were devoted to the university and spent their waking hours serving it.

Under Cheadle's tutelage I learned what it took to be a chancellor in the University of California and within the larger complexities of UC's nine-campus structure, including dealings with regents, legislators, donors, the executive branch of the United States government, governors, and others having an interest in the university, for example, local officials, journalists, alumni, parents, and the public.

Concerned that I might fail to complete my dissertation with all I was doing in his administration, Cheadle gave me permission to take every Wednesday afternoon off and two months during summer 1965, in order to accelerate my research and writing. Without his support and encouragement, I would have taken at least another full year or two to complete my writing, or at the worst, I would never have finished, working as I was at nights, on holidays, and most Saturdays to get it done.

On the completion of my dissertation, the awarding of my Ph.D. in June 1966, the publication of my dissertation by the University of California Press in 1967, and the favorable reviews of the book that followed, I was appointed assistant professor of education in the Graduate School of Education at UCSB half-time along with my administrative appointment, which was then designated as assistant chancellor, also at half-time, but with essentially the same range of duties as before. In practice this meant a 150 percent workload. I did not mind, however, because I was making headway both as an academic and as an administrator, as Vice President Kidner years earlier had encouraged me to do. This dual track enriched my understanding of both areas, given that my area of academic interest was higher education.

Owing to our home's close proximity to the campus, our family took full advantage of the university's recreational, athletic, cultural, and intellectual life, thus helping to mitigate the otherwise negative aspects of working long hours both at home and on campus. Our children were young, mobile, and not yet encumbered by school, and Libby and I had a set of friends in the neighborhood, at church, and on campus whom we enjoyed and whose friendship we shared.

Our third daughter, Lisa, was born at Cottage Hospital in Santa Barbara in 1966, and our fourth daughter, Marci, in 1969. We had our hands full at home, Libby especially, although I helped in every way I could; and we were busy on campus, Libby assisting there any way she could.

We learned in those years how to help each other at home and at work. It was a pattern we developed in our Santa Barbara years, setting the style for our responsibilities not only at home and at work but also at church and in the larger community as well. We did not allow these demands to separate us or to create resentments or to otherwise impair our relationship. Instead, we turned them to our common advantage and were much the better for it, not only then but even more when I served as president of the University of Utah and later as president of the University of California.

When Cheadle was appointed chancellor in 1962 the campus enrolled 4,700 students, 7,900 when I joined his staff two years later, and nearly 14,000 in 1970, my final full year at UCSB. This was dramatic growth, especially for a research university and one expected to meet UC's exacting standards both for faculty appointments and for students seeking admission. An overwhelming need for student housing, both on campus and in the Goleta Valley, gave rise to the uncontrolled growth of privately developed student housing in adjoining Isla Vista. This mostly student-populated community was bounded on three sides by university-owned lands and on the fourth by the Pacific Ocean.

During the period 1964–67 the campus prospered. New academic programs were added, the campus was in demand from students throughout California, the graduate school was growing, the two professional schools—engineering and education—were thriving, new facilities were being built, student housing was being constructed on campus, additional campus lands were acquired, excellent faculty members and talented members of the staff and administrative team were recruited, the cultural and intellectual life of the campus flourished, relations with the press and community were respectful, and Berkeley's problems with the Free Speech Movement—that now famous FSM—hardly touched UCSB, except generally as to public opinion. Times were good, and we were happy with our work, friends, family, community, and church. I wondered how long it would last.

The answer came on January 20, 1967, when the Board of Regents summarily dismissed our president, Clark Kerr, essentially for his handling of events in 1964–65 and their aftermath; California's newly elected governor, Ronald Reagan, had run for office in no small measure on a platform of "cleaning up the mess at Berkeley." It was at Reagan's first meeting as governor and, therefore, as a UC regent that President Kerr, who on that day had twice been asked to resign and had refused, was dismissed by the board on a vote of 14–8, with immediate effect. As Kerr put it later, he left the position as he had come into it, "fired with enthusiasm!"

Nothing was quite the same at UC after that, not just because of Kerr's departure, although it had a telling effect, but because of the regents' shabby treatment of him as well. The turbulence that led up to his dismissal and the action by the regents reflected shifting values and priorities within the larger society: the political balance in the state, the social attitudes of students and faculty members, and the interplay between state government and the university. All these factors heightened tensions between the university and the public and within the UC community itself. As ideas and actions took on a more adversarial and confrontational character, the campus was becoming a less civil and respectful place. Kerr's dismissal and the FSM also helped illuminate the very wide net of social, sexual, indeed cultural revolution that was ensnaring young people and their universities in Europe and the United States. The effects are still unfolding.[1]

As my duties evolved with the changing times, my job title went from assistant to the chancellor to assistant chancellor and lastly to vice-chancellor-executive assistant.

A Changing Campus: 1967–1971

This progression of duties was tied to increasing levels of student unrest. From 1967 onward the chancellor grew increasingly alienated from what was happening and less willing to deal with it; and as a staffer in my early thirties, I was willing to help in areas he found unfamiliar and off-putting. As a member of the cabinet, I was kept informed about all matters of interest to the central administration and the president's office as well. I attended meetings of the Board of Regents from 1968 on, accompanying Chancellor Cheadle on a regular basis, helping him at the board meetings and also on campus as our student problems grew and evolved during the years 1967–70.

A glance through the student yearbook offers a visual perspective on how UCSB changed from the early to the late 1960s. Through 1965 *La Cumbre*, as it was called, depicted a campus that was indistinguishable from most middle-class, modest-sized universities and colleges in the intermountain West, the Midwest, and the South. As in the conservative 1940s and 1950s, it displayed fraternities, sororities, student clubs and organizations, intramural and intercollegiate sports, and homecomings. It featured administrators and faculty members who enjoyed the special regard and respect of students and praised them for their accomplishments.

The first crack in this culture was evident in *La Cumbre* of 1966–67 and again of 1967–68, which reported on President Kerr's ouster and a student march on the state capital to protest his dismissal in which UCSB students had a consequential role; Governor Reagan's first budget for UC (1968–69), which proposed to raise student fees and reduce UC expenditures, and the ensuing student protests; and speakers on campus such as Bishop James A. Pike, the outspoken and left-leaning Episcopal bishop of San Francisco, and Linus Pauling, a Nobel chemist whose views on everything from vitamin C to nuclear weaponry were thought by many to be left of center. These speakers contrast with those in previous years as reported in *La Cumbre,* such as the theologian Paul Tillich, Kenneth Clark, a British man of letters and historian, and Robert Hutchins, head of Santa Barbara's Center for the Study of Democratic Institutions and former president of the University of Chicago.

While not too much should be made of these differences, they at least reflected a perceptible shift in students' interest in such matters and a more lively expression of students' concerns about politics and social issues than had been typical. There was also a somewhat greater range and intensity to students' political activity, with campus protests over the granting of academic credit for ROTC courses, against the draft and war in Vietnam, and against Dow Chemical Corporation, for its production of armaments used in Vietnam by the United States.

The Beginning of Student Protests

The campus remained more or less free of exceptional or even markedly untoward student behavior or protests during my early years there. All that ended with the fall term of 1968 when our comfortable, congenial, and somewhat insulated campus was catapulted into the mainstream of minority aspirations and anti–Vietnam War protests that over the next two to three years would change UCSB almost beyond recognition. The events on campus were in important ways an extension of, or at least linked to, social and political forces operative both within the United States and, concurrently, in Western Europe, Latin America, and East Asia.

Within Europe there were common themes and characteristics: the overcrowding of universities nearly everywhere, with students' attendant frustrations and perceived diminution of individuality; the democratization of formerly elite institutions under government prodding or coercion, with admissions policies and teaching methods and practices more suited to mass than elite higher education; the addition or increase of student fees and tuitions as an offset to government funding; and the perceived irrelevance of curricula to the personal and professional interests of a dramatically changing student body.

In the United States, more to the point, the widespread involvement of thousands of university students in the civil rights movements of the early 1960s, especially in the South, not only heightened student interest in such issues but also stimulated a broadened and growing awareness of social conditions within the nation as a whole. The assassinations in 1968 of Martin

Luther King and Robert Kennedy and the street warfare at Chicago's Democratic National Convention that summer only aggravated the tensions and taught many students political tactics calculated to advance the civil rights of disenfranchised minorities. With an invigorated political and social consciousness and a heightened commitment to direct political action, many students brought these tactics back to their universities as the preferred means to advance their political or ideological commitments.

Hence events in the early to mid-1960s laid the groundwork for the troubles that were to follow, especially bearing on the older generation then governing and managing the universities: regents, trustees, administrators, and faculty members alike. An activist and ideologically intolerant minority of the younger generation was impatient for change and lacked sympathy for the norms, customs, and underpinnings of American academic life. This subset of student activism was brutal and costly, brutal as to the unforgiving and insistent threats and rudeness with which it denounced contrary views and advanced its own, and costly as to the human wreckage—mostly among students and their families—it left in its wake, however today's recollections of these times mythologize and make it appear otherwise.

The contrasts were stark, the implications for all parties grave, and the university's very raison d'être was put at risk: direct action versus contemplation and reflection; ideology versus evidence, especially negative evidence; advocacy versus impartiality in teaching and scholarship; incivilities and crass personal behavior versus personal restraint, tolerance, and respect for the views of others; free speech for those whose views accorded with "truth" or "right" thinking and interrupted or suppressed speech on the part of those who disagreed. These were fundamental issues about which the older generation cared deeply and about which much of the younger generation seemingly cared very little or not at all. Such "old-fashioned views" were to be subordinated to the means and ends to which the new generation, or least a noisy share of it, appeared to be committed.

I first sensed a change in climate at Berkeley in the late 1950s and early 1960s when I was both a staff member at Alumni House on campus and a graduate student. By the early 1960s it was apparent in the dress, conduct, and interests of students, in the growing presence and clustering of former students and others south of the campus, especially on Telegraph Avenue, and at the southern points of campus ingress and egress where community and city boundaries collide.

Few, however, anticipated the sharp turn of events in fall 1964, when the Berkeley campus erupted and the FSM overwhelmed not only the campus but eventually both the Berkeley administration and the university's president. It was, in a way, an unintended "dry run" for the real thing later in the decade when the antiwar protests at UC gathered force and momentum, as newer minority issues appeared.

Minority Issues

The University of California was one of the first major public universities to take affirmative action to increase the representation of minority students on its campuses when its Educational Opportunity Program (later called the Early Academic Outreach Program) was launched in 1964. The assumption was that by merely recruiting to the campus historically underrepresented minorities, the university would carry out the major part of its job. To call that assumption ineffectual and wrong-headed would be to understate its impact. The assumption failed to account for these students' differing levels of preparedness, motivation, or financial and moral support from their families, in contrast to those UC was used to seeing in its incoming students. It also allowed insufficiently for how abrupt a change it was for students coming mostly from their own ethnic communities to find themselves as distinct minorities within an overwhelmingly white student body. To aggravate the culture shock, very few of their own race or ethnicity were to be found on the staff, on the faculty, or within the administration.

Protests: 1968–1969

During the early morning hours of October 14, 1968, sixteen members of the Black Student Union, many of them freshmen and some nonstudents, entered North Hall, the main computer center on campus as well as a major UCSB classroom and office building. They ejected the employees working on the first floor of the computer center and secured two wings of the building from within by chaining the doors and locking the windows. Monitors were ready to alert those in the computer center to the entry of any persons intending to hamper the takeover. They threatened immediate damage to computer instrumentation and irreplaceable files if university or civil authority tried to remove the group and stationed students with wrenches and other tools at the computers to carry out the threat.

Lyle Reynolds, dean of students, and his assistant, Gary Peyton, entered the building through an overlooked open window and encountered the students, who handed them a list of demands. "The mood of the black students was one of great excitement," Reynolds later reported to Chancellor Cheadle. There was "a keyed-up anger, and a determination to hold the building at great personal sacrifice. It was also apparent that some of the younger ones did not have a strong stomach for the event. Also it was evident that they had selected the biggest and strongest Blacks that they could find."[2]

Dean Reynolds tried to get the students to call it off, indicating what the event would do to UC's educational opportunity program and to them as individuals: perhaps suspension or dismissal, even the end of their education. Since he knew some of their parents, he mentioned the parents' possible views. But, he noted, "The students indicated that they had considered all these probabilities and in their frustration, their anger, and their deep feelings of injustices being perpetrated on their race, they were willing to sacrifice themselves, completely if necessary, to draw attention to their plight in the university and elsewhere."[3]

Reynolds and Peyton worked hard to reduce tensions, to persuade the police to make no efforts to enter the building forcibly, to protect the computer center along with administrative, academic, and research data that were then irreplaceable. Reynolds also believed that such forced entry would result in physical harm being done to "many policemen and students alike. The policemen I saw," he added, "were soft and overweight, while the students who outnumbered them were young, athletic, and armed with wrenches (at least those stationed at computers)."[4]

By 9:30 A.M. a large crowd of students had gathered, including some of the more radical white students who had managed to secure a position close to the building. They were raising quite a ruckus, thus complicating (because of their numbers) the prospect of any police action. The black students' demands were very much within the context of other such minority protests made within UC and across the country in the ensuing years. For example, they sought the dismissal of certain campus staff; the creation of a college of black studies, with black instructors, and a graduate program in African American studies; an investigation of racism on campus; the hiring of blacks in UC's upper management, black counselors, and black coaches; and the development of a more effective community relations effort of special interest to black students and black members of the Santa Barbara community.

In preparing a comprehensive report of the incident for the chancellor (at his request), to use on campus and to inform the president, the regents, and the larger community, I tried to make sure the incident would not be reduced to mere sound bites.[5] I quote at length because it reports not only what happened that day but also the approach the UCSB administration took in dealing with this and related protests over the ensuing two to three academic years:

> The administration had one of two viable alternatives from which to choose: the first was (a) to discuss the grievances with representatives of those holding the building; (b) to seek additional time in which to reduce the emotion and tensions of the moment; and (c) as a result of a and b to persuade the blacks to leave the building peaceably. The second alternative was to clear the building by force. . . .
>
> The administration decided in favor of hearing out representatives of the black students while at the same time alerting sheriff's officers and highway patrolmen from the Santa Barbara area so that the building could be cleared and secured by nightfall if the black students refused to leave before then. Uni-

versity police were already on the scene. (Later in the day, sheriff's deputies from adjoining counties were alerted and ordered to the campus.)

The Chancellor asked selected members of the faculty, administration, and student body, including the President of the Associated Students, to join him during the late morning hours in a meeting with representatives of the black students holding the Hall. With the exception of the first demand—to dismiss the Director of Intercollegiate Athletics and the Chairman of the Department of Physical Activities—which was rejected at the outset—the remaining seven demands were answered by the Chancellor in terms acceptable to all interested parties [he would make a good-faith effort to accomplish several of the demands, but without a timetable or commitment as to the particulars, and to refer to the Academic Senate those demands that pertained to UCSB's educational and academic programs].

. . . [Invoking standard procedure, the chancellor asked the Associated Students Judicial Council to review violations of university regulations. The council] concluded its deliberations by recommending suspension from the University of the students who were occupying North Hall, with the provision that the suspensions be deferred pending good behavior. While the Judicial Council was conducting its hearings, the Chancellor and other administrative officers, in cooperation with the County Sheriff, made plans to secure the building before nightfall, by force if necessary, if the students had not left voluntarily by then. The task was especially sensitive, as by late afternoon several hundred students had formed outside North Hall, some hostile and others sympathetic to those inside. This meant that not only would the element of surprise be critical if the Computer Center was to be secured free from destruction, but that the crowd outside would have to be moved or contained before the building proper could be secured.

Fortunately, the use of force was not required. When informed of the Judicial Council's recommendation to the Chancellor on disciplinary action, the black students left North Hall on their own initiative and without damage to the equipment, furnishings, or, structure except for two broken windows. Several of them came into the Administration Building to await the Chancellor's decision on what discipline would be taken against them while a crowd of some 400 sympathizers gathered in front of the building to wait for the decision on discipline.

Following an hour's discussion with his principal administrative advisers, key members of the faculty, and officers of the Associated Students, the Chancellor accepted the recommendation of the Judicial Council and directed that the students involved in the sit-in be placed on suspended suspensions at once [i.e., on probation, to be suspended only if they violated university regulations]. The decision was immediately reported to the black students affected and to the news media.

As the day closed and the campus returned to normal, the news services erroneously reported (1) that the black students involved in the sit-in had been granted amnesty by the Chancellor; (2) that the Computer Center had been badly damaged, with the loss estimated at $3,000,000; (3) that the campus had not functioned during most of the day. While the wire service reports were grossly inaccurate, they were, nevertheless, widely believed and they probably never were corrected in the public's mind, in spite of university efforts to deny the inaccuracies by reporting the true facts in detail. . . .

Why did the black students lock themselves in North Hall?

The blacks wished to dramatize their deep feeling of resentment at the treatment of their race and other minority races in American society. The small numbers of blacks in the universities and colleges in California and in other states were just one reflection of the issues they hoped to dramatize. Black students at UCSB constituted a very small proportion of the student body, both in absolute terms and in percentages. At UCSB the number was about 200 out of an enrollment of 12,600, a percentage of 1.6. Most of them had enrolled between the years 1966–1968. The sit-in was an attempt to startle the campus into recognition of the black perspective and to dramatize their frustrations and expectations. It was also true that some part of their purpose was motivated by power seeking. . . .

By its actions that day, the administration earned the confidence of the larger and moderate elements of the student body and the greater number of the faculty who clearly favored the course of action pursued by the administration. Thus, the campus as a whole—students, faculty, and administration—was better prepared to move justly and quickly against any further willful and deliberate violation of University regulations than would have been true had the administration moved in harsher ways against the black students. For example, three previously announced illegal demonstrations and sit-ins planned by SDS for the week of October 14, 1970, were cancelled as a result of the administration's handling of the Monday sit-in, cancelled it should be said, because there was no general support remaining among the student body and faculty for further demonstrations. (Even the black students who were involved in the sit-in opposed any further political action that would have disrupted the campus or violated University regulations and worked with the student body officers to discourage the SDS actions.)[6]

Although most of the students, faculty, and staff believed that this matter had been well handled and that the outcome was both just and fair, the public in Santa Barbara and around the state had very different views and so too did Governor Reagan, who coincidentally was scheduled to speak the next week at Santa Barbara's Channel City Club, the day the essential parts of the above report were released to the public.

Backlash

The governor had attended a meeting of the Board of Regents at UC Santa Cruz the previous week and spent most of the early part of his remarks in Santa Barbara railing against the students and also members of the faculty and administration at Santa Cruz who had acquiesced in or otherwise accommodated or failed to challenge unlawful conduct by students directed against members of the university's governing board. The regents' meetings had been interrupted, he reported, several regents had been pushed and jostled, and obscenities had been shouted against members of the board along with a variety of gross incivilities directed against individual members.

Although I had not been at Santa Cruz for these meetings, several friends of mine, both on the faculty and in the administration there, confirmed the essential accuracy of the governor's account.

Reagan was angry and so was the audience, animated in particular by the governor's reference to the computer center incident at UCSB the previous week. "Here in Santa Barbara," he went on, was another episode "at which administrators once again capitulated to the threat of force and once again assured our students that violence and coercion work. We are told by the Chancellor that some expensive equipment would have been damaged, but what is the cost of selling out sanity and due process, the values of the majority of persons on the Santa Barbara campus and our society?" he asked. And he asserted, "The people have not turned this institution over to the faculty to rule by insubordination, or to administrators to rule through appeasement and capitulation, or to students to rule by coercion."[7]

While I could more than sympathize with the governor's agitation at the events on the Santa Cruz campus, I thought he was quite wrong in judging the Santa Barbara incident as he did. His reaction hurt us in the Santa Barbara community, and we paid a price in community goodwill because of it, in spite of an excellent editorial in the *Santa Barbara News-Press* that contrasted Reagan's assessment to Cheadle's and came down on Cheadle's side.[8] Here was the "great divide" in thinking about such campus protests and how to handle them, between those on campus responsible under law for dealing with them and those off campus who, as elected public officials, infused their own views with the burden of the broader mandate and wider moral authority of the body of citizens they were elected to represent.

In a strange way, the coercive character of the new student activism and the familiar coercive nature of government are much alike: each relies on direct political action to achieve its respective objectives; each is as ready as the other to distort truth and misrepresent facts to secure its purposes; each finds it convenient to make simplistic assertions about highly complex, nuanced, and subtle events and ideas; each is by and large uncaring about the effect its actions have on the university; each is unremorseful about the means it uses to reach its ends; and each in approach, behavior, means, and tactics is at fundamental odds with the norms, customs, beliefs, and principles of free universities everywhere, relying as the latter do on evidence, reason, reflection, respectful tolerance, civility, and the commonly accepted ways of knowing, whether it be in theoretical physics, philosophy, genetics, law, history, entomology, or medicine. But universities are much more adept at dealing with external political forces, with nine hundred years of experience in doing so, than at dealing with comparably crass intrusions and pressures from within.

In the coming years we were to learn what was needed to deal with such political activities driven mostly from within. But in 1968 we were less ready, less able, and less experienced in doing so. For my part, I was not a key player in the computer center incident; the chancellor was the key player, ably aided by Vice-Chancellor for Student Affairs Steve Goodspeed, a senior member of UCSB's faculty and administration (his father had been a distinguished member of the Berkeley faculty for many years) who never shirked his duty and who paid dearly for it (in health, regard, and standing) during the years 1968–70 and afterward; and those in the dean of students' office, Lyle Reynolds and his colleagues, who knew the students and liked them and who had a very tough time when sandwiched between the contending forces. They paid too in diminished morale and relationships among students and colleagues alike.

As a member of the chancellor's cabinet, I was present outside the computer center during the morning, learning what I could, informing Goodspeed and Cheadle throughout most of the day of the relevant events, and then deliberating in the afternoon with the cabinet when the chancellor made the key decisions. As earlier mentioned, he later asked me to prepare a comprehensive report on the incident for the regents and the president, to prepare a general communication to the campus on what occurred, and to salvage what I could of the needed goodwill of our alumni, community leaders, the media, and the public generally. It was not an easy assignment, but from that time on I was in the mainstream of events relating to the antiwar demonstrations, ethnic study issues, minority concerns, and other volatile issues.

Reactions

The computer center was our first major incident. It was very instructive.

The media could be trusted to misreport the facts and to continue to do so even when corrected as to the facts (the *Santa Barbara News-Press*, a Pulitzer Prize–winning and independently owned newspaper, was a notable exception, reporting accurately and fairly in its news pages and evenhandedly in its editorials), and the television coverage was the worst (I never could decide if the miserable reporting of these events by the media in general was due to malice or incompetence or both).

The public could be trusted to believe the media even when it knew better.

The students could be trusted to respond to manipulation by any number of parties wishing to do so, especially when the objectives were contradictory.

The staff could be trusted to do their jobs.

The faculty could be trusted to think otherwise.

The administrators could be trusted to be wrong, whatever decisions they made.

The politicians could be trusted to praise or find fault according to the latest polls, usually rewarding the guilty and punishing the innocent.

While there were notable exceptions, these generalizations were mostly on target, and they have not changed much since. My respect for Chancellor Cheadle and his handling of this matter was unbounded, and not just because I agreed with his decisions. He was available, forthright, respectful, diligent, conscientious, unintimidated, and determined to do his job as best he could in the university's service. He was guided consistently by the operative principles of academic life, whatever others may have thought of him or his decisions. If Governor Reagan had seen him in action under the realities he confronted, perhaps he would have been less ready to judge him so harshly and might have been more sympathetic to the problems university administrators confronted, not only in California but across the country; but alas, it was not to be.

This incident was for the chancellor the first major "shot across his bow." Others were later to strike amidships, and as with Vice-Chancellor Goodspeed and others, he was to pay a heavy personal and professional price for being steadfast and honorable throughout the next two to three years as he faced attacks on the one hand for being indifferent to student views, aspirations, and desires and on the other for capitulating to student pressures and failing to discharge even the most elementary duties of the position he held.

But he was not guided or indeed influenced by these judgments, although they hurt and he felt them deeply. Despite vicious criticism, he remained committed to the tenets he had always lived by and would live by throughout his tenure as chancellor, best expressed in the final paragraph of his order placing twelve UCSB black students on suspended suspension for the remainder of the fall quarter in 1968:

> It is my firm resolve to maintain on this campus conditions that assure reason and persuasion as against coercion and intimidation in the work of this university. Our regulations are fair and reasonable and have been constructed over the years out of experience and in collaboration with students, faculty and administration. It is my earnest hope, in the spirit of free inquiry and the reasonable exchange of ideas that this university community can undertake to resolve its differences, its imperfections and to deal fairly and progressively with the special problems of our minority groups.[9]

And try he did, until engulfed by events, particularized to UCSB, when during the 1969–70 academic year our world seemed to have fallen utterly apart and the chancellor's ability to deal with these events and pressures was much reduced. But we first had to get through the remainder of the 1968–69 academic year. This was no small task. As the winter ended and on into spring 1969 not a week went by without hostile rallies, mini-riots, vandalism, mass arrests, marches, and bomb threats.

Trends and Trouble

None of these issues amounted to much in the larger scheme of things, although for those of us involved in dealing with these matters on a daily basis they seemed consequential enough. At San Diego, Los Angeles, Santa Cruz, Riverside, and Berkeley there was real trouble, especially at Berkeley, which at this time found itself in the throes of the People's Park riots and other such volatile and violent matters, resulting in the governor's declaring a state of extreme emergency on the Berkeley campus.

The regents and president were also now beginning to divide on issues of how to deal with the protests raging across the state. The governor and legislators, reflective of public opinion for the most part, were also expressing their dismay at and concern with the protests and demanding that the university administration take more aggressive and affirmative steps to deal with them, as Reagan's remarks in Santa Barbara made clear.

We, of course, were not insulated from the public backlash now sweeping the state with even greater intensity than when Governor Reagan was first elected. Awareness of the public's outrage about happenings at most of UC's nine campuses infected everything we did at UCSB. Being responsible for our relations with the community, alumni, and press, my work had taken on a new and wholly unexpected turn.

Fortunately, Stuart Taylor, editor-publisher, and Paul Veblen, executive editor of the *Santa Barbara News-Press,* were ethical and capable journalists with whom I could talk and share confidences. I met with them regularly pointing out where their accounts were fair and accurate and where, at least in my view, they were not. I explained what we were doing and why, what our guiding principles and operating procedures were, and what we understood to be the activists' objectives.

These "backgrounders" and the honest give-and-take helped enormously in getting our side of these controversies into the hands of responsible journalists, getting timely feedback, and checking our sense of public opinion with their own. In retrospect, I believe that Chancellor Cheadle and perhaps others might not have survived the years 1968–70 without these efforts and our good fortune in the presence of such responsible journalists for the region's leading daily newspaper.

As we moved into spring 1969, there was a good deal of probing by the students of the administration's line on protests, our weaknesses and strengths, and the calculation of these judgments projected onto the upcoming spring term and the 1969–70 academic year. Those of us in the administration were fine-honing our policies, procedures, rules, and regulations so as to be certain they were fair, administrable, and, if challenged, sustainable, both within the university and in the courts.

We also made real progress in responding to the concerns of minority students, whose agenda, if not their tactics, at least possessed a strong element of reasonableness, in contrast to the mostly middle- and upper-class white radicals drawn from one faction or another of the Students for a Democratic Society (SDS), whose purposes I saw as principally scapegoating the university for problems they had at home, with the draft, with the Vietnam War, with social or governmental policies, or with other issues that were disturbing or complicating their lives. Whereas the minorities not only had a greater moral base for their demands (aside from the war) but were also more single-minded in seeking their objectives than were the Radical Student Union (a spin-off from the SDS) and other mostly white organizations whose tactics were as random as their issues.

While the cognizant committees of the Academic Senate had responsibility to review and act on such matters, I had been asked by the chancellor to meet privately with representatives of the student Chicano organization in an effort to help them prepare and propose a department and center of Chicano studies that both in language and substance might enjoy the Academic Senate's favor and ultimate support.

My objective was to make certain that the proposal was viable, well conceived, and educationally compelling so that it could not be turned away on technical or frivolous grounds. I worked mostly with Fernando de Necochea, Jr., a counselor in the College of Letters and Science, who proved to be a reasonable, articulate, and fair-minded person. Our work stretched over several weeks, as we met privately in various places on and off campus, and eventually bore fruit with an approach and philosophy that proved to be transferable to the black student's program being worked on by the black students and their advisers. Thus in fall 1969 we set up the Department of Chicano Studies and an accompanying research center and a corresponding Department of Black Studies, also with its center for interdisciplinary research. I was proud of our efforts. They helped demonstrate to the minority community, on and off campus, that there were alternatives to political action, political rhetoric, and nonviolent but unlawful activity in seeking change. Nevertheless, we confronted major problems in mounting these programs on such an accelerated time scale: the need to recruit faculty members for the new departments, intragroup rivalries, and the ongoing commitment of the early advocates, some of whose level of interest appeared to be in inverse relationship to their successes.

Because of our success with the minority students and faculty in the academic year 1968–69, when 1969–70 began the minority students were mostly on the sidelines, leaving a much reduced field of open issues for the white radicals to protest than would otherwise have been the case. I do not intend to deal with the numerous other skirmishes and protests that we confronted in 1968–69, except for two that captured the national spotlight.

The Flacks Case

The first occurred on April 3, 1969, when on recommendation of the Department of Sociology of the College of Letters and Science, Chancellor Cheadle offered an associate professorship in sociology to Richard Flacks, an assistant professor at the University of Chicago. He accepted the UCSB offer in early May, but his appointment set off a flurry of public criticism and acrimony, as Flacks was much involved in the founding of the SDS in the early 1960s and was a well-known scholar dealing with student movements, attitudes, and behaviors. A near-fatal attack on him in Chicago that spring had made national news and drew even more attention to his appointment.

The chancellor's initial report to the Board of Regents on his offer to Flacks was received with much suspicion and poorly concealed hostility. Cheadle defended his decision on traditional academic grounds, pointing out that whatever affiliation Flacks had earlier maintained with the SDS had ended, that his behavior at the University of Chicago was beyond reproach, that the quality of his scholarship was respected, even by his critics, and that his appointment had enjoyed an exacting review consistent with UC's rigorous standards for appointment to its faculty. But while the appointment held, the chancellor received another round of virulent criticism, frustrating and demoralizing him at a time when he was in need of encouragement and support, which all of us in his administration sought to provide.

The second issue was a tragedy.

Violence

A bomb planted by an unknown party in the inner courtyard of the faculty club on campus—and triggered to explode if moved—blew up at 6:29 A.M. on April 11, 1968, when Dover Sharp, the club's custodian, discovered the box and tried either to move it or to determine its contents. He was mortally injured by the ensuing explosion. Wounded, with his clothing on fire, he struggled to reach a wading pool some 75 feet distant to extinguish the flames, and students ran to his aid from a nearby dormitory. He was rushed to the Goleta Valley Community Hospital with burns over 80 percent of his body. In spite of surgery and heroic efforts to save him, he soon died.

I received a call at home early that morning informing me of this tragedy and went immediately to the faculty club. I was sickened by what I saw: the explosion had left parts of Mr. Sharp throughout the courtyard and on the surrounding walls. I was furious and inwardly raging at the inflated political rhetoric, idle threats, bombastic demands, and grossly unreasonable and churlish behavior to which we had been continuously subjected by many of the activist students who, in my view, had made it possible through their words and actions for a disturbed person to "go over the line" and engage in murderous action, while they themselves were unaware of or indifferent to the terrible implications their behavior carried for others. It changed my attitude toward some of the more aggressive and irresponsible activists and hardened me toward them in ways that caused me to recall my days in Korea ten years earlier.

The perpetrator has never been identified, and no one has come forth to confess or share any information that proved helpful to the police.

Modus Operandi

During the 1968–69 academic year the chancellor was advised in these difficult matters by Russell Buchanan, vice-chancellor for academic affairs, Raymond Varley, vice-chancellor for business, Lyle Reynolds, dean of students, and many others, including senior members of the faculty, but most especially by Vice-Chancellor Goodspeed, his associate George Smith, Assistant to the Chancellor for Black Affairs Preston Dent, Assistant to the Chancellor for Chicano Affairs Ralph Herrera, and myself. Professor Robert Kelley of the Department of History took account of Goodspeed's and my role in his 1981 book, *Transformations,* the most accurate and complete account of the student unrest at UCSB during these years, as follows:

> In January, 1969, a United Front formed by the Black Students Union, the Students for a Democratic Society, and UMAS (Mexican-American Student Association) demanded that the promised increases in minority enrollment and faculty be speedily put into effect. Now, as later, leadership in the ensuing negotiations came from a calm and reasonable man, Assistant Chancellor David Gardner (who would later become President of the University of Utah), and from Vice Chancellor for Student Affairs Stephen S. Goodspeed, who by his retirement in 1978 would spend almost twenty years at the top levels of the UCSB administration. Both made remarkable contributions, sometimes separately, sometimes together. Indeed, the entire administration was plunged into almost continuous internal dialogue over what to do in these difficult circumstances. There was an inescapable suspicion, impossible fully to dismiss, that the leadership of the protesting groups was not in fact interested in settlements, but in a continuously unsettled campus in which student leaders and their cause, nationally, could garner high off-campus visibility. On their side, the minority students regarded the administration's refusal instantly to give in to all demands, many of them impossible to grant, as institutional racism. Meanwhile, Gardner and the Chancellor paced the fifth floor of the Administration

Building, and the living room at University House [the chancellor's on-campus residence], debating possible solutions. Moving ahead in the midst of angry confrontations and mutually exclusive demands from extremists on both sides, on and off-campus; remaining calm and taking the reasonable course despite the most violent and abusive provocations and incessant misrepresentations of motives: these were the essential tasks given the Chancellor, his advisers, and the leadership of the campus Academic Senate.[10]

The spring and summer of 1969 had witnessed the further escalation of the Vietnam War and the enactment of a plethora of laws throughout the country, and especially in California, seeking to restrict various forms of student protests by strengthening the authority of university administrators while reducing their discretion. Tensions continued to build across the country as student protests, violence, and bombings on and off campus escalated, as did public outrage over these events. UC administrative and faculty leaders were seeking to understand better and to prepare more completely for what everyone knew would be an academic year full of troubles, while knowing that their actions would be subjected to intense and withering criticism by the protesting students on the one hand and the elected public officials on the other, exhausted and out of patience after the events of the year just past and wary of trouble sure to come.

At UCSB, the Department and Center of Black Studies and the Department and Center of Chicano Studies had been approved and were nominally under way. More minority students, especially Chicano students, had enrolled. More minorities had been appointed to staff and faculty positions. New and important academic buildings had come on line, and what came to be the campus landmark, Thomas Storke Tower and Plaza, had been dedicated by Chief Justice Earl Warren. Yet state appropriations had been cut, student fees raised, and funds for future UC buildings slashed, while a bond issue for funding new UC buildings had been defeated by a vote of the people whose anger toward UC and its students was like a dark cloud hanging over all we were striving to accomplish as the students returned for the fall term of the 1969–70 academic year.

The Momentous 1969–1970 Year

The term began well enough. Campus enrollment was up about 1,000 students, to 13,654 (including 2,000 graduate students). New buildings were coming on line. The departments of black and Chicano studies had admitted their first students. Six hundred and fifty of the new freshmen students had been admitted through the educational opportunity program. The Education Abroad Program, administered for the entire university by UCSB, was both growing and expanding. New research institutes were under way in education, the environment, the behavioral sciences, and black and Chicano studies. Off campus, however, the state was punishing UC: operating budgets were slashed, tuitions and fees were increased, and faculty salaries were singled out for punitive action all owing to the public's distaste for the students' protests occurring on all nine UC campuses and the handling of them by the faculty and administration, the former thought to be complicit and the latter considered to be inept.

The autumn term of 1969 at UCSB, however, was characterized more by skirmishes and positioning than by major protests or disturbances. The groundwork was being laid for more intensive protests for the winter and spring of 1970.

The Allen Case

On June 1, 1969, an assistant professor of anthropology by the name of William Allen was informed that his two-year appointment would not be renewed at the end of the 1969–70 academic year. This decision provoked a pronounced and adverse response not only from Allen himself but also from some of his students who were allied with the black and Chicano student organizations, the student government, the student newspaper (*El Gaucho*), and the Radical Student Union, among others.

Allen appealed the decision in two ways: by seeking a reconsideration of his department's decision through the university's established procedures, and by encouraging student demonstrations for his cause in a series of events in early 1970 that gave rise to the academic year's first major demonstrations on campus. He demanded not only a hearing on his case by the Academic Senate review committees and by the administration, but also an "open" hearing rather than a "confidential" one, the latter being consistent with university policy and practice and the former not. Petitions for this purpose were circulated throughout the fall and presented to the Academic Senate and administration in early January 1970, with some 7,700 signatures (the number was never verified, only asserted).

Chancellor Cheadle was in Europe and Africa on education abroad business for the university at this time. The acting chancellor was Russ Buchanan, a professor of history who had played only a nominal role in the events of 1968–69, except as his duties for overseeing UCSB's academic programs had involved him. In this instance, as vice-chancellor for academic affairs he was both responsible for dealing with the Allen case and the acting chancellor during Cheadle's absence. This was a structural and procedural defect in UCSB's management, as it removed the second review of the case that would otherwise have involved the chancellor himself, just as it circumvented the procedures Cheadle had put in place to advise him about matters that bore on the problems we were having generally.

Nevertheless, Buchanan conducted himself with dignity throughout the coming travail that enveloped not only him but the campus as well, making a series of courageous decisions and standing his ground under difficult and intimidating circumstances. Student protests, incivilities, bad manners, and boorish behavior were not his "cup of tea," and he rejected them as a substitute for reasoned and respectable dialogue. He simply took the issue at hand, considered it as he usually would, rejected the demand for an "open hearing" in Allen's case, and referred the matter to a faculty committee, consistent with established and long-standing university policies. But in making the correct decisions, he did not take account of the volatile and highly charged political context on campus. Hence the announcement of his decisions triggered a series of events, one leading to the other, that turned the winter and spring terms of 1970 into a nightmare for the campus, including most of its students, faculty, staff, and all of us in the administration as well.

On January 29, in reaction to Buchanan's decisions of four days earlier, roughly 1,500 noisy but orderly students rallied in the plaza between the administration building (now Cheadle Hall) and Campbell Hall, vehemently protesting Buchanan's decisions and demanding an open hearing for Allen. The crowd shrank to 200–300 determined protesters as the afternoon wore on, and the dean of men, Bob Evans, attempted to disperse the smaller crowd pressing insistently on the front doors (glass) and windows of the building. When some students pushed him hard, he shoved back. The police then interceded to protect the dean, who was quickly surrounded by protesters. Ground-floor windows fronting the plaza now began to break. Rocks were thrown and more windows shattered, with glass flying everywhere. All personnel were evacuated from the front offices, the doors secured, and additional efforts made to disperse the crowd. The few remaining at the close of the day encamped that night on the plaza, warmed by a bonfire they had lit.

The next day several thousand demonstrators (three to five thousand) blockaded the administration building. Arriving staff members received verbal and some physical abuse as they sought to enter, as I did. Buchanan judged the conditions to be sufficiently disruptive to university operations, as well as threatening, that at 10:00 A.M. he asked for local police forces to be dispatched to the campus to restore order and to open the administration building, which was by now fully blocked and barricaded. The police arrived at 2:00 P.M., and the protest's leaders duly noted the four-hour lapse between the call and the arrival: it confirmed for them the realities the administration faced in seeking a timely police presence in an unincorporated section of a rural county, in marked contrast to the ready availability of specially trained riot police in the state's urban communities. This reality helped define the administration's options in dealing with protests at UCSB, deprived as we were of the discretion to call for police assistance and to be able to count on it both in terms of its timeliness as well as of its effectiveness. This was no one's fault, just the realities confronting us in a rural county with widely dispersed policing capabilities and neighboring cities with few police officers.

The three hundred police comported themselves in a very professional way, sweeping the area of protesters, reopening the building, and dampening the demonstration to the point that by 5:30 P.M. only the police remained. The police were on campus until February 4, and they were needed. UCSB was hit with bomb threats (the library alone was ordered evacuated due to such threats over 100 times during the 1968–70 period), the faculty club was vandalized, the ROTC building was attacked, windows of many buildings were broken, graffiti was everywhere, and a comparable series of harassing activities were carried on around the clock both on campus and in Isla Vista. The police left the campus at the end of the day February 4, 1970, as things seemed to have calmed down.

Between the first demonstrations on January 29 and the departure of the police on February 4 Buchanan had rightly, in my view, rejected the demands for a joint faculty-student review committee to hear Allen's case, concurred in the Academic Senate's action on February 3 not to make the Allen hearing public, announced that nineteen more students had been arrested for their participation in the ensuing unlawful demonstrations, barred these nineteen from campus, and suspended them from the university pending judicial hearings on their conduct. Buchanan also turned away a demand for amnesty for the nineteen accused students along with an assortment of other "demands" intended to absolve the accused students of any culpability and to make them whole as to their student status.

On February 4 the senate committee hearing the Allen case rejected his appeal by a vote of 6 to 1. Allen then "took charge" of the demonstrations himself by leading some 1,000 demonstrators on a parade through campus, disrupting classrooms and labs and the library, calling for a student strike, and otherwise seeking to engender support for his cause. The day ended quietly enough. The strike did not materialize in spite of Angela Davis's appearance the next day at a rally for Allen (she was well known within the UC community and nationally as an African American activist; at the time the renewal of her academic appointment at UC Los Angeles was under threat). Allen was then charged by the administration with unprofessional conduct, and the charges, except as to minor issues, were found to be meritorious by the faculty hearing committee later that spring.

On February 8 Chancellor Cheadle returned to the campus from his extended trip abroad and gave a public and unqualified expression of support for Buchanan's decisions. The campus continued to rumble, but not at the earlier level of intensity. The Allen case gradually faded away, although student resentments and grievances about it did not. Twelve students and three police officers had been injured in the course of these demonstrations. The campus was in the national news, and the public was infuriated, not only with

UCSB, but also with the university's other campuses where even more frequent and dangerous protests were under way. UCSB was catching up, however, and fast.

In the chancellor's absence, I had not been centrally involved in these matters, though I took part in the discussions that led to most, but not all, of Buchanan's decisions. These decisions would have been better accepted and more widely understood if they had been accompanied by a greater sensitivity to their political and community relations dimensions, if the local press had been briefed privately before announcing the decisions publicly, and if the administration had bought space in the campus newspaper to explain these decisions more completely. We should also have touched bases with key constituencies, both within and outside the university, as soon as possible. And we should have secured concurring statements from the university's president.

These and other steps were not taken either before or after the decisions were announced. They might have made no difference whatsoever or could have caused the political middle at least to pause. In my view, their absence made the ensuing demonstrations more intense and larger than they needed to be. I regret that I was not more insistent about pressing for these measures at the time the decisions were about to be made even though I was not included in the decision-making process under Buchanan as I had been under Cheadle.

The Kunstler Affair

The next burst of protest, however, was a function of what was happening not at UCSB but in a courtroom half a continent away in Chicago, where seven of the leaders of the infamous protests at the Democratic National Convention in Chicago were on trial, defended by William Kunstler.

In mid-February 1970, with the Allen matter phasing down, the protesters' attention turned to the Chicago Seven (as they came to be known), seeking to draw parallels between those seven and the nineteen UCSB students arrested for their part in the late January and early February demonstrations on campus. Kunstler was invited to speak on campus by the Radical Student Union, a recognized student organization under UC policy with the right to invite and to compensate outside lecturers from funds derived from the student government. The Kunstler invitation was reported by the campus newspaper on February 19.

The chancellor received a telephone call the following day from the FBI indicating that UCSB was to be the object of demonstrations tied to Kunstler's appearance on February 25. If we said he could come and speak, then his presence or remarks would be construed as the trigger for the planned demonstration. If we said he could not come, that decision would be regarded as a sufficient reason to provoke a disturbance. So in either instance the public would be critical of, if not enraged by, the protests and we would suffer another loss of public goodwill. But if we denied Kunstler the right to speak, we would lose not only public support over the ensuing disturbance but credibility on campus over denial of access to UCSB facilities for Kunstler's speech. We needed leverage to pick up the pieces afterward and decided to allow him on campus, hoping that the decision would help preserve our position internally even though we knew we would be savaged by the larger community for having done so.

I was in full accord with the chancellor's decision on this but wondered how much of the impetus for this event was local. I concluded in my own mind that parties and forces not at UCSB but from elsewhere had set it up. Why else the call from the FBI? And why, following Kunstler's appearance, and all the trouble that followed it, did some individual members of the Radical Student Union leadership come to see me privately, wondering aloud what had happened? They had planned for the usual protests, but not for a riot.

We worked with law enforcement as best we could to mitigate matters and to prepare for the protests, but it was not easy, given the overlapping of interested jurisdictions: for example, the FBI, county sheriff, California Highway Patrol, campus police, and others. Being located in a rural county, we depended on "mutual aid" from other jurisdictions at the very time law enforcement was contending with large-scale student protests throughout the state.

Kunstler spoke on campus to a large crowd of students and others (three or four thousand), playing to their all too evident sympathies, working emotions to a higher and higher pitch with great skill in the words he employed as well as the manner of his speaking, stopping short of language construable as having incited a riot. I attended the speech, sensed the mood, and braced for the consequences.

After Kunstler's speech the large and restive crowd moved into Isla Vista for a rally at Perfect Park (Santa Barbara's rough equivalent of Berkeley's People's Park). Rocks were thrown at police cars, the realty office was broken into, other store windows were broken and vandalized, and some sniping was reported. The protest had given way to a full-scale riot.

By 6:30 P.M. milling crowds are breaking windows of realty company and other business establishments. Between 6:30 and 7:30 P.M., fire is set in trash bin at Bank of America. Sheriff orders crowd to disperse or be arrested for unlawful assembly. 150 officers make first sweep on the crowd and are repulsed with rocks. A patrol car is overturned and burned. A later force of 80 law enforcement officers running single file to the bank, reported to rescue a guard, remain only a few minutes before being driven off by the hostile crowd. Gas is used on the crowd. At times, greatly outnumbered groups of police isolated, surrounded and nearly overwhelmed. Police withdraw and set up roadblock into Isla Vista. Fire is enlarged; flames leap 40 feet high by 12:30 A.M., completely destroying bank. County fire equipment parked nearby not able to be used because of hostility of crowd. Rioting continues until about 2:30 A.M. when police return. A final sweep disperses the remaining 200 or so. Crowd uses heavy missiles (concrete chunks, etc.) later found to have been projected from previously manufactured "launcher." 116 police reported injured, several severely.[11]

In a setting of confused violence so dangerous that sheriff's deputies finally withdrew, advising firemen to stay away also, the Bank of America building in Isla Vista was set in flames, after three attempts, and burned to the ground. Governor Reagan flew to Santa Barbara to declare a state of extreme emergency, and rioting continued, forcing police out of Isla Vista. National Guard troops were then mobilized and sent in and order was restored. Meanwhile, more than a hundred people had been arrested for widely varying alleged crimes and misdemeanors.[12]

The presence of the National Guard in the early morning hours of February 27 to enforce the anti-loitering ordinance and the curfew ordered by the county in effect from 6:00 P.M. to 6:00 A.M. helped calm the area. With unloaded weapons the guard together with local deputy sheriffs patrolled Isla Vista without major incident. A steady rain helped. Some vandalism, rock throwing, and catapulted ball bearings harassed the officers and the guard, with the commander of the guard being struck by one of the ball bearings. One UCSB employee was also wounded by a bullet in the arm, the source being contested, as he drove between a group of student protesters on the one side and police on the other. The bullet, it was later discovered, was a smaller caliber than from any police weapon then in use.

The guard finally withdrew on March 2. The anti-loitering ordinance was suspended the next day. In the course of these events some 115 persons were arrested, 47 of whom were not students (not a surprising number). Of the students arrested, eight were from other university or college campuses, including two "journalists" from the university's Riverside campus student newspaper who, instead of covering the protest, took part in it, one consequence being that the UC Riverside car they had used to drive to UCSB was burned and gutted.

Once the guard had withdrawn, we were then merely contending with the expected guerrillalike hit-and-run tactics—a bomb threat here, a fire there, arson here, vandalism there. Not that these were trivial or inconsequential. They were not, especially for the small businesses in Isla Vista whose livelihoods were so compromised by the earlier riots that bankruptcies were now being filed.

Governor Reagan's appearance in Santa Barbara on March 18 for a downtown speaking engagement was another excuse for the protesters to trash parts of downtown Santa Barbara. Nineteen persons were arrested, including Professor William Allen for driving through the area with a shotgun displayed in his car. Allen was suspended from all his duties on the faculty three days later by the chancellor pending a review of his case by the Academic Senate's Committee on Privilege and Tenure, which committee, a few days later, took the chancellor to task for his "unwarranted" suspension of Allen prior to a final determination of the charges levied against him. The chancellor rejected this argument, and I might add, in language not includable within this account. The Allen case lingered throughout the spring but in a much-muted state, called out on "slow news days" to keep things going when not much else was happening.

The Rubin Incident

The campus was then being set up for another unwelcome event, this time courtesy of Jerry Rubin, one of the Chicago Seven, who had been invited to speak at Isla Vista and/or on campus April 16. The chancellor denied him the right to speak on campus, and the county denied him the right to speak in Isla Vista. The chancellor had consulted with President Hitch, several chancellors, and legal counsel before acting and then acted decisively.

This decision, of course, did not sit well with Rubin and his supporters. He chose to have his wife, Nancy, represent him instead. She spoke, both on campus to over 1,800 persons and at Isla Vista's Perfect Park, unhindered. Her remarks and those of Stu Alpert, a Berkeley radical and also one of the Chicago Seven, managed to stir trouble up once again. By late afternoon crowds were once again roaming Isla Vista, throwing rocks and smashing storefronts, and another curfew was declared by the county board of supervisors in effect from 6:00 P.M. to 6:00 A.M. the following day.

In the hours following the lifting of the curfew the morning of April 17, demonstrators were out again drawing an assortment of adherents as they moved through Isla Vista, concentrating their attentions on the newly constructed temporary offices of the Bank of America being built on the same site as the old one, which only weeks earlier had been burned down. We could not win, it seemed: riots when we allowed Kunstler to speak and riots when we refused Rubin. This tended to confirm my suspicion that we were less the object of random protests and rioting, locally planned and driven, than an exceptionally vulnerable pawn used by others for whatever objectives they were seeking. There was, however, a new dimension to these dynamics. Students were now in conflict one with another for the first time with significant numbers of students opposed to the random and gratuitous trashing of property. They were now willing not only to speak out but to act as well.

Several fires were already burning when a concentrated attack on the temporary Bank of America began, with Molotov cocktails and burning debris being thrown or pushed into the bank through broken windows and opened doors. These fires were being extinguished by several students actively opposed to these actions, one such being Kevin Moran, a UCSB student who had left his apartment to help maintain some order in the community. He was on the porch of the temporary bank, along with a handful of others doing his best to extinguish the fires, when two trucks of armed police arrived, teargassing the crowd and seeking to disperse the rioters.

Within a minute or two Kevin Moran lay mortally wounded on the steps of the bank, a victim of a police bullet accidentally discharged that apparently ricocheted and struck him.[13] This death did nothing to deter the rioters, as they were out again the next night attacking the bank and adjoining structures. Police this time in larger numbers, equipped with and firing bird shot along with teargas canisters, quickly moved against and dispersed the crowd. Each escalation was getting nastier, and feelings were running even stronger. The early evening to early morning curfew was suspended on April 21 as Isla Vista finally calmed down.

The Anti–Vietnam War Riots

Protests returned to the campus shortly thereafter, precipitated by U.S. military actions in Cambodia. They escalated quickly: attacks on the ROTC building on campus, bomb threats, very large rallies, buildings entered and vandalized, including the administration building; the Student Union was looted along with the cafeteria. The size, frequency, and character of these demonstrations were soon well beyond the capacity of the campus itself to manage, and police were once again called in from the outside to help.

On May 6, 1970, with the UC campuses alive with large-scale protests and unlawful activity that appeared even with UC resources and outside police to be uncontainable, and with some campuses of the state colleges in roughly the same situation, and against the backdrop of the Kent State killings the previous day in Ohio, Governor Reagan ordered all the campuses of UC, the state colleges, and the community colleges to be closed until May 11.

I recall the conversations among and between the president and the chancellors about the governor's intended but not yet announced order. The chancellors were not happy with this decision, as they would have preferred to tough it out, believing that while it was easy to close a campus—we had thought of doing so ourselves twice that winter and spring—it might prove harder to get the campus open again. Moreover, it would give the radicals as much time to recoup as it would us. But we closed on a Wednesday, not to open again until the following Monday. In retrospect, I believe the governor's decision was the correct one, and in reality, we might have had to close down for the rest of the academic year if things had gotten much worse.

Once closed, however, we bent ourselves to the task of opening five days later. All the usual precautions were taken, the expected plans prepared, and the policy and procedures determined. But in reality, we did not know what we could expect on the following Monday morning. Goodspeed and I, with the now seasoned help of the dean of students and his staff and Vice-Chancellor Varley, worked the problem. On Sunday night the chancellor and his advisers met in his office to consider the prospects for the opening the following morning: the leaders of the radical group were holding forth in the Student Union, haranguing a small crowd about the need to keep the campus closed (perhaps they and Reagan had been in partnership all along, I remarked). The activists indicated their intention to keep it closed with a massive sit-in at the two points of ingress and egress to the campus, among other things.

In listening to this rubbish, Vice-Chancellor Goodspeed smiled, got up, telephoned the student radio station, and told its personnel to get over to the Student Union building and transmit the discussions into Isla Vista and on campus residence halls. He then had his staff call the fraternities and sororities, residence halls, and student organizations on and off campus, urging them to tune into the campus radio station.

Within a matter of minutes, hundreds of students were streaming to the building, filling it, and expressing their views on this matter. For example, they asked, "If the campus is not going to open tomorrow, when will it open?" They had term papers they needed to write and couldn't finish without access to the university's library. Laboratory assignments could not wait any longer as time made a difference with many of them as well.

The radicals had been trapped by their own rhetoric as they could not advocate "participatory democracy" on the one hand and simply ride roughshod over majority opinion on the other. The feeling in the now packed Student Union building was unmistakable: the campus would open the next day, and it did without significant incident.

The campus then quieted down, except for the routine prattle about revolution in the daily campus paper, the paper being a bit of poison spread around the campus every morning of the academic year 1969–70. Even Jerry Rubin was allowed to speak in late May. Two-thirds of the students left before his "speech" concluded. It was a big flop.

The Convocation

Shortly after the campus reopened, the chancellor had set aside a portion of an early afternoon for a general campus convocation at the stadium, so that issues related to the Cambodia incursion and the Vietnam War could be considered by the students. Some six to seven thousand students attended. Speakers from mostly the left spoke and the usual rhetoric was heard once again. Bob Kelley recounts, very accurately, what happened next:

At length the Chancellor himself rose to speak, at which point some thirty to forty militants, painted and attired in bizarre costumes, began to heckle him. He had given them time to speak, the Chancellor burst out, thoroughly aroused, and now he wanted his own moments—at which point the six thousand students in the stadium roared their approval. The heckling nonetheless continued as he spoke. Then militants began moving up and around the platform, in so threatening a fashion that David Gardner and others moved down with them to protect the Chancellor. Once again the Chancellor pleaded for free speech, once again the crowd responded enthusiastically, and suddenly cherry bombs were exploding beneath his chair, making many think that shots were being fired, and transfixing everyone in their places. As Cheadle was later escorted from the stadium, it was plain that a virulent shift in mood against the most radical militants had occurred among the students.[14]

Goodspeed and I went to the chancellor's campus residence immediately after the speech. He was preparing to leave for medical treatment in Santa Barbara, having been burned by the cherry bombs that had been thrown directly under him on stage. They were not inconsequential burns, and he was in pain, although he never flinched on stage when they went off and never once complained subsequently.

The Chancellor

I thought of Cheadle's sturdy character and sense of duty exhibited in such a public and awkward setting and how, in spite of his being attacked, maligned, and otherwise abused throughout the past two years by parties both on and off campus, how privileged I was to serve under him and to learn from him during six years at Santa Barbara; and conversely, how cowardly, cynical, hypocritical, manipulative, and duplicitous were the worst of the radical students we were dealing with. I found myself regarding them only with contempt.

When the chancellor handled problems like these a year earlier, his questions of us were to the point, his reactions clear, and his decisions crisp. As the year wore on, however, his responses had less preciseness and confidence, which I attributed to his fatigue and to unrelenting pressure, from Governor Reagan and those who agreed with him on the one hand, and on the other from the radical elements on and off campus, the objectives of these warring factions, of course, being mutually exclusive. Little by little our conversations with the chancellor changed, and by fall 1969 Goodspeed and I would explain a problem to him, share our analysis, and select a preferred option from among the many under consideration. Instead of waiting for the chancellor's decision, we now said that unless the chancellor was to instruct us otherwise by, say 10:00 A.M., the preferable option, as described, would be his assumed preference as well and we would proceed accordingly.

The chancellor took no exception whatsoever to this subtle but significant change in decision making. Neither Goodspeed nor I welcomed it, as we held the chancellor in the highest regard, knew what he was going through, and supported him throughout. But he was at the eye of the hurricane. He was chancellor. We were just there to help him. Being chancellor, especially under these conditions, was a lonely and vulnerable position.

The Final Riots

The final saga of 1969–70 played out from June 4 until mid-June, before the students had completed their studies and left campus, some for the summer and others, thankfully, forever. It started when a grand jury indicted seventeen persons accused of having participated in the burning of the Bank of America on February 25. Two days after the grand jury indictments, a protest rally of about two thousand was held on campus. Here was another and final chance for the radicals to cause trouble, and they did. The rally led directly to a series of events in Isla Vista that night, with the bank once again the magnet of protest and attack. Adjoining buildings were not spared.

A series of major skirmishes took place in Isla Vista over the next several nights between police and rioters (not protesters), with injuries on both sides and a marked escalation of numbers and a hardening of hearts and tactics. A curfew was once again ordered by the county, but this time the Los Angeles County Special Forces unit, not the National Guard, was called in to restore order, and things went from bad to worse in a hurry. Members of the administration, faculty, and staff were present in appreciable numbers trying to cool things down, and members of the Isla Vista clergy, working with their parishioners and others who had chosen to come into this volatile and risky environment, helped as they could.

One problem was the curfew itself, which took effect at 7:00 P.M. As this was in early June, and the academic year was on a quarter system, finals were scheduled and went until 10:00 P.M. Well into the night and early morning hours we talked with law enforcement officials about the best way to handle the protests and rioting while maintaining the schedule for finals, and deliberating from midnight to 3:00 A.M., as we so often did, took its toll. The administration had been on a round-the-clock schedule for months; we were not only exhausted, but nerves were raw and patience thin. After all, we also had our regular workloads. As evidence of the exceptional level of stress we all experienced, I had already been hospitalized for two weeks earlier in the spring, having contracted an acute and enduring bronchial infection by burning the candle at both ends. But this time we were not just dealing with rioting students and malcontents; we were dealing with rioting police as well, as Kelley reports:

Suddenly, a new element entered the scene: the Special Forces of the Los Angeles County Sheriff's Department. They arrived to join local police in a major effort to impose order through the massive use of force.

These new arrivals were under no local control, they had no local loyalties or ties, and they interpreted the curfew, which referred to loitering near "public places," to mean that everyone in Isla Vista was to remain inside their dwellings, with doors and windows closed. In effect, they were imprisoned after 7 P.M. People were arrested in their yards and on balconies; in scores of instances doors were broken down without warning in "hot pursuit"; property was maliciously destroyed; people were beaten with nightsticks, thrown against walls, dragged by the hair, and sexually molested. More than thirty people who were beaten were not even arrested, in circumstances when hundreds were being detained. Gas canisters were freely thrown into yards and dwelling places, and arrested persons were subjected to physical abuse, especially in crowded jail circumstances. (The Los Angeles Special Forces, after massive public criticism of their grossly illegal violence on this occasion, were later quietly dissolved, though all official investigations were quashed.)

During all this disorder, many UCSB students were jailed, and both Assistant Vice Chancellor Gardner and Vice Chancellor Goodspeed nightly visited them, to stay in touch and offer assistance. Then it became apparent that a new crisis was approaching. There was no way for students to take final examinations during the nighttime hours and still be back in their Isla Vista apartments before the 7 P.M. curfew. A meeting was convened between University administrators and the sheriff's forces and those of the Highway Patrol in which, after two hours of discussion, the police agencies finally agreed to allow the University to transport the students back to their homes by bus. On the night of the 10th of June, ten school buses lined up at Robertson Gymnasium, ready to depart in convoy at 10:15 P.M., and 700 students got on board. With Goodspeed in a leading Highway Patrol automobile, Dean of Men Robert Evans in one following, and a monitor in each bus, all of them equipped with walkie-talkie radios, this extraordinary procession began its slow movement through Isla Vista, stopping at designated corners to let students disembark. Helicopters circled overhead, and burned-out automobiles from the days of violence littered the scene.

By now, almost 300 people had been at various times arrested, and the *Santa Barbara News-Press* was calling for an end to the curfew and to the arresting of innocent persons, the illegal entering of homes, police terrorism, and widespread violations of civil rights. When hundreds of people, including the newly elected Isla Vista Community Council and members of a faculty-clergy observers group, gathered in a massive sit-in protest against such lawlessness in an area by the bank called "Perfect Park" in Isla Vista, the climax was reached. Several hundred people submitted nonviolently to arrest. Then, without warning the crowd was suddenly instructed to disperse and attacked with clouds of gas and flailing nightsticks.

Chancellor Cheadle issued a statement implying that a closing of the campus was imminent. Tension was greatly eased when Vice Chancellor Goodspeed was able to get through to a friend in the Governor's office in Sacramento, and persuade the authorities there to authorize a lifting of the curfew until 11:00 P.M. in the evening, thus allowing students to return to their apartments after nighttime examinations. On June 12, 1970, the curfew was finally lifted entirely.[15]

A modest elaboration on Kelley's excellent account may help further illuminate some of these events. Goodspeed and I would routinely be in Isla Vista at night and on campus, dividing our efforts so as to spread our observations of these events. Following the arrests (and there were hundreds of them), we would visit students in the crowded county jail in Santa Barbara, taking notes that seemed to be urgent, admonishing and comforting where that seemed to be right, and doing what we could to help both the students and the officers guarding them to get along.

One night as we entered, a young woman shouted for our attention. As we responded, she said that the teargas in the area had forced her out of her second-story apartment and into the courtyard below. Not knowing what was really happening but curious to know, she left her sleeping baby under the stairwell and stepped out onto the sidewalk just in time to be caught up in a police sweep.

"Would you please check on my baby," she asked, and see that the baby was taken care of until she could obtain bail the next day. We did so immediately. The baby was still there, sound asleep, and we had her brought to the jail for her mother's care. In the chaos of such events, the innocent get swept up as easily as the guilty, and the police under enormous pressure, stress, and public expectations do their best while being subject to the worst kinds of verbal abuse and physical danger throughout (but I do not mean to excuse the behavior of extremists on both sides, who it seemed could hardly wait to get at each other night after night).

I also recall being with the convoy of buses that went into Isla Vista. Goodspeed was in the lead. The dean of men was next. I was in the last bus. All the streetlights were out. Helicopters lighted our way with searchlights. Police cars flanked, preceded, and followed our route. Trash bins and cars were on fire at many of the intersections, thus the need for a preceding truck with a large blade to push these obstacles aside. Teargas was everywhere as were police in full riot gear, at once on edge and tired, tending to overreact as the evening went on and concrete, rocks, nails, and other missiles and hard objects rained down on them not only from the streets but from apartments and balconies as well, or even catapulted from considerable distances with devastating effect. In the middle of this near war scene, we stopped every other block to let students get off and run for their apartments. Each student whose final was scheduled after the curfew received transportation into Isla Vista and a pass authorizing him or her to move between the bus and his or her apartments within a five-minute period or risk arrest.

It was such a nasty scene and the students on my bus were so distraught that Goodspeed and I went straight to the commander of the special forces. We explained our concerns and proposed that some "give" by the county on the curfew would help dampen the crisis; and would he support such a move? We thought this was essential or the next night was going to make the evening just passed seem like a picnic. We got nowhere! Instead we were lectured, as though we were children, about this being an insurrection and they had been called in to put it down and they intended to do so.

Goodspeed and I then drove to the chancellor's house on campus. We woke him up, it being about 12:30 A.M. We told him how the convoy and the evening in Isla Vista had gone, the police commander's reaction to our suggestions, the large number of arrests made, the mood of the contending parties, and the need for the curfew to be put over until after the close of finals the next night or, in our opinion, we could expect and would face a very real disaster.

I also remember adding that if I were a parent and really knew what the conditions were, I would pull my son or daughter out of the university first thing in the morning; and that we had a duty to the parents who were not present to secure the safety of their students studying at UCSB. Thus, if we could not get an extension of the curfew, I argued, we should close the campus the following morning. We could work out the academic consequences later. Goodspeed agreed and so did the chancellor.

Early the next day, through a series of conversations with President Hitch and key people in the governor's office, the last one involving President Hitch, Chancellor Cheadle, Goodspeed, and myself with the governor, Reagan agreed to intervene and do what he could to persuade the county board of supervisors to move the curfew to 11:00 P.M., to replace the Los Angeles County Special Forces unit with the California Highway Patrol, and anything else within his authority that we thought needed to be done. As our conversation concluded, Reagan said with a laugh that while he was happy to help us, if anything went wrong it would be on our heads, not his. We said that was fair enough as he was responding to our request, we were not responding to his, and that we would shoulder the full responsibility for the outcome.

The start of the curfew was put back from 7:00 P.M. until 11:00 P.M., thanks to the intervention of the governor and the insistent efforts of Vice-Chancellor Goodspeed, the chancellor, and others working with the county board of supervisors. The extension was announced about 6:00 P.M. Thus, there was no need for a second convoy into Isla Vista. Students returned to their apartments after finals with little incident. I was present in Isla Vista, of course, just before the curfew went into effect. The California Highway Patrol was in place in a single file around the commercial district. Large numbers of students were across the street from this thin line of police. One or two of the officers, about the age of most of the students, cracked a couple of jokes. The students responded in kind, the curfew came, the students left, and the year 1969–70 was over, commencement excepted, which proved to be as pleasant and as uninterrupted an occasion as possible under the circumstances.

I told Libby as it all ended, "If I had wanted this kind of life, I would have gone to West Point or accepted one of the multiple offers the CIA made on my return from Korea." Those two academic years stood out as the most consequential in my brief service with the University of California, not the most pleasant, satisfying, or rewarding ones, in which I gained an uncommon level of real work experience in a very politicized, charged, unrelenting, and unforgiving administrative and media environment.

During the protests the lives of thousands of students were stimulated and invigorated. But the lives of thousands more were bruised, battered, harmed, and bewildered and often enduringly. The professional careers of capable, long-serving, and often distinguished academic administrators and some senior faculty members were also prematurely concluded, often under sad and unforgiving circumstances. Because of these protests, the politics of the state changed, the attitudes of the California public hardened against the university, and the norms of academic life were fundamentally and permanently altered. Whatever the gains, the costs were dreadful and yet rarely mentioned, it should be added, as the recollections of these times have come to be memorialized in mostly self-congratulatory assertions as unbalanced as they are unaccountable.

Those indelible events remain etched into my consciousness and burned into my memory. I learned how very much alone the person is who carries decision-making authority under conditions such as those we confronted; how confident and unforgiving the views and judgments of noncombatants and "Monday morning quarterbacks" can be when they know nothing of the facts and the real world with which we were dealing; how reluctant most faculty members are to get mixed up in matters of this kind; how readily students believe the worst of authority and the best of those challenging it; how easily misled the public and how willingly misleading the media. I came to recognize how important it was to have advisers who would speak their minds; how crucial it was to explain decisions to all interested parties in a timely and open manner; and how an administrator working under these circumstances and looking for any acknowledgment of a job well done would be as well advised "to go buy a dog," or so my friend Derek Bok, president of Harvard, later told me at the time I was retiring from the University of California in 1992.

On the more positive side of the coin, I learned once again that the political center of gravity fits between the opposite ends of the political spectrum and how crucial it was, therefore, that the center hold during times of stress. Otherwise, the pressures from the opposite extremes will weaken the center and thus destabilize the consensus of views and opinions upon which rest the means of settling disputes and managing or resolving conflict; that most students, faculty, staff, alumni, and the public were well intentioned even when misled and that you simply had to work harder to gain their confidence; that persons of goodwill could be very much at odds, one with another; that to reconcile differences without compromising either of the contending parties or those whose counsel and advice you had sought and whose judgment you respected was crucial; that there is a difference between finding an answer that satisfied and discovering a solution that worked; that after most controversies had ended there is a rush to penalize the innocent and reward the guilty; and that the world at large is not nearly as rational as those within the academy prefer to believe and, of course, neither are they.

Isla Vista

Some general observations about the "student ghetto" of Isla Vista are now warranted, for its peculiarities played a marked and consequential role in the political activities and violence that came to characterize the academic year 1969–70.

Isla Vista—or IV, as everyone called it—encompassed an area of nearly 350 acres, with a population of some 13,000 persons in 1969, of whom some 9,000 were enrolled students. Most of the remaining residents were late-stage teenagers and twenty-somethings. There were some families, but even fewer mature adults having more than a transitory stake in the community. Except for roughly a hundred single-family homes, its residents lived in multiple-unit housing. County services were sparse to nonexistent, except for infrequent police patrols. Landlords mostly lived elsewhere. IV had no local government, few sidewalks, and no parks or other urban amenities characteristic of the average community of this size; its mobile student population (new freshmen, graduating seniors, transfers, and so forth) and transient population of other youth came and went as events unfolded and interests attracted. These conditions, with the added complication of highly concentrated drug usage within that age group, was tinder for the slightest spark.

The excessive rate of UCSB's growth between the years of 1958, when the student body numbered 1,450, and 1970, when enrollments reached nearly 14,000, drove IV's development. Neither the county nor the university was willing to accord IV's buildup a priority high enough to change this dysfunctional "community." Both bore sufficient responsibility for its haphazard growth as to make their respective burdens unavoidable. I recall many a discussion of what the university might do to help with planning and implementing a reasonable set of civic and cultural amenities within IV—or even to acquire the area—but the talk went nowhere, the conclusion being that the university had no authority beyond its boundaries. The county and the developers did not welcome any such expansion of university interest, and the students seemed to prefer the personal freedom IV offered to the more guarded character of university-owned housing on campus. As things fell out, the price paid by IV residents, UCSB students, faculty and staff, the University of California, and the larger Santa Barbara community proved to be very high indeed.[16]

These impressions of IV and the others noted above were what I took away from my UCSB years, grateful for the colleagues and friends with whom I had worked and played, deeply appreciative of the chancellor and his wife for all they had done for Libby and me and our family. And I was keenly aware of how young and inexperienced I really was when President Hitch asked me in fall 1970 to join his staff in Berkeley, as the university's newest and youngest (at thirty-seven) vice president and university dean for extension and summer sessions. The chancellor urged me to accept, but with very mixed emotions, as we had come to work together both well and closely. With the family's support I accepted, and we moved over the Christmas holidays from our home in Santa Barbara to a new one just east of the Berkeley hills in the small town of Lafayette, then twenty minutes by car from my new offices in Berkeley.

A NEW ASSIGNMENT: WORKING WITH HITCH

Charles J. Hitch was a Rhodes scholar at Oxford University in 1932. Subsequently Hitch was asked to join the Oxford faculty, the first American Rhodes ever so chosen. He served at Queens College from 1935 to 1948 with leave for wartime services in the Office of Strategic Services, the Central Intelligence Agency's predecessor, with major responsibility for conceptualizing the strategic bombing of Europe by Allied forces. Later he joined Robert McNamara as one of his key advisers in the U.S. Department of Defense under Presidents Kennedy and Johnson before joining Clark Kerr's administrative team as vice president for administration in 1966.

President Hitch was a brilliant, soft-spoken, somewhat retiring, and reflective person, albeit not in the least unsociable, who exhibited time and again an uncommon level of integrity and resolve. He succeeded Harry Wellman, the acting president of the university, in 1968 and served as president until 1975. His calm, fair, honest, and open way of dealing with everyone served the university admirably during the turbulent years of 1968–70 and thereafter as he sought to reunite a Board of Regents bitterly divided over the dismissal of Kerr and the ensuing turmoil and student protests raging acutely and visibly on the University of California's nine campuses.

This was no easy task, seeing as how Ronald Reagan was governor and, therefore, a regent and one who attended board meetings quite often, unlike his predecessors. Other ex officio regents chose to attend mostly because the governor did: the lieutenant governor, the Speaker of the state Assembly, and the superintendent of public instruction, all elected politicians and each with his own political agenda. As to the appointed regents, they too were a mixed group, by and large doing the best they could under difficult and stressful conditions and caught up in the same crosscurrents of public opinion, student unrest, faculty restiveness, and national distress about the Vietnam War as everyone else. Nearly all came to respect and support Hitch.

During the storms of student unrest, political intrusions and pressures, public alienation, fiscal exigencies, and low morale that characterized the university during most of his years as president, Hitch managed to bring UC into the security of a breakwater so that in the mid-1970s the university was once again able to think more about its future and less about the debilitating events of the immediate past.

The Extended University

One of the initiatives that Hitch pushed and supported was the development of what is today called "distance learning," and what in the University of California was then called the "extended university."

The idea of an *extended university*, to facilitate and expand enrollment in degree programs for adult, part-time students studying away from campus and at times more convenient to them, had been considered at an all-university faculty conference on the Davis campus in spring 1970. This particular conference (I attended as one of the Santa Barbara representatives) concluded its deliberations by endorsing the extended university in principle and charged the president and Academic Senate with the responsibility of determining the university's interest and readiness for this initiative. This idea was a rather radical one for a university that until then had been quite willing to support off-campus courses offered by University Extension to some 325,000 persons annually, so long as it was self-supporting financially and did not confuse courses being offered with degrees being awarded.

This was not a California movement, nor a regional one, but a national effort being made by colleges and universities elsewhere and encouraged by foundations and national commissions. The objective was to take account of the new technologies available for teaching, the changing lifestyles and work habits of the American public, the unrelieved pressure for greater access to higher education and more equal educational opportunity, the desire of government to reduce higher education's unit costs of instruction, especially in consideration of enrollment increases then being contemplated, the unmistakable preference of some full-time students to mix part-time study with work, and the growing desire of the fully employed to combine work on the job or at home with periodic full-time or part-time study. A report on this subject by the Carnegie Commission on Higher Education, chaired by Clark Kerr, endorsed a mix of ages "on the job and in the classroom" and pointed out that "sharply compartmentalized roles" isolated students versus workers.[17]

UCLA's dean of extension, Leonard Freedman, a nationally respected figure in extension work, was appointed by Hitch in July 1970 to chair a universitywide task force on the extended university; and I was appointed as university dean of extension and vice president for the extended university and public service in fall 1970 with effect from January 1, 1971.

The basic organizational arrangements for the extended university were assigned to me to work out. Funds for pilot programs were authorized by the president and passed to me for handling. My office undertook studies to determine the university's capabilities to mount these programs, and a special review committee of key members of the Academic Senate formed to review the task force report and expedite the Academic Senate's response. We also set out to assess the impact of this initiative on the university's several libraries, to survey the attitudes of potential students, including the university's undergraduates, to plan for and implement pilot programs on several of the campuses, and to plan our approach to the State of California for both immediate and longer-term state funding.

I was responsible for coordinating and overseeing all these endeavors both within the Office of the President and across the university's nine campuses and for representing Hitch in the Academic Senate's review of this matter, in the legislative hearings in Sacramento, and in our dealings with the Educational Testing Service, the Corporation for Public Broadcasting, the U.S. Department of Education, and the executive office of the president of the United States.

I mention this set of interested parties, and it is not exhaustive, to point out how complicated, time-consuming, and constituent-driven is any effort by a large and influential university to try something—anything—new, as almost any one of the parties can by its opposition or its silence bring the endeavor to a halt or at least slow it down to the point of freeze-frames. But the flip side to the problems of dealing with a multitude of constituencies and a large bureaucracy is working with coalitions and gaining leverage for trades and nuanced understandings. Taken together, the positives more than overcome the negatives. There was support enough for the extended university to permit us to get under way and not enough opposition to prevent it, as favorable an outcome as could be expected in this contentious and difficult environment.

The Academic Council's report was favorable and set forth agreeable conditions for our proceeding. The president included a request for state funding for the next fiscal year (1973–74). In July 1972 the university's consortium for the extended university appointed to oversee this work was activated by Hitch, and with the consortium's advice and the president's support we got under way.[18] During the 1972–73 academic year we were able to secure approval for ten new degree programs to be offered as part of UC's extended university. They were campus-specific, campus-determined, and campus-controlled. The extended university was *not* a tenth campus but a means for campuses to experiment with efforts to offer older, part-time students the chance to earn a UC degree, off campus and at convenient times. These ten programs, one on each campus except for two at Riverside, enrolled 601 students. Eight of them started in fall 1972, and two were to begin in winter 1973. Five were professional master's degrees, and five were for junior and senior students.[19]

Some of the chancellors and the deans of university extension on the nine campuses were not confident that the extended university would complement rather than constrict their own highly successful extension and adult education programs. Thanks to the unqualified support of Hitch and that of Chester McCorkle, the university's lead vice president, I was able to deal with the chancellors and deans and with the Academic Senate at the statewide level throughout these first eighteen months. Chet was committed to the extended university, having worked at Davis, a campus featuring the university's principal agricultural college and the cooperative extension activities supporting them, including agricultural field stations and experimental stations sprinkled across California.

As a vice president and university dean, I came to understand the workings of a multicampus system, to appreciate the complexities of decision and policy making within the overall university, to apprehend both the need for and the difficulty of seeking counsel and advice from all the major stakeholders, and to glimpse the intricacies and interplay of power among and between the university's own extensive bureaucracy and the state's bureaucracies as well. I found the challenge of this tutorial, however formidable and risky, to be an altogether agreeable one and that I was giving as well as I seemed to be taking.

I was also making many friends throughout the university's nine campuses and in state government as I tried to generate support for the extended university or, at least, to mute or to otherwise mitigate outright hostility. I am especially proud of having persuaded Governor Reagan, principally through his education adviser, Alex Sherriffs, UCB's much-criticized vice-chancellor for student affairs in 1964–65 during the FSM, to support the university's proposal for the extended university in the governor's 1973–74 budget, the only new UC program the governor funded during his early years in office ($1.5 million).

The role of the faculty in the university's system of shared governance also became clearer to me. I found that members of the faculty, while not always sympathetic to this effort, were always courteous and made their views known in thoughtful and reasoned ways. I was also learning a great deal about the university itself, quite apart from the extended university, as a member of the president's cabinet and, thus, involved in nearly all the issues confronting the university from 1971 to 1973. Two examples will perhaps suffice.

Lessons from Hitch

Hitch invited me into his office one afternoon to check on some marginal notes I had made in the draft of a speech he was preparing. He was relaxed, sitting back in his chair and enjoying a huge cigar. His desk was free of paper or clutter of any kind, and I asked, how could he maintain such a clean desk? He laughed, stubbed out his cigar, leaned forward with a smile, and said, "That's why I have you and the other vice presidents around."

As we were working on the draft, a telephone call came in from one of our representatives in Sacramento. Hitch relit his cigar, asked one or two questions, confirmed the $10 million figure they were discussing, thanked the caller, and hung up. "Well," he said, "our operating budget was just cut $10 million by the legislative committee hearing our budget in the State Assembly. The cut came because we refused to admit to UC San Francisco's Medical School the son of a prominent contributor to one of the state's most powerful politicians. I want you always to remember, Dave," he went on, leaning forward for emphasis, "that this is the price we have to pay to maintain the university's independence from these and other kinds of untoward political pressures." I said I would remember it.

The second example was at a midyear meeting of the Board of Regents at UCLA, in 1971 or 1972. The president was reporting the outcome of the state budget. When he got to the university's portion he noted, as Governor Reagan sat next to him, that whereas the governor's budget for UC had been woefully inadequate, Regent Robert Moretti, then Speaker of the Assembly and a Democrat, had persuaded the legislature to improve it dramatically, and how "appreciative we all are of Regent Moretti's efforts."

During Hitch's report, I noticed Governor Reagan frowning and just barely able to hold back what he was thinking. Moretti, sitting directly across the table from Reagan and Hitch, was beaming. Hitch went on, "There is language in the Budget Act, however, and inserted with Regent Moretti's concurrence, that directs the Board of Regents to rescind its action of last year to close the School of Criminology at Berkeley and that the regents' failure to do so would result in major budgetary penalties being levied on UC's budget."

Hitch looked up at Moretti who was sitting directly across from him, smiled, and said, "This budget language is, of course, unconstitutional. It is for the regents, not the legislature, to decide such matters and I have no present or future intention of inviting a reconsideration of this matter by the board." Now Moretti was frowning and Reagan was beaming. I remember thinking to myself, this is *exactly* the way to handle the matter—or even to manage and govern the university. And both Reagan and Moretti will respect him for having handled it this way.

TO UTAH

My involvement in the extended university came to an end in summer 1973 when I was offered and accepted the position of president of the University of Utah. This was a very hard decision for our family and for me to take: another move in barely two and a half years, and away from our native California.

Hitch urged me to take the job. "We'll get you back eventually," he said, "and meanwhile you'll gain experience of a kind you will need with your own campus and at a respected and growing university." So accept we did, leaving behind a fine staff to carry on the extended university's work—Keith Sexton, Bob Jones, Pat Johnson, Irma Smith, and others—and our many friends and colleagues throughout the university, on the Board of Regents, in the president's office, and on the campuses. As with Santa Barbara, it was a new chapter in our lives and, while we turned the page with much sadness, we also did so with much excitement about what it would all mean for our family.

The extended university helped UC probe its opportunities in distance learning at a time when most others were just starting to think about it. UC missed a very real opportunity in deciding to drop this program after Hitch's retirement in 1975. We missed the chance to be on the cutting edge of the changes in higher education that our country's colleges and universities today are considering and adopting nearly everywhere, using new technologies to change the way students learn, both on campus and off. Instead of being at the back of the curve as the university is today, it could have been one of the national leaders.

In early August 1973 we set out for Salt Lake City and the University of Utah and our new state of residence. Leaving California was not easy, nor was it easy to leave the University of California, with which we had been affiliated for fifteen years. What we did not know was that we were on our way to a university that we would also come to love, were privileged to serve, and where for the next ten years we would enjoy an uninterrupted honeymoon.

THREE

SERVING THE UNIVERSITY OF UTAH

ANOTHER TRANSITION

The decision to step away from my position at the University of California and into the presidency of the University of Utah may seemed to have been a perfectly logical step, but it was not. We would be leaving our native California, family, and friends as well as the university that was such an enriching part of our family's cultural, intellectual, and social life. Moreover, our four daughters, ages four to twelve, would be changing schools, adjusting to new friends and home circumstances; and Libby would be setting up our new home in Salt Lake City, having just done so in Lafayette after our move from Santa Barbara.

We knew very few people in Utah, apart from several hundred relatives. We were not professionally or socially acquainted with anyone either on or off campus. We knew none of the state's leadership in government, business, academic, or religious circles. We had only our childhood recollections of the state that were as limited as they were dated. And for me, as for most men, it was going to be much easier moving into a new position with its built-in support and in-place colleagues than for Libby, who was more on her own, regardless of how much help I tried to be.

And yet we knew Utah's history, understood its culture and values, recognized the changes that were occurring in the state with its growing prosperity and substantial in-migration, and appreciated the warm and generous outpouring of goodwill that attended my appointment and our arrival.

My memories of Utah had always been warm and full of respect for a people who made the most of what little they had, worked hard for what they earned, regarded education as a right and accepted their responsibility to support it as a duty, nurtured the arts, and loved and valued family and friends.

A Place to Stay

The only glitch was our decision on housing. The university owned a modest home not far from the campus, where one of the university's vice presidents and his family had been living. It was offered to our family to serve as the President's House, there having been no official home for the president for decades. The size and internal design of the home, however well suited to a couple with one or at the most two children, were not right for us. We proposed that the home be sold (it was, and at a gain), and that a larger one be acquired in the general neighborhood, which we liked very much. A house to fit our family *and* serve as an official residence for purposes of entertaining and university functions was found and purchased at a cost of $125,000 (it had 4,500 square feet). This transaction captured the media's interest, and critical articles on the cost of the home appeared in the city's two major and competing newspapers. All this preceded our arrival in Utah and, fortunately, was complete before I took office on August 1, 1973.

In the latter part of July 1973 I attended a Board of Regents' meeting in Cedar City, Utah, for the purpose of becoming better acquainted with the regents and the Utah commissioner for higher education, Dr. G. Homer Durham, former president of Arizona State University and a distinguished and well known Utah educator. Much to my surprise, the issue of the house was scheduled for discussion by the regents. Peter Billings, the regents' chairman and a prominent Salt Lake attorney, casually mentioned to me as we were heading into the afternoon board meeting that as the President's House had been the object of not inconsiderable public interest and criticism, the regents intended to discuss the matter briefly and then table any action on it until "the furor died down."

I was startled, to say the least, and observed that we had sold our California home and planned to leave for Utah within a week, so what should we be planning to do in light of the board's apparent intentions; and "why was I seemingly the last to know when I was the most affected?" He said, "Well, you'll just have to find another place to stay until this matter can be worked out" and ignored the second part of my question. My reaction, however injudicious, was appropriate. I responded, not only did "I have no intention of moving my family twice, but no intention of moving it once unless this matter is resolved today one way or another." He looked at me incredulously and, without further comment, walked into the meeting. Commissioner

Durham then came over to assure me that "this would all work out in good time and that I should be patient."

I said in a very calm and steady voice just what I had said to Regent Billings and added that the members of the university's Institutional Council—a local board with limited but important governing authority, which had bought the house under delegated authority from the state Board of Regents—would not take kindly to this delay, as it would reflect on their judgment and authority, that the press rather than allowing this issue to die down would choose instead to build it up if action on the matter was delayed. Moreover, being unable to count on the board's goodwill, especially at the outset of my work in Utah, I felt more than mere disquietude. I asked that the matter be voted up or down before the day's business was done. He said, "You really mean that, don't you?" I assured him I did.

The issue was approved by a voice vote. It was not tabled and it was not debated. The commissioner explained to the press the history of the house purchase, why this was an altogether reasonable outcome, that the regents and the Institutional Council were of one mind and that the matter was not going to be reconsidered at a later date under any circumstance.

It was very interesting to observe in Utah, and later in California, how much stock others placed on where our family wished to live: they seemed to feel entitled to assert their preferences over that of the governing board and the president. Others were not living there, we were. No two president's family circumstances are the same, yet the President's House is what it is. An incoming president, therefore, is not uncommonly subject to criticism or resentment if remodeling or new furnishings are thought to be needed; and similarly resented, if the university president's house should be found incompatible with the needs of the new president's family.

No small number of university presidents have either lost their jobs or have chosen to leave their posts over matters of where and under what circumstances other people (regents or trustees, alumni, donors, legislators, faculty members, staff, and interested others) expect the president and his or her family to reside, regardless of the myriad circumstances that obtain. If I had it to do all over again, I would buy my own home, finance it through a conventional mortgage arrangement with a bank or mortgage lending company or mortgage broker, and negotiate a base salary and housing allowance sufficient to cover this increment of my living costs.

THE UNIVERSITY OF UTAH

The University of Utah's 1,500-acre campus sits astride Salt Lake City's east bench, looking west to the Salt Lake valley and beyond to the Great Salt Lake and east at the Wasatch Range of the Rocky Mountains that rises abruptly from the university's easternmost boundary. The site is breathtaking and the campus handsomely laid out with an impressive mix of old and new buildings, roughly half of them constructed between 1960 and 1973. Another major spurt in building was to occur during my tenure, when we were able to increase the campus's capacity by about one-third as well as to secure additional lands for the university's long-term needs.

Founded in 1850 as the University of Deseret, it is one of the oldest universities west of the Missouri River. Its founding was an audacious act of faith for the small Mormon pioneer community, then housed mostly in small log cabins and barely meeting its most elementary needs in the heart of the nearly unpopulated Great Basin and western desert. But education counted in that community, not only for its intrinsic worth but also because it was the only way up for a people who had been driven from their homes by mobs from Ohio to Missouri to Illinois and then west in the harsh winter of 1846, crossing the frozen Mississippi River into Indian Territory in February of that year. They subsequently blazed the Mormon Trail across the Great Plains the following year to the heart of the Rocky Mountains, with the first wagon trains entering Salt Lake valley on July 24, 1847. As a desired, indeed needed, dimension of this remote territory's educational, intellectual, and cultural life, a university was rated as a high priority even then.

Utah's people are proud of this early commitment to education, and not only of their history but also of the fact that Utah today ranks nearly at the top of all fifty states in the percentage of young people completing high school, the percentage of high school graduates going on to college or university work, and the percentage of those entering higher education who complete it. As a Mormon, I was well aware of this history and these values. My job, therefore, was not to promote these values or encourage these attitudes, but rather to maintain the quality of Utah's education in general and that of higher education in particular and to hope to improve it over time. This would be an expected role for me to play, as the University of Utah was the state's "flagship" university and its most important and influential educational institution.

My knowledge of the University of Utah's reputation, however, had been gained not from any personal contact or association, but rather from the opinions of national leaders in the professions and in academic circles. I knew the university to be a well balanced teaching and research-oriented institution and headed for first-tier ranking at an accelerating pace. When I was invited by the regents to become the university's tenth president, everything I learned only strengthened my opinion of its standing and prospects.

I was especially impressed with the breadth, depth, and balance of the academic program. The university's financial resources, historically sparse by comparison with most institutions of similar reputation, character, and scale, had been effectively deployed and prudently administered. Its laboratories, libraries, clinics, and museums were good to excellent but also needing further development. The campus was stunningly beautiful, well planned, and brought to a state of harmony and coherence by people who obviously cared.

I found members of the faculty to be fully deserving of their national reputation for teaching excellence, albeit with considerable unevenness in the quality and scope of the research. The students were to be a source of enduring pleasure. The staff was loyal, competent, and hardworking, and the alumni and major donors were both supportive and anxious to assist in the university's further growth and development.

There was also an acceptable balance among and between the university's sources of funding. The dependence on federal dollars was disproportionate in some areas, but the state's share of total expenditures, as compared with the share the students paid in tuition and fees, was reasonable. The auxiliary agencies, self-supporting parts of the university's program, were fiscally sound. The level of private giving in absolute terms needed some tending, but as a proportion of total university income, gifts represented a not unreasonable share.

Since Salt Lake City is both state capital and home to the university, I found a disquieting level of distrust between several powerful legislators and the university, a less than fully committed relationship between the business community and the campus, an uncomfortable level of tension between the university and the state's other colleges and universities, and a sense of unease between town and gown generally.

While community and governmental relationships needed tending, the task seemed to me to be attainable as people *cared* about the university, rejoicing with it on some occasions and expressing their concern on others, but never indifferent. Thus, with any degree of luck and the right kind of committed effort, the outlook for continuing qualitative as well as quantitative growth was favorable.

In 1973 the U, as it is commonly referred to, was one of roughly fifty to seventy-five major American research universities, depending on the criteria employed. It enrolled 21,000 students drawn from all of Utah's twenty-nine counties, all fifty states, and more than fifty foreign countries. The academic program was housed in a graduate school, three colleges, and eleven professional schools, including one of the nation's most esteemed medical schools and health science centers. Bachelor's degrees were offered in sixty-four fields of study and there was a rich array of programs offered at the master's and doctoral levels throughout the university's curricula, both in letters and science and the professions.

The teaching faculty of roughly 2,500 persons included approximately 1,600 on the professorial scale. The campus is within five minutes of downtown Salt Lake City, with its symphony, ballet, theater, dance and opera companies, its galleries, shops, and restaurants. Several of North America's premier ski resorts are thirty to forty-five minutes to the east, and the adjacent mountain wilderness reaches north to the Idaho and Wyoming borders and east to Colorado. To the west is the Great Basin Desert, shared with Nevada, whose western boundary touches the eastern foothills of California's Sierra Nevada. It is a spectacular setting for a university, and the University of Utah made the most of it in recruiting distinguished scholars and scientists and outstanding graduate students to the campus from throughout the world.

The Utah System of Higher Education

Utah's nine public colleges and universities—from Utah State University in Logan, near the Idaho border in the north, to Dixie College in St. George, at the border with Arizona to the south and Nevada to the west—are governed by a system of dual boards, one for the system as a whole (then the state Board of Higher Education and later the state Board of Regents) and one for each college and university (the Institutional Council and later the Board of Trustees), both the regents and trustees being appointed by the state's governor to four-year terms.

The presidents are appointed by the Board of Regents, whose executive officer is the commissioner of higher education. He is not the *system's* chief executive officer but the *board's* chief executive officer. The presidents work with the commissioner but not for him. They report directly to the regents, as does the commissioner. This somewhat awkward structure is inherently susceptible to various interpretations about who had what authority and who decided what. But it worked in Utah because the people involved got along and wanted it to work. In California it would not have worked for a week.

The state's population in 1973 was 1.2 million, concentrated along a thin urban strip running between Utah Lake and the Great Salt Lake to the west, the Wasatch Range rising out of the valley floor on the east, and from Provo in the south, home of Brigham Young University, to Ogden, 45 miles north of Salt Lake City. The state's population was roughly 70 percent Mormon with the rural communities being populated mostly by persons of that faith. Salt Lake City was roughly one-half Mormon and one-half persons of other faiths. The politics of this needed to be understood, but once understood could be handled.

The Politics

The legislature, unlike California's nearly full-time and unrelenting law-making machine, met for only forty-five days a year. Its members were ordinary men and women—teachers, farmers, ranchers, technicians, electricians, carpenters, homemakers, lawyers, doctors, and almost all Caucasian. The Senate was dominated by members of the Mormon faith and was more conservative than the House, whose members reflected the region's diverse interests.

The Mormon Church, a dominant influence in the state with its own university in Provo (BYU), took not just one but two steps back from the public colleges and universities' affairs to avoid even the least hint of pressure, thus setting the norm for other constituents' interaction with the state's public colleges and universities.

I had the privilege of serving in what may have been the freest public university in America, free in the sense that I suffered almost no political interference from any quarter in the internal affairs and inner workings of the University of Utah during a full decade of service. On my return to California in 1983, in stark contrast, I experienced in one month more political forces seeking to work their magic on the University of California than in the entire ten years I had spent at Utah.

The Students

The university's students were mostly upwardly mobile middle-class students, coming from large families with modest resources, commuting to campus, and working part-time, determined to succeed. I liked and enjoyed working with them throughout my ten years at Utah, seeking to improve their opportunities, to keep their tuition and fees down, and to provide them with on-campus employment. Aside from occasional outbursts of adolescent exhibitionism in the student newspaper, untoward behavior and/or language at basketball and football games (especially when playing BYU), and weekend frivolity on fraternity and sorority row, just north of the campus, students at the U took their course work seriously.

The notable exception occurred during "the streaking craze" of the mid-1970s, when students would run naked through the campus, usually at the least propitious of times, for example, at homecoming, alumni and donor gatherings, Founders Day, or at commencement. All this started in the southeastern part of the country, as I recall, and knowing that it would hit conservative Utah in about two weeks, I visited with Wayne Shepard, our chief of campus police and security.

I asked Wayne to work up a plan for dealing with the inevitable streakers and report back within the week. He did and with a plan that resembled the D-Day landing of the Allies on the beaches of Normandy in World War II. I looked at it and finally said, "Wayne, let's keep this simple: If the person is streaking, let him or her run as they are more streakers than exhibitionists; but the minute they stop running, arrest them—then they are less streakers and more exhibitionists." He liked that and that's what we did.

Within a day or two I had a call from Dallin Oaks, president of BYU, a friend of mine and former classmate at BYU in the 1950s. He had a real concern about streakers appearing at BYU (understandable), and asked how we were planning to handle it at the University of Utah. I told him. He thought that was the perfect answer, but if challenged by his board (the leaders of the Mormon Church) he would refer them to me for guidance.

Student life at Utah was sheer pleasure. We dined in the residence halls, held receptions for new students each fall, attended the athletic events (football, basketball, women's gymnastics, and men's and women's skiing for the most part). I met regularly and often with the student body presidents and their associates and included the students in key decisions about buildings being renovated or constructed principally for their benefit and in which they would be financially implicated (e.g., residence halls, intramural athletic fields, the stadium, the field house, recreational facilities, the student union, the student services buildings and associated landscaping, and the foot, bicycle, and vehicular traffic patterns under consideration). The students never disappointed me, were invariably responsible, helped in substantive and critical ways, and never backed away from the ensuing financial obligations they and/or their parents were assuming or the advice they had offered.

The university had a very well organized and active student government, a campus newspaper, full of surprises and inherently unpredictable, but never grossly malicious or abused by the paper's editors, as was the case at UC Santa Barbara in the late 1960s. Fraternities and sororities played an important but not overriding part in the life of the campus, and in my view served a very useful purpose.

There was one early incident I have always recalled with a smile, involving the U's football team. I had arrived on campus in August 1973, and my secretary, Lillian Ence, said, "You know it's customary for the president to visit the football team during fall practice. They'll be expecting you within the next two weeks." I said, "Good. Please get me a copy of the upcoming season's program and I'll review the names of the players and learn something about the team." I went to the practice field two weeks later, having done my homework, watched the team from the sideline for a while, and, with a growing apprehension about the upcoming season, introduced myself to the coach. He whistled for the team, one young man arriving well ahead of the rest.

I recognized this young man from his photograph in the program because he was from Berkeley (he later played for the Green Bay Packers). So I said, "Good afternoon." He said, "Good afternoon." I said, "You are Steve Odum, aren't you?" He responded affirmatively, and I said, "And you're a graduate of Berkeley High School aren't you?" He said, "Well, yes." I said, "Well, that's great. I'm a graduate of Berkeley High School too." He said, "Oh yeah? Who the hell are you?" They knew how to keep presidents humble at the University of Utah.

The Tenure Issue

The state's very popular third-term governor in 1973 was Calvin Rampton, a prominent Salt Lake attorney and a likable and effective governor. We became and have remained good friends with him and his talented wife, Lucy Beth (recently deceased). My first introduction to Rampton had been arranged at the governor's request. But, he said much later, when I walked into his office on that day he thought I was a graduate student and discreetly consulted his calendar to be sure there had not been a mix-up. I felt grown up, of course, and found the governor to be every good thing I had heard about him, except that he could be as tough as he wished to be, a quality that on more than one occasion I came to observe and respect.

Following a brief conversation, the governor indicated that he had two purposes in asking to see me. The first was to get acquainted, and the second was to inform me of his intention to submit legislation at the upcoming session that would do away with tenure in Utah's public colleges and universities. He indicated that he did not wish to surprise me and would welcome any views that I had, including objections.

I asked, "Will your proposal be welcomed or will it be rejected?"

"No question that it will go through," he said and then added, "without any problem at all."

"I can answer you one of two ways or both, if you prefer," I responded. "One way is to recall how tenure arose in the Western university, why it arose, the purpose it serves, and the difference between freedom of speech and academic freedom, both historically and within a contemporary context."

He said, "Please spare me the lecture. I gather you take exception to this bill. What is the second reason?"

"The second reason," I said (somewhat taken aback), "is less elegant, but perhaps more pertinent. The fact is you can't take a group of professional people, highly educated and capable people at that, strip them of rights they have enjoyed for most of this century, cast a cloud over their freedom to share what they have learned with their students and colleagues— or with the public either—because they now might jeopardize their university position or even their jobs, and replace these protections with nothing at all. The American university community, like its European counterpart, is well aware of what happens when scholars cannot seek or teach or publish the truth as they apprehend it within the norms and customs of their professions." And I added, "If you take away tenure, you will also take away much of the culture that allows the faculty and the administration to share in the governance of the nation's better universities. And, if you choose not to have tenure, you will come to have in its place either a unionized faculty or one protected by the state's civil service laws. At least with tenure, unlike with the civil service or unions, you can make and act on timely judgments as to the promise, performance, and capability of faculty members."

I then described the university's personnel system and how the administration of tenure actually worked. I concluded by pointing out that my comments should not be regarded as "anti-union," as most of the U's staff was unionized and I had no concern with that whatsoever.

"Well," he said, "I hadn't thought about these points." After we discussed it further he observed as I was taking my leave, "I think I'll drop the bill."

It occurred to me then, and from time to time since, that much of the success of any university president is the result of what doesn't happen as much as of what does. The governor proved not only to be supportive but a joy to work with, as was his successor, Scott Matheson, also a Democrat, who served for two terms following the completion of Rampton's three-term incumbency.

The Agenda

I had been appointed in April 1973, with effect from August 1, 1973, and had taken the intervening months to wind up my work at UC and inform myself about the U. I went on a nearly weekly basis to Utah, meeting with the university's officers, regents, members of the Institutional Council, deans, and senior members of the faculty so that on taking office I could move quickly to get my team in place. These meetings were very helpful, so much so that I followed the same format ten years later when I returned to UC as its fifteenth president.

All these meetings took place in the other person's office. I made a point of going to them, one-on-one, not asking them to come to me. As a result of these conversations, I was able within the first month of taking office to restructure the central administration, to devise a working relationship with Commissioner Durham, to know the key regents and members of the Institutional Council, to meet and learn from the academic and staff leaders, and to establish my priorities, which included

Strengthening the U's ties with the legislature, which had suffered during the preceding two years

Strengthening the U's position within the state system of higher education, the challenge being to run the system without appearing to do so, and to make all the colleges and universities of the state winners

Improving faculty salaries dramatically, so that we could compete with the nation's twenty-five to thirty-five leading research universities

Reducing the size of a top-heavy administration

Acknowledging the work and needs of the staff, most of whom were
    unionized

Supporting students' interests and championing their needs, but without
    pandering to them or accommodating their every want

Winning back and then holding a broader swath of public goodwill than
    I found when I arrived, when people often compared the U and
    BYU in terms unfriendly to the U and unfair to the realities of both
    places, and to do so in alliance with BYU, or at least in friendly
    competition

Attracting into the central administration the most able, confident, com-
    mitted, and intelligent people I could recruit

Increasing our financial support from the legislature and from the founda-
    tions, alumni, and friends, whose support had been episodic and
    mostly unimaginative

Keeping a healthy and reasonable balance between my professional duties
    and my family obligations

    The first step was to reorganize and shrink the size of the university's ad-
ministration, to recruit capable people to work with me and with one another, to reduce the cost of the central administration, and to make it clear
that there was a new administration in place and ready to start work with the
commencement of the new academic year. I did so on August 20, 1973, less
than three weeks after taking office: the number of vice presidencies dropped
from ten to five, with their functions consolidated and redistributed. I asked
four of the ten vice presidents to remain, although with different titles and
duties, and added a fifth. In addition, I brought in two special assistants, Arvo
Van Alstyne, a distinguished professor of law, first at UCLA and at this time
at the University of Utah's College of Law, one of the nation's premier professors of law and a leading scholar in his specialty, and R. J. Snow, whom I
had come to know and respect when serving at the University of California,
Santa Barbara. I recruited him from his duties as director of the University
of California's Education Abroad Center at the University of Bordeaux,
France. It was a great team and a stable team and no president could have
been blessed with more able and committed colleagues than these. Just as
significantly, they were respected by the faculty, staff, and students and also
by the university's major constituent groups, including the governor and the
legislature and our governing boards.[1]

    My next move was to become acquainted with Utah's legislative leaders.
I met one-on-one with over sixty of them, either at their homes, ranches,
schools, farms, or places of business, at breakfast or lunch, wherever and
whenever it was convenient for them, during my first five months of employment. I asked them to share with me what they liked about the U and

what they didn't, where they thought our strengths rested and where our weaknesses lay, what I could do to help improve relations with the legislature and what they could do to learn more about the U. These were invaluable meetings and put me on a first-name basis with each of them, to share confidences, seek advice, hear them out, and become friends with many of them.

My next step was to visit every public college and university in the state: five community colleges, two comprehensive four-year colleges, and one university. The eight presidents were very welcoming of this initiative, took pride in showing me their campuses, sharing their problems, and affirming their desire for better relations not only with the U, but also within the system of higher education as a whole.[2]

I then sought to improve faculty salaries to a point that would make us competitive with the nation's second-tier research universities. The U had been unsuccessful in maintaining competitive faculty salaries because the Utah County legislators (BYU territory) had a lock on the key committees and an alliance with the rural counties, especially in the Senate. These more conservative rural legislators served longer than urban ones and therefore had greater seniority, which in turn led to their holding a disproportionate share of key chairmanships and positions in the legislative leadership. They were mostly members of the Latter-Day Saints (LDS) Church (and, being Mormons, cheered for BYU during BYU and Utah games even if they were Utah alumni). I knew that we could hold the Salt Lake County legislators' votes, but these were not enough. How to break this potential stranglehold was the challenge.

I resolved to visit with my friend from BYU days, Dallin Oaks, then president of BYU and a fine person, a former and respected professor of law at the University of Chicago, and legal scholar and teacher of considerable reputation.

"Dallin," I asked, "What is the most difficult single problem you have here at BYU?"

"Faculty salaries," he responded. "I cannot seem to persuade my board to improve faculty salaries at BYU to the levels we need, both to recruit and to hold people of the kind our board of trustees is asking me to recruit."

I said, "We have the same problem, but neither of us can solve it without the other."

I then noted that we had been blocked in our efforts to improve faculty salaries by legislators from BYU's home county but that if our faculty salaries rose, his would too. "After all," I said, "your board compares BYU's salaries with ours." He agreed and we struck a deal: he would help persuade the Utah County legislators on the merits of our need, and I would work with legislators from Salt Lake County to the same end. In addition, I promised to visit Glenn Taggart, then president of Utah State University, whom I knew well and respected, to secure his support (he was having the same legislative problem as I was), believing that if we could secure Taggart's support for legislators from Cache County, where his university was located, together with those from Salt Lake and Utah counties, we would have votes sufficient to accomplish our purposes and no one could stand in the way of our legislative success in this area.

I also indicated that if we proved to be successful, faculty salaries across the state system of higher education would also rise, enabling them to attract and hold the talent they were seeking, and would make the state more attractive to business and to persons of ability in the scholarly and scientific communities, the professions, and elsewhere. Our success would also make clear to the other colleges and universities that the U could help them, rather than confirm their belief that the only way they could help themselves was to hurt the U by shifting resources intended for the U to themselves through legislative influence. The plan worked. Faculty salaries rose in low double digits over a two- to three-year period and sufficiently to put us squarely in competition with Category A Research Universities as reported annually by the American Association of University Professors, the gold standard of rank in the scheme of things.

The Development Effort

The private sector was also becoming increasingly important to the university, as it was throughout the nation's system of higher education. Our first real opportunity to involve private donors in the U's development came with our decision to expand the hospital and medical school, a $50 million project undertaken in the mid-1970s. It would require general obligation bonds of roughly $40 million from the state and another $10 million from the private sector. This was a great deal of money in 1975–76 in Utah. No university had ever raised $10 million from the private sector in Utah for a single project. I thought the arrangement was fair enough, however, as it represented a stretch for the state as well as for the university. In any event, the facilities were desperately needed if the University of Utah's health sciences were to sustain their quality.

Salt Lake City's principal banker was George S. Eccles, one of a line of community-minded members of the Eccles family not only to build their banking empire (the First Security Corporation) but to render consequential public service, his older brother being Marriner Eccles, chairman of the Federal Reserve Board under President Franklin Roosevelt. George Eccles was committed to the University of Utah, and a leading figure in the state's business and philanthropic circles, but, I can assure the reader, he was no pushover. It took me several meetings to persuade him to chair the capital drive for $10 million and an even longer period to persuade him to give the first $1 million as our lead gift. I felt I had earned every dime of it, but once committed, he delivered.

We directed our effort to secure a second and equal contribution from the LDS Church, as its support would be critical to many other potential donors. Note that in the 1970s the idea of a $1 million gift from the LDS Church for any purpose was unheard of, and especially for a purpose not obviously related to the direct interests of the church itself. Eccles asked me to arrange the meeting, and I did so through the efforts of Arch Madsen, president of the Bonneville International Corporation, the holding company of LDS Church–owned businesses and a neighbor of ours. John Dixon, the university's vice president for health sciences and dean of the medical school, and I met with the president of the Mormon Church, Spencer Kimball, and his two counselors, President N. Eldon Tanner and President Marion G. Romney, in Kimball's office along with Eccles and Madsen.

Madsen explained the general purpose of the visit and then turned it over to me. I described this project and why it should be supported not only by the state but also by the private sector, including the LDS Church, given the medical center's reach into the surrounding states of Idaho, Wyoming, Colorado, Arizona, and Nevada, these areas each having consequential LDS populations, not to mention Utah. I pointed out the high percentage of LDS doctors who had been and were being educated at the medical school and at the U's other health science colleges, and that the overall quality of health care on which the people living in this rapidly growing part of the United States depended was centrally influenced by the U's medical center.

Dixon then explained the project in detail, what the expansion meant in terms of hospital care, the training of physicians and other health care professionals, and medical research. Eccles then asked for the $1 million and concluded his direct but well-spoken appeal by indicating that he had told me that "if the church were to make a gift of $1 million, he would match it." This was a startling comment, as his pledge of $1 million made to me the previous week did not assume a required match from the LDS Church or any other consideration of any kind whatsoever. I thought it best, however, to reflect on this incongruity privately rather than openly.

President Kimball, who was the decision maker, was a humble and kind person of unqualified goodwill, truly beloved by all who met him. He was taken aback by the magnitude of the request and not quite sure how he should respond. He turned for advice to President Tanner. A Canadian by birth, Tanner had been president of TransCanadian Pipeline and more recently was instrumental in revitalizing Salt Lake City's downtown and bringing new businesses to Utah. He too was a well-liked and highly respected person, as was President Romney both within and outside the Mormon community.

Tanner's immediate response to President Kimball's question was one I shall never forget. "Well, President Kimball," he remarked softly but with a smile on his lips and a sparkle in his eye, "I believe that unless we are going to say yes we should pray about it." All of us nearly fell off our chairs laughing, including President Kimball and especially President Romney, who observed that President Tanner's comment "was as good as he had heard." Once we were composed, President Kimball said, "Well, I guess we'll have to say yes or pray about it, but we'll decide which it is to be and let you know."

The church came through with the entire amount, as did Eccles with his gift, and with $2 million in hand we were able to move forward to secure the rest. We raised over $13 million for this project in about a year's time. This success buttressed our development efforts in general and the university's fund-raising program overall: the campaign had set a new standard and higher expectations.

Of Government and Politics

We also had to persuade the Utah State Legislature to commit the amount of roughly $40 million in general obligation bonds needed for this project, as noted above. Dixon and I worked the legislative halls as best we could, with forty-five minutes remaining before the annual budget session ended. We were worried because some powerful senators opposed this project for a number of mostly unrelated reasons: several didn't like bonding for any purpose, others didn't believe a public hospital should compete with the private ones, and one or two didn't believe more hospital beds were needed in any event.

Dixon and I did all we could but fell short by a mere handful of votes. Senator Hughes Brockbank, a friend of the university's and a personal friend of both Dixon and me and a neighbor to us both, was carrying the bill in the Senate. He came out of the Senate chamber into the hall with a discouraged look on his face and said, "I am three votes short. Which do you want: the hospital expanded or the medical school enlarged? I can get one or the other, but not both."

Dixon turned visibly white and started to say something. I cut him off and turned to Brockbank with an argument along the following lines: "Senator, John and I have pushed this through the labyrinth of university reviews and politics, got support from the university's two governing boards, persuaded the governor to support this bill, and helped move it through the House of Representatives. George Eccles is raising the money and made a gift of $1 million from his personal assets, so has the LDS Church. We've done our job, now it's time for you to do yours. It's hard for me to imagine that senators who oppose this bill will want to be remembered for damaging the quality of health care in Utah, not to mention the hurt done to Utah's young people interested in studying medicine, nursing, and pharmacy. They can count on our making clear to the public, regardless of how it comes out, the role each senator played. If we could have managed with either the expansion of the hospital or of the medical school, we would have proposed it. So the answer to your question is, we need both or we want nothing. What can we do to help? And, if nothing, good luck." He smiled and said, "I'll try my best," and walked back on the Senate floor.

Dixon, now looking ashen, said, "Gee Dave, don't you think we should have taken something instead of risking everything?" I said, "No," and swallowed hard, my heart racing.

Twenty minutes later Senator Brockbank delivered the bill with a margin of one or two votes. The margin counted for nothing. The bill had passed, and the university's health sciences would continue to grow and develop, laying the groundwork for what is now one of the nation's most formidable centers for teaching, training, and research in the health sciences.

This exercise was most instructive. As with the governor's bill on tenure, much of any university president's success occurs in private, keeping bad bills from passage and securing the enactment of good ones. The tenure bill never saw the light of day (as noted), and no one knew how much risk was involved in seeking full rather than partial funding for the expansion of the university's medical center in the mid-1970s.

I also had to push hard for our capital needs with the Board of Regents itself. For example, on one occasion the board seemed unwilling to fund the full cost of a proposed library for the university's College of Law. They were willing to fund it at about 75¢ on the $1.00. Having argued unsuccessfully for the full amount, I proposed to withdraw the request in its entirety until the board could see its way clear to fund it properly. This provoked them some, but we got it funded in full.

Another example was in the operating budget in the mid-1970s when our enrollment had dropped nearly 10 percent (the economy was very good at this time and students needing money had dropped out to work while the times were favorable). Some regents wanted to reduce the number of authorized faculty positions at the U by a percentage comparable to the enrollment drop (around ninety-five faculty positions). As the regents were about to vote on the motion, the chairman finally realized I had chosen to say nothing and asked what problems I would encounter if the motion to cut ninety-five faculty positions was approved. I said very quietly, "I would have no problems whatsoever, but I would be pleased to inventory the problems my successor would face." I then went on to point out, really to remind them, of how hard it is and how long it takes to build a faculty of real distinction, to develop a balance as well as a critical mass of talent across all disciplines: to build a great faculty is to build a great university. "It is not just turning a faucet on and off, and such irreparable harm would be done to the university if the motion were to pass that I would be compelled to resign in protest."

And I would have. In any event, I concluded, "the regents would seek to re-store these positions within two years when the economy cooled, and the students returned to their studies. And what," I asked, "would have been ac-complished in the meantime? The cost benefits are all negative." I urged them to table the matter, and they did, much to my relief.

But these were atypical incidents. The governing board proved to be a pleasure to work with. The members were dedicated to the institution, gave freely of their time and talent, supported me, and helped fight for the re-sources needed by the university. I discovered that they had more respect for presidents who were prepared, forthright, professional, honest, and com-mitted than those who tried to read the board's intentions, to bend to the political winds, or to seek undue notice for themselves or exceptional ad-vantage for their institution (this was also true in California).

Legislators too had little patience with self-seeking, weak, and unreason-ably accommodating university and college presidents. Fortunately, in a state as small as Utah, hiding places were few and far between. I knew most of the legislators by their first names, knew who had influence and who only thought they had, who were sophisticated and who were not, who respected the uni-versity and who only appeared to, and who were unfriendly to the university, while wishing to appear otherwise. I knew who could be counted on under pressure, who would stand up to the governor and/or the legislative leaders, and who could count votes.

We were always open and straightforward advocates for the university but sympathetic to our colleagues at the state's other eight colleges and univer-sities as well. We were supportive of the commissioner of higher education, never surprising him, keeping him timely informed, and respecting the role Commissioner Durham played. While we were strong advocates for the uni-versity, I always tried to keep in mind the problems with which each legisla-tor was contending, always seeking to reconcile our differences and/or find a solution acceptable to both of us so that neither felt let down or used by the other. Two examples should suffice.

During my first legislative session, the Senate committee hearing our budget had a motion on the table advanced by Senator Dixie Leavitt from southern Utah, to reduce from 14 percent to zero the overhead on contracts and grants that the university could retain rather than remit to the state. Over-head funds accompanied direct grants for research and helped defray the indirect cost of doing the research, that is, the provision of laboratory space, the cost of utilities, the custodial and maintenance work required, library resources, administrative support, and the like. The university kept only 14 percent of its earned overhead at this time, 86 percent of it being folded into the state's coffers. Senator Leavitt believed that by reducing the uni-versity's percentage even further, the state could collect the 14 percent by crediting it to the university's share of state appropriations but then reduce the university's overall budget from *state* funds by that amount *and* shift the 14 percent of state monies that would otherwise go to the U to other colleges in the state, especially those in southern Utah, in which the senator had a vital interest. Facing a new and presumably inexperienced university president, Senator Leavitt saw his chance to capture the remaining 14 percent. But I knew that UC kept roughly 50 percent of its overhead and was determined, therefore, to move the University of Utah's percentage above 14 percent or in any event not to allow it to drop any further.

I managed to get the matter put over until the next day. On returning to campus that afternoon I called Willem Kolff, a member of our faculty world famous for his original work in dialysis treatments and protocols and later for the work he did in developing the world's first artificial heart. I asked Kolff if he could help me the next day. "What," I asked, "would someone who lost an arm in a haying accident a hundred years ago be wearing on the stump of his arm?" He said, "A leather pouch with a small spoon and fork attached, and a hook at the end." "What," I then asked, "would such a person be wearing today?" Aware that his research unit had a prototype of an artificial arm that worked off electrical impulses and signals rather than more conventional means, I asked if he and Steve Jacobson, who was doing most of the work on the artificial arm, could accompany me to the legislative hearing the next day; and would they please bring both the pouch, utensils, and hook and the prototype of the arm they were working on.

The next day I introduced Dr. Kolff and Dr. Jacobson to the committee and asked them to explain what someone who lost an arm in a haying accident a century ago would be wearing (three of the legislators were ranchers or farmers) and what such an injured person today would be wearing. Kolff explained the matter in general, and Jacobson demonstrated the new arm while passing the old leather pouch, utensils, and hook around the table.

I then indicated that the new arm was the result of research during the intervening years in materials science, engineering, anatomy, neuroscience, physiology, and so forth, and that Senator Leavitt's bill, however well intentioned, would do real harm to the university's research capabilities, surely not what the senator would knowingly propose. I went on to point out that 14 percent was in itself woefully low, drawing comparisons with the percentages retained by other major research universities in the United States, including the University of California, and suggested that a substitute motion be considered and acted on before Senator Leavitt's main motion came up for a vote.

The substitute motion proposed was to increase the 14 percent retained overhead to 25 percent in lieu of Senator Leavitt's motion to reduce it from 14 percent to nothing. One of the senators with whom we had discussed this problem the night before offered such a substitute motion, and it passed overwhelmingly, thus supplanting Senator Leavitt's motion. After the motion passed, Leavitt laughed, the other legislators smiled, and they all went on with their business.

The second example occurred during the last night of a legislative session two or three years into my work. As things were looking good at the capitol, my family and I were attending a basketball game on campus with R. J. Snow and his family. Just before halftime, the public address system announcer said I was wanted at the capitol. Snow and I left immediately. Twenty minutes later we were there talking with the university's legislative representative, Bob Fox, well liked and respected among legislators and very good at his job. Our budget had support in the Senate, Fox said, but had turned into a disaster in the House as a coalition of interests led by Democrats from Weber County (just north of Salt Lake City) had significantly reduced our budget and redistributed the reduced amount to other colleges and universities within the state. Moreover, this was the Democratic caucus position, and caucus positions were extremely difficult to break. Indeed, I thought it was probably impossible, with only 105 minutes remaining before the legislature adjourned for that year.

Snow and I were wearing red coats, crimson and white being the university's colors, as we had come directly from the basketball game. We stood out in these red coats wherever we went, in the corridors and halls and offices just off the House floor. We were also highly visible to the television cameras that were covering the final hours of the session live, and much in evidence to legislators who for years afterward would say in mock horror when they saw us, "The redcoats are coming! The redcoats are coming!"

The three of us literally ran between the Senate and House leadership seeking to put a deal together. We succeeded with the Republicans in both chambers and with the Democrats in the Senate as well but not with their counterparts in the House, who were in a majority. There was some movement, however, and a growing unease on the part of many of the House Democrats about their caucus position when they observed how hard we were working and how unhappy we were. Our effort had also become the focus of the television coverage (we saw to that, I might add) and the message coming over to viewers was that the Democrats were doing great damage to the University of Utah and doing so for the express purpose of advantaging every other college and university in the state, which, of course, was exactly what was happening.

At our request the sergeant at arms, a friend of Bob Fox's, distributed our proposed budget amendments to members of the House as the proceedings drew to a close. Naturally, the higher education budget required a vote in both chambers, but it had to occur soon if we were to get the House bill over to the Senate for a vote before the clock ran out. We were nearly out of time.

The Speaker of the House was Ronald Rencher, a Democrat from Ogden in Weber County, a University of Utah alumnus of great personal integrity and, we discovered, considerable courage as well. He agreed to step out of the chambers, and we explained to him what the caucus position would mean to the university, how grossly, indeed, how fundamentally and pointedly unfair it was, how we were going to deal with it publicly and politically if the House enacted the caucus position since both parties in the Senate were supporting our proposed amendments.

The problem was that he, Rencher, was head of the Democratic caucus and in an impossible position. Thus we stopped short of pressing him for a definite response. Instead we asked that he promptly call the higher education appropriations bill to the floor for a vote one way or the other and in a timely way; and if it should go our way, then at least we could still get it to the Senate before it was too late.

He promptly called the bill up for a House vote as the next item of business. The vote was taken electronically, and the lights flashed, showing how each member was voting (some members, taking account of the pattern of voting, changed their votes two or three times). Finally the voting ended. It was a draw, and Speaker Rencher would have to break the tie. He did so by voting for our budget amendments. The House erupted: threats of betrayal were hurled at the Speaker from the floor by members of his own party, and in the general confusion that ensued we had just enough time to get the amendments over to the Senate, where they easily passed.

I asked Bob Fox if in view of the turmoil still going on in the House, "we should thank those who supported us or wait for a more propitious time." He said, "You must be kidding! Where's the closest exit? We're out of here."

We worried about the fallout from this successful but contentious outcome. What price were we to pay for our efforts? What enemies had we made? What friends had we hurt? We had no reason to be concerned, I discovered much to my astonishment, as the legislators themselves, however unhappy or resentful they may have been, knew that we had won fair and square, that we had more clout than they had fully realized, and that our position was not unreasonable. As a result of our work they would be far less likely to try such a maneuver in the future.

It was a highly instructive experience and a most encouraging outcome. I can still hardly believe that we had the audacity to try, much less the fortitude to succeed. Rencher was defeated at the next election, and his days in the state legislature were over. He later served for many years and with great distinction as the United States attorney for the State of Utah. He and his wife were personal friends, and I remain in awe of the courage he exhibited that evening.

DOWN TIME

With only 1.2 million people in Utah, and given the prominence and visibility of my position, Libby and I looked for some place we could vacation with the family, a place we could grow into, a place we could afford, and a place outside Utah. Otherwise, there would be no end to friends and strangers approaching us to complain about the U's football team or about the "godless" professors at the U or about "a lazy" professor who lives next door and mows his lawn at 3:30 P.M. instead of working, or teaching loads or administrative salaries or tuition or admissions or why didn't my kid get into your medical school, and so forth.

Thanks to our friends Joe and Barbara Bentley we found a magical place on Wild Horse Island on Flathead Lake, on the Indian reservation of the same name, in northwestern Montana just south of Glacier Park, between Missoula on the south and Kalispell to the north, and flanked by the Mission Range of the Rocky Mountains and the Bob Marshall Wilderness to the east and the Bitterroot Mountains to the south and west.

We built a small cedar cabin for our family on our 750 feet of lake frontage. With no electricity available from elsewhere, the pump house held a generator, water pump, and water pressure tanks; the Flathead is the largest freshwater lake in the western United States, and its unfiltered water is safe to drink. All the comforts of home. We shared the 2,500-acre island with about 125 Rocky Mountain big horn sheep, fifty to sixty deer, enough coyotes to keep it all in check, occasionally a visiting mountain lion and bear or two, ducks of every kind, geese, osprey, bald eagles, and a handful of neighbors scattered mostly along the southern shoreline. We spent a score of summers at our cabin, and our daughters and their families use it even today. The crystal-clean air, scent of pines, clear water, wildflowers and wildlife in abundance, including a handful of wild horses on the island itself, make it a special place. We would return to Salt Lake City and campus at the end of each summer, ten pounds lighter and feeling ten years younger.

The University of Utah also had a most enlightened leave policy for its president, as well as a generous sabbatical program for its faculty and key academic officers. After three consecutive years of service, the president is expected to leave for three months with pay. I did so twice, first to finish our cabin in Montana and second as a visiting fellow at Clare Hall, Cambridge University. Each was a memorable experience for the whole family.

BUILDING EXCELLENCE

I made strenuous efforts to strengthen the humanities with fellowship and sabbatical support and with study grants for faculty members as needed. Similar but not identical efforts focused on the social and behavioral sciences, the Colleges of Health and Nursing and Pharmacy, and selectively across the university's many disciplines, as opportunities offered themselves. I appointed Pete Gardner (no relative), a chemist and the respected dean of the college of science, to serve as my senior academic officer, vice president for academic affairs, and to help me with the appointment of the deans of our colleges and schools.

My work with the Academic Senate at Utah was uneventful, Pete Gardner doing most of the work. I, of course, brought the perspective of UC's shared governance to the table, which assumed a much higher level of Academic Senate involvement in the university's governance than was customary at the U. The faculty were open to new interdisciplinary initiatives, already much engaged in teaching yet also determined to broaden and deepen their research endeavors, which they did. I worked to provide the libraries, laboratories, computer facilities, and research instrumentation and other intellectual resources they needed as quickly as possible.

I have already mentioned the growth and expansion that occurred with the funding of the medical center and its various health science schools and colleges. The efforts of Chase Peterson also improved the quality, breadth, and scope of these programs when he succeeded John Dixon as the university's vice president for health sciences in the late 1970s. We recruited Chase from Harvard University, where he had served under Derek Bok as a vice president for many years and earlier as dean of students during the chaotic late 1960s. Chase's father had been president of Utah State University and both were well known in Utah. His undergraduate and medical degrees had been taken at Harvard, and he brought new ideas and an energetic style to his new position. He succeeded me as president of the U in 1983, when I left for the presidency of the University of California.

As vice president, Peterson took the occasion of the medical center's expansion to embark on a long-term and strategic effort to make the University of Utah the nation's foremost center for research, teaching, and training in the area of genetically implicated diseases and related areas as well. He set about to build faculty capabilities in these areas, both in the health sciences, in the basic sciences on lower campus, and in physics, chemistry, and the life sciences in their many forms. Disciplines were reorganized in the School of Medicine to facilitate this purpose, and research grants were sought from both federal and private sources. The LDS Church worked with Peterson and his colleagues to link significant parts of the research effort with the church's health and genealogical records, which were remarkable for their completeness and accuracy. And it should be noted that polygamous marriages among some church members in the latter half of the nineteenth century added much that was unique to this remarkable database.

As president, Peterson interested the Howard Hughes Medical Institute in this opportunity and the medically unique research it offered. The institute later came to establish one of its major research centers at the University of Utah in the area of genetic research, as did the George and Dolores Eccles Foundation of Salt Lake City, which helped fund a major laboratory and research facility to house these programs and to fund visiting scholars and outstanding graduate students wishing to study at the U. In the mid-1990s Jon and Karen Huntsman and their family, friends of ours for a quarter of a century and former neighbors during our years in Salt Lake City, provided over $200 million in gifts to create the Huntsman Cancer Institute to further genetic research.

I follow this example in some detail because it points out how high-quality academic programs are developed: a supportive state government providing mostly for the physical facilities, equipment and labs, and basic operational support; a private sector, both within the state and outside it, recognizing promise, ability, and competence and wishing to build on them; a federal government willing to pay both the direct and indirect cost of the research it funds; and, critically, faculty members of reputation who are committed to building not just another research program but a world-class research endeavor, sufficient to attract to the U the best minds and most promising young people together with scientists, clinicians, scholars, technicians, and health practitioners. While the administration plays a crucial role in identifying the opportunity, securing the resources, setting priorities for campus programs and budgets, and helping to negotiate the appointment of new faculty members, gifts, and state appropriations, it is clearly secondary to the role played by the faculty themselves: the real work depends on their creative powers, dedication, education, and training. Fundamental genetic research was and remains a striking accomplishment for a university so geographically removed from the nation's principal centers of intellectual strength.

The world also heard much of the University of Utah's medical school and research endeavors when the first artificial heart was implanted in Dr. Barney Clarke at the University of Utah Hospital in December 1982. Research on this heart was under way at Utah when I arrived in 1973 and continued at an accelerated pace throughout the 1970s, reaching its culmination with the actual implantation of the heart in a human being. Knowing that this event would attract worldwide attention both to the university and to the state, we laid very careful plans to ensure that the media briefings were timely, forthright, and complete, that the key players were reasonably available, and that the significance of the event was neither understated nor exaggerated.

The operation did grab the world's attention: from the four corners of the globe the press descended on the University of Utah by what seemed the thousands. There were gasps of approval and harrumphs of disapproval by researchers elsewhere and an unrelenting inquisitiveness by people who saw this operation offering hope beyond their wildest dreams. I called on Chase Peterson to handle all the publicity, which he did with great care and much success. This was not an uncomplicated assignment, given the personalities of the three principal figures in the development of the artificial heart: Robert Jarvik, after whom it was named, Willem Kolff, to whom I have already referred, and William deVries, the lead surgeon. To say that these three persons did not get along would be a gross understatement. I recall asking Peterson to take responsibility for briefing the media about this event, and under no circumstances to bring all three principals together to talk with the media.

Peterson performed superbly in every respect, and the principals proved to be unexpectedly civil to one another. Barney Clarke survived 112 days (12,912,499 heart beats) before succumbing, and the medical and scientific communities were forced to reconsider some of their assumptions about this matter. So too did the researchers at the University of Utah, as the device proved to be only partially successful, albeit implanted in an already desperately sick patient.[3] The university had every reason to be proud of this accomplishment, as I was too. Barney Clarke's heroism and courage, and that of his wife who was with him throughout, can hardly be overstated.

Following the operation and after some of the furor had died down, Libby and I hosted a dinner party at the Alumni House on campus for all the key players on Jarvik's team, Kolff's team, and deVries's team. During the dinner Dr. deVries observed that he had brought a seven-minute videotape with portions of the operation and would we be interested in seeing it. I thought to myself, "I'm not really sure I wish to see this while eating dinner," but I could hardly refuse. We agreed and the video began, after a short introduction. Seated next to deVries, Libby was looking a bit pale. When the video reached the point when Barney Clarke's natural heart had been removed and placed on a metal tray, Dr. deVries turned to Libby and whispered, "This is the part of the operation when I knew there was no turning back." Libby, somewhat ashen, nodded her assent.

The truth is that I had very few faculty problems or problems with our academic programs. It was a matter of gathering the resources the faculty needed for their work. Once they had them, and they got much of it during my decade at Utah, their efforts moved the institution forward. Thus, as this chapter suggests, a disproportionate part of my time went into securing the needed resources, and this in turn required the goodwill not only of the decision makers in the state, but of the average citizens as well.

NEW STANDARDS FOR ADMISSION

Unlike the University of California—which drew its entering freshman class from the top 12.5 percent of all graduating high school students—in 1973 the University of Utah for all practical purposes had no admissions standards other than high school graduation. There was no required set of courses on which admission depended, no minimum grade point average required in such courses, and only a gesture made in applying minimum scores to national achievement and aptitude examinations.

As a result, a very high percentage of students admitted as freshmen either failed to complete their first year or chose not to go beyond it. This experience was both traumatic and expensive for the students and their families and, in my view, wasteful of scarce university and state resources and faculty time and effort as well. But I was unable to do anything about admission standards for several years, knowing that any move by the U to set higher standards would be vigorously opposed by the other colleges and universities. It might also be regarded by the legislature as an elitist move and viewed with suspicion by the regents. I believed—correctly, as it later turned out—that the public, the schoolteachers, and the media would favor such a move.

In the early 1980s, when Terrel Bell was Utah's commissioner of higher education, I was serving on a number of national commissions concerned with educational issues, was better known out of the state than when I had arrived in 1973, and was more secure in my position. Confronted with the dramatic increases in enrollment estimates for Utah's system of higher education projected through the 1990s but with little optimism that the state could afford it all, I decided to take up the issue.

I had in mind several steps to redistribute students from the university and four-year colleges to the community colleges. This cascading down of enrollments to the community colleges would match students' readiness for higher education with that segment of the system best able to take account of their individual needs and ready them for transfer at the junior level to one of the four-year institutions. Such a move would also reduce the average unit cost of instruction to the state for students enrolled in its public system of higher education (higher average costs in four-year institutions than in community colleges). It would lower the cost of providing higher education capital facilities, as building costs are on average also greater per student for the four-year institutions than for those at the community colleges.

To succeed with an admissions policy, I knew that the university would have to prepare the plan itself and move it forward on its own. Allies would be few and enemies abundant. An Academic Senate committee was quietly appointed to draw up a set of course requirements for freshman admission to the University of Utah. The usual reviews were arranged, and I was personally involved from the outset. The heart of the new admissions policy was embodied in the newly required courses for admission, grades nine through twelve. No minimum grade point average for admission was deemed appropriate, in part because it would merely provide another target for unfriendly voices to call out their criticism, thus unnecessarily jeopardizing our initial steps.

We (the Academic Senate and the administration) were ready in 1982 to move forward with our new admission requirements. The problem then was not with the new course requirements, but the question of who had authority to act on them: the legislature or the Board of Regents or the Institutional Council, or all three. Systemwide, the policies were ambiguous on this point, and ambiguity served us well here. I concluded that it was as rational as it was reasonable to fix the Institutional Council with the authority rather than any of the other interested players.

At a regularly scheduled morning meeting of the Institutional Council in 1982, this matter was put on the table, discussed at some length, and acted on promptly and favorably. The representatives of the Academic Senate spoke encouragingly, as did members of the administration. I supported this move without qualification and urged it on the council with as much insistence as I could, having spoken privately with each of its members ahead of time. It passed unanimously. That evening and the morning following, the editorials appearing in the state's principal newspapers and on the state's three main network television channels were all laudatory. They believed that the university had taken the correct step, as this move would help strengthen the state's public schools, offer teachers a more confident standard to measure both their success and their students', provide counselors leverage to encourage students to take the more demanding rather than the easier courses, and strengthen the overall quality of the entering freshman class at the of University of Utah. And it would reduce the rate of first-year student attrition.

The Utah community of teachers and administrators from kindergarten through grade twelve was also enthusiastic, although the state superintendents of the larger school districts thought they should have been consulted. Actually, we should have consulted with and notified them, but if we had done so we would never have succeeded in getting the new policy in place: too much politics, too many moving parts, not enough time.

The meeting of the Board of Regents was scheduled the next day, on a Wednesday, at the College of Eastern Utah. I knew the regents would not be happy with the Institutional Council having acted as it had on Monday and would be especially critical of me as the council had acted on my initiative and on my recommendation. The regents, of course, had to take account of all nine institutions, not just the University of Utah; and here we were, using our admissions standards to differentiate ourselves from the other eight.

I had talked with Commissioner Bell before the meeting, explained what we were doing and why, and had confided in him as to why we had proceeded as we did. I said, "Ted, can you just remain silent, don't do anything. I'm not asking for your support but I would not welcome your opposition." He said, "That's the easiest request I have had for some time. I'm not getting into this," he concluded, although I believed Bell was basically in favor of this move.

I had a very difficult time at the meeting. Some of the other presidents were not happy because they thought this move would give the University of Utah a certain standing and reputation that they did not have and could not get. Of course they were right. As the meeting wore on, the regents were most unhappy with me but not inclined to be overly explicit about it, as the press was both there and had editorialized favorably, as noted above. The chairman of the board was Don Holbrook, a committed supporter of higher education in the state, a prominent graduate of the University of Utah's Law School, and a friend. He was not happy with me either, but he was not uncivil and strove to maintain a reasonable balance in the conversation as the day went on.

When the matter came up for action toward the end of the day, the regents moved to delay board action on this matter to a later meeting. They assumed that they, not the Institutional Council, had the authority in this matter and that their vote would be required to confirm and make legal the vote of the Institutional Council. The motion appeared to have considerable support, so I asked to speak. I explained why the University of Utah felt the need to put these admission standards into place, how they would strengthen the quality of public education in Utah and signal a readiness of our freshman students for university work, how well the teaching profession and the media alike had received them.

In my judgment the Institutional Council *had* the authority to act, and therefore, I argued, the regents must first withdraw that authority and then reserve it to themselves before they could act on our admissions policy. And unless they did so, I explained, I planned to mail already prepared letters over my signature to Utah's superintendents of schools the next morning, enclosing copies of the new admissions policy for entering freshmen. Thus "you also need to direct me by a vote of the board not to mail these letters tomorrow morning, if it is your intention to withdraw authority from the Institutional Council and defer this matter to a later date."

This was a risky maneuver, but I thought in the end the regents would not want to take this issue on, because the people of the state had responded so favorably and members of the press, then present, would have been severely critical of the board for having undone something that the media itself so supported. The motion to defer was tabled. No further action was considered, and the matter was settled.

This single decision, to put course requirements in place for freshman admissions to the university, did more to improve Utah's public schools than anything that otherwise could have been done, given the state's large school population and its modest tax base.

The teachers were thrilled, and so were the parents. The students grumbled. The superintendents of schools felt slighted, as did the presidents of the other eight colleges and universities. The regents were aggrieved. The Institutional Council was happy. The legislature had no view of it, as it was not in session. The press was ecstatic. So was I, even though the regents should have taken me to "the woodshed" for the way I handled it. But it could not have succeeded any other way, and everyone knew it.

More high school students immediately enrolled in the courses now required for admission to the university. High school counselors were now able to persuade their students to take the more demanding courses, rather than the easier ones. The university's prestige rose. The students subsequently enrolling were proud of having taken a more rigorous set of courses and felt better about themselves; and they performed better once they were students at the university. I count the enactment of these new admissions standards as one of the most important contributions I was able to make while serving at the University of Utah.[4]

The others worth noting during my presidency include our having put into place employment packages for members of the faculty that brought the U into the mainstream of the nation's leading research universities (average faculty salaries rose from 30 or 40 percent of our leading competitors' to 70 percent) and enabled us to hold on to our best faculty members and to recruit to the University of Utah faculty persons being sought after by the country's leading universities, including UC; having obtained unprecedented levels of private-sector support for an array of academic and student-centered programs and facilities (from $3 million per year in 1973 to $15 million in 1983); and having improved the levels of alumni, legislative, and public regard. We also refreshed and energized relations with the LDS Church, helped bring about a harmonious set of relationships within the Utah system of higher education, including excellent relationships with our governing board, and made strides in the development of the university's academic programs, especially in the health sciences, the basic sciences, and in the fine and performing arts, together with the facilities needed to implement them. The U's math and physical science programs were ranked second nationally as the most improved; federally sponsored research rose from $27 million in 1973 to $60 million in 1983; student-faculty ratios over the same period improved from 21:1 to 16:1; and the percentage of teaching assistants in our undergraduate classes dropped from 25 percent to 16 percent.

This list of achievements was all made possible by the hard work and skilled efforts of leading members of the faculty, key administrative officers, the commissioner for higher education, selected members of our governing boards, friendly governors, certain legislative leaders, and the media, which, in contrast to California's, looked at least as hard for positive as for negative things to report about the work of the university and its leadership.

In short, I regarded these ten years at the University of Utah as a professionally and personally satisfying ten-year honeymoon full of accomplishment, friends, and colleagues in abundance.

UC KNOCKING AT THE DOOR

I had been at the University of Utah for just over a year when President Charles Hitch announced his intention to retire as UC's president, effective June 30, 1975. The search committee looking for his successor contacted me to determine whether or not I would be willing to be considered as a successor to President Hitch. I told the committee that I really could not be considered as a candidate as I had been at Utah for such a short time, I think fourteen months at that point, and that if I were to go to California my successor at Utah would be the fourth president in five years. Alfred Emery, a professor of law at the U had served as interim president of Utah for two years before I was appointed in 1973, having succeeded Jim Fletcher in 1971, who had left Utah to serve as the director of NASA in Washington, D.C. "The regents would never have hired me at Utah if they thought I would be leaving so soon," I explained, "and I regarded myself as having a moral obligation to remain in my present post."

UC's search committee did not want to hear about all that but did not challenge it. One member simply said, "Would you be willing to help us sort through the qualifications of people whom we are considering and to help us better understand the position itself?"; in other words, "please give us a hand in the search." I said that I would be very happy to do that so long as it was clear that I was not a candidate for the position itself.

I flew to the San Francisco Bay Area in fall 1974 and met with the search committee for two to three hours. The conversation was a constructive one, and the committee appeared to be honoring the terms of my participation. When the meeting concluded, Governor Edmund G. "Jerry" Brown, who was a member of the committee, walked out with me and said, "I really enjoyed your answers to our questions," which surprised me because I thought his views and mine were very much at odds. He then said, "I would like to talk with you at greater length. Are you free for dinner tonight? I would like you to join me at the Zen temple in San Francisco." I said, "Well, I appreciate your invitation, would ordinarily be delighted to accept it and would welcome the opportunity to talk with you further, but my wife and I have already accepted for dinner at the president's house in Berkeley." The governor said, "Break it." I said, "I can't do that. We've accepted it and the Hitches are expecting us." "Can you have breakfast in the morning with me?" he then asked. I said, "Sure, just let me know where and when." "I'll call you tonight," he said.

As we finished our dinner at the Hitches' that evening, I mentioned my conversation with the governor. Hitch said, "You should have broken your dinner commitment with us. The governor of the state wanted to meet with you." I said, "The governor didn't seem troubled." Shortly thereafter the governor called. Charlie Hitch handed me the telephone and said, "The governor is on the phone for you." Brown said, "I can't meet you for breakfast as I had thought. Can we have lunch together?" I said, "Lunch won't work. My father is very ill in Walnut Creek, we have a late afternoon flight back to Salt Lake City, and the only time I can see him is in the afternoon." Hitch was aghast at my response. "What are you saying?" Charlie mouthed silently. But the governor said, "Oh, I see." He was very good about it; no problem with the governor. "Can you meet me at 10:00 A.M." I said, "Sure." We agreed to meet at a private residence in Berkeley.

He was on time, which was a good sign, and we met for two hours at a small home in north Berkeley, sitting on a king-size bed in a room that afforded no other option, nor, would it seem, did any other room offer more. Much to my amazement, the governor and I got along quite well, even though we seemed to differ on almost everything regarding the University of California. When our conversation concluded, Libby and I visited my father and flew back to Salt Lake that evening.

Shortly afterward, I received a call from the secretary of the regents, Marge Woolman, whom I knew well. She was calling for the search committee and asked if I would meet with the entire Board of Regents for the same purpose as I had met with the search committee. I reemphasized that I was not a candidate for this position, that I could not be a candidate for this position, and that I could not take the position even if it were offered. "We know that," she said, "but your earlier visit with the search committee was much appreciated and a comparable visit with the full board would be especially welcomed. Would you be willing to come?" I said, "Of course, under those conditions, I would be happy to do it." I flew down to San Francisco and met with the UC regents for two hours.

I had to leave the meeting before it concluded as I had obligations early the next morning in Salt Lake City. As I was walking out, Regent Dean Watkins, of whom I thought very highly and who surely would be counted among the most intelligent and effective members of the Board of Regents, and a highly successful businessman, said, "Dave, you need to know that the full board is meeting tomorrow. I know that you're not a candidate but I am asked to tell you that if you do not withdraw your name and do so officially, you are going to be elected tomorrow as the university's next president."

I said, "Has there been some misunderstanding here? How could have I been clearer about this matter?" and then reiterated why I could not accept, honored and appreciative as I was with his and the regents' confidence and regard. He said, "Well, Dave you either send us a letter to that effect to be received by tomorrow morning, or you're going to be elected. I sincerely hope you will reconsider."

I wrote my letter on the plane returning to Salt Lake that night indicating my reasons for being unable to consider serving as UC's president. The next morning I prepared the letter, signed it, sent it by overnight mail (there were no faxes in those days), and then called and read it to Marge Woolman. I asked that she read my letter, immediately, verbatim, to the chairman of the board, which she did.[5]

When the regents read the letter, I am told that there was wonderment as to how I could refuse an invitation to serve as president of the University of California. They deferred any further action on the matter for the rest of that day. Throughout the day and well into evening I received a series of telephone calls from board members I knew encouraging me to reconsider my position, pointing out that the University of Utah would succeed in finding a replacement for me, that the qualities they thought I possessed fitted the needs of the institution and wouldn't I please take account of these matters and reconsider my position.

I recall especially my conversation with William French Smith, who was the board's vice chairman and who later served as attorney general under President Reagan. We had known each other from my days at UC Santa Barbara and in the Office of the President. Smith said, "No one can believe you are unwilling to accept the presidency of the University of California. We must be missing something." I said, "You're not missing anything. It's just as I described it to you." He then said, "Dave, I don't think you understand. You have nineteen out of twenty-six votes on the first ballot. Jesus Christ wouldn't get more votes than that from this board." I indicated how honored and appreciative I was of the board's confidence but added that I could not change my mind for the reasons that I had already given.

While my overriding concern was an obligation I felt toward the University of Utah, I was also concerned about our family. I understood Utah and the job was manageable. It was one campus in a small state. In contrast, the University of California had nine campuses, five major medical centers, an agricultural empire (it was the state's land-grant institution), worldwide interests, and an annual operating budget of roughly $5 billion. The UC president's public position and what I knew of the state's politics at the time meant that I would be away from our young family at least 50 percent of the time. Even so, the personal issues were subordinate to the professional ones: I simply could not look my colleagues at the U or on the board or any of the U's many constituents in the eye and tell them I would be leaving after they had been so supportive and encouraging about my work. I did my best to make my views understood by friends among the UC regents and other friends and colleagues at the University of California who were also calling, but with very uneven success.

I also told Libby "an offer of that kind comes only once in a lifetime, it will never come again." She said, "That's okay, it won't be our last opportunity for you to be president somewhere else if you believe it would be more agreeable than what we have now."

I have sometimes wondered how I would have managed as president in the later 1970s with Governor Jerry Brown and what came to be his quite unfriendly views of the University of California, and with the other problems the university was confronting within the legislature and the state. There is, of course, no way of knowing. In 1983 I *was* willing to listen to an invitation from UC—not because of any unhappiness or sense of lethargy at Utah, but because the reasons in 1975 no longer pertained.

During the later years of my service at Utah I was much involved at the national level, serving on various national commissions and committees, study groups, and task forces of higher education associations headquartered in Washington, D.C. These assignments concerned student financial aid policies, the financing of our nation's colleges and universities, research policies, higher education legislation under consideration by the Congress, and national higher education policies and strategies. But the one that engaged most of my attention and came to count for more than all the others combined was my service as chairman of the National Commission on Excellence in Education.

Our ten-year honeymoon at Utah never ended, but life moved on.

FOUR

A NATION AT RISK

AN UNLIKELY PROSPECT

Ronald Wilson Reagan was elected president of the United States in November 1980. To the astonishment of his party and perhaps himself as well, in the latter part of his first term he traveled to public schools across the nation, advocating their cause and seeking to improve both the work of and support for education in kindergarten through grade twelve. He abandoned the Republican Party's education platform and his own electoral campaign commitments to abolish the U.S. Department of Education, to return prayer to the schools, and to enact tuition tax credits and/or school vouchers. How this unlikely prospect unfolded is the subject of this chapter.

The president's personal involvement in and commitment to the nation's schools and the vital work in which they were engaged came about during his first term from the surprising choice of Terrel H. Bell to serve as the secretary of education, the last and thirteenth cabinet member to be appointed.

The Secretary of Education

Ted Bell was a very humble person but had very little to be humble about. He was a seasoned and knowledgeable educator, sophisticated in the ways of the nation's capital and capable of making hard decisions. Much to their later dismay, his critics and detractors often mistook his self-effacing manner for weakness at best and ineptitude at worst.

In the four years he served as U.S. secretary of education, he managed against all odds to increase the presidential, congressional, gubernatorial, and legislative interest in and support for American public schools. He helped to move education to the top rungs of the country's domestic agenda, bested only by public concern for the then high levels of unemployment. And he launched a broad-based and long-lasting effort to improve the nation's schools and the quality of education offered to America's young. This remarkable outcome startled Reagan's more conservative White House advisers, who were in an intense struggle with Bell throughout his four-year tenure for the ear of the president and even more for his heart. Bell won in Reagan's first term, and his antagonists in the White House did in the second.

Bell had been a leader in Utah education for more than three decades, serving as Utah's superintendent of public instruction and as commissioner of higher education. When he was commissioner for higher education and I was president of the University of Utah, we worked well together. Even when we disagreed, I liked and respected him not only for what he had accomplished, but also for his fairness and honesty when he made a decision. He was always willing to listen to reason rather than worry about whose influence was the most telling or whose threatened sanctions were the most onerous or who made the most noise.

The president's invitation to Bell did not surprise me, but given the Republicans' agenda for education, his acceptance did. Bell was a moderate Republican in disagreement with much of the party's views on these matters. He was, however, no novice when it came to understanding the machinations of Washington, D.C., having served under both Presidents Richard Nixon and Gerald Ford, first as deputy commissioner for education and then (1974–76) as commissioner of education, in which position his responsibilities encompassed the "education" in HEW. He reported to the secretary of HEW, Casper Weinberger, who was later to serve as Reagan's secretary of defense.

When Ted had been offered the secretary's position but before he accepted it, he called me seeking advice and information about Reagan, whom I had known during my years at UC. He was also interested in whatever information I could share with him about several of the president's top aides and advisers and members of his "kitchen cabinet": I knew UC Regents William Wilson, later U.S. representative to the Vatican, William French Smith, later Reagan's pick for U.S. attorney general, and Glenn Campbell, director of the Hoover Institution at Stanford University, who also served on Reagan's intelligence advisory committee.

I told Bell that Reagan would be quite easy to work with, but only if he could get to him. I explained that Reagan was an honest person who believed in his principles and was committed to the rightness of his views, that he was approachable and willing to listen if you could be brief, helped along with some humor and an anecdote or two; and I said that he was more adaptable than most people supposed, that his political instincts and skills were uncanny, and that critics consistently underestimated his intelligence and common sense, which is why he generally prevailed and they did not. And the best way to work with the president was without airs or impressions of self-importance or arrogance or sense of mission. These would not do. "Just be yourself, Ted, it's more than enough," I said in closing.

Bell met the president-elect for the first time at Blair House before the inauguration. Bell's account is worth remembering:

> The president-elect was warmly attentive. I found myself very comfortable in my first conversation with him. I knew that his quest for this last member of his cabinet had been delayed because of lack of conviction concerning its importance. But he displayed interest in and concentration on what I had to say. He explained his concern about a cabinet-level Department of Education. He emphasized his interest in schools and colleges and his firm conviction that education should be primarily a state rather than a federal responsibility. He expressed fear of federal control of education.
>
> The most surprising and encouraging thing to me was the fact that Ronald Reagan showed none of the scorn or bitterness toward federal financial assistance programs that I had heard from [Edwin] Meese. . . . The president didn't sound like an enemy of the schools. I was even more encouraged by what he did not say, because I knew he was choosing his education chief and this was his chance to warn me about what must be done. . . .
>
> When I reminded the president-elect that I had testified in support of the bill to create the department [of education], he asked if I could support an alternative. I said I was willing to consider establishing an independent federal agency of lesser status than a cabinet department, but I also explained my opposition to placing education back in HEW.
>
> I then told the president-elect that if I were selected to be his secretary of education I would want the responsibility of supervising the staff work that drafted alternatives to the department structure. The president-elect answered, "Well, okay, let's go for it!" And with that casual response I became a member of the president's cabinet.[1]

The First Year

Bell's first months in office were trying. There was a fierce pull and tug between the secretary and his more moderate friends and the Edwin Meese wing of the White House. One of the president's closest and most trusted advisers from his days as governor of California, Meese was thought to represent the more conservative of Reagan's closest advisers and those of comparable persuasion in the West Wing of the White House.

The early battles dealt with Bell's nominees to key appointments within

Education. The political litmus test Bell's antagonists in the White House applied to these nominees came up negative, while their suggestions were no more welcome to Bell. The secretary was not making much headway or friends in high places during the early months of his tenure.

Craig Fuller, a young and personable UCLA graduate, was then serving as the White House director of cabinet affairs. Fuller reported to Meese and also to Jim Baker, Reagan's chief of staff. Both Fuller and Baker came to Bell's aid, providing a counterweight to Meese's influence. With some give here and take there, Education's key posts were finally filled. The entire exercise, apart from the appointments themselves, was a most instructive baseline for the contending parties.

The country was not in a happy mood in the late 1970s and very early 1980s: inflation and interest rates were in double digits, an especially insidious form of "taxation," hitting people on fixed incomes, among many others. Unemployment was high and spreading, and the middle class was restive. Those below it were increasingly unemployed, and those above it were seeing their businesses, farms, and ranches "going on the auction block."

Abroad, America's stance seemed far less predictable and far less confident, with the effects of the 1973 oil imbroglio still very much on people's minds. There was also the nightly televised spectacle of our embassy staff in Tehran blindfolded and bullied by mobs for the world to see, a further extension of the nation's malaise at home and of its perceived decline abroad. There was widespread criticism not only of government in these times but of established institutions generally, including the nation's public schools and the performance of their students.

The Problem

Adverse findings of student performance in America's schools were being reported as early as the mid-1970s. These increased as the 1980s approached. By 1981 the National Assessment of Educational Progress reported dramatic ten-year declines in the writing and thinking abilities of our students. The National Science Foundation, in the same year, reported that one-third of the nation's high schools were requiring only one year of mathematics and one year of science to graduate. Foreign language studies had dropped dramatically, and many of our universities and colleges had eliminated foreign languages as a requirement for admission. In short, school achievement in the United States did not equal that in many developed and developing countries alike.

The education establishment had no effective or credible response to these and numerous other and similar findings. Moreover, the nation's colleges and universities chose more often than not to complain about these trends on the one hand and to accommodate rather than to resist them on the other. Rather than working with the schools to help correct these adverse trends, much of higher education chose instead to move more and more high school courses into the collegiate level and not infrequently grant such classes graduation credit, thus undercutting efforts in K–12. Our expectations for student achievement were also steadily declining—how else to explain that as grades were rising, actual student achievement was falling. We were expecting less of our students, and they were giving it to us.

Secretary Bell, of course, was keenly aware of the nation's growing unease and decided to appoint a panel to appraise the condition of the nation's schools:

> I hoped to get such a panel charged by the president himself to perform the task of appraising the condition of our schools and reporting to the nation on what should be done to give us a first-rate education system. But when I took this idea to the White House it was met with diffidence or scorn. . . .
>
> So I decided to appoint my own commission. A cabinet-level commission would not carry the prestige of a presidential appointed panel, but it was apparently my only option. If the commission had any impact at all, it would seem worthwhile. . . .
>
> I wanted a commission whose membership would command respect and be beyond reproach. It had to be balanced; I wanted liberals and conservatives, Republicans and Democrats, males and females, minorities, educators and noneducators. Most of all, the panel's words had to be powerfully convincing to the American people. . . .
>
> From the outset I knew that I must have David Pierpont Gardner, president of the University of Utah, as the chairman. . . . He is a brilliant, articulate, personable man. He would be strong. He would not be overpowered by anyone in the federal government nor would he tolerate any interference with the work of his commission.[2]

The Beginning

In March 1981 Bell called me at my office at the University of Utah, asking first for help in staffing his department, which I felt could only be marginal. He then asked if I would be willing to chair a task force charged to examine options to the Department of Education as he was under substantial pressure to move forward with the president's desire to abolish it.

What Bell had in mind was an independent agency within the government able to carry out the tasks then assigned to Education. I told him I reserved "twenty-foot poles" to maintain my distance from such endeavors. He groaned but then went on to ask if I might be willing to chair another of his initiatives, this one to assess the performance of American schools and find ways to reverse its decline; his plan was not yet far enough along to discuss it at the time. I said that such an effort would interest me, depending on the arrangements and the specifications of his plan.

The next time I heard from Bell was by letter on April 10, 1981, in which he set out his ideas on a special national commission:

> As I see it, David, the prime problem rests with our secondary schools, but our colleges and universities need to set standards and lead out in directions that will encourage reform. Contrary to what you have been doing at the University of Utah, some institutions have been accommodating without protest or visible concern, each cohort of high school graduates entering the world of academe. I do not believe that this trend will reverse itself until we rally the support of the entire American education establishment.[3]

Within a few days Bell and I discussed the matter again. I was, of course, complimented that he would ask me to serve in this capacity but had a number of concerns. The first was that at the time I was one of twelve members of the National Commission on Student Financial Assistance, along with Senators Robert Stafford and Claiborne Pell, some higher education representatives, and members of the House I also knew: John Brademas, Democrat of Indiana, and Bill Ford, a Michigan Democrat who was chairing it. I had accepted this assignment and could not just walk away. Another committee I chaired had just gotten under way, a National Collegiate Athletic Association's study of athletic concerns in higher education, with leading coaches and university and college presidents from throughout the country. These and other national and regional obligations coupled with my work as president of the University of Utah gave me considerable pause. Bell was undeterred.

The commission would be "the most important initiative" of his service as secretary, he went on, because he saw the country as having "one last real chance to galvanize support for the public schools by improving and/or reforming them lest a wholly disenchanted public were to abandon the public schools in favor of tuition tax credits and/or school vouchers that would hasten the current trend to transfer increasing numbers of students from public to private schools." We exchanged some further views, and I said I'd call him back within the week.

When we spoke again, I had looked carefully at my calendar and commitments, had visited with key regents and members of the university's most immediate governing board, the Institutional Council, and had talked with Scott Matheson, then Utah's governor, and with Libby.

I had decided to accept Bell's offer, but only if Bell would provide the political cover and financial support needed to do the job. In some strange way the stars were aligned for such an undertaking: a former Utah commissioner of higher education was secretary of education, Senator Orrin Hatch of Utah was the ranking Republican member of the cognizant committees of the U.S. Senate, Governor Scott Matheson of Utah was to be the upcoming chairman of the national governors conference, and I was president of the University of Utah. I was also enough of an acquaintance of the president so that we could not be easily undermined, and well enough known by leaders in both the House and the Senate that we could count on a fair hearing.

Conditions

I also understood that Bell needed to break the political mold in which he found himself, that the issues with which he was concerned were troubling to me as well, and that Ted was right as well as courageous in trying to tackle these problems. After informing Bell that I would be willing to serve as chairman of what was to become the National Commission on Excellence in Education, I asked if the following conditions were agreeable:

- We two would have to agree on the commissioners to be appointed (12–20), and either could veto the other's candidate;
- There would be no "political litmus test" for candidates, because education should be a nonpartisan issue;
- Bell would apply no pressure directly or through surrogates on any member of the commission in any way whatsoever as to the report's substance; this was to be the commission's report and we were to be uninstructed in the matter except as to our charter, on the language of which Bell and I would have to agree;
- Funding for the commission's work would be sufficient to do the job and without my having to come back and beg for more;
- The commission would complete its work in eighteen months;
- The president would receive the report, if Bell could persuade him to do so;
- Bell would publish the report on his own authority whether or not he or the president liked its substance;
- We would have to agree on the executive director of the commission's staff; and
- Bell would take appropriate steps to disseminate the report as widely as possible.

Bell accepted and so did I.

THE COMMISSION

Dr. Milton Goldberg, acting director of the National Institute of Education, the Department of Education's research arm, and former associate superintendent of the Philadelphia schools, was recommended by Bell to serve as the commission's acting executive director pending my approval. It was a brilliant choice and a shrewd political maneuver by Bell because it finessed the political test that would otherwise have applied to a "permanent" executive director subject to the customary White House review and concurrence.

I not only agreed to Goldberg's appointment as the executive director but felt quite blessed to have a person of his experience, insight, and integrity to help with our work. His service proved to be invaluable, and it was a joy to work with him. Except by reputation, neither Bell nor I was acquainted with Goldberg, but his leadership of the institute had come to Bell's attention because Bell was uncommonly interested in its research. I was able to make some inquiries of my own, and the answers more than confirmed Bell's judgment.

Over the next few weeks, Goldberg and I worked hard to vet prospective commissioners. We had essentially the same criteria, but the political pressures were on Bell and Goldberg, not on me. We were looking in various parts of the country for persons to serve who knew the schools—as school board members, teachers, administrators, politicians, professors, and business leaders—who collectively would bring to the commission the depth and breadth of needed experience, respect, and credibility. Before too long we had settled on a first list and another of alternates. By then, we had also decided on an eighteen-member commission, I having preferred fifteen and Bell twenty.

As this process was moving forward, Bell asked if I would persuade Glenn Seaborg to be a commissioner; he had tried but failed. Seaborg, a world-famous chemist and Nobel laureate, had been one of my nominees. Reagan knew and respected him, and his stature was very great indeed. I knew him well and was confident that he would bring just the right mix of both substance and standing to our work. He also knew his way around Washington, having served under several presidents as chairman of the Atomic Energy Commission and as one of Berkeley's best and most beloved chancellors. I called Glenn and he accepted, much to Bell's and my relief. He contributed immeasurably to the commission's work and the regard in which it came to be held in Washington, throughout the country, and by Reagan.

Another call came from Bell shortly thereafter, a somewhat sheepish call, I should add, as he had been directed by the White House to ascertain my political affiliations and activities as a condition of my appointment. In Utah I was thought to be a Democrat and in California a Republican. While I voted and was registered as a Republican, I was not bound to either party, had never contributed to a political campaign, and had never endorsed a candidate at the local, state, or federal level. My political views were as eclectic as they seemed to be enigmatic to those interested in such matters.

As Bell already painfully knew, the question was contrary to our understanding. If I answered it, I said, the White House would be emboldened to expect a response from everyone on our list—was he going to ask Seaborg, who had served under Republican and Democratic presidents alike what his political affiliations and activities were? I told him I couldn't answer. Political tests ran wholly contrary to the spirit of the work we were about to undertake, and in the end the White House could not prevail without some consequential risk of its own were the use of such a political test to be known publicly.

My refusal to answer would jeopardize my appointment not only as a commissioner but certainly as chairman, Bell said. In turn I noted my unwillingness to serve in either capacity under the conditions being imposed. He said he'd do his best, but could not be confident of the outcome. My refusal turned out, however, to be a blessing in disguise, as when he called back within a few days there was triumph in his voice in reporting that the White House had chosen to waive its usual political test, that our list was fine, and that we should proceed without further White House consultation. He then added, but "they were not happy about it." I congratulated Bell and said, "They don't have to be happy about it for us to do our work, and this vignette will, ironically, provide us enhanced not diminished political cover as we go forward."

Our commission was empowered, our charter was approved (Bell had found this to be more difficult than expected as the White House budget office had been "nitpicking" this document), the money was allocated, the staff was chosen, and we were ready to go by midsummer 1981, with a tight eighteen-month schedule to do our job. Members of the commission were:

David P. Gardner (chair)
president
University of Utah
Salt Lake City, Utah

Robert V. Haderlein
immediate past president
National School Boards
   Association
Girard, Kan.

Yvonne W. Larsen (vice chair)
immediate past president
San Diego City School Board
San Diego, Calif.

Gerald Holton
*Mallinckrodt Professor of Physics
   and Professor of the History
   of Science*
Harvard University
Cambridge, Mass.

William O. Baker
chairman of the board (retired)
Bell Telephone Laboratories
Murray Hill, N.J.

Annette Y. Kirk
Kirk Associates
Mecosta, Mich.

Anne Campbell
former commissioner of education
State of Nebraska
Lincoln, Neb.

Margaret S. Marston
member
Virginia State Board of Education
Arlington, Va.

Emeral A. Crosby
principal
Northern High School
Detroit, Mich.

Albert H. Quie
former governor
State of Minnesota
St. Paul, Minn.

Charles A. Foster, Jr.
immediate past president
Foundation for Teaching
   Economics
San Francisco, Calif.

Francisco D. Sanchez, Jr.
superintendent of schools
Albuquerque Public Schools
Albuquerque, N.M.

Norman C. Francis
president
Xavier University of Louisiana
New Orleans, La.

Glenn T. Seaborg
*University Professor of Chemistry
   and Nobel laureate*
University of California
Berkeley, Calif.

A. Bartlett Giamatti
president
Yale University
New Haven, Conn.

Jay Sommer
*national teacher of the year,
   1981–82*
Foreign Language Department
New Rochelle High School
New Rochelle, N.Y.

Shirley Gordon
president
Highline Community College
Midway, Wash.

Richard Wallace
principal
Lutheran High School East
Cleveland Heights, Ohio

My reaction was a mix of hope and apprehension, as I knew only Bart Giamatti, president of Yale University, and Glenn Seaborg; but I had confidence in Goldberg's and Bell's judgment to settle on a panel of persons with whom I could work.

I was aware of some but not all the problems Bell and Goldberg confronted in distilling a long list of potential commissioners to only eighteen persons. Yvonne Larsen and Annette Kirk had been strongly recommended by the White House. I had strongly recommended Seaborg and Giamatti. Baker had helped to secure a reluctant Gerald Holton's acceptance. The national education associations housed in the nation's capital all had their candidates as well, each having been asked by Goldberg to nominate five persons from their respective organizations (we chose one from each).

In the end, the details of our selection made no difference. We represented our own knowledge, our own experience, our own biases, and our own consciences, no one else's. No commissioner sought to dominate. Previously prepared statements of position were quietly shelved as our discussions ensued. Caution melted into collegiality and later into friendship. The "chemistry" of the eighteen was remarkably good, and I have nothing but admiration and respect for every one of the commissioners who served on the National Commission on Excellence in Education, 1981–83.

On August 26, 1981, Bell announced the appointment of his commission and the charge he had given to us. We were to examine student performance in America's schools and colleges with an emphasis on teenage youth and compare this performance with that of other countries; to study the interaction between K–12 and higher education, especially with respect to admissions criteria; to examine the K–12 curriculum and academic standards; and to seek out and to study all other matters related to the quality of public and private education in the United States.[4]

The commission's first meetings were held in Washington on October 9–10, 1981. Only Giamatti was absent. We met as strangers come together in behalf of a worthy endeavor to render our country what service we could. I wish to stress this point, as certain critics of our report seem to be convinced that this was a grand conspiracy of the Reagan administration, that we were surrogates for the Republican Party's right wing, that the outcome was predetermined, and that the commissioners were all in collusion.

In fact, not only was the commission appointed over White House objections, indeed irritation (a courageous act by Bell), but the commissioners could not be easily defined as right, left, liberal, or conservative. They were well-educated, thoughtful human beings who were respected and accomplished in their respective spheres. The commission's report undid rather than advanced the Republican Party's and the president's education agendas, and it stimulated a level of public interest and attention to education unknown in this country since shortly after the Soviet Union launched *Sputnik* a quarter of a century earlier but still present today. For example, President George W. Bush advanced his candidacy in no small measure because of his desire to be the "education president." He led the effort to enact the No Child Left Behind legislation in 2001. This was one of the nation's most dramatic expressions of federal interest in education, calling as it does for report cards on the performance of America's schools and school districts.

We began by introducing ourselves, and then Bell "swore us in." He infused our task with the seriousness it deserved, explained the process and criteria by which the commission had been selected, and pledged his good offices in support of our efforts. As Bell himself recalled, "The press came to the commission's first meeting, and my commitments were reported to the public. I was on the record now. There could be no backing down on what had been agreed to. This satisfied the commission members, and they took up the challenge."[5] On October 9, 1981, early on in our work, we traveled to the White House for the only meeting the full commission was to have with the president. We met in the cabinet room. Bell introduced the commissioners to the president and he to us, following which Reagan began his remarks by looking around the table and across it at Seaborg, Baker, Kirk, Larsen, and Albert H. Quie, all of whom he knew, and noting with a smile that he was feeling quite nervous about "meeting with such a highly educated and impressive group of people." We all laughed. He then thanked Bell and all of us for the work we would be performing for the country. His remarks were friendly and nondirective, although his underlying principles were apparent throughout:

> The first and most important of those principles is that education does not begin with Washington officials, or even State and local officials. It begins in the home, where it is the right and the *responsibility* of every parent. Our educational institutions—both public and private—exist to assist families in the instruction of their children. . . . A second principle, true in education just as in our economy, is that excellence demands competition. Competition among students and among schools. . . . A third principle is diversity, which is absolutely essential to the American way of life. Nowhere is this more important than in education. Pluralism in American education has always been one of the strengths of our society and we welcome the recent resurgence of independent schools. . . . Finally, let me just say a word about our fourth kind of principle—the one that teaches us there really *is* a difference between right and wrong. I think it's time we too have a good look at this moral side of contemporary schooling. How, for example, can we expect to restore educational excellence in schools still plagued by drug abuse and crime and chronic absenteeism?
>
> And if we want to strengthen our children's sense of honesty, discipline and direction, can we not begin—just as we do on our coinage or in the halls of Congress—by allowing God back in the classroom and by striving in our own lives to abide by His 10 Commandments? That, at least, would be a start. Of course some people insist there are *no* simple answers to *any* of the problems that plague our society. I disagree. Many of the answers are simple—they're just not easy.
>
> None of you has chosen the easy road. And with a lot of work and dedication and cooperation, I know you'll help many of our children to get back on the right road.[6]

It was my job to respond to the president's comments, and I observed at the outset "that if the president thought he were nervous how does he think I am feeling, with him sitting next to me and my esteemed colleagues surrounding us?" He and the commissioners laughed appreciatively, and I went on to offer remarks appropriate to the occasion:

> The betterment of education in our country should expand individual choice, tap unrealized promise and potential, enliven our sensibilities and understanding both at home and abroad, inform our civic discourse, enrich our lives, restore confidence in and support for our schools, colleges and universities, invigorate our economy, improve our security and help assure our future as a free people.[7]

Following my brief comments we had a relaxed, cordial, constructive, and unexpectedly lengthy conversation with the president. It was a good start.

As our visit concluded, the president turned and privately thanked me for serving as chairman, as he remembered my work at UCSB in the late 1960s and with Hitch's administration in the early 1970s, mentioning the favorable accounts of my service he had received from mutual friends on the University of California's Board of Regents. He also said that he knew how difficult and contentious the task I had accepted was going to be and then said, "Just do your best and don't worry about the consequences."

These comments were not only unexpected but gracious as well. They were also encouraging, as detractors on his staff and in the White House would have to be more than careful when seeking to deprecate the commission's work or its members, given not only his opinion of our acquaintance but also his long-standing personal friendship with several of the distinguished citizens who were serving as commissioners.

The Work Begins

At the outset I resolved to take a very low profile and concentrate on chairing, not guiding the commission. My decision reflected

- The complexities of the issues with which we would be dealing;
- The political environment and high visibility of our work;
- The need for the commissioners to become acquainted before they locked themselves into the corners of their several and varied opinions; and
- The need to arrange our agendas and schedules of meetings to maximize the flow of information to us and minimize the flow of viewpoints and opinions among the commissioners and to the public.

I insisted that we needed to think first about what we didn't know rather than what each of us thought we knew and to consider the testimonies and opinions of others before offering our own. My rationale was this: The commissioners were knowledgeable and perceptive observers and practitioners of what we were studying. Naturally, they would have developed views and opinions over the years, based on their own experience and contacts; certainly I had.

What I wanted us to avoid at all costs was taking positions *prematurely*, settling into a particular point of view, and seeking like-minded colleagues "to outvote" those of contrary persuasion. The commission would fail embarrassingly, and without effect, if we did. Moreover, we all had much to learn from what others were scheduled to tell us, which I was confident would oblige all of us to reconsider our own opinions or at least rearrange our individual biases.

This tactic of discouraging commissioners' exchange of views, although I did not mention it to anyone other than Goldberg, seemed somewhat puzzling to the commissioners and provoked a mild complaint or two. But it was what we did; and it was the right way for us to proceed, with the commissioners learning, sharing impressions, and keeping us on schedule for the April 7, 1983, deadline for the delivery of our report to the secretary.

The commission relied on five principal sources of information:

Commissioned papers (44, subsequently available on the ERIC system)
The testimony of scholars, practitioners, teachers, students, administrators, public officials, business leaders, and parents at eight plenary meetings and six regional meetings, all of which were open to the press
Extended readings in already available literature
Public reports, letters, and other forms of communication from interested citizens and educators
Examples of notable programs and approaches already under way to improve education in individual schools

The full commission met three times between October 1981 and February 1982, again in May and September 1982, and finally four times between November 1982 and April 1983, when the report was officially approved and submitted to the secretary. Six separate hearings were also held between April and September 1982 on subjects the commissioners believed to be especially noteworthy:

- Science, mathematics, and technology education—at Stanford;
- Language and literacy: skills for academic learning—at Houston Independent School District;
- Teaching and teachers' education—at Georgia State University in Atlanta;
- College admissions and the transition to postsecondary education— at Roosevelt University in Chicago;

- Education for a productive role in a productive faculty—at St. Cajetan's Center in Denver;
- Education for the gifted and talented—at Harvard.

Our hosts at each of these regional meetings were themselves well-known and respected educators, for example, Donald Kennedy, president of Stanford; Derek Bok, president of Harvard, and Patricia Graham, dean of Harvard's Graduate School of Education; Billy Reagan, superintendent of the Houston schools—the presence and support of all our hosts gave increased standing and credibility to these meetings.

Several other panel discussions and symposia were also scheduled on relevant but narrower subjects. I asked individual members of the commission to attend and chair these sessions, thus engaging them even more directly in our ongoing work. Special subcommittees also dealt with certain issues we had trouble discussing in a full commission meeting, for example, the report's format and title, or the issues of character or moral education in the schools.[8] And as the individual commissioners or subcommittees reported on each session to the full commission at our next meeting, their "findings" paid rich dividends.

With each passing meeting, and with each increment of information and fresh perspectives—as I observed the evident and growing desire of the commissioners to converse among themselves, and not just at meals but after hours as well—I was glad to loosen my restraint on their exchanges. But by then people were better acquainted, their common and mutual respect was apparent, and the commissioners and the staff were in the process of examining their earlier opinions and views; so was I. By fall 1982 we were well into the substance of our discussions and later in the year were able to sort out the issues we regarded as central or marginal.

We Debate About a Format

The staff, of course, were helping with all the agenda and monitoring our discussions in the hope of offering suggestions for the report itself: substance, format, length, style, content, data, and so forth. I shared two or three of their early efforts with the full commission. Clearly, the staff envisioned a very different kind of report than the one forming in my mind, theirs being a more familiar format for commissions: scholarly in tone, jargon filled, lengthy, and, in my view, of interest to almost no one, regardless of its careful and thorough preparation. Their drafts read more like master's theses than what I believed Bell needed to provoke the public and media to take note, to move education up the domestic agenda, and to galvanize and focus the nation's interest on the issues we were addressing. I shared these concerns with several commissioners in private, not wishing to embarrass or discourage our staff but hoping to test an idea I had been considering.

At about this time we set out entrance requirements for freshman admission to the University of Utah. We had publicized this move in a full-page advertisement purchased by the alumni association in the *Salt Lake Tribune*'s Sunday edition of February 7, 1982, listing the new course requirements and defining what we meant by them subject by subject (as noted in chapter 3, n. 4).

This direct communication to Utah's citizens proved to be very effective, and I wondered if we might consider a similar approach to our upcoming report. I asked Seaborg, Holton, Larsen, Baker, Quie, and some others what they would think of submitting our report to the secretary in the form of an "open letter" to the American people. Were we to do this, the entire character of the report would change: it would be written in plain English, it would be brief, it would be less official and more open, it would be less encumbered by political sensitivities. And it would affirm my view that when the American people become interested in an issue, so too would the government, while the reverse is less true. They liked the idea; so too did Goldberg, and with some refinements we set ourselves on this course in late fall 1982.

With information from our commissioned papers, panels, hearings, symposia, and subcommittees coming in at a rapid pace, the seriousness of our discussions increased correspondingly. My job was not to guide this conversation but to facilitate it, making certain that everyone was heard, that no one person or like-minded group of commissioners engaged a disproportionate share of our meetings, that the more reserved commissioners were invited to comment and to contribute, that we stayed on rather than strayed from the subject at hand, and that we completed our work on schedule.

Things Coalesce

As our meetings moved forward, I shifted my role from facilitator, scheduler, and organizer to more active chairman, summarizing lengthy discussions, calling out points of argument, identifying unresolved issues, making distinctions between answers and solutions, and quickly moving the commissioners toward a consensus about the content, organization, length, tone, title, and format of our report to the secretary. We took no votes. Everyone knew when we had a solid consensus on any issue, and after noting it, we simply moved on to the next issue. No one felt a need to formalize their views at such times. The only vote I recall taking on a substantive rather than on a procedural matter was when we unanimously voted to submit the report to Bell in April 1983.

We settled on an open letter to the American people, addressing them through Secretary Bell. The report was not to exceed forty pages. It was to be highly readable with an uncomplicated design and format. The report was to be written in plain, straightforward English with an urgent tone and five subject areas within which our recommendations would be made, sandwiched between a succinct description of the problem and the results of our findings at the start, and a letter to parents and students at the end. We spent nearly three hours discussing the actual design of the report and its title. In early 1983 we settled on *A Nation at Risk: The Imperative for Educational Reform;* and it was to be this title, not the Gardner or Bell commission's report, that Bell and I later strove to sell to the press and to others, believing that its public impact would be much greater.

The commission coalesced early around five subject areas for its recommendations:

- The curriculum or *content;*
- *Standards and expectations*—academic standards in the schools, admission standards of our universities and colleges, linked to the irony of rising grades reflecting declining student performance and achievement;
- *Time*—length of the school day and of the school year, and use of time in the classroom as well;
- *Teaching*—preparation of teachers, their further education, terms of employment, and circumstances of their professional lives within the schools; and
- *Leadership and fiscal support*—role of principals and superintendents, elected public officials at all levels, educators, parents, and others in advocating for the schools and seeking public support for their needs.

The staff was preparing drafts of a report for our consideration as these conversations moved from the general to the particular; they followed the points of agreement but fell short of what we were after: a hard-hitting, succinct, clear, articulate, and compelling case for what we found and what might be done to improve our nation's schools.

We Assign Tasks

As we moved into early 1983 with this set of key findings, I was becoming increasingly concerned about our seeming inability to resolve our particularized differences. Unresolved, they would trigger minority reports and, in my opinion, detract from and defuse the report's impact. I was also concerned with the continuing gap between the substance and tone of the drafts being prepared by the staff and what some of us were looking for in the report.

Gerald Holton, a distinguished professor of physics at Harvard, had been reluctant to accept Bell's efforts to recruit him as a commissioner, having little reason to believe that the report would amount to more than most such reports. Bill Baker's intercession persuaded Holton to accept; and he did so reserving his discretion to write a minority report. It had been my impression all along that he intended to do just that. Holton had turned out to be an indispensable member of the commission, respected and liked by all, honest and forthcoming in his views, likable and fun to be with, highly intelligent, broadly knowledgeable, and an active, constructive participant. I was determined to capture his talent and abilities and surmount his early reservations about the commission by asking him, rather than the staff, to write the next draft for the full commission's review.

I appointed a subcommittee of the commission to invite Holton to prepare such a draft and to vet it, as appropriate. Holton agreed and wrote what was to become the first real draft of the commission's report; it had just the right tone, included nearly all the main points, allowed for the diversity of opinions on major issues, but managed to employ language that permitted the commission to coalesce. It also included some of the views he might otherwise have insisted on putting in a minority report. As soon as I read Holton's draft, I knew we were on our way. At that point it was just a matter of getting everybody aboard. I did not underestimate the effort required but had an inner confidence that it was possible, if not probable.

Goldberg liked the Holton draft as well, and it served as the basis for our final meetings in early 1983, both of the full commission and of the subcommittee I had appointed to help prepare the report itself, chaired by Yvonne Larsen, our commission's vice chair.

The Hard Part Begins

In preparing the final report, I faced several major problems: within each new draft I had to narrow our differences and defer consideration of any remaining differences until we reached agreement on all other points; I had to honor the decisions that had been made about tone, length, format, brevity, and style; and I had to dissuade the four commissioners who seemed determined to write minority reports on views to which they alone were particularly attached—all this by our deadline of April 7, 1983. And finally, I had to honor commitments I had made to the commissioners that the preparation of a final report would enjoy their full review and involvement and would harbor no surprises.

As January slipped into February Goldberg and I were working with increasing intensity and determination to bring this effort to closure. My life was especially complicated in January and February 1983, as the Utah State Legislature was in session and I had the duty to protect and advance the University of Utah's interests during those always difficult and stressful months. I was also being actively recruited by the search committee responsible for finding David Saxon's replacement as president of the University of California.

Bell had followed our work closely, but without any interference of any kind. He was acutely aware of the deadline:

> As the charter deadline approached, I realized that before many months, we would be involved in the 1984 election campaign. I wanted the report out and the dissemination completed before the election season descended on us. Given our appallingly prolonged election campaigns, I knew we could tolerate no delay.[9]

We Make Adjustments

As the due date for the report approached, it was clear to Goldberg and to me that we were not going to make our deadline of April 7. There were still too many issues to hammer out, four or five minority reports to discourage, and the language of the report to be made just right. Goldberg and I were working together in my office at the University of Utah when in early February we both realized that we were not going to be ready with our report when Bell expected it. Goldberg laughed when I said that we should call Bell and tell him, suggesting with a smile that I should call. After all, he said, "you don't work for him, but I do." So I picked up the phone. Bell's account of the call follows:

> [We] had scheduled the release of the report at the White House for late March. Since the commission was looked on with scorn by the rightists who populated many White House offices, I felt it was a stroke of luck to have gotten on the president's calendar at all. If we tried to reschedule, I was far from sanguine about the prospect of presidential participation, and without the president, we would lose the attention of the huge White House press corps. We needed network TV, the wire services, and the giants among the nation's newspapers to cover this event if we were to get our message out. Everything we hoped to attain rested on this, and it in turn rested on the president's presence.
>
> "Dave, we can't get the president. At least, I don't think we can if we put this off another month," I protested.
>
> "We need [the] unanimous support of all commission members [for] every aspect of the report," David replied, "I can get the four or five who are in disagreement to join the majority, but it will take me more time to mediate the differences." . . .
>
> With [late April as a new target], I called White House Chief Jim Baker to plead my case for a delay. He was very understanding and sympathetic. He and Cabinet Affairs Director Craig Fuller seemed to appreciate the significance of the commission's work. This support was the only reason I have received any attention from the president in the first place. . . .
>
> A few days later he [Baker] called with a commitment of April 26 on the president's calendar. I was elated. We agreed to make our release on that date. Would the commission members still be hung up? On that note, I called Dave Gardner to tell him the good news.

"How are you coming?" I asked.

"We're coming along," he replied a bit evasively.

"I can't delay again," I warned.

"Don't worry, Ted, We'll make it."

And they did. The report was indeed adopted by unanimous action of all the members of the commission. David Gardner had performed a miracle.[10]

Witness Bell's courage, if not daring, that he was willing to plead for a new due date and to reschedule the president of the United States without knowing what was to be in our report or if we were really going to make the new deadline. He relied on our word, and we did everything we could to honor and acknowledge that trust.

The last full meeting of the commission before our report went to the secretary was at the Chicago Airport Hilton Hotel on March 24, 1983, one month before President Reagan was to receive it. This informal meeting did not go well. Members were making a final effort to include points of particular interest to them, and instead of moving forward, we actually began to slip backward. For example, Seaborg wanted our recommendations to include a fourth year of science and math for high school graduation, another wanted to soften some of the stronger language, others wanted to strengthen it, some thought we should include issues of moral and character education, others didn't. As each issue of contention arose, others would surface. It became contagious. The report was due at the printer in Washington on April 17 so that it would be available for the White House ceremony on April 26 when the president was calendared to receive it. Goldberg and I were getting nervous.

I cut the meeting short by deciding to catch an earlier flight back to Salt Lake City, as I did not wish to prolong or be caught up in what was proving to be the only really unproductive meeting in one and one-half years of work (it was also my fiftieth birthday, so everyone was understanding). Goldberg walked out with me, and on the way to the departure gate I said, "Milt, we've just had the last meeting of the commission until this report is in final form. We can't afford to start going backward after having gone forward these past eighteen months; and, besides, we don't have the time. Clear your calendar, as I will mine, between now and the end of the month and the first week of April. Arrange the dates that will work for you to come to Salt Lake City and we'll finish writing this report."

He agreed. Between then and early April Goldberg and I spent many hard and stressful days writing and rewriting the report. Little by little it began to fall into place. We contacted members separately by letters and phone calls and got prompt responses to our revisions. Members of the commission seemed to sense that their report was going to make a difference and was actually looking good, and they wanted to be both supportive and helpful in facilitating the preparation of the final draft, which was mailed to them on April 5.

As our irrevocable April 17 deadline approached, we intensified our efforts. With a request for their prompt and final response, Goldberg persuaded one or two commissioners to accept the final draft without the need to prepare a minority report as they had earlier intended. I did likewise with a couple of others, pointing out in one instance that if the commissioner was determined to write a minority report, then another commissioner, more famous and better known, would write a contrary one on the same point and would carry more weight and significance than the commissioner with whom I was speaking.

At the end Goldberg and I were scrutinizing each word, nuance, and paragraph to assure their conformance with commitments we had made, calling commissioners to satisfy last-minute compromises on language, and making arrangements for the White House ceremony and for the report's publication in time for its presentation to the president on April 26, 1983.

Goldberg returned home two weeks before the April 26 due date. I sent the final report by overnight mail to all commissioners, asking for their signature, on April 12, 1983, with the following comment:

> As we are all well aware, each one of us might have written a report that would differ in some respects from the one enclosed. The strength of the final draft, however, rests principally upon the efforts each of us has made to accommodate one another's views so that a unanimous report could be made to the Secretary and the American people. Such a report reflects how well intentioned and thoughtful people, holding differing views on issues of central importance to the country, could discover ways and means of reaching essential agreement on these issues.
>
> Any suggestions that you have for changes at this point must obviously be at the margin and of nominal significance. They should be called in to the Commission's staff no later than noon on Friday, April 15.[11]

We received additional comments and expressions of concern from a handful of commissioners, but most signed promptly. Goldberg and I spent the weekend of April 16 and 17 working on outstanding issues. My final call was to Seaborg from my home in Salt Lake City on Sunday night, April 17, around eight (MDT), the final changes to the report being due in Goldberg's hands two hours later, by midnight (EDT), to make our schedule. Seaborg was still pressing me for certain changes in language and emphasis, certain paragraphs to be moved, changes to be made in high school graduation requirements, certain points to be stressed, others to be de-emphasized.

I did what I could but finally said, "Glenn, you sound like you're negotiating the nuclear test ban treaty with the Soviet Union [as he had]; this is your old friend Dave Gardner talking with you." There was a pause, and he responded, "Well, what is it that you want me to do?" I said, "I want you to sign this damn report!" "Well, why didn't you just say so. No problem, you may regard me as having signed," he said laughingly. With Seaborg's approval, all eighteen commissioners had signed off, and no minority reports were written.

I called the final changes into Goldberg at 11:30 P.M. (EDT), he being much on edge when receiving my call, and we were on our way. I telegrammed each member of the commission on April 19, informing them that the final report had been forwarded for publication and asking them not to discuss its contents.

Goldberg shared the final draft of the report with Bell on April 20. Bell read it with Goldberg and Mary Jean Letendre, Bell's capable political operative with the Congress and White House, who had helped us in so many ways; indeed, her help had been indispensable. Gary Jones, Bell's undersecretary for education, and Tom Anderson, Bell's legal adviser, were also present. Jones and Anderson had been a real help throughout and afterward as well.

Bell's response was that the report was as powerful as it was brief. He was astonished that it could have been written so completely and compellingly in so few pages in light of the many hearings, commissioned papers, research, public testimony, and other input the commission had relied on. He also expressed surprise that the report was in the form of an open letter to the American people, a most unorthodox form of reporting officially to a cabinet secretary.

By the next morning, Bell was convinced that "A Nation at Risk" was "right on the money" and would be a powerful force for change that would capture the nation's attention. He began plans for a major PR effort to achieve these objectives.[12] Bell's enthusiasm for the report was not diminished, it needs to be mentioned, even though it took no account of the key points in the president and the Republicans' education platform: prayer in the schools, tuition tax credits or vouchers, and abolishment of the department itself.

The Report Goes to Bell

We held the last meeting of the commission over lunch on April 26, 1983, in Washington. The commission approved the report for the record, reflected on our eighteen months of working together and the enduring friendships made, thanked the staff for its excellent work, and commended Secretary Bell, who was with us, for his courage and perseverance in appointing the commission and the protections his office had afforded us so that the commission's report was its own and no one else's.

The report was addressed to Secretary Bell in the form of an open letter to the American people, as noted. The text was thirty-six pages, with a one-page transmittal letter signed by me, a three-page introduction, and twenty-five pages of appendices. The prose was tight, direct, and hard-hitting and the substance of the report hit Washington and the country like nothing since the shock of Russia's *Sputnik* twenty-six years earlier.

Our report's recommendations keyed off the five subject areas referred to earlier in this chapter, the recommendations themselves being driven by our findings. Neither the findings and recommendations nor our judgments about the nation's schools required lengthy explanations. Hence when we released the report we prepared a very brief press advisory but no executive summary. The report is its own summary.[13]

The Press Reacts

Earlier that morning Bell, our vice chair, Yvonne Larsen, and I had informally presented the report to President Reagan in the Oval Office of the White House. Vice President George H. W. Bush was also present, as were Ed Meese and Craig Fuller.

The president was in a good mood, looking forward to the formal presentation of the report later that day in the State Dining Room and warmly welcoming of us all. I could tell, however, that he had not yet read the report, not surprisingly given the lateness of its publication. We thanked him for his support, acknowledged our debt to Bell for this initiative, and shared with him the unified views of the commission that this report should and would make a difference in the education of America's young. We did not discuss any of the details.

Following our meeting Bell, Larsen, and I met with the White House press corps in the briefing room of the White House for about forty-five minutes. The press had received early but embargoed copies of the report the day before. Still, the media turnout astonished us: there were two full rows of television cameras, and the crowded room was alive with energy.

Given the brevity of our report, we had chosen not to prepare a detailed and lengthy press release. We believed that if the press could not capture the story from a release, then the reporters might choose to read the report itself; and they had. As I looked over the milling and restless crowd, I thought to myself that our report was going to be reported with a vengeance across the nation and abroad as well, because most of the reporters were of an age that they would most likely have children in school, as I did.

Bell welcomed the press, recalled his decision to appoint the commission, commended the commissioners for their honest, nonpartisan, and committed effort to render a constructive and forthright account of the quality of education in the country and what could be done to improve it, introduced Yvonne Larsen, and then turned it over to me.

After a few brief remarks, I invited questions. They were fast in coming, insistent but friendly. The answers were easy to give, as we had been dealing with the issues both in our professional lives for years and in our work on the report for the last eighteen months. It was very clear as the conference came to a close that the reporters had not only read the report but liked it as well.

The education editor of the *New York Times,* Edward B. "Ted" Fiske, asked the last question. He prefaced it with a reference to the nation's response to *Sputnik,* orbited by the Russians in 1957, which had shocked the country, stirred up debates about American education, and provoked Congress into enacting legislation intended to do something about it. Fiske went on, "I certainly don't see any appeal for any strong symbolic act by the White House to exercise this kind of leadership. In other words, it seems to me that it's not a terribly profound document [the report] and I just wonder whether you would have any comments on either the philosophy or the need for a strong symbolic—not necessarily financial leadership—by the White House?"[14]

Bell turned to me and, to the amusement of the press, suggested that perhaps I would wish to answer Fiske's question. I did so as follows, in part:

> Whether or not one tends to think that this is a profound document is a function of how you see society functioning. . . .
>
> We have addressed this in the form of an open letter to the American people. We hope they will read it. We hope you will all report it. We hope it will evoke discussion and controversy so that some attention will be brought to these problems. If, in fact, at the local level, in the school boards, in the parent-teacher organizations, in the admissions offices of universities and colleges, at state school boards' levels, in the various committees of the state legislatures concerned with this problem these issues bubble up and there's an expression of concern and desire to improve the education that we offer to our young people, it won't be long before the political leadership is aboard that wagon.
>
> My own view is it works better that way than the other way. Now, the other way works if you have a crisis because you can get some prompt and immediate, albeit brief, response. We don't think this is a crisis. We think it's a problem that's been coming for years and we think we'll be years getting out of it. And we tend to think that what it is that government pays attention to floats with what the people are concerned with.
>
> Our need is to get the people concerned about this issue. If that works, it will [take] root in this country and the political process will flow from it. So we've taken a completely different approach. Whether it will have success or not, time will tell.[15]

That response ended the press conference as reporters swamped Bell, Larsen, and me with questions they could not ask in the conference itself.

While we had all hoped for media interest, and a friendly and informed response from the press, none of us had any idea how consequential it would be or how telling our report would be on the American people, on their

elected officials, and on President Reagan. We went from the press conference to the commission's luncheon exhilarated by what we had observed
and anxious that our presentation of the report to Reagan that afternoon
would work out as we'd hoped.

As Bell and I were finishing our lunch and thinking about that official
four o'clock meeting, we were notified that the president's remarks prepared
by his staff for the ceremony bore little relationship to the commission's report and its recommendations. We were asked to come to the White House
immediately to help turn things around.

On arriving at the White House, I was reminded of the last-minute efforts
several years before to secure amendments to Utah's budget for higher education when the outcome would otherwise have been devastating to our
cause. But this was a different arena, and the stakes were now nationwide.

What we discovered was that the remarks prepared for the president were
"everything we didn't want them to be," as I remarked to Bell, who was doing a slow burn. Working with Craig Fuller and other White House staffers,
we managed to rewrite most of it, although intense and insistent counter-
pressures were being waged by Meese and his cohorts. Bell finally reported
back that the speech was now "good enough" and that "the most erroneous
and misleading statements had been rewritten or excised." Bell observed
"that the president was being ill-served by his 'ever vigilant' staff seeking to
include in the president's remarks statements that were simply untrue, and
not they but the president would pay the price." Believing that we had been
successful, however, we relaxed some and reviewed the protocols for our
meeting with the president in the State Dining Room.

After brief remarks by Bell and by me, the president arrived nearly twenty
minutes late and quipped on his somewhat embarrassed and belated entrance that "he could have been introduced as the late president of the
United States." Reagan knew how to soften an audience.

THE PRESIDENT RECEIVES THE REPORT

Reagan took note of our commission's findings, affirmed his interest in education, linked the quality of education to the country's social and economic
strength, expressed concern about the apparent decline in student performance, and then to Bell's dismay, my disappointment, and the commission's
astonishment—easily observable since the commissioners were sitting directly in front of the podium—the president read two paragraphs we thought
had been removed from his remarks but had now miraculously reappeared:

> Your call for an end to federal intrusion is consistent with our task of redefining
> the federal role in education. I believe that parents, not government, have the
> primary responsibility for the education of their children. Parental authority
> is not a right conveyed by the state. Rather, parents delegate to their elected

school board representatives and state legislators the responsibility for their children's schooling.

In a 1982 Gallup poll, the majority of those surveyed thought Washington should exert less influence in determining the educational program of public schools. So, we'll continue to work in the months ahead for passage of tuition tax credits, vouchers, educational savings accounts, voluntary school prayer and abolishing the Department of Education.[16]

Our report, of course, had made no mention of tuition tax credits, vouchers, educational savings accounts, voluntary school prayer, or an end to the department; and for the president to intimate that it had was as unfair to the commission as it subsequently proved to be embarrassing to the president.

Bell's revelations of this singular event deserve to be remembered:

The president fished into his pocket for the note cards he always used when speaking, apologized for his lateness, and then started on the remarks that had been prepared by his staff. It was almost identical to the speech that I had read and rejected. The words that I thought Jim Baker had gotten excised from the script came off those cards with the usual Reagan eloquence and style. . . .

I have been a champion of private schools and colleges in my life. I had no objection to tuition tax credits for parents who sent their children to private schools. But the purpose of the meeting was to present the commission's report, and this was not the time or the proper setting for this issue any more than it was the proper setting in which to emphasize the issue of prayer.

To my relief, the audience knew this. They were glancing sideways and giving each other knowing looks.

As the president launched into that part of his speech that treated the prayer issue I looked over into the foyer just off the State Dining Room to see Ken Cribb give a congratulatory gesture and victory sign to his fellow defenders of the right. Ed Meese was standing there with a big smile on his face.[17]

The press sensed a story as they watched the commissioners react to Reagan's remarks and enveloped them as soon as the president had departed. Commissioner Holton, whose reaction to Reagan's remarks was not altogether inaudible, recalls this event: "'They just stormed over to us,' said Holton. 'One guy grabbed me and said, "I am from the *New York Times* and I must have dinner with you. You must explain to me what's really in this report.""'[18]

It was a great irony that the president's untoward remarks, coupled with the obvious distress of the commissioners, should have helped publicize a report the more conservative wing of the White House had hoped to suppress. Reagan's remarks met with critical publicity throughout the country, driven home by editorials and cartoons panning his speech while praising the report.

Bell became an instant celebrity with *A Nation at Risk*, it being the lead story reported nationwide that evening and on the front pages of virtually every newspaper in the country the following day. His memoirs recall his reaction and the nation's response to our report. As he noted, "We had hit a responsive chord. Education was on everyone's front burner."[19]

Bell and I made the rounds that night on the major news programs, for example, David Brinkley's show, Ted Koppel's *Nightline,* McNeil-Lehrer, National Public Radio's *All Things Considered,* and many more. The next morning Bell and/or I were on *Good Morning America,* the *Today* show, and others. Bell was the featured personality on the following Sunday's morning news shows, and he and I taped television and radio interviews for distribution throughout the country and gave interviews with the major national news magazines, including *Time* and *Newsweek.* I delayed my return flight to Salt Lake City two days because of the media's interest.

On April 30 the president addressed the nation by radio, as he did weekly, and his subject was the commission's report. The tone had now changed, and although the president once again mentioned his "agenda" he now stressed the commission's findings and recommendations and highlighted the historical and contemporary relevance of education to the nation's well-being. In the course of these remarks the commissioners were amazed to hear that the president, not Bell, had created the commission:

> You may have heard the disturbing report this week by the National Commission on Excellence in Education that I created shortly after taking office. Their study reveals that our education system, once the finest in the world, is in a sorry state of disrepair. . . .
>
> . . . Parents who never finished high school scrimp and save so that their children can go to college. Yet today, we're told in a tough report card on our commitment, that the educational skills of today's students will not match those of their parents. About thirteen percent of our seventeen-year olds are functional illiterates and, and among minority youth, the rate is closer to forty percent. More than two-thirds of our high schoolers can't write a decent essay. Our grade is a stark and uncompromising "U" for unsatisfactory. We must act now and with energy if we're to avoid failing an entire generation.[20]

A *Washington Post* piece by Bill Peterson retraced the familiar events that allowed the commission to reach accord. It concluded:

> At the long-embattled Education Department, the report is regarded as a major victory for Bell. "He knows the administration has given the department to the New Right," said one longtime department official. "But he really wanted to do something besides carrying Reagan's water to the Hill, which he thinks is his duty. I think he feels better about this than anything he's done since he came to town."[21]

Bell had committed himself early on to hold twelve regional meetings throughout the country, to share the report with the education community and interested community leaders and state and federal officials. These were very successful regional meetings attended by over 10,000 people from every state in the union, from the first in Hopkins, Minnesota, to the last in Indianapolis, Indiana, attended by 2,000 policymakers including governors, members of Congress, state legislators, educators, and other leaders.

President Reagan attended several of them. I joined him for the first and the last, and for the one at Pioneer High School in Whittier, California. Just before the first forum meeting in Minnesota, I received a call from the White House asking if I would accompany the president to the meeting on Air Force One; and if I could do so, the president would welcome the chance to discuss the report with me en route. Naturally, I accepted.

The President Converts

Once Air Force One was airborne, the steward asked me to join the president in his cabin. I had prepared for a ten- to fifteen-minute meeting, believing I'd be lucky to get that much. On entering the president's cabin, I was greeted not only by the president but also by Craig Fuller and James Baker, Reagan's chief of staff, who proved to be very helpful in all we were seeking to do.

The president reached for a legal-size yellow tablet, placed it on his desk, asked me to join him, and started down two pages of written questions, prepared in his own handwriting, questions he said that "had occurred to him as he was reading our report." He said that he wanted to finish our discussion during Air Force One's flight to Minneapolis, that we would not be interrupted except for some soup and a sandwich, and that I should not feel rushed. He wanted a thorough and candid conversation and asked Fuller to take notes.

His questions for the most part were ones I would have asked as well and some others I wouldn't have thought to ask. He had obviously read the entire report and read it carefully. There would be no 3×5 or 5×7 prompt cards for this discussion. Our conversation continued throughout the flight. I did the best I could to answer the president's questions, and he seemed more than satisfied. As we finished, he said, "I really like your report and intend to 'sell' it to the American people." He asked for my help in doing so and thanked me both for my work and for taking the time to join him on Air Force One.

As I stood up to leave, he asked with a smile, "if I would answer three questions he had not yet asked," as he "was unable to find any reference to them in the commission's report." The first question was, "May I have your views on my intention to abolish the Department of Education?" I answered by suggesting that my views were not really important, but "that if I were you I would use the department for constructive and useful purposes just as Secretary Bell had with the appointment of our commission, as the votes were not in the Congress to abolish the department in any event." Baker said, "I agree, Mr. President."

The second question was, "May I have your views on tuition tax credits and vouchers." I demurred again as to any personal views but noted that "any proposal by the administration to the Congress for such legislation, however well conceived and compellingly argued, would be perceived not as an effort to strengthen but to weaken public education; and might it not be better to focus on getting our report in front of the American people than concentrating on just one aspect of a much larger and more complex picture." Baker again said, "I agree, Mr. President."

"My final question," the president said, with a smile, "goes to your view of prayer in the schools." I observed, "The plane appears to be on its final descent into Minneapolis." Everyone laughed, including the president, who said as our meeting ended, "Okay, I think I know your answer. See you at the forum later today."

The president's appearances at Hopkins, Whittier, and Indianapolis can only be described as very successful for him and very good for education. He was saying all the things I hoped he would, was enthusiastic about these meetings, and especially enjoyed being with the students. Some viewed his involvement as strictly self-serving and entirely political. I did not then and do not now. The answer as to how his interest in education appeared to flag in the second term is not to be discovered in the first one.

In addition to his participation in these regional meetings, the president devoted nearly sixty speaking commitments over the next twenty months to education, keying off *A Nation at Risk,* including an address to the American Federation of Teachers, headed by Al Shanker, a progressive and courageous union leader who embraced the report and championed its recommendations until his death.[22] Two of the president's Saturday radio addresses were devoted to this subject, as were portions of his 1984 State of the Union message. Siri Voskuil takes note of this activity:

> Twice, the President made education the subject of his weekly radio address to the nation. He frequently used the White House as a backdrop: he held a luncheon for State Teachers of the Year; he awarded medals to presidential scholars; and twice representatives of national education organizations were brought in for publicized consultations with the President. In late September 1983, he gave awards (including a four-by-six foot flag of excellence) to 152 winners of the new federal Secondary School Recognition Program. In October, he proclaimed 1983–84 the National Year of Partnerships in Education and announced his intention to sign a memorandum directing all federal agencies to "adopt" a school. At a ceremony in August 1984, he announced that a teacher would be the first private citizen to fly on a space-shuttle mission.[23]

The Nation Reacts

However well and enthusiastically the report may have been received, it was not welcomed by the nation's principal and most powerful teachers' union, the National Education Association (NEA). The NEA regarded the report as an attack on teachers, on the public schools, and on the professional capability of its members (the organization had little respect if not outright hostility toward Reagan). Before the commission started up, Goldberg and I met with several of the NEA leaders and staff for lunch in Washington. We explained what the commission's work was to be, how the members were chosen, that we had "a clean slate" as we began our work and intended to make the most of the possibilities inherent in Secretary Bell's charge, and that our work would be ours alone but informed by the counsel, opinions, and perspectives of a wide swath of interested parties. I asked in particular if, as a valuable source of information and insight about and experience with the issues, the NEA staff would offer us their counsel, informally or officially, in writing or by a series of personal and private visits if they preferred. They chose not to help.

The next we heard from them was when the report was released, eighteen months later. They were nearly the first "out of the gate" in publicizing their criticism of the report. The NEA's reaction stood in stark contrast to the nation's second-largest and most consequential teachers' union, the American Federation of Teachers, whose views of the report were carefully considered and, on balance, constructive even as to those aspects of our report with which they took issue. I understand that the NEA leadership now believes that the report should have enjoyed NEA's support in 1983, rather than its scorn. Think what might have happened to help improve K–12 education in this country if Reagan and the NEA together had taken the lead. Regrettably, such opportunities come along only rarely.

But we had addressed our report to the average American, not to the country's political, business, or academic leaders, although we welcomed not only their interest but their constructive response and involvement as well. The media helped, as did governors such as Graham in Florida, Clinton in Arkansas, Riley in South Carolina, Keane in New Jersey, Alexander in Tennessee, Matheson in Utah, and Hunt in North Carolina, among others. Legislative leaders throughout the country, including my "home states" of California and Utah, supported our work, as did the publication of some thirty books and major reports following ours. The creation of well over three hundred task forces at the state and local levels to pursue the commission's findings and recommendations were also of major importance.

By February 1984 *Newsweek* reported that unemployment was the only issue ranked higher than education in its national survey of public concerns, higher than inflation, relations with the Soviet Union, protection of American jobs, or the federal deficit. And as Voskuil notes, the report—widely reprinted and translated into many languages, among them Italian, Spanish, Arabic, Chinese, Japanese, and Korean—"has become the benchmark against which education reform efforts (and education commission reports) continue to be measured."[24]

Yet some in the academic community criticized the report for the use of "superficial" findings, the misuse of data, the absence of footnotes, and the fact that we were associated with President Reagan's administration and thus somewhat tainted. We were also accused of undermining public regard for teachers and the public schools in general, and the lack of a more expansive treatment of minorities in our education system was also asserted.

I readily acknowledge that there were issues and data we might have included or treated more expansively and agree that it was not a "scholarly" work. The early drafts prepared by the staff fit the critics' hopes more than our intentions did. But a formal report much longer than thirty-six pages would have been a "turnoff" for the audience we had in mind; had we adopted one of those drafts instead of what we did, I wouldn't be writing this chapter about *A Nation at Risk,* as our report, like those of most other government commissions, would have gone unnoticed, shelved indefinitely and attracting little comment.

In any event, all our reference materials, all the data and published works, commissioned papers, and studies on which our findings were based were cataloged and made publicly available at the National Institute of Education's office in Washington. Our commission could hardly be faulted for serving the Reagan administration's interests, as our report derailed its education agenda. We took special care to protect the teachers from being scapegoated in the report and also addressed issues of differential readiness to learn and of equity in our nation's schools, all contrary to our critics' assertions that we failed to do so.

And finally, I do not believe that our report harbored misleading or erroneous data or findings. Several members of the commission (I was one) went over these very matters in great detail with our staff. Criticisms aside, the report galvanized a nationwide effort to reform the schools, especially at the high school level, our primary focus. While it is certainly true that many of these reforms were under way before our report was issued, it is also true that *A Nation at Risk* added both weight and substance to their efforts and those that followed.[25]

In 1989 the nation's governors held a National Education Summit in Charlottesville, Virginia. The summit, the first of its kind in the history of the country, was convened by President George H. W. Bush, with Governor Bill Clinton of Arkansas in a lead role for the governors. (The only other presidential efforts akin to Bush's initiative in the nation's history occurred when Theodore Roosevelt convened a meeting of the nation's governors to consider environmental issues and Franklin Roosevelt met with the governors to discuss the economy.) The summit endorsed six national education goals and engaged the governors and the federal government in common cause to advance the interests of education in America.

Over the next several years, the Congress enacted the Goals 2000: Educate America Act in 1994, and in 1995 the closely allied Improving America's Schools Act. The most recent legislative extension of this trend was in 2001 when under a Republican administration (George W. Bush), the boldest and most extensive legislative interest in public education by the federal government in the history of the country was enacted: the "Leave No Child Behind" legislation. And, it should be made clear, this was very much a bipartisan issue in the Congress. Comparable efforts were also made by many of the nation's governors, as noted.

On April 26, 1988, five years following the submission of our report, Secretary of Education William Bennett and President Reagan observed this anniversary at a ceremony in the East Room of the White House. Under the headline "35 Pages That Shook the U.S. Education World," Ted Fiske of the *New York Times* called the report "one of the most significant documents in the history of American public education" and touched on its effects:

> The results of the movement started in part by "A Nation at Risk" are widespread. All but five states have raised graduation requirements, and more than two dozen have passed comprehensive educational packages. . . .
>
> Skeptics viewed the drive for school reform as a passing fad, but the movement has become self-renewing, constantly darting off in new directions. . . .
>
> The first wave brought the sort of "input-output" changes that come naturally to politicians. State legislators appropriated new resources, such as money to raise teacher's salaries, and set new standards, like tighter curriculums and competency tests for teachers.
>
> But the question inevitably arose: How do better-paid teachers help students meet the new standards? This led to a second round of changes aimed at understanding and improving the teaching and learning process itself. States like California began systematic reviews of their curriculums, and teacher training became a popular issue.[26]

The American business community was late to react, but once it made a commitment in 1990, it had a major and positive impact on the movement, mostly at the state and local levels, being taken up as a major issue for American business by the National Business Roundtable, the Business–Higher Education Forum, and later the National Alliance of Business.

I wish to note here the debt of gratitude I continue to carry for my fellow commissioners. The members of the commission were among the most dedicated, informed, and intelligent people I have been privileged to work with. They were also "good people," determined to do a proper job in their assigned task, and as willing to learn as to teach. I was blessed to have had the opportunity to work with each and every one of them in a common effort to improve our country's schools and the education of our nation's school-children.[27]

Bell too worked hard and long not only to advance *A Nation at Risk* and spread its message but in a number of other and creative ways as well. He developed a state-by-state comparison of student scores and college entrance examinations, ranking them by state along with the percentage of high school graduates taking the examinations. The "evaluation wall chart," as it came to be known, also gave the state-by-state statistics for the percentage of the school-age population living in poverty, the percentage of minorities enrolled in school, the percentage of students completing high school, and per capita income, teachers' salaries, and expenditures per child.

Bell drew up the chart at the request of the nation's governors, who gathered in summer 1983 at Vice President Bush's vacation home in Kennebunkport, Maine. The chart got mixed reviews but served to open up for public scrutiny comparisons of student performance, and their social and economic context for all to see.

Bell also launched a Secondary School Recognition Program to honor outstanding schools. This was a most sought-after honor by the schools, and the program was another boost to the commission's report. Bell recalls one such recognition ceremony at Pioneer High School in Whittier, California, just south of Los Angeles, which the president asked me to attend. Its students came chiefly from low-income Hispanic families, and their achievements were outstanding. At the award ceremony's most dramatic moment, Bell relates,

> the president and I proceeded to unfurl the Excellence in Education flag and hold it up before the audience and all the TV cameras. Because of the way the banner had been folded, and because I didn't check it prior to our displaying it, the president unfurled a flag that was not only upside down but also backwards.
>
> Naturally, the audience laughed at the goof. Even after we corrected the upside-down display, the flag was backwards, and the audience roared again. But Ronald Reagan, always poised and unflappable, turned the whole episode into an opportunity to help everyone laugh some more. It was an incident that demonstrated why he is so popular and why so many people esteem him even when they disagree with his policies.[28]

Bell also recalls the formulations of the Republican Party's education platform of 1984, on which the commission's report had such a major impact.

> *A Nation at Risk* placed educational reform high on the public opinion agenda, and this had its political payoff for the president. He stole the issue from Walter Mondale, and it cost us nothing in the budget. It was simply a splendid issue to use in the domestic affairs arena, for it obscured concern about cuts

in welfare, aid to dependent children, Medicaid, and other social program reductions. It had such broad-based national and popular support that by the time the Republican Platform Committee addressed the issue, it was clear that any move that even hinted it might be anti education was doomed.

Given this, the far right did not have a chance. The platform committee wanted no part of a move to put abolition of the Education Department back in the 1984 platform. Republican delegates who were serving in the U.S. House of Representatives deserve most of the credit for rejecting any push to put the abolition of ED back on the list of campaign planks. Many of them were solid, responsible conservatives who had the wisdom to know that the party would be hurt. We won by an impressive vote of six to one when the matter came up. It was a victory to savor, and I enjoyed it thoroughly.[29]

THE TIDE TURNS: REAGAN'S SECOND TERM

Bell mentioned to me several times as we were working to advance the report and its visibility that many of his friends believed that Reagan was "just using you and the report for his own political advantage." Bell's usual response was to say, "He may be using me, but I am doing all I can to use him for my cause and to take advantage of his great popularity."

But with the reelection of the president to his second term in fall 1984, things changed dramatically for Bell. His budget was once again under downward pressure from the White House budget office, leaks to the press of Bell's confidential memoranda on his budget priorities were complicating his life, and a certain coolness was seeping out of previously welcoming offices in the West Wing of the White House. Bell's support and his cause were clearly slipping, and in spite of his willingness to continue the fight, the doors were closing, as Bell recalled:

> What had changed so suddenly? How could the so-called sensitive area of education become such a low priority in such as short time? The only difference was that the election was over. We had won our mandate from the people for a second term. *A Nation at Risk* had served its purpose: Our campaign for nationwide school reform movement to implement the report's recommendations helped in the campaign for reelection. . . .
> I remembered words of Voltaire I had read long ago: "Every success sharpens the sting of later defeats." In politics and in Washington, I decided, this was all too true.[30]

On November 8, 1984, Bell submitted a terse, four-paragraph letter of resignation to the president, effective December 31, 1984. His resignation shocked and disappointed me, as did the circumstances of his resignation as he recounted them. As to my own view, I did not then and do not now regard the president's involvement in this endeavor as duplicitous, although the circumstances surrounding Bell's departure and his view of it make such a conclusion plausible. Having spoken with the president at length about the report, as noted and on other occasions, I do not myself arrive at so harsh an opinion. Of course Reagan did calculate the political implications of whatever he decided to support or oppose, as any president would, but I do not believe that his involvement was a charade.

The Meese faction simply moved to adjust things after the election faster than Bell did, and his faith in the president made insufficient allowance for the role Reagan's key staff played in almost everything he did. The Right, stung by the defeat of their education platform at the Republican National Convention, reacted with renewed vigor and aggressiveness to recapture the president for "their education" agenda in his second term and to undercut Bell. They did so quickly and arranged for the appointment of his successor, knowing that the president depended heavily on his work being staffed and that Bell's agenda was incompatible with their own.

William F. Bennett was soon nominated as Bell's successor. Bennett remains a very articulate and intelligent spokesman for the more conservative faction of the Republican Party, well able to advance his views and influence. I had never met Bennett until invited by the president to join them for lunch at the White House shortly after Bennett's nomination. I called Bennett to see if we might meet privately before our luncheon. He agreed. We met in the White House.

I did what I could to acquaint him with the work of our commission, explained the rationale for our report, detailed the progress we had made, and, most important, called out the momentum already in place, not only federally, but at the state level as well. Knowing of Reagan's reliance on staff work, I emphasized how important it would be if he, Bennett, were to sustain the president's interest in advancing *A Nation at Risk,* consistent with Reagan's involvement the past year and a half.

Bennett was having none of it. His answer was that I was discussing Bell's agenda with him and he had a different one, namely, to put pressure on the universities and colleges of the country to improve and strengthen their work and role. I responded by pointing out that the president had also endorsed and advanced Bell's agenda and that if he didn't stay the course our momentum would falter and the efforts of the past would fall well short of their intrinsic potential. He was unmoved.

In our February 1985 luncheon with Reagan, therefore, I did what I could to strengthen the president's resolve to sustain the momentum that he himself had contributed to so positively and with such effect. Bennett was no help. I knew right then that we had failed or would at least fall well short of what was well within our grasp. On June 5, 1985, I wrote a personal letter to the president urging him to remain engaged in the reform effort. In essence I argued:

[I am] increasingly concerned that the reform movement you so spectacularly started your first term appears to be losing some of its force. The reform movement need not and should not lose ground. This movement is nationwide, yet local in its manifestations; it involves our national interest, yet is best dealt with by the states and local school districts; and it affects the nation's security, economy, and civility, yet requires no major new Federal initiative for it to succeed. What it does need is your continuing personal support and involvement—not necessarily at the same level of intensity or frequency as in the past, but enough to insure that the effort is both nurtured and sustained.

I am fully aware of how insistent are the demands on your time; you had already given generously of your schedule and leadership skills in behalf of the cause about which I write. But we still have some distance to travel before we are home. I write, therefore, to urge that you and those who advise you on this matter find a way to recapture your participation and active involvement in this effort.[31]

He responded on July 12:

Thank you for your letter of June 5.

I believe that *A Nation at Risk* may well prove to be a turning point in our educational history. The Nation owes you a debt for chairing the National Commission that produced it, and I intend to continue supporting actively and enthusiastically the educational reform movement it helped to advance.

As you suggest in your letter, the reform movement is currently focusing its efforts at the State and local level. This is entirely proper. My role must primarily be to encourage the efforts of parents, teachers, principals, communities, and States to transform the rising tide of mediocrity, identified by your Commission, into a rising tide of educational excellence.

I appreciate your reminder and encouragement to do even more. Let me also encourage you, in turn, not simply to continue your own active role, but to remind others outside the Federal government to join in the movement for educational reform. I can assure you that I, along with my Secretary of Education, Bill Bennett, and others in my Administration, will continue to be enthusiastic partners in this citizens' movement for educational excellence.[32]

Opportunity Lost

The president, however, came to follow Bennett's lead, encouraged by his more conservative advisers and Bennett's own preferences. Higher education came under attack by Bennett, but with negligible effect. Reagan neither joined in this broadside against our colleges and universities nor sustained his interest in the K–12 reform effort, although much of the initiative was by then shifting to the governors.

Bennett did not wholly ignore our report or what it had accomplished. Indeed, he made favorable reference to it from time to time. He just decided, it would seem, not to spend much of his or the president's time on it, although I think he warmed up to *A Nation at Risk* toward the latter part of his tenure, as reflected in *American Education: Making It Work,* his report to Reagan in April 1988, on the occasion of a White House ceremony linked to our report's fifth anniversary, and later in a 1998 publication entitled "A Nation Still at Risk."[33] But it was too late, both for Reagan and for the country. What could have been was not to be. A critical chance to help the country improve its educational system was largely lost, or at the least its momentum was seriously impaired.

The most conservative faction of Reagan's advisers had managed to recapture both the president and Education, thus removing at the national level the one person, a very popular president, who could have kept the nation's eye on education and move the reform efforts forward to a more mature and enduring conclusion, collaboratively with the states.

I thought back to my days at Santa Barbara and how important it was there for the center to hold. Here the center was losing to the most conservative elements of the White House on one side and the liberal-leaning teachers' union (NEA) and some educational researchers on the other, and all for their own but different purposes wanted none of what *A Nation at Risk* was proposing. Common ground is what our report symbolized, whatever its imperfections. But neither extreme was looking for common ground to help the country move ahead in improving its schools. Instead they pushed for their respective and more constricted views of what seemed best for them.

Under these conditions, checkmate occurs. Thus the great middle, searching desperately for common ground, loses, and little to nothing gets done. And so it was here, reports as recently as 1998 discouragingly resembling our earlier findings of the realities of K–12 education in the United States.[34] Edging into the new millennium, in 2002 the United States Supreme Court has judged vouchers to be constitutionally permissible, as the encouragement and support for this movement come in no small measure from our country's minority communities who despair over the public schools their children attend.

Bell really did have it right in 1981 when he asked me to chair the National Commission on Excellence in Education. "David," he said, "we have one last chance to galvanize support for the public schools, to improve or reform them, lest a wholly disenchanted public abandon the public schools in favor of tuition tax credits and/or school vouchers, thus hastening the transfer of students from public to private schools."[35]

But we lost that chance at the federal level, and America's schoolchildren were the losers. Bell's view of all this concludes his memoirs:

> We would have changed the course of history in American education had the president stayed with us through the implementation phase of the school re-

David's father,
Reed Snow Gardner,
on the range, Pine
Valley, Utah, circa
1916.

David as an infant
with his mother,
Margaret Pierpont
Gardner, Berkeley,
California, 1933.

Lynn Gardner,
cousin, with David
in hat, collecting
eggs on the farm,
Delta, Utah, 1941.

With Bill Underhill,
Echo Lake in back-
ground on the way
to Desolation Valley
for trout, 1950.

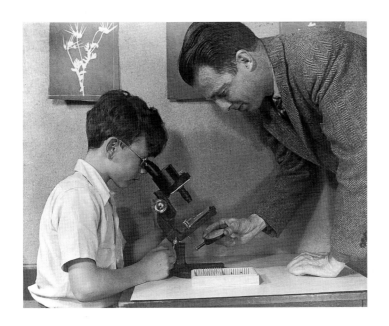

With sixth grade teacher, Mr. Turner, Cragmont Grammar School, Berkeley, California.

David and Libby (Elizabeth Jane Fuhriman) at their wedding reception, Alumni House, UC Berkeley, June 27, 1958. Photo: Arthur Odell Studio, Oakland, California.

The Gardner daughters, Flathead Lake, northwest Montana, July 1982: Marci, Lisa, Karen, and Shari.

The Gardner family at their ancestral home in Pine Valley, Utah, 1980: bottom row from left, Allie Dixon Gardner (stepmother), Reed Snow Gardner, Vilate Gardner Trussel (sister); back row, David and brothers, Reed and Jim.

Presenting a university souvenir to an incoming Berkeley freshman at a student orientation party hosted by the California Alumni Association at the home of Mr. and Mrs. David Bohannon, Woodside, California, 1960. Photo: Ted Streshinsky.

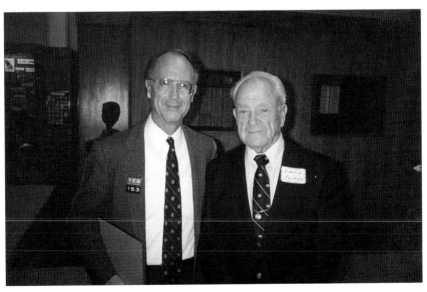

With Emery Curtice, UC Berkeley athlete and alumnus, friend and mentor, circa 1988.

Mary Cheadle and Chancellor Vernon Cheadle, University of California, Santa Barbara, 1977.

The commander of the National Guard and officers at UC Santa Barbara, called to Isla Vista in spring 1970 to control rioting. Photo: 1970 *La Cumbre*/ASUCSB. Used with permission.

The Isla Vista branch of the Bank of America the morning following its burning during riots at UC Santa Barbara, spring 1970. Photo: 1970 *La Cumbre*/ASUCSB. Used with permission.

Inauguration as the tenth president of the University of Utah, Salt Lake City, November 19, 1973.

Members of the administration serve ice cream to students during homecoming activities at the University of Utah, 1980. Photo: Special Collections, J. Willard Marriott Library, University of Utah. Used with permission.

The University of Utah men's ski team celebrates its 1983 NCAA title, Deer Valley, Utah.

Libby and David visiting with Her Imperial Majesty Empress Farah, Saadabad Palace, Tehran, Iran, 1977.

Party for Gardner by his University of Utah staff, just prior to his leaving for the University of California, 1983. Photo: University of Utah Public Relations.

Trustees of the Tanner Lectures on Human Values meeting at the University of Utah, June 1982. Clockwise from left, President Donald Kennedy of Stanford; President Emeritus O. Meredith Wilson of Oregon and Minnesota; President Harold Shapiro of Michigan and later of Princeton; Gardner; President Derek Bok of Harvard; professor, former Master of Clare Hall and Vice-Chancellor Emeritus, Lord Ashby of Cambridge University; Professor O. C. Tanner of Utah; and Professor H. L. A. Hart, Master of Brasenose College, Oxford. Photo: University of Utah Public Relations.

President Ronald Reagan receiving the report, *A Nation at Risk: The Imperative for Educational Reform,* submitted by the National Commission on Excellence in Education, in the Oval Office of the White House, April 26, 1983. Left to right: Craig Fuller, secretary to the cabinet; Edwin Meese III, counselor to the president; Yvonne Larsen, vice chair of the commission; President Reagan; Terrel H. Bell, secretary of education; Gardner, chair of the commission; and Vice President George H. W. Bush. Photo: Courtesy of the White House.

President Ronald Reagan and David Gardner following the president's receipt of *A Nation at Risk*, the Oval Office of the White House, April 26, 1983. Photo: Courtesy of the White House.

THE WHITE HOUSE

WASHINGTON

July 12, 1985

Dear Dr. Gardner:

Thank you for your letter of June 5.

I believe that A Nation at Risk may well prove to be a turning point in our educational history. The Nation owes you a debt for chairing the National Commission that produced it, and I intend to continue supporting actively and enthusiastically the educational reform movement it helped to advance.

As you suggest in your letter, the reform movement is currently focusing its efforts at the State and local level. This is entirely proper. My role must primarily be to encourage the efforts of parents, teachers, principals, communities, and States to transform the rising tide of mediocrity, identified by your Commission, into a rising tide of educational excellence.

I appreciate your reminder and encouragement to do even more. Let me also encourage you, in turn, not simply to continue your own active role, but to remind others outside the Federal government to join in the movement for educational reform. I can assure you that I, along with my Secretary of Education, Bill Bennett, and others in my Administration, will continue to be enthusiastic partners in this citizens' movement for educational excellence.

With my warm best wishes,

Sincerely,

Ronald Reagan

The Honorable David Pierpont Gardner
President
The University of California
Berkeley, California 94720

Clark Kerr, twelfth president and Charles J. Hitch, thirteenth president, at David Gardner's inauguration as fifteenth president of the University of California, UCLA, April 12, 1984.

Berkeley Chancellor I. Michael Heyman and Governor George Deukmejian at Gardner's inauguration. Photo: UCLA Photography.

Principal speakers at the inauguration: from left, Harvard President Derek Bok, Gardner, and Lord Ashby of Cambridge University. Photo: UCLA Photography.

Libby and David Gardner. Photo: Joseph A. Ochoa.

President Gardner, Jack Peltason, and UCI's founding chancellor Daniel G. Aldrich, Jr., at Peltason's inauguration as chancellor of UC Irvine, March 1985.

At the inauguration of Chang-Lin Tien as Berkeley chancellor, Charter Day, the Greek Theatre, UC Berkeley, March 22, 1991. Photo: Peg Skorpinski.

form movement. And this would have won a place in history for Ronald Reagan as the man who renewed and reformed education at a time when the nation was, indeed, at risk because we were not adequately educating our people to live effectively and competitively in the twenty-first century.[36]

Nevertheless, *A Nation at Risk* had remarkable staying power and a part in the improvement our schools have made in the intervening years. And perhaps Commissioner Emeral Crosby, principal of Northern High School in Detroit, had it right when he suggested that our report "is like the baton in a relay race. It doesn't determine the race but it's the thing that keeps the runners going." In light of what has happened in the intervening years, I also believe that if Bell had not suffered an untimely death in 1996 he would have been more upbeat about his own contributions and the results of our report than his quoted comments here suggest. In any event, I am proud of my role in making it all happen and of the privilege of working with so many dedicated and wonderful people.[37]

This experience also helped ready me for the convoluted and sometimes barely believable world of California politics, as I moved in August 1983 into my new responsibilities as president of the University of California, the nation's most distinguished public research university within the most populous, diverse, wealthy, and enigmatic state in the union. I discovered that everything I had done professionally was a mere warm-up for the next nearly ten years I was to serve as UC's fifteenth president. I would have to "earn my degree" all over again.

FIVE

BACK TO THE BLUE AND GOLD

RETRACING FOOTSTEPS

At the dinner table shortly after my appointment as president of the University of California in early March 1983, the family was talking about what this would all mean especially for our daughters: Karen, a senior at Stanford; Shari, a sophomore at the U; Lisa, a junior in high school; and Marci, who would be entering high school in the fall.

The conversation was a mix of excitement, sadness, crosscutting feelings, and some apprehension with everyone seemingly speaking at once when, during a brief interlude between eating and talking, Lisa looked at me and said, "Well, Dad, you will soon be a 'lame duck' in Utah and a 'sitting duck' in California." While everyone laughed and appreciated Lisa's way of always saying just what she thought and usually as it occurred to her, time proved her to be prescient.

This next adventure in our lives had been occasioned by UC President David Saxon's announcement in fall 1982 that he would step down as president on June 30, 1983, after eight years of service. At the time I felt apprehension, ambivalence, and uncertainty, all traceable to what Saxon's retirement might mean for our family and my career. In one sense, it was presumptuous to suppose that it carried any meaning whatsoever for me, but in another I knew—even if I were only a candidate for his post—that it involved an inner struggle between the pull of Utah and the tug of California.

The Search

The familiar and well-tried processes for finding a new president mandate a faculty committee to help identify and vet candidates; a regents' committee to oversee the search and to recommend one candidate to the Board of Regents for election; and an array of alumni, students, and staff to be involved and/or consulted as appropriate. And then there are interested others whose views and preferences would be gladly proffered if invited, or more insistently offered if overlooked: the presidents of leading American universities, the chancellors and other key officers within UC's nine campuses and the Office of the President, donors, the governor and key legislators, and those within the minority, educational, business, agricultural, and labor communities whose opinions mattered.

Saxon's decision to retire made me think of my decision seven years earlier to turn away the offer to serve as UC's president. I wondered who would take Saxon's place, since I had burned my bridges in 1975; or had I? The question lingered, unshared and unspoken, but omnipresent in my own mind, nevertheless. I was soon receiving calls from friends at UC, members of the faculty and staff, alumni and donors encouraging me to express my interest, offering to write or gather support for my appointment.

My response was consistent and unequivocal: "Please do not do anything." First of all, I knew that I might have to rethink the matter again and did not, at that point, have a confident view. Second, the family would need to be supportive. Third, I would have to be certain that what I had to offer was what the search committee wanted. And fourth, and perhaps most important, on grounds of both principle and practice I would not seek such a position and appear to equate the settled, studied, and careful process of selection for a nonpartisan, nonpoliticized position with that of a political campaign or put myself in the debt of those who helped, not to mention the awkward and unsettling implications of an incumbent president appearing to seek another post and falling short. Hence if the UC search committee wanted to contact me, it would do so. And its approach would be both timely and appropriate, unencumbered by any third-party representations about my perceived interest in the position or lack thereof. As far as I know, that is what happened.

In early 1983 the search committee approached me through the regents' secretary, Bonnie Smotony, who asked if I would be willing to meet with the committee in Los Angeles. I asked: "How many candidates are on the short list, but no names, please?" "Three or four," she answered.

This then was a serious call, which made it all the more unsettling. "Could this really be happening?" I asked myself and next, thinking of the impact on my family and me, "Do I really want this to be happening?" I said I would call her within two days, intending to use the intervening time to seek Libby's views and insights as well as those of our daughters before taking even the first step.

Libby had a different view in 1983 than in 1975 and recalled that I had turned away the UC position once before, but "for reasons that no longer pertain." She said that as to the family, I should be free to consider the position if I wished, and at the least I should accept the invitation to visit with the search committee. In her usual diplomatic but straightforward way, she neither urged me to look favorably or unfavorably on the prospect but did encourage me to take the first step so as not to miss the chance of taking the subsequent others if thought to be desirable by all parties.

As for myself, I was well into my tenth year at Utah, had accomplished much of what I had set out to do in 1973, and judged that if I were to remain in my Utah post I would enjoy several additional years of professional accomplishment and personal satisfaction but at a somewhat diminished rate, owing to the encumbrances borne by ten years of decision making on the one hand and an overly familiar and mostly predictable personal and social environment on the other.

While I knew the University of California well, had followed its fortunes under Governor Jerry Brown and President David Saxon, had many friends throughout the university, and was aware of its triumphs and travails, I also knew that its president, unlike the chancellors, was one step removed from campus life. I had always cherished my daily contact with colleagues and students at Berkeley, Santa Barbara, and Utah, being directly connected to the university's work and raison d'être. Would I like equally well being one step removed from campus life? This issue and many others engaged my thoughts over the next two days as I considered my answer.

If I accepted the search committee's request to meet with me, feeling complimented by the mere fact of the invitation, and even more so against the backdrop of exchanges in 1975, I decided to reserve my discretion to stand or not to stand for appointment just as the regents were doing in interviewing three or four candidates and not just one. With that understanding, I returned Secretary Smotony's call and accepted the interview.

My friend of many years Regent Dean Watkins was chairing the search committee. We met at the Airport Marriott Hotel in Los Angeles several days later, passing through the "service delivery" entrance and the kitchen to the meeting room so as to maintain the confidentiality of the interview. I walked into the room not knowing who else was being interviewed, not knowing most of the regents present, and not being privy to the questions to be asked or the dispositions and inclinations of most of the questioners.

After introductions, Regent Edward Carter asked the first question. He was the board's most senior member, a leading businessman from Los Angeles, a person of marked influence within California, a personal friend of President Reagan's, someone deeply devoted to the university, and a very tough and exceptionally blunt individual for whom I retained respectful recollections from my work both at UC's Santa Barbara campus and as a vice president of the university.

But Carter's question stunned me. "You're a Mormon, are you not?" he asked. Taken aback, I said "yes" but nothing more, even though I could tell he was looking for a more elaborated response. In the next instant I thought of the army sergeant at Fort Ord who had approved of me because of my religious faith, the Berkeley draft board that had held it against me, and decided that I was going to say nothing more.

After an awkward pause, another regent put the second question: "I would like to know your position on the Equal Rights Amendment."

This question, really the same as Carter's but now couched in political rather than direct religious terms, gave me serious pause about the intent of the interview within the context of its presumed purposes. I wondered how best to respond and finally said something along the following lines: "These two questions are, in the first instance, legally impermissible and, in the second, wholly inappropriate unless it's your intention to apply a religious and/or a political test to the appointment of the university's next president contrary to the express provisions of the state constitution charging the regents to keep the university free of political and sectarian influence in the administration of its internal affairs. I will, therefore, not respond to your second question nor elaborate on your first."

I let my words sink in for a moment, turned to the questioner, and said, "Why don't you rephrase your question? Ask me about my views of the educational and employment opportunities women should expect to find or would hope to find at UC. Phrased that way, I will be happy to answer." She said, "All right, what are your views?"

With some brief mention of my having four daughters and being keenly aware of the implications attending her interest, I said that "women should have the same freedom over their lives as men do, including, and not by way of limitation, their personal and professional lives, and that neither the law nor university policies and practices should impede or otherwise interfere with the exercise of that discretion." I also noted my twenty years of administrative experience, ten years of prior service at UC, and ten years at Utah, where my actions, not just my words, were on the record.

"Well, that's a good answer," she said, and we moved on.

This exchange had its uses for it made clear that I was not importuning the board for this position, that I was not one to accommodate questions impermissible under the law or by custom, and that what they saw was what they would get if they offered me the position. The remainder of the uninterrupted three hours' interview was uneventful and involved the standard questions that interviewing committees ask. Nevertheless, the exchange identified the tensions of the fault line dividing the liberal and conservative board members, the former not appearing to favor my "candidacy" and the latter seemingly determined I should be theirs.

My religious faith doubtless contributed to those perceptions, as would also my ten years of service in conservative Utah. And perhaps so did the fact that I was then completing my work on a commission for the Reagan administration. Some of the longer-serving liberal regents may also have recalled my days at UCSB where I was much engaged in dealing with the student radicals, and not in ways they would necessarily have preferred. And I was thought to be a conservative in California and a liberal in Utah. All this, I believed, resembled a micro-McCarthyite approach to judging people by their perceived associations. Not a good idea. Yet this troubling thought did not rise to the level of an overarching concern: I was confident that I could work with both sides, given that each tended to exaggerate my views by assuming they were more left or right than they actually were.

As the interview concluded, Regent Carter asked the last question: "Are there any peculiarities about your administrative style or your personal commitments that we should know about?" I said, "Yes. You should know that throughout my working life I have sought to balance my professional obligations and my personal and family life, determined to succeed in each rather than to sacrifice one for the sake of the other."

"What do you mean by that?" Carter then asked, somewhat surprised. I answered by describing our "not more than two consecutive nights out and nothing on Sunday rule" and added that Libby and I believed deeply that no success outside the home could compensate for failure within it.

Carter's answer came swiftly. "Well, that might have worked for Utah—it is a single-campus university and a much less complicated place than UC. Utah has a small population and is only a fraction of California's size. Here we have nine campuses, not one, and some twenty-five million people. You can't possibly do here what you did there and meet your responsibilities as president of UC." "Well," I answered, "if you really believe that to be true, then you should not be interviewing me. You should be interviewing someone else."

There was no response for several seconds when Regent Frank Clark said, "Ed [Carter], why are we asking these questions? If we hire Dave or anyone else, how they do the job is their business. Our only concern is that the job gets done. If the job gets done, fine. If not, we fire him." Clark then turned to me and said, "Isn't that right?" I said, "That's exactly right." And that was that. The interview was over.

On my flight back to Salt Lake City, I thought that my candor had probably not advanced my chances of serving as UC's next president; but I felt just fine about it because my answers were truthful and not calculated to win me either votes or regard. Besides, if by chance I were to be offered the position and accepted it, the regents who had interviewed me would know the ground rules between us; and, I should add, as will be made clear later, this proved to be a very important consideration.

Between my meeting with the search committee in late February and my election as president on March 2, 1983, with effect from August 1, 1983, I received several calls a day from friends in California encouraging me to take the position, warning me of the pitfalls, informing me of the politics within UC and in the state capital regarding this appointment, and encouraging me to believe that the task at hand was tailor-made for a person with my experience, character, and personality. By and large, I simply listened to these calls, but I also made a handful of calls myself to check on points raised in the interview and to learn about the regents' political dynamics.

The calls were stimulated by newspaper articles appearing throughout California speculating about the search and naming candidates, for example, Chancellor Charles Young of UCLA, Chancellor Ira Michael Heyman of UCB, President William Gerberding of the University of Washington, among others. I personally knew and respected all these men and was pleased to be in such company regardless of the outcome. These articles and calls merely reconfirmed the correctness of my earlier decision not to seek this position nor to invite others to do so on my behalf, especially if I were to be appointed and, thus, needful of cordial relationships with all the university's nine chancellors, not just seven of them.

Meanwhile, my situation at the University of Utah was becoming increasingly awkward. We were in the middle of our annual session of the state legislature, and I was the university's lead player, not only for budgets but also for legislation we favored or opposed; and naturally, whatever the California papers were saying, the Utah papers carried too, thus provoking speculation about my intentions.

I was also trying to meet my obligations as chairman of the National Commission on Excellence in Education while being unclear about my professional future on the one hand and on the other wondering how Secretary Bell, President Reagan, and the American public would receive *A Nation at Risk* the next month. I had the energy, interest, and patience both tasks required and was happy with my personal and family life but, if asked, increasingly ready to accept a new challenge at UC or content to serve the University of Utah for a more extended period as circumstances dictated. In addition, I was increasingly confident that our commission's report would prove to be a positive and constructive force in the service of American education. With all these forces swirling around me, oddly enough, I was in a state of equilibrium, not really anxious or threatened or full of misgivings about any of these matters that came to have such a profound effect on my life and family and on countless others as well.

As February 1983 came to a close, I received a call from Regent Watkins, advising me of the search committee's intention to put my name forward to the Board of Regents with the unanimous recommendation that I be elected as the university's fifteenth president. "Would you be willing to have your name put forward, and would you be willing to serve if elected?" he asked. The answer to these questions depended on a number of matters:

- Is the committee submitting only my name to the board?—Yes.
- When will I meet with the full board?—Before your name is formally submitted, for breakfast on March 2 in Berkeley, with the closed meeting of the regents to follow, convening for the single purpose of electing you.
- What will be the full board's reaction to your committee's recommendation?—Favorable, probably unanimous. Depends on how you do in your breakfast meeting with them.
- What will be the reaction to my appointment within UC?—Favorable, disappointed candidates and their champions excepted.
- What will be the reaction in Sacramento?—Governor George Deukmejian is supportive. The legislature will reflect many opinions, regardless of who is appointed.

We discussed these and related university matters, including my starting date, major issues of concern to the regents, the chancellors, the vice presidents, and the Academic Senate, and not only Watkins's views about these concerns but also his insights as they bore on the workings of the board, the university administration, and the faculty leaders. We then reviewed procedures, protocols, and press relations about which I needed to be informed; I said I wished to talk with the family before giving him a definitive response and would call him the next day with my answer, which I did: it was positive, with the entire family rallying around in support.

Terms and Trouble

My acceptance, however, was conditioned on two points: I needed to discuss the terms of my employment (I did not seek a formal contract), and I wanted my election to be by a unanimous, or nearly unanimous, vote of the regents. He agreed with the second point and said the university's general counsel, Don Reidhaar, would call to discuss the terms.

Reidhaar and I had been friends for many years. He knew the university intimately, possessed unquestioned integrity, and was anxious to help. I received his call within five minutes of concluding the one with Watkins. Our discussion was uncomplicated and unexceptional except for two issues: first, my salary, which the regents had discussed (*without any* involvement or participation by me, indirectly or directly), had been fixed at $150,000 a year, compared with Saxon's $95,000; and second, the concerns I had about living at Blake House, the president's official residence in north Berkeley (Kensington), which was in a poor state of repair. The Saxons had mentioned that whenever it rained, they and those helping them had to put containers throughout the house to catch the leaks; water damage was evident on the western walls, and the house was settling, badly. And since the surrounding ten acres of formal gardens were open daily to the public, the Blake House residents lived, as it were, in a public park. Libby and I would often be away on university business and worried about the security of our two teenage daughters, living alone in this very large and at once quite secluded and public home. Reidhaar agreed that I should discuss these two matters with Watkins.

Watkins and I did so that very night. As to the $150,000 salary, I was concerned that the differential between the salary of the outgoing president and the one incoming would prove to be politically and, perhaps, publicly awkward. His response was quick: the problem would be short-lived because—as comparisons with salaries for presidents of other major U.S. universities showed conclusively—"we are dramatically behind. We need to be competitive with the president's salary or we cannot hope to argue that we should be competitive for the university's chancellors, vice presidents, and other officers, or for our faculty and staff as well. Their salaries are not competitive either. The board is determined to fix this problem for the good of the university. Saxon's unwillingness to allow his salary to rise above its current levels, comparisons notwithstanding, has in part put us in this bind. We should have overruled his preferences in this matter and we now are unwilling to fix your salary at less than the level indicated."

Even so, I noted, there was a very real prospect that "once the regents put me on point with this level of salary, I, not they, would pay the political price," in Sacramento and on the campuses as well, and certainly from those faculty and staff who instinctually view administrators and their compensation with suspicion, if not outright hostility; and their numbers are not small. Watkins ended this part of our discussion by saying that "the regents would back this up and deflect any criticism from you to the board." However well-intentioned, these words proved to be without effect.

Although this decision unsettled me, I knew Watkins was right as to its positive effect on compensation within the university as a whole. But, as I had feared, my salary came under attack after my appointment, in criticisms by Assemblyman John Vasconcellos, among others. He was chairman of the Assembly's Education Committee, which heard and acted on UC's budget, and proclaimed to *Newsweek* his distress "that UC is not more responsible with its money," calling my $150,000 a year "highly outrageous." Others chimed in and before long a concurrent legislative resolution was introduced, not carrying the effect of law, but intended to be heard, nevertheless, criticizing the Board of Regents for its actions on my salary and demanding that it be rescinded.[1]

Compensation had already become a sticking point for me. It was prejudicial to my relations in Sacramento and hurtful in my dealings with the faculty, staff, and unions then representing over 40,000 of UC's nearly 100,000 employees. Moreover, if this legislative resolution passed, the faculty, staff, and students would attribute every subsequent hostile or unfriendly act of the legislature directed at UC to the compensation issue. I conveyed my feelings on this directly to Steve Arditti, UC's representative in Sacramento, advising him as I also did Saxon that if this resolution were to pass my willingness to come to UC would be highly problematic. With no small measure of effort, the matter was finally killed in committee.

The second issue had proved to be unexpectedly difficult when Watkins stated the regents' decided preference: "that you live in Blake House." I asked, "Is living there to be a condition of my appointment?" He said, "No." I asked if it were an implied requirement. "No," he answered. "Then," I said, "we will not live in Blake House but prefer to buy our own home in Orinda under the same terms and conditions as housing had been provided for us by the University of Utah."[2] He agreed and said he would see to it as part of the regents' action on my appointment. We later came to use Blake House intensively for meetings of the chancellors, receptions, dinners, entertainment, and faculty, staff, and student functions. We just didn't sleep there.

The controversy over both issues was attributed to my "typical Mormon greed," in "demanding" a high salary when Saxon had been willing to serve for one-third less, and in expecting the state to pay for two homes rather than one. These comments came principally from UC faculty, at least the ones I know about, and especially from the Berkeley campus. Never mind that I never asked for $150,000 or in fact had an opportunity to fix my salary otherwise; never mind that the salary was what people in this post were paid at major universities nationwide; never mind that Blake House repairs would have cost hundreds of thousands of dollars, which expenditures would themselves have provoked comparable levels of criticism; never mind that we used Blake House extensively for university functions; never mind that the repairs were made over time, rather than all at once (the house was not refurnished until just before Libby's death in 1991); never mind that it would have been my family living there while these repairs were being made, not my critics'; never mind that no state funds were used to meet the cost of operating Blake House (approximately 8,500 square feet) or in my housing allowance for our Orinda home (3,200 square feet); and never mind that when it comes time for faculty members to negotiate with UC about coming or staying, many negotiate much more insistently than I have ever done. In any event, I was not the first president or chancellor not to live in official housing but in my own home: President Clark Kerr and Chancellor Glenn Seaborg also did. And finally, to vilify my religion and its members in such a bigoted and crass fashion evoked less than kindly thoughts about such colleagues.

The regents' breakfast meeting in Berkeley on March 2, 1983, proved to be uneventful except for the choice of the university's next president. I knew seven of the twenty-six regents, knew something about some of the others, and knew almost nothing at all about the rest. Based on my meeting with them at breakfast and on Watkins's subsequent account of the board meeting, I was encouraged to believe that our relations and theirs with one another were agreeable enough, even though the conservative/liberal divisions were omnipresent.

Even so, everyone seemed clearly committed to the university's well-being, its mission, and its importance to the state, while expressing time and again a fear for the university's immediate and prospective fiscal health. The fear was well founded, owing to the deteriorating base of UC's funding from both state and federal sources, the reduced state of affairs for the university's five medical centers, and low morale within the university as a whole, weary from fighting with California's governors for sixteen years, eight with Ronald Reagan and eight with Jerry Brown.

Appointed

Following breakfast, the regents convened in closed session for less than an hour, and my appointment was made official. A press conference followed with warm remarks being offered by Saxon and several regents, but most particularly by Regent Watkins, who had chaired the search committee. The following are the most salient portions of my prepared response:

> I am keenly aware that this is a public, secular University whose charter, obligations, and protections are embodied in the State's highest law. The university has consistently striven to be worthy of this trust, and the record over the past 115 years has been one of civilization's truly great achievements. . . .
>
> I am also well aware of changes that are taking place in California—in its population, economy, social structure, and character. The University will be obliged to allow for these changes in its planning and in its educational programs, securing on the one hand the academic standards and educational expectations that have been historically characteristic of the university, and on the other, doing everything within its influence and capability to enroll in its student body and to engage on its faculty and staff persons whose race or sex are less fully present in the University than one would both expect and hope to find.[3]

The newspaper and campus coverage of my appointment was most revealing, the headlines referring as much to my compensation as to my appointment and in the early paragraphs to my religion. The newspapers in southern California and the Central Valley accorded prominent and serious coverage to my appointment. The San Francisco papers did not (the *San Jose Mercury News* excepted). Generous and supportive articles appeared in the alumni and other university publications on the university's nine campuses.

The *Sacramento Bee* editorial was especially welcome, setting forth as it did what I was confronting but assuming that I would do well enough just to stay UC's present course when, in my own mind, I had already decided to alter it:

> There have been far better times to begin a term as president of the University of California or, for that matter, most other institutions of higher education. The challenges of the next few years—to use the most optimistic phrase—are more likely to be concerned with protecting the quality and strength of existing programs, and of finding money in an arid economy, than they are with the heady activities of growth, innovation and educational experimentation. If anything, they are more difficult, require more of the incumbent and offer fewer rewards even for the man or woman who succeeds brilliantly.
>
> Given these challenges it's impossible to know how well anyone can succeed, but there is little question David P. Gardner, whom the regents the other day selected to be UC's next president, is as qualified as any person to take them on. An experienced university administrator, both in the UC system and, for the past 10 years as president of the University of Utah, Gardner appears to have the combination of fund-raising, administrative and academic experience—and the patience and perseverance—that the next few years are likely to demand not only from UC's president but from most college presidents in this country.[4]

All in all, my appointment was well received, the editorials were favorable, and letters of congratulations poured in as did telephone calls from friends throughout the country as well as from colleagues within UC. It was a good start, compensation and religious issues notwithstanding.

Transitions: Utah and California

As I had done ten years ago—but in reverse—after my appointment (and the expected round of press interviews), I visited California frequently between my appointment on March 2 and the effective date of my appointment August 1, 1983, meeting with key university officers, faculty members, and some regents. I hoped to reorganize the Office of the President promptly, not only because it needed reorganization but also because the key people I wanted to keep needed to know and others needed as much time as I could give them to find another position, within UC or elsewhere. These fruitful meetings served me extremely well, though I had to refocus my energies on *A Nation at Risk* and the University of Utah's budget as I brought my administration at the U to an orderly close.

It was not easy for us to leave Utah after ten years and the many friends and colleagues we had gained both at the U and in the state, especially given the disappointed but gracious way everyone treated us during our final months. Fortunately my successor, Chase Peterson, was already in place at Utah, serving as the university's vice president for health sciences. We had recruited Peterson to Utah in 1978 from his position as a vice president of Harvard University. He walked into the president's office at Utah on August 1, 1983, as I was the same day walking into my new office in Berkeley. The transition at Utah was cordial, mutually respectful and supportive, timely, and conclusive, but less so in California, where even the simplest things, it seemed, were made complicated. I was pleased by the warmth of the send-off from Utah, especially as reflected by the state's major newspaper in its editorial two days following my UC appointment.

> We have no doubt that personable David Gardner, who within months after accepting the University of Utah presidency had reversed deteriorating public support for the school, will be more than equal to whatever demands arise at California's renowned but often troubled university system.
>
> In Utah, Dr. Gardner displayed unusual talent in quickly establishing and then maintaining friendly relations with the Legislature and with the state's business, education and religious establishment.
>
> From this carefully cultivated foundation of support, Dr. Gardner directed his energies to expanding the university's physical plant and enhancing the quality and variety of its instruction. . . .
>
> The most fitting tribute to David Gardner's service to Utah would be to replace him with an individual capable of sustaining the momentum for excellence and innovation he leaves behind.[5]

In spring 1983 I received a call from Celeste Rose, education adviser to Willie Brown (later serving as an intern in my office, and now as a vice-chancellor at UC's Davis campus). Brown was the powerful Speaker of the Assembly, second only to the governor in terms of political clout and influence in California. Rose was asking if I could meet with the minority caucus—some fifteen or twenty legislators, most of them black and Latino—within the next few days. "They would," she said, "like to meet and welcome you and be afforded the opportunity to express themselves on certain of their concerns regarding UC's operations and policies." This was one of those offers I could not refuse, and in fact, I welcomed it. The sooner the better, I thought, to discuss their concerns about minority interests and gender in UC personnel and admissions policies and practices before such issues came up in the context of specific and tangible legislative or budgetary differences. I accepted but, reading their unexpressed intent, realized that if I were a Catholic, a Protestant, a Jew, or a Muslim they would never have thought it right to inquire into my religious faith; and it was always the same with the press as well: "Gardner, a Mormon," but never "Smith, a Catholic," or "Jones, a Baptist," or whatever.

Throughout my life I experienced a double standard, including what I knew were reservations by many within UC about the regents having appointed a Mormon. These reservations, I also knew, often existed in those who most professed to be free of prejudice and full of goodwill toward others and who, under other circumstances, would condemn any McCarthyite effort to judge an individual's views, beliefs, and character because of his or her associations. But when it came to my religion, these same people thought it to be perfectly acceptable, indeed compellingly correct, to wonder about my views, beliefs, and character because of my religion and/or to ascribe certain generalized moral deficiencies to me and to members of my faith, such as "Mormon greed." The world is a strangely hypocritical place.

The meeting with the minority caucus was held in Speaker Brown's office, although he was not present except to introduce everyone. There were some fifteen people present and from both legislative houses, and both sides of the aisle. Elihu Harris was the "designated hitter" (later mayor of Oakland and a friend later in my administration).

He started by reading from what appeared to be a five- or six-page document covering the usual issues: affirmative action in admissions, personnel, contracting, and purchasing, the "disgracefully low" level of minority representation in UC's student body, and the like. After about one and a half pages of this, I intervened politely, but firmly, and said in effect: "Assemblyman Harris, perhaps we can save everyone's time today if you would allow me to read this document myself later rather than your reading it to me now. If so, we could then address the real issue that occasions this meeting, namely, my religious faith and its widely perceived unfriendliness toward African Americans and women; and if you would be willing to check my record of twenty years, ten at UCSB and the office of the UC president combined, and ten at Utah, as the basis for confirming or challenging my comments and observations this morning, we can have a more productive morning." He said, "Fine, let's get at it."

The ensuing conversation was substantive, insightful, helpful, and cordial, laying the groundwork for a constructive set of relations with these legislators throughout my tenure (the South African divestment issue excepted). Arditti told me that as the meeting ended one of the senators on the way out said to him that it was the first time she had found herself "acting as though she were the 'bigot' rather than attacking those who were."

While in Sacramento for this meeting, Saxon accompanied me (but not to the minority caucus) as I visited with key legislators, including a luncheon for the leadership of both houses hosted by Senator John Garamendi, majority leader of the Senate, a UC Berkeley alumnus and former football player at Cal later to become a good friend. These meetings went extremely well and helped in any number of ways to allay people's concern about my religion, my politics, my experience, my intentions, and my ideas. The day ended in a visit with Governor George Deukmejian, the just-elected Republican governor of California and the state's former attorney general.

Those at the meeting included the governor, Steve Merksamer (his chief of staff), Saxon, Arditti, and me. Saxon registered his alarm at the governor's recent decision to make a midyear cut in the current state budget (including UC), and the conversation deteriorated from there. But this was a Deukmejian-Saxon conversation. I said nothing but observed the governor's irritation at Saxon's blunt but clear expression of disappointment at this budget action and the harm it would do UC. The same points subsequently and publicly were widely reported in the media and attributed to Saxon. In spite of the awkwardness, I liked how the governor handled it: cautious, attentive, understanding, and firm. Merksamer and I communicated without exchanging a word.

It was not hard to conclude that the governor was a man to be worked with not criticized, to be cultivated not confronted, to be prepared for meetings and not to be surprised. Besides, he had an informal way and very genuine style that I liked, was straightforward, sparse with words, and, as I suspected and later learned, was a person of great personal integrity whose word was sufficient and who was inherently trusting of others until disappointed, after which the offending party was "out."

I also noticed how much he respected Steve Merksamer and how much he appeared to count on his judgment. Merksamer was a brilliant, tough, driving person who was unwaveringly loyal to the governor and was up-front and honest in his dealings. As with the governor, his word was sufficient. I liked both of them instinctively and looked forward to working with them.

The last major incident to engage my interest before I took office came in June when Regent Glenn Campbell, director of the Hoover Institution at Stanford, a staunch conservative and something of a curmudgeon and a strong advocate for my appointment, was not elected to a second-year term as chairman of the Board of Regents, an action ordinarily taken in deference to the serving chairman.

By a split vote of sixteen to eight the regents picked Regent Yori Wada, a liberal from San Francisco and a longtime champion of human and civil rights in the Bay Area, the split being mostly but not entirely along ideological lines. Regent Stanley Sheinbaum, a well-known and respected member of the liberal establishment and a generous supporter of various philanthropic and nonprofit organizations in Los Angeles, was elected vice chairman. The liberals had chosen to assert their numerical majority. I wondered if this action had anything to do with my appointment, thought by some to have been the preference of the board's more conservative members. Regent Watkins called me the night of Campbell's unseating to assure me that the board's choice of Wada related only to the board's internal dynamics, but I still wondered about it.

These several events, coupled with the governor's announcement three weeks after my March appointment that the State of California would be paying its personnel and vendors with IOUs instead of cash because of declining state revenues, caused me to wonder if California had always been this way or had I merely forgotten. How, I asked myself, could I have come to be comparably comfortable in Utah and California, two states as different as any in the country? No answer came to me.

California's Master Plan for Higher Education

The rapid growth and development of the University of California to the rank of the world's most preeminent, distinguished, and best-balanced public university is one of the most dramatic and telling events in the annals of American higher education. The university was founded on March 23, 1868, chartered by the state as an educational nonsectarian land-grant institution.[6]

UC's first students entered in 1869. The first class (of twelve students) graduated in 1873. By the early twentieth century UC was a founder, along with a handful of the nation's other leading universities, of the American Association of Universities. By 1923 UC led the universities of the United States in enrollment with 14,061 full-time students studying mostly at Berkeley. In 1934 the American Council on Education's episodic survey of the quality of graduate schools in the United States obliged the Ivy League universities to take account, for the first time, of a serious competitor rising on the outer edge of the West Coast.[7]

The enrollment bulge hit UC hard following World War II and forced the state to take important additional steps toward organizing its public institutions of higher education to remain qualitatively superior but still accessible to students and affordable both to the taxpayers and those wishing to study on one or more of its many campuses, all three being consensus goals for this fast-growing and highly mobile state. Governor Earl Warren played a key role in this planning effort, collaborating with his former classmate at Berkeley, UC President Robert Gordon Sproul. Sproul served during the crucial years 1930–58, dealing in turn with the Great Depression, World War II, the spurt in enrollments following that cataclysmic conflict, the dramatic in-migration to California during the 1930s and 1940s, mostly from other parts of the country, the rise and ambitions of the state's expanding community colleges, and the growing number of state teachers' colleges.

Until the late 1950s California's public system of higher education was, as to number of campuses and their location, mostly about local community ambitions, regional economic interests, and provincial pride. Almost every session of the legislature witnessed unplanned, nearly random, and highly politicized decisions to locate a new community college here and a new state college there. There was no underlying state policy about such matters or framework for more reasoned and conceptually coherent decisions. Clark Kerr's appointment to succeed Sproul in 1958 as UC's president changed all of that.

Kerr was a highly respected member of the Berkeley faculty, a famed arbitrator of some of California's and of the nation's most consequential labor-management disputes, and well regarded by many regents (but not all) for the moderate but principled role he played in the early 1950s during the UC loyalty oath controversy. In 1952 he had become Berkeley's first chancellor. The idea of chancellors for the university's campuses was not a welcome turn of events for Sproul, who ran a highly centralized university administration, and with phenomenal success, for twenty-eight years. But the times were changing, and Kerr, as president, faced the need to decentralize this already very large and complex institution, to plan for a doubling of its enrollments in the 1960s, and to bring some order to the structure of California's quite random and disparate "system" of public higher education; many of his initiatives would overlap.

On taking office in 1958, he dramatically reduced the size of the president's office, delimited the authority he wished to retain, and parceled out the remainder to the chancellors, and in some instances to vice presidents. The decentralization of the university's administration continued throughout Kerr's term of office and, more or less, during the service of his successors as well.

Kerr also gathered together California's leading educators to take on the issues of growth in the public and private segments of higher education in California. They studied the expansion of existing campuses, the adding of campuses, the governing structures of the community colleges, the state colleges, and UC and the distribution of students across them, the assignment of institutional missions, admission standards, and related matters.

The result of their effort was to be a treaty of sorts, drawn up by the principals of the state's public and private colleges and universities, with the state legislature's imprimatur in 1960 as the now famed but then quite radical Master Plan for Higher Education. Thus California led the nation in developing a three-tier system of higher education that has been studied worldwide as a model for those states or countries wishing to increase access to higher education while improving its overall quality. With minor changes, the plan remains in force to this very day. Though not perfect, it works remarkably well: the rationalized and reasonably funded system allowed the state and its public and private colleges and universities to prosper as they grew.

In essence, the Master Plan assigned an academic mission to each of the three parts of California's public higher education system, while encouraging the further growth of the state's private colleges and universities. It also defined the pool of students eligible for admission to each segment and differentiated the expected sources of funding for each, roughly as follows:

- The two-year community colleges were to be open-door institutions offering a general education to students wishing to transfer to one of the state's four-year institutions as juniors and providing programs for those interested in technical, vocational, and other skill-related fields. The adult learner was also to have a call on these colleges, which were to be open not only to high school graduates but to anyone eighteen years or older who might benefit from attending. They were to be essentially cost-free to students and funded from a mix of state and local sources. The system was to be overseen by a board of governors, whose members were to be appointed for six-year terms by the governor with the Senate's concurrence.

- The California state colleges, then part of the state's Department of Public Instruction, were now to draw their students from the top 33.3 percent rather than from the top 50 percent of California's high school graduating seniors. The California state colleges became an independent system, the California State University. The colleges were to offer a full range of undergraduate programs leading to the bachelor's degree and a select number of offerings at the master's level in certain professional fields such as education and engineering. Research was to be more applied than basic and tied to the institution's comprehensive teaching function. Funding was to be provided chiefly by the state, and the system's governance was vested in a board of trustees, appointed for six-year terms by the governor with the concurrence of the Senate.

- The University of California's place in the scheme of things was confirmed by reference to the provisions for governance embodied in the state constitution and the derived authority of the regents (who either served ex officio or were appointed by the governor for sixteen-year terms with the Senate's concurrence). The pool of students eligible for admission was modestly reduced from the top 15 percent of California's seniors completing high school each year to 12.5 percent. UC was to offer comprehensive undergraduate curricula leading to the bachelor's degree, a corresponding array of master's degrees, and doctoral-level work for the Ph.D. in all fields, including tertiary degrees for the professions. UC was to be the state's primary agency for research and a provider of public service to the society at large, a role also reinforced by UC's being the state's land-grant university. Funding was to come, albeit not in any specified proportions, from the state, the federal government, student fees, and tuition for nonresidents, self-supporting operations, university hospitals and clinics, private gifts and grants, income from endowments, and an array of miscellaneous sources.

The University of California played the critical and leading role in negotiating this plan and thus had a special obligation to honor it; and so would I as president. Fortunately, the ground rules were in place, subject to only nominal interpretation.

The Challenge

The university was also the most distinguished public university in the United States, and the Berkeley campus, the best-balanced and most distinguished campus in our country. My challenge would be to keep it that way and see to its ongoing growth. A dramatic slippage in funding over the previous sixteen years had led to low morale, an ill-maintained and inadequate physical plant, poor legislative relations, rising student fees, and noncompetitive salaries across the board, an especially severe problem for UC in its efforts to attract and retain faculty members.

When I was born in Berkeley in 1933, California's population was roughly 6 million; fifty years later when my service as president commenced in 1983, it was 25 million; and on my retirement nine years and two months later California's population was estimated at 31 million. In 2002 it topped 35 million, a nearly sixfold increase during my lifetime.

But mere numbers do not reflect the full story of a changing California. The ethnic mix of its population shifted, with dramatic increases in those of Mexican and Central American heritage and those of Asian descent, while African Americans' share of the population held steady for the most part and whites' share was in marked decline. Hence the proportion of ethnic minorities on UC campuses would rise inexorably, albeit at differential rates as to numbers, ethnicity, and status.

So the question was, would UC plan intelligently for this numerical growth in its student body, staff, faculty, and administration? Would we lead the effort to effectuate the accompanying social and ethnic transitions while maintaining our obligations under the Master Plan, our relations with both public and private higher education, UC's constitutional autonomy, our legislative and gubernatorial support, and the confidence and support of the regents and of the public, free of undue or implicitly controlling political or governing strictures? No small task. To tackle it, I required a strong hand internally: supportive administrative and Academic Senate colleagues within our expected and much-commended consultative culture, and either a benignly accommodating or affirmatively supportive Board of Regents.

Owing to their complexity, their inherently controversial character, and the politically charged environment, the issues of UC's growth and ethnicity would be hard to deal with. But these issues were *central* to both UC's and the state's long-term economic growth, cultural coherence, and social and civil order and, therefore, unavoidable.

In contrast to these complexities, the money issues were more immediate and their consequences more readily observable, though the politics were more perceivably entangled and unpredictable. UC's place in the higher education community was also more vulnerable if funding for its role and the maintenance of its excellence in teaching and research were not forthcoming. But this was an arena I knew well. I understood university budgets, was experienced in working with legislators and governors, and had experience in the byzantine politics of seeking and allocating funds.

One friend asked on learning of my appointment at UC, "How will you cope with a nearly $5 billion budget when at Utah your budget was only some $275 million?" Well, I said, "the consequences of good or bad budgets are wholly predictable and most of the personalities and issues and problems are much alike; and as to the dollar difference between California's and Utah's budgets, you just change the first number and add three zeros." Budgeting issues were not the problem. Funding was.

UC's funding had suffered badly under Governor Reagan's eight years of nearly unrelieved hostility, mitigated only by the intercession of key Republican-appointed regents who helped argue UC's case in his second term, for example, Regents William French Smith, William Wilson, Dean Watkins, Edward Carter, and Glenn Campbell. It also suffered under Jerry Brown, who succeeded Reagan as governor, and who exhibited for another eight years a nearly equal lack of regard for or interest in UC, I could never tell which. His animosity, it seemed, derived at least as much from his view of UC as an "elitist" institution (although he had been a student there) as from the support of his late father (Governor Pat Brown) for UC during Kerr's presidency (1958–67), which the second Brown chose not to emulate.

Ironically, UC was hurt because Reagan saw it as an institution that should enroll those not able to gain admission to or pay for the "better" private universities and colleges and, as a public institution, should not qualitatively compete with the privates. He felt UC should be an extension of the state's "welfare" program.[8] Moreover, he perceived it as being generally liberal/radical in its politics and irresponsible in its administration. Brown felt UC's high standards for admission, excellent faculty, world-class research, and vast intellectual, cultural, and creative resources were an unreasonable burden on the state. If UC wanted to seek and to attain those levels of excellence, he believed, then it could get the money from sources other than the State of California's taxpayers, which, of course, is exactly what UC had been doing for decades and does today.

UC couldn't seem to win: too good for one governor who saw it as part of the welfare program and too good for another who thought the state should not be responsible for fostering or, if you wish, paying for excellence at these levels. In a strange way, both Reagan and Brown had concluded that UC shouldn't be as excellent as it had become, at least not on the taxpayers' dollars, and had arrived at these views for quite different reasons (or perhaps their views were more fundamentally alike than may appear on the surface).

Having encountered the same views in Utah many times, from Republicans and Democrats alike, I concluded that unfriendliness to real accomplishment and excellence in public universities crosses state boundaries and is a nonpartisan issue. It is an obstacle to contend with in securing proper levels of funding from the state. In Utah I had always directed my political efforts toward the people, and I also would in California. But in California the governor had the authority to veto any item he didn't like in the state's budget. In Utah, he did not. Thus we and our friends (and I personally) had to make every effort to have a strong, positive working relationship with California's new conservative governor, George Deukmejian. He and the liberal Democrat Willie Brown, Speaker of the Assembly, held the political cards in California, and each could, although in different ways, help or hurt us irretrievably.

The governor and the Speaker were poles apart in politics and in personality. But they had known each other for many years; both were also self-made men from minority backgrounds who had confronted prejudice of an especially virulent kind. I resolved to work straightforwardly with each, to earn their trust and confidence and, I hoped, their respect. Whatever their differences about K–12 education, welfare, health, prisons, highways, or other state interests, what counted for me was their view of UC. I learned long ago that both donors' and politicians' views of universities settled nearly as much on their opinions of the university's president as on the institution itself. This may seem to be unreasonable, but it is the reality, and I had to allow for it.

I decided on the problems I needed to solve at UC, some soon and others later. These included renewal of the physical plant and its expansion, support for our operating budget, low staff and faculty morale, and uncompetitive salaries for our faculty, staff, and administration. I was determined to improve the university's overall quality and capability on all nine campuses, not at just two or three. I wanted also to give some serious and creative thought to our changing student body and how students learn best, distance learning opportunities, lower-division education, the growing globalization of the U.S. economy, and California's strategic position with long and useful ties to Asia and Latin America, among others. All this would depend *very* heavily on whether or not I could play an instrumental role in restoring the university's long-lost fiscal health. If I succeeded, all else was possible; if not, I would not be asked to serve overly long, nor would I wish to.

My First Budget: A Risky Venture Considered

A plan was forming in my mind (as early as May 1983, after my visits to California) about how to accomplish the singularly important and indispensable objective of obtaining proper levels of support for UC from the state. It would not happen unless I took a risk against all odds, experience, and reason. I concluded that it was either this approach or a steady, long, and dreary effort to recover over five to ten years what we had lost during the previous sixteen at best; and just as likely, the continuing slippage in our fiscal health would lead to a much-diminished University of California, unable to accommodate the upcoming generations of students, and unable to retain the university's faculty, a cadre of more than six thousand scholars and scientists as exceptional and brilliant as had ever been gathered under the tent of any single university. The risk was worth it, and I intended to take it.

The university's lead budget officer was William Baker. Bill and I had grown up in Berkeley two years apart and had been acquainted for many years. We had also served in President Hitch's office, he in his budget role and I as a vice president. Baker knew the university as well as anyone. He was well connected throughout the university and in Sacramento and was energetic and committed to UC. His father had also served UC for forty-five years. Baker's assistant was Larry Hershman, an extremely bright and articulate person, fully knowledgeable about UC and its fiscal affairs, as sophisticated a practitioner of budgeting within both the bureaucratic and political arenas as I had ever met.

Baker and Hershman came to see me in Salt Lake City in July 1983. They pointed out that UC's budget procedures required them to put the finishing touches on UC's 1984–85 operating and capital budgets before I would have much chance to review them. They were well along and wanted my advice before completing the budget documents for the regents' October meeting. They would, in any event, already have begun their discussions with the state's Department of Finance well before that date.

They gave me the bad news up front. UC's fiscal condition was worse than I had been told; the backlog for maintenance and repair of buildings was now interfering with normal operations; plans for new buildings for teaching and research were prepared but awaiting funding; faculty salaries were 16 percent below our comparison universities; staff salaries were similarly depressed, and administrators' salaries were the worst of all on a comparative market basis. Undergraduate enrollments were expected to decline between 1983 and 1992 (I didn't believe this prediction then or later and said so when the regents saw our enrollment projections in late summer 1983. As it turned out, my estimates and UC's official enrollment projections were both low). UC was losing faculty at an alarming rate (Utah had been recruiting some of them), and the budgets for travel, supplies, computers, utilities, and libraries were inadequate in the extreme.

Baker and Hershman's approach was consistent with the chancellors' agreement one month earlier: to fashion a budget proposal to the state that would marginally reverse the adverse trends of recent years, seek some modest advantage for the coming year (1984–85) over the one just started, and seek a substantial bond issue in order to make some real and needed headway on a capital budget for our building needs.

We discussed this plan at length along with Baker and Hershman's own preference for a modestly more aggressive stance than the chancellors'. The chancellors favored an operating budget increase of about 3 percent and an improved capital budget. Baker and Hershman preferred something closer to 5 or 7 percent. We also discussed the probable likelihood of success with each increase. As I listened, I became increasingly restive. This was going to be *my* first budget, and I would be held to account for it.

I also knew that such a modest proposal—even if an improvement over those of recent years, and even if successful—would not do much to restart the university and would not give me the leverage I needed to carry out my larger agenda. So I asked, what increase in our 1984–85 operating budget would allow us to recover *in one year everything* we had lost under Reagan and Brown, during their combined sixteen years as California's governors? The answer was 21 percent for the base operating budget (12 percent for nonpersonnel costs, plus 9 percent for personnel costs) and another 11 percent for the retirement plan for a total increase of 32 percent. We then looked at this figure in very general terms and assessed its chances.

On that point, Baker and Hershman were unequivocal and straightforward: "No way." "What are you thinking?" "We'll be lucky to get 3 percent." "How will you look asking for 32 percent and getting 10 cents on the dollar?" But the plan I had been forming in my mind anticipated, indeed required, not a prudent or even a reasonable course of action. It required a change in direction. Baker's and Hershman's views, sound and judicious as they were, underplayed the level of support I hoped to receive from the governor, the legislature, the regents, and the staff and faculty during my "honeymoon" year. It would also put off any real efforts to restore our funding to its proper levels.

So I asked Baker and Hershman to draw up a budget that would increase our base operating budget by 21 percent and restore full funding to UC's retirement fund by another 11 percent. They assured me that to make such changes at this late date would not only be extremely difficult but would divert much-needed staff time at a crucial juncture in the budgetary process.

Instead, they said they would prepare a budget for increases at the 3 percent, 5 percent, and 7 percent levels and meet again. By this time I knew what I wanted to do and said they were welcome to prepare budgets at whatever level they thought appropriate, but what I wanted to see shortly after my arrival in Berkeley the next month was a budget showing the 32 percent increase.

Our conversation ended with those instructions and with my comment that in recent visits to California I had sensed a "survival mode" at UC and, in my judgment, "that won't do any more. I had heard," I went on, "that the best we could do was to hold on until better times," akin to the *Sacramento Bee*'s editorial of the previous March. "This was a self-fulfilling way of looking at our responsibilities," and I added, "it was no wonder morale was low, that at Utah we were on the move, recruiting out of UC's several campuses, including the Medical Centers, and that I intended to start my administration with a new approach." I asked as they were leaving, "Bill and Larry, do you believe the university needs to be turned around and set on a more positive and promising path to the future?" "Yes, of course," was their answer. I then observed quietly, "I only know of one way to turn the university around, and that is to turn it around: 32 percent will do it, 3 percent won't. See you next month." I can just imagine their conversation en route to Berkeley that night after our meeting.

Baker and Hershman and their staffs, of course, had been fighting the good fight for years, doing all they could in the face of unfriendly governors. They dealt on a daily basis with the adverse consequences of these regrettable circumstances and heard the frustrations of the regents, the expressed concerns and complaints of the chancellors and leading faculty members, the staff's array of grievances, and student resentments engendered by rising fees and tuitions. I had not. But my high-stakes move carried profound implications for UC's present and future, as well as for my own tenure and effectiveness as president. The 1984–85 budget was to be my first step.[9]

THE UNIVERSITY OF CALIFORNIA: PRÉCIS AND PROFILE

The University of California is one of the world's most complex and sophisticated institutions, the largest and best of its kind. It is a formidable enterprise to govern and manage, not only because of its public character but even more because of the work it does and the highly educated and independent people who carry out the work and on whom its reputation rests.

The university does not welcome much management and regards the exercise of administrative "leadership" as an oxymoron. Its internal affairs are exquisitely balanced within a well-tested and much commended system of "shared governance," shared between the administration and the Academic Senate. Each of these bodies possesses authority independent of the other, derived by way of direct delegations of authority from the Board of Regents, the university's ultimate governing body under terms of the state constitution, which provides not only for executive, legislative, and judicial branches of government but also for a fourth: the University of California.

The university's founders vested in the Board of Regents the unqualified authority to govern the new university and fixed on the board a constitutional mandate to keep the university free of sectarian and political influence in its internal affairs. They were equally determined to put as much distance as possible between the university's constitutional autonomy and the legislature's judgment about the university's operations, programs, policies, teaching, research, and public service.

In other words, the university was to be insulated from the swirling winds of partisan politics that, for the most part, define the actions of legislatures. These constitutional provisions have been honored over the years, both by the regents and the legislature, and while differences between the two have not infrequently been litigated, the founders' purposes adhere. This single protection and provision for UC's autonomy is shared with only a handful of other American universities, and in the instance of UC, is the *first* reason accounting for its rise to eminence, especially within such a brief time.

The *second* was the regents' decision in 1920, buttressed by language embodied in the Organic Act chartering UC in 1868, to delegate direct and full authority to the Academic Senate over courses of instruction and curricular requirements, and for the setting of UC's academic standards for student admissions, subject to regental concurrence. In addition, the Academic Senate has a major but not a final role in academic personnel decisions, working collaboratively with the academic departments, schools, and colleges and with UC's senior academic officers. The discretion of these senior academic officers may in the end be absolute but is exercised with great, nearly unexceptional, deference to faculty judgment in the proposed appointments, promotions, demotions, and terminations of individual faculty members. The Academic Senate also has the right to organize itself and its committees as it sees fit and to elect its officers and committees as it collectively chooses without interference from either the university's administrative officers or the regents.

While not a complete account of the senate's role, this quick summary expresses the spirit of the regents' intentions, and it is the fact of a strong Academic Senate and a strong administration, working with separately delegated authority within UC's labyrinth of overlapping but distinguishable processes and policies, that explains the second reason for the university's strength, resilience, and quality.[10]

The *third* reason lies in the Board of Regents' willingness to delegate nearly all its constitutional authority to the president, and the president, in turn, at least since 1958, to the chancellors of UC's nine (now ten) campuses. It cannot be said that UC's administrative officers lack authority. They possess it in abundance and, tempered by the realities of shared governance on the one hand and a strong, independent Board of Regents on the other, have come to act in a deliberative, consultative, professional, and collegial fashion that has steadied the university during times of travail but not hindered its forward momentum when more favorable conditions prevail.

The *fourth* reason is the Board of Regents itself. Individually and collectively, over more than thirteen decades the regents have been champions and protectors of the university, dedicated to its welfare, jealous of its autonomy, demurring to presidents and the Academic Senate on most matters, and asserting their constitutional role when needful in encounters with governors and legislatures, notable and recent exceptions to the contrary notwithstanding, for example, the loyalty oath controversy of 1949–52, the decision on divestment in 1986, and the abandonment of affirmative action in 1995.

The *fifth* reason is the steady and diligent commitment to the University of California as a *single* university, operating on its then nine and now ten campuses: In the corporate sense, it is a single entity governed by a single Board of Regents possessing nearly unqualified constitutionally derived authority, adopting its own bylaws and delegating what authority it chooses through its standing orders. There is one president, appointed by the regents, to whom sufficient authority is given to exercise UC's central executive authority. There is one Academic Senate operating on each campus but also universitywide as required, whose members (essentially the professoriate and key administrative officers) comprise a unified and comprehensive, not representative, Academic Senate. There is a single, consolidated university budget for the state's share of UC funding, submitted by the regents to the legislature and governor that, when acted on by the governor and legislature, comes to UC as a "block grant," allocated within UC by the president, not by the regents, and according to policies worked out by the university administration. There is a single set of personnel policies, salary schedules, and policies for UC faculty and other academic personnel, universitywide negotiations with the unionized staff, and common fees and charges for students, except for some campus-specific programs or facilities. There is a single official university voice speaking for UC in the state capital, under direction of the president, involving members of his staff in Sacramento and others from throughout the university and helping to insulate the campuses from direct political interference.

The *sixth* reason pertains to the common university standards for admission at the freshman level (12.5 percent of California's graduating high school seniors are eligible for admission to one of UC's campuses).

The *seventh* reason for UC's worldwide standing is its relationship to the people of California. Californians are proud of its accomplishments, appreciative of its role, and honored to be a part of its success and/or to have studied on one or more of its campuses. The public on balance and over time has been willing to pay for UC's overall excellence and ambitions, even when furious with its tolerance for protest—in 1964–65 during the Free Speech Movement and from 1965 to 1971 in demonstrations against the Vietnam War—or with its apparent unresponsiveness to public concerns about the nation's security, in the McCarthy era during the loyalty oath controversy. Understandably, parents are less happy when their own sons or daughters fail to be admitted to the campus of choice and/or the major of preference, as are many alumni when the football or basketball teams are not winning more than they are losing and the like.

The *eighth* reason has been UC's steady development of multiple sources of revenue rather than a simple reliance on state funds for its operating and capital budgets: federal funds for research, public service, and student financial aid; student tuitions and fees for an array of student-focused programs and activities; private support for scholarships and fellowships, endowed chairs, library and museum collections, intercollegiate athletics, and a range of non-state-funded capital needs; and revenue from self-supporting auxiliary operations.[11]

These were all matters with which I was well acquainted from my previous work with the university. My task was to arrange the university's top administration so as to confirm, not confound, any of the crucial reasons for UC's success, especially those central to its role as a single university with several campuses, a concept with which I not only agreed but to which I was strongly committed. I also needed to organize the Office of the President to fit my style and my intentions.

Profile of UC as I Take Office

How did the University of California look in the year I became president?

Twenty-six regents governed the university, eighteen of whom were appointed by the governor with the Senate's concurrence for twelve-year terms (reduced by constitutional amendment in 1974 from sixteen years); seven served for so long as they held the office of governor, lieutenant governor, Speaker of the Assembly, superintendent of public instruction, president of the alumni association, vice president of the alumni association, and the president of the university; a student regent was appointed by the board for a one-year term. All twenty-six had the right to vote on any and all issues coming to the board for action. Nonvoting members with the right to sit with the board and to comment but not to vote on all issues under discussion included two faculty representatives (the chair and vice chair of the Academic Senate). The three officers of the regents reported directly to the board and not through the president: the general counsel, treasurer, and secretary of the regents.

The chancellors, vice presidents, and directors of the national laboratories also attended meetings of the regents, and almost all these officers would participate in one or more meetings of the board and its committees.

The university enrolled 141,099 students on its nine campuses, of whom 25,575 were graduate students and 12,308 were enrolled in the health sciences and professions. Of this total enrollment 26 percent were minorities. And 52.5 percent were male; 47.5 percent, female. Annual student fees and expenses totaled $5,800 to $7,000, depending on the campus, field of study, and related matters. Nonresidents paid an additional tuition of $3,500.

In addition to the students noted above, UC enrolled 360,000 adult, part-time students through its nine-campus university extension network, most studying off campus. This program was entirely self-supporting, that is, no state funds were used to support it.

UC students came from every county in California, all other forty-nine states, and over one hundred foreign countries. And 83 percent were California residents. The Education Abroad Program arranged for seven hundred UC students to study in forty-five foreign universities in twenty-six countries each year.

Instruction was offered in more than one hundred schools and colleges on UC's nine campuses in virtually every field of knowledge, from freshman up to and including postdoctoral education and training. All the professional schools were represented, but not on every campus. Fourteen health science schools were on six campuses, including five major medical centers. The libraries housed some 20.5 million volumes.

The university received roughly $500 million in federal contracts and grants for research, or roughly 10 percent of all federal dollars granted for this purpose to the nation's colleges and universities.

UC managed for the federal government the Los Alamos National Laboratory, the Lawrence Livermore National Laboratory, and the Lawrence Berkeley National Laboratory. These three labs conducted basic and applied research in nuclear science, energy production, national defense, and environmental and health areas, although no classified or weapons research was performed at the Lawrence Berkeley Laboratory as it was at Los Alamos and Lawrence Livermore.

UC also had on its nine campuses over 150 specialized laboratories, centers, institutes, and bureaus in partial satisfaction of its role as the state's primary agency for research, ranging from the Scripps Institution of Oceanography at UC San Diego in the south to the agricultural field and experiment stations mostly headquartered at UC Davis in the north. UC was the state's land-grant university and, as such, in addition to its research endeavors in agriculture, also managed the Cooperative Extension programs in every county and in most communities in California sponsoring, for example, 4-H youth programs, education programs for adults, and nutrition programs for low-income and disadvantaged individuals and families. It also researched California's forests, woodlands, wetlands, rivers, and coast, especially within UC's own natural reserve system encompassing 100,000 acres of environmentally sensitive sites throughout the state.

This vast enterprise employed 97,964 persons, with an additional 18,961 at the national laboratories, for a total of 116,925. Of those serving on the nine campuses, 69,110 were on the staff or in the administration; another 22,307 held research, teaching, and other positions tied directly to UC's academic work; and 6,547 were on the faculty as assistant, associate, or full professors.

The university's operating budget was $4.437 billion per year; university operations cost $3.1 billion, 40 percent of which came from the state and 60 percent from other sources; and the national laboratories managed by UC for the U.S. Department of Energy cost $1.337 billion, all of which came from the federal government.[12] Its size and complexity were both a burden and an advantage, the former because of the enlarged pool of possible sources with which UC needed to stay in touch, and the latter because of the flexibility the university possessed in preparing its budget, and the corresponding diminution of its dependence on any single provider of monies, which increased its discretion and enlarged the scope of its autonomy.

Here was an enterprise with an array of problems rivaling its successes, and how to solve the first and sustain the second was the challenge. I would need all the help I could get and the best and most experienced colleagues I could find.[13]

Reorganization

My experience at Utah in reorganizing the president's office was most instructive: do it quickly, humanely, and confidently. Intent on doing the same at UC, I began this task on my arrival in Berkeley on August 1, 1983, with the September 16 meeting of the Board of Regents as my target date for action. A flurry of discussions ensued between the officers of the Saxon administration and myself. August, being a slow month, allowed me the time needed to accomplish this important but sensitive task.

I regarded decisions about personnel and structure to be clearly within my discretion, under authority delegated by the regents. So discussions proceeded, and I formed my views. Just before the September regents' agenda I did talk with our new chairman, Yori Wada. I expected the Board of Regents to support me in my reorganization and recommendations for new appointments of the key people. I was not disappointed.

Here, in a summary but accurate fashion, is my report to the board. I explained that I had cut the number of personnel who directly reported to the president from thirteen to seven, identifying those people who could carry out regrouped assignments and distributing organization charts that noted the changes. As the regents' minutes reflect, I further noted that, as the second phase of this administrative reorganization, each vice president and the executive assistant will evaluate and reorganize, as warranted, their respective areas of responsibility.

> President Gardner reported that funds released by abolished positions total approximately $650,000, and that, after funding salary augmentations required by the reorganization and reserving funds for further possible reassignments, he anticipates a net salary savings of at least $400,000 resulting from the reorganization.[14]

Chapter 6 discusses the reorganization in more detail, including the individuals involved. The conversations I had not only with the persons appointed to serve in my administration but with those who were not asked to stay were professional, civil, and respectful but hard nevertheless. I regretted some of the disappointments that occurred. After all, persons at this level are accomplished people; they had been fully engaged in doing the university's work, and at the highest levels. I had not been. Moreover, nearly all were older than I (at fifty), and this was a factor in the equation as well.

Reorganizing UC's central administration within a six-week period was not easy, but the regents received my recommendations well. It encouraged me to hear the board's senior member, Ed Carter, with thirty-one years of service, commend me on developing in such a short time what he believed "to be the best organizational structure of the president's office in the history of the university";[15] Regent Campbell concurred.

It was especially pleasing to me that I could both reorganize and staff the Office of the President with such capable people—all from UC. As far as I could tell, those views were shared by the chancellors, the Academic Senate's leadership, and the university community as a whole, albeit with some understandable reservations expressed by those dislocated (I did my best to facilitate their transfer into other positions within UC). It was a very good start and the second step of the course I had set upon. I only wish the rest of the September meeting had gone as well.

A DIFFICULT BEGINNING—PERSONALLY AND PROFESSIONALLY

Libby and our daughters (now twenty-two, twenty, seventeen, and fourteen) had remained in Salt Lake City during August while I took up temporary residence in Blake House, pending their move over the Labor Day holiday when our new home in Orinda would be ready for occupancy. I commuted to Salt Lake on the weekends, leaving Friday afternoon and returning first thing Monday morning.

I had been extremely busy at my office in Berkeley, working up the reorganization, arranging for the new appointments, shuffling both the table of organization and offices in University Hall (the Office of the President), directly across the street from the western entrance to the Berkeley campus. Nancy Nakayama, who had been serving as Saxon's executive secretary, agreed to remain on, as did Gloria Copeland, Saxon's, and before him, Kerr's, executive assistant. This was wonderful news for me as I had known both of them from my prior UC experience and was keenly aware of their hard work, loyalty, dedication, intelligence, judgment, tact, and discretion. We were working long hours. They were briefing me on personalities, politics, and persons I would soon be encountering. It seemed they knew *everyone*, knew who to put through on the telephone, how to assign my correspondence for staffing, who to schedule and who to direct to others, and so forth. Each was always gracious, never overbearing, and always one step ahead of me. I counted heavily on Copeland until her retirement in the mid-1980s and on Nakayama throughout my tenure as president. After Copeland's retirement Janet Young assumed much of her work and remained throughout both my administration and my successor's, Jack Peltason, rendering us all the support and dedication that either of us could have hoped for.

The agenda for the September meeting of the board was already well under way when I arrived, being handled by Assistant President Dorothy Everett and her associate, Ruth Byrne, both very experienced people, along with their seasoned staff. Most of my time was spent becoming acquainted with the issues and the key players in my office, responding to requests to meet or interview, to speak or do this or that, almost all untimely, and preparing for my budget to be discussed in October with the regents. The press was also intent on meeting with me, and I responded as I could.

No sooner had our family arrived in Orinda over Labor Day 1983 than we received word that my stepmother had passed away quite unexpectedly. She and my father were living with my younger brother, Jim, and his family in Manhattan, Kansas. Neither she nor my father had been well for several years. Jim is a medical doctor and his wife, Martha, an experienced surgical nurse. My father and mother, therefore, were well looked after during their last months in Kansas.

As I was the closest family member present, and Mom was to be interred at our family plot in Sunset Lawn Cemetery, just below Blake House, it fell to Libby and to me to make the funeral arrangements and handle all the associated details and planning.

Ten days later my father died, just as unexpectedly, and once again we sought to cope with the shock and sadness of a parent's death while being obliged to make all the arrangements, on top of everything else then going on, and all within a two-week period of having arrived in California. My father's funeral—scheduled in the East Bay at 1:00 P.M. on September 16, the board's second day of meetings—was the backdrop for my first meeting with the regents as UC president.

I was in an ambivalent and uncommonly pensive move on September 15 as the first day's meeting began: still shocked by the proximate death of my parents, exhausted from the events of the previous several months and of our family's move and the disruption to our family in making this move, wondering how the reorganization and several other items on the agenda would go. I decided that I was not very happy about it all when I should have been excited and anticipatory. I was in a sour mood, not usual for me.

Thursday meetings of the board were for the committee, and Friday morning was for the full board. On this occasion, the first committee meeting was of the board's Subcommittee on Officers' Salaries. This was the subcommittee that recommended to the board salary adjustments for the university's officers, namely, chancellors, vice presidents, directors of the national laboratories, legal counsel, the treasurer, the secretary of the regents, and a host of others, including the president. They were all *merit*-based adjustments. As president, I served as an ex officio voting regent, on all committees of the board, except audit.

The subcommittee made its report, a motion to adopt was made and seconded, and the vote was a tie. Everyone looked at me as I, under the circumstances, held the tie-breaking vote. Being in an uncommonly grumpy mood and very tired at the time, I said, "You must not look to me for this decision. I have no firsthand knowledge of the work or the performance of these officers, whether the proposed merit increases are deserved or not, fair or not, or otherwise [these were Saxon's recommendations, not mine]. Moreover, this is September and action on these items was scheduled for July but put over for reasons about which I am uninformed. You will have to settle this matter without my participation. I am abstaining." They worked it out but didn't like my refusal to vote.

This was even more evident as the day went on, as the regents made oblique references to my comments and aimed pointed remarks at one another, coloring nearly every discussion with animosities provoked mainly by the June action to unseat Regent Campbell as chairman. I had thought I was the only one in a sour mood but soon discovered that my mood was better than most.

The next morning, when the board's closed session business had concluded, Chairman Wada indicated that we would then move into open session. I asked if he could delay the closed session a bit longer as I wished to share my impressions of the previous day's meeting. They agreed.

I said, in effect, that I had been reflecting on the Thursday meetings and, while I was not well known to most members of the board, and they not well known to me, that perhaps it might be useful if I shared my disquietude about and disappointment with the first meetings I had experienced as president (as far as I knew the board was not aware of the recent death of my parents and I said nothing, as I did not want that knowledge to be factored into their response to my comments).

I observed that the ill will generated in June and the ensuing unfriendly personal feelings and animosities were getting in the way of their judgment and the university's best interests, that I should never have been asked to participate in setting the salaries of UC's officers at this point, much less be criticized for not doing so. Therefore, before we went into the open meeting of the board, I wanted to know what it was I was being asked to do as president: "seek to harmonize your differences as a condition of moving forward with the university's business—since a divided board with a new president wouldn't work—or do the job you said needed doing when I interviewed with the search committee and with the full board? As I couldn't do both, which was it to be?"

This is my best recollection of what I said, direct and, I suppose, presumptuous, but I was in no mood to play these games. I had a huge job awaiting me, they had just hired me, and I expected their support, not next year, but now, and unequivocally.

Following perhaps ten or fifteen seconds of awkward silence (a long time, I assure the reader), Regent Carter said: "The president is absolutely right. As far as I am concerned we should start fresh today with one another and accord the president our unqualified support, unencumbered by our individual differences." Carter spoke for the conservatives. Regent Sheinbaum then spoke in much the same way. He spoke for the liberals.

I thanked the board, regretted the need for my perhaps unduly blunt expressions of concern, but now felt able, with their evident and now tangible support, to move confidently to deal with UC's problems that were as vexing as they were profound. The rest of the meeting was uneventful.

In retrospect, my spontaneous decision to raise this issue, emboldened by my disquietude and awareness of my father's funeral scheduled for later in the day, helped bring the board together, gave notice that there was a new president, and dealt with a nagging problem. If addressed later than sooner, that backlog of ill will would hamper my ability to take some hard decisions about the university's future, including the 32 percent increase in our base operating budget due for the board's consideration the following month and now set in my mind, though in no one else's. Lisa had it right, from lame duck to sitting duck.

All that aside, I remained keenly aware that the University of California was a noble institution and had been entrusted to my care in the very special role I was about to play in its life and history. I was glad to be there, doing what I could, back to the blue and gold.

SIX

THE WORKINGS OF THE UNIVERSITY
AND THE CRUCIAL FIRST YEAR

GOVERNANCE AND MANAGEMENT STRUCTURE: BALANCING AUTHORITY

The role of the president of the University of California is pivotal to the sustainability of UC as a single institution, the effective functioning of the university's Board of Regents and of the Academic Council, the securing and allocation of UC's resources, the appointment of its key officers, the coherent exercise of its executive powers, the preservation of its constitutional autonomy, and the discharge of its ceremonial and symbolic obligations both domestically and internationally. The president holds the single position within the university that is accountable for the totality of its endeavors, the chancellors and vice presidents being responsible for a single campus or specialized functions respectively.

The president is the one who promulgates universitywide policies consistent with delegated authority or formulates and recommends to the Board of Regents the enactment of new policies or the revisions to or rescissions of ones already in place. Under the university's administrative structure and system of shared governance with the Academic Senate, the president is both the university's chief executive officer and its chief academic officer but exercises the former function in full and the latter only rarely, given the authority of the Academic Senate and the need for the university's faculty to make professional judgments in matters more properly within their purview than within the administration's orbit of responsibilities.

Who is president, therefore, makes a difference in the university's work and fortunes. Its purposes, culture, and values depend on wise decisions, insightful and clearly articulated policies, and a light management touch. In particular, the public university needs an effective and supportive governing board, a friendly state government, and protection against sectarian or political interference with its internal operations and against external attacks on its academic freedoms.

Hence a balance of authority among and between the governing board, the president, the chancellors, the vice presidents, the general counsel, the treasurer, and the secretary of the regents is crucial to the effective conduct of the university's operations. The University of California has done as good and as sound a job of this as any university with which I am conversant, not perfect, of course, but a superior job nevertheless. The dynamic of these relationships remains fluid and adaptable to changing times, conditions, and personalities. But at any given point the distribution of authority—along with built-in ambiguities that form an essential part of any managing structure—is remarkably clear, comprehensible, and mostly honored by those involved. There is and needs to be room for some deliberately worded ambiguities, ambiguities having their place in any such large-scale complex organization, especially in a university wherein authority is so widely shared and broadly distributed. Ambiguities afford both faculty members and administrative officers the discretion to employ commonsense judgments in seeking solutions rather than being held to a single "one fits all" standard so often encountered in encrusted bureaucracies.

Virtually *all* the regents' delegated authority vests in the president (except authority they delegate *directly* to the Academic Senate). But the regents retain the authority to appoint the president, and on the recommendation of the president, to appoint the university's vice presidents, chancellors, and directors of the national laboratories managed by UC for the federal government (whose directors report to the president).

The regents also reserve the authority to recommend UC's state-funded operating and capital budgets to the governor, to approve the functionality of buildings and their design over a certain cost, to accept gifts and contracts and grants over a certain amount (both $5 million when I served), to fix tuition levels for out-of-state students and fees for all students, to close or approve new campuses, schools, and colleges, to adopt resolutions for or against ballot initiatives or propositions of vital interest to UC, to judge the performance of their officers and fix their compensation, to oversee the audit function, and to amend their bylaws and standing orders.

There was a time when the president redelegated only nominal authority to the campuses. Even with Kerr's appointment in 1952 as Berkeley's first chancellor, very little changed; but on Sproul's retirement in 1958 Kerr put in place a dramatic and still ongoing decentralization of the university's administrative structure along with substantial delegations from and by the president to the chancellors (the vice presidents are principally staff to the president and not line officers, as are the chancellors). This delegation was driven by the university's increasing complexity and unceasing growth—in students, faculty, and staff and in needed infrastructure: facilities, land, equipment, and intellectual resources.

Naturally, there has been and remains a pull and tug within UC's administration about where the balance and division of this authority should rest at any given time, such judgments being a reflection of growth, opportunities, available resources, rivalries, ambitions, and personalities, and delegated authority coming at times—mistakenly—to feel like entitlement.

The exercise of formal authority relies for its legitimation on the reasoned and culminating expression of a settled set of well-understood processes and procedures and expected conversations among and between those who do the university's work: members of the faculty, staff, and administrators, as well as the students and sometimes the labor unions. The president and the regents need always to keep this "culture of expectations" in mind. This is as true for the fixing of admissions standards and the submission of budgets as it is in the forming of organized research units and the establishment of new campuses.

My sketch here and in chapter 5 of how UC is governed and managed and how it works focuses on its remarkable institutional framework within which the rough-and-tumble debates, politics, and conflicts of the university take place. These were matters I both understood and had at the forefront of my mind as I began my work. They helped inform the steps I was taking to clarify my relations with the regents, to structure my office, to recommend the appointment of certain key officers and not of others, and to establish my position with the chancellors of the nine campuses who reported to me but who also had the delegated authority to operate and to administer their respective campuses.

The chancellors commanded both visibility and regard within their campus community and in the city or community hosting it; they had access to an extended family of interested parties and constituents such as alumni, donors, local legislators, the professional and business interests within the service and commercial radius of the campus, and, of course, the students studying on their respective campuses and their parents. The university's principal constituents tended to identify with a campus—where they had been students or where their children or parents had studied, whose athletic fortunes they followed—whereas the president, one step removed from the university's real work, had collective responsibility for all nine campuses.

The Chancellors

How I arranged my relations with the chancellors, therefore, was of central concern to me. Fortunately, when I began my service as president I had known five of the nine, most for many years: Mike Heyman at Berkeley, chancellor since 1980, a professor of law at Boalt Hall and vice-chancellor for several years on that campus, and a candidate for president of UC at the time of my appointment; James Meyer at Davis, chancellor since 1969, a professor of animal science, and a major figure in the early development of Davis as a general campus of the university; Daniel Aldrich, Jr., at Irvine, founding chancellor of the campus since 1963, a professor of soils and plant nutrition and in his twenty-second year of service as chancellor (having previously worked under Clark Kerr as a universitywide vice president and dean of agricultural sciences), and a neighbor when we both lived in Berkeley in the late 1950s; Richard Atkinson, chancellor at San Diego, in his third year at the campus, having come to San Diego from his post as director of the National Science Foundation, and a nationally known and respected psychologist; and Charles Young, chancellor at Los Angeles, a political scientist appointed in 1968, having earlier assisted Kerr in the formulation of the California Master Plan and, like Heyman, a candidate for the UC presidency when I was appointed.

I did not know Tomás Rivera, chancellor at Riverside since 1979, a writer and poet of considerable reputation, and UC's first minority chancellor; Julius Krevans, just appointed chancellor at San Francisco, UC's only campus devoted exclusively to the health professions and health sciences, a professor of medicine and former dean of the medical school on that campus; Robert Huttenback, chancellor at Santa Barbara since 1977, a professor of history at UCSB and a former dean at the California Institute of Technology; and Robert Sinsheimer, chancellor at Santa Cruz since 1977, a professor of biological sciences and leading American microbiologist, also drawn to UC from the California Institute of Technology.

These were colleagues to be taken seriously, given their well-established positions, the breadth and depth of their complex and demanding administrative assignments, their experience and acquaintance with the regents, and their visibility both within California and in the larger university community, nationally and internationally.

The campuses, however, were *all* known to me, because I had had frequent occasion to visit them in my previous positions.

The Campuses

The campuses were very different one from another—size, program, location, student body, character, culture, history—but were also much alike: each a UC campus and each having a common purpose, common policies, rules and regulations, common standards for admission, common tuition and fee structures for students, common values, common minimum standards for the appointment, promotion, and termination of faculty and staff, and a common administrative structure. But there were important differences among the campuses in the administration of these policies; for example, the average grade point and SAT scores of entering freshmen varied from campus to campus, as did the judgments made about new faculty members being recruited and the promotion of others and at what level to fix their appointments for purposes of rank and salary. Each had its own distinctive history, culture, personality, and identity:

- Berkeley (Cal or UCB), the university's founding campus, *was* the University of California when established in 1868, its first courses being offered in Oakland. Its operations at Berkeley commenced in 1873, on the completion of North and South Halls, the latter still in use. The breadth, depth, and excellence of its academic programs and work are well known at the undergraduate and graduate levels and in its professional schools. It was at the time of my appointment and remains today the nation's most distinguished, best-balanced public university. In 1983, 30,009 students were studying at Berkeley, with little anticipated growth, thus setting the challenge to innovate and adapt to changing times and opportunities within the constraints of an established size and fixed but spectacular site looking westward to San Francisco Bay, to the Golden Gate Bridge, and to the Pacific's far horizon.
- Davis (UCD) was established in 1905, as the applied counterpart to the more "academic" College of Agriculture at Berkeley. It served as UC's principal campus for the agricultural fields of study and especially the applied aspects so crucially relevant to what was then, as in some ways remains today, California's largest single industry, comprehensively described. UC Davis is sited in California's Sacramento Valley, a short distance west of the state capital and in some of the world's richest and most productive agricultural lands. In 1959 Davis was made a general campus within the University of California's changing structure, with a College of Engineering, a Graduate Division, and a School of Law soon following. Since then, Davis developed as a comprehensive UC campus with a full undergraduate and graduate program and an array of professional schools including medicine and UC's only School of Veterinary Medicine. It retained its unique character as a campus mostly residential in character and proud of its roots as a premier center for studies in the agricultural sciences, enrolling 18,969 students in 1983 and poised for substantial growth throughout the 1980s and into the late 1990s, perhaps even beyond.

- Irvine (UCI), founded as one of three new general UC campuses in the early 1960s, opened its doors in 1965 with an entering class of some 1,600 students. It grew rapidly as a comprehensive research and teaching university within the boundaries of UC's norms and standards, including the full development of its undergraduate and graduate programs and an array of professional schools, medicine included. The Irvine campus, a few miles inland from Newport Beach on the southern California coast, enrolled 11,908 students in 1983 and, like Davis, was expected to grow well into the twenty-first century.
- Los Angeles (UCLA), founded as the Los Angeles Normal School in 1881, became a part of UC in 1919, with construction starting in 1929 on its present site in Westwood, not far from Santa Monica Bay and the Malibu coast. Like Berkeley's, UCLA's academic program was comprehensive and at all levels, including both professional schools and a major medical center (which Berkeley lacks). Tension between Berkeley and UCLA had been a way of life for decades, and I would be obliged to allow for those points of stress in my dealings with both chancellors. Its enrollment in 1983 totaled 34,751, UC's largest.
- Riverside (UCR), founded in 1907 as a Citrus Experiment Station and located ninety minutes east of Los Angeles in the rapidly growing sections of Riverside and San Bernardino counties, established its first undergraduate liberal arts college in 1954; it was designated in 1959, with Davis, as a general campus of the university. It came to offer a comprehensive program of undergraduate and graduate instruction, accompanied by the development of major research centers and institutes concerned with pollution, environmental issues, and agriculture. In 1983 Riverside enrolled 4,706 students and was expected to grow well into the twenty-first century.
- San Diego (UCSD), first established as a marine station on the Pacific Ocean in La Jolla, became part of UC in 1912, evolving into the Scripps Institution of Oceanography. In 1959 San Diego was designated as one of three new general campuses of UC to be built in the 1960s, opening its doors in 1964. It had grown rapidly and well, strengthened by the cadre of world-class scientists already affiliated with the Scripps Institution and a magnificent and ample site within blocks of the Pacific Ocean, just northeast of La Jolla. In 1983, 13,468 students were studying at San Diego. The campus had developed a comprehensive set of offerings at the undergraduate and graduate levels and in the professional schools, and was set to grow well into the twenty-first century.
- San Francisco (UCSF), UC's only campus given over exclusively to the health sciences, began in 1864 as a private medical school, affiliating with UC in 1873 and later adding dentistry, nursing, and pharmacy. In 1964 UCSF attained the same status as the other eight UC campuses

with the appointment of its own chancellor. The campus was then and is now a world-renowned center for advanced study in virtually all fields pertinent to the health professions and sciences. In 1983 it enrolled 3,644 students pursuing these fields of study while operating not only major hospital and research facilities but also clinics both on campus and in the city; it thus formed a critical part of the health care available to residents in and around San Francisco and, like Davis, for residents of northern California as well (the coastal counties). UCSF was not expected to grow much, if at all, except for facilities needed for its research.

– Santa Barbara (UCSB) became a UC campus in 1944, as noted in chapter 2, developing first as a liberal arts college and later as a general campus within UC when so designated by the regents in 1958. Over the years the campus evolved into a comprehensive university for teaching, research, and public service, including professional schools. In 1983 it enrolled 16,752 students, studying in virtually every field at both the undergraduate and graduate levels, as the campus attained earlier than expected standing among the leading research universities in the United States. Modest growth was expected for the Santa Barbara campus.

– Santa Cruz (UCSC), the third new campus to be built by UC in the 1960s, was designated as a general campus of the university in 1961, with instruction beginning in 1965. Located in the coastal redwoods north and just east of the City of Santa Cruz, the campus overlooked Monterey Bay, housed most of its students on campus within a college system, and offered undergraduate and graduate studies in nearly all fields except the health sciences. It was a campus with an emphasis on teaching, expected to make the students feel that as their campus was getting larger it would, nevertheless, appear to remain small. The organization of the academic program, provision for on-campus student housing, location of the physical plant, and administrative structure and faculty reward systems were all calculated to attract more serious undergraduates. Santa Cruz enrolled 6,892 students in 1983 and was slated for modest future growth.

The campuses were serious institutions, each with a proud history. They and their chancellors were respected within UC and by the larger higher education community. The chancellors were experienced enough and talented enough to do any number of other things if they so wished. They were already in place, known to their colleagues, the regents, legislators, alumni, and donors; two of them had hoped for appointment to my job. I, having been away for ten years and being the youngest one of them all, was relatively unknown.

The chancellors would be friendly, wishing to help, and so forth, but mostly waiting to see how I would react to and interact with them, the vice presidents, regents, and the Academic Senate leadership, how I would get along with the governor and key legislators, and what I intended to do, when I intended to do it, how I intended to do it, and why. I was under no illusions about the work awaiting me in this exacting and often contentious arena.

The President and the Chancellors

As a vice president under Hitch, I had attended meetings of the Council of Chancellors (COC) on a regular monthly basis, as did the other vice presidents. While the same format had been followed during Saxon's tenure, during my visits to California after my appointment but before I took office I had been told that these meetings had become quite difficult and that from time to time the chancellors would meet without the president.

I was determined to invigorate the Council of Chancellors, which as president I would be chairing, to enhance the collegial nature of our relationships, to include the chancellors and vice presidents in the fixing of our monthly agendas, to end the meetings of chancellors without the president, to convey my desire that COC meetings be forthright and collegial, and to make it clear that the decisions were to be made by the president and not by a vote or a consensus of the participants: the chancellors were not a legislative body and I was not a governor. I discussed all the above issues with the chancellors, individually at first and then collectively later. Not one chose to break away; everyone chose to cooperate and help. I was very gratified with the outcome. I succeeded here because there was consistency between what I was saying and what I did and because I made effective use of the COC as promised. And in fact the COC played a critical, indeed, an indispensable role in my administration. It helped facilitate effective, respectful, and productive relations among us, or at least as much as could reasonably be expected given the strong-willed nature, egos, and experience of those involved.

These monthly meetings focused on such matters as UC's budgets, pending legislation at both the state and federal levels, major policy issues, affirmative action, student fees, state politics, educational policy issues (including admissions policies), and new academic programs. We discussed faculty recruiting and compensation, use of university facilities for other than teaching, research and public service programs, and union issues. We were also concerned with government policies and programs, such as Medicare funding for our hospitals and clinics, student financial aid, research policies, indirect cost reimbursement issues, nondiscrimination regulations, and so forth. We reviewed the major universitywide issues being prepared for the upcoming monthly meetings of the Board of Regents to make certain that what we were recommending, informed by past and ongoing conversations with campus personnel, including the chancellors, still sounded "right" to everyone and that the timing was propitious.

I enjoyed these meetings. They were an intellectual challenge; we were dealing with very complicated, sophisticated, and often politically charged issues. They were fun because the people around the table possessed wit, intelligence, charisma, strong personalities, and a proclivity for debate; and they were stimulating because each chancellor was used to making final decisions on his campus, and prevailing.

I recall that Chancellor Young of UCLA, not one renowned for reticence or indifferent opinions, would ratchet up the volume of his comments in proportion to his level of agitation, culminating in a stroll, or perhaps it was more a parade, around the room where his gestures could be more appreciatively linked to the points he was making, all the while with one chancellor or more, and usually Heyman, offering either comments about or judgments concerning his line of reasoning or conclusions. After this had gone on a while, I would quietly ask if he, Young, was nearly finished as we did have a larger agenda to consider. He would laugh, offer a quip or two directed at one or more of the chancellors, and sit down, having expressed himself in a fashion calculated both to influence views and to make it clear that his opinions were to be considered.

I recall on one occasion when meeting at Blake House we were unable to arrive at a reasonable decision on an intractable subject now forgotten. Sinsheimer remarked, "Dave, I don't know why this is such a problem. The answer, at least it seems to me, is readily apparent." He then proceeded to define the problem as he saw it, arraying the factors to be considered such that they yielded a comprehensive answer to the problem. "Bob, do you know what's wrong with you scientists?" I asked with a smile and in the most friendly way possible. "No, what?" he asked, I believe somewhat taken aback. "You tend to think about a problem in mostly linear terms, and thus you think you have resolved it when you reach a rational outcome that on the surface appears to be *the answer*. I agree that you have shown us the way to the *right answer*, but the trouble is, an unworkable *answer* is *not* the *solution*."

I then went on to explain why his answer wouldn't work, for example, timing, politics, personalities, precedent, and so forth. Everyone laughed at this exchange, and everyone understood it. Two or three months later Sinsheimer was the commencement speaker at Cal Tech and in his opening remarks recalled this incident and urged the graduates always to remember "this lesson" that he had recently learned.[1]

Another example of how we worked through tough issues occurred near the end of my service. We were discussing another problem, comparably resistant to a solution because of its complexities and internal inconsistencies, and equally now lost to my memory. None of us could discover a workable course of action with which we were comfortable. Heyman then offered an analysis of the problem, proposed a solution, and explained why he thought we should proceed accordingly.

It sounded pretty good, others agreed, and with Heyman's skills of reasoning and his strong personality, we were moving toward what seemed to be a viable solution. The issue was important enough, I remember thinking, that I wanted each chancellor on record, along with the vice presidents, before expressing myself in a definitive way about how we would proceed.

Everyone in the room supported Heyman's proposal until we got to Vice President Brady, the last person to be asked. His answer was straightforward and simple: "It won't work! Too many moving parts." There was a prolonged silence, and as I reflected on Heyman's "solution" it was evident not only to me but to everyone else in the room that Brady was right. We all then worked to simplify Heyman's idea, did so, solved the problem, and moved on. What he meant by "too many moving parts" was that the proposed solutions involved an excess of interdependent actions that would fail to link up if even one should fail or fall short of what was needed. Our solution was to craft a solution dependent on fewer such interactions, and to provide for backup lines of decision making if our critical expectations proved unavailing.

I mention these examples to give the reader a flavor of how the COC worked, how we got along even given the disparate and diverse nature and personalities of the players. The chancellors' administrative responsibilities appeared to be quite similar but were really not, given the differences among and between the histories, sizes, cultures, budgets, locations, and differential levels of programmatic maturity of the nine campuses, as well as the native competition that both campuses and chancellors would have one with another and with me, individually and collectively. I respected the chancellors' very different personalities and wanted us all to get along.

These were important meetings. Much of the university's success depended on our understanding of major matters, our creativity and skill in thinking through and sorting out our options and then making the right choices, securing a favorable response to these decisions from within UC and from the Board of Regents, and determining how they would be received by the full panoply of UC's many constituents. We were keenly aware of the possible consequences our decisions would have on public higher education elsewhere, and in certain instances on private colleges and universities as well, given UC's prominence and reputation.

The result of this time-consuming, but necessary, effort was better but certainly not perfect decisions, a mostly cohesive, usually cordial, and generally cooperative Council of Chancellors, few surprises, and a sense of our working as a real team in behalf of a larger common cause we all respected— although our discussions didn't always sound so altruistic or harmonious, I hasten to inform the reader.

The regents understood the COC's role, which enhanced their confidence in the items coming to them, knowing that the process was sound and the university's historic culture of consultation and collegiality had been honored. It also strengthened my hand with the regents, as they knew that the administration was unified and, therefore, less susceptible to board manipulation.

The Vice Presidents

The university's five vice presidents, while not line officers, were an indispensable part of UC's administrative structure. Their roles, under my general guidance, were to assist the chancellors with their interpretation or administration of universitywide policies, to work with the campuses in the preparation of items for regents' meetings, to advise me on issues within their respective areas of responsibility, to communicate with regents as required, and to oversee the operations and the work of their staffs in the areas assigned to them by the university's management structure:

- William Frazer, senior vice president for academic affairs, a theoretical physicist from the San Diego campus and former provost of UCSD's Third College, was an important member of the Saxon team and a highly respected faculty member. Within the new structure, he was to carry the responsibility for UC's academic programs and personnel, educational policy, relations with the Academic Senate, the state's public schools and California's other colleges and universities (public and private), the operations of the three national laboratories, the University of California Press, UC's Education Abroad Program, UC Extension, and a host of related duties.
- Ronald Brady, senior vice president for administration and finance, an economist and a seasoned, tough, and brilliant administrator, former vice president of Syracuse University and the University of Illinois, carried much of the same portfolio of duties under Saxon. He was responsible in my administration for UC's financial and management information systems, audits, human resources, the retirement system, contracts, union negotiations, coordination and preparation of materials for regents' meetings, security, and an array of related functions.
- William Baker, vice president for budget and university relations, a civil engineer, was Saxon's budget officer and a lifelong friend from Berkeley. During my service he was responsible for the preparation of UC's budgets, both operating and capital, governmental relations both in Sacramento and Washington, D.C., press relations, public information, and alumni relations and development, as well as a number of special assignments from time to time: for example, overseeing California's proposal for the Super Conducting Super Collider in 1998, and leading the search to locate UC's tenth campus.

- James Kendrick, vice president for agriculture and natural resources, an agricultural economist, carried most of the same duties in the Saxon administration as in mine. He was charged with overseeing UC's responsibilities as the state's land-grant university with its vast network of cooperative extension offices and field and agricultural experiment stations, farms, and ranches and its vast holdings of environmentally sensitive and research-rich lands, waters, wetlands, and forests throughout California.
- Cornelius Hopper, vice president for health sciences, a medical doctor and a former assistant to Saxon, was a former vice president of Tuskegee Institute. He was responsible in my administration for staffing issues related to UC's five major medical centers, its hospitals, clinics, and health professional schools, the administration of state-funded programs for AIDS- and tobacco-related research, and other important functions within the university's array of health-related professional schools, hospitals, clinics, and research in this vital and costly area of university operations.

These capable and respected professionals knew the university well and had the skills, imagination, knowledge, and personality to work within UC's complicated structure while commanding the regard of their colleagues and those with whom they interacted outside UC. Each had worked for Saxon in related capacities, but in my administration each carried additional duties, since I had eliminated two vice president positions and several assistant to the president positions as well.

I held individual and collective meetings with the vice presidents each week. The one-on-one time I reserved for problems and issues best considered in private, and the collective meetings obliged each vice president to take account of and acknowledge his colleagues' work. The meetings also facilitated their work with the chancellors and with their campus counterpart vice-chancellors, not only fostering a high level of formal and informal communication among and between my key officers but also keeping to a minimum the inevitable differences and misunderstandings that form a part of any enterprise so vast, complex, and visible as was and is the University of California.

The Academic Senate

The university's Academic Senate, so unique in its role and organization in American higher education, was, of course, critical to the university's governance. While not technically part of management, the senate played an indirect part in virtually every major decision: funding for new academic initiatives, funding for the construction of new or for the renovation of older facilities for teaching, research, and public service, libraries, computer centers, clinics, hospitals and the like, issues of compensation for all academic personnel, support for and allocation of faculty positions across UC and for fellowship funds for graduate students, study leaves and sabbatical policies, and the allocation for research-related purposes of the university's very substantial indirect cost reimbursement funds and monies earned on royalties and licenses.

While I had earned my Ph.D. in higher education at Berkeley seventeen years earlier, had taught at Santa Barbara, had authored a well received scholarly book and numerous articles in the leading journals and periodicals in my academic field, and had been promoted to the rank of full professor within UC before leaving for Utah in 1973, I was not perceived as a traditional University of California faculty member as Clark Kerr and David Saxon were. Yet the examples of Robert Gordon Sproul and Charles Hitch offered ample precedent for the appointment of UC presidents who were selected for other qualities deemed to be sufficient. I was not overly concerned about my standing or my acceptance by the faculty. Deep down I knew, however, that I would have to earn their respect as the president of the University of California, my work as president of the University of Utah notwithstanding.

I also knew that the University of California, like any great university, could not rise to levels of excellence and distinction that reached beyond the collective brilliance and performance of the faculty: those who taught in the classrooms and worked in the laboratories, hospitals, and clinics, those whose research pushed back the boundaries of what is known, and whose public and professional services in the larger community so enriched and elevated the quality of life for peoples everywhere. Hence, it was a matter of central importance that I work closely with the university's Academic Senate *and* discover the resources so desperately needed to retain members of UC's faculty (some 6,550) and to recruit those we were seeking from throughout the world. This task, in the end, was the most important, bar none.

The universitywide Academic Council, composed of an elected chair and vice chair and the chairs of the senate's standing universitywide committees, was the Academic Senate's vehicle for connecting with my office and coordinating its efforts within the context of UC's elaborate decision-making process. Those serving were all members of the university's professoriate— bright, interested, dependable, but variously conversant with administrative matters. This last point was not a real problem as I wanted their advice as faculty members, not as part of the administration.

Vice President Frazer and his staff worked closely with the Academic Council and was respected by them. I, of course, had full confidence in Frazer's ability to represent me in this capacity. Once a month I would meet with the council and review matters of mutual interest and concern, for two or more hours. This connection with the senate was supplemented three times a year by meetings with the Academic Assembly, the senate's legislation-making arm, whose members were elected by each of the senate's nine divisions, campus by campus.

With the council, Frazer and I discussed UC's budgets, pending legislation in the state legislature or before Congress, upcoming matters on the regents' agenda, policy issues then under attack or review, and trends, problems, and opportunities for the university in general. I did not discuss campus-specific issues unless they carried implications for the university generally.

These were meetings that I welcomed, from which I always learned, and at which I was able not only to share information and seek advice but also to take a rough and present measure of faculty opinion(s) on short- and long-term issues. They gave me an informal means of broadening my personal acquaintance and friendship with members of the faculty, dispersed as they were among all nine campuses. They were professionally and personally satisfying occasions, and I believe the faculty felt the same way.

It should also be noted, contrary to popular belief, that the faculty almost invariably acted and advised in the most thoughtful and rational of ways, respectful of both their role and mine, and that of the regents too. While this was not necessarily the same judgment I would make about some of the opinions and counsel received from individual faculty members, some invited, others offered, it was true of the interaction I had with the Academic Senate, in its many forms, during my nearly ten years as president.

I also met monthly with the chair and vice chair of the senate, some of whom I had known, including personal friends of many years standing, especially Neil Smelser and Martin Trow, both of the Berkeley campus, both leaders in their respective fields and well-known scholars in the United States and abroad. The chair and vice chair and I would explore more deeply and more directly many of the same issues that were to be covered with the Academic Council and Academic Assembly and such additional items as might also be scheduled for the next or upcoming meetings of the Board of Regents.

Both the chair and vice chair of the Academic Senate were nonvoting faculty representatives to the Board of Regents, who sat at the table during meetings of the board with the right to speak as freely as any voting member on whatever issues were before the regents. The senate, many years ago, had been offered a voting seat on the board but chose instead the arrangement just described, preferring to participate in regents meetings as a "representative voice" for the university's faculty rather than as indistinguishable, voting members of the board obliged, by custom and expectations, to take a broader view of matters coming to the regents. Those representing the senate at the Board of Regents' meetings were well prepared, respected, and influential, never abusing their position but always making certain that when faculty interests and educational policy issues were under discussion the senate's view was heard.

The Staff

I also met with the staff assembly, representing the university's nonacademic personnel. That a high percentage of the university's staff was unionized constantly constrained me from communicating as freely and as directly with them as I was able to do with the faculty and others. I much regretted this circumstance; though I did the best I could, I could not really alter or overcome the conventions of union/management cultures and obligations that, at least in university settings, get in the way of real collegiality.

The Students

Finally, but certainly not least, were the relations I had with the council of student body presidents, one from each of the nine campuses, with whom I would meet three to four times a year, usually at Blake House.

These meetings were essential, although some chancellors did not welcome them, fearing end runs. But they signified my regard for the students' role and made evident my desire to have their opinions and advice. These meetings also enabled me to share the facts of pending issues, to explain changes in university policies, rules, and regulations, and to listen to their views on student fees and financial aid policies and about their educational experience both in and out of the classroom or on any other matter they wished to raise. They believed in the usefulness of these meetings, for the most part, as at the least it gave them and me a chance to hear opinions free of their being filtered through what they saw as the university's "forbidding bureaucracy."

The Regents

How the regents met their responsibilities, interacted with the president and key administrative officers, organized their work, and made decisions also needs to be understood. I had to allow not only for the ideologies and personalities of each of the twenty-five regents, not counting their president, but for the procedures they followed and the governing precepts they honored. These I had to understand as completely as possible, or I would be incapable of commanding either their confidence or the chancellors', vice presidents', or faculty's regard.

Roughly 100 to 125 items appeared on the regents' agenda for each of their nine yearly meetings, putting aside special meetings, unscheduled committee meetings, and the like. These items would be referred to the cognizant committees, for example, educational policy, hospitals, grounds and buildings, and finance, for handling on Thursday during the full-day session. The meeting scheduled for Friday morning was reserved for the full board. Except for the closed meetings, which were held prior to the open portion of the meetings and were reserved for such issues as litigation, contracts, real estate transactions, investments, personnel, and compensation, the regents' meetings were open to the public as permitted under California's open meeting laws to which the board voluntarily adhered.

The board's president was the governor of the state, and the board's chairman was elected by the regents annually. The president of the university was an ex officio voting member of the board, as were the governor, lieutenant governor, state superintendent of public instruction, Speaker of the Assembly, and president and vice president of the alumni associations (rotated through the campuses annually). A student representative, appointed by the regents from a slate submitted by the student body council, represented all nine campuses and served as a voting member for a one-year term. The term for regents other than ex officio members and the student representative was twelve years on nomination by the governor and with the consent of the state Senate.

In the course of my service, I proposed a number of changes in the regents' schedule and procedures, which the board welcomed as making more effective use of its time. The regents began to meet on the campuses on a rotating schedule, having not done so for years because they were apprehensive about protests disrupting the meetings. The regular business meetings were reduced from nine to seven, plus two one-day meetings six months apart dedicated to issues of strategic policy only. A consent agenda was instituted to collect the more routine items and act on them with a single motion. I also preferred not to introduce most items, as had been customary for many years; instead, issues of universitywide import were introduced by the cognizant vice president, and campus-specific matters, by the interested chancellor.

Further delegations of authority were made to the UC president. The president was responsible for fixing the agendas (a not-to-be-underestimated consideration) and for ordering the business. I took this duty very seriously, not wishing to place on the agenda items for consideration by the board before they were "ripe" or if I thought them untimely. Depending on the issue and where we were in dealing with the subject internally, I calendared items for information, discussion, or action, seeking to keep the regents informed in a timely way about items of interest (the information items); to provide the board a timely opportunity to discuss and debate items before being asked to act (the discussion items); and to ask the regents for a decision when we knew what we as an administration wanted, what we thought we could get, and what was timely and ready for a board decision (the action items).

The preparation and coordination of the regents' agenda was a complicated, sensitive, and difficult task. To follow the preparation of an item would require charting the university's deliberative, consultative, and decision-making process, involving staff, faculty and sometimes students, administrators, and university officers throughout UC. In their subject matter, items would often cross campuses (e.g., faculty salary scales and university policies), administrative boundaries (e.g., hospitals and audits), and functional divisions of labor (e.g., management information systems and budgets). They were often complex and contentious and required substantial lead time and multiple levels of review before reaching the Council of Chancellors' agenda and/or my desk for final consideration and approval for calendaring as an item for regental information, discussion, or action.

Because these items would quite often be of public and, therefore, of media interest, it was a challenge to keep media and public attention off the process: premature discussion of an item, perhaps barely formed as an idea or only sketchily prepared for purposes of discussion, if reported, could well mislead the public into supposing that decisions had been made or that intentions or directions had been determined when that may very well not have been the case at all. Mischief, ambitions, and ill as well as goodwill were an inevitable part of this process, especially on issues that engendered ideological or politically partisan feelings.

It was truly amazing that the system worked so well, especially given the decentralized nature of UC's operations, the breadth of review and consideration such matters received, and the complexity of the items themselves. It is a tribute to the intelligence and competence of those on the campuses and in the Office of the President on whom we so heavily depended to prepare these materials in ways that deflected unreasoned criticism, personal aspiration, ideological and politically partisan commitments, and such other intrusions calculated to advance individual or special interests at the expense of what was best for the University of California.

The preparation and coordination of the agenda, shortly after my arrival, was assigned to Senior Vice President Brady, whose attributes were noted earlier in this chapter. Brady was a problem solver par excellence, acknowledged as such by his friends and critics alike; but he was, if I may put it gently, more attentive to the task at hand than to the sensibilities of those doing it, especially if they required more direction or explanation than Brady thought necessary. He contributed immeasurably to the effective conduct of UC's business, although not without arousing irritation about his style and personality from some, and resentment toward him from many, to which he paid no attention whatsoever. The items being prepared for the COC's consideration and for my approval for submission to the board came in on time and were properly vetted, well written, and ready for both my final review and the regents' consideration.

Brady's work was effective, innovative, and directed toward finding solutions to problems that others could not. I counted heavily on him in this arena, especially as the items going to the regents not only carried my signature but were the basis for decisions that would either help improve, merely sustain, or permit slippage in the excellence of this most remarkable of public universities. He got along very well indeed with the chancellors, somewhat less evenly with the vice presidents, and only sporadically with the faculty. Some regents thought Brady walked on water. Others wished he would slip and go under. He treated all equally, being "no respecter of persons" in the biblical sense, a much-commended attribute in the spiritual world but not altogether welcomed in ours. In any event, I not only respected but liked him, and I appreciated his hard work and the remarkable contributions he made to the university.

One of the challenges we faced was a Board of Regents whose members, while supportive of and committed to UC, expected to be doing something as regents, not just listening to us or approving whatever we sent forward to them. They were accomplished, successful people in their own right, holding views and opinions borne of their own experience, trials, and tribulations—the very kind of people we wanted to serve as regents, but it made for something of a challenge.

The regents, of course, did not live in our world. Most of them lived in a corporate-legal culture, and the university's academic culture sometimes produced impatience, lack of understanding, and therefore unneeded controversy. Moreover, they were political appointees, except for the ex officio members, but at the same time were expected to safeguard the university's political neutrality even though being beholden, at least in part and early on, to the political forces that had led to their serving as regents. Time tended to socialize regents to their duty, with the longest-serving regents often being the most independent and for that reason the most effective.

Before I placed an item before the board, it had undergone the most careful and rigorous internal scrutiny imaginable. If the item was for board action, I expected, indeed obliged, to formulate the motion for enactment of the item as its lead paragraph. My decisions were taken only after I had carefully read the results of our internal reviews, considered the opinions of the chancellors and vice presidents, the senate, and others, read contrary opinions, talked personally with the chancellor(s) or vice president(s) most implicated, consulted with the university's chief legal adviser (the general counsel), sounded out certain regents either directly or through a vice president and/or chancellor, and, if it was a politically sensitive issue, discussed it with our representative in Sacramento, Steve Arditti, and sometimes with the governor's chief of staff, the education adviser to Willie Brown, and, as needed, with Speaker Brown, Governor Deukmejian, and others.

Thus, for the board to return an item for further study was virtually a request to start over, unless in the language of the referral I could deal with it under delegated authority, or with only modest consultation required. Of course the board had the absolute, legal, and moral right to do as it wished, and I always respected that. But if too often "corrected" by the board, my position would be weakened over time as well. So I worked very hard not to submit items that were going to be defeated or that would require a direct regental action to correct. I do *not* mean by this that I neglected my duty to advance the university's agenda consistent with my obligations, only that I gave much and careful attention to the timing and means employed in settling on a decision and advancing the item to the board.

My staff and I did our homework, ensuring that we knew more about the item than anyone else—the points of contention and the views of interested parties—because we personally and informally talked with those regents thought to be most interested, the vice presidents making most of these calls in my behalf and at my behest. In this fashion, we took the regents' "temperature," learned of their views, understood how an adjustment here and a change there would make the item more agreeable (without changing its purpose or substance), and determined to repackage it, to keep it on, or remove it from a regents' agenda.

This process worked miraculously well and, in nearly ten years as president, the board sent back, amended, or defeated my recommendations not more often than two or three times a year, if that. One of the unexpected and negative consequences of this seemingly seamless commonality of views between the regents and the president was that the board was perceived to be unduly under my influence. This view grew among Democratic circles in the state legislature as regents' expired terms, deaths, or resignations, in tandem with Deukmejian's appointments, lowered the percentage of liberals on the board. For my own part, I was also anxious about this trend as we needed to work with both parties in the legislature, not with just one, and we counted on the regents to help us in this effort. A politically unbalanced board would not be helpful, but that is what we eventually got in spite of my efforts to persuade Governors Deukmejian and Wilson otherwise. (Our critics in the legislature, of course, had no idea how the university functioned or how much informal effort was expended by my colleagues and by me, and by the regents themselves, to make this huge system work for the university's overall good.)

At the meetings of the board I kept a low profile, asking vice presidents and chancellors, as earlier noted, to present the items on our agenda for which they were responsible, to respond to questions, to guide the discussion, and to move the matter forward for board action; the formal aspects of this process, of course, were handled by the chairman of the board, not by me. I sat on the chairman's left and to the right of the secretary, sometimes offering a suggestion to the chairman, and other times a point of clarification to the secretary, but always and with singular concentration on the course of the discussion or debate, observing the body language and informal exchanges between certain regents, with accompanying facial expressions; sensing as best I could the tenor of the discussion, its present and probable direction; and counting votes if necessary.

If the matter was proceeding without undue difficulty, I said nothing. If it was going less well, I also remained silent except for entering a point of clarification, an interpretation of policy, or a factual correction and, sometimes, a brief observation to help complete the turn onto a straight road leading to the desired end. If it was going badly, I would intervene and withdraw the item on my own initiative before the discussion went any further. If an amendment was required or seemed desirable, I would speak promptly in support of such an action; or if the item was clearly headed south contrary to my desires, I would listen to the arguments, calculate their impact, count votes, discern the forming coalitions, and consider my own remarks.

At what seemed to me to be the most propitious time, I would seek the chairman's recognition and summarize the strengths and weaknesses of the arguments advanced by individual regents, explaining why the alternatives being discussed had been rejected by our internal reviews in favor of the proposal I had made and why their approach might appear to be the "preferable answer" but was not the "solution," as it wouldn't work. Then, and with due regard for their sensibilities and the merits of their arguments, I strove to secure their support for our solution, which we regarded as the one most desirable for the board to support, all things considered.

I feel somewhat awkward about sharing any assessment of my working style and its presumed effectiveness, as I can hardly be regarded as a disinterested observer and fully acknowledge that self-delusion may color these descriptions a bit. But I can hardly omit any reference to this part of my work as president, because much of my success or failure depended on securing the cooperation of the board, helping bring them to the actions needed by the university without dividing the board itself, or alienating it from the rest of the university community or any of its parts.

I cannot really know whether others regarded my work in the same way as I did (self-insight has a way of being frail and unreliable—a lurking problem with autobiographies, I openly acknowledge). For what it is worth, however, two others who have had the opportunity to observe my work closely, and over an extended period, have described my work with the regents. The first is Jack Peltason, chancellor at Irvine from 1984 to 1992, former president of the American Council on Education, chancellor of the University of Illinois, my successor as president of the university in 1992, and a close friend of many years standing, who recalled these meetings and my approach in his introduction to my oral history:

Before David dealt with any issue, he did his homework and knew more about the subject than anybody else. So whether he was dealing with students, faculty, other administrators, regents, or politicos, he won almost all the arguments by the power of his logic and the persuasiveness of his reasoning. He was always sensitive to the tactics and politics of a situation but after listening to the discussions, he would summarize the advice he received, make sense out of incoherence, and work to build consensus for action that would serve the best interest of the university.

Watching him at a Regents' meeting was seeing a virtuoso at work. Regents have strong opinions and are not reluctant to discuss them. Their convictions were often conflicting and the board would be deadlocked. Then, without benefit of notes, David would summarize the various positions, put the issue into context, make a recommendation which, on its merits, would receive a vote of all the regents. In fact, he was so persuasive that the regents found themselves accused of being rubber stamps. They were not; they simply were persuaded by David to do what was best for the university.[2]

Professor Martin Trow of the Berkeley campus, an internationally respected scholar and in the later years of my administration chairman of the Academic Council and, thus, the senate's representative to the Board of Regents, who was a friend and colleague of many years' standing, also commented on my work with the regents in most interesting fashion in his oral history:

> I've had a fair amount of experience in public life and on committees. . . . But I've never seen anybody manage a body as effectively as Gardner did the Board of Regents. And that was made possible by his personal qualities, one of which is that he is almost always simply smarter than anybody else in the room.
>
> But I've been around a lot of smart people, so that is not enough. Gardner is extremely smart, but he is also very, very keenly analytical, which isn't quite the same thing. He can take a problem and break it down into its component parts, which already suggests a solution—his solution. . . . At meetings he tends to wait for everybody else to speak and then sum up what has been said or else make reference to it in his response. In this summing up it is clear that he has been listening, and his summaries are very fair to what has been said, including those who hold opinions differing from his own. But then he also has no hesitation about dealing very sharply with people who are criticizing something that he or one of his staff people have done, simply by producing a body of evidence and facts and packaging them in a way that overwhelms the critic. . . . Most of the time I think he simply persuaded people that he had thought the matter through, he had a lot of facts and information and that he had a better solution than everybody else. In addition to which, if anything important came up, he had talked it through with every member of the Board on the telephone beforehand. . . . [H]e also told them what was on his mind so there were no surprises. No surprises. They knew where he stood, and he knew where they stood. . . . He always had to take their views into account, but he'd take them into account, on the whole, before the meetings.[3]

These sketches convey something of the intricacies of UC's governing and administrative structures, the role and organization of the Academic Senate, and, to a lesser extent, how the staff and students fit into the larger structure, as well as my administrative style. As to the last point, I would at least like to think that my work with the board approximated the kind and generous assessments of Peltason and Trow.

MOVING FORWARD

The task that lay before me in the early months of the fall semester of 1983 was as formidable as it was unavoidable: I had to earn the confidence and support of the regents, the chancellors, and the Academic Senate, to restructure the central administration, to staff the key positions, and to forge an effective working relationship with the governor, the legislative leadership, and the congressional leaders overseeing matters of interest to UC, many of whom I already knew, as I was already widely acquainted with the Reagan administration.

I also needed to visit all nine campuses of the university, the three national labs we managed for the federal government, and other parts of this sprawling and fascinating institution, while learning everything I could about university policies, practices, customs, rules and regulations, problems, opportunities, and issues. And I was to be formally inaugurated as president, consistent both with custom and expectations.

Inauguration

My inauguration as president was scheduled by the regents for the morning hours of Thursday, April 12, 1984, on the Los Angeles campus. The inauguration of a UC president had also taken place at UCLA in 1968 when Charles J. Hitch was invested as the university's thirteenth president. I had attended Hitch's inauguration as a faculty delegate from UC Santa Barbara and had been impressed with how well UCLA had managed the entire affair.

Chancellor Young of UCLA had expressed a desire early in my administration to host the inauguration once again, this time in the newly renovated Royce Hall, a beautiful complex for the performing arts that was a famous UCLA landmark and one of the university's most handsome buildings. Berkeley had made no such gesture. I accepted UCLA's invitation. The great majority of the state's population lived in southern California, five of the university's nine campuses were in the south, the state's major newspapers and main media outlets were in Los Angeles, the governor was from there, and I knew that UCLA would do it right. I believed that such a ceremony, bringing to bear the full and impressive force of the entire university on a single and time-honored tradition, was important. This was an uncommon and infrequent ceremony consistent with Western practices and in keeping with UC's own traditions.

In 1983 the university was experiencing financial hard times, had suffered grievously under Governors Reagan and Brown for sixteen years, had alienated much of California's citizenry during the Free Speech Movement and the subsequent antiwar demonstrations of the 1960s, and was much in need of a boost in public regard and esteem. I hoped the inauguration would help, drawing to the university as only an inaugural could do leaders of the state, leaders of American higher education, foundations, and scientific and scholarly societies, and the faculty, students, and staff of all nine campuses including many of their most prominent alumni and key donors.

I also believed that we needed to make not just a gesture but a full and complete ceremony, worthy of UC's traditions and its place in the top ranks of universities worldwide. Why would we want to do less? It would offer UC a rare opportunity to express itself as a single institution—formed from its many parts but a single university, nevertheless. As to my own involvement, I regarded myself more as a prop or totem than as the object of personal attention, as the means whereby this highly public and widely reported occasion could be justified and an opportunity for the university to shake off its problems and celebrate its accomplishments.

Chancellor Young and members of his staff, assisted by members of my staff and others drawn from the Berkeley campus much experienced in such events, worked very hard to plan and accomplish the favorable outcome we all envisioned. We were not disappointed.

The academic procession moving through the center of campus and into Royce Hall was a colorful affair, with academic robes and hoods from many of the world's universities worn by members of the university's faculties and by the 120 delegates from universities and colleges from throughout the United States and abroad who were in attendance. Representatives of UC's staff and students from all nine campuses were also included among those who preceded the official party into a filled to capacity Royce Hall.

The last to enter were led by University Marshal Ralph H. Turner of UCLA, chair of the Academic Assembly of the Academic Senate, and Marshal Neil J. Smelser, chair of the Academic Senate at Berkeley. Following, in turn, were Governor Deukmejian and me; then the chairman of the Board of Regents, Yori Wada, and Lord Ashby of Cambridge University, our speaker of the day; and other speakers, followed by the members of the Board of Regents, the chancellors of the university, the officers of the regents, the student body presidents from the nine campuses, and honored guests.

I had invited Lord Ashby, a dear friend of many years, former vice-chancellor of Cambridge University and master of Clare College in that ancient university, to be our speaker of the day. Derek Bok, president of Harvard University and also a good friend of many years, spoke as the representative from American universities and colleges and the nation's learned societies, foundations, and associations. Greetings were extended by several speakers representing the faculty, administration, staff, students, and alumni of the university. Governor Deukmejian spoke in behalf of the state.

These remarks were, of course, fitted to the occasion with Deukmejian referring to UC as "one of our state's proudest achievements and one of our most precious resources"; and Bok, in like fashion, referred to UC as an "authentic national treasure" and "a leader among American universities in an era when American universities are preeminent in the world."[4] And Ashby's remarks were, typically, quite wonderful, warm, elegant, full of wisdom, laced with humor and optimistic:

> Your new President stands before you like a brand new automobile, shining, immaculate, not a scratch or dent on the coachwork. He knows, as well as any of us, that it will not stay that way. Even in the parking lot, so to speak, when the car isn't occupied, the coachwork gets scratched. But it's the strength and durability of the engine that matters, and we have a guarantee of that from your President's record in Utah and before that in this university. . . .
>
> The cliché for describing universities is to call them communities of scholars. It is surprising how few people realize what peculiar communities they are. One of your own faculty, Burton Clark, has called them institutions for the management of knowledge. Unlike workers in industry, each worker creates his own product. Unlike strategy in the armed services, those in command do not set one goal by orders from the top. The essential work of the university goes on at the frontiers of knowledge. That's where the experts are, eagerly pushing the frontiers outwards. All the action that makes universities exciting in teaching or research is along the frontiers. In the middle of all this excitement, in the eye of the vortex, sits the president. He was at one time at the frontiers himself, but now he can no longer work there. The most junior faculty member is better qualified than the president, when it comes to oncogenic protein sequences, or interstellar scintillation, or tribal law in New Guinea, or medieval Greek. It may be—as Burton Clark suggests—that the medievalist can get on perfectly well without a biochemist on the campus. The paradoxical thing is that neither of them could get along without the president (though some may think they could). For he represents the force of cohesion, compensating for the centrifugal forces along the frontiers, preventing the great institution from flying apart. No wonder the president has to be durable.

During the formal investiture my own academic robe and hood were, as was the UC custom, replaced with those worn by Benjamin Ide Wheeler, the university's president whose long tenure (1899–1919) played such a pivotal role in the shaping and development of the University of California. A portion of my inaugural remarks follows:

> [U]niversities exist for many purposes and they serve many ends. One of those purposes is to remind us of what has lasting value, of what endures beneath

the currents and eddies of everyday life. We would do well to adopt what Lord Ashby once called an "attitude of constructive defiance" against the times, especially when those times are demanding and difficult, such as the period through which we have just come. English history illuminates the point. I draw from J. R. Green's *Short History of the English People*. The year is 1648. In that year we are in the midst of the Puritan Revolution, of civil war in England, and we read of the outbreak of the Royalist revolt in February, the revolt of the Fleet and of Kent in May, of the campaigns of Fairfax and Cromwell in Essex and Wales in June and July, of the Battle of Preston and the surrender of Colchester in August, and of Pride's purge in December. And at the end of a gloomy, bloody recital, we come to this entry in italics: *Royal Society begins at Oxford.*

In the midst of all that is transitory in our age, may we yet discern something permanent, something that will outshine and outlast all the violence in our contemporary struggles for power. I believe that the University of California bears the standard of significance in a world awash with trivia. It is one of civilization's authentic triumphs. While conserving the past, it helps mold the future—a wellspring of ideas, beneficial to our society and the world of which it is so pivotal a part. With your help, and that of our alumni and friends throughout the globe, we shall keep it that way. It is my pleasure and my great privilege to be in its service.

I also took note of the initiatives I intended to take, as already discussed in earlier chapters of this book.

The inauguration went very well. Its purposes were achieved and there was good feeling about it by most, but not by all. At Berkeley, and perhaps elsewhere, although I didn't hear about it, there was some grumbling that I had chosen UCLA rather than Berkeley, that the ceremony was overly elaborate, that it was self-serving and not appropriate for today's world, and that it cost too much money. Yet the inauguration paid handsome dividends for UC, helped tie the governor even closer to the university and other influential persons who were also present, honored a tradition worthy of UC and academe, and brought to the university Bok and Ashby, two internationally known and highly respected personages whose expressions of respect and admiration for the university were widely noticed. But I was not surprised at the grumbling. I had heard it when both Hitch and Kerr were inaugurated.

Berkeley had, in any event, not been particularly welcoming of my appointment nor hospitable in the early years of my presidency, although this changed for the better as time went on. Compared with the steady stream of invitations received from the other eight campuses, I was not made to feel welcome at Berkeley, officially or otherwise.

I was determined not to have any of this coolness affect me, but in all honesty it did. I had grown up in Berkeley, knew the campus intimately, and had nothing but the utmost respect and regard for the excellence of its programs, the brilliance of its faculty, the dedication of its staff, and the liveliness and capability of its students. Many of its faculty leaders and members of its staff, as well as of its alumni, were personal friends of mine. Not to feel welcomed, indeed, to feel only grudgingly received on campus, was a very sad thing for me to experience.

Perhaps this went with the job, as Berkeley never had thought the president's office itself very friendly to Berkeley's perceived needs and position, helping as it also did eight other campuses, and often against Berkeley's wishes. Perhaps there were other, more personal reasons. But I had little time to reflect on this disappointment as I needed to concentrate on laying the groundwork for my upcoming budget proposals that, as previously mentioned, were being completely reworked consistent with the instructions I had given to Baker and Hershman at our July 1983 meeting in Salt Lake City.

I had to inform myself about the budget itself, not just the 32 percent increase in the operating budget that I had decided to seek. I also needed to learn more about how the regents preferred to do their business. Finally, and most urgently, I had to estimate the probabilities of this budget succeeding or failing. It was, after all, a radical proposal and a high-risk venture for a first-year president, and I needed to be alert to efforts to neutralize or undercut this budget, whether prompted by concern about its impact on the viability of my presidency, its impact on the university, or both.

The 1984–1985 Budget

The university's budget was remarkably difficult to amend or redirect in the later stages of its preparation. The budget for 1984–85 was begun in the early fall of 1982, with extensive campus discussions involving Baker's and Hershman's staffs and their campus counterparts. It was given more definitive direction as the legislature discussed the university's 1983–84 budget in spring 1983, and even more guidance as that budget was approved in June. The president, while being kept generally informed of these budget discussions, would not really get involved until early summer, as I had done while still in Salt Lake City. *Final* decisions were to be made in August or early September 1983 for the 1984–85 budget year.

My decision to change that budget fundamentally only three months before the regents were to consider it and four months before its adoption by the board violated the consultative processes within UC. It preempted the discussions that had been under way for nearly a year, caught the chancellors by surprise, and caused many a sleepless night for those in my office and on the campuses who were scrambling to do in sixty to ninety days what would ordinarily have taken six to twelve months. To add to the complexity, UC was administering the 1983–84 year while settling on its proposals for 1984–85 in August and September 1983, in the middle of a transition from one president to another. My decision, therefore, was not one to be taken lightly.[5]

But I couldn't help it. I had not been contacted until midsummer, even though I had been appointed on March 2, and much of my effectiveness as president would rest on restoring the university's budget to levels more consistent with historical norms than those that had prevailed during the sixteen years of Governors Reagan and Brown. Moreover, I believed this was the right course for the university, and I was going to take it, unless directed otherwise by the regents.

It was not surprising that the chancellors and vice presidents were not overly pleased. At COC meetings, they clearly communicated their concerns about the "unreasonableness" of my decision to seek in one fiscal year to recover what we had lost over the past sixteen years. No one took exception to my analysis of the need for this budget, only my judgment in seeking such a radical budget my first year and under a new governor.

The regents were also hearing about this budget in the normal course of their individual calls to the vice presidents on other matters, at social occasions on the campuses, and at the September meeting of the board. As a result, I received a series of phone calls asking about my intentions regarding the budget presentations in October and November, and expressing no little alarm about the rationale for submitting a proposal for such a dramatic increase in the state's share of our operating budget. The regents' questions, which were much the same as Baker's and Hershman's, reflected not only the probable embarrassment the regents would suffer if these proposals were turned away, with the predictable charges of irresponsibility and harsh cries about their judgment, but also their concern about the impact on me if we failed.

I assured them that these were all matters I had pondered at length and that I had discussed them with the chancellors and vice presidents, whose views substantially echoed those of the regents. But I argued, "I would have no more favorable time to take such an initiative, as the state's economy was already rebounding contrary to news reports about its ongoing financial difficulties; the university needed a jump-start, not just a routine turn of an ignition key driving on a weakened battery; and if we succeeded the university would be energized beyond description, with morale restored and the future made brighter than it had been for nearly two decades."

I then shared with them what my Grandfather Pierpont observed one day, in frustration with my seeming lethargy: "Well, David, if you want to sit back and watch the world go by, it will go by." I suggested that UC for too long had been mired in a survival mode, imprisoned by low expectations as self-fulfilling as they were self-defeating. Moreover, if the proposal wasn't accepted, they could blame me. If it was, they could take the credit. After all, "I only propose, you dispose. It's your budget, not mine, but it is the one I intend to recommend for your consideration and action. I will have done my job. You would then have to do yours." While I believe the chancellors, vice presidents, regents, and Academic Senate leaders believed me to be "courageous," they saw that as little different from suicidal.

In all truth, I did not know how I was going to get this budget approved, either by the regents or by the governor and state legislature. I knew the economy was moving into high gear, I believed my relations with the governor, the board, and, I hoped, the legislature would be very good to excellent, and I knew that our case was easy to make given the demonstrable deterioration in our physical plant, libraries, faculty and staff salaries, and our capital and operating budgets.

All the negative responses I was receiving, however, made me begin to wonder if my enthusiasm for the prospect of a 32 percent increase in our operating budget was warranted. Had I misjudged or dismissed without justification the cautions and reservations of my administrative colleagues and members of the governing board? Would my proposal trigger divisions within the regents at the very time they seemed willing to come together? Would such a budget provoke a civil war between the state's other two public systems of higher education and the University of California, as neither of them shared our budgetary ambitions or had knowledge of our intentions? Would failure in this risky effort damage my credibility with the governor, as well as the respect and regard that I enjoyed from my colleagues in the administration and on the faculty, and with the governing board that had so recently hired me?

I concluded that the odds were even and decided that if I were to be criticized I preferred that it be for failing to get what we needed, after having asked and fought for it, than for failing either to ask or to fight.

When making this decision, I was reminded of a conversation four years earlier at the Rockefeller Center in Bellagio, Italy, at a conference of Middle Eastern university presidents and provosts convened by the University of Utah. Among those attending was the then provost of the American University of Beirut, who had been caught up in the Lebanese civil war. One day, he told me, they were visited by representatives of the political left who told them that they regarded the university as an outpost of American imperialism and its corrupt culture and demanded that the university be closed on pain of death for failing to do so. The political right, hearing of this demand, expressed their support for the university, emphasized its importance to the country's future, and threatened death to those who did not keep it open.

I inquired about the process that led to their decision, all the while thinking how fortunate I was to be at the University of Utah where strong feelings were mostly confined to our athletic contests and the student newspaper.

He answered, "It was an easy decision. We decided that if we were going to be killed in either instance, we preferred to be killed striving to keep the university open rather than working to close it down."[6]

Governor Deukmejian

In either late September or early October I received a call from Kenneth Khachigian, one of the governor's political advisers, a Reagan speechwriter and a well-respected and successful political consultant from San Clemente, California. I had known Ken and his wife, Meredith, at UCSB in the mid-1960s, when he was student body president and Meredith had run his campaign.

Ken asked if I would meet with Governor Deukmejian in Los Angeles, along with himself and the governor's chief of staff, Steve Merksamer, to get better acquainted and to discuss UC. I was delighted to say yes, and the meeting was arranged at the Windsor Restaurant in downtown Los Angeles. It was to be informal and low key, with no formal agenda. "Do you want to bring anyone with you?" Ken asked; and I said, "No, I would prefer that the meeting be just as you described it."

I had not seen the governor since the very awkward meeting with Saxon several months earlier (described in chapter 5). I had intended to seek an appointment with him in the early fall to share my impressions of UC's condition and my plans to respond, hoping for at least a glimmer of hope that our interests and commitments would be congruent.

There were just the four of us, and we were together for only two hours, including lunch. The meeting changed the university's fortunes and trajectory in historic ways, much to my amazement and great relief, and I believe to the governor's as well.

After lunch, we discussed our family, mutual friends, and some issues confronting the state, with my offering some recollections of my days at Santa Barbara with the Khachigians, with much joking at Ken's expense. The governor, who was impressed that I had come alone and with no notes, asked, "What is the condition of the University of California now that you have had at least some chance to consider it?" I explained, in turn, the problems that I had found, inventorying them as succinctly and clearly as I could, and as comprehensively as possible without losing focus or belaboring the answer. The governor was most attentive, and Merksamer and Khachigian took notes.

He then asked: "What does all this mean for the university's quality and future?" I again responded by tying the problems we faced to the adverse consequences they carried—adverse, if not corrected, both in the short and long term, and to the state as well as to the university.

His third question made no reference to my first two answers: "How long do we have to correct these problems?" I said, "Two to three years, after which, if uncorrected, the downward spiral will be so intense and driven with such momentum, that neither you nor I can do anything about it."

He asked a fourth question, again without commenting on any previous answers: "I don't understand what you mean. Please explain further." I told him I was then scheduling visits to the university's nine campuses, to be made during the current academic year. These would include meetings with the chancellors, members of the administration, leaders of the faculty, representatives of the staff, students, alumni, donors, friends, and the leaders of the various support groups for athletics, the libraries, the museums, and so forth. I would also be meeting with editorial boards and representatives from the minority communities, the professions, and the business community.

"I will be asked by all of them," I said, "to indicate my sense of the university's present and hopes for its future, my estimate of how UC was going to pull out of its fiscal problems, and how encouraged they should be." I then asked, "What should be my answers? What am I to tell them? What can I say?" Before he could answer, I went on: "If I cannot give people reason to be optimistic, if I cannot represent that our budgets will improve, especially for the faculty, if I cannot give them hope about having the library resources they need, the computers they require, the equipment needed for their laboratories, and the facilities within which they can pursue their teaching and research—if I cannot give them this positive assurance about UC's future under what will be regarded by them as the most favorable set of circumstances for us in nearly two decades, then they will conclude that if, under these most congenial of conditions, UC cannot make headway, then there are no future conditions under which UC can be expected to do so."

The result, I explained, is that they will vote with their feet, moving away from UC (as had already been happening, as I knew personally from the experience of Utah), away from the state. There would be a general flight of faculty, in other words, to universities that were unwilling to remain content with their all-too-familiar set of problems and perceived barriers to change. "By hospitable and favorable conditions," I went on, "I mean a new governor whose public speeches and informal comments give clear evidence of your appreciation for the place and value of education at all levels in our society and its relevance to the quality of life, cultural vitality, scientific and scholarly progress and economic strength of California; a new university president who brings no baggage to the table and desires to work in partnership with you, and, as possible, with the legislature; an improving economy; and campuses that are uncommonly quiet. We will never have a more favorable set of conditions and we need to take full advantage of it and without losing a moment in doing so."

I made these points with a determination and commitment in my voice and demeanor that reflected the depth of my concern and the genuineness of my feelings.

The governor reflected at some length and then asked: "Give me an example of what we can do." He had moved from passive to active questioning, and I felt a flicker of real hope.

My answer was quick and definitive. I explained how UC's faculty's compensation as a matter of state policy was fixed at the average of the nation's four leading public and four leading private universities. While the policy was still in place, the funding was not, and the most important single thing he could do would be to close that gap, which in fall 1983 was 16 percent. The gap in staff salaries was 10 percent.

He turned to Merksamer and said, "Steve, maybe we could do this over a two- to three-year period." Merksamer agreed. I shared my appreciation for his understanding of the importance of this issue and told him "how grateful the whole university would be if he could see his way clear to propose this to the legislature." I then said that if he wanted to signal his unmistakable intention to restore the university's fiscal health, to affirm his confidence in one of California's most genuine and enduring successes, then why didn't he "close the gap in one year? No one would be expecting it. Everyone would be startled and appreciative beyond words." (Actually, I could hardly believe I said this after he had already offered to close the salary gap in two to three years.)

He turned to Merksamer, who had some budget data with him, and we briefly consulted and readily arrived at a dollar figure the governor could count on if he wished to move more quickly on this issue. He said to Merksamer, "Let's see if we can't do this," but, I emphasize, he did *not* commit to it.

This one instruction, this single expression of serious intent, this wholly unexpected but deeply gratifying response moved me to express not only my thanks but also my belief that such "an action by you would serve as a shot across the bow" of the nation's leading universities that "UC was coming back, that we would soon be after their most talented faculty and that they might just as well look some place other than UC when they came raiding." He liked the comment.

Naturally, such a decision would create for the governor a number of problems with the California State University system, the community college system, and other parts of the state budget with which we competed. While his intentions were clear, no definitive and conclusive judgment could be made on the basis of this one meeting.

For my part, I made it clear that I would not share this information except with Baker and Hershman (he knew Baker personally). Also, if circumstances were such that this plan could not be in his proposed budget to the legislature in January, we would work with him to determine the next best move. I said that I would do nothing to discomfort him in any way as he worked his way through the state's budget, even if he needed to modify the outcome for which we both now hoped.

He appreciated this approach very much, indeed; it prompted him to then suggest that I should work with Merksamer on a three-year plan to fund

UC, as needed, to attain its optimal strength and capability. And with that comment the meeting ended.

It was the single most important and telling meeting of my years as president, leading as it did to unprecedented budget increases for UC and equally unheard-of capital budgets, not only for 1984–85 but for several subsequent budgets as well. It also engendered a level of mutual and unqualified respect between the governor and me, really an easy and confident friendship, that was sustained throughout his two terms as governor. We were both straightforward, up-front people, more quiet than charismatic in our personalities, private in our personal lives and respectful of our different roles.

I never surprised the governor, nor did he surprise me. I never sought to manipulate our relationship in any way whatsoever. He was as good as his word and so was I, and each accepted what the other said at face value. I did not bother him unless it was unavoidable, and I never sought advantage or used our relationship for any interest other than the university's. I was blessed to have such an honest, decent, and capable person with whom to work, and the university was benefited in ways both unforeseen and nearly without precedent.

Steve Merksamer, who played a key role in fostering this relationship, was my best and most effective adviser on many matters, working unceasingly for the university's good and defending us when needed. He recalls in his oral history this Los Angeles meeting and the relationship that evolved between the governor, Merksamer, and me:

[I]t was clear that everything flowed from this meeting during the rest of Deukmejian's term in terms of the University of California—was Gardner saying, "I'm different than my predecessors. UC is going to be conducted differently, managed differently than the way it's been managed in the past. We're going to work with you. We're going to be more politically adept. We understand the real world and we want to be a partner." And the governor said, "I agree with that. I'm glad you understand my problems. And I understand your problems. And once we get my problems taken care of, as a partner, we will fulfill our end of the partnership, and we will restore together excellence to higher education in this state." . . .

There was a bonding that took place certainly between David and the governor, but also between David and myself. He had an extraordinary relationship with George Deukmejian, but he worked through me during the whole period of time. Although he could see the governor whenever he wanted, and did! . . .

That is remarkable for a governor, and I frankly think remarkable for a university president. So many people at that level let their egos dominate, but I never saw that in either David Gardner or George Deukmejian. Both, at the end of the day, would put the public purpose and the public interest ahead of anything personal. And that's one of the reasons why I think they both made a significant difference in California history and why they both got along so well.[7]

The governor also recalls our first meeting and the way we worked in his oral history:

> I had a very good first impression. He's an individual who you immediately recognize as very articulate. He is very organized. He's very personable, and he makes an excellent impression. . . .
>
> [H]e explained to me what the difficulties were for the UC system, having gone through that prior sixteen years where they had not had very much support. And that made me much more aware of the difficulties, and the fact that it was becoming exceedingly difficult to attract and to retain a lot of the good members of the faculty, and so forth—and a number of other issues. . . .
>
> He just always had a very persuasive and significant way of focusing on the key issues, and always did it in a way as demonstrating his willingness and his helpfulness in dealing with our budget concerns, as well.[8]

I flew home from Los Angeles invigorated and excited about what now seemed to be just the right move on my budget proposal. No more second-guessing, no more reservations, no more hesitancy. We were going to do it!

Baker and Hershman, of course, could hardly believe my report, but once it was confirmed by their counterparts in the state's Department of Finance, the ball began to roll.

I never told the chancellors or vice presidents of this meeting with the governor, until early in the new year, nor did I inform any regent, not wishing to appear to put the governor in a corner if he ran into insuperable obstacles, not wishing to cast any doubt on our relationship, and wanting to be absolutely certain that no press reports, issued prematurely, would complicate or undermine our forward momentum.

The 1984–1985 Budget in Play

The budget went forward to the regents in October and was acted on by the full board in November and proceeded without incident, reservations, or concerns, muted in deference to my first budget and my brief service as president. Once the regents acted, the university came alive with the possibility of a forward-looking and major budgetary move by the president and the board, even though the prospect for its final disposition by the governor and legislature was not assured.

It was clear that our discussions with the state's Department of Finance were being guided by Merksamer, in consultation with Deukmejian, and, as the Christmas season approached, we were optimistic about the outcome. Sure enough, the governor's budget, when issued in January 1984 (this document being the point of departure for the legislature's review of UC's budget), was everything we had hoped for and more: the governor even included a request that the fees paid by students at UC be reduced by $75 and that the legislature make up the loss with an additional appropriation to UC's budget. Our capital budget was also intact. Not a building was lost.

No one could believe this budget: regents, chancellors, vice presidents, budget officers, faculty, staff and administration, and the students gave me credit for the fee reduction in spite of my disclaimers that I had nothing whatsoever to do with what was a singular initiative by the governor himself.[9]

As earlier mentioned, we had an experienced and respected staff in residence in Sacramento, under the direction of Steve Arditti, who reported to Baker. Arditti, a UCLA graduate, was a veteran in the state capital and was well known throughout UC and in the agencies of state government, as well as by legislators and their staffs and by the governor and his staff. He knew the university intimately, worked unceasingly in its behalf, and was remarkably effective, partly because he was so well liked personally by legislators, and entertained them on a regular basis with his wife, Melva, at their home on the Sacramento River, in the course of which many a breakthrough for UC's interests was negotiated or arranged.

Baker, Hershman, Arditti, their staffs, and others from throughout the university carried the university's ball, and they did so brilliantly. They used me sparingly, but at timely and critical points in the process, to visit with one legislator or another, to seek a compromise when needed, to persuade as necessary, and sometimes just "to show the flag" and also to help in our negotiations with Mike Franchetti, Deukmejian's first director of the state's Department of Finance, who also came to play a very important role in our 1984–85 budget and in preparing the three-year plan for restoring UC's fiscal health as directed by the governor.

When the dust had settled, the governor's budget was approved virtually *in full*, and the capital budget as well. The risk and the hard work had paid off. The governor was very happy, the regents ecstatic (and doubtless relieved). My colleagues were unbelieving (but soon got over their incredulity and began spending the allocated funds). I counted my blessings and was thrilled for all that this represented for the University of California.[10]

The faculty was energized, as was the staff, and the students felt someone really cared about them. Legislators wondered what had happened and how (as other legislators had in Utah when a last-minute effort rescued the University of Utah's budget from the House Democratic caucus), and the larger university community and its extended family of alumni, friends, donors, and well-wishers not only took note but showed their approval with levels of private support that grew every year thereafter.

Arditti's comment expressed at the end of this rigorous and demanding process of working with the legislature bears noting: "I remember one thing we said to ourselves at the end of that year—two things: 'Gee, isn't it great to get a good budget! And getting a good budget through is just as hard as getting a bad budget through.'"[11]

My position within the university was demonstrably strengthened as it also was with the board. I could not have been more encouraged or gratified by the outcome. The visits to the campuses had gone well, and also to the national labs. I was on a first-name basis with the legislative leaders of both parties and in both houses; my relations with the governor and with Merksamer as well were unimprovable. I was already well connected in Washington, D.C., but my first year didn't hurt in drawing federal attention to what was now happening at UC.

All in all, I could not have hoped for a more satisfying start, personally or professionally; and for the university, which is what it was all about, the positive implications were enduring, as Clark Kerr notes in his foreword to my oral history:

> It was his first (1984–85) budget as president of the University of California. It was the most risky, most venturesome budget prepared in the history of the university—and the most needed both then and later. . . .
>
> Gardner won his chancy proposal, and in its entirety. This erased the deficits of the prior sixteen years. Beyond that it established a position of strength that made possible a survival in the early 1990s. From 1990 to 1993, state general fund support for the university fell 24 percent in real terms. Had this percentage been added to the prior 32 percent, the university could hardly have recovered for many years, if at all. Instead the university moved into the academic rankings by the National Research Council in 1993 with four campuses ready to be rated among the top twenty in the nation in terms of the proportion of "distinguished" programs. Herodotus once wrote that "great deeds are usually wrought at great risks." So it was here.[12]

NEXT STEPS

The objectives I had sought to accomplish my first year were now largely in hand. The groundwork had been laid, the Office of the President reorganized, the regents won over, the council of chancellors and vice presidents working well, the campus and lab visits completed, the resources obtained, and new levels of confidence reached. It was now time to move the university forward on other fronts.

It was time to secure the buildings, equipment, and allied and additional resources required to expand not only our enrollment but our research and our public service. We needed to increase the enrollment of students from communities that were poorly represented in UC's student body, especially black and Hispanic students. It was time to take account of California's favored position on North America's western coast, as the countries of the Pacific Rim were coming increasingly into their own. We could now plan for our future by reformulating UC's long-range planning for its academic programs, its physical plant, and its fiscal requirements. It was now timely to review the balance within our academic programs to be certain that the humanities, arts, and social and behavioral sciences, then receiving only a very modest share of UC's research dollars, were properly cared for and encouraged. Our standards for admissions needed to be studied in light of California's changing public schools and the state's evolving demographics. We needed dramatically to improve funding from the private sector, and finally we needed to plan our financial affairs, taking account of our immediate past and remaining aware that if we were to have good times we should also surely experience bad ones.

The university was now positioned to move forward, and it did, not just at one, two, or three campuses but at all nine.

SEVEN

THE UNIVERSITY ON THE MOVE

ACADEMIC INITIATIVES

As noted in chapter 5, the University of California in 1983 was a complex
and far-flung enterprise. Its nine campuses stretched the length of California, carefully sited and planned, housing a world-renowned professoriate
numbering some 6,550, employing nearly 100,000 others, and teaching more
than 141,000 students. In addition to its five major medical centers and associated clinics, and more than 150 organized research institutes, bureaus,
and centers, the university had agricultural lands and 100,000 acres of natural reserves across the state, all used for teaching and research as were the
astronomical observatories and a fleet of oceangoing ships from the famed
Scripps Institution of Oceanography at the San Diego campus. In addition
to facilities for teaching and research, most campuses also had stadia, playing fields, sports arenas, bookstores, residence halls and cafeterias, concert
halls, theaters, and museums. Over 20 million books, manuscripts, documents, journals, periodicals, maps, rare books and archival collections were
housed in a vast network of general and specialized libraries. And the university had agreements with forty-five of the world's leading universities for
faculty and/or student exchanges. The world had never seen anything quite
like it.

UC also managed three national laboratories owned and funded by the

U.S. Department of Energy but operated by UC as a public service to the country. This relationship began at the close of World War II, when UC professors such as Glenn Seaborg, Robert Oppenheimer, and Edward Teller were central to the work of the Manhattan Project, which, of course, produced the atomic bombs that brought the war to an abrupt conclusion when used against the Japanese cities of Hiroshima and Nagasaki. Mindful of their role in beginning the nuclear age, after the war the government invited UC to manage the laboratories to conceive the succeeding generations of nuclear weaponry and to design but not to produce the U.S. stockpile of strategic nuclear weapons. UC agreed; the work was done mostly at the Los Alamos National Laboratory in New Mexico and at the Radiation Laboratory on the Berkeley campus.

Over time the radiation laboratory (now known as the Lawrence Berkeley National Laboratory) divested itself of this and other classified work, which was transferred to a new facility, the Lawrence Livermore National Laboratory (founded in 1952), southeast of Berkeley. More recently, Livermore and Los Alamos have been central to the technical verification of nuclear disarmament as both the former Soviet Union and the United States undertook to shrink their nuclear weapons stockpiles.

Both within the university and elsewhere, UC's uninterrupted management of these two "weapons" laboratories from the close of World War II until the present day has been strongly supported by some and vigorously opposed by others, the former seeing the university's involvement as being central to the nation's security and the latter viewing it as wholly incompatible with the work and function of a university (see chapter 8). I was expected to oversee our management of these complex and important places and to advise the regents periodically on whether UC should continue to manage them.

The University of California, taken as a whole, was one of the world's, and certainly the nation's, most important and esteemed institutions. It was also true, however, that the university had been sorely tested in recent decades, first with the loyalty oath controversy of 1949–52, second with the Free Speech Movement at Berkeley in 1964–65, and third by major student protests against the war in Vietnam during 1965–71, internationally reported events with significant public and political backlash. The latter two were, in part, linked to the studied fiscal neglect of the university by Governors Reagan and Brown for sixteen years (1966–82).

As I had been an avid student of the university's history, I knew how remarkably resilient, creative, and adaptive UC had been over the years. I had no doubt that UC would rise to its opportunities and surpass what seemed possible if given budgetary encouragement and an administration respectful of its traditions, culture, high standards, and system of shared governance.

The university's previous administrations had never slighted their respect but had not always been blessed with sufficient political, governmental, or budgetary support.

Once the university's 1984–85 budget had been enacted and signed by the governor, however, the stars were all aligned in UC's favor. We had just received an increase in our operating budget of roughly one-third from 1983–84 to 1984–85 and some $200 million for new construction. We also had a very friendly governor and a supportive legislature. Public and student interest in the university was growing, as expressed by an unexpected but increasing demand for freshman admission; and my administration was deeply committed to the university's well-being and willing to work as hard as was necessary to shift the university from low gear into overdrive.

My opportunity to test the mood and attitude of the chancellors, vice presidents, faculty leadership, and regents, once our 1984–85 budget became reality and provided double-digit salary increases for both faculty and staff, came sooner than I had expected.

The World's Largest Optical Telescope

As Saxon was briefing me in June 1983 about the university's problems and opportunities, he devoted a disproportionate share of the time to a proposal he had received two years previously from several campuses and the Lawrence Berkeley National Laboratory to construct the first of a new generation of optical telescopes. Try as he might, though helped by some well-placed regents and prominent alumni, the $70 million needed to pay for the construction of such a telescope had not been found. He urged me to keep at it and "to bring the chancellors along who tended to see the project as a competitor for university research funds they wished to use in different ways."

Saxon was a highly respected physicist, and his commitment to this project was therefore driven by professional as well as university interests; he enthusiastically brought its promise and potential into vivid and vibrant relief. I didn't require much pressing of the point, however, as it sounded right to me that UC should be on the cutting edge in this academic arena. One of the university's established strengths was in astronomy and astrophysics, and for decades UC had operated the Lick Observatory with its 36-inch refractor atop Mount Hamilton near San Jose, California.

The history of the project dated back to the early 1970s when it became evident that efforts to improve the light-gathering capabilities of optical telescopes to move research in this field to higher levels had pushed the instruments to their physical limits. The problem confronting astronomers was to build a larger telescope whose massive bulk would not cause distortion or a collapse under its own weight.

No resolution was in sight until 1979, when Jerry Nelson, a young scientist working at the Lawrence Berkeley National Laboratory on the Berkeley campus, suggested that instead of fabricating a single mirror 10 meters in diameter (which no one knew how to do), thirty-six hexagonal mirrors, each measuring 1.8 meters in diameter, be arrayed in honeycomb fashion and made to function as though they were a single mirror 10 meters wide. With each of these lightweight hexagonal mirrors continuously aligned by computer to account for movement, temperature changes, wind, and other threats to their stability, they could function as one. This ingenious approach was then modeled and, when thought to be theoretically sound, was designed and proposed through the usual layers of faculty and scientific review to Saxon and the regents. The telescope was to be built over a period of five to six years and housed in a new observatory to be constructed on top of Mauna Kea on the island of Hawaii, the highest point on the Hawaiian chain of islands, and the most favored viewing site in the Northern Hemisphere (the best in the Southern being located in Chile).

The 10-meter telescope (TMT), as this project was then called, was to be eleven times larger than UC's Lick Observatory telescope and would have twice the diameter and four times the light-gathering capacity of the Hale telescope at Palomar, Cal Tech's observatory in southern California, then the largest optical and infrared telescope in existence. It would see twice as far into space as the Hale and explore a volume of space eight times greater. It was expected to produce images of exquisite clarity and detail, to see galaxies in their formative stages, to discern the chemical composition of the nearest and most ancient of stars, and at infrared wavelengths to probe nearby interstellar clouds of dust and gas—all contributing to the formulation of new theories about time and space while testing those already proposed.

I shared Saxon's views of this project with the chancellors at one of our early meetings in fall 1983 and found that Saxon's comment to me that they held a reserved view of it to have been a marked understatement. At that point, of course, our budgetary circumstances were very difficult, and the chancellors were sensitive to any big-ticket item that could conceivably hamper their desperate search for funds. They encouraged me to defer the matter to better times.

I responded by indicating that this advice, however well intentioned, would not stand the test of practicality or desirability. First, it would give the appearance that I was abandoning a major initiative much desired by the scientific community both within and outside UC, after Saxon's hard fight in spite of budget problems. Second, the project would help the university take the needed step of shaking itself out of the survival mode of thinking, as my budget proposal intended to do. And quite apart from these considerations, this was a project that UC should be doing, consistent with its purposes, history, and intellectual capabilities—and the most important reason why I wished to proceed.

While most of the chancellors were unfriendly toward this project, they took no steps to undermine our effort to fund it. Chancellor Sinsheimer, in contrast, championed this project throughout with help that was critical in any number of ways. Our successful effort to raise $70 million and build the TMT was, as I had expected, a very difficult challenge; but it also turned into one of the most complicated, even bizarre, fund-raising adventures in the history of American higher education.

The newspapers would periodically inquire about this project and occasionally write a feature article dealing with it. On August 16, 1983—at the urging of Professor Harold Ticho, a physicist and vice-chancellor from the San Diego campus, and Joe Colmes, on loan to the Santa Cruz campus (the lead campus for this effort) from the university's nearby Lick Observatory— the *San Jose Mercury News* carried a story about the 10-meter telescope and the university's inability to find funds for it. This story was read by Edward Kain, the brother of Marion O. Hoffman, who, he said, was looking for a means of memorializing her late husband, Max Hoffman of New York City. UC development officers at Santa Cruz and in the office of the president followed up with Kain and then pursued this possibility directly with Mrs. Hoffman at her winter home in Beverly Hills.

When she had been informed about this project and was ready to discuss the partial funding of it, I traveled to Los Angeles to meet with her personally on December 15, 1983. She was a lovely and gracious person wishing to memorialize her late husband, a successful businessman who had been much interested in things mechanical and technical. She believed he would have had a special interest in the 10-meter telescope because of its engineering, mechanical, technical, and scientific sophistication; and she was interested in helping UC fund this project.

I had been accompanied to this meeting by Brad Barber from the president's office on loan to the Santa Cruz campus, who had been much involved in fund-raising for the project under Saxon's and Sinsheimer's direction, and by Eugene Trefethen, a famous Berkeley alumnus, Napa Valley vintner, and San Francisco Bay Area businessman who, at Saxon's urging, had been chairing the volunteer committee seeking funds. The three of us reviewed with Mrs. Hoffman what we were trying to do, stressing that this would be the world's largest optical telescope, that its work would enjoy international attention, interest, and support, and that it would be a unique and an appropriate means of memorializing Mr. Hoffman and his distinguished career.

As our midday meeting concluded, she expressed her intention to make a gift of $36 million to fund roughly half of the cost of constructing this telescope, in consideration of its carrying her late husband's name as a memorial to his life. We also discussed the possibility (and I encouraged her to consider this) of making this a memorial to both herself and her late husband as a testament to their lifelong marriage. She demurred but did not object. She said the papers would be drawn up promptly and that she would sign them the following afternoon.

The following day Mrs. Hoffman died unexpectedly, the papers prepared but not signed. I was saddened because I had liked her very much, her death was so untimely, and our prospects for accomplishing her intended memorial were now thrown into doubt. I was also concerned, of course, for the TMT and its prospects.

Within a matter of months, however, Ms. Ursula C. Niarakis, who had been Mr. Hoffman's personal secretary for many years before becoming Mrs. Hoffman's as well, acted in her capacity as executor of the Marion O. Hoffman Trust. Knowing of Mrs. Hoffman's intentions and wanting them to be fulfilled, she entered into an agreement with the regents to transfer $36 million from the trust to the University of California for the partial construction of the TMT in satisfaction of Mrs. Hoffman's desire to memorialize her late husband.

Mrs. Hoffman's sister, Ms. Doris Chaho, who along with Ms. Niarakis was a trustee of the foundation into which the Hoffman estate would ultimately flow, questioned the appropriateness of Ms. Niarakis having made this gift. A legal hearing on the matter was expected in probate court in New York. The university accepted the gift, however, as the trust had legal title to the assets, Ms. Niarakis had lawfully passed the assets in her capacity as trustee, and the gift was entirely consistent with Mrs. Hoffman's stated intentions.

As these discussions with the Hoffman interests proceeded, I was faced with securing the difference between the $36 million Hoffman gift and the $70 million cost of building the TMT.

Vice President Frazer and Chancellor Sinsheimer at Santa Cruz were a very great help in this effort. They helped me in understanding the scientific and technical import of this project and in our construction and operation of it later on. We also discussed how to raise the additional monies and concluded that we needed a partner. The California Institute of Technology in Pasadena was the logical choice, given its capability and experience in this area. Frazer, Sinsheimer, and UCLA Chancellor Young laid the groundwork at Cal Tech in anticipation of my call in spring 1984 to Murph Goldberger, the university's president.

Goldberger was a scientist and I was not, but Frazer covered that part of it for us. I explained to Goldberger the history of our fund-raising efforts (he already was well informed about the TMT project itself) and of the Hoffman gift, which at that point appeared to be secure although subject to some minor negotiations.

"Would you like to partner with UC in this effort?" I asked. "We have raised $36 million. If you can raise the same, we can be proportionate partners in the construction, operating costs, and ownership of the TMT, the shares and details to be worked out by our respective staffs." The University of California would, in addition, contribute our $6 million cost of development and dedicate the entire Hoffman gift to this project. The answer was "yes" and he would proceed accordingly, subject to his board's approval. Goldberger moved expeditiously and his fund-raising had considerable success over a relatively short time.

Meanwhile we were having more and more difficulties with the Hoffman interests, who, it seemed, were now divided on how best to proceed and, I suspected, whether to proceed or not, even though $36 million had already been gifted to us for the project.

Our family was vacationing in midsummer 1984 at our cabin in Montana when Frazer reached me with the news that Cal Tech had uncovered a donor whose interest went well beyond being merely a participant in this effort: he wanted, instead, to contribute the entire $70 million on condition that the TMT carry his father's name as a memorial. Would I call Goldberger immediately? I did so from a pay telephone next to the highway encircling Flathead Lake, as logging trucks and other uncommonly noisy and fast-moving rigs of one kind or another made a quiet conversation nearly impossible. But I got the message anyway.

Howard Keck of the Los Angeles–based Keck Foundation wanted to memorialize his late father, William M. Keck, founder of the Superior Oil Company. He liked this project very much and wanted to pay not for some of it, but for all of it. Ironically, the University of California had earlier approached Keck with a proposal seeking funding for the TMT from the Keck Foundation, but the policy of the foundation at that time barred giving to public universities. Naturally, we could not break our commitment to the Hoffmans, nor did Goldberger suggest or hint that we should do so. This was a dilemma of no small consequence for both of us.

Goldberger then went on to explain that there had been some earlier discussion between UC and Cal Tech scientists about building two 10-meter telescopes and positioning them some 100 yards apart. This would permit them, acting together, to focus on a single target and thereby greatly enhance their light-gathering capability. These conversations had not been pursued, however, given the difficulty UC was having in finding monies for even one TMT.

As we talked about this possibility, it seemed to both of us that it would be scientifically desirable if two telescopes, rather than one, could be built, thus securing Cal Tech's and UC's dominance in the field of astronomy for the foreseeable future. We agreed that the Hoffman name would be carried on the first and the Keck name on the second. We also agreed that the scientists from both institutions should consult once again on the desirability of this plan before any consideration of next steps.

The next step came quickly, as both faculties and the Lawrence Berkeley National Laboratory displayed much enthusiasm for building two TMTs rather than one. The question was, would Keck and the Hoffman interests agree to this arrangement? Goldberger was to talk with Keck and I with the Hoffman people. Keck readily agreed. The Hoffman interests were divided.

Nevertheless, the regents indicated their willingness to proceed with the Hoffman TMT pending Cal Tech's decision on the second telescope. This plan was to be formally presented to both the Cal Tech board and to the Hoffman trustees, and a report made at the next meeting of the Board of Regents on our progress.

By November 1984 the Hoffman trustees had advised us that they were not interested in further exploring the construction of a two-telescope facility. Their decision was tied to the name recognition aspects of the proposal. In other words, Mrs. Hoffman, we were advised, had intended to affix her late husband's name to the world's *largest* optical telescope, *not* one of two of identical size. They offered UC the choice of proceeding with the single TMT, carrying the Hoffman name, or returning the $36 million with the possibility of gifts subsequently being made to UC for other purposes. The message was communicated to Frazer and to me in person by the Hoffman's attorney, Edward Cox, the son-in-law of former President Nixon; he was gracious but clear that were we to proceed with the building of the Hoffman Telescope with the Hoffman money, and were Cal Tech also to build one of equal size with funds from its donor, the ensuing litigation would be awkward for everyone and would indefinitely delay the construction of the TMT.

With this response in hand we proceeded to fashion an arrangement with Cal Tech for the joint construction of one 10-meter telescope to carry the Keck name and deferred any response to the Hoffman trustees pending a meeting on December 10, 1984, of the Cal Tech Foundation trustees, whose acceptance or rejection of the terms would be pivotal.[1]

Following the affirmative response of Cal Tech's board, UC returned the $36 million to the Hoffman Trust. It had been made crystal clear by the Hoffman trustees that to do otherwise would have caused us considerable delay and significant cost increases. Moreover, their funds would still have left us short $35 million, as the events noted above had delayed any further fundraising for nearly nine months. With Cal Tech, in contrast, in a partnership that linked much of the nation's intellectual talent in this field in a common endeavor, we had the full cost of the project in hand, and the scientific work of the university could go forward without delay. The chancellors were also content with this outcome, for self-evident reasons, and we promptly moved forward with this exciting project as rapidly as possible.

The UC/Cal Tech partnership, the Keck Foundation gift, and the science to be done were announced at a press conference on the Cal Tech campus on January 3, 1985. I recall walking across the campus after the announcement with Howard Keck and telling him how sorry I was not to have succeeded with the Hoffman trustees in my effort to gain their support for one of the two telescopes we had hoped to build, but how appreciative we all were for the support of the Keck Foundation for the construction of the one, adding that perhaps, over time, the second might also be built. He urged me not to worry about having lost the Hoffman support, "because if the first one works, my foundation may very well pay for a second."

Ground was broken for the first telescope in 1985. It was dedicated in November 1991. It performed as promised, and now there are two, the second also a gift of the Keck Foundation. Together, they are like a pair of binoculars probing the heavens for new knowledge and understanding, not only of space but also of Earth's small place in its black vastness.

Even setting aside all the legal and other complications of this saga (largely omitted here), our construction of these two telescopes was an improbable outcome, as the world's leading telescopes are elsewhere funded by national governments, and sometimes more than one. Not here. The Keck Observatories were the result of American enterprise led by two of the nation's greatest universities, one public, the other private, and with the full cooperation of the University of Hawaii, which controlled the site on Mauna Kea. The money came from the private sector with only modest but very useful help from the federal government and the states of Hawaii and California. It was a great success, and I was honored to join with others in making it happen.

Shortly before its dedication I recall a question asked at a regents' meeting addressed to Frazer along the following lines: "Will the Keck telescope be making discoveries that could have practical value?" Frazer, who had been a tenacious and committed champion of this project throughout and who had played such a key role within UC and between Cal Tech and UC during the telescope's construction and the early years of its operation, paused for a moment and then answered that he thought "there would be no practical applications." Everyone laughed. Here was a real university at work. Knowledge for its own sake. Intellectual inquiry its own justification. New ideas sufficient in and of themselves. But when I heard Frazer's answer, something Seaborg had once told me was in the back of my mind: "the only difference between basic research and applied research is a time lag." All this reminded me of the toasts of old at Cambridge University following dinner at high table, which included "God bless the Higher Mathematics and may they never be of use to anyone."

Happy as I was, in the end I felt very sorry for Mrs. Hoffman. Her desire to find an appropriate means of providing a permanent tribute to her husband was lost in the scramble for position and advantage following her death. But it is also true that her commitment, compromised by her untimely passing, set in motion a series of events that resulted in there being built atop Mauna Kea not one but two telescopes, the largest of their kind in the world. She surely shares in the good that has been wrought. Without her act of generosity in 1983, who knows what would have happened with the TMT and what would have come of all that these two telescopes have come to signify in the world of science, as evidence of mankind's thirst to learn and will to know.

Nota Bene

Some of the academic initiatives taken during my nearly ten years as president were new, others an expansion of well-known and respected programs, and others, as in the instance of the Keck Observatories, long-simmering but unfulfilled ideas merely awaiting the resources to bring them to life.

This chapter will cover examples of each of these in which I was directly involved, focusing on their success. They illustrate how the president of the university could make a difference in the university's academic programs if actions are taken carefully, indirectly, and with a scrupulous regard for the role of the Academic Senate and with a capable and competent chancellor. I reserve for chapter 8 tales of how difficult it really was to succeed with such initiatives: the inter- and intracampus rivalries, the conflicts of turf and personality, the politics within and between the campuses, the disagreements between my staff and the campuses, the problems with certain regents who had their own interests to pursue, and many other troubles. Thus the reader of this chapter should not assume that these accomplishments were easily attained, nor, in the next, that I am there exaggerating the difficulty of pursuing and achieving the matters reported.

Enrollment of Minorities and Women

The university had made a sustained effort over the previous twenty years to attract young people from California's minority communities to its undergraduate student body, for example, UC's Educational Opportunity Program, outreach programs, affirmative action programs, and an array of subject-specific efforts to improve the preparation of middle and high school students in English and math. Much less effort, however, had been made in recruiting graduate students holding special promise and potential for enrollment in UC's Ph.D. and postdoctoral programs, especially from the minority communities; and the same was true for women, who were nearly as poorly represented in many fields of study.

As this issue was part of my "need to improve" agenda, I decided to move as soon as possible, not only to maximize the educational opportunities at the graduate level for women and minorities, but to do so on our initiative and not wait to react to the pressures of others.

Frazer had responsibility for working up a comprehensive plan with his colleagues in academic affairs, especially Professor Eugene Cota-Robles, after whom one of these programs was subsequently named, and he proposed a plan with several components:

- The Graduate Outreach and Recruitment Program (established in 1984–85), intended to recruit and financially to help promising minority and women students hoping to pursue their advanced studies on a UC campus.
- The Graduate Research Assistanceship/Mentorship Program (established in 1984–85) to provide minority and women graduate students in their second, third, or fourth year of graduate work with half-time research assistance, and to link them more directly to members of the faculty engaged in related areas of research.
- The President's Postdoctoral Fellowship Program (established in 1984–85), which offered two years of support for postdoctoral research for each of twenty-three new fellows annually. Each fellow had a faculty sponsor who mentored and assisted the fellow in gaining visibility among colleagues, not only at his or her home institution but across all nine campuses. The monetary value of the support was competitive with fellowships at the nation's other leading universities.
- The Dissertation-Year Fellowship Program (established in 1989), which provided one year of support to minority and women Ph.D. candidates in writing their doctoral thesis, and additional financial support and nonresident tuition waivers as needed.
- The Eugene Cota-Robles Fellowship Program (established in 1989–90) to provide mentoring and two years of financial support to minority and women students at the beginning of their doctoral work for sixty-seven fellows annually, again at levels of support highly competitive with the nation's leading research universities.

Hundreds of talented women and minority students who would otherwise have not found it possible to pursue their advanced studies at UC, if at all, were, with these programs, able to take all or a portion of their advanced studies as graduate students or as postdoctoral fellows at one of the University of California's campuses. The campuses, of course, pursued their own program initiatives tailored to their individual needs.

Most of these programs were voided with the regents' action to end affirmative action at the University of California in 1995. I thought this was a great loss, not offset by any corresponding benefit. These programs cost relatively little money, targeting very bright and accomplished students whose presence in many of the university's programs was dramatically low, for example, women in engineering and African Americans in mathematics. Moreover, many of those recruited remained in California, thus enriching our state and the communities in which they resided. These programs, in my opinion, were conceptually sound and beneficial both to the students and the university, and their elimination in 1995 represented a real loss to the students themselves, the University of California, and the state.

Graduate School of International Relations and Pacific Studies

In early 1984 Chancellor Richard Atkinson approached me after a chancellors' meeting at Blake House, asking if I would support a new MBA program for the San Diego campus.

UCSD's world-famous reputation rested principally on a well-deserved regard for the distinction of its faculties in the natural and physical sciences and for the work of the Scripps Institution of Oceanography, with strengths in many other parts of the academic program. Atkinson was looking for opportunities to build not just the depth of his campus but also its breadth, especially in the social and behavioral sciences and the humanities. He was also hoping to increase the number of professional schools at San Diego, although he had an excellent school of medicine and university hospital on campus.

Atkinson is a very bright and able person as an academic as well as an administrator, having held both faculty and administrative positions at Stanford and having served as director of the National Science Foundation for the United States government, in which capacity he and I had first met. He has an exceptional eye for quality and was building his campus into one of the top universities in the country. UCSD had momentum, and I wanted to and did, throughout my tenure as president, help San Diego all that I could.

Despite my confidence in Atkinson, I was not enthusiastic about another MBA program within UC, at least not at that time. We had enough of them. He was disappointed to hear my response and began to lay out the other side.

I said, "Dick, I know the arguments you are going to make and they are not compelling. Why don't you do something new, something that is unique to UC and just right for your campus?" I had been thinking well before his visit about California's favored position on the western coast of North America; the border with Mexico was just a few short miles from his campus, with Central and South America stretching southward. He looked west to the Pacific Ocean from his office near La Jolla, and the next landfall, islands excepted, was East Asia—the Far East. But in relation to California, it was our Near West.

There were no schools of international relations in the western United States, the Jackson School at the University of Washington excepted; the Thunderbird School in Arizona was really a specialized business school with an international curriculum and focus.

"Dick," I said, "why don't you establish the first school of international relations in the University of California?" I then went on to inventory UCSD's favored geography, the absence of such schools in the West, and the need for the University of California to offer students more opportunities for advanced work in international relations. I asked him to consider the positive impact this would have on departments in the social sciences and the humanities at San Diego and on the work of Scripps in the Pacific Basin and the opportunities it would open up for students and faculty alike for exchanges with universities in Latin America and Asia. "You would have the lead in this area," I continued to argue, "and instead of following with just another MBA, you would be leading with a program unique to UC, and one needed nationally. Most schools of international studies and international relations, as you know, are focused on the Atlantic Rim countries, not on those contiguous with the Pacific Ocean, namely the westernmost countries of South America as well as Central America, Mexico, and North America including Canada and Alaska, and the great swath of countries stretching in the north from the Russian far east and in the south to New Zealand and Australia."

Atkinson accepted my comments about the MBA and seemed to be intrigued with what I had suggested. We agreed that he would sound out the faculty in San Diego about this prospect and get back to me.

The rest is history. The faculty reacted favorably to these ideas, especially Professor Roger Revelle, a revered member of the faculty and former director of Scripps. They formulated an academic plan for the development of such a school, passed it through the usual stages of campus and Academic Senate review, and submitted it to me for recommendation to the Board of Regents. My recommendation was favorable, and Atkinson's presentation to the board stressed the points already noted above and emphasized that the existing area studies programs, though outstanding, did not treat the Pacific Basin as a whole or provide the professional training needed for most jobs in the region.

Following Chancellor Atkinson's presentation, the regents acted on January 17, 1985, to approve the School of International Relations, as follows:

> The proposed School of International Relations envisions three teaching programs: a Master's degree program in International Relations and Pacific Studies, with about 250 students in a two-year program; a small doctoral program of about 20 students; and several advanced certificate programs of one year or less. The total enrollment in all of these programs is expected to be about 400 students per year. About seventy-five percent of the enrollment is expected to be from California, ten percent from other states, and fifteen percent from foreign countries.
>
> Faculty members will hold primary appointments in the School, with the possibility of joint appointments with other schools and colleges as appropriate. The faculty will be led by a dean. The School will develop two advisory committees: one for academic specialists on international relations and Pacific studies in the University and outside, and one for members of the state, national, and international communities. The School proposes to admit its first cohort of students in the fall of 1987, reaching full strength in five years.

Chancellor Atkinson concluded by noting that requests for approval of specific curricula and degree programs will be proposed later, after the appointment of a dean and key faculty members. The general nature of the program has been described so that Academic Senate and other reviewers could evaluate the academic merit of the proposal.[2]

The school, designated as the Graduate School of International Relations and Pacific Studies, was unique in the country and within the university. I gave it priority funding in our operating and capital budgets: for faculty positions, library resources, support staff, and so on, and for funds to construct the buildings needed to house the new school. I supported this initiative on its merits, but also to signal to the other campuses that I favored new and bold ideas. This was the first new professional school in the University of California to be approved in nearly two decades.

Professor Peter Gourevitch was appointed dean of the school within the month and had a major and salutary impact on its early development and future prospects. The regents approved the granting of graduate degrees effective with the fall quarter of 1987, when the first students and faculty members arrived. The school was dedicated on March 10, 1988.

But not everyone was happy. The Berkeley campus had great depth and breadth across many disciplines in area and language studies and could have rearranged these in order to create such a school, but had not done so. I was visited by senior faculty members of the Berkeley campus soon after the regents had acted on the new school at San Diego and was criticized for not having placed it at Berkeley instead. I reminded them that it was San Diego that had proposed the school, not Berkeley, and that even if Berkeley had chosen to consider this opportunity, it would still have been deciding whether or not to proceed at the time the first students were going to be graduating from the school at San Diego.

Berkeley was a mature campus. Its enrollment had essentially topped out, and space was at a premium. To do something new and important would require an adjustment of budgets, faculty positions, and space that would meet the fiercest resistance from those who perceived themselves to be discomforted, threatened, or underappreciated. San Diego had no such constraints. Enrollments were growing, and so too would their space and budgets. This new school was a net gain, with no corresponding dislocations elsewhere or diminution of other programs or activities required.

Moreover, I wanted to foster competition among and between the campuses not just for budgets and buildings, as was already common, but also for academic programs, believing that it would strengthen the university. Indeed, Berkeley did rearrange its international and area studies programs in ways that improved both their visibility and capability, chiefly because of the San Diego initiative.

The UCSD initiative also prompted me to think more broadly about UC research programs concerned with the community of nations rimming the Pacific Ocean. Many of these were in need of additional support, and there were deficiencies in our curricula and study abroad programs that also needed to be addressed.

My interests in this respect were informed and helped along by Professor Robert Scalapino, director of Berkeley's Institute of East Asian Studies. Scalapino was one of the world's leading and most astute students of matters Asian. He and his remarkable wife, Dee, were personal friends of many years, and he helped me grasp the totality of the global forces influencing this region of the world. From 1984 onward, I encouraged the university to position itself for a more pivotal academic role in the area.

The Graduate School of International Relations and Pacific Studies at UC San Diego was a solid first step. So also was UCSD's Fifth College, which later fixed on comparative culture and international education as the focus of its curricular emphases. In 1986–87, funding was also provided for UC's new Pacific Rim research initiative with the goal of fostering and enhancing research on the economic, political, social, trade, finance, cultural, security, and related issues pertaining to this region and to its interactions with the world.

I focused on this issue personally throughout my presidency, authoring op-ed pieces for newspapers and articles in periodicals and emphasizing this theme in a series of major speeches to service clubs, alumni clubs, professional organizations, and various academic audiences, such as my Earl V. Pullias Lecture in Higher Education at the University of Southern California in 1988.[3]

Education Abroad

I then turned to UC's highly regarded and well-established Education Abroad Program, created by Clark Kerr in 1961, headquartered at UC Santa Barbara, and directed by William Allaway. Bill and I had been friends since my days at Santa Barbara in the 1960s. I was fully conversant with the program, which aimed at providing meaningful and academically reputable study abroad for UC students, usually in their junior year.

The first UC study center abroad was in France, pursuant to agreements negotiated between the University of Bordeaux and UC in 1961. By 1983 some 700 students were studying abroad at forty-five host universities in twenty-six countries, mostly in Europe. And unlike most such programs elsewhere, UC provided no separate facilities for its students, no separate program, and no special treatment. We wanted our students to receive the same treatment as all others studying in the host university. The same was true of the students coming to UC from universities with which UC had agreements.

Allaway and I talked at length about expanding our Education Abroad Program within the Pacific Rim universities, without shrinking our programs elsewhere, indeed expanding them as possible. We both agreed that such an expansion of the Education Abroad Program should take place. I assured him that the resources would be forthcoming. He moved as quickly as possible to effectuate these additions with universities in China, Japan, Korea, Australia, New Zealand, Mexico, Chile, Peru, and other countries. I also provided the funds, including scholarship support, for students wishing to but financially unable to participate.

Our study abroad enrollments doubled during the time I served as president. Research arrangements were also being made for faculty members interested in Asian and Latin American studies. The flow of students from these countries to UC enriched not only those who participated but also the campuses, both abroad and at home, in which these students were studying.

When I left office in 1992, some 1,450 UC students were studying at 104 host universities in twenty-nine countries, and UC was receiving 400 foreign students as part of these agreements, mostly from universities in Pacific Rim countries.

I wish also to make clear that my international interests were global, as UC's interest and involvement should also be. We made headway virtually everywhere in seeking out opportunities for our students and faculty members, for example, as the first American university to formalize student and faculty exchanges with the Leningrad State University in the then Soviet Union (Rector Stanislav P. Merkur'yev and I signed the agreement at Blake House). We also reached out to promising universities struggling against previous or present oppressions of one kind or another, for example, helping the fledging American University of Armenia (AUA) get its footing with the advice and involvement of members of the university's faculty, staff, and administration. As UC's signatory to our agreement in 1991, I was asked to participate as the principal speaker at AUA's tenth anniversary celebration in San Francisco, on December 7, 2001. It was very gratifying to see how far AUA had come in a decade, to recognize what enthusiasm there was for AUA's future, and to realize that we had helped make it all happen.

Center for German and European Studies

In early 1988 I received a call from Richard Buxbaum, a professor of law at Boalt Hall and a leader of Berkeley's Institute for International Studies, asking if I would be willing to join with the presidents of several other American universities at meetings in Bonn, Germany, with the chancellor of the Federal Republic of Germany, Helmut Kohl, for two and a half days. He explained, "Chancellor Kohl's concern is that the ties between Europe and the

United States, which were so wide and deep following World War II among government officials, business heads, and academics, were weakening as the earlier generation was retiring or dying." He wanted the advice of a handful of America's most respected university presidents on this issue and asked the heads of several German private foundations to join him and us for these discussions. I said that if my schedule could be arranged to allow it, "I would be honored to participate."

On March 9, 1988, I received the official letter of invitation from the chancellor, which began:

German-American relations are of an exceptionally good quality and they are very close. On my recent visit to Washington I found impressive confirmation of this partnership and friendship, which has developed steadily since the Second World War. All the same, we should not overlook the fact that on both sides of the Atlantic positions of leadership are being occupied by people from generations that do not share the common experience of the postwar era. Against the background of this generation change it is apparent that in the academic field in the United States, particularly in the humanities and social sciences, interest in Europe and Germany is declining. We also note the same tendency here in the Federal Republic of Germany with regard to the United States.[4]

The meetings were held at the Chancery in Bonn and hosted by the chancellor July 6–8, 1988, against the background of the central question regarding the future of German-American relations: "How can we maintain the cultural links between our two countries in the long run?"

These were interesting and challenging meetings. The discussion encompassed events and issues that had tied Europe and America so closely together since World War II and those that were now seemingly forcing us apart: for example, the Pacific Rim pulling the western United States toward Asia, and the Soviet Union and unrest in Eastern Europe drawing Germany and Europe's attention to the east. In addition, the academic and cultural exchange programs between Europe and America were of smaller scale and less significance than in earlier years. There was a growing hostility in Europe toward the United States, with its pop culture and movies depicting crime and violence at home and in the streets. Changing patterns of trade, migration, and demographics in both Europe and North America were also mitigating against the German-American relationship with which Kohl was concerned.

The chancellor spent the equivalent of an entire day with us and joined in the conversation as though he were just another participant rather than being head of the German state. He was a serious man in these discussions but a charming and very social and friendly person after hours, especially when he and Mrs. Kohl entertained us at the chancellor's official residence that night along with Germany's president, Richard von Weizsacker. The chancellor and I discovered we had several mutual friends and interests. He had been advised by his staff of my work as chairman of the National Commission on Excellence in Education, knew of our report, *A Nation at Risk,* and asked me to join him after dinner for an extended discussion of K–12 education in the United States.

Kohl's idea was to help found and fund American Study Centers in Germany and German Study Centers at three American universities, along with a scholarly journal dealing with American and German issues. He also wished to foster international conferences, meetings, seminars, and symposia—all calculated to help improve the relationship between the two nations while broadening and deepening their range of contacts. The centers were to be the centerpiece of the effort. They would provide research funds for visiting students and scholars, and for the publication of their findings, as well as fellowships, study, and travel grants. They were to be funded for the first ten years by the German government, and subsequently by the host universities. When our meetings concluded, we were asked to submit proposals for these centers through Professor Werner Wiedenfeld, Kohl's coordinator for these and related matters, for review by his office; they would then be passed on to Chancellor Kohl for his decision.

In the course of these discussions, I urged the chancellor to consider broadening the scope of his concern from German studies to European studies. I argued for this modification believing that the growing interdependency of European countries, the patterns of trade, the role of NATO, the prospective integration of the European community, and the structure of European studies in American universities all pointed toward the need for a broader conceptualization.

After some discussion, he agreed; and the German Study Centers, to be funded by the German government at Kohl's express behest, became the German-European Study Centers.

On my return home I called Donald Kennedy, president of Stanford University, who had been invited to these meetings but who could not attend. I filled him in where others, who had also briefed him, had left gaps and asked if, in light of our two universities being the only ones invited in the western United States, we might jointly submit a single proposal, thus compounding our academic strengths and improving—in my view, to the point of certainty—the probability of our success in the competition. Kennedy was not interested in a joint proposal. Stanford was going to submit their own.

I asked Buxbaum to oversee the preparation of our proposal as a universitywide program, involving faculty members from the university's other eight campuses but housed at Berkeley, which was Chancellor Kohl's decided preference. He did so and admirably. Our proposal was excellent, enjoyed widespread support throughout UC, and was ready on time.

In November 1989 the chancellor approved one center for Harvard, one for Georgetown University, and one for UC. Stanford was stunned, believing, as I later understood, that their excellent contacts in the German Embassy in Washington, D.C., would give them some advantage, or that their individual proposal would more likely win on its merits than a joint submission with UC. In any event, we were elated, and as this grant from the German government ran for ten years, we would have sufficient time to fund its continuance from other sources. The agreement between the German government and the University of California was signed in the German Embassy on November 1, 1990, with the German ambassador to the United States hosting the ceremony.

After the grant was announced, Chancellor Young of UCLA approached me between committee meetings of the Board of Regents at which I had just reported this grant. Young was clearly agitated, asking, "Why did Berkeley receive this center? Why didn't you put it out for the campuses to compete? Why was this done so quietly and so quickly?" Every time I tried to answer, he had another question. When finally, in exasperation, he concluded, I simply said, "Well, Chuck, the center is at Berkeley because that's where Chancellor Kohl wished to put it." "Oh," Young said. "Why didn't you just say so?" I pointed out that I had said so as quickly as his unrelenting questions had allowed. We both laughed and that was that.

Buxbaum, of course, deserves most of the credit for bringing the center to UC, but it would not have happened without my involvement and commitment as UC president. The bureaucratic in-fighting among and between the interested German ministries was fierce, as the money to fund these centers was coming out of their budgets; but it is hard to imagine that the competition was greater than between the interested American universities. Buxbaum skillfully and effectively protected UC's position while I sought to inform Wiedenfeld and he, Kohl, about the superior position of the University of California, all nine campuses taken together, compared with others.

The Humanities

In 1985 Frazer and I were allocating funds from overhead earned by the university on its federally supported research. We were approving $500,000 for a lab in physics, $750,000 for one in chemistry, $1 million for another one in biology, $2.5 million for a piece of equipment at one of the medical schools, and the like. These were all worthy requests, and I only wished that we could say "yes" to all that we were reviewing and then acting on.

In the course of these decisions, I turned to Frazer and wondered aloud about how much good we could do for the humanities by redirecting the funding of just one of the pending requests for this piece of equipment or for that lab for some deserving scientific endeavor. We both believed that for between $2 to $4 million a year a great deal of good could be done for the humanities, for example, faculty study grants, graduate student fellowships, conferences, symposia, seminars, and the like—and universitywide. I asked Frazer to sound out the senate leaders informally for a sense of their views on the matter and, if favorable, to return with a plan for considering this possibility seriously.

Not long afterward Frazer reported that the faculty would be supportive of such an initiative and urged us to explore it further. Frazer arranged for the appointment of a universitywide ad hoc committee of faculty members chaired by Professor Stanley Chodorow, dean of arts and humanities at UC San Diego and later provost of the University of Pennsylvania. I had known Stan from my days with the extended university under Hitch. Chodorow had been open-minded about that initiative and helped me with our efforts at San Diego. He was well respected as a scholar, liked as an administrator, fair, and thorough.

I was very concerned with the long-range viability and adequacy of funding for the humanities given the declining enrollments in these disciplines as student demand for professional schools and business, engineering, and science programs was growing, the very modest funding for research in the humanities at the federal level ($139 million), and the lack of any state funding whatsoever. A 1980 report by the Rockefeller Commission had expressed similar concerns about the levels of support for the humanities nationwide.

I took the occasion on May 31, 1984, in delivering the first David P. Gardner Lecture in the Humanities and Fine Arts, an endowed lectureship at the University of Utah that Obert C. Tanner, professor emeritus and founder of the Tanner Lectures on Human Values, had created in my honor when I left the University of Utah, to share my concerns and to affirm my interest in, and support for, the humanities. In "Humanities and the Fine Arts: The Soul and Spirit of Our Universities," I said, in part:

> I chose my title, first of all, to underscore the profound importance of the humanities and the arts to the intellectual life of universities and to the activities for which universities act as patrons. Literature, history, archeology, philosophy, languages, linguistics, drama, dance, music, art in its various forms—these and related disciplines help form the great cultural stream of humane learning and scholarship that constitutes our most precious legacy. The arts and humanities are linked by their common desire to understand human beings in all their complexity and contradictions; their capacity for pleasure and pain in expression and gesture; their potential for good and evil; their instinct for play and their thirst for meaning and purpose. As disciplines, they have a central place in education because they are devoted to the task, as Ben Morris puts it, of "discovering what it means to be human." . . .
>
> [T]he humanities and the arts confront a great challenge, in that the val-

ues and approaches to knowledge that they embody often appear to be at odds with the dominant mode of thinking in our society today: that of science and technology. . . .

. . . I am troubled that we seem to be, by nature, so competitive a society that we feel obligated to pit different ideas and processes against one another rather than focusing on their intrinsic worth and on their interconnectedness. The sciences and the humanities are, in many respects complementary and supplementary. Each helps us understand our world and ourselves. Each illuminates the other, and when the light from one casts a shadow on the other we should remember that light and shadow require one another for either to have meaning. In other words, we should focus our attention on their shared elements rather than on what is popularly thought to be their mutual exclusivity. . . .

To experience the arts, to study the humanities, is to add height, depth, and breadth to our living. It is manifest in the simplest forms and in the most mysterious complexities. The arts and the humanities provide inward awareness and outward sensitivity. They evoke a response, a physical, emotional, and intellectual blending, that is unique in our lives.

. . . They bring the riches of the past into the present, provoking us to admiration and wonder, about both our world and our individual place in it. Who could have expressed this point better than did T. S. Eliot, with whose profound and beautiful lines from *Four Quartets* I conclude my lecture:

> We shall not cease from exploration
> And the end of all our exploring
> Will be to arrive at where we started
> And know the place for the first time.[5]

These were matters about which I felt deeply and wished very much to address. Thus I waited with only nominal patience for the advice of the Chodorow committee, whose meetings proceeded apace throughout 1985 and spring 1986, when their report was ready and forwarded for review by the cognizant committees of the Academic Senate and subsequently to me for action. I relied on Frazer, with the help of his colleagues, to follow the work and to arrange for recommendations that would respond to the concerns he and I had earlier raised. I was not disappointed.

The committee included within its purview the study of modern and classical languages, linguistics, literature, history, jurisprudence, philosophy, archaeology, comparative religion, ethics, the history, criticism, and theory of the arts, and those aspects of the social sciences that have a humanistic content and employ humanistic methods. It recommended that a new University of California humanities research institute be created to host scholars in residence, to convene symposia, conferences, seminars, and the like on the humanities and on humanistic themes, and to publish the proceedings thereof.

The models were the Institute for Theoretical Physics at Santa Barbara and the one for Mathematical Sciences at Berkeley. Funds would also be provided to support research fellowships for faculty members, predoctoral fellowships for graduate students in the humanities, and the allied and ancillary costs of making these initiatives as viable as they were expected to be exciting. All these grants and fellowships were to be made available across all the university's campuses.

The report was well done, well received, carefully reviewed, and approved, and in summer 1986 five campuses vied to house the new institute. The competition was intense, and I was under considerable pressure from each contending campus to favor it and reject the others, although each marshaled different arguments. I turned this matter over to Frazer and the Chodorow committee for their counsel and recommendations.

The recommendation came in early 1987 and favored Irvine. I concurred, although Berkeley and UCLA had been lobbying hard. Each was unhappy with the Chodorow committee's recommendation and even more upset with me for having accepted it. The Irvine campus, of course, was delighted. I made a $3.5-million allocation to Irvine's base budget for this new universitywide endeavor, the Humanities Research Institute, and appointed Professor Murray Krieger to serve as the founding director. Krieger was a very distinguished and admired University Professor of Humanities whose home campus happened to be Irvine. His appointment was made on recommendation of a search committee and of Jack Peltason, who had succeeded Dan Aldrich as UCI's chancellor in 1984.

Another way that presidents can help promote the university's academic work is to engage the influence of well-known and respected members of the faculty. Two illustrations will make the point.

Undergraduate Education

On October 17, 1985, Frazer reported to the regents that a major review of UC's lower-division programs (freshman and sophomore years) was being undertaken and that I had asked Professor Neil Smelser to chair a task force for this purpose. Smelser was a Berkeley professor and a University Professor of Sociology, one of the nation's leading sociologists, a prolific author, and one of the university's most popular teachers. He was also well known to the regents, having been Acting Chancellor Martin Meyerson's assistant in the FSM era and during part of the anti–Vietnam War protests that subsequently wracked the Berkeley campus (Meyerson left Berkeley in 1966 to become president of the University of Pennsylvania); he was later an assistant to Chancellor Roger Heyns for educational development. I had known Smelser for many years, especially given his scholarly interest in higher education. He later served from 1987 to 1989 as director of the Center for Studies in Higher Education at Berkeley.

Smelser is a highly intelligent, intellectually honest, knowledgeable, and insightful member of the faculty, esteemed by his colleagues and by me, and I was confident beyond doubt that he was the one to review the education we were offering our freshmen and sophomore students. He was also soon to be one of the faculty representatives to the Board of Regents by virtue of having been elected by the senate to chair the Academic Council. Smelser later came to serve as director of the Center for Advanced Studies in the Social and Behavioral Sciences at Stanford.

The task force was charged to examine the lower-division curriculum, the quality of teaching, the role of teaching assistants, patterns of student enrollments, and the quality of academic support services. The report was due in mid-1986. My interest in this aspect of UC's teaching was of long standing, as I believed that the university, while doing a credible job in this area (better than the public generally supposed), could do a good deal better but was hampered by the structure of UC's faculty reward system, by the heavy emphasis on research and graduate education, and by custom and complacency. Moreover, three national reports, highly critical of undergraduate education in the United States, but from different vantage points, had just been released, authored by members of the National Institute of Education, the National Endowment for the Humanities, and the Association of American Colleges. The time for a review was ripe.

I was also aware that the Academic Senate had made a report to the regents on general education in the university as recently as 1984. Six of the campuses had also changed and/or strengthened their general education requirements between 1979 and 1984, and Santa Barbara and San Diego were each in the final stages of changing or reviewing their general education requirements.

The task force was not meant to intrude on these campus initiatives or plans, but to benefit from the work recently done on the eight campuses offering lower-division work and to take a less particularized and more broad-ranging view in assessing UC as a whole. Such an endeavor would help inform the eight campuses and the regents themselves about what was happening in general education across the university. It would help sustain a universitywide interest in this important but commonly neglected part of our work. And it would signal my interest in discovering ways by which UC's education, especially of our freshman and sophomore students, might be improved.

It would also respond, in part, to legislative and other external judgments about the university's commitment to these students, and the perceived overuse of TAs and underuse of the professoriate at this level of instruction. This was important, as whenever I met with the university's alumni, state legislators, donors, service clubs, and the editorial boards of newspapers, I heard the complaint that as a research university we were less interested in undergraduates than either CSU or the community colleges were.

The Smelser report was made to the regents at their meeting of October 16, 1986, at which time I devoted most of the meeting to Smelser and the report of his task force.[6]

Smelser called attention to the task force's recommendations, discussed each, and stressed the need for us to offer some portion of our students' first two years of university studies in seminar format rather than relying unduly on lectures. The seminars were to be taught by those holding professorial rank, and the numbers of students in each seminar would be limited, consistent with established practice. He also stressed the need for the TAs to be better trained and better prepared for their assigned teaching duties than was currently the case. I committed funds to accomplish all of this, and the Academic Senate's committees on academic personnel and educational policy took these issues under active consideration, and with favorable outcomes. I also appointed a presidential advisory committee on undergraduate education to follow up on these recommendations, with Professor Joseph Watson, a vice-chancellor and a professor of physics at San Diego, as its chair.

Watson's committee was my means of tracking the Academic Senate's and campus responses to the Smelser report, of sharing these initiatives throughout UC in a timely and consistent manner, and of keeping my office and the regents informed as well. The Academic Senate made its report directly to the regents and to me.

The ensuing discussion was intriguing and stimulating. The regents liked the Smelser report, hoped it would have an impact, sought clarification, and urged me to keep them informed of our progress. The conversation then moved away from how UC could do a better job in teaching its lower-division students to what should be taught at that level—a question argued for about eight hundred years, and never settled. I welcomed this conversation and remained silent until the end, preferring to hear out the individual regents, who had unexpectedly strong feelings on this matter.

Smelser had his hands full. But he was fully up to the task, as he conducted a "regental seminar" on the subject. In particular, he engaged with Bill Honig, California's State Superintendent of Public Instruction and, therefore, an ex officio member of the Board of Regents. He and Smelser went at it for nearly 45 minutes of uninterrupted debate. In broadly oversimplified terms, Honig argued for an emphasis on content in the lower-division curriculum, and Smelser, for process. The minutes report their exchange (somewhat sanitized):

> Regent Honig thought that the Task Force had evidenced first-class work, but expressed his concern that it had dealt with educational policy at the university in a technical and specific manner rather than addressing the broader question of what should be expected in a graduate of the University of California. He then proposed some issues for consideration in addressing the quality of undergraduate programs [including questions of the individual vs. society, questions

of democracy and government, and understanding economic systems and internationalization]. . . .

Professor Smelser believed the common core of Regent Honig's questions was the issue of what constitutes an educated person. Dr. Smelser believed the educated person was a process rather than a product, which he inferred to be the expectation of Regent Honig. Further, he stated that the Task Force had not addressed the questions raised by Regent Honig because it did not have a specific product in mind, which Professor Smelser felt to be consistent with the ideals of freedom, democracy, and toleration in the same sense as that mentioned by Regent Honig. . . .

Regent Sheinbaum returned to the issue of values discussed earlier by Regent Honig and faculty representative Smelser. He understood Professor Smelser to indicate that he did not wish to have Regent Honig's values imposed on students, and he noted that the issue of teaching values is appearing more frequently. Regent Sheinbaum believed that the general fear of someone else's values being instilled obscured the point Regent Honig was raising as to how students learn to think about these values, rather than what they thought about them. Regent Sheinbaum agreed with Regent Honig that the report addressed process and structure at the expense of addressing how to ensure that students think about issues one believes to be critical to an education.[7]

Other regents also wished to be heard, and the board members had an honest-to-goodness debate about the educational work of the University of California instead of about budgets, contracts, real estate, personnel, politics, affirmative action, legislation, buildings, and other such matters that customarily consumed their time.

Regent William French Smith, President Reagan's attorney general, was in attendance at this meeting, participated fully, and at one point, while acknowledging the distinguished makeup of the task force and the quality of the report, wondered whether the "net result of the self study is as valuable as an external review in guiding the hard choices such a review raises." Rather than deflect the conversation I decided to defer my response to this comment to my summation at the close of the meeting, as the minutes recall:

President Gardner thanked all participants in the morning's discussions and cautioned against underestimating the complexity and challenge facing the University as it moves forward in this area. He noted that the University is a derivative of what it has been and where it has been, and the concerns it now faces are the result of forces which have been at work over the last eight centuries. Dr. Gardner recalled the slow changes within universities since the eighteenth century. . . . He described the mission of the American university as being, in part, self-contradictory. It must accept some as freshmen students who are eighteen years old, some well prepared and some less well prepared, and do for two years what is done in Europe at the high school level, then move them into their specialties and into their major as juniors and seniors, and then get more serious with them at the graduate level. The university in America must hire faculty to teach both undergraduates and graduates and to advance the frontiers of knowledge in their respective disciplines. . . .

Finally, President Gardner addressed Regent Smith's question of whether an outside entity less infused with self-conflicting problems should perhaps review the institution. He noted that Oxford and Cambridge universities had been reviewed by royal commissions about every two hundred years, and that that was about right.[8]

My comment about Smith's suggestion that we consider an external review brought a hearty laugh from him and the rest of the regents, and those attending, including the press. The meeting ended, and it was, for me at least, not the end but the beginning of a continuous effort to keep the issue of undergraduate education front and center throughout my tenure as president.

Faculty Reward System

A universitywide Task Force on Faculty Rewards was also appointed by me in September 1990 and reported its findings in June 1991. I asked Professor Karl Pister to chair this task force owing to its importance and sensitivity. Pister, a professor of engineering at Berkeley and a longtime dean of the College of Engineering on that campus, and I had been well acquainted for many years. If ever there was a good university citizen it was Pister. He was respected throughout the university for his commitment to UC, his success as dean at one of the nation's leading colleges of engineering, and his intimate acquaintance with the Academic Senate and the inner workings of the university. He was also a person of unimpeachable integrity. (These very qualities prompted me to appoint Pister as interim chancellor at Santa Cruz on the unexpected departure of Robert Stevens in 1991. Appointed permanent chancellor in 1992, he served with distinction in that post until his retirement in 1996.)

The charge to the task force was to "review current academic personnel policy on the criteria for advancement and to review current practice in the implementation of this policy to determine if the reward structure in the professorial series is consistent with the mission of the university." In other words, was teaching being honored in practice as well as in theory when the performance of faculty members was assessed?

The university's stated policy in this respect was clear and had been judged by the task force sufficient for its purposes: "Superior intellectual attainment as evidenced both in teaching and in research or other creative achievement is an indispensable qualification for appointment or promotion to tenure positions." But the 1991 report also faulted the language, when put into practice, as failing to take sufficient account of "changes in emphasis and interest that will naturally occur in an academic career." In other words, at some times in one's professional life research played a more dominant role; at other times, teaching. The unwavering and uniform application of the policy for the review of faculty performance, usually every third year, was therefore thought by the committee to be unduly stringent, and it urged instead that a more extended period be considered when faculty performance overall was being judged.

Not everyone agreed. There was considerable resistance within the faculty to the appointment of this task force as well as to its report, some believing that it was an effort by the administration to "weaken UC's academic standards for review of faculty performance."

I did not see it in that light at all, although the concerns came as no surprise given that faculty members are instinctively and not without reason self-protective whenever an issue of this sensitivity is raised. The report bore directly on the values and priorities that form the basis for judging academic work within the university and therefore, by extension, on how members of the faculty arrange their own work and academic lives to fit these expectations. This was no small or trivial matter.

Frazer and Pister worked very closely and effectively together in moving the work forward. I stayed out of it, receiving periodic reports and making it clear both that I did not want to anticipate the outcome or fix a set deadline for the report. Good progress was being made, faculty concerns were dying away, and it seemed that we would be receiving yet another boost to our effort to strengthen teaching at UC.

The final sticking point came on the language for promotion to Step VI of the professorial scale, which required "evidence of international distinction in research" but was silent on teaching. I could not reconcile this silence with the university's consistent argument that teaching and research went hand in hand, that our faculty reward policy made provision for both, that one's teaching counted and not just one's research. Thus, I shared with Frazer and Pister my belief that some adjustment in the controlling language should be made but did not specify any preference, leaving the wording entirely to the task force to consider and recommend.

Not surprisingly, this request created quite a stir within the faculty. It was hotly debated, and for some time. But for the same reasons noted above, I did not rush the process, having every confidence that Frazer and Pister would find an appropriate and balanced response; and they did. Following the recommendations of the task force and with the concurrence of the Academic Senate, I revised the salient section of the university's academic personnel manual: advancement to Professor VI was to be on the basis of "great distinction, nationally or internationally recognized in either scholarship or teaching."

This was progress and, in the end, was recognized as such by the faculty. The outcome would have been very different if the faculty had seen me as seeking a particular result or specific language or as reaching across the line of shared governance in ways that violated university policies or customs. I did none of this, of course, and the faculty as usual, and in their own time, found just the right solution. It might appear at first to be a modest or even self-evident response to my earlier expressed concerns, but it was not, as Frazer and Pister's report to the regents on July 16, 1992, made clear. Frazer explained that every faculty member had received a copy of the task force's report, which had been debated on all campuses, and that he and Pister agreed that the new policy, which "improve[s] the university's ability to reward exceptional teaching," is in the spirit of the report's recommendations.[9]

A Direct Effort to Strengthen UC's Undergraduate Teaching

On February 7, 1992, I sent a letter to the chancellors of the eight campuses with undergraduate programs calling for a phase-in over three years of efforts to improve the education of our undergraduate students. This letter built on the work of the Smelser and Pister committees and the efforts that the campuses themselves already had under way.

I asked that by July 1, 1992, the chancellors submit to me their plans for implementing the following four objectives:

- Increase the number of freshman and sophomore seminars.
- Reduce class size when and wherever possible.
- Increase the range and number of opportunities UC's undergraduates have for supervised research.
- Increase the numbers of courses and sections offered by the campuses so that students can more easily make normal progress toward their degrees.

These objectives enjoyed the endorsement and support of the Academic Senate; and the Academic Council said it would help in any way possible even in the face of UC's new financial difficulties.

These steps were to be taken within UC's existing resource base. In other words, I made no effort to use funding as bribe or punishment. In the end, the faculty must itself desire such action.

The faculty response was very positive and so was that of the chancellors. Class schedules were reworked. Senior members of the faculty taught lower-division students in larger numbers than before. Freshman and sophomore seminars flourished. On the Berkeley campus, for example, 184 seminars were offered for the 1992–93 academic year beyond those already scheduled as part of Berkeley's ongoing efforts to improve undergraduate education. These changes resulted not only from my letter and from the campus chancellor and his colleagues, but most essentially from the faculty members themselves. The program was originally called the "Hundred Seminar Program." As of 2002, Berkeley offers two hundred such seminars each year, enrolling nearly 3,500 students; since 1998 participating faculty have received a modest stipend of $2,000 a year in recognition that this additional seminar is on top of their normal teaching loads.[10]

It is simply wrong to assume that the faculty are not interested in their undergraduate students, wrong to suppose that research is their sole interest, wrong to believe that only monetary incentives are needed in this area of the university's work, and mistaken to think that some overarching bureaucracy is needed to oversee and guide such initiatives. The way of the academy is not the way of the world. That is why these institutions need to be overridingly self-governing rather than subject to the less informed and more coercive nature of government's many forms and facets.

The effectiveness of such self-government was illustrated on July 1, 1992, when the state's Senate Education Committee killed Assemblyman Tom Hayden's bill to increase the teaching load of UC's tenured faculty members to two courses per quarter or semester. Knowledge of these new seminars for freshman and sophomore students at Berkeley (and perhaps elsewhere within UC as well) was the trigger for defeating this proposed legislation, which was as intrusive as it was ill informed.[11]

My letter looked not only backward to the Smelser and Pister reports, but also forward to the upcoming All-University Faculty Conference on Undergraduate Teaching to be held during the next few weeks. This effort to sustain regental, faculty, and general university interest in undergraduate education was held in early 1992, the second such conference I had convened; the first, in 1990, was on affirmative action. All-University Faculty Conferences had been held annually at UC, under the sponsorship of the presidents, from 1947 to 1976, when they were discontinued. I had attended several of them myself over the years and believed that they were very useful. They fostered a wider sense and appreciation for the university in its totality, stepped outside the confines of each campus, and provided the president and senate leadership with faculty views on important and pressing matters of interest to the entire university. The 1992 conference went well and gave further impetus to our efforts to improve undergraduate education at UC.

LONG-RANGE PLANNING FOR UC

Finally, I wish to share my experience in developing the long-range academic, physical, and fiscal plans for UC's nine campuses in light of marked changes in UC's enrollment expectations and other trends.

On my arrival at UC in 1983, I was told that the university did not anticipate enrollment increases for several years. The 1980s were expected to give us a welcome breather, enabling UC to rebuild both its capacity and capability, which had been so badly damaged from the late 1960s to the early 1980s. But these enrollment estimates proved to be quite wrong, the difference arising from the percentage of UC-eligible California high school graduating seniors not just choosing to apply to UC but actually intending to enroll.

Our enrollments rose every year from 1983 until my retirement in 1992, increasing from 102,000 to 125,000 undergraduates. Graduate student enrollments for that period held steady at around 25,000, as did those in the health sciences at about 12,000. The actual head count of students enrolled in 1992 totaled 164,000, up from 141,000 in 1983, an increase of over 16 percent. These increases came because the percentage of UC-eligible high school students choosing to enroll in the University of California rose from 5 percent in the mid-1970s to 7.9 percent by 1986. This represented a jump of about 50 percent, in contradiction of UC's own 1983 estimates. By 1988 UC's enrollment had reached levels predicted for 1995–96.

These unanticipated increases together with those projected into the first two decades of the coming century prompted a fresh look at the university's long-range planning, first campus by campus and then for UC as a whole. As I reviewed the situation in 1987, I wanted to undertake such planning sooner rather than later: at the time, we had excellent operating and capital budgets, faculty salaries were competitive, and buildings were going up at an unprecedented rate with a substantial and fully funded backlog. Student demand was increasing, and it would take considerable time first to project enrollments by campus and then negotiate them across campuses. The environmental issues that would be raised by the expansion of our existing campuses, most of which were located in prime coastal locations and/or in growth-conscious communities, were also a pressing concern. I thought that we should begin the process of planning the university's future anew with the needs of a new century and a demographically changing and growing California at the front of our consciousness, and I wanted the regents to review these long-range plans by no later than fall 1988.

The first task was to seek the advice of the chancellors and vice presidents on how to proceed. By this time, some of the chancellors on campuses when I began my presidency had retired or resigned. Dan Aldrich at UCI retired in 1984 and was replaced by Jack Peltason, whom I had recruited from his presidency of the American Council on Education. His return to Irvine was a homecoming in a way, as he had served under Aldrich in the early years of UCI as Aldrich's academic vice-chancellor before leaving for the chancellorship of the University of Illinois, Urbana-Champaign.

Tomás Rivera had suffered a fatal heart attack in 1984. It was a great shock to us all. I asked Dan Aldrich to serve as acting chancellor at Riverside until we could find a successor, which we did in the person of Theodore Hullar, a rising star at Cornell who joined us as Riverside's chancellor in 1985.

Chancellor Robert Huttenback at Santa Barbara resigned his post in 1986 following irregularities in expenditures from state funds on his personal residence in Santa Barbara. He was replaced by our "utility chancellor," Dan Aldrich, who once again came to our rescue, serving for one year as acting chancellor at UCSB until Barbara Uehling arrived to take up her duties as chancellor in 1987. We had recruited Uehling from the University of Missouri at Columbia, where she was serving as chancellor of that university. She and Rosemary Schraer, who replaced Hullar at Riverside when he became chancellor at UC Davis after Jim Meyer's retirement in 1987, became the first women chancellors to serve in the University of California.

In 1992 Schraer suffered a fatal stroke, and we once again had both the sadness of a death at Riverside and the need to find a new chancellor, which we did in recruiting Ray Orbach to succeed her. Ray was a distinguished physicist and a long-serving and highly respected dean of UCLA's College of Letters and Science.

At UC Santa Cruz, Bob Sinsheimer retired in 1987. He was succeeded by Robert Stevens, president of Haverford College in Pennsylvania, former provost at Tulane, and former faculty member at the Yale School of Law. Stevens resigned in 1991 (he was later elected master of Pembroke College at Oxford University in England). He was succeeded at UCSC by Professor Karl Pister, as earlier noted.

And finally, when Mike Heyman retired at Berkeley and moved to the Smithsonian as its new secretary in 1990, we recruited to succeed him the first Asian American to serve as the chancellor of a major American research university, Professor Chang-Lin Tien. Tien had been a Berkeley faculty member for over a quarter of a century, was a former vice-chancellor for research at Berkeley, and was serving at UCI as Peltason's academic vice-chancellor when Heyman resigned.

Thus, within five years there were new chancellors at Riverside, Irvine, Santa Barbara, Santa Cruz, and Davis, and two years later at Berkeley. But while the team changed the work went forward.

The Planning for New Campuses Begins

Our efforts began with proposals from each of the nine campuses for enrollment growth, disaggregated by lower division, upper division, master's level, and the doctorate, including professional schools; the health sciences were planned for separately. These estimates were not easy to make, as they affected every part of campus life: the prospective size and character of academic programs, the recruitment and retention of faculty, and the hiring of staff, along with the associated land, buildings, and infrastructure needed to support these programs. On environmental matters—particularly the impact that the California Environmental Quality Control Act was expected to have on the process, substance, cost, and time of any development—we sought the advice of the general counsel.

Naturally, the requests of the several campuses, taken in their entirety, exceeded the carrying capacity of the university as a whole, anticipated unreasonable growth rates in some instances, and went well beyond the expansion that the host communities would be willing to tolerate in others. There was also an excess of ambition with respect to new graduate students and programs and proposals to establish new professional schools already adequately represented within UC. All this was to be expected.

The vice presidents and their respective staffs studied these proposals, making sense of them within the context of the university as a single institution, arranged them to facilitate decision making, and offered judgments of their own about their merits. It was, in fact, a very orderly process accompanied by a minimum of contentiousness. Once our conversations had gone as far as they could, I then proceeded to vet each campus proposal one at a time with each chancellor.

One example of such negotiations should suffice to illustrate the nature and character of these discussions.

The Berkeley campus enrolled 30,576 students in 1988. This level of enrollment exceeded the reasonable carrying capacity of the campus in virtually all respects, including laboratory, research and clinical space, student housing, libraries, and buildable land; and this level of enrollment was also regarded by the City of Berkeley as adversely affecting the city itself.

The problem was that dollars followed enrollments, both up and down. How could Berkeley reduce its enrollments without losing significant state funds? Chancellor Heyman was willing to reduce enrollments, but not to take the accompanying hit on his budget.

Thus, I proposed that undergraduate enrollment at Berkeley be cut by 2,018 students and graduate enrollment increased by 900, for a net reduction of 1,126. While not a major reduction, it was enough to take some of the enrollment pressure off the city and off the campus infrastructure—utilities, student housing, parking, and the like—as well. This change would have no affect on Berkeley's budget, as 900 graduate students, on average, cost what 2,018 undergraduates did. While Berkeley's state funds would not be affected, the ratio of graduate to undergraduate students, which had fallen significantly in recent years, would be improved.

Heyman agreed.

I succeeded in working out most differences with all the campuses; however, the twenty-year campus enrollment projections remained unresolved for some campuses, the ratio of graduates to undergraduates on others, and the ultimate size of the campus at still others. It thus fell to me to make decisions that in some cases I knew would not be welcomed by the chancellors or their campus colleagues, certainly initially. But this is why there was a president. My final decisions were taken on a long night flight from Europe to San Francisco in the late spring of 1988 and communicated to all interested parties promptly on my return. When UC was viewed as a whole, the decisions were right. Those on the individual campuses were not so sure, but these inevitable disagreements were manageable.

I scheduled a series of meetings with each chancellor in spring 1988 for the purpose of sharing my reasoning with them campus by campus, and then again with all other chancellors and the vice presidents present. Once I had walked them through my decisions and my reasoning, they were by and large satisfied, or at least persuaded that I had been fair, acknowledging that in my shoes, they would have done much the same. The only exception was Riverside, which wanted to grow at a rate I regarded as excessive; I could not accept it, out of concern for the ability of the campus to recruit faculty members in sufficient numbers to match the proposed growth, for the impact this rate of growth would have on the city of Riverside, and for the effect that such substantial proposed numbers of freshmen students would have on the social cohesiveness of the campus. Riverside was not happy with me.

Our presentation to the regents of this long-range enrollment planning was placed on the agenda for the October 20, 1988, meeting of the board, a policy meeting given over entirely to this subject. I introduced the item by emphasizing the assumptions behind the analysis: "that the University's assigned mission under the California Master Plan will remain undisturbed, that our standards for freshman admission will continue to qualify the top $12\text{-}\frac{1}{2}\%$ of California's high school graduates, and that our commitment to enroll UC eligible California residents seeking undergraduate admission will be honored." During the planning period, 1988–89 through 2005–06, we expected "demand for enrollment to exceed the capacity of our existing campuses," and how that excess demand can be accommodated would be discussed. Our best estimate of campus enrollments to 2005–06 was then presented to the board (see appendix 1).[12]

I then indicated that of the total enrollment growth of some 60,000 expected by 2020, all but 20,000 could be accommodated on our existing nine campuses. The remainder would necessarily be enrolled on one or more new campuses—up to as many as three in the early years of 2000 to provide not only for the 20,000 students who could not be accommodated by our nine campuses but also for those to come later, our existing campuses then being essentially full. The alternative was to allow UCLA and Berkeley to reach 40,000 each and to permit a rate of growth at Riverside, Santa Cruz, and Santa Barbara that would be unwise on its face and most likely resisted by the host cities. The other campuses at Irvine, San Diego, Davis, and San Francisco were already projected to grow at a rate and to a size deemed to be appropriate.

Our report went on to take account of the need for each of the nine campuses to prepare and submit to the regents during the next two to three years a long-range development plan, at which time the regents could take another look at the numbers and either confirm or revise our estimates. We could then also discuss the resource implications of this growth for UC's operating budgets, capital budgets, and debt capacity, faculty recruitment problems, faculty housing issues, the planning process, environmental issues, and related matters.

The only decision I wanted in October was to put any decision over until November. Only then would I seek authorization from the board to proceed with the long-range planning of the University of California, including the possibility of new campuses—no sites suggested—and the long-range development plans for the existing nine campuses within the general limitations put forward in our plan, subject to later regental review and revision. At the November 1988 board meeting, the regents authorized the administration to plan for one new campus in California's Central Valley, to open by 2000, and to reserve its judgment about two others until early in the twenty-first century.

Between 1989 and 1991, all nine long-range development plans were submitted to the regents and approved. These plans inventoried the academic ambitions of each campus, the rate of enrollment growth, the ultimate campus size, the resource implications, the land and building requirements, and the environmental mitigations to be taken. The mere preparing of these plans compelled each campus to look hard and comprehensively at where it had been, where it was, and where it was going. It also required each campus to forge a consensus among all interested parties on campus, negotiate an agreeable outcome with the host city and/or county, and discover creative solutions to the associated environmental impacts.

This was a very large and difficult task, and every campus managed to do it. I was proud of my faculty and administrative colleagues, and the very talented staff (including mine and those of the vice presidents) that provided the technical and research support required. An indispensable contribution was also made by our legal advisers in the Office of the General Counsel, headed by James Holst following Don Reidhaar's tragic and untimely death in 1985.

Our estimates of enrollment growth proved to be remarkably accurate, at least to 2001–02. For UC as a whole, we estimated that total enrollment would then reach 193,585 students, from an enrollment level of 153,881 in 1988–89, reflecting a growth of 39,704 students (head count). Actual enrollment reached 186,083 in 2001–02, or 7,502 fewer students than anticipated; most of the disparity occurred during the first half of the 1990s, when the state and the university were preoccupied with a dip in state revenues that rivaled those of the Great Depression in the 1930s, and steps were taken to restrain our enrollment by some 5,000 students (see chapter 10). Our estimates of enrollment for the existing campuses, however, were right on the money at 186,815 (estimated in 1988 for 2002).[13] The shortfall for UC as a whole was fortunate, as the university's new campus at Merced is not expected to open until 2005.

Once we were under way, I arranged to meet with the legislative leaders for dinner in Sacramento, and some fifteen to twenty members of the Assembly and Senate attended. When we presented the same report, more or less, as we had to the regents, it was very well received. We were complimented on its thoroughness and the foresight we had shown but warned that we were much ahead of the state itself with these plans.

I was also concerned by the comment one senator made as we were leaving the dinner party. He said in an unfriendly tone, "Well, I see you are setting about to extend UC's empire even further." I responded by taking issue with his judgment of our motives. "Senator," I said, "all we are trying to do is to make certain that the doors of the University of California remain open, as open to California's next generation of students as they were open to you and to me. If you don't want us to plan for that, but instead wish to reduce the percentage of students eligible for UC, then you need only to tell us." He just walked away.

I finally concluded that the pressure on state resources was just reaching the point that our share of the state budget might very well soon go down, and that the series of propositions and initiatives recently passed by the voters that earmark parts of the state budget—for example, Proposition 98, which constitutionally reserved a fixed percentage of state general funds for the K–12 schools and California's community colleges (see chapter 8)— would shrink higher education's share even further. These were realities the legislators did not want to face, at least on their watch; and here we were obliging them to face up to them. As things turned out, this analysis was exactly right, and as we moved into the 1990s, these realities became inescapable for everyone.

Other Initiatives Emerge

In any event, the long-range development plans for each of our campuses were approved. The search for a new campus in California's Central Valley, a proposal I had made in 1988 and the regents had approved that same year, began. The university was moving forward, guided by our collective efforts and informed by the plans we had so meticulously put into place.

The fact that these plans all struck a fiscal brick wall in the early 1990s, owing to a national recession whose effects were especially pronounced in California, does not detract from our long-range planning efforts or the positive effect they had. They helped carry us through the early half of the 1990s and the state's worst fiscal crisis since the Great Depression with a minimum of friction and intercampus rivalries. Our building programs carried on well into the 1990s because of the long construction times required and because funding had been included in previously approved state building bonds. And the university survived those difficult years much better than we otherwise would have, not only because we had planned well but also because we had gone into the recession better funded and more fiscally secure than at any time in UC's history. The tenth campus, not incidentally, began construction in 2002 near Merced in California's Central Valley, just short of the foothills leading to Yosemite National Park; it is already enrolling students ahead of its planned 2005 opening.

Other major academic initiatives included three new professional schools in addition to the Graduate School of International Relations and Pacific Studies at San Diego: the College of Engineering at Riverside, the School of Environmental Sciences at Santa Barbara, and the School of Social Ecology at Irvine. But my involvement in these schools was minimal, the initiatives being driven by the faculties and respective chancellor of each campus.

New articulation agreements were negotiated between UC, CSU, and the community colleges, at my instigation and in response to legislative unhappiness about the sometimes inexplicable unevenness in UC's treatment of courses taken at the community colleges.

A center for faculty and students in Washington, D.C., to house and support those involved in the array of UC activities in the nation's capital was also fully planned, though lack of funding led me to pull it back in mid-1992. It was subsequently constructed under President Atkinson's leadership in the late 1990s. The California Council on Science and Technology was created to enable UC, along with the private research universities of the state, namely, Stanford, USC, and Cal Tech, to advise the state legislature and the governor on such issues and to seek interinstitutional opportunities for fostering research and interaction with the private sector. It has helped the state a great deal. Various initiatives to assist faculty members in financing and securing their personal residences were also put into place. Not all the initiatives succeeded—for example, an effort was made to secure for California the Superconducting Super Collider, but it went instead to Texas (where the project was killed by the U.S. Congress in 1993)—but many did.

Countless other new programs were also approved in the normal course of the university's work by the academic departments, schools, and colleges and by the chancellors. The president is very little involved in such matters. The university works best that way, as it makes for less bureaucracy, affirms UC's decentralized system of decision making, and ensures that decisions are taken by those best and most credibly able to make them.[14]

I emphasize these points, and have included the examples in this chapter, in part because one often reads in the literature on higher education that university presidents are powerless, that the faculties are hopelessly resistant to change, that the unions have immobilized the staff, that the students attack whatever the administration does, and that the governing boards afford the president precious little discretion while holding him or her responsible for virtually everything.

I did not find these pessimistic, if not cynical, assertions to be in the least bit true. Not at Utah and not at California. University presidents not only have very substantial authority but also possess abundant influence and power—though none of these attributes makes much difference if not boldly exercised or fully engaged.

These claims assume that the incumbents are self-starters, willing to act, conscious of the strengths and weaknesses of others (just as they need to be aware of their own), content to internalize their successes and absorb their failures, willing to take advice or turn it away, happy to work long hours and able to walk away from the job for the sake of the institution, willing to say no or yes according to their best judgment, willing to endure a certain isolation and bear the disgruntled and faultfinders, willing to balance personal life with the demands of the job or lose one or the other or both, and deeply committed to the purposes, values, and culture of these rare and remarkable institutions that form so crucial, indeed, so indispensable a part of modern civilization.

This is not to say that things work well all the time, or that mistakes are not made, or that poor choices do not have enduring consequences, or that there are not ample bumps and barriers along the road, or that presidents do not err or fall short of expectations, as the events described in the following chapter help illustrate.

EIGHT

BUMPS AND BARRIERS ALONG THE WAY

This chapter's title intentionally distinguishes among and between *bumps,* by which I mean uncommon digressions and unforeseen interferences amenable to resolution with little more than careful and persistent attention to the personalities and problems presented; and *barriers,* by which I mean not mere inconveniences but real and persistent obstructions to the resolution of differences, impervious to the usual problem-solving processes.

Within UC's governing structure, the president's office is the lightning rod. As a result, it registers most of the serious bumps and barriers. It is, for example, the nodal point for resolving issues that involve conflicts among chancellors that cannot be reconciled at the campus level. It is the designated office for communicating with the legislature and the governor (designed partly to protect individual campuses from particularized conflicts or pressures). It is the locus of *legal* responsibility for the university's involvement in all conflicts that have legal or possible legal implications. It is the office on which the regents depend for the integrity and credibility of their work, and the one to which they have delegated most of their authority. It is the office responsible for allocating UC's budgets and for determining most of its policies. To understand this complex function is to appreciate, therefore, how much is riding on the president's decisions and how much on the what, when, where, why, and how of the president's involvement. Substance, sequence, timing, and communication are all factors in this equation, along with a little luck, good and bad.

The examples of bumps and barriers are intended to illustrate the bewildering array of matters engaging the president's time and energy. Some of these are internally generated, others governmentally induced, and still others are the work of external interests having a stake in the university's policies, practices, and purposes; a few simply wish to use the university for their own purposes, whether or not they have a stake in the university. Rather than order these examples by their importance or their themes, I describe them more or less randomly, to give the reader a sense of how disparate and diverse and often unexpected were the issues I dealt with on a nearly daily basis, such matters coming to my desk comparably devoid of order. How and when I dealt with them, of course, is another matter, but this is how they came. These bumps and barriers with which we were expected to contend, and the publicly charged environment within which we were working, should make clear to the reader that every decision we made earned an enemy as well as a friend, the former tending to have longer memories and more intense recollections than the latter.

BUMPS

As with its faculty, the university's students are drawn from throughout the world, each bringing a unique set of beliefs to this demanding "marketplace of ideas" where contrary and competing viewpoints thrive. The university, therefore, is inherently unpredictable, as alive to its future as to its past, a source of chronic, systemic tension that helps explain both its role and its contributions, the ideas and culture of the world informing and enlivening its daily discourse.

California is itself a remarkably modern society: multiethnic, multiracial, multicultural, socially pluralistic, entrepreneurial, in motion. It attracts immigrants from throughout the globe, mostly from Mexico, Central and South America, and East and Southeast Asia, with new ideas, lifestyles, social arrangements, and religions. Like UC, the state too is unpredictable and discomforting. But in virtually all other ways, they are stunningly unlike.

The state is a political entity with defined geographic boundaries. Those making the policy decisions and the laws are elected by the citizenry. The responsibility of state government is to protect persons and property, to secure civil rights, to administer justice, to provide a range of needed educational and social services, to promulgate rules and regulations, to establish the basic ground rules, and to fix the taxes by which the state and its subordinate governmental jurisdictions are to be funded and rendered functional. The state relies on coercion as much as on persuasion to carry out its functions, and its elected representatives are "accountable," in some gross but well-understood sense of the term, at election time.

The University of California, by contrast, is an institution dedicated by custom and law to the discovery, organization, study, and transmission of knowledge. It is merely one part of a global community of scholars whose values and norms are more universal than parochial and whose interests and experience, therefore, are by definition international. Unlike officials in an elective democracy, UC's key officers, administrators, faculty, and staff are appointed, as are its regents (most ex-officios excepted). Students seeking admission are accepted or turned away according to norms and judgments of the faculty whose views also prevail in the setting of courses and standards for the awarding of degrees, their authority being rooted in nine hundred years of Western tradition. Not surprisingly—given the differentiated basis of authority the state and the university legitimately claim—their principles, issues, and interests often collide.

The University and the State

The well-known issues of state/UC conflict include the loyalty oath controversy (1949–52), the Free Speech Movement (1964–65), and the Vietnam War demonstrations (1967–71). I had my share of clashes between 1983 and 1992, over divestment (1985–86), affirmative action (1986–87), and UC's management of Livermore and Los Alamos National Labs (1983–92), among others. Controversy was most pronounced during the annual sessions of the legislature and the U.S. Congress. Legislation dealing with nearly every aspect of university operations was proposed every legislative session, the "hammer" being the budget, and wielded as often, as directly, and as firmly as was thought necessary to bring UC into line with the prevailing political winds and or party platforms, for example, admission standards, student fees, courses of study, union interests and labor relations, minority rights, building codes and environmental regulations, graduation requirements, nondiscrimination legislation, faculty and staff compensation, genetic engineering, faculty teaching loads, AIDS and tobacco research, and animal rights.

The university had an excellent team in Sacramento. I counted on its members to carry UC's interests and, all things considered, we were generally successful. Our success was usually judged on how well or poorly we had done with our operating and capital budgets whereas some of our most difficult, sensitive, and time-consuming efforts were committed to defeating legislation we judged to be prejudicial to UC's interests or inconsistent with its constitutional protections.

The regents had delegated to the president responsibility for deciding UC's position on legislation considered by the state legislature or the Congress. I, in turn, expected the heads of our offices in each of these capitals to make the necessary judgments and keep me informed. Occasionally, the issues were important enough or the decision "to support," "to oppose," or to "take no position" was so close that I would ask the Board of Regents for guidance.

On the more sensitive and unforgiving of issues when the staff and individual legislators had been unable to reconcile contending views, I often found that a personal visit by me, a change in a word here or an added or deleted phrase there, a bartering of a word here for a sentence there, took care of the problem. But sometimes if a legislator was interested in another piece of legislation as well, we could help him or her with that something else in exchange for relief on our differences. Or we might indicate that the legislator did not have the votes for what she or he wanted us to do to, or that we could seek, and would mostly likely secure, a gubernatorial veto; or if the issue impinged on UC's autonomy, we indicated that we would either litigate the matter if enacted or ignore it. This was the usual "stuff" of making legislation or defeating it, and our team did a wonderful job. I helped as I could.

Animal Rights and AIDS Research

We dealt with many such bumps in this fashion. I recall Steve Arditti describing his experience one day at the legislature when a legislative committee was hearing complaints from a certain legislator and from animal rights advocates about UC's use of animals in research. Nothing the UC representative could say helped either with the legislator or our critics: it was a decidedly unsatisfying experience. The same afternoon another hearing was scheduled on UC's research efforts on AIDS. The room was full of AIDS activists, as the morning had been of animal rights advocates. Our principal critic, who berated us for not doing enough research in this area (no one was doing more), was the same legislator who had condemned us that very morning for using animals in research.

After the hearing, Arditti cornered this legislator in the corridor and pointed out the inconsistency of his morning comments with his criticisms in the afternoon. After all, he noted, "research on AIDS required the use of animals." The legislator stopped Arditti with a smile: "I know all about that, but many of my constituents were in the audience both this morning and this afternoon. Several had come from long distances to be here and I couldn't let them down. Don't worry about it. You're doing a great job. Now, about my son's application for admission to Berkeley . . ." (Such inquires from legislators, donors, and others of influence were as frequent as they were unavailing.)

In the mid-1980s the state was beginning to respond to the growing incidence of AIDS in California and elsewhere. Substantial funds were being appropriated by the legislature to UC for research in this area, which we supported. UC Vice President Cornelius Hopper was handling this for us and had already formed an advisory committee of leading scientists from UC and other leading research universities and entities in California to peer-review the research proposals. Once the appropriation had been made, Hopper was under intense pressure from certain legislators, including Speaker Willie Brown, to direct no small part of the monies to certain researchers the legislators thought to be especially worthy (research pork barreling, I called it). Hopper came to see me, distressed that such pressure was being applied and knowing that it would be unthinkable for us to have acceded.

Hopper and I agreed that such legislative pressure was not only inappropriate but unsustainable as well, and that we would not under any circumstances allow those who were to do this research to be chosen by other than through peer-review. Moreover, if the conditions insisted on by the most interested legislators were so at odds with our own peer-review processes, then we should advise them to appropriate the funds to someone else. Otherwise, if they were determined to appropriate the money to us with unacceptable conditions, we would ignore their stipulations or simply not spend it.

Hopper had a very tough time working the state capital under the burden of these instructions, but in the end the money came to UC unencumbered and was carefully deployed to those researchers thought by their peers to be the most qualified, ready, and able to use it.

Even our decision to move the Office of the President away from Berkeley in the mid to late 1980s was the object of much legislative interest.

Office of the President—Outside Berkeley?

The president of the university had maintained his office in Berkeley since the university's founding because Berkeley was where it all began. As UC became a multicampus university in the 1920s and, most expansively so after Kerr took office as president in 1958, the Berkeley campus became increasingly resentful and/or jealous of the university's new campuses. It also came to regard the president, whose office was adjacent to the Berkeley campus, as exerting a disproportionate influence on or at least evidencing an inappropriate level of interest in the Berkeley campus *and* to Berkeley's detriment. The other eight campuses were convinced that the very opposite was true. Moreover, every political protest at Berkeley spilled over and involved the president's office in University Hall on Oxford Street, immediately opposite Berkeley's main West Gate entrance. Though the protests were usually about Berkeley campus issues, they occupied an unreasonable amount of my time and attention; the official presence of both president and chancellor in the same city also tended to confuse the students about who the real "culprit" was. All things considered, Chancellor Heyman must have found my presence in Berkeley to be more of a burden than a blessing.

My office and staff were housed not only in University Hall, but also in costly leased offices throughout the city. At first we hoped to improve our operations and reduce our costs by making a major addition to University Hall, my main office. No plan we could devise, however, was acceptable to the city, which on the one hand seemed to resent our presence and on the other appeared fearful, but skeptical, at the prospect of our moving out of Berkeley.

After several months of dithering by the city, with one complaint after another about every plan we put forth, I decided, with the concurrence of the regents, to relocate our offices to the Kaiser Center on Lake Merritt in adjoining Oakland. Here we could house all our offices and at a substantial savings, while relinquishing University Hall to the Berkeley campus for much needed administrative space, since the campus also had an excess of leased space throughout the city. The Kaiser Center was much more convenient, both for UC personnel flying into San Francisco or Oakland airports for universitywide meetings at my offices and for key members of my staff who often visited our nine campuses and other university operations throughout the state.

The decision met the cost and functionality tests, but not the emotional or political ones. As to the latter, Mayor Loni Hancock and her colleagues in the Berkeley city government—consistently unfriendly and uncooperative—were now "outraged" that we should be leaving Berkeley, our historic home, for Oakland a city they deemed unworthy of housing our offices. And prodded, I assume, by local merchants unhappy at the prospect of 1,500 professional and staff employees shopping and eating in Oakland instead, the city of Berkeley now belatedly sought to wrap its arms around us.

Tom Bates, the assemblyman for Berkeley and environs in the state legislature, also began to make unfriendly comments about our decision. Speaker Brown, who favored our move to Oakland, however, dealt with that matter. My staff was divided, the half living in Berkeley being mostly unhappy, and the half living in Oakland being mostly pleased. Yet in the end, as Bay Area residents, an off-campus site did not draw them away from the university's real work.

The California Agrarian Action Suit

One of the many changes in California's socioeconomic and demographic characteristics occasioned a bump that spanned three administrations—Hitch's, Saxon's, and mine—a lawsuit filed in 1979 against UC and finally settled in UC's favor in 1989.

The California Agrarian Action Project's lawyers argued that UC research related to agricultural mechanization (one example is the tomato harvester developed by UC Davis and the tomatoes developed, also by UC Davis, so that their shape was made congenial to the mechanical requirements of the harvester) was of benefit only to large agribusiness and harmful to all other segments of society, particularly small farmers and farm workers. Such research, they alleged, violated the regents' trust obligations and constituted a gift of public funds, contrary to the intent of pertinent federal legislation, especially the Hatch Act.

Shortly after I got to Berkeley in midsummer 1983 Donald Reidhaar, the university's general counsel, brought the matter to my attention. At that point the issues in this litigation had been narrowed to one major demand, namely, that UC research in agriculture be made subject to an existing procedure that would require UC to do a "socioeconomic impact report," as Reidhaar described it to me, "akin to an environmental impact study, on any agricultural research if it drew, in whole or in part, on funds derived from the Hatch Act." While Reidhaar did not advocate that we settle the suit on these grounds, neither did he seek to dissuade me.

Our meeting did not last very long. I pointed out that the demand was, in principle, no different than insisting that we carry out such an analysis on any research before its publication or on any class before we offered it to our students. "This condition strikes at the very core of the intellectual freedoms the academic community worldwide had struggled for over nine hundred years to ensure, and we will not be a party to such an agreement, however long the litigation takes or whatever it costs."

Reidhaar seemed somewhat surprised at the finality of my instructions but was understanding. He and his colleagues battled long and hard for six more years before the issue was finally settled by the courts, in our favor and on every count.

"Hate Speech"

In addition to pressure from the legislature, local politics, and changes in the larger society, UC was also affected by the actions and policies of other leading research universities as in the instance of the "hate speech" policies enacted by many of the nation's universities in the 1980s. "Hate speech" gave voice to racial and ethnic prejudices and long-standing divisions within the larger society that had spilled over into campus life in quite unexpected ways. University policies on affirmative action, admissions, housing, employment, and student financial aid that favored minority students triggered resentment among many other students, especially those not comparably benefited.

Such language and its accompanying behavior were deeply offensive and troubling to minority students and damaged the sense of community on many campuses. In trying to deal with this problem, some universities adopted "hate speech" policies. But judging that such policies intruded on

First Amendment protections, the courts struck down the University of Michigan's, for example, even though they were intended to discipline or otherwise punish students who employed language and/or exhibited behavior thought by the university to interfere with the minority students' work and sense of acceptance on campus.

This issue arose within UC late in the game, as I had been of the view that the enactment by UC of such policies would raise as many practical and legal questions as they hoped to resolve. But in early 1989 I discovered that the previous year Chancellor Heyman at Berkeley and Chancellor Young at Los Angeles had promulgated their own policies on "hate speech" for their respective campuses, and that Chancellor Uehling at Santa Barbara was about to do the same. I was astonished. UC was a single legal entity: only the president had the authority to enact or amend such policies. The chancellors' actions were anomalous.

I instructed Chancellors Heyman and Young to suspend any enforcement of their individual campus policies and told Chancellor Uehling not to consider them at Santa Barbara as well. This was an unwelcome set of instructions, and I received no little criticism for it. But I was no less unhappy than the chancellors and thus not overly sensitive or concerned about those on the campuses who found fault with this decision.

I promptly raised this issue with the vice presidents for their advice and then with the chancellors. Given its complexity, the matter unsurprisingly generated as many different points of view as there were vice presidents and chancellors, ranging from Heyman who "wanted to push the legal envelope" with a strong and encompassing set of regulations at the university-wide level, to Chancellor Atkinson at San Diego who wanted to do nothing, and to Chancellor Jack Peltason at Irvine who worked hard, along with me, to find a consensus.

I will never forget our last discussion of this intractable matter. It was on a Wednesday night in mid-1989 just before a two-day meeting of the regents at UCLA, and the chancellors and I were having dinner at the nearby Regency Club. This issue was the last item on our agenda (not by inadvertence). By the time we reached this final item for the evening, most of the chancellors were feeling "little pain," having partaken with uncommon pleasure from the generous provision of California wines that had accompanied dinner.

The ensuing discussion should have been videotaped for historical purposes. It was as full of emotion as it was unhelpful and collapsed amid an unusual (and actually quite humorous) exchange of comments by chancellors about one another, more than on the issue before us. Finally, when it was clear that no consensus could be forged among us, I told the chancellors that I needed to proceed but "they would be the first to hear of the new regulations—I knew I could count on their complete cooperation."

With that they all relaxed, urged me to move forward, and with waves and expressions of goodnight jostled their way out the door and into the warm, fresh air of a Los Angeles evening. I was left to decide the issue, a complex and politically difficult one, with a "divided house," an uncommon outcome during my administration.

On September 21, 1989, I issued an amendment to the student conduct policy applicable to all UC students and all campuses, adding to the university's list of prohibited student conduct the use of "fighting words":

> personally abusive epithets which, when directly addressed to any ordinary person are, in the context used and as a matter of common knowledge, inherently likely to provoke a violent reaction whether or not they actually do so. Such words include, but are not limited to, those terms widely recognized to be derogatory references to race, ethnicity, religion, sex, sexual orientation, disability, and other personal characteristics. "Fighting words" constitute "harassment" when the circumstances of their utterance create a hostile and intimidating environment which the student uttering them should reasonably know will interfere with the victim's ability to pursue effectively his or her education or otherwise to participate fully in university programs and activities.[1]

The amendment, which by definition revoked the recently issued policies at Berkeley and UCLA, was well received in general (in my cover letter I made clear that the change was not intended to limit students' protections of free speech under the law or applicable university policy). It was noted nationally and compared with the more aggressive policies that were being adopted elsewhere. The American Civil Liberties Union, however, took a very dim view of my actions, as did Tom Hayden, chairman of the Assembly's Subcommittee on Higher Education, the former concerned that we had overreached and infringed our students' First Amendment protections and the latter concerned that we had not gone far enough.

The ACLU official response, however, was slow in coming because of differences within the organization itself. Finally on August 8, 1990, in a letter to me from ACLU directors in California, the ACLU stated, "If the current student code harassment policy remains in effect after August 31, 1990, the ACLU intends to initiate legal action on behalf of a broad range of University of California students who believe, as we do, that the student conduct harassment policy infringes on their constitutional rights."[2]

I believed that we had done our best to balance the rights and interests of all parties, that we had adopted a restrained and yet sufficient and enforceable policy, that we had not jeopardized anyone's constitutional protections but had taken appropriate steps to discourage verbal and behavioral abuses that might otherwise threaten the ability not only of minority but of other students as well to remain at and fully participate in UC's academic, residential, and extracurricular activities and programs. I advised our legal team "to respond to whatever questions ACLU asked but not to speculate about our handling of hypothetical cases, and if the ACLU chose to litigate, so be it." As it turned out, the ACLU decided not to litigate.

Propositions

Numerous propositions are presented to California's voters for their consideration at election time, the procedure completely bypassing the people's elected representatives in Sacramento. Some in the form of statutes and others as amendments to the state constitution, the propositions are mostly the work of special interests in the state who seek support from the voters when they fail to get relief from the legislature. The work of the legislature, of course, also involves pressure from special interests, and if the lawmakers too often thwart the will of the people, the electorate can at least use propositions to effectuate legislation themselves and vote the measures up or down. California law has been protective of such direct expressions of public will. Were it not for the common sense of the average voters, who generally manage to understand what they are being asked to approve and thus defeat the worst of them, California would be an even greater enigma that it already is.

When these measures were placed on the ballot, and UC's vital interests were implicated, the regents would support or oppose them or take no position at all, the first two options triggering a determined effort by the UC administration "to inform" the public about UC's concerns but not "to advocate" for the passage or defeat of any particular ballot measure. State law required this distinction to be made, and every reasonable effort was taken to honor the distinction.

Several of the bumps encountered were the result of such propositions, for example, the Gann Spending Limit on State Appropriations, the Gann Limit on Public Salaries, and Proposition 98 (to reserve for public K-14 education in California a predetermined share of the state budget), among many others. To illustrate the nature and character of these always sensitive and usually critical measures with which we were concerned and which consumed no small measure of our time, I will deal only with Proposition 98, an initiative sponsored by the K-14 (public schools and community colleges) establishment for the purpose of securing a constitutionally assured share of the state's general fund budget. This proposition had the effect of providing funds for K-14 before anyone else's budget was considered by the state. Its share of the budget was to be fixed without regard to the state's overall fiscal condition or the essential requirements of any other part of the state budget, including the California State University and the University of California. If Proposition 98 were to be enacted, when coupled with the other existing constitutional or federal protections for other portions of state government, nearly 85 percent of the state's general fund budget would be committed by law, and not subject to the legislature's discretionary action. This remaining 15 percent was to fund every other part of the state, including UC. On top of this, the state was obliged to adhere to the spending limit provisions of a previously enacted proposition, namely the Gann Spending Limit, which capped state spending regardless of circumstances, but with adjustments that failed to take account of the state's changing personal income or demographics.

Proposition 98 passed by a very small margin in 1988 and guaranteed to the K-12 schools and community colleges roughly 40 percent of the state's general fund budget, or their prior year's budget, adjusted for enrollment growth, whichever was greater. Other provisions further strengthened the schools' call on state general funds whenever revenue exceeded the state's spending limits.

The regents had decided to take no position on Proposition 98 for fear of being seen as hostile to California's public schools. The state superintendent of instruction was Bill Honig of San Francisco, who also served as an ex-officio regent. He and I had some sharp exchanges at the March 16, 1989, meeting of the board as I tried to identify the proposition's long-term adverse implications for UC. It proved to be as threatening to UC as we had feared, and in consort with other interested parties we sought in 1989 to secure amendments to Proposition 98 as well as to the Gann Spending Limit that would mitigate their most harmful and unreasonable parts.

Both propositions were eventually amended, but they together with other restraints on the exercise of legislative discretion, not only eroded the effectiveness of state government in general but reduced the discretion of the legislature and the governor to act in accordance with the state's immediate and long-term needs. Subsequent state and private commissions helped some, but these concerns washed away in the early 1990s as the recession set in. This issue has yet to be dealt with, the problem being hidden and submerged in a sea of budget surpluses attendant to California's spectacular economic recovery in the middle to late 1990s, but ever more apparent with the dramatic slippage of state revenues since 2001.

BARRIERS

Quite unpredictably, however, issues of this kind would often evolve into powerful forces for change or politically charged and emotionally driven controversies: highly visible, ongoing, and resistant to solution, or even accommodation. They were consequential barriers in our path. The four barriers I will describe reflect the range and character of problems with which we were concerned, often simultaneously: affirmative action, especially in undergraduate admissions; UC's management of the "weapons" labs at Livermore and Los Alamos; the California Public Interest Group and its mechanism for raising monies from UC students; and the call for divestment of UC-owned securities in companies doing business in what was then apartheid South Africa.

UC and Affirmative Action

As early as 1964, UC mounted determined and organized efforts to attract more minority students to its campuses. Driven by the challenges of the civil rights movement, federal legislation encouraging and/or requiring affirmative steps, and California's own rapidly changing demographics and what these portended for UC's and the state's future, UC's efforts were well intentioned but often naive. As I noted briefly in chapter 2, the initiatives were rooted in the assumption that all that was needed was to identify reasonably promising minorities early in their high school years, to enroll them in the courses required for UC admission, to assist them in finding campus housing, employment, and/or financial aid, and otherwise to facilitate their application for admission and on-campus course selection and registration. Though necessary, these steps fell well short of making UC's growing student diversity a positive factor in the education of minority and nonminority students alike. A heavy price was paid in the mid to late 1960s, and even beyond, for this flawed assumption.

There remains a continuous push and pull between public universities and the country's major minority communities over access to higher education. Tensions center on the appropriateness of the standards for admission, the fairness of national examinations that form part of those standards, the pertinence of the general education requirements for lower-division students, and the "relevance" to minority interests of some courses of study offered or omitted. The ethnic and racial composition of the staff, and especially of the faculty, also play a part in the controversy, as do the arrangements for student housing, the funding of student organizations, the provision for financial aid, and the applicability of the student codes of conduct to perceived or asserted cultural differences (including "hate speech" policies).

Of lesser relevance to undergraduate admissions is the issue of gender, though it figures in the debates over admission to graduate education and training and to the professional schools. Yet no other issue trumps the controversy over undergraduate admissions, especially at the freshman level. This is as true at UC as at any other leading research universities, public and private, throughout the nation. But at UC it is an especially significant matter given the university's exacting standards for admission, the state's changing demographics, the generally contentious nature of California politics, and the exceptionally highly charged nature of higher education in California.

Every UC president from Kerr on has dealt with this issue. They still do. None has solved it, nor has the Board of Regents, nor will they. I was well aware of the history and the issues, and did the best I could, which was thought by some to be quite enough, others not enough, and others too much.

But this was an issue with which the president and chancellors and the regents were obliged to contend. And, I should add, they should have been obliged to contend. It was critically important to the long-term aspirations of all Californians, the particularized needs of the many minority communities, the provision of educated and trained people throughout our society, and the fulfillment of America's generalized hope and desire that talent should have its chance and that the opportunity for further education should be available to those who have prepared themselves and are willing to work for it.

In the early years of my administration I sought views, criticisms, advice, and impressions from an array of interested parties within the minority communities, the majority community, within and outside the university, and within state government, especially among the most concerned members of both houses of the state legislature. I informed myself of policies and practices elsewhere. I made certain that our student services and outreach programs were properly funded and staffed. Annual reports of our progress were made to the regents in open, public meetings, and great pains were taken to be certain that the media had the correct data and the whole picture. I addressed this issue in my remarks when appointed, in my inaugural address, in meetings throughout UC, in my speeches to service and alumni clubs and organizations, and in other ways, not only to demonstrate the sincerity of my interest but my commitment to it as well, and I did so throughout my tenure.

We were making solid but not spectacular progress from the early 1980s right up to and through the last year of my service as president, an average increase of 1 percent for each year in historically underrepresented minorities enrolling at UC. Some slippage followed, owing principally to the state's dramatic economic turn down in the first half of the 1990s.[3]

Asian American and Latino Complaints

In 1986 we suddenly came under sharp attack by California's Asian American community, especially in the San Francisco Bay Area, when UC was accused of discriminating against Asian Americans in its admissions policies and practices. These criticisms focused mostly on Berkeley's admissions practices for first-year students and arose for several reasons: the 1984 removal of Asian Americans from the target group of Berkeley's Educational Opportunity Program; UC's success in enrolling larger numbers of historically underrepresented minority students in the 1980s; an unexpected demand for UC by students graduating from California's secondary schools; and a percentage drop (not a numerical one) in the proportion of Asian Americans admitted to Berkeley in 1986, even though there had been a dramatic increase in the previous years both in applications and admissions of Asian American students to UC. (White students would have been as credibly concerned about the fairness of their admissions, but they had not organized either to protest or to litigate.)

With these charges of discrimination levied at Berkeley, and in a very public way, politics took over the debate: the state auditor general got in the act, studies by the Berkeley administration were undertaken, analyses were exhaustingly pursued, the legislature wanted to know what was going on, so did the public, and so did the regents. So did I.

These charges were the object of extensive national coverage. Everyone had an answer, no one had a solution. Political rhetoric soared in Sacramento about the unfairness of UC admissions policies, especially for Asian Americans, and the concomitant need for a redoubling of our efforts to enroll more historically underrepresented minorities, all this, of course without prejudice to any applicant regardless of race or ethnicity. Within this overheated climate, we tried to set out the facts. Here they are.

UC's freshmen admissions responded to the requirements of the California Master Plan for Higher Education, which fixed the pool of UC-eligible high school graduates at the top 12.5 percent of the state's high school graduates. At that time, students reached this goal by taking the courses required for admission, grades nine through twelve; by earning a 3.3 grade point average (B+) in the required courses taken grades ten through twelve; and by taking the SAT I (aptitude) and SAT II (achievement) tests. These requirements would qualify them for freshman admission on one of UC's eight undergraduate campuses, but not necessarily at their campus of first choice or in their major of preference. The SAT scores had meaning only as a further refinement when we reviewed applicants competing for freshman admission to a given campus or major. If a particular student's grade point average was less than 3.3, then a higher than average SAT score could offset the difference (there was an index that calculated all this). Alternatively, a poor score on the SAT I or SAT II could *not* keep a student otherwise academically eligible (through high school courses and a 3.3 GPA) out of UC.

Each campus administered its admissions programs under a broadly worded universitywide admissions policy the regents adopted in 1988.[4] In addition to the criteria noted above, it provided that campuses should admit the first 40 to 60 percent of the entering class strictly on the basis of the academic record: courses in high school, including extra credit for advanced placement courses and honors courses, grade point average, and SAT scores; the exact percentage would depend on the size and character of their applicant pool, the characteristics of the existing student body, and such other considerations as were thought to be pertinent to the admissions process for that year, campus by campus.

In considering students for the balance of the class to be admitted, all of whom needed to be UC eligible on academic grounds, we used additional criteria: we wanted students from every county in California, from the farms, suburbs, metropolitan areas, and inner cities; from different socioeconomic backgrounds; and from different races and ethnicities. We also wanted students with leadership promise and creative inclinations. We were not just admitting individual applicants. We were admitting a *class* that under our policy—and consistent with the master plan and prior legislative resolutions—was not to mirror but to *encompass* or take account of contemporary California's social and cultural diversity. Quotas were *never* part of this plan, and I was vigorously opposed to them. Each campus would assign a numerical weight to these "subjective" or nonacademic criteria, but with no single criterion outweighing the others.

In the middle to late 1980s UC enrollments were growing well beyond earlier expectations, Asian American applicants dramatically so, and black and Hispanic or Latino applications and enrollments were also steadily rising, as noted earlier. The competition for first-year undergraduate admission was especially intense at Berkeley and UCLA, and growing elsewhere within UC's eight undergraduate campuses.

In reporting to the regents on November 20, 1987, on the complaints then being registered by the Asian American community, I sought to make clear the dimensions and complexity of the problem being raised, not just for Asian Americans but for everyone, and predicted that the problem would be getting worse rather than better (as it surely did): the university was caught in an admissions trap that was really worse than the zero-sum situation I described to the regents—"the University can admit only a certain number of students, so if one group gains then another group will appear to lose"[5]— that looks at the issue from the simple mathematics of who has what percentage of the total 100 percent. Of course, from the numbers point of view it was zero sum. But from the social-psychological standpoint (using the logic of relative deprivation) it was a situation of every group feeling it was losing, no matter what. And I was also facing the social-psychological dimensions of this issue, not merely working with the numbers.

At about this time I met with several representatives of the Asian American community who had been pressing me for changes in our admissions policy, especially at Berkeley. Chancellor Heyman was present, at my request. The Asian American representatives argued against our use of *subjective* criteria—geographic, socioeconomic, racial—for the second round of freshmen admittees. "Is it not true," they asked, "that by adding these subjective criteria to the purely academic ones that fewer of our students are being admitted than would otherwise be the case if you instead relied only on the academic criteria?" I said yes and noted that a campus-by-campus analysis showed that their argument applied to Caucasians as well. Then I countered with a question: "Are you saying we should admit the entire class based solely on the objective academic record?" Though phrased ambiguously, their answer was "yes, except, of course, for underrepresented minorities."

I explained that UC's policies were essentially the same as other public and private universities of our kind around the country (though we sought to explain our policy and private universities didn't at all). But UC was admitting a *class,* not just *individuals,* and the class should bear some rough resemblance to the demographics of California's high school cohort. With 27,000 applicants who all met UC's basic admissions requirements seeking admission to Berkeley, 25 percent of them with perfect high school records, the freshman class of 3,500 would be nearly exclusively Asian Americans and Caucasians if we went strictly by academic records. I pointed out a simple fact: "There is a finite number of spaces to be filled on a given campus and when one is admitted others who want it just as badly are turned down."

I finally suggested that, as with beauty, fairness is in "the eye of the beholder." "We are doing the best we can," I said, "and we must be doing something right because everyone is mad at us."

I was not far off in making that comment, as within weeks I was meeting with representatives of the Latino or Hispanic communities. They had taken note of the Asian American arguments but felt the subjective criteria were fairer, because many of their young people had to change high schools three or four times a year as their families moved with the crops, and because of poverty, language problems, and low levels of parental education. They were arguing for proportional representation. "We are 26 percent of the state's population, and growing, and we expect to be 26 percent of the entering freshman class." As I did with the earlier group, I explained our admissions policies and practices in some detail and heard them out. The meeting ended cordially.

In summary, I am very proud of our progress in making UC a more diverse place, and pleased that the academic achievements of our entering students rose instead of falling. Yet the time was fraught with strong feelings and a sense of relative deprivation from virtually every racial and ethnic group on and off campus, not just the minorities. There is no solution to this problem, at least at the moment. California's graduating high school seniors still have large differential rates of UC eligibility by race and ethnicity, and each group starts from a different set of assumptions about what constitutes fairness.

The Weapons Labs

The second barrier concerned UC's half century of management of the government's nuclear weapons labs, the first at Los Alamos, New Mexico, and the second at Livermore, southeast of San Francisco Bay. The third, the Lawrence Berkeley National Lab, is on UC land in the Berkeley hills, adjacent to the campus. A source of concern for some during WWII when it was much involved in classified research, this lab then slowly decanted its classified weapons research to the Lawrence Livermore National Laboratory.

There had been no real controversy about the Berkeley lab for many years, but it was linked to the other two by way of the contract UC had with the U.S. Department of Energy (DOE) to manage all three. And, unlike other government-owned or contract-operated labs around the country, those at Los Alamos and Livermore were designing the nation's nuclear weaponry. Thus, we were lightning rods for antinuclear groups in the society and on the campuses who believed that the university should not manage these labs, as their purpose and work were fundamentally at odds with UC's cherished academic and intellectual freedoms and made the university complicit in a "morally repugnant" defense strategy.

The other side of the coin was that UC had helped found Los Alamos, and the university's scientists—among many others Lawrence, Oppenheimer, Teller, and Seaborg—led in developing the first atomic bomb and the others to come. Moreover, UC did 11 percent of the nation's basic research funded by the federal government, not counting the research at the national labs operated by UC, and it knew how to manage large-scale organized research better than any other university or government-owned laboratory. In accepting this management role, UC had made it consistently clear that it was doing so in the nation's service, our fee for managing the labs for nearly fifty years being very modest (approximately $12 million annually).

Nevertheless, UC's on-going management of the labs remained a major point of dispute within the university. The chancellors were not of one mind any more than the vice presidents or the regents were, or the faculty or staff, or the students, or the alumni.

Not only was the university's extended family at odds with itself but so too were members of the general public and, naturally, their elected representatives in the legislature. UC's president was the direct focus of forces on both sides of the debates. I had no confident position about the university's management role when appointed president in 1983, but I had to have one soon because the five-year contract was up for renewal in 1987, with UC obliged by 1985 to express its intention to renegotiate a renewal or not. I set about to learn all I could and as quickly as possible.

With help, my "education" on these matters proceeded apace. Within a matter of weeks after I took office Professor Edward Teller, former professor of physics at Berkeley, former director of the Lawrence Livermore Lab, then a senior fellow at Stanford's Hoover Institution, and especially known for the lead he played in developing the world's first hydrogen bomb, came to see me.

Teller wanted to be certain that I knew of UC's critical role in managing the labs. He hoped that I would be a stalwart in defending their work and UC's management role and told me that I could count on his support. He also took nearly one full hour to explain the missile defense system (known then as "star wars") that he had persuaded President Reagan to support, and the indispensable role the Los Alamos and Livermore labs had in its development. Teller was a formidable man, and age had not slowed him down. As our meeting concluded, I had greater insight into why people *on both sides* of these issues felt as strongly as they did.

My next visitor was Professor Glenn Seaborg, one of the world's leading twentieth-century scientists, Nobel laureate in chemistry, the co-discoverer of plutonium (on the Berkeley campus) and of several other elements in the periodic table of elements, including seaborgium, named in his honor. As noted in chapter 4, Seaborg and I had been friends for over a quarter of a century, first when he was chancellor at Berkeley, later as head of the Atomic Energy Commission under several U.S. presidents, and even later as a member of the National Commission on Excellence in Education.

In 1983 Seaborg was chairing Berkeley's Lawrence Hall of Science. He was a force to be reckoned with at Berkeley and one to be welcomed at our side on any number of issues of interest to the state legislature, such as research policy, graduate education, science policy, teaching load issues, and especially on matters affecting the national labs.

Seaborg was a strong proponent of UC's management of all three labs, not as much for the university's sake as for the nation's security. His arguments were uncomplicated and straightforward: no one else, he believed, could do as good a job, and the job had better be done as well as the country could do it. Scientists, he said, would come to these labs and not to others, because here they were UC employees. Moreover, the labs offered multiple opportunities for campus-based faculty and graduate students to engage in the labs' cutting-edge, *unclassified* basic research in environmental, public health, and other research arenas. The directors of the labs were appointed by the regents on the recommendation of UC's president and reported to him, and not to a political appointee, another advantage of UC management, Seaborg pointed out. He concluded by noting that the labs assumed a critical role in securing the nation's defense in a dangerous world, and that fact could not merely be wished away by those who found fault with the work of the labs and UC's management of them.

I took Seaborg's views as my point of departure in exploring the pros and cons of this arrangement. I discussed it with key figures at the labs, in government, various nonprofit organizations, or associations of one kind or another, including clergy, and members of the faculty, staff, and administration both within and outside UC.

The first real decision I had to make about this issue came in 1984, when the director of Los Alamos Lab, Donald Kerr, chose to step down from his position. It fell to me to recommend his replacement not only to the regents but also to the secretary of the Department of Energy, John Herrington, whose concurrence was required.

Secretary Herrington sent a list of a dozen names to me for consideration. These were scientists with lab and/or government experience, steeped in the work, and possessing a deep knowledge of U.S. nuclear defenses. They were all highly respected people but were also in their sixties and up. I thought we should reach down in the organization for fresher faces and new ideas, and at the very least to compare them with those suggested by the secretary.

Senior Vice President William Frazer, a professor of theoretical physics from the San Diego campus, was of inestimable help in the search and in meeting our oversight role of these labs as well. Frazer knew the labs, and had, as did I, the clearances necessary to know of the work going on and why we were doing it.

I asked him to seek out some younger candidates from the lab itself or from Berkeley or Livermore for us to consider along with the names offered by the secretary of DOE. Sig Hecker emerged, a highly respected materials scientist at Los Alamos in his early forties. Herrington had been initially taken aback by our recommendation but on meeting Hecker came around quickly and enthusiastically. The regents appointed Hecker as the new director, where he served until the mid-1990s with great distinction. He was a major player in helping the nation's policymakers devise the security policies and posture of the United States during these years. He also had a lead part in advising the Russians on how to reduce their nuclear arsenal pursuant to agreements reached between Russia and the United States after the collapse of the Soviet Union and the end of the cold war in the early 1990s.

The results of my inquiries and growing acquaintance with the labs persuaded me that Seaborg was essentially correct in his analysis. But it was in a way a grudging conclusion. I knew how prickly the DOE could be, how bureaucratic it truly was, how much time this would consume, not only for me but for Frazer and Ronald Brady as well (Brady negotiated the contracts with DOE and worked with their respective administrators; Frazer oversaw the scientific work).

The directors of the three labs reported to me, and that also took time. So did the protests registered on almost a weekly basis by those who wanted us to end our management role. Most of these protests were entirely within the law and, I should add, within the bounds of civility as well. They occurred at nearly every meeting of the Board of Regents, outside my offices in Berkeley every Wednesday, and often in Sacramento or elsewhere when I was testifying or appearing. Some regents were also unfriendly toward our management role, although a decided majority favored it, as did the governor.

I concluded that while the nation was well served by our management of the labs, UC's interests were on balance not, though in the larger scheme of things our concerns were mere inconveniences measured against the magnitude and significance of our contributions to the nation's defense and strategic security requirements.

The DOE appeared at the first negotiating session in 1985, following the regents' decision to renew the contract, with a stack of brand new contracts intending to free the DOE from limitations on its oversight role that had been embodied in all the previous ones. I asked Brady to advise DOE's negotiators that we were not in a position to start over and to explain that these matters were hard enough for a new UC president to deal with in any case. To seek to rewrite the contract in ways that would be perceived as shifting authority for some aspects of the management from UC to the DOE would undermine the already tenuous hold I had on this entire relationship. We prevailed.

The need to negotiate a renewal of these contracts arose once again five years later, in 1990. Admiral James Watkins, former chief of the nation's nuclear submarine forces, former chief of naval operations, and a fine man, was serving as secretary of DOE. At that point the entrenched bureaucratic forces within DOE and certain congressional interests were actively pushing for DOE *not* to renew UC's contract but to invite others to bid on it, along with UC, of course.

We had heard rumors to this effect for some time. Sure enough, I received a call from Admiral Watkins in early 1991, shortly after the regents' decision to enter into negotiations with DOE to renew the contracts. He said the DOE had decided to place the contracts for managing the three national labs out for bid. He then explained the political pressure he was under from the Congress, whose constituencies were in some instances pressing for this outcome as they wanted the business. These included nonprofit research institutes, and various consortia of universities. The purpose of his call, he said, was to give me a heads-up before the matter was officially decided and/or before the press reported it.

I stated that if in his considered judgment as secretary of DOE a change would strengthen the country's strategic defense position, then that is what he should do. But I pointed out that for the Berkeley lab, being both a special case and so woven into the fabric of Berkeley's scientific and creative endeavors, the contract should unquestionably remain with UC. As to the labs at Los Alamos and Livermore, however, I added, "UC would register no objection to his decision" (there might, of course, be others who object, e.g., the governor, certain regents, congressmen, and so forth), but he should also know that "the university would *not* be among those bidding to manage the two labs."

He was shocked, thinking, I believe, that this was a mere ruse to provoke his reconsideration. It was not. As I told him, "UC had managed these labs as a public service for nearly fifty years. We had done so with only the most nominal financial consideration, had endured on-going, even growing, controversy about our role, on campus and off, and that we could not possibly be seen as chasing after the business. It simply wouldn't do, and he should neither misunderstand nor miscalculate our intentions."

His answer was to the effect that DOE would therefore not place the contracts out for bid, that too much of the nation's defense rested on these contracts with UC to disturb them now. He said he would require some time "to work" the matter at DOE and in the Congress before this judgment could be publicly confirmed. When in Washington shortly thereafter, I discussed the matter with the White House chief of staff, Don Regan, who confirmed what Watkins had told me.

Watkins was as good as his word and in July 1991 announced DOE's intention to negotiate with UC for the renewal of the contracts by September 1992. The contracts were finally renewed by the regents in November 1992, after a slight delay owing to my retirement on September 30, 1992.

When it came to the matter of UC's management of the national labs, I had received plenty of advice, as had my predecessors: special faculty committees, for example, the 1969 Zinner committee, the 1977 Gerberding committee, the 1985 Littlejohn committee, and the 1990 Jendreson committee, all except the last affirming their support for UC's management (a majority of the Jendreson committee had urged a termination of the arrangement over time). I also had the ongoing advice of my Scientific and Academic Advisory Committee, comprised of some of the nation's leading scientists and arms control experts. And at each regents' meeting just before the key decision dates we heard from a parade of persons testifying before the regents.

There were subtleties to the management of these labs that received much less attention than the grosser forms of expressed support or opposition, subtleties best expressed by Seaborg and Herbert York, former chancellor at UC San Diego, a distinguished American scientist and leading arms control expert and negotiator for the U.S. government, who also at this time headed my Scientific and Academic Advisory Committee. York's comments came at the Board of Regents meeting of June 15, 1990, when this issue was once again being hotly debated:

> During the Reagan administration, government officials, including President Reagan, believed that the Soviet Union was cheating on the threshold test ban. The laboratory directors repeatedly testified before Congress and elsewhere that there was no evidence to support that conclusion; Professor York noted that this was done without fear of reprisal from the government. More recently, the laboratory directors have taken very definite public positions relating to

nuclear weapon safety, in direct opposition to views held within the Department of Defense. Professor York also recalled the tremendous amount of controversy surrounding the Strategic Defense Initiative and the fact that long-time members of the Lawrence Livermore National Laboratory had taken positions strongly promoting this strategy. In response, a group of scientists, including many representatives from the University of California and the laboratories, issued a report opposing the initiative; these scientists have retained their relationships with the laboratories, without fear of censorship. He noted that this is due in large part to the policies and procedures of the University of California in its management of the laboratories.[6]

In the end I found the views of Seaborg, York, Frazer, Teller, and many others more persuasive than arguments to sever the arrangement. In arriving at this conclusion, I also knew I would be subject to intense criticism; and I was. As I summarized my thinking about the labs for the regents on September 20, 1990, I recommended that we once again enter into negotiations for the renewal of these contracts but seek to improve our oversight. And with the pending close of the cold war, I proposed that we take a more aggressive position with the DOE so as to include a higher proportion of non-classified research in its budgets for the labs:

I also am persuaded by the conviction of the nation's policy makers that the laboratories over the years have served the vital interests of the United States, contributed to the preservation of peace, and helped advance the cause of democracy and individual liberty throughout the world. Since World War II, the security of the United States has depended in no small measure on the committed and competent work performed by our scientists and engineers at these laboratories.

The excellence of the scientific and technical staff is remarkable by any standard and derives principally from UC's management. The University's management of the laboratories is, therefore, performed as a service to the nation, even though it yields no significant monetary rewards, requires considerable time and effort of the University's management, and, often occasions criticism both from within and outside the University. It surely would be easier both for this Board and for the University's management were we not to accept this responsibility. We do so, however, in response to the nation's call, and in recognition of the special role this University can play in securing our nation's independence and the freedoms from which flow both the civil liberties we all enjoy and the academic freedoms so crucial to the work of our university and others like it. . . .

The significant changes taking place in the Soviet Union and Eastern Europe and the concomitant easing of East-West tensions open the possibility for material redirection in the [Livermore and Los Alamos] programs. This rapid realignment among nations has presented the University a unique opportunity to assume a broader and more beneficial role in the management of the laboratories. It would be particularly ironic to relinquish the University's management responsibilities at the very time we are able to bring the full benefit of the University's ability to bear on the range of new programs and research initiatives that will be developing, e.g., the nation's need to develop a secure, sufficient and reliable supply of energy; remedy significant environmental matters; secure advances in biological and bio-medical sciences; and enhanced national economic competitiveness.[7]

Over time the scientific, engineering, and technical talent at the labs, the sophistication, depth, and breadth of their equipment and facilities, and the half century of UC oversight will surely yield dividends well beyond the defense-related contributions achieved during WWII and the era of the cold war. I believe this would be a shared goal by all those who have contended over this issue, one with another, these many years.

California Public Interest Research Group

The third barrier to be recalled in this chapter, the extended conflict between the university's administration and Board of Regents on the one hand and on the other the California Public Interest Research Group (CALPIRG), was one in which many students, legislators, environmentalists, and consumer advocates had a significant interest.

Several states had their own counterparts to this organization, and college and university students were the "foot soldiers" for the various public advocacy and public policy issues it pursued. CALPIRG was a private, nonprofit incorporated entity, wholly independent of the colleges and universities from which it drew many of its workers and volunteers. It was free of any accountability whatsoever to those institutions that agreed to collect much of the money on which CALPIRG depended, at the state and national level alike. Many people perceived it as having a significant role to play in the environmental movement, in an array of other socially sensitive issues, such as those of special interest to Ralph Nader, the country's best-known consumer advocate, and in the political campaigns of legislators whose purposes and policies were consistent with those pursued by CALPIRG.

In mid-1987 I received a note from Regent Dean Watkins, sharing a letter he had just received from Consumer Alert, a Modesto, California–based nonprofit organization, which called Watkins's attention to the method used to collect membership fees for CALPIRG from UC students enrolled at Santa Cruz, Santa Barbara, Berkeley, and UCLA. The method was a negative checkoff system: it collected students' "contributions" to CALPIRG unless students chose not to pay them. Unlike a positive checkoff, in which students paid only when they acted to do so, the negative checkoff meant that students automatically paid unless they acted *not* to do so. For example, those four campuses required all students to pay certain university fees as a condition of enrolling in and being admitted to courses. Along with these *mandatory* university fees, the fee card included an amount for CALPIRG in the total dollars to be paid *unless* students indicated a desire not to contribute to CALPIRG and deducted the specific amount from the listed total of mandatory fees (or if they paid the listed total, they could request a refund from the appropriate university office).

On learning that the arrangement persisted, Watkins urged me to issue a "cease and desist" order. Orders, of course, are a last resort in a university setting, as they tend to induce something of a boomerang effect when tried. I decided to find out what I could about this matter before doing anything.

The student services office provided me with the details, and even though the formats and procedures varied slightly from campus to campus, the essence of it was that UC was collecting money from its students by means of a negative checkoff and remitting it to CALPIRG (less nominal administrative costs incurred by UC). CALPIRG used it for its varied purposes without any accounting to the university that I could trace even though the terms of the UC-CALPIRG agreement did require such an accounting.

The regents had rejected the arrangement in the late 1960s, but Saxon had approved it in 1976. Since then, procedures for collecting the fee had been put to a vote of the students on four campuses, at one time or another, and had been approved by them as well. Nevertheless, the arrangement troubled me. I had rejected a similar proposal at the University of Utah many years earlier by the Utah counterpart of CALPIRG. Why, I wondered, did this organization rely on a negative checkoff instead of the positive checkoff that all other nonprofits, charities, or churches seeking voluntary contributions from their supporters or members used?

The answer was obvious. They got more money this way. It was not worth the bother to seek a $2 or $3 refund, or to read the small print on the fee card. Or perhaps students or parents simply didn't read the fee card and its bill of particulars, looked at the bottom line, and wrote a check accordingly. Carelessness also counted. I thought it odd that an organization given over to social advocacy and consumer interests should find a more indirect than forthright way to collect its own money.

Before I got around to doing anything about it, Chancellor Heyman at Berkeley asked me to put the matter on the Council of Chancellors meeting scheduled for September 2, 1987. The ensuing discussion was fascinating. Five chancellors whose campuses did not have this arrangement didn't want it, and the chancellors of the four campuses that had it didn't like it. Yet none wanted to do anything about it, the first group for fear that it would stimulate a drive to expand the practice across UC, and the second from concern at the irritation that this issue, if raised, would engender. Ergo we did nothing.

Two years later I received another letter from Regent Watkins, in which he forwarded a copy of a letter from a UCLA student objecting to UCLA's practices in collecting this fee and once again asked that the matter be investigated. I replied that I would review the practice with the chancellors. For the same reasons as before, the chancellors were still reluctant to do anything about the negative checkoff. Someone pointed out that it was not illegal (a pretty weak defense, in my view). But I took note of the more determined if unorganized student effort, at least at UCLA, to do something about this practice.

At the next COC meeting on December 6, 1989, the majority of the chancellors and I concluded that the issue was of sufficient concern to warrant a more complete analysis. We would devise a broad universitywide policy on collecting voluntary fees from UC students and would ask the regents to approve it.

Now that the wheels were in motion, it didn't take long for the counterforces to react. Letters began to come in, mostly from legislators sitting on the committees of crucial interest to UC's budget and related matters, troubled that *we* were troubled by the negative checkoff. In similar phrasing they extolled the virtues of CALPIRG and equated the loss of a negative checkoff with the loss of CALPIRG funds in their entirety: we were "defunding" CALPIRG, they alleged. They urged me to back off and leave the matter to the students, campus by campus.

None of us had called CALPIRG's virtues into question or objected to a positive checkoff method to fund the organization. But since we were collecting money from students, we were responsible for the design and use of the university's registration fee card. Once again we found ourselves in the arena of political spin, misrepresentation, conclusions drawn from one set of facts applied to another. Headlines in some student newspapers, for example, trumpeted any change in the method of fee collection as causing a total loss of funding for CALPIRG, though no other organization anywhere within UC relied on a negative checkoff for voluntary student contributions.

After the first alarm sounded, the issue turned partisan in Sacramento, with pleadings from Democratic legislators to keep the negative checkoff and from Republicans to end it. So much for nonpartisan social advocacy. And the tone of the letters changed to one of suggesting that "we" and "they" had much more important issues to deal with than the "small matter" of how fees were being collected for CALPIRG on UC campuses. I thought to myself that if this was true why are *they* spending so much time on it?

As the winter term moved forward, it was clear to me that this issue had been blown entirely out of proportion. While doing what we could to temper the more extreme expressions, our discussions with the students proceeded apace as we sought common ground. By early March I concluded that the chancellors on the four campuses having CALPIRG fees should work together, with their student governments and representatives of CALPIRG, to find a new approach that would take us out of the political cauldron.[8]

By summer 1990 the controversy was in full swing: the legislature included language in the budget act for UC directing that I not take this matter to the regents for a decision but continue CALPIRG's negative checkoff. I found this to be absolutely astonishing! It is the regents' job, not the legislators or mine, to decide on fees that students should pay and the method of collecting them. This egregious example of unconstitutional legislative microman-agement came on behalf of an organization with nothing whatsoever to do with the university. CALPIRG was a privately incorporated nonprofit entity. Its only link to UC was that UC students were involved in CALPIRG's leg-islative programs and the campaigns of legislators they supported—the two major political parties could as easily make comparable claims.[9]

Letters were coming now from the lieutenant governor of California, Leo McCarthy, and from members of Congress, among others Ronald Dellums. It was the most intense political effort to influence UC on what was basi-cally an internal matter that I had observed during my nearly ten years as UC's president, divestment excepted. And as the Board of Regents was plan-ning to consider and act on the issue in September, a flurry of letters ar-rived, including one to me by Ralph Nader under date of September 19, the day before the regents' meeting and the first communication I had received from him.

The general thrust of Nader's somewhat rambling and untidy message was to assert UC's intention to destroy CALPIRG indirectly through the fund-ing mechanism. He compared the board's pending decision with adminis-trative actions in the 1960s that had provoked a free speech movement and wondered why, in the face of UC's many problems, we should be spending so much time on this matter. He even recalled, with no little resentment, my unfriendly response to the proposal for a negative checkoff in Utah years before. And finally, he observed, this would be my decision even more than the regents', and my responsibility in the months ahead.[10]

The regents considered this entire matter at length on September 20 and 21, 1990. After reviewing its history, along with the procedures for collec-tion on all four campuses, and listening to the views of CALPIRG's repre-sentatives and others, they decided against negative checkoffs for *any* pur-pose in the collection of student fees. The board did authorize the use of a positive checkoff consistent with regulations to be promulgated by the cam-puses. I recounted the outcome to Nader by letter on October 4 and enclosed for his information the copy of an editorial from the UC Santa Barbara stu-dent newspaper that disagreed with his view (the student newspaper at Berke-ley also vigorously opposed it).[11]

Nader then appealed to California's attorney general, John K. Van de Kamp, to investigate the regents' denial of CALPIRG's right to use a negative checkoff system to collect fees from UC students for its programs. He suggested that CALPIRG's support of Proposition 128, the "Big Green Initiative," had influenced UC's policy decision, but as no evidence existed to support his complaint, the attorney general set the complaint aside.

As we moved into 1991, the issue continued to fester. Legislators who were supported or otherwise helped by CALPIRG, both with their interests and in their campaigns, wanted to punish me for having raised the issue (in fact, students and a nonprofit consumer rights' organization had raised it). Or they wanted the issue just to go away. It didn't, so they threatened in the Assembly version of the 1991–92 UC budget bill to cut $1 million from my administrative operations unless UC and CALPIRG reached an agreement before June 30, 1991.

On June 5 I addressed this matter in a letter to the legislature's Joint Conference Committee on the Budget. The critical portions follow:

> Last fall, the Regents adopted a policy requiring that any mechanism used for collecting voluntary fees from students as part of UC's registration process be in the form of a voluntary, positive check-off in order to give students a clear and unmistakable choice voluntarily to pay *nonmandatory* fees. . . .
>
> The use of the Registration Fee card is a matter of internal UC governance and, therefore, fully within the Regents' scope of authority. Thus, we regard the action proposed by the Assembly as inconsistent with the spirit and letter of the Constitution and, therefore, purely punitive in nature. The transfer of $1 million from the Office of the President to student financial aid would require the layoff of approximately 25 people in the Office of the President. This is a consequence that is completely irrelevant to an honest disagreement over how most fairly to collect voluntary fees from UC students.
>
> It is worth noting that CALPIRG is a private, nonprofit California corporation. The university exerts no influence over CALPIRG's organization, structure, purposes, or expenditures. I find it to be unprecedented, therefore, that a private corporation has persuaded the Assembly subcommittee responsible for acting on UC's budget to take this action because of the university's unwillingness to collect fees from its students in ways deemed by the Regents to be deceptive and for the benefit of this private corporation. Indeed, the Assembly's action raises, in my view, very significant public policy issues.[12]

This threat was never effectuated, but efforts at compromise on the checkoff seemed to be at a standstill. Our proposals to the local CALPIRG representatives would seem at first to take hold and then shortly thereafter be rejected. Unless something more was at stake, I felt sure the matter would have been settled long before. This assumption was confirmed when Nader came visiting in late September 1991.

I knew Nader and his sister, Laura Nader, a professor of anthropology at Berkeley and a leader in the anti–weapons labs group, slightly because we had mutual friends in Berkeley. My meeting with him lasted about an hour and a half. Even though we had clear and straightforward differences on the CALPIRG issue, our talk was cordial. I did what I could to persuade him that his earlier assumptions about our motives and intentions or our perceived distaste for CALPIRG's bent on social and political issues were entirely without foundation.

He seemed more ready to believe me than when we had last corresponded, but funding for this organization was a concern that for him tended to subordinate every other consideration. He insisted on the fact that the students had voted to put this arrangement into place and argued that neither the regents nor I had any right to revoke it. In turn, I observed that some students voted for it, and some years back, and asked what, in any event, distinguished the worthiness of CALPIRG's endeavors from those of other worthwhile and useful efforts carried on by the Salvation Army, Catholic Charities, the American Red Cross, or the American Cancer Society, and others like them. They, like any other nonprofit I knew about, had to persuade people to make a positive decision to contribute voluntarily, in stark contrast to the plan CALPIRG insisted on for itself.

Nader's answer was roughly as follows: the alternatives would cost them money, and if UC did manage to put a positive checkoff in place of the negative, it would be a contagious act and most likely spread throughout the country. In closing, he noted that he had heard rumors that I might possibly be stepping down as president owing to my wife's death earlier in the year. And if so, for me to leave with the regents' reputation and mine in a shambles would be too bad. Nader said flatly that the regents and I had declared political war on CALPIRG and that he was declaring political war on us.

As 1991 moved into 1992 this issue persisted, though with some positive exchange of ideas. But with the pending conclusion of the 1992 legislature as we came into summer, there was another flurry of letters pressuring us to keep the waivable fee. At this point my patience was nearly exhausted, and so was I. I was leaving office on September 30 and seemed unable to close on a solution.

A letter to me from Assemblyman Robert Campbell, who chaired the state assembly's key committee hearing our budget, put the burden of finding a solution on UC and complained of our "inaction." I wrote to him on September 4 to protest the charge:

> This is not a matter of "inaction"; rather it is a matter of fundamental disagreement, as you well know. You attribute to the University "a lack of visible results" as though the burden is entirely on the University for there not being an agreement. It takes two parties to agree. CALPIRG is one of the parties and we are the other. We are seeking to discover an arrangement to which both parties can agree. CALPIRG has made its proposals, we have made ours; and we continue to discuss them.[13]

My final involvement in this seemingly endless controversy came on the same day as I answered Campbell, in the form of a letter to the chancellors. I sent them each a copy of my proposed guidelines for implementing the voluntary student fee pledge with CALPIRG and referred the matter to the president-designate, who took office October 1. In the ensuing months these guidelines proved to be the basis on which the campuses effectuated agreements with CALPIRG; but it occurred under Peltason's presidency, not under mine. It provided, in short, that all first-year students wishing to contribute to CALPIRG—or to any comparably qualified organization—could ask that their contribution be included on the registration fee card for the time they were enrolled at UC, unless revoked by them subsequently. Thus, a positive decision to contribute was required, but students did not have to make that election each time they paid fees. I thought this was reasonable enough.

To this day I know of nothing I could have done to conclude the controversy before leaving office other than to accede to CALPIRG's demands. This I would not do. I regarded this funding scheme as a deliberately deceptive means to raise money in which the university had come to be a complicitous partner. Far from wishing to harm student rights, I regarded myself then and now as having *championed their* rights. If I had done nothing about the issue, UC would have continued to participate in a ruse to raise money from them for CALPIRG without students' having chosen affirmatively to contribute. CALPIRG, and those who fought so hard to keep the waivable fee, in my view, were hypocritical at best and cynical at worst.

The fourth and final barrier presented substantive moral challenges to the university, unlike those of CALPIRG, whose demands on the university were just political and self-serving.

Divestment

The issue of *divestment* brought demands that the regents dispose of any equities, bonds, or other securities held in UC's investment portfolio of companies "doing business" in South Africa. These demands arose because of the South African government's policy of apartheid that most of the international community had condemned for many years and that persons of all races and ethnic groups within South Africa had challenged for its gross discrimination against nonwhites and mainly black South Africans in education, employment, housing, government services, and civil rights in general.

Most people in the United States roundly condemned this policy. America's black citizens felt a particular abhorrence for apartheid, given their own history in the New World. Black and civil rights advocates in the United States, therefore, had taken a proactive role in seeking economic and diplomatic sanctions on South Africa by the U.S. government, the global corporate community, and other major institutions in our country, including our leading colleges and universities.

As recently as the mid-1970s, these forces had found potentially fruitful support in America's universities and colleges whose investment policies they were seeking to influence, either by "cleansing" the portfolios of companies doing business in South Africa or, failing that, by imposing nondiscrimination policies on companies implicated through their South African operations.

The University of California's first official encounter with these forces was in 1977, when the regents were requested to divest their holdings in such companies (most of which derived 1 to 3 percent of their revenues from South African operations). To do so at that time would have required the sale of 50 percent of the equities and over 40 percent of the bond holdings in UC's portfolio, plus transactional costs, and would have left a much reduced pool of securities subsequently qualified for UC's acquisition. The board declined to do so and cited its duty as a fiduciary of the endowments, pensions, and other trust funds whose assets were the regents' responsibility to invest for the well-being of the beneficiaries, be they retirees, faculty members with endowed chairs, students with scholarships, fellowships, or loans, creditors for UC's debts, or others.

UC's general counsel, Don Reidhaar, also advised members of the board in 1977 that, in his opinion, any action to divest ran the risk of the regents' breaching their fiduciary duty under pertinent state laws. Regental actions short of divestment were however available to the regents, should they wish to consider them.[14]

Other universities in the United States were also being asked to divest. Some did and some did not, with the legal interpretations of fiduciary duty, it would seem, depending on the ideological inclinations of lawyers and the courts, as well as on the members of the universities' governing boards and their administrations. The legal basis for divesting or not divesting came to seem more elastic than earlier supposed.

The first hint that this issue would again appear on a regents' agenda was evident in early fall 1984, when inquiries regarding UC's previous actions on this issue were being made of my office, of the general counsel, and of the treasurer. Individual regents were also asking about it (especially those who had not been serving in 1977), and the student newspapers were active in discussing this issue in their news sections and op-ed columns. I was neither experienced nor knowledgeable about apartheid or South Africa or the extent and character of U.S. corporate operations there.

Fred Gaines, a law school student at UCLA, had been elected by the regents in fall 1984 to a seat on the Board of Regents as the voting representative of the student body from all nine campuses. He was determined to engage UC in a debate on the divestment issue. The South African government was cracking down on dissenters within the country with renewed intensity.

Protests against the system were becoming more violent and widespread. The advocates of apartheid in South Africa's ruling party, while very much still in control, appeared to be more on the defensive than earlier. And as the issue heated up in the United States, the advocates for divestment were adopting a more aggressive tone and were becoming a more insistent factor in U.S. domestic politics.

Gaines advised me of his intentions in fall 1984 and asked that I calendar this item for the January 18, 1985, meeting of the Board of Regents. I would not agree to do so, however, as it was my practice not to place any item before the regents without evident cause and until my colleagues and I had examined the matter ourselves, as noted earlier. I would have responded to any other regent the same way.

Gaines then sought direct regental support for a reconsideration of UC's investment policies at the January 1985 meeting, having worked the more liberal members of the board between meetings. He proposed that the treasurer give the regents at least three options on investment to consider at their June meeting, along with an analysis of the regents' record of socially responsible investing, the shareholder proxy voting system, and the activities of other institutional investors with holdings in South Africa.[15]

I remember observing in the course of the debate that the regents' approval of this motion would also be a decision to commit a substantial portion of the university's administrative time and energy to this task, rather than to other UC matters. But I said I would not object if they believed this issue rose to as high a level of priority as Gaines was proposing. The motion passed unanimously, with seventeen regents present, the last unanimous vote the board would cast on this matter in the ensuing eighteen turbulent months. Here is another example of how easy it is to get into a situation and how unexpectedly hard it is to get out of it.

With the decision of the board to revisit this issue, the politics commenced, with much skill and forethought by the students and faculty members who were giving it shape and direction. If one was *not* for divestment, then one must surely be *for* apartheid. This was a standard and well tested political strategy to drive out the middle, demonize those at the opposite end, and delegitimize any real discussion of either the South African situation or the basis of any corporation's decision to remain in South America or to depart. It also tended to preclude any discussion of alternatives to divestment that fell short of "full divestment now," which was argued principally as a moral act when it was at its core a political one.

This strategy eventually worked, of course, because the political approach when exerted principally from within paralyzes as it also corrupts the intellectual process and the academic norms and values of the university, just as the FSM and Vietnam War protests of a generation earlier did and the debates over UC's admissions policies do today. By politicization I mean the substitution of a fixed view for an inquiring one, and of implicitly coercive means for persuasive ones.

UC had been softened up by such tactics in the 1960s and was therefore more accepting of the divestment protests in the mid-1980s: to "persuade" if possible, to "harass" where necessary, to "intimidate" as needed, and to "coerce" as required those who sought to have a broader discussion of this matter or to entertain any view other than the single-minded approach taken by those leading this movement.

I was determined, regardless of what the politics proved to be, that I would do everything within my authority to consider this issue fairly, thoroughly, at our own pace, and in ways consistent with the norms of both academic life and the expectations of our governing board. Thus I scheduled a series of meetings in the winter and spring of 1985, at both special and regularly scheduled meetings of the Board of Regents, to allow the advocates *for* and *against* divestment to be heard. We heard from persons who were expert on South African affairs, gave the regents ample opportunity for debate among themselves, and informed them about their legal, fiscal, and investment duties and options, including potential conflicts of interest. I was also resolved to carry on these discussions in an environment as free from disruption as possible.

If I may understate it, those who would subordinate any process or oppose any delay to the ends they were seeking did not welcome my intervention. I couldn't help how they felt, but I could do what we had decided to do. It was not easy, as during the next several months our daughter Lisa, an undergraduate student at UC Davis, was threatened with kidnapping and I was required to have security for most of the time whenever I was on campus, and often at home as well.

Knowing that there would be major ongoing protests over this issue within UC, just as there were at most major universities from 1984–86, I advised Vice President Brady, who was responsible for security, to proceed as follows: "if the protests are on campus, it is the chancellor's responsibility to deal with them. If they occur at our offices then we have an affirmative obligation to protect those protesting from their detractors, and the reverse, so long as the protesters and detractors are acting in accordance with the university's time, manner, and place regulations *and* so long as they are within the bounds of applicable laws. If they were violating either, they should be subject to university discipline in the first instance and/or to civil authority in the second. And if the call was close, err on the side of a more generous rather than a more strict interpretation of the applicable rules, codes or statutes." In other words, protect the protesters and their detractors in their civil rights and cite and/or arrest them when they, or their detractors, violate the rights of others. And that is what we did.

I never worried one minute about those instructions, as I thought them to be eminently fair, even though many arrests eventually occurred (over one thousand outside my office alone in an eighteen-month period). Violations of our student code and of the law proved to be overwhelmingly non-violent, at least by our students. The usual crowd of persons off-campus, especially at UCLA, San Francisco, and Berkeley, however, showed up to make trouble whatever the object of student concern. In the process they exploited both our students and UC and—in the depictions of these protests on nightly TV—confounded the public about who were students and who were not.

I was also aware that UC was to be a very important test case, as were the Ivy League schools, Stanford, and select others in Texas, the Midwest, and the Northwest. Thus we settled in for what we knew was to be unrelenting and unforgiving political pressure from some of our students and many of the faculty, from Democrats in the legislature, and from large numbers of our alumni as well. Through the remainder of the 1984–85 academic year regents' board meetings were attended by vigorous protests. Individual regents were the object of intense lobbying, as was I. All our actions throughout the winter and spring, as we moved toward the June 21, 1985, decision date, were thought worthy of prominent coverage by the media. Three or four incidents will help illustrate the scene.

The student organizations leading the movement for "full divestment now" were clustered, not exclusively, but primarily at Berkeley. The Berkeley student organizers had scheduled a forum on South African investments for the Berkeley campus on April 24, from 1:00 P.M. to 4:00 P.M. The regents, including key administrative officers in my office and I, received written invitations to attend. I thought we should be there, wrote to the regents on April 22, 1985, to that effect, and followed the letter up with a phone call urging them to accept, to be present, and to participate, as appropriate. Nearly half the board came, and on short notice and to their credit. The forum was held in Harmon Gym (Berkeley's well loved basketball pavilion with poor acoustics). All things considered, it went pretty well. The regents and I were seated in the front row of the audience, not on the platform, which I thought both fair and to be preferred in any event.

As it was getting under way, I remembered that Lieutenant Governor McCarthy was coming and had saved him a seat next to me. When he got there somewhat after the starting time, the crowd was stamping its feet rhythmically on the wooden bleachers, evidencing support for divestment. Several thousand students stamping their feet in an old barnlike structure, on fragile wooden bleachers, made quite a din. The lieutenant governor appeared to be somewhat shaken by the noise and the scene in general. I waved him over and said, "Relax, Leo, think of this as though it were a basketball game." He laughed and then settled down.

The speakers, of course, were all prodivestment. This was not so much a forum as a rally, and the students seemingly appreciated the presence of so many regents. Without prior notice three or four regents were asked to speak, the first two favoring divestment. Their comments were received with thunderous applause. The next speaker opposed divestment. His comments were received with thunderous boos. The fourth speaker was Regent Jack Henning, longtime leader of California's AFL-CIO, a formidable orator, an intelligent and knowledgeable man, an excellent regent, and a person I had come to admire. His remarks too were warmly received by the audience as he favored divestment.

But before Henning sat down, he gave the students a lesson I hoped they would remember. He acknowledged the warmth of student reaction to his comments but also took account of the remarks of the regent who had just preceded him, who had been so vigorously booed and heckled. Henning then said that the sponsors had invited the regents to attend the forum as their guests. And by definition a forum meant that several views would be explored, not just those with which the students agreed. Thus, to boo and attempt to shout down views at odds with their own was wrong. Henning concluded, "in my business, when we have an agreement with management, we live by it; we don't break it, and they owed the regent to whom they had been so rude an apology." After a few moments' silence, stunned silence, I should note, a general and warm applause rippled with increasing intensity throughout the audience.

My invited comments were brief. "I am reserving my final views until I am confident of holding them," I said. Then I told them about what I had been reading and those with whom I had been speaking and from whom I was seeking advice; I described what the regents were doing to learn what they could about this issue and summarized what remained to be done before the June 21 decision date. My comments were not welcomed, but I received somewhat more muted expressions of unhappiness than had the regent who had earlier opposed divestment.

In the course of the protests during spring 1985 Bishop Desmond Tutu of South Africa, a well-known, indeed quite famous figure in the fight for human rights in South Africa, visited California for a series of student-sponsored prodivestment lectures on several UC campuses. He is a thoughtful, intelligent, and kind person whose moral core is as strong as it is steady. He finished his visit with a speech to the California State Legislature, which I viewed on TV. Speaker Brown and Bishop Tutu then appeared at a press conference, also well covered by TV news. Willie Brown commended the bishop for his appearance, his message, and his cause. Then, holding a Coca-Cola can in one hand, he brought it down hard on the lectern, observing as he did that he "would never have another Coke until the Coca-Cola company had withdrawn from its South African operations."

The president of Stanford, Don Kennedy, and I had earlier arranged to meet with Tutu in Los Angeles the following day to discuss the divestment issue with him personally. As the meeting got under way, the secretary came into the room (this was at the famed Melvin Belli's law offices in Los Angeles) and asked what we wished to drink. Kennedy said, "I'll have a mineral water," I asked for the same, Mrs. Tutu, who was also with us, had something else, and the good bishop said, "I'll have a Coke." With some amazement in his voice Kennedy said, "But Bishop, I saw you on TV last night and you said you'd had your last Coke until the company had withdrawn from South Africa." The bishop laughed, observing that Brown had so resolved, not he. "Moreover," he said, "I like Coke." The meeting then proceeded and was very helpful.

The next encounter with a South African leader was at a special regents meeting at UCLA in early June. We had invited (among many others both favoring and opposing apartheid) Chief Minister Buthelezi, chairman of the South African Black Alliance and the leader of South Africa's Zulus, who observed that not all expressions of moral indignation against apartheid in fact assisted the black struggle there. He advised Westerners to use nonviolent means and negotiation to bring about radical change and pointed out that black-white economic interdependency in South Africa, along with blacks' growing consumer power and higher levels of education that followed employment, all argued for more investment in that country, not less.[16]

Speaker Brown, as an ex-officio regent, was present at this meeting, and the ensuing encounter between Buthelezi and Brown was decidedly unpleasant and painful to observe. As a backdrop to this discussion, and others like it throughout the day, major demonstrations took place immediately outside Royce Hall, although the conditions within were entirely orderly.

Chancellor Young, who is a tall and very athletic man, not known for his reticence or patience, had been outside the hall trying to keep reasonable order within a very large, noisy, and hostile crowd of students and other protesters. He had been jostled and nearly punched several times and had periodically reported to Vice President Brady on what was going on. A few individuals had managed to get to Speaker Brown (or an aide) during a recess and had complained about the chancellor and his use of campus police. Brown in turn complained to the chairman of the board, Vilma Martinez. She not only defended Young but agreed to join Brown outside to assist the chancellor if Brown thought he could do any better. The meeting then resumed with Brown present and Martinez in the chair.

At our regular meeting of the board on the Berkeley campus in May 1985, a significant portion of our meeting had been set aside for taking public testimony on divestment. The meeting was held at Berkeley's Lawrence Hall of Science at the east end of the campus, up the hill and adjacent to the Lawrence Berkeley National Laboratory. While on the campus and in the City of Berkeley, the Hall of Science was also immediately adjacent to the City of

Oakland. The roads that provided access to the site were Oakland's, not Berkeley's. In any case we had not wanted to hold this meeting in the center of the campus (it would have effectively resulted in the closing of the campus given the 4,000 to 5,000 persons who came to protest, and many violently in this instance); earlier in the year Berkeley officials had made it clear that we could not count on the city's help if there were protests on the divestment issue—a far from impartial stance. Therefore we scheduled the meeting at a site that would not fundamentally disrupt the campus and where we could count on police help from Oakland both to maintain order and get us all out after the meeting.

I had been bitterly criticized for this decision by certain legislators who would have preferred a major disturbance that made national news and caused regents to be "detained," if I may put it euphemistically. Actually I didn't care about their criticism, because they weren't going to be there. We were. And they weren't responsible for the meeting. We were.

This proved to be one of the most difficult and threatening of meetings I attended of the Board of Regents, including the antiwar demonstrations of the late 1960s. I recall Chancellor Heyman in midafternoon coming up and whispering to Chairman Martinez that he wasn't sure how much longer the large crowd outside could be contained, and "couldn't we move the meeting along." She turned to him and said, "Chancellor Heyman, this is a duly constituted meeting of the Board of Regents of this university. We have the public's business to accomplish and we intend to complete it." Heyman looked at me. I suggested to Martinez that as much as we could condense aspects of the meeting, we should do so, and glanced at Heyman to let him know I would try to help. I appreciated his predicament, having been in that position myself many times as well, just as I very much respected Martinez for her response.

As it was, we were lucky to finish and to get out at all. We helicoptered the governor and his aides off the roof/and were forced to rely on Oakland's motorcycle police to get the rest of us out in vans. Speaker Brown and I were in the last van. As the motorcycle police moved forward in a V shape, the first vans had no trouble exiting. But the last one or two did. Our van was pummeled pretty roughly as we swung out of the grounds and on to the road. Sitting next to Brown, I said, "Well, Willie, some of your supporters must not realize that you are in the van." He said, "My supporters? Who the hell are these crazy people?"

While all this was going on, of course, we were receiving great pressure from the Democratic leadership of both houses to divest, sooner than later, in the course of which I was asked to testify at a special legislative hearing in Sacramento. Of course, I accepted. The hearing was held on May 14, 1985, in the largest hearing room in the Capitol. It was overflowing with people. Even Jane Fonda, then married to Assemblyman Tom Hayden, came from

Los Angeles to listen, as did other Hollywood notables. As Speaker of the Assembly, Willie Brown dominated the questioning. William Pickens, an impartial observer and later director of California's postsecondary education commission, recalled the hearing, as follows:

> The hearing room filled gradually, as one committee dissolved into another and the serious order of business drew near. Assembly Speaker Willie Brown, Jr., had darted in and out of the subcommittee meeting, and while in the room padded about like a cat in a cage. University President Gardner sat impassively for ten minutes amidst this, as one committee reconstituted itself into another. Finally, the horse-shoe table was full of legislators—the Speaker at its front in a luminous, tan, Wilkes/Bashford suit.
>
> Gardner began by explaining the University's process for considering the South Africa issue. . . . A dramatic pause followed his initial remarks. Everyone knew that no one would speak—not even the subcommittee's chair—before the Speaker.
>
> Then began a crisp interrogation, half a dramatic personal statement by the Speaker and half a Socratic probing of the President. One could imagine the same oral artistry in a sweltering Tennessee courtroom so long ago as Clarence Darrow and William Jennings Bryan clashed over evolution.
>
> The Speaker fixed Gardner in his sight and held him there—almost unblinking it seemed—for nearly an hour. "Now, Dr. Gardner. . ." he began each sentence, and then followed with some statement succeeded by a barbed question.
>
> Gardner answered each question patiently—something like a watchmaker meticulously organizing tiny parts scattered around a table. . . .
>
> Details dominated the first hour. Then the Speaker turned to what was really on his mind. "Dr. Gardner," he began slowly, his voice gradually rising to a crescendo, "we are very concerned by the University's attitude. Specifically, I want one scintilla of evidence that the atrocities of the South African regime present a problem to you personally, not as President of the University, but as a human being."
>
> The question, or something like it, had been anticipated by Gardner. He paused before answering, and then leaned forward as if to be face to face with the Speaker.
>
> Tersely, Gardner explained that the Presidency required a separation of responsibilities and personal values in the conduct of most business; that many groups constantly pushed him to take up their worthy causes; that he was the only one who could try to forge some consensus among contending groups on the Regents and within the University as a whole—and no President could if his personal values were proclaimed at every step.
>
> Now, Gardner was emphatic to say, that did not mean he would never speak out on social injustice or persecution. "Mr. Speaker," he said, "my great grandfather was driven from Canada because of his religion; he settled in Nauvoo. Then, a mob burned his house and drove him to the West. After several years and more bloodshed, he came to Utah but this was no sanctuary. In fact, the bones of my ancestors are strewn throughout the western United States, and

I have personally known discrimination because I am a Mormon. Therefore, Mr. Speaker, I abhor oppression whether it occurs in South Africa, or in Iran, or in Russia. But I do not choose to advertise it."

"Furthermore, the university and I as its leader, because of its public service as an educational and research institution, must take a different posture toward activism and justice than does government whose role is primarily coercion."

But the Speaker was not to be denied—he cut immediately to what [was] most important in his mind: "you can end discrimination against you by changing your religion. Blacks in South Africa cannot do that. They cannot speak to a University President in the way I am to you. They can't be philosophical about discrimination. They can't change the color of their skin. And so it goes in this country as well: Willie Brown cannot change his skin as he could his religion. Nor can Gwen Moore. There are no Utahs for Bishop Tutu."[17]

This assertion stirred thoughts in us all. Certainly in one sense it was true: skin color is more apparent than religious convictions. But, in another sense, it was not true. In Gardner—from his bearing, his instincts, his convictions—religion reached deep into his being, and it could not be changed casually. No, whatever physical, social, emotional and spiritual forces had shaped both these men during life's journey had left an imprint beyond anyone's power to change.

Each man, of course, was most memorable in representing the quintessential expression of his profession, or—in a larger sense—of his "calling." The Speaker is the consummate American politician: a mixture of evangelist, revivalist, debater, and moralist, man of action. His thoughts are charged with emotion, a call to belief, a message aimed at conscience. One invariably listens to him with a growing fervor and animation—on whatever side of the issue. The President is different: everything about him bespeaks discipline, order, reason, and temperance. He is a man of immense and critical intelligence whose judgment appears to result more from a process—turning over facts in his mind—than from some pre-existing conceptions.

But both have certain qualities in common: both have pondered the major questions of life, bringing to bear the enormous personal resources given to each. Both have come to different conclusions about life, but in ways that catapulted them to leadership in institutions among the most powerful in our nation.

No one could be declared a winner or loser in this confrontation: no one's will was bowed; no opinions were changed; no decisions emerged. We all left, though, with a profound sense of having witnessed a singular event on the jousting field of politics and education.[18]

I seemed to be earning no friends in Sacramento and, some suggested, implacable enemies; but as it turned out, and thanks mostly to Chancellor Krevans's friendship with both the Speaker and myself, Speaker Brown and I had breakfast together the following September at Krevans's official residence at UC San Francisco.

It was in a way similar to my first meeting with Governor George Deukmejian. Thereafter, and right through to the conclusion of my service as president, Brown and I got along extremely well. The Speaker was responsive, supportive, and personally friendly. His help, together with the governor's, made for an unbeatable combination at the very heart of political power in California, thus dramatically helping to advance UC's agenda. Other legislators did not hold my views on divestment against me either, probably for much of the same reasons Brown didn't. He had concluded that my views were my own and that the process and procedure leading to the regents' decision had been fair to all parties. I also believe it was tied to my willingness to stand up to him rather than to cave in as most people did, and to the fact that I never attacked him or personalized our differences.

But it was not just legislators, students, and various activist groups interested in pushing both UC and me, it was also some faculty members, though as best as I would discover the faculty was pretty much divided on this issue. Just before the June 1985 vote on this issue by the regents, I agreed to meet with a dozen or so Berkeley faculty members to explain my views on divestment. At my request Neil Smelser joined his colleagues, as he was then chairman of the university's Academic Council and one of two faculty representatives to the Board of Regents. Smelser's account in his oral history is worth remembering:

> A group of really strong, ideologically committed faculty members, mostly from Berkeley, who were almost all in my recollection from the anti-lab contingent, came and requested an audience, a meeting with David right in the heat of the divestment furor before the regents' meeting. David agreed to meet them in University Hall, I think against his better wishes, because he just knew he was going to get beaten up. There wasn't going to be a dialogue; there was going to be a lot of shouting. David asked me as president of the senate to come and sit with him in that meeting, to be present. And I was present, and I knew all these guys. I had been a faculty member with them for a long time, I had been with them through the FSM, I had been with them through the lab debates—I just knew the whole cast of characters. It was Leon Wofsy, it was Larry Levine, it was Robert Bellah—my colleague in sociology—I remember those faces. . . . It was in fact a kind of shouting contest. In fact, I got kind of angry; I did not express my anger during the meeting. I was sympathizing with David, because he was the one person taking all the heat, and the group was not interested in hearing his opinions. . . . They wanted him to change his mind and to go along with their side. And he didn't do it, and he defended himself perfectly well, but the thing became a very heavy meeting. The only time I expressed my irritation was at the end when I leaned over and said to Larry Levine, but in such a way that everybody heard, "I really have to congratulate you guys: you are the world's leading experts on moral blackmail." Levine just totally froze. Later he wrote me a letter saying I should apologize to that group. . . . I wrote him back later saying that if apologies are due it's from you people. And that was the end of it. David never forgot my comment. . . . He came to me afterwards and said, "You could say that, but I couldn't say that." . . . It was a very nice moment in my relationship with him.[19]

The June 21, 1985, meeting of the board was the day of decision. We had moved the meeting from Santa Cruz to San Francisco, both to accommodate those members of the public wishing to be heard and to take advantage of the additional security that the San Francisco Police Department was willing to provide and that Santa Cruz's could not.

Our discussion on divestment alone ran over four hours and was broadcast live by public television (KQED). It was an orderly meeting and not disrupted (with very tough going on the streets outside, but well contained by the San Francisco police, including their mounted unit). I was proud of how the regents comported themselves, not only at this meeting but throughout our five-month odyssey. Divestment of course was and always had been an issue about which moral and reasonable human beings would differ, and no one sought to put anyone else down or to subordinate anyone else's moral center to their own.

The debate was intelligent, everyone was heard, various proposals were advanced and amendments voted, and at the end of the day the regents voted *not* to divest. Instead—and on my recommendation—they put into place a structure for reviewing, on a consistent and constant basis, the quality of corporate citizenship in South Africa of UC-held companies doing business there. The Sullivan principles were invoked as a standard for judging such corporate behavior. I was to report on a regular basis to the board the findings associated therewith and, in short, was charged to be certain that UC played an affirmative and proactive role rather than merely sell our holdings and thereby remove ourselves from the arena altogether.

Regent Brown had come prepared with a substitute motion to accomplish the full divestment he was seeking. But after an extended debate and an unsuccessful effort to take some portions of his amendment and add them to the main motion, his amendment failed. Before the meeting I had talked at length with every single regent in an effort to understand their respective views and to accommodate as many as possible within the purview of my own remarks and recommendation.

This effort was noted at the close of the meeting by several regents. I recall especially Regent Yvonne Brathwaite Burke's commenting on how much "she had appreciated my efforts to be responsive, fair and thorough in the face of the pressures I had been under," even though she favored divestment and had voted against my motion.

All of us were under pressure with legislation pending in Sacramento at the time of the vote, to punish the university in various ways if the regents didn't vote to divest: to eliminate UC's capital budget, to delay transfers of the state's share of funding for UC's retirement plan, to divert faculty and staff salaries, and other such bludgeoning tactics to assert the legislative will over that of the regents, which body was constitutionally commanded to keep the university free of such political partisanship in the administration of its affairs. None of these threats were ever carried out.

For myself, I found this to be a profoundly trying experience. I had colleagues and friends, on and off campus, on both sides of the issue. I did not want to damage our relations in Sacramento. I did not want to be at odds with the faculty who, while also divided, were moving increasingly toward a posture of favoring divestment. I did not want to be at odds with two or three chancellors who favored divestment. I found, of course, that I simply had to do what I thought was right. An excerpt from my comments to the regents on June 21, 1985, explains why—since I personally believed that opposition to apartheid was better expressed in other ways—we could not permit the university to be used in support of a particular set of political views:

> One can criticize how this debate has been carried on within the University, for it has not infrequently taken on more of a political or coercive character than a reasoned and analytical quality. However, one should not fault, in my opinion, the concern for social progress and the cause of individual and personal freedom that has activated and enlivened student, faculty, and staff opinions in recent months. People do care deeply about this issue.
>
> The University, of course, must also be cognizant of and sensitive to its own traditions, customs, and purposes. The issues before the Board this morning encompass more than the injustices of apartheid, divestment of the University's interest in companies doing business in South Africa, fiduciary duty, investment options and legalisms; they also reflect a dispute about the nature of the university itself and how it is to respond to injustices in the larger society.
>
> The University of California, like all universities in America, is committed to the established values of academic life: patient inquiry; the sequential development of ideas; the emphasis on reasoned discussion and criticism; and the continued reference to evidence. These values affirm the University's faith in intelligence and knowledge and its obligation to ensure the conditions for their free exercise. Ideas are to be welcomed, exchanged, critically examined, freely debated, and respected.
>
> These values are the means by which the cause of truth is carried forward. They are the values that distinguish the university from governments, churches, business and other institutions, parties, groups, and associations in our society. They form the core of the enterprise and the basis of whatever respect and freedom the university can hope to command from the larger society. They should be nurtured and protected, not contravened; and these values stand in contrast to economic sanctions, boycotts, institutional pressuring, and similar means of effecting change which are more coercive than they are reasoned expressions of the human will.
>
> I believe that we as Regents should not permit the University to be used in support of one particular set of political views. This principle would be perfectly clear if, as a Board, we were to support a candidate for public office or

lend our support or opposition to a partisan political position or apply political or religious tests when appointing members of the University's faculty and staff, admitting students, or selecting university officers; the principle also applies to the issue before us. Moreover, we were not elected nor appointed as Regents to make public policy on a wide range of public issues. We have, on the contrary, a rather narrow charge, and that is to exercise ultimate authority and to bear ultimate responsibility for the University of California, an institution for the advancement of learning and teaching in all its forms. Our steady concern is and ought to be the welfare of the university and the cause it represents. And in the management of the university's funds, we have a fiduciary responsibility, characteristic of trustees, to manage those funds prudently and in the service of the activities and purposes of the institution we are honor bound to serve. But it is also proper that a university should speak for, and embody, the values of freedom, justice, and racial equality; and it is right that the Regents express our common detestation of political and racial oppression wherever it may exist. It is right that we do so because such practices are a threat to free universities everywhere and because they constrain rather than liberate the human spirit, the informing and freeing of which form the most basic of the university's purposes.[20]

My motion passed 16–10. It was a policy of selective investment and selective divestment. And the response of the most vocal students and faculty members to the June 1985 action of the board was expectedly hostile, but muted with the summer months on us. The reaction of the press was mixed, of the legislature mixed but predominately unfriendly, of the alumni mixed, as with the staff. Our actions encouraged some other universities across the country and complicated the lives of others. The decision was noticed nationally and editorialized on by the nation's media, and, in general, the matter was thought to have been settled at UC. It was settled but not ended.

I moved promptly to establish a universitywide committee to implement our course of action, including the oversight of companies doing business in South Africa in which UC held a financial interest, asking Chancellor Young at UCLA to chair it. He and other members of the Committee for Investor Relationship went about their work promptly, were diligent and faithful in meeting both the spirit and letter of the regents' resolutions of June 21, and were making substantive headway throughout the 1985–86 academic year.

At the same time, however, this issue was becoming an even greater point of contention within the United States itself, domestic politics now eclipsing what were the presumed basis of people's concern to start with. Divestment was once again being pushed on the campuses as the new academic year began. We witnessed a rerun of the 1984–85 year: campus protests, petitions, legislative threats, civil disobedience, and "shanty towns" constructed during the day on our campuses by prodivestment students and torn down at night by antidivestment students. The regents and I were vilified throughout, regardless of the substantive progress Young's committee was making. In fact, no one seemed to care about the committee.

What the critics wanted was the symbolism of UC's voting for full divestment, especially as they had hit a wall in their efforts at Stanford, Harvard, Princeton, and other leading American private universities not dependent on state funding for their core budgets.

In the end none of these protests, petitions, and threats made very much difference: we were used to dealing with them and had done so for years. What did count, however, was the decision Governor Deukmejian made in late spring 1986 to change his mind and favor divestment.

The first word I had about this was in May or early June 1986 when Steve Merksamer, his chief of staff, called. He said the governor was rethinking his position and asked if I would join him and the governor in the latter's office to discuss it. The meeting was scheduled immediately. Deukmejian was up for reelection in fall 1986. His chief opponent was Tom Bradley, mayor of Los Angeles. Bradley, a well-known and much respected mayor who was black, was making an issue of the governor's vote the previous June to support my motion and not Brown's. Some observers believed that Deukmejian was changing his position because of Bradley's criticism and his own prospects for reelection. I knew Speaker Brown had been privately working with the governor to change his mind, but I never believed this was the principal reason. As he told me when we met, he had become increasingly troubled with the news accounts coming out of South Africa.

All this killing and violence, directed mostly against blacks, reminded Deukmejian of the Turkish massacres of Armenians in World War I, "in which my family was caught up and suffered terribly." He had been wondering for some time about the correctness of UC policy and had concluded that, "whereas I had supported your motion the previous June, I cannot now, eleven months later, any longer do so."

As he intended to propose to the regents at the upcoming meeting that the policy be amended to bring about full divestment over time (the upcoming meeting being in Santa Cruz on July 18, 1986), he wanted not to surprise me but to afford me the chance to make my case once again. The governor and I were friends; we respected and cooperated with one another. We helped move the university forward together, and I regretted that on this issue we could not agree.

I summarized my views once again (he already knew them), brought him up to date on the work of Young's committee, and indicated that he needed to do what he thought was right, and if in doing so resolved to make his motion to divest at the July meeting, then he should know that I would have to vote against it.

He answered by saying that I should feel free to vote as I thought best, that it would have no adverse bearing on or consequences for our relationship and his support of UC whatsoever. And he would make this point clear to the media after the meeting, regardless of the outcome. The meeting ended cordially, as always.

We were each as good as our word, and when he made the motion to divest, I voted no. The motion passed thirteen to nine with one abstention. Three new regents had been appointed by Deukmejian since the vote thirteen months earlier, all three of whom voted to support the governor's motion, and a new alumni regent elected since the previous vote also voted for the divestment. These four votes along with the governor's swung the majority to that side of the controversy.[21]

My single comment in the debate was that my views were well known and that I could add nothing to them. I could count however. While I respected the governor's sense of conscience, I felt that the new regents who had not been a party to the previous year and a half of controversy did not really understand the issue or the significance of their votes but were merely supporting the governor. All these persons became very good regents over time, and most of them became my personal friends as well. But as I left our July meeting, I really did wonder if our vaunted constitutional protections meant as much as I had always supposed (it was just as well that I left for our Montana cabin for a needed several weeks' rest immediately after the meeting, when I was in a negative and sour mood; I was in an upbeat and positive one on my return).

Remarkably enough, this vote was a great anticlimax. No protests had accompanied the meeting, and few people were clamoring to be heard there (Mayor Bradley did attend and address the board). Even Speaker Brown did not attend. The results were reported but less prominently than the previous year. The campuses were surprisingly quiet: almost nothing was said about a "great victory" for divestment. By this time the issue and action had moved to the U.S. Congress, where it should have been centered all along, at least in my view.

The Young committee was disbanded; the treasurer commenced the sale of over $3 billion of UC assets with the transactional costs incurred reaching into the millions of dollars. Within a relatively short time UC's interest in South Africa faded away entirely. We had sold our holdings in companies having South African operations to others who presumably had no interest whatsoever in the apartheid question, and with our sales we thus abandoned any claim to assert an interest in corporate operations in South Africa as they affected or otherwise implicated blacks in that country.

It was the last we heard of student concerns for blacks in South Africa, as economic sanctions took hold and some U.S. companies sold or closed their operations there in the following years. It was also the last time the issue came to the regents' attention, except for their taking notice of the legislature's vote to indemnify members of the board against charges of having breached their fiduciary duty (1987), and, several years later with the end of apartheid, being asked to revoke UC's policy on divestment and to encourage U.S. companies to reenter South Africa.

In a very real way, I believe we failed our students in this debate. It was not a "bumper sticker" issue even though advocates for divestment had treated it as such—if you opposed divestment, you were for apartheid, or if you were against apartheid, you were for divestment. We made mostly half-hearted efforts on some campuses to engage the student body in a discussion of this complex and multifaceted issue, but in the end advocates for divestment took it over. Our faculty possessed some of the world's experts on South Africa and its troubles, but their expertise was overlooked or expressly discarded. That the university should have been so willing to allow this opportunity to help inform and educate our students about this part of the world to pass us by because it would have invited even more disruptions and drawn even more ire from the "true believers" than most on the campuses thought was worth it, says much about the state of UC and other American universities (we were not alone) and the level of political correctness we have in recent years come to accept.

In any event I did what I could, but in the end it was not enough.

NINE

THE PUBLIC AND DIPLOMATIC LIFE

THE TASK

The presidency of the University of California set me on a large stage. Its domestic and international cast included government officials and legislators, alumni and donors, diplomats and heads of state, scientists and scholars, business leaders and heads of the nation's major foundations, presidents, vice-chancellors, and rectors of the world's leading universities. To interact with these accomplished people in their diverse settings was an engrossing task. And, as president of a famous and respected institution, I was privileged to take a consequential role. Character and preparedness were also factors not to be underestimated, for they counted in the interplay of personalities and ideas that were germane to all that I strove to do in my public and diplomatic endeavors on the university's behalf.

Foremost in my mind was the cause of free universities everywhere and the essential values on which their well-being depended. I opposed the growing politicization of universities and the use of religious and/or political tests in the appointment or advancement of faculty members, the enhanced role of government and governing boards in unversities' internal affairs, the suppression of ideas and academic freedom, and the relentless shrinking of public funding for universities everywhere.

To understand the winds of change blowing across the social, political, religious, economic, educational, and cultural landscapes of our world, and to apprehend their causes and consequences, was an essential part of this task: the diminishment of the nation-state, the rise of tribalism, the growth of civil disorder, the changing nature and meaning of sovereignty, the weakening of civil authority, the ascendancy of fundamentalist religions, and modernity's effects on developing countries—the globalization of ideas and trade, the industrialization of labor, urbanization, science, technology, and the mass migration of peoples. All these affect the universities, their freedoms, and the level of support they can expect to receive, sometimes for the better and sometimes for the worse.

I read widely and learned from well-informed visitors or hosts. It was also my good fortune to have academic and administrative colleagues who brought superior intellects to the table, along with experiences rich in life's vagaries, seasoned by extensive travel and other university assignments. They were sophisticated observers of our own and other cultures as well as the subtle inner workings of large-scale, complex institutions, especially research universities.

I benefited from the many opportunities I had to travel throughout the world. Adding to my widening circle of colleagues and friends, I served as the nation's fortieth-anniversary Fulbright lecturer to Japan, received honorary degrees in Asia and Europe, represented our nation's public universities at the nine hundredth anniversary of the founding of the University of Bologna and at Harvard University when celebrating its three hundred fiftieth birthday,[1] visited China, Japan, North Korea, South Korea, and the Soviet Union on assignment with a small team of other Americans under the auspices of the Asia Society, and gave papers at various international conferences.

Within this country I served on several national commissions, the boards of several professional and nonprofit organizations, and various corporate boards; and was elected as a member or a fellow of the American Academy of Arts and Sciences, the American Philosophical Society, the National Academy of Education, and the National Academy of Public Administration.

During these trips and engagements I worked to broaden my understanding of American higher education by comparing and contrasting other systems with our own, and to establish a professional and institutional network helpful to our university's many and varied international interests.

AT THE UNIVERSITY OF UTAH
Iran

This story of international engagement began with my early years as president of the University of Utah, long before my return to California. The U and Utah State University both had a long-standing relationship with Iran, in part because the topography, hydrology, soils, minerals, flora, and fauna of that nation—defined by high mountains in the north and high desert plateau country to the south—much resembled Utah's. Scientists from Utah had traveled to Iran for decades, well before the region's petroleum deposits and radical fundamentalists achieved prominence, assisting Iran in its efforts to modernize its agricultural practices and water systems. They also helped modernize its environmental management and its mining and other extractive processes. In turn, Iranian professors and students had been researching and studying at Utah universities in significant numbers for decades. As president of the University of Utah, it was my responsibility to look after this relationship.

Three extended trips to Iran took place during my ten years at Utah. I hoped to negotiate exchanges with several universities, but principally with Tehran University, to increase the flow of students, scholars, and scientists between their universities and ours, to arrange for access to their superb collections of Islamic and Persian art and artifacts and to their libraries and other intellectual resources. This we did with the assistance of the chancellors of their leading universities and Iran's Ministry for Science and Education.

In the course of these negotiations Libby and I traveled throughout the country, from Shiraz and Persepolis in the south to Isfahan at the center and to Tehran in the north, including a three-day trip to the Caspian Sea at the country's northern boundary. We traveled variously under the protection of the crown, the government, or Tehran University, depending on the country's political temperature. This country with its rich religious and secular history, its magnificent art and elegant poetry and literature, its architecture and cultural treasures impressed Libby and me very much. So too did the working of modern Iran, occasioned by my first experience during the 1984 visit to Utah of Ardeshir Zahedi, Iran's ambassador to the United States. The ambassador had studied at Utah State University as a young man, was married to the shah's daughter, and was a person of consequence both within Iran and in Washington's diplomatic circles.

His visit to campus had been well publicized, given the prominence of our Middle East Library and Center for Middle East Studies, and the surprisingly large number of Utah students interested in this region. The ambassador was to pay me a courtesy visit in the late afternoon of the first day. We had arranged the usual dinner on campus in Zahedi's honor with faculty and students followed by a breakfast with community leaders in downtown Salt Lake City the next day.

The notice of the ambassador's pending visit and public lecture on campus had brought Pete Gardner, vice president for academic affairs, to my office: a number of the faculty hoped I would give Zahedi a petition asking about the well-being of a colleague from Tehran University who had been a visiting professor at Utah the previous year. On his return to Tehran the previous summer, Gardner went on, he had been arrested for undiscoverable reasons and was still in prison. But if I was unwilling to present this petition personally to the ambassador on their behalf, the most interested faculty members would try to get maximum publicity for their own protest of Zahedi's campus visit.

I told Gardner that they had every right to protest, to circulate petitions, and otherwise to express themselves within the bounds of the law and university policies, but that in my opinion such gestures—by them or by me in their behalf—would be counterproductive. Moreover, the ambassador was our guest and should be treated as such. Finally, I promised to raise the issue informally and personally with Zahedi if the faculty members would agree not to behave in ways that would make it difficult for our guest or me.

Gardner called a couple of hours later with their concurrence. Thus, when the ambassador came for his visit later that day, I would be expected to fulfill my end of the agreement. But if my effort failed, try as I might to enlist the ambassador's interest and support, I told myself no one would credit the attempt. Even so, this approach was preferable to the actions my colleagues had proposed: they were merely going to confirm their friend's indefinite incarceration.

With the pleasantries out of the way and most of our discussion about student and faculty exchanges complete, I asked the ambassador if he would do me the favor of inquiring after the circumstances and condition of one of the university's former visiting professors, now a professor at Tehran University (but also in jail); he had been a temporary but esteemed member of our faculty the previous year. Rather than petitions and protests about our incarcerated colleague, "the most interested members of our faculty hoped I would inquire directly of the ambassador about their friend's status and the well-being of his family." The ambassador wrote down his name and said he would inquire of the appropriate parties and get back to me.

"By the way," Zahedi told me in the morning at breakfast, leaning over so as to speak softly, "your friend has been released from prison, the charges have been dropped, and he has been reunited with his family, all of whom are well." He added that this result came in response to my "very correct inquiry and out of respect for the University of Utah."

I expressed astonishment as well as appreciation for how promptly and with such effect he had acted on this matter and thanked him very much. "No problem," he said, "easy in, easy out." This incident was highly instructive, confirming as it did my mostly untested assumption that a president's quiet use of office not only is an asset but also works much better than public pressure, which tends to rigidify things.

During our final visit to Iran just months before the fall of the shah and his government, Libby and I entered the expansive campus of Tehran University to meet with our friend Chancellor Houshang Nahavandi for lunch before I delivered a lecture. Security was much in evidence, but the campus

seemed oddly quiet. Yet the windows on the first two floors of every building were broken or were then being shattered by small bands of students
roving the campus with apparent impunity.

Security was very tight at the chancellor's second-story office too, but we
were graciously received. In the course of our lunch, loud and boisterous
noises were heard outside in the alleyway below Nahavandi's office. The chancellor waved us over to his balcony, and we all looked down on two to three
hundred students chanting slogans, carrying placards and signs, and running or jostling their way along the narrow alley. Behind them, moving at
the same pace and at a discrete distance, were large numbers of riot-attired
police with the usual helmets, visors, shields, and assorted weaponry.

When this parade had passed, the chancellor said that we were witness-
ing an annual campus ritual to memorialize an event of many years ago when
police had come on campus to control a major protest, in the course of which
several students had been killed. The students we had seen were surrogates
for other students, and for the larger society as well, pretending to riot just
as the police pretended to arrest them—all this for nationwide TV consumption that night. The windows that had been broken or were being broken
were all part of the game. No one would be held culpable for shattering windows on the first two floors; their replacement cost was part of the university's annual operating budget. But there would be arrests if anyone broke
windows at the upper levels.

Putting my astonishment aside, I decided that in some peculiar way this
ritual was more efficient and civilized than our student protests at home,
which were often more random and opportunistic, and which both sides
tended to take literally.

Cambridge University

In 1979 I accepted an invitation from Clare Hall, a graduate college at Cambridge University, to serve as a visiting fellow for the Michaelmas term. The
University of Utah granted me a three-month leave, which, combined with
earned but unused vacation, gave us nearly four months of memorable experiences in Cambridge. The Ashbys introduced us to the leading lights of
Cambridge, helped us make the most of our visit, and eased negotiations between Cambridge University Press and the University of Utah Press to publish the Tanner lectures.

While there I also arranged for several students from the University of
Utah to study each year during the summer months at Cambridge University and for some continuing education adult learners to enroll as well. These
arrangements have remained in place. Other mutually beneficial agreements
were also worked out between our two universities during my brief stay.

Before leaving Cambridge, I prepared an article on the first of many unfriendly initiatives by the then newly elected prime minister, Margaret Thatcher, toward Britain's colleges and universities, especially those creating financial barriers to the enrollment of overseas students at British universities, which my article criticized (it appeared in the *Times Higher Education Supplement*).[2]

I returned to the university full of enthusiasm, rested and ready to deal with problems that had appeared intractable when I left.

The Tanner Lectures on Human Values

This now quite famous and much respected series of lectures was founded in 1978 at Clare Hall, Cambridge University and, as I noted earlier, funded by Professor Tanner of the University of Utah's Department of Philosophy, a successful entrepreneur in Salt Lake City's business community and one of the most kind, gracious, and philanthropic persons I have ever known. He was a remarkable human being, as is his wife, Grace. I served for several years as the founding chairman of the trust. Lectures are now delivered annually by leading scholars, scientists, and statesmen at American and British universities (at the U, Stanford, Cal, Michigan, Harvard, Princeton, Yale, and Oxbridge, respectively). The presidents of these universities (or heads of colleges at Oxford and Cambridge) serve as trustees along with the Episcopal bishop of Utah, Carolyn Irish Tanner (the founder's daughter), and two or three others, with Chase Peterson and myself as permanent trustees.

The purpose of the Tanner lectures is "to advance and reflect on the scholarly and scientific learning relating to human values and valuation [embracing] the entire range of values pertinent to the human condition, interest, behavior and aspiration." They have become a valued part of the intellectual life of the universities fortunate to be included.[3]

"Showing the Flag" at Home and Abroad

Just as we viewed trips to the Middle East, Europe, and Asia as occasions for "showing the flag"—to broaden the University of Utah's visibility and scholarly affiliations, to enlarge the study abroad opportunities for our students and the research possibilities for our faculty—we enjoyed regular visits by leading academics, government officials at the cabinet level, ministers of education and science from several countries, usually with the presidents of their leading universities in tow, foundation heads, ambassadors, artists, authors, musicians, and other persons of standing, position, and reputation. During his term in office President Gerald Ford paid us a welcome and successful visit as well.

Libby and I hosted many such visits and, as appropriate, included our daughters among the guests. We remembered most such events with pleasure. They marked the steady building of goodwill for the university—a consequence not to be underestimated in an area geographically remote from the centers of wealth and learning in the nation's northeastern corridor and on the Pacific Coast—but otherwise, few of them were noteworthy. But two occasions were well worth remembering.

The first arose shortly after our arrival at the U when the board of the Carnegie Corporation of New York chose to meet in Salt Lake City. Sterling McMurrin, then dean of our graduate school, was a Carnegie trustee and had served under President John F. Kennedy as United States commissioner of education. McMurrin called to ask if Libby and I would host the Carnegie board, along with leading members of our campus and the Salt Lake communities. We accepted gladly, planned for cocktails and hors d'oeuvres at the Hotel Utah's Empire Room (alcohol could not be served on campus by state law), then dinner on campus in one of the galleries of the university's Museum of Fine Arts.

Our guests would come from the academic community, business, the major nonprofits, Salt Lake's major religions; the list would also include some of our leading alumni and most noteworthy donors, along with civic leaders, the governor, and key legislators. I had met three or four leaders of the Mormon Church and planned to invite them as well. But I knew that the church frowns on the consumption of alcohol. So I called McMurrin, explaining that I did not want to put the church leaders in a quandary or find myself in one either. So could we invite them for cocktails as well as dinner? His response was unexpected: "What's the problem?" he asked. "After all it's in their saloon." Of course; as I should have recalled all along, the church owned and operated the Hotel Utah where the cocktail hour was to be held. The invitations went out and were accepted, and everyone had a good time. I am sure McMurrin was wondering if the university had chosen its new president wisely.

The other outstanding incident occurred in Moscow during the International Association of Universities' meetings of university presidents, rectors, and vice-chancellors, some 700–800 of them, in the mid-1970s. The rector at Moscow State University, site of the first plenary session, not only welcomed all of us but, more significantly, remarked on the happy congruence in the then Soviet Union between the academic majors offered by their universities, the majors chosen by the students, and the manpower needs of the Soviet economy and larger society.

At lunch I was seated next to the rector and, as conditions permitted, referred to his earlier address and expressed my surprise at the "efficiency" of interests served by the conditions he had so thoroughly and with such apparent pleasure shared with our colleagues that morning. Making certain no one was listening to our conversation, he lowered his voice and said, in perfect English and with a gentle laugh, "Oh, the system I described this morning doesn't work worth a damn. I was handed these remarks by the ministry last night and told to read them." We then went on to other matters we could discuss more comfortably.

In general, I found a remarkable frankness and an unexpected level of trust among the delegates. There were more similarities than differences among us: we were committed to our respective institutions and the underlying values of academic life; we valued our exchanges at international meetings. Under these conditions the normal rigidities and formalities gave way to an openness and generosity of spirit and forthrightness that I had not fully anticipated. I enjoyed the Soviets, mostly Russians, who were seeing to our needs and making every effort to guarantee the success of these meetings.

The Soviet Union's leading government officials as well as the heads of its leading universities were all present at the reception that evening. It was held in one of the most beautiful buildings I had ever visited, St. George Hall of the Great Kremlin Palace. Inscribed on the white pillars of this fabulous room were columns of names in gold leaf, listing the nation's most honored military heroes from earlier wars. The floor was inlaid in striking patterns with woods from throughout the country and served as a warm accent to the crystal chandeliers that hung from the great room's domed ceiling. Tables set in a horseshoe around the room for this memorable occasion held bottles of wine, vodka, and other drinks suited to the Russian palette. And each table was laden with fruits, meats, fish, fowl, vegetables, and pastries along with a profusion of desserts and chocolates. In this historic and magnificent setting I easily imagined the Russian czars and wondered to myself if things had changed that much after all.

When the evening with its seemingly continuous toasts ended, I and a very few of my colleagues were the only ones able to maneuver out of the room on our own and down the grand staircases without placing ourselves in harm's way.

AT THE UNIVERSITY OF CALIFORNIA

My later experience in California unfolded on a grander scale than in Utah. It was more complex, and fraught with problems that seemed perhaps more predictable in California. And California's great university system held a leading position among the very best of universities everywhere, buttressed by the state's famous and magical influence.

When traveling for the University of Utah, I was graciously received wherever I went. As president of the University of California, I was accorded treatment that, except for issues of security and honor guards, resembled the courtesies extended to a head of state or governor. I was expected to visit leading government officials, often including the head of state. Both government and the universities arranged elaborate dinners in my honor. Visits to the host nation's most treasured, scholarly, and well-known sites were arranged. In nearly every instance the doors swung open for anyone I asked to see.

While Utah had helped prepare me for these experiences, some time passed before I came to feel completely at ease and able more effectively to advance the University of California's interests around the globe.

Education Abroad

As noted in chapter 7, I was desirous of enlarging the scale and scope of the university's already highly regarded Education Abroad Program, especially into Asian universities. Bill Allaway, the founding director, and later his successor, Professor John Marcum of the Santa Cruz campus—both superb leaders—undertook this initiative. But I did not mention the several trips to Asia our initiative required and the ensuing experiences.

Libby and I visited the leading universities in Japan, South Korea, China, Taiwan, and Hong Kong to explore possibilities. What impressed me most of all was the large number of UC alumni then in positions of academic or administrative leadership at the major universities or in key government positions everywhere we went. These were capable and talented people, often working under conditions not altogether friendly or supportive (the hard sciences and engineering were general exceptions). They enrolled only the brightest of their respective nation's youth, sought advanced study opportunities for their most intellectually gifted students at the best American universities, and were eager for enhanced faculty and student exchanges between their universities and the University of California, where they often had many friends among the faculty. Thus the timing of our initiative seemed to be propitious—and in each instance both sides benefited in ways consistent with our respective institutions' purposes and underlying values.

Over the next few years we helped establish new study centers for UC undergraduate students wishing to study in Asia, encouraged reciprocity agreements, and facilitated similar faculty and graduate study and research opportunities. In short, we managed to give more balance to our Education Abroad Program by opening Asia more completely, just as President Clark Kerr had done earlier in Europe and Africa. Later we increased education abroad opportunities in Latin America as well. Scholarship support for needy students was also significantly increased for UC students wishing to study abroad.

I made many friends throughout Asia in the course of these visits, especially among the leaders of Asia's major universities. Several opportunities also arose to discuss the role of government and of universities within both open and less open societies with my friends as well as with ministers, vice presidents, and heads of state. I not only sought to understand the boundaries and constraints within which they worked but also tried hard to help them under-

The Council of Chancellors of the University of California, tired of posing, 1988. Left to right: Jack Peltason (Irvine), Barbara Uehling (Santa Barbara), Ted Hullar (Davis), Charles Young (Los Angeles), Gardner, I. Michael Heyman (Berkeley), Julius Krevans (San Francisco), Richard C. Atkinson (San Diego), Robert Stevens (Santa Cruz), and Rosemary Schraer (Riverside).

The vice presidents and president of the University of California, 1992. Left to right: Ron Brady, Gardner, Kenneth Farrell, William Baker, William Fraser, and Cornelius Hopper.

Presidents Emeriti David Saxon and Clark Kerr, President David Gardner, and Presidents Emeriti Charles J. Hitch and Harry W. Wellman (acting) at Charter Day, the Greek Theatre, UC Berkeley, March 22, 1991. Photo: Peg Skorpinski.

The spouses of UC's president and chancellors, at UC Santa Barbara, spring 1987. First row from left: Mary Regan-Meyer (Davis), Suzanne Peltason (Irvine), and Patricia Krevans (San Francisco). Second row from left: Jean Aldrich (Santa Barbara), Libby Gardner, Sue Young (Los Angeles). Top row from left: Therese Heyman (Berkeley), Karen Sinsheimer (Santa Cruz), Rita Atkinson (San Diego), and Joan Hullar (Riverside). Photo: Ric Lopez/UCSB.

Gardner with President Mihran Agbabian and officers of the American University of Armenia and UC commencing the partnership between the two universities, 1991. Photo: Jeanne Gardner.

Gardner with Rector of Leningrad State University, Stanislav P. Merkur'yev, signing an agreement for student and faculty exchanges with Education Abroad Director William H. Allaway (far left) and a member of the Soviet delegation (far right), Blake House, February 1988. Photo: Richard Whittaker (courtesy of the UC Office of the President).

With Philippine President Corazon Aquino at the Greek Theatre following her remarks and concluding her visit to the Berkeley campus, October 1986. Photo: Gordon Stone/*San Francisco Examiner.*

King Juan Carlos I of Spain receiving the Berkeley Medal from Chancellor I. Michael Heyman, October 2, 1987. Looking on from left: Gardner and Queen Sophia. Photo: Ron Risterer.

The visit of German Chancellor and Mrs. Helmut Kohl to the Berkeley campus, the Greek Theatre, September 1991. Photo: Peg Skorpinski.

Unexpected musical talents at work, the Blake House gardens. Left to right: Chancellor Kohl, Cal's Straw Hat Band student leader, Gayle Wilson, Gardner, and Governor Pete Wilson. Photo: Peg Skorpinski.

The visit to UC San Diego of Mexico's President Salinas, fall 1991.

UCLA Chancellor Charles Young, Charles University (Prague) Rector Radim Palouš, Czech Republic President Václav Havel, and UC President David Gardner on the occasion of Havel's 1991 Tanner Lecture at UCLA.

With President George H. W. Bush following planning meeting for 1989 Education Summit of the nation's governors, convened by President Bush. Photo: Courtesy of The White House.

Gardner with Harvard President Derek Bok, chairs of the Commission on New Possibilities for the Admissions Testing Program for the College Board, presenting revisions to the SAT, New York City, March 1991. Photo: Joe Wrinn/Harvard University Office of News & Public Affairs. All rights reserved, © President and Fellows of Harvard College. Used with permission.

On the occasion of Stanford University's convocation celebrating its 100th anniversary, Gardner compliments the Stanford band on its "unique brand of football" as Stanford President Donald Kennedy looks on, May 20, 1987. Photo: Ed Souza/Stanford News Service.

With Clark Kerr when dedicating the Clark Kerr Campus at UC Berkeley, November 1986.

Chancellor Emeritus Glenn T. Seaborg, Oski, David and Libby Gardner at a fundraiser for Cal, fall 1990.

The divestment controversy under discussion at a regents' meeting, May 17, 1985, at Berkeley. Left to right: Gardner, Governor Deukmejian, Regent Sheldon Andelson, UC Treasurer Herbert Gordon, Regent Edward Carter, and Regent Dean Watkins. Photo: AP/Wide World Photos.

University of California Board of Regents, 1992. Front row from left: Governor Wilson, Chairman Khachigian, Gardner; second row from left: Regents Yeager, Hall, Anderson, Watkins, Johnson, Gonzales, Campbell, del Junco, Bagley, McCarthy, and Wada; third row from left: Faculty Representatives Trow and Brownlee, Regents Brophy, Stoney, Williams, Darnell, Kolligian, Leach, Burgener, Ochoa, and Hallisey.

The Gardner family, Blake House gardens, November 1985. From left, Libby, Shari, Lisa, Karen, David, and Marci. Photo: Barry Evans.

With daughters, Shari on left and Marci on right, following regents' meeting of November 1991, when Gardner announced his resignation as UC president. Photo: *Oakland Tribune*.

A memorial to the life of Libby Gardner in the Family Garden of Clare Hall, Cambridge University, England, 1997.

David and Sheila upon their engagement, Park City, Utah, October 1995. Photo: © Busath Photography, Salt Lake City, Utah. Used with permission.

Sheila and David
fishing the Strawberry
River, central Utah,
1998.

Matthew Rodgers
and Sheila at a mothers'
luncheon hosted by the
2001 Serra High
School football team,
San Mateo, California.

Sheila and David at home in Park City, Utah, November 2002. Photo: Stuart Ruckman, Salt Lake City, Utah.

stand how liberating for the society as a whole and how intellectually invigo-rating it is for the universities, and those who labor in them, when such insti-tutions are freer to choose how, when, and what to teach and, similarly, when faculty members are free to pursue their intellectual interests and free to share openly with their students, colleagues, and the larger society what they learn.

I made clear that the awkwardness of dissent or the expression of contrary views or the seeming threat of new ideas and fresh ways of looking at estab-lished norms were all essential to academic life. Such intellectual freedom not only invigorated the classroom, the students, and their teachers but also helped inform and renew the larger society as well, thus permitting evolu-tionary rather than a less desired abrupt or even revolutionary change in the larger society. These arguments were met courteously but with uneven effect.

On several occasions I remarked that large numbers of their best students and faculty members yearned for universities more akin to the American model than their own. While any country's universities reflect its own cul-ture and progressive impulses, I emphasized, at their core they and all other universities worldwide are committed to the common underlying values of academic life. Hence the modern world marked the evolution of these uni-versities as critical to the evolution and progress occurring within their host country. These comments were politely received, but their effect was never easy to discern.

Shanghai

Our Asian friends, of course, were not short of advice for the United States and the University of California. One incident I recall vividly was at a din-ner in our honor hosted by the president of Fudan University in Shanghai, Xie Xi De. In the course of dinner the president leaned over and quietly ob-served that reports had been coming from California that the Berkeley cam-pus was discriminating against Asian Americans seeking admission at the freshman level.

I had not expected this issue to arise in Shanghai, but I explained as care-fully and as thoroughly as I could what our admissions policies were and how they were administered (noted in detail in chapter 8). We tried to admit a class that encompassed the diverse backgrounds, socioeconomic profiles, ge-ographic characteristics, and exceptional talents of candidates who were, I added, also at the upper reaches of academic preparedness for study at the University of California. My words did not persuade the president. "No," she said, after listening most attentively, "only the best [academically the best] should be admitted." But Berkeley, I explained, had well in excess of 27,000 applicants, and roughly 10,000 of these had perfect high school records while we had only 3,500 freshman spaces.

"Why is that a problem?" she went on. "Why don't you simply admit those whose high school records are perfect and whose test scores are the highest?" In response I pointed out that the University of California's policies were not dissimilar from those in place at America's other leading universities, which did not rely on objective academic criteria alone for the first-year class.

She remained unmoved and explained how the leading Chinese universities, including her own, "admitted only those students who scored highest on the national exams." I thanked her for the explanation, indicated my admiration for her university and its students and faculty, and in conclusion observed that the United States had no national examination (though at any university's discretion it could use the SAT exam offered nationally), and that her admissions problems were perhaps less complicated than our own. Our conversation then moved on to other topics.

Pacific Rim Relations

My Asian contacts and experiences also led to the formation in 1989 of an organization to advance the common interests of the leading university in each country bordering the Pacific Rim, including North America, Mexico, East Asia, Southeast Asia, New Zealand, Australia, the Philippines, and Fiji. This organization was the idea of Ambassador Hayden Williams who had also served for many years as president of the San Francisco–based Asia Foundation. He asked if, together with his help, the University of California might wish to lead in forming such an organization.

Yes, I said with enthusiasm. The first meeting was held in San Francisco in 1989, the second eighteen months later at Chulalongkorn University in Thailand, and the last in spring 1992 in Seoul, Korea. Only the presidents of the leading university in each country could attend. No substitutes.

The only problem we had at our first meeting was our strong desire to invite both the president of National Taiwan University and the president of Peking University. The Chinese consul general in San Francisco (whom I knew) called in some embarrassment to indicate that the president of the University of Peking could not attend if we were also to invite the president of National Taiwan University, as China regarded Taiwan as part of China, and not as an independent state since each country was to have but one representative, as he understood it.

I pointed out that we were inviting university heads, not government officials, that they would be representing their respective universities, not their respective countries, and wondered if this explanation would serve. "Sorry, it just won't do," he said.

If the Chinese government would not cooperate, the question for us was, which university president would we invite: National Taiwan University's or the University of Peking's? Not wishing to consider that choice and wanting both presidents to join us in any event, I then said to the Chinese consul

general, "how would it be if in all our publications, in all our public statements, in our roster listing the participants, on our name tags, and on our
conference table identifications we refer to our guests by university title *alone*
without affiliation to a country?" "That would work," he said. "I know I can
count on your word. Please proceed to include Beda [the University of
Peking's more frequently used title]," and we did.

These three conferences were excellent. We made and cemented friendships and put in place Pacific-wide computer and telecommunication systems to facilitate our interactions. We arranged cultural and intellectual exchanges on an ad hoc basis and freely acknowledged the commonality of
our interests as well as our differences. The conferences were an example
of what universities can do together despite their countries' differences to
enlarge the scope of their influence and take advantage of scarce intellectual resources. And for me they were another example of UC's influence,
especially in Asia, because no one turned our invitation away.

Hong Kong

In late 1988 Professor Chia Wei Woo, newly elected vice-chancellor and
president of Hong Kong's just chartered and newly forming third university, called to see if I could find the time to assist him in planning for and
then helping build the Hong Kong University of Science and Technology
(HKUST). Woo and I had known each other when he served as president of
San Francisco State University in the early 1980s and I was still at Utah. We
had traveled together throughout Israel for nearly two weeks with a visiting
group of American university presidents.

Hong Kong University, the first and best known university in the then
British colony, had held sway in higher education circles for many decades.
It was joined in the early 1960s by the Chinese University of Hong Kong,
ably assisted by UC's president, Clark Kerr, and I was being asked to do the
same in a parallel case a quarter of a century later.

After consulting with the chairman of the Board of Regents and other
key members of my board, I accepted. Thus began one of my most interesting of international assignments that ran from 1988 to 1996, with three trips
to Hong Kong each year, and sometimes more. I also took an administrative
leave of five weeks during March and April 1989 to help HKUST at a critical time in its development. I served first as an adviser to the planning committee and later as a member of the governing board, the University Council in British parlance.

HKUST opened its doors at its spectacularly sited campus at Tai Po Tsai
on Clear Water Bay Peninsula, overlooking the waters of Port Shelter on the
South China Sea, on August 10, 1991, only forty-eight hours after the architect certified the completion of the project (Phase I), and six weeks after

originally planned. The construction of 152,424 square meters of academic and residential space (Phase II) was completed in late 1992 and took only twenty-three months. The pace was amazing, especially given the difficulty of the site and its distance from the heart of Hong Kong. But this was and remains the Hong Kong way, as I discovered early on in my service.

The Hong Kong government had decided to build the university in 1986. It was to open in 1994. In 1988 the government changed its mind and asked the planning committee and the university administration to move the opening date up to 1991. I was at the meeting where this was discussed and remember it well. In addition to several prominent Hong Kong leaders on the committee—including Anson Chan, who later held the number one governmental position in the Hong Kong civil service, the general secretaryship, where she served with great distinction during the British turnover of the territory to China in 1997—the members also included Michael Birt, vice-chancellor of the University of New South Wales in Australia, Peter Moore, head of the London School of Economics, and Sir Gordon Higginson, vice-chancellor of the University of Southampton, also in England.

This collection of able and interesting people was overseen by our chairman, Sir Sze-yuen Chung (everyone addressed him as Sir S. Y.). He was a leading businessman and a former legislative leader in Hong Kong, where he had lived all his life. As chairman, he was invariably correct in making sure the council worked and its members were heard.

The group was both alarmed and excited about the government's edict on the opening date of the university. I harbored real reservations about the decision, but as an American and newly involved I chose to listen instead of to speak until the end when Sir S. Y. asked for my views.

"The government's action is problematic," I suggested, taking primarily into account what seemed to be possible from the standpoint of construction and therefore allowing insufficiently for the university's academic requirements. What was to be built depended on the uses to which the facilities were to be put, I explained. For ordinary classrooms and administrative and infrastructure requirements, this was not a problem. But for the laboratories, clinics, library, and computer and other complex teaching and research space, it was quite another matter. "Moreover, the design and functionality of such facilities could not be left to the more generic responses of the architects and engineers. These decisions needed the input of the faculty members who were to use them, few of whom had been hired." As I elaborated these points, I stopped just short of suggesting a later date or confirming the earlier one.

Sir S. Y. thanked me for my comments and the insights they provided but then observed with a smile that I had forgotten to allow for just one thing: "This is Hong Kong," he said, "not the United States." Everyone laughed, as did I. For he was right and I was wrong. The university was built on schedule (by contrast, UC took seven years to choose a site in the Central Valley for its tenth campus). The academic departments, schools, and colleges were staffed with an excellent faculty drawn from Europe, North America, China, Taiwan, Singapore, Australia, New Zealand, and Hong Kong. The students were admitted amidst great competition for the few spaces. On October 10, 1991, the university ceremonies formalizing the opening were held in the great court with both colonial and Chinese university leaders and governmental officials present and others representing universities from around the world.

The great and gala opening day, however, featured a decidedly Hong Kong ceremony with Lord Wilson, the governor of Hong Kong and the queen's representative, giving the principal remarks of the day and a band from the local Ghurka regiment of the British garrison in Hong Kong providing the music. Within the first ten years, HKUST was ranked seventh among Asian universities. The business school was named number one in Asia by *Asia Inc.*, and among the top fifty in the world by London's *Financial Times*. It was and remains a remarkable achievement, as, of course, is Hong Kong itself.

This assignment was the single most insightful and informative experience I had in Asia and the most helpful, as HKUST was being followed by the Chinese universities in the hope that China would itself try something new, and my colleagues in China all knew I was involved. We in America have a great deal to learn from others, as they do from us.

The Asia Society Mission

The second most interesting experience was a trip under auspices of the Asia Society of New York to North Korea, South Korea, China, Japan, and the then Soviet Union in May 1991. Professor Robert Scalapino of Berkeley headed the small team I was privileged to join, and its other members were a journalist, several scholars, an educator, a corporate CEO, a retired admiral formerly in command of all U.S. forces in the Pacific, and fellows from the Asia Society staff, twelve in all.

Scalapino was a friend of many years. When we first met in the early 1960s I was a young staffer at the California Alumni Association, and he was in demand as a speaker for our many alumni and student groups who admired and respected him, or as the nominee for critical and sensitive assignments by the university administration and Academic Senate, as during the Berkeley Free Speech Movement. At the time of this trip in spring 1991 he was a valued adviser to the incumbent president of the United States, to the State Department and our diplomatic corps in Asia, knowing as he did every major leader and figure throughout Asia and being one of the world's most highly regarded and authoritative authors of historical and contemporaneous events and trends in Asia.

Our team had been asked to do what we could to persuade the North Koreans to apply for their own membership in the United Nations (which the United States would support) rather than oppose South Korea's pending application for admission to the U.N. With the encouragement of China, Japan, and South Korea (the Soviet Union had not at that point been willing to express itself, being preoccupied with its imminent demise), our efforts were successful. The U.N. acted not long afterward to admit both the Koreas to membership.

Our second assignment was to persuade the North Koreans to abandon their well-known efforts to develop not only nuclear weapons but the capacity to deliver them across great distances as well. Despite early signs of agreeing, North Korea demurred, and its announcement in October 2002 of further plans to develop its nuclear capability only confirmed its intent. Though everyone in the United States government seemed to be surprised by this "news" in 2002, it had been obvious over eleven years ago, and our visit was entirely overt and disclosable.

I had visited the four other countries several times by 1991 but never North Korea, except clandestinely during my army days in the mid-1950s. The nation's president was Kim Il Sung, the "Great Leader," and his likeness was omnipresent wherever we traveled. Pyongyang, the capital city, was rich with parks and public spaces, intersected with major river systems, and marked by wide boulevards and a deeply carved and tunneled subway system. It was impressive at first glance, as were our accommodations in a special government compound, but on gaining greater familiarity and understanding we drew contrary conclusions as well. What appeared to be a building boom was, in fact, a mirage: nearly all the large cranes observable on the horizon in all directions next to countless high-rise concrete apartments stood motionless; the buildings were mere shells (the army began work on them, having little else to do, but funds were lacking to finish them). Signs everywhere lauded the patriotism of those who ate once or twice instead of three times a day. Unexpectedly few people were on the streets, and they averted their eyes until we had walked by them, when they turned to have a good look, as we noted in the storefront reflections of display glass.

I recall the rantings of the announcer at Pyongyang's major outdoor stadium (seating more than 125,000 persons) during a soccer match between the North Korean and South Korean teams (the players intermingled so as to eliminate the loss of face attendant on a national loss). Before a stadium filled to capacity the official propagandist lauded the prospect of a reunification between the two Koreas, which his government opposed (though not transparently), because its reality would overwhelm North Korea's political and economic systems. South Korea too opposed reunification while appearing to favor it; the costly German reunification not long before cast up the specter of economic burdens in the poverty-ridden north. Some Eastern

European diplomats sat in the stands with our team from the United States, a total of twenty-five Westerners in a sea of North Koreans who were visibly stirred and excited by this prospect of reunification. The entire event was a political rally masquerading as a soccer match. I was somewhat uneasy, all things considered.

On our trip to Wonson—from Pyongyang across the entire width of the country to this eastern port on the Sea of Japan—we noticed that the land had been tilled right up to the roadbed. And the lower portion of the mountains had been stripped of vegetation and farmed without terracing: these were all signs of a country desperate for food. In the course of this half-day drive from the capital and back plus the similar trip south to the Yellow Sea port of Kaesong, we saw only eight passenger cars, all Mercedes, the remaining vehicles being either buses or military trucks, roughly 20 percent of which were apparently disabled for one reason or another or out of fuel.

Back in Pyongyang we toured Kim Il Sung University. It was surprisingly well planned and had a reasonable mix of facilities, grounds, and student housing. During our visit to the main library I asked the lady at the reference desk for the most recent issue of *Foreign Affairs Quarterly*. To my astonishment, she readily produced it and handed it to me. Leafing through it, I noticed that certain portions of the text had been blackened out, censored, in other words.

As I returned the periodical to the librarian, I asked her about this. She observed quite matter-of-factly that the censored parts were of no interest to the students anyway and that the blackened portions would facilitate their reading of this periodical. I then asked who decided what the students were interested in. Somewhat taken aback by the question, she said with no apparent awkwardness, "Why, I make the decision. I'm the librarian." I was glad to get an answer.

I also remember the expressed hostility of their deputy foreign minister toward the West and the United States in particular during our two meetings with him. These were the least congenial of our meetings since they focused on returning to U.S. hands the remains of U.S. soldiers killed in the Korean War. Karen Elliott House of the *Wall Street Journal*, an experienced, smart, and sophisticated journalist responsible for the *Journal*'s international operations, was a very effective member of our team. She kept pressing the deputy foreign minister on this issue. Finally, in exasperation (I do not believe he had had much experience with the free Western press) he said, "Well, why won't you just receive these remains over time as we have proposed? What are we supposed to do with them anyway, eat them?" This subject was then concluded and we went to another.

The North Koreans wanted to repatriate remains a few at a time; in the eyes of interested parties they thus accrued maximum and ongoing benefit. The United States wanted them returned at once. The result was that nothing happened, although I note that in early 2004 the two countries apparently reached an agreement on this issue—thirteen years later. And as the five-day visit to North Korea came to a close, tensions had eased somewhat. The North Koreans were, of course, always civil and courteous outside our formal meetings.

One story comes closest to encapsulating our experience in North Korea. We were being shown some of the major public buildings in downtown Pyongyang, one of which was the very impressive National Museum. An acquaintance of Scalapino's escorted us through the museum, a very interesting tour indeed. When we had seen what they wanted us to see, the tour ended.[4] Scalapino asked if we could also see the Korean War exhibit rooms. The answer was "No; and in any event we would be late for our next appointment if we did." Scalapino then ascertained that the appointment was in thirty minutes. "Well," said Scalapino, "you better call and tell them we are going to be late because we are not leaving here until we see the Korean War exhibit." Our guide, the director, hesitated but then agreed.

The exhibit alleged that the United States had started the Korean War in 1950, invading the North Koreans' homeland unilaterally and without provocation; we had used chemical weapons on their troops, and in the end their armies had vanquished ours. Never mind that everyone in the room knew otherwise on all counts. Finally someone in our group asked why the exhibit was silent about the massive intervention of Chinese troops, after the decimation of North Korea's armed forces during MacArthur's advance to the Yalu River (the northern border between North Korea and Manchuria). The director laughed and said, "We have a separate museum for our Chinese visitors."

We thanked the director and moved on to our next appointment, after Scalapino drew our attention to a very large and prominently displayed photo of the Great Leader and his generals that he, Scalapino, easily recognized. "But it's odd to see the photo in its present form," he remarked to the director, "with the Russian generals who were standing next to your distinguished government and military leaders painted or airbrushed out or otherwise excised from the photo." With a smile and a good-natured wave, the director bade us good-bye.

These Asian experiences were not unique to my service. Clark Kerr was an internationalist too. Charlie Hitch, who succeeded him, had been an Oxford don for thirteen years and actively engaged with the Asia Foundation during his tenure as president. UC's worldwide interests are little understood at home but widely known and valued abroad. Serving in the footsteps of those who had themselves contributed so much gave me much professional and personal satisfaction.

The public and diplomatic portfolio for the domestic agenda was no less demanding and expectant than the international, and often the two intersected so as to make the differences indistinguishable. One example should suffice.

Chancellor Kohl of Germany

As described in chapter 7, when I visited Bonn at the invitation of Chancellor Helmut Kohl, he and I spent considerable private time together discussing the proposals in *A Nation at Risk*. We talked on the patio of his official residence overlooking the Rhine River until late in the evening, and I found myself liking this person very much. I resolved then to invite him to Berkeley as a Tanner lecturer.

After nearly two years of negotiations, he timed his visit to the opening of the Center for German and European Studies on the Berkeley campus, the tangible result of my earlier trip to Germany and UC's excellent proposal that resulted in German support for one of three such centers in the United States.

His visit in fall 1991 was a great success. He lectured to an overflow crowd at the Greek Theatre on the Berkeley campus, dedicated the new center, met with leading UC scholars in German and European studies in general, and dined at Blake House as my guest with some of the university's regents, vice presidents, chancellors, and leaders of the Academic Senate, the German ambassador to the United States and his entourage from Washington, D.C., along with Chancellor Kohl's from Germany. Two other guests at Blake House were Governor Pete Wilson and his wife, Gayle, who came early at my invitation to visit privately with Chancellor and Mrs. Kohl and remained for the reception and dinner.

September in the Berkeley hills is usually a delight: warm, clear, and free from the fogs of summer. Our evening was thus blessed, and the reception was held in the spacious grounds fronting the entrance to Blake House. I had invited the Straw Hat Band, a small group of Berkeley students with musical talents who enjoyed playing university music and songs, to perform for our distinguished guests during the reception.

When the band arrived, the wine was flowing freely. The director of the band, a student, asked me if Chancellor Kohl might enjoy conducting one of the numbers they were scheduled to play. "No musical talent was required: the band knew what to do, and would begin and stop on beat regardless of what the ad hoc conductor might be doing," he explained.

I said I could not speak for Kohl as this was a unique American expectation for a German head of state and perhaps it would be best if we did not pursue the matter. I then volunteered Governor Wilson, a Berkeley graduate, and a very informal, easy-going person who, I surmised, would be far more likely to accept. So he did, putting on a straw hat that settled onto the tops of his ears and nearly hid his eyes as he got ready to perform.

Kohl was standing next to me, saw Wilson, and asked, "Is Governor Wilson going to conduct the band?" I said, "Yes, it would appear so at least." Much to my astonishment Kohl then added, "I want to conduct the band too and I want one of those straw hats as well." We responded immediately. There we were, with the governor of California and the chancellor of the Republic of Germany, the former with a straw hat too large and the latter with one too small, perched on his hand actually, flourishing a baton in front of one of Berkeley's most cherished student musical organizations. The German newspapers the next day carried the chancellor's picture engaged in this musical frenzy. I never knew if this was a plus or minus politically for him back home, but I think he didn't really care: he was having a good time.

Several other heads of state also visited UC during my tenure: François Mitterand of France, King Juan Carlos and Queen Sophia of Spain, Corazon Aquino of the Philippines (all at Berkeley), Carlos Salinas de Gortari of Mexico (at UCSD), Václav Havel, head of the then Czechoslovakia Republic, and soon-to-be-elected President George H.W. Bush of the United States (both at UCLA).

President Mitterand of France

While many stories bear remembering, I call out only two. Mitterand was to visit Berkeley for most of one day in 1984. He and his entourage were to arrive at the base of the Campanile. Chancellor and Mrs. Heyman, Libby, and I were to take him to the top, show him the campus and the Bay Area from that spectacular vantage point, accompany him to Wheeler Hall for his scheduled lecture, and then drive the official party to the chancellor's residence for lunch. Governor and Mrs. Deukmejian were to join us for the entire time to help host the president of France.

For starters, the governor's plane was grounded in Los Angeles owing to fog. Thus the chancellor and I were on our own, along with our spouses. We met Mitterand as scheduled, admired the view from the top of the Campanile, as expected, and then began the 40- to 50-yard walk to Wheeler Hall for Mitterand's lecture. The walkway was lined on both sides, five or six deep, with a crowd of somewhat hostile, often rude, and very loud protesters, most of them (as the police later told us) nonstudents who had come from San Francisco.

The object of their scorn was Governor Deukmejian because he had vetoed a gay rights bill the day before. Uncertain what the absent governor looked like, the crowd took its hostility out on poor Mitterand, who wondered what he had done wrong, just as the French and U.S. Secret Service were doubtless wondering what they had missed.

Being a real pro, Mitterand walked directly up to the loudest protester and stopped. He addressed him in a low voice in French, inaudible and unintelligible to most of the onlookers, and everyone quieted down so they could make out the translation into English. Mitterand then moved on, stopping five or six times in this fashion, so by the time he reached the doors to Wheeler the protest had lost its edge.

After the lecture we avoided the expected crowd outside by walking out a back door to the cars waiting to take us to University House. But it was a beautiful Berkeley day, and Mitterand decided he preferred to walk, wishing to see the campus once again. The security personnel from both countries objected vehemently but to no avail, and off we went.

The security detail matched Mitterand's leisurely pace, with barrier ropes about 10 yards long on both sides of the path to keep spectators at a respectful distance. Iranian students were there to protest, furious with the military aid France was providing to Iraq—their country's opponent in a protracted and bloody war—and eager to express their anger to Mitterand directly. All he wanted, of course, was to enjoy a brief stroll through campus. So Mitterand ignored the protesters completely and directed his questions to Chancellor Heyman and to me about campus landmarks he remembered.

As we approached the chancellor's residence amidst all this hubbub, several Iranian students broke away and ran toward the house and up on its lovely lawns to the left of the entrance, in order to carry their protest right to the front door. By then Chancellor Heyman was at the end of his patience. He is a very large man and commands attention especially when his displeasure is directed your way.

"You over there!" Heyman shouted to the students. "You are on my lawn and I want you to get off my goddam lawn right now." And move they did. Mitterand's admiring smile and friendly comments to Heyman eased the tensions of the moment, and we moved into University House without incident. We were glad to have lunch and end the day with the usual pleasantries between hosts and guests.

The King and Queen of Spain

One of my fondest such memories involves the visit to Berkeley of King Juan Carlos and Queen Sophia of Spain. The king was scheduled to speak on campus at Zellerbach Auditorium just after a luncheon hosted by the Heymans and Gardners. It was a very warm day, and we were anxious to make our guests as comfortable as possible during and after lunch. We had asked that only the best California wines be served and that the menu be light and more sparse than expansive. All the doors and windows of University House were opened to increase the flow of fresh air, and the chairs and tables were not overcrowded. The considerable security accompanying their visit (the Bay Area has a significant Basque population) was as discrete as possible.

The king and queen were a delight. They were enjoying their visit to the campus immensely and looked forward to the rest of the day, and to meeting our invited guests who included Governor and Mrs. Deukmejian, several regents, distinguished scholars of European history from the Berkeley faculty especially specialists on the Iberian Peninsula, and several university officers.

The king was at a faraway table to Libby's right, and the queen was likewise to my left at my table. The waiters saw to the needs of our guests, who were thoroughly enjoying our state's best wines; they also knew to pour apple or white grape juice in my wine glass. As it was very warm, I had several glasses of apple juice. The queen apparently took note of the frequent refills and midway through lunch turned to ask what I was drinking. I said, "apple juice," and explained why. Seemingly relieved, she turned the conversation but shortly thereafter quietly asked if she too could have some apple juice, as wine at midday gave her a headache, but in consideration of the Spanish vintners she disliked saying so.

As lunch was coming to a close, I prepared to offer the first toast of the meal in honor of our special guests. "How do you give a toast with apple juice?" the queen asked. "Oh," I responded, "it's easy. First of all, the juice is in a wine glass, second it looks like wine, third our guests have been enjoying their wine throughout the meal and are somewhat less observant than they might otherwise be, and it is a warm day. No one will notice." With that she laughed and said what a good idea this was, that the king had the same problem with wine midday as did she, and, if I did not object, she intended to share this alternative with him.

The lecture was well received, and Spain's leading couple, he a bold and courageous leader and she a much admired and hard-working partner in the Spanish cause, were a pleasure to have as guests. And UC held its own.

Alumni

Alumni relations and the accompanying advocacy and fundraising efforts pursued by UC were uncommonly complicated but not particularly difficult, given the high levels of loyalty and commitment to UC of the alumni and the university's many friends. This positive support was interrupted from time to time by such divisive issues as the loyalty oath controversy of 1949–52, the FSM of 1964–65, the Vietnam War protests of 1967–71, the South African divestment controversy of 1984–86, and the affirmative action disputes of the mid-1990s—an average of one major controversy per decade.

The alumni are ideologically and politically diverse, but for the most part they care very much about their alma mater's well-being and prospects. They are actively interested in what is going on at UC, and especially at the campus from which they earned their degree(s) or at least studied. Alumni indifference has never been much of a problem. Thus, when controversies of the kind just noted arise, they regard themselves as stakeholders, and, of course, they are. After all, they knew the university well when they were students, followed its successes and trials, contributed their money to it, attended the athletic, cultural, and intellectual events scheduled on campus, provided scholarship support for students, helped with student orientation programs, assisted in UC's legislative efforts, operated and paid for the alumni associations on UC's nine campuses, and published magazines to keep the alumni informed about the university.

In short, they are vested in UC, and when they don't like what is going on, the university needs to have an open ear and understanding attitude, as I tried to do throughout my service.

William Baker, my vice president for budget and university relations, was the officer responsible for overseeing campus and Office of the President alumni programs, the former administered by each of the nine campuses and the latter by his office, which was mostly legislatively linked. The chancellors, sometimes overseeing and other times cooperating with their respective alumni associations, were responsible for the usual range of alumni activities, for example, student recruitment, scholarship programs for entering students, alumni clubs, and alumni publications. Mercifully, alumni focused their dissatisfactions with intercollegiate athletic programs on the chancellors. I was not involved in the athletic programs in any direct way, as much as I enjoyed attending the games and supported them as part of the legacy of American colleges and universities.

All nine alumni associations had formed a confederated union and hence spoke with one voice in UC's behalf, to the legislature, the governor, and Congress. They were effective. "Alumni day" at the state capital was held annually and attended by several hundred of our leading alumni from every campus throughout the state. Following a breakfast meeting where I would inform the alumni of our legislative problems, they would fan out, visiting legislators they knew personally, advancing UC's cause, urging its support, and wielding what influence they could. Their personal influence, and related efforts throughout the year in Sacramento and in the district legislative offices of members of the state Senate and Assembly, paid off for UC, and handsomely.

Development

The division of labor for UC's alumni programs and its fundraising efforts was comparable. Except when a chancellor invited me to help close a gift, I had little part in UC's efforts to secure private support. Or I could help with contacts chancellors didn't have but wanted when individual donors or foundations asked for my involvement or when the object of our private support was to fund a universitywide project or program, such as the 10-meter telescope in the early to middle 1980s.

The chancellors, therefore, had both the function and the accountability for our development efforts, campus by campus, and they were remarkably, almost unbelievably, successful. Private gifts to UC, taking the campuses collectively and including those that came to UC without campus designation, rose from $157 million annually in 1983 to $433 million in 1992, for a total of $3,109,616,845 during my tenure. And drawing on my significant fundraising experience at the California Alumni Association and as the first director of the California Alumni Foundation as well as at UC Santa Barbara and as president of the University of Utah, I was able to advise, indeed even occasionally to help, some of the less experienced chancellors as they positioned their respective campuses to seek the private support essential to realize many of their aspirations and plans.

To the credit of the governor and the legislature, both in Utah and in California, they made no efforts to offset state support against private support coming to either university. Thus, as state support increased in Utah and California for their respective universities, so too did private support and so too did federal contracts and grants for research and public service. The result in both places was a prolonged period of institutional prosperity, lasting for ten years in Utah during my tenure and nearly nine years in California.

THE LEGISLATURE

Student tuitions and fees had risen inordinately in the 1960s and 1970s, especially in the leading private universities and some of their public counterparts. The faculty's teaching loads had declined during the same period, thus increasing the real unit costs of instruction, principally as faculty shifted more of their teaching to research (this generality applies most to the hard sciences and engineering and less to the humanities, arts, and social and behavioral sciences). There had also been a corresponding rise in the proportion of undergraduate teaching by teaching assistants and part-time and auxiliary faculty, whose numbers had risen dramatically both in absolute terms and as a percentage of the teaching staff as a whole (though from 1973 to 1983 we were able to bring the student-faculty ratio at Utah down from 21:1 to 16:1).

Students' discontent translates into legislative sympathies not for the universities but for their students and leads to sharp criticisms of the universities' teaching loads and the diminished percentage of the full-time faculty teaching freshman and sophomore students. Thus, legislators tend to put downward pressure on both faculty salaries and student tuition and fees, and vent their criticisms by attacking universities' "bloated bureaucracies" (note that bureaucracies grow every year principally in direct response to the seemingly endless demands and increasing regulations of the federal, state, and local governments for greater accountability and oversight of these institutions: laws or regulations on privacy, the environment, civil and animal rights, workplace conditions, collective bargaining, and so forth).

In my experience, legislators usually have only two enduring interests in the university: to keep fees and tuitions low and to make certain that all eligible students wishing to enroll are able to do so. This is what their constituents want and what they try to give them. What happens to the students once they are enrolled at modest to low levels of tuition is of lesser concern, and the criticisms noted above serve to justify adverse university budgets during tight budget years.

I believe my general assessment is valid, but not in every instance. For I met legislators from both parties in Utah and in California who were truly committed to the well-being and further development of the public colleges and universities and who worked hard and effectively to secure the resources needed to advance their work. Thus our job was to cultivate and inform such legislators and to be wholly open with them and rely on their integrity and goodwill to help carry the day. In parallel we tried to neutralize the least supportive, usually by engaging friends of theirs who were also our champions, mostly in the private sector, on behalf of our cause. The great middle was harder to get at, but we worked this arena as best we could.

Speaker Brown

The leadership in the legislature was the most critical element, and its views of Utah or UC really counted. In Utah, as I related earlier, it required less tending, but in California, its structure was both more pronounced and dominant: Willie Brown essentially controlled the Assembly throughout my tenure. A small number of senior members who were for the most part very friendly to UC similarly controlled the Senate.

As in Utah, I managed in California to get along with the leaders of both parties (in general) and in both houses. Once the South African divestment issue was behind us, the Speaker and I enjoyed an excellent relationship. He was readily accessible, personally or by phone, his word was good, and our conversations were open and direct. And he was of enormous help to UC throughout my presidency. However different we were in background, race, religion, and life experiences, he and I were the same age and worked hard on the way to our respective positions, suffered setbacks, but were both committed to and respectful of the public trusts we held. Besides, I liked Willie. He was fun to be with. He was politically savvy and had a fine sense of humor. He was highly intelligent, always one step ahead of the game.

Not all members of the California Assembly were as friendly, but enough were that with Brown's expertise we did extremely well there and in the Senate, where Senators Nick Petris, John Garamendi, Gary Hart, Diane Watson, Becky Morgan, Al Alquist, and others always helped when we needed it.

Assemblyman Vasconcellos

In the Assembly we had the most trouble with and sometimes also the most help from John Vasconcellos of San Jose. Vasconcellos was a long-serving and intelligent but somewhat unpredictable person, if I may understate it. He had a love-hate relationship with UC, and with me as well. His views counted as chairman of the Assembly's Committee on Ways and Means, thus influencing but not controlling UC's budget in that house. Brown helped as best he could, but Vasconcellos marched to his own beat.

On some days he was friendly and supportive and on others just the reverse. I never knew why; and, given my more steady and even-tempered personality and more systematic and analytical ways of dealing with issues, I suppose he found me trying as well. I heard that he thought me lacking in passion; I, in turn, thought he had an excess of it. His attitude was most friendly when others were giving us a hard time, and the least friendly when we were doing well. But however random and erratic the objects of his affections, in many ways I admired his independence and courage. He is now serving his final year as a state senator.

I recall one occasion when he congratulated me for my success with Governor Deukmejian on UC's budget and then proceeded to criticize me for not persuading the governor to do as well for K-12. I reminded him that I was representing UC, not K-12, and that the K-12 lobby was not only more powerful than UC's but vastly better funded and with a very large staff. "Why are you criticizing me," I asked "instead of those responsible for K-12's interests?" "Because," he answered, "you have the governor's ear and they don't."

Assemblyman Hayden

Tom Hayden was a member of the state Assembly whose influence was slight but whose profile was high. Again, he was not easy to understand, though less unpredictable but not less passionate than Vasconcellos. Hayden had a real interest in higher education, since his days as one of the founders of the Students for a Democratic Society in the 1960s. His view of UC's role in California and the nation was fundamentally at odds with my own. We skirmished on other than the fundamental issues but were still able to maintain a dialogue with each other, though he seemed not disinclined to take an unwarranted shot at UC if it helped him politically while tossing off its significance and his intentions when challenged later.

Like Vasconcellos, Hayden was smart and fortunately never took himself too seriously. He could also be very warm and friendly, as he was when Libby died. All things considered, Vasconcellos and Hayden, difficult or unpredictable or critical of UC as they could be, did care about the university, informed themselves about it, and when it really counted were with us more often than not. Besides, they made for a much more colorful set of experiences than I would otherwise have had.

SUMMING UP
Two Legislatures

All in all, legislators in California were pretty much representative of those who elected them, as was true in Utah. But in Utah they were 70 percent of one religious faith, almost all Caucasian, middle or working class, teachers, farmers, craftsmen, and some professional and business people as well, more homogeneous in every respect than their counterparts in California. Here the legislature was more of a free-for-all than a deliberative body, especially in the Assembly. Its members were as diverse as the state's citizenry—multiethnic and racial, all religions or none at all, boisterous, marginally disciplined, politically striving, and welcoming of publicity, whatever its character or color. It reminded me of the Pierpont family reunions when I was young.

After all, whereas Utah's legislature met for only six weeks, California's worked full time. Bills would be introduced to achieve certain social objectives that were barely believable, for example, when Willie Brown and others sought to enact legislation that would require UC *to graduate* the several racial and ethnic groups within its student body at exactly the same rate. Yet our legislative relations were very good, as were our relations with Governors Deukmejian and Wilson. Both were Republicans, and the Democrats held a majority in both houses of the legislature during my tenure. Actually, this arrangement was more of a help than a hindrance given its inherent checks and balances, including a Republican governor's budget line-item veto authority.

Since both parties dealt the political cards, UC had ample discretion to "play" in this game. We formed countervailing coalitions to defeat unwelcome legislation or enact bills UC favored, found common ground between the governor and legislative leaders or used the one to check the other, enlisting our friends, alumni, and regents from both parties as needed, and affirmed UC's political neutrality and nonpartisan approach to other issues of interest to the lawmakers.

Whatever problems I had with the four governors and two decades of legislators with whom I worked in both states, none rises to the high level of appreciation I have for these experiences or for the support they provided the universities I served and me personally. I have no complaints. It was a great run.

The Media

My relations with the media in general, on balance and over time, were also very favorable. The media showed its ugly and grossly unprofessional side during the last months of my service at UC, the next chapter's subject. That and my experience with student unrest at UC Santa Barbara aside, I have no complaints about the basic fairness or professionalism of the publishers, editors, and reporters with whom I interacted. While they didn't always get it quite right, neither did I. By and large, they reported and interpreted my actions as president both at Utah and California with reasonable accuracy and fairness, choosing to report as many favorable things about the university's work as inherently controversial ones.

In Utah the higher education beat was covered by mature and responsible reporters. In California, as with most things in this enigmatic state, there was a mix of both senior, informed, and mature journalists covering UC with junior journalists, whose stories occasionally resembled adolescent exhibitionism. The southern California newspapers seemed to have a preponderance of the former, and the San Francisco Bay Area, a disproportionate share of the latter. This advantaged our campuses at Los Angeles, Irvine, Riverside, San Diego, and Santa Barbara and hurt the campuses at Berkeley, San Francisco, Davis, and Santa Cruz, but only generally speaking. All things considered, the coverage was not much better or much worse than that of most other urban newspapers nationwide.

In the north I found the *San Jose Mercury News* had it right most of the time, with the *Sacramento Bee* and its affiliates in California's great Central Valley a close second. The *San Francisco Chronicle* was a mix, very much depending on the reporter assigned, but pretty solid on its editorial pages. In the later years of my service I came to regard the then *San Francisco Examiner* as a journalistically challenged newspaper, although in the early years of my administration I had little reason to complain.[5] And in the south the *Los Angeles Times* dominated and usually assigned very competent people to the UC beat. I thought the *Riverside Press,* the *San Diego Union,* and the *Santa Barbara News-Press* were all also very good newspapers and tried hard to be fair.

Nationally, I found the *New York Times* to be a remarkable newspaper, with great news-gathering capabilities, competent reporters, and well-written editorials, reflective, however, of its more general left-of-center position. The *Washington Post* was as reliable as any and was a diligent newsgathering and reporting institution with intelligent and informative news columns and editorials. Frankly, it is hard for me to imagine how the *New York Times* and the *Washington Post* and the *Los Angeles Times* actually got their work done each day in such prodigious fashion, given the complexities and nuances of the world they report on and attempts by every self-interested party (including higher education) to use and influence them. I always found the *Wall Street Journal's* news reporting and editorial pages to be exceptional (though I seemed most often to be impressed with its editorial opinions on matters I knew very little about, and less impressed on things I knew a great deal about).

My Portfolio

I was also active with various professional associations such as the American Association of Universities, the American Council on Education, the National Association of State Universities and Land-Grant Colleges, and various national commissions and special assignments from the National Collegiate Athletic Association, the College Board, and the Business Higher Education Forum that I chaired from 1988 to 1990.

I close this chapter, however, with one final story that I cherish. Shortly after President George H. W. Bush's election in 1988, the American Council on Education asked me to join with eleven other university presidents for a private meeting with the newly inaugurated president; Benno Schmidt, then president of Yale University, Bush's alma mater, led the group. We met in Bob Atwell's office, the council's president, to discuss the issues to be raised and to assign the responsibility for asking them. I was to share with President Bush my experience with Chancellor Kohl as a lead into discussing the need to strengthen graduate studies and student and faculty exchanges in the American research community. At that time considerable strain existed between the universities and the federal government on these and a number of other issues, including student financial aid and the indirect costs of doing government-sponsored research.

As we entered the room and were greeted by the president, a large body of reporters gathered there asked what the meeting was about, and why we were there. The president offered some generalities and then showed them out.

Schmidt introduced each of us to the president (I had met Bush during the campaign when he debated with Governor Dukakis at UCLA, and remarkably, he remembered our talk then as well as the day *A Nation at Risk* was released). We then expected to go directly to our questions. The president, however, chose otherwise. He started the questioning. "I am aware of some differences between the nation's universities and the federal government," he said, "but it has been my view that our partnership over the years has worked pretty well, both for your institutions and for the nation. So, what's the problem?"

We had been prepared to ask questions, not answer them. So we just all sat there like mutes (much to our later embarrassment). After a prolonged and awkward silence, the president then said, "Let me rephrase the question. Why are you people so pissed off at us?" That broke the ice and off we went for an hour of very constructive discussion with President Bush.

The public and diplomatic parts of my portfolio were demanding, but they were also pleasurable, an important part of the satisfaction I have derived from my professional life over nearly four decades. This chapter dealt with only some of them. This aspect of the responsibilities carried by presidents of America's major research universities, however, is hardly known, much less acknowledged by the universities we serve or by their governing boards for that matter.

The governing boards fix their sights on issues of interest and concern to the university for which they are ultimately responsible. The faculty, themselves active in their own world of scholarship and research together with teaching, obviously have enough to think about. The students, if not traumatized by the amount of work the faculty ask of them or otherwise distracted by the pleasures and hazards they choose to seek out, have no idea about a president's global role, and neither does the generally overworked and underappreciated staff.

But the president knows, recognizing where his or her intervention in the public and diplomatic arena can advance the interests of the university, assist the faculty, and provide new and different opportunities for its students. In dealing with government the president must know how our system and the accompanying politics actually work, just as in working with business leaders and foundation heads, she or he requires reasonable insight into the world of international business markets and the economic, social, cultural, demographic, and religious forces that influence them.

And in a way it hardly matters whether anyone else does know about the importance of these activities. The president can proceed pretty much alone. But the students, staff, faculty, and governing board surely *would* know if the president of one of our country's leading universities chose *not* to play on this stage.

TEN

TRAGEDY AND TRIBULATION

As the twentieth century's final decade began, life was good for me both at work and at home. The University of California was moving forward on all its nine campuses and planning for a tenth. UC's academic reputation was on the ascendancy. Students were enrolling at unexpectedly high rates. And considering all sources of support, funding for the university had never been higher than in 1989–90:

State funding per student—in real terms and on a weighted full-time basis—was at near-record levels;

Gifts from the private sector were without precedent and growing;

Federally funded contracts and grants for research and public service were at their all-time highs;

Student fees remained remarkably low, compared to tuitions and fees at other major public universities nationwide;

Staff and faculty salaries had been competitive within their respective marketplaces since UC's budget of 1984–85. Those for UC's most senior administrators were less competitive, taking into account salary, benefits, housing, and deferred compensation (the differences were modest to significant);

Our state-funded capital budgets had reached unprecedented levels. The legislature had also enacted laws allowing UC to borrow for construction of research facilities and repay the costs from overhead earned on the research conducted in such facilities;

Students were willing to assess themselves or otherwise to be charged for
    building student unions, recreational facilities, athletic fields, health
    centers, student service buildings, and residence halls;
Our five medical centers were in the black though struggling (as usual); and
The budgets of our self-supporting auxiliaries were in balance—parking
    services, bookstores, cafeterias, intercollegiate athletics, residence
    halls, and the like.

In addition to the budgetary and funding issues, the university was well positioned in other ways as we came into the 1990s:

All nine campuses were completing their long-range academic and develop-
    ment plans;
We were recruiting to our faculties most of those we wanted while generally
    holding on to those being recruited by others, although California's
    high cost of housing was a growing problem;
New academic majors and departments, professional schools and colleges
    were forming across all nine campuses, as were several newly orga-
    nized research units;
Relations with the governors (both Deukmejian and Wilson) were excel-
    lent, as were our relations with the key players in the state legislature;
    and
Our central administration had experienced no turnover in seven and a
    half years, except for the death in the mid-1980s of my close friend
    and colleague Vice President Jim Kendrick. He was succeeded by
    Kenneth Farrell, who ably carried on the work critical to the univer-
    sity's obligations under the federal land-grant statutes and to the
    well-being of California's agricultural sector.

On the home front, our family was healthy. Two of our daughters were
caught up in university studies: Marci was an undergraduate at Berkeley, and
Lisa was a graduate student at the University of Washington. Shari and Karen
had completed their graduate studies, one at UCLA, the other at Queens
College, Cambridge, and both were soon to be married. Libby was heavily
involved in representing UC not only in this country but abroad as well (as
noted briefly in chapter 9 and earlier), and we enjoyed the increase in discretionary time that came with a smaller household. Thus as the eighties
faded into the nineties, the prospect furthest from my mind and imagination was that my world—both personal and professional—would come
crashing down within twelve to eighteen months, devastating me personally
and demoralizing me about my work and service as UC's president.

These events are hard for me to write about. They bear on three of the
four most important parts of my life: my marriage to Libby, our family, and

the University of California (leaving aside my religion). The resulting fusion of the institutional and the personal makes objectivity uncommonly difficult to achieve, but I intend to back off from praising or blaming others and defending or justifying myself. Still, in the nature of the case I cannot hope to be completely neutral.

ADVERSE TRENDS
California's Economy Heads South

As the nation moved into the 1990s, we began to see the first signs of a weakening economy. The cold war was in its final stages and as the Berlin wall came down, along with the Soviet Union, so too did much of California's highly profitable defense industry. The state was rich in military bases sprinkled throughout its Central Valley and coastal regions. These too felt the ending of the cold war, as little by little their size and numbers shrank. These body blows to California's economy came so abruptly and with such intensity that they triggered an economic depression in California second only to the Great Depression of the 1930s.

UC's Political and Social Climate Darkens

The Gulf War of early 1991 rallied the country long enough to defeat Iraq and free Kuwait but not long enough to earn President Bush a second term; the declining economy, not the victorious war, held sway in the minds of the electorate. The presidential and congressional campaigns of 1991 and 1992 were about people losing their jobs or going bankrupt, businesses failing, farms foreclosing, all in an economy that appeared to be weakening every day. The politics of race and class complemented the economic issues: the Democrats argued for taxing the rich and helping the poor, and the Republicans argued for lowering taxes and boosting business incentives and national security (which, as it turned out, people cared less about).

The mood of the country was uncommonly ugly. Bush was out, Clinton was in, and the class warfare rhetoric translated into a promptly enacted tax increase, one of the largest in American history, especially for the upper-income earners who, exultant critics knew, deserved it. As the political and social agenda of the early 1990s preoccupied and further divided people, American business and government at all levels took the biggest hits. And the nation's colleges and universities came a close third.

As California's economy declined, this mood was starkly evident in our discussions with key legislators from 1990 through 1992. Once again UC was portrayed as an institution of privilege, enrolling only the "elite" young people of the state. Moreover, the average cost to the state for students enrolled at UC exceeded the cost for students in the California State University system and the community colleges—their distinct missions aside—a point of vulnerability for UC as we moved into an extremely difficult period of declining budgets.

In the 1980s UC had been much more successful at getting state funding than had CSU and the community colleges. Somehow we were to blame for this, not advocates for CSU and the community colleges. Similar resentments were stirring within the community of K-12 supporters and for the same reasons.

Legislators repeatedly admonished us to allow for these resentments in our budget negotiations. They also wanted us to know that as state revenues declined they would look after K-12 first, then health and welfare (for the Democrats) and prisons (for the Republicans). Higher education and unprotected state operations were to be a distant third for both political parties.

The university's plans for expanding the number of campuses by three over the next thirty years to accommodate forecasted enrollment demand (considered by the regents in 1988) were now being described by some legislators as just another aggrandizement of UC's power position within the higher education community.

Fees and tuitions had changed little during the mid to late 1980s, but now students perceived a threat to their pocketbooks. They took steps in Sacramento to make certain that their pockets were to be the last ones picked in the scramble to make up for shrinking state revenues; so did the unions representing large numbers of UC staff. The faculty tended to believe that things would just go on as usual, and of course it was my job, not theirs, to make it so. Yet another factor in the equation that yielded such an unhappy period for UC and for me was that my relationship with the regents came under fire.

Resignations, illness, or expiring terms had led to an unusually high rate of turnover among the regents in the late 1980s, disrupting the familiar and predictable relations that marked the board's work early in my administration. As positions on the board fell vacant, Governors Deukmejian and then Wilson appointed only Republicans. The resulting imbalance made the board an easy partisan target for the legislature, since Democrats controlled both houses. Though in fact nearly all the regents supported me, liberal legislators resented my "excessive" influence over the board's conservative elements. And the legislators' perception of my role undercut my ability to get the university's business done with a minimum of controversy and a maximum of effect.

Thus imbalances in both board and legislature deprived us of the ability to play the political game in Sacramento that a more evenly divided legislature and a more politically balanced Board of Regents would have allowed.

The political priorities and system of social and economic values embedded in the ideologies of the two parties, and within the personal commitments and motives of each legislator, were now going to play themselves out in California and in a very public, contentious, and volatile setting. No scenario any of us could construct in the very early 1990s gave reason for encouragement.

My own view, both then and now, was that legislators knew only too well where the state was headed economically and didn't know what to do about it. They had failed to address the fact that federal law, the State Constitution, and some politically "unchallengeable" state statutes, enacted both by the legislature and directly by the people in propositions, left them with discretionary control over only 15 percent of the state budget. UC was in the 15 percent, and the legislators were looking for ways to explain or otherwise justify the actions they were contemplating; and these actions did not favor higher education.

Thus, I knew there would not be enough state money to go around in the early years of the new decade. At that point, however, UC was fiscally strong, and we were reasonably confident that we could cope with a modest downturn, for a year or two. No one, including us, however, foresaw a five-year downturn or the depth and suddenness of the decline, and not surprisingly. After all, California had not suffered such a precipitous loss of state revenue for over sixty years.

In point of fact, I was more concerned at that juncture with the 15 percent problem, which I had made a major effort to correct, both in Sacramento and with the regents. For the most part my concerns and warnings fell on deaf ears. We had had a great run from 1983 on, and no one, it seemed, wanted it to end. In such instances, of course, denial takes over. And it did for us and for the state, and its government as well.

As events unfolded, I was reminded once again of what I already knew: money makes the "wheels" mesh and move with little noise, maintenance, or repair, but in its absence the same wheels grate, grind, and break down, commanding an uncommonly high level of care and commitment from those who are held responsible for their workings. Putting it another way, in times of prosperity, conflicts have to do with the play of greed in the context of opportunity, whereas in tough times conflicts grow more bitter and desperate.

The Budget Dips

UC's 1990–91 budget was the first to feel the effect of the state's fiscal problems, both as Governor Deukmejian proposed it and midyear, when he ordered a further reduction in levels of authorized expenditure (the 1989–90 budget was tight, but nothing then pointed to an extended problem). Our response to the governor's cuts was well within the bounds of conventional budgeting, like that of any university faced with not immodest but time-limited cuts in its budget. Our budgets for state-funded research, public service, and administration all absorbed 5 percent cuts. But support for our teaching programs, UC's consistently highest priority for state-funded accounts, remained intact. Student fees rose by 10 percent and nonresident tuitions by 10.6 percent. We deferred graduate enrollment increases, made salary adjustments for faculty and staff effective January 1, 1991, rather than when the fiscal year started July 1, 1990, and froze salaries for our senior administrative officers at their 1989–90 levels.

Between the 1990–91 budget and the one proposed for 1991–92, Governor Deukmejian's term expired. After his eight successful years as California's governor and equally unwavering years of support for the University of California, we found ourselves in fall 1990 working with a new cast of characters in Sacramento to negotiate the 1991–92 budget. Pete Wilson, California's junior senator, had prevailed in his run to succeed Deukmejian.

Wilson was a graduate of the Boalt School of Law on the university's Berkeley campus. He remembered those days with pleasure and nostalgia; he possessed not only an appreciation for the University of California but a great respect for it as well. Hence Wilson was disposed to support UC as best he could.

A New Governor Takes Over

As Deukmejian had, Wilson had served in California's legislature for several years, knew the state well, and enjoyed widespread support. When it appeared that Wilson would run to succeed Deukmejian on the Republican ticket, Bill Baker and I met with him for lunch in the Senate Dining Room in Washington, D.C.

I recall the conversation well, as both Baker and I asked him why he might run for governor now, given the growing indications of a significant downturn in the California economy and his emerging influence in the U.S. Senate. He said he had been briefed on what would be a difficult period, but "the California economy would pick up soon, as it always had." Neither Baker nor I thought that he had been briefed enough, and even we were overly optimistic, for events engulfed projections. In any case, we felt confident we could work with Wilson should he be elected, and that was what counted.

For the most part our impression proved accurate, and throughout my administration Wilson was supportive of UC and of me. Of course, where Deukmejian had been blessed with adequate state revenues, Wilson was not: we all confronted a very discouraging fiscal picture.

We did not, however, have as close and confident a relationship with Wilson and his chief deputies as we had with Deukmejian, because they did not give the legislators quite the same impression that the legislature was *not* to play with the governor's budget for UC but approve it essentially as he wished.

In California this expectation is of no small consequence, given that the governor has the authority to line out of the state budget any part of it he disagrees with and to keep its other provisions and the budget as a whole intact.

In any event, I have no complaints about either Wilson or his key deputies and advisers and remain grateful for the steady and assured support they and he gave me throughout my final year, when I was under such intense and barely believable pressure over the terms of my retirement benefits.

Our Budget Woes Grow

Wilson's 1991–92 budget for UC hit us hard, but not disproportionately. Baker and I had talked with Wilson before his final decision on it. We had also talked at length about UC's budget with Wilson's new director of the state's Department of Finance, Tom Hayes. He too was both friendly and supportive but faced a steadily worsening fiscal picture.

Wilson knew how difficult fiscal 1991–92 was going to be but did not anticipate how bad 1992–93 would be. Thus, he was determined to make the hard cuts in 1991–92, to "get them behind him" and to lay the groundwork for his agenda and near-normalcy in 1992–93. He wanted no new taxes, intended to bring his 1991–92 budget to the legislature in balance, and planned real cuts, not just ones his analysts or the legislature imagined or otherwise manipulated. We had no real reason to fault this approach and we didn't.

The regents met at our Riverside campus on January 18, 1991, to discuss the governor's proposal for 1991–92. It made the midyear cuts ordered for our 1990–91 budget permanent, with a corresponding downward adjustment in the base budget for 1991–92. It made no provision for adjustments in salary for faculty, staff, or administration but instead proposed major reductions in our overall support costs. Student fees were to rise by 20 percent and nonresident tuition by the same percentage. The equipment budgets and infrastructure requirements were to be significantly lower as well.

In sum, the difference between what the governor proposed and what the regents had requested was $295 million, an amount roughly comparable to the combined state-funded budgets of two of our nine campuses, one modest size (Irvine or Davis) and one small (Riverside or Santa Cruz).

At the February 1991 meeting of the board, Tom Hayes and Elizabeth Hill, legislative analyst for the state, addressed the board. As the minutes of the meeting make clear, the only real differences about the economy and its effect on the state budget these two best informed people in the state found were the size and scale of the red ink then engulfing California. Hayes was more optimistic, Hill less so. They also disagreed over the time projected for the end of the economic downturn, Hayes being much more hopeful than Hill. We should have paid more attention to Hill's estimate. The board took no action at this meeting because the budget picture remained too fluid to make any confident decision whatsoever.

The winter and spring of 1991 came and went as we pondered the course of the state's economy and what it would mean for UC. The usual approach to budget cutting was no longer adequate. Where else could we cut? No one seemed to know, unless we harmed our teaching programs, compromised our research capability, impoverished some of our students, or hurt our faculty, staff, and administrators. None of those prospects appealed. As matters actually worsened, the governor and the legislature made deeper cuts in UC's budget. This was a full-blown crisis, and there was no use deceiving ourselves into believing otherwise.

Late in summer 1991, when the budget was finally approved (well after the mandated June 30 deadline), we were facing a gap of $312 million in our state-funded operating budget and had to make it all up in the fiscal year that started two months earlier. Moreover, the base budget kept the previous year's consequential cuts. And in taking those cuts for 1991–92 we had to allow for a 1992–93 fiscal year that looked no better.

As we were preparing for the fiscal year's unavoidable and hurtful decisions, Vice President Ronald Brady proposed a voluntary early retirement incentive plan (VERIP), the first such plan in UC's history. Funds for this plan would be drawn from UC's retirement plan reserves, which were very strong, so much so that neither the state nor UC employees had contributed to the plan for several years (the state had earlier and quietly folded the appropriations otherwise reserved for this purpose into our base operating budget and without prejudice to any other state funds appropriated to UC).

We directed the early retirement plan at staff and faculty members in their middle to late sixties. For them, it sweetened the calculated length of university service and the three highest years of salary by 10 to 20 percent, which would add materially to their retirement income from UC's defined-benefit pension plan (appropriately, senior administrators were not eligible to participate). Approved as a one-time offer, VERIP made all the difference between our surviving 1991–92 and not. Moreover, those on the staff or in the faculty who took the early retirement option could, at the university's discretion, be called back to their respective or related position, but at less than half-time. The result of this plan, along with other major cuts and increased fees, allowed us to balance our budget for 1991–92, but just barely:

- Reductions from the staff totaled 1,000 full-time-equivalent positions throughout the university, mostly by virtue of VERIP, along with a hiring freeze and some layoffs;
- Reductions from the faculty and other academic positions totaled 700 full-time-equivalent positions (almost all through VERIP), along with a part-time, temporary callback to ensure staffing for our courses so

that students could make normal progress toward their degrees. We saved the difference between a retired senior professor's salary with benefits and a newly hired junior professor's, less the cost of the callback—in all, tens of millions of dollars—and thus also kept UC's 17.6:1 student-faculty ratio intact during the early years of these deep cuts;

- A freeze in cost-of-living and merit increases affected all personnel (faculty, staff, and administrators);
- Student fees rose by 40 percent and nonresident tuition by 20 percent;
- The 1990–91 freeze on additional graduate admissions now applied to 1991–92 as well;
- Cuts of 5,000 in undergraduate admissions still honored our obligations under the Master Plan for Higher Education;
- Cuts of 5 percent applied to funds for administration and deferred maintenance, for institutional equipment, and for research and public service activities; and
- The shift of some state-funded positions to self-supporting auxiliary budgets increased charges to the users of auxiliary activities (parking services, bookstores, residence halls, and the like), thus reducing our reliance on state funds.

Throughout this process I made every effort to keep the university community fully informed of our actions. We worked hard in Sacramento to staunch the hemorrhaging of our budget and consulted extensively about our options with leaders of the Academic Senate, the student body, and union representatives, consistent with our contractual obligations. Nevertheless, our budget problems were as real as they were unexpected to the university community. The necessarily draconian cuts at once irritated, demoralized, and blackened the mood of the students, staff, and faculty who, as I was the one making UC's budget decisions, not unsurprisingly assumed I was somehow implicated or enmeshed in the events that gave rise to the budget's effects on our programs and personnel.

Once again there were many answers throughout the university to the budgetary problems we were having, and few solutions. Everyone's answer was to transfer the cut to someone else or to another program: anywhere save to the person offering the advice. This instinctive response meant, of course, that every budget decision I made earned me resentment and criticism from people who would have decided otherwise. This rule held true for decisions in Sacramento as well, though legislators could and did seek refuge in the "misjudgments" or "ill will" of their legislative colleagues, whereas the governor and UC's president could not.

The governor's budget proposal for UC's fiscal year 1992–93 was made in early January 1992. Essentially a rerun of his proposal for 1991–92, it was worse because the cuts were piled on top of those already taken in the two previous budgets. Along with a 25 percent cut in state funds for the Office of the President, it anticipated further cuts in UC's administration and a continuing freeze in senior executive salaries (at 1989–90 levels). It proposed another voluntary early retirement plan for faculty and staff who did not take the first offer, moving down the age scale while moving up the "sweetness" level. It planned to raise student fees by 24 percent, put additional limits on undergraduate admissions, and made other reductions similar in character and scale to those outlined above for 1991–92.

As we expected, Governor Wilson's budget proposal in January 1992 for the 1992–93 fiscal year was too much to hope for: state revenues continued to fall and budgets with them. In late August 1992 the legislature finally approved UC's 1992–93 budget, and it went to the regents in mid-September. The difference between the proposed total in January 1992 and what UC received for 1992–93 was $255 million. During the three fiscal years from 1990 through 1993, the difference between what UC needed—to fund undergraduate admissions, to keep our competitive salaries and benefits for university personnel, to limit fee and tuition increases to legislative guidelines (a yearly maximum of 10 percent under state policy, which the regents ignored), to maintain the physical plant along with our research and instructional equipment, to sustain our libraries and museums, and to adjust our fixed costs for inflation while meeting our regulatory obligations under federal and state laws—approximated $650 million, or in real terms some 24 percent of our base operating budget.

We could not meet our obligations to UC students and those who funded our research if we cut deeper into our operating budget. We were still significantly short. Hence we arranged to borrow $70 million for our operating needs from uncommitted balances within UC's own nonstate accounts (to be repaid from state appropriations over ten years, through 2002). Our acts reflected our long-term intent:

- While student fees and tuitions rose dramatically during 1990–92, UC's fees and tuitions at the close of 1992 remained well below those of comparable public universities nationwide and—as a percentage of family personal income in California—at about the same levels as those UC students paid in the early 1970s. *And* we managed to keep UC's student-faculty ratio at 17.6:1 throughout these years, just as it had been when I took office in 1983.
- Salaries and benefits for faculty, staff, and administrators were very competitive when the cuts began but suffered real comparative losses by the time the cuts ended, though on my recommendation the regents acted to soften the loss in 1991 by setting up a form of deferred compensation for all employees within UC's self-administered retirement plan (an annual payment roughly equal to the amount they would have

received if UC's state-funded budget had permitted it. The total deferred income with interest would be paid out and taxed on retirement).

– Our creative and unique voluntary early retirement plan worked, relieving UC of making other budget decisions that would have been even more hurtful. Moreover, UC was able to reach into the marketplace (when other universities were not) to recruit junior faculty members to its campuses from among the country's most talented and promising young academics. And finally, hundreds of faculty and staff who took VERIP returned to their positions part-time, to the benefit of UC and at a savings of tens of millions of dollars. Individual faculty members' and staff's decision to retire fell unevenly on the university, even from one campus to another, thus creating strains and controversy we sought to mitigate but with only partial success.

– While UC did its job throughout these difficult years, and at its standards, it also took significant steps to improve undergraduate teaching throughout the university as—without coercion or reward—the faculty committed to offer more classes of smaller size, including seminars at the freshman and sophomore levels; to offer more sections of required and heavily enrolled courses, thus facilitating students' steady progress toward their degrees; to increase the number of UC's most distinguished faculty members, including senior professors, who taught introductory courses to freshmen and sophomores; and to broaden opportunities for research relationships between undergraduate students and their professors. (UC's work on these changes reflected recommendations in the Smelser report of 1986 on undergraduate education, the Pister committee of 1991–92 on criteria to strengthen the teaching share of a professor's work, and an all-university conference on undergraduate education that I convened in the early spring of 1992).

– Throughout those problematic times and at historically high levels we sustained our capital budgets, funded mostly from bond issues voted on by the people biannually, and by contributions flowing from the private sector at record levels regardless of the state's economic downturn.

The University of California owed its ability to absorb these enormous cuts without irrevocable harm to the embedded resiliency of UC, its adaptive capacities, its fundamental strength and professional pride in its accomplishments and standing, the skill, experience, and effort of the staff on the campuses and in my office, the cooperative and respectful relations between the Academic Senate and the university's administration, and the regents' unwavering support for our budget proposals and actions.

Yet, as Clark Kerr noted in his introduction to my oral history, if UC had not secured a 32 percent increase in its operating budget in 1984–85—offsetting in full the combined losses incurred under the administrations of

Ronald Reagan and Jerry Brown—the debilitating effects of the additional cuts in the early 1990s would have placed UC at mortal risk:

> From 1990 to 1993, state general fund support for the university fell 24 percent in real terms. Had this percentage been added to the prior 32 percent, the university could hardly have recovered for many years, if at all. Instead, the university moved into the academic rankings by the National Research Council in 1993 with four campuses ready to be rated among the top twenty in the nation in terms of the proportion of "distinguished" programs.[1]

I now step back from fall 1992 to fall 1990, to recount the most wrenching and devastating trauma of my life, which ran concurrently with the university's problems recounted above.

LIBBY'S ILLNESS AND DEATH

Libby, my wife for thirty-one years, the mother of our four daughters, the companion who had not only sustained me with love and sound counsel but helped make those years successful, fell ill with a suddenness that stunned us both. It cost her her life and changed mine forever.

Always steady, confident, and capable, Libby was raised in a loving home. She was well educated, expected to do no less than her share and to make the most of her opportunities. She was a loving, conscientious, and spiritual wife and mother. Rather than complain when things weren't going her way, Libby went about her life with an uncommon equilibrium and a matter-of-factness that fit her Swiss heritage. She treated everyone the same: with courtesy, care, and kindness; as a human being first and anything else—as a famous or obscure individual—last. And for all this she was widely admired and loved. No small measure of the success I have had in life rests squarely on my good fortune in having found and married Libby Fuhriman in 1958.

We traveled extensively together as time and circumstances allowed, right from the first years with the California Alumni Association. We made many friends as we visited alumni clubs and scholarship committees throughout California. We attended and participated as we could, mostly together, in the cultural, social, athletic, and intellectual life of Berkeley and Santa Barbara, and again on our return to the Bay Area when I served as a UC vice president and university dean of extension under President Hitch.

During our decade at Utah, Libby had a heavy responsibility on campus as well as in the community, Salt Lake City being the state capital and the headquarters of the Mormon Church. I honestly do not know how she did all this with four young and growing daughters at home. But she did. She saw to it that we had a circle of friends with whom we felt comfortable and that our family had a steady and loving environment. And I knew that the "home front" was covered while I persevered at the university.

I also helped with the raising of our daughters as best I could, attending their school functions and taking family trips. I made sure I was home for our family dinner whenever possible (most of the time). I encouraged Libby to believe that 68-degree water at Flatland Lake in northwestern Montana was not as cold as it sounded and to commit to build our summer home there. We agreed: money was to be spent carefully and prudently, mostly on our home and family, and elsewhere to enrich our community and university ties. Thus we managed a reasonable balance between work and play, never drifting into separate, less overlapping lives.

Libby's role as the spouse of a university president was in many ways akin to the services rendered by others (usually women) comparably situated. The place and service of such spouses, even today, is either not considered or is ill considered. It tends to be respected and appreciated or demeaned as being anachronistic and sexist. I can't help what other people may think, but I can say that Libby's role was one she wished and was happy to play; and that in my life she was an indispensable force for good, a dependable and honest friend, and a loving and nurturing wife and mother.

Libby and I once estimated that we had personally entertained or hosted some 140,000 to 150,000 persons during our eighteen years together at Utah and California: students, parents, faculty, staff, regents, donors, alumni, legislators, governors, ambassadors, Nobelists, heads of state, presidents of foundations, and heads of universities and their senior academic staff from throughout the world.

But when we returned to UC, with the correspondingly increasing demand on Libby to host this group or that, to speak, to visit, to travel, to help, to lend her support here and there, I started to think about how to recognize her and the wives of our nine chancellors as well, assuming they too rendered equally indispensable services to the university. The real incentive for this idea, however, came from Sue Young, whose husband was UCLA's Chancellor Chuck Young. With the regents' support and suggestions made collectively by the spouses, in November 1987 I issued a policy "to reflect and to recognize the contributions and services to the university of [the president's/chancellors'] spouses when acting as official agents of the university." It acknowledged their significant role in planning, arranging, and hosting university functions and appointed them Associate of the President or Associate of the Chancellor. It also gave them certain rights and courtesies.[2]

The reaction among the spouses of university presidents nationally was very favorable, as we were clearly in the lead on this issue. For years it had been the object of no little discussion among spouses and some presidents, but almost no action. Yet feminist voices pointed out that UC was rewarding voluntary rather than encouraging paid employment for women and, by subordinating their role to their husbands', making women correspondingly more vulnerable and less independent. My view was that the critics were not doing this work, our spouses were, and doing it willingly.

Libby's illness first manifested itself in October 1990, when we were attending meetings of the American Association of Universities at the University of Pennsylvania in Philadelphia. She collapsed in the shower early one evening as we were getting ready for dinner. Her pain persisted all night, and the next morning we decided to leave for home, believing that a degenerative disc problem she had was acting up again. On our return home, the doctor ordered her to bed for ten days in hopes that that her back, once rested, would return to its earlier, livable state. It did not, and as time went on she developed breathing problems and other symptoms that could not possibly relate to the lower back.

In late November she was admitted to Berkeley's Alta Bates Hospital for more extended tests. After a series of nondirective tests over several days, a bone biopsy and symptom-specific blood tests revealed multiple myeloma with complications. This form of cancer affects the bone marrow and, in her case, was also producing an aberrant form of the amyloid protein that circulates through the blood stream and attaches itself to vital organs, in her case the heart and kidneys.

She was subjected to the usual radiation treatments in December and very low doses of chemotherapy in early January, but to no avail. Her heart had been so weakened that an increase in chemotherapy to levels that would affect the cancer would provoke cardiac arrest.

Throughout Libby's hospitalization, I was in her room from early morning until midnight, assisting her with the doctors, nurses, aides, technicians, and other staff and providing what support and encouragement I could. My office set up a courier service to this busy urban hospital so that I could work in her room, and a phone for meetings by conference call. Everyone at the office was quite wonderful, not bothering me unless absolutely necessary and covering for me as needed. Libby was in the hospital from late November until just after Christmas of 1990. When she came home, all four of our daughters were there, albeit briefly. From January on they alternated being with her at home, and their help was indispensable. January was the only point of light during this period: our family had a chance to be together once again, and Libby's energy levels had improved some.

Nevertheless, the rate at which her illness proceeded shocked me. She said nothing, trying instead to cheer our daughters and me up. At night I saw to her needs and was able to capture three or so hours of sleep, as I had been doing since late November. Dr. William Parmley, our good friend of many years and head of the cardiovascular department at UCSF, was a consultant in Libby's case. He and other UCSF physicians contacted the leading doctor for this disease at the Mayo Clinic, who said whatever could be done for her there could be done just as well at Alta Bates: her weakened heart put a bone marrow transplant out of the question.

When Libby's condition worsened as the month wore on, her primary physician, Morton Meyer, a senior physician at the Berkeley clinic, insisted that she return to the hospital for critical care. Thus she reentered Alta Bates for the last time in late January 1991. I was beginning to lose hope, but neither she nor I had given up.

After several days Dr. Meyer said that I should have the daughters come, as Libby would not last much longer. But before they saw her, Dr. Meyer wanted Libby to know everything. And I wanted Bill Parmley to explain matters to Libby: she was not going to die of cancer, but of congestive heart failure. I reached Bill in the early hours of the morning at a medical meeting in Washington, D.C. He said he would be on the next plane to San Francisco and Dr. Meyer and I should meet with him in Libby's room that night.

When we met at 10:00 P.M., Bill told Libby in plain words what she was facing and said her death could occur at any time. She listened to Bill without tears or outward emotion, asked a few questions, and added, "I want to be certain I understand what you are telling me. I am going to die of heart failure but not of my cancer. Is that correct?" Bill said, "Yes." "Well, that's good," Libby said without hesitation. "I wouldn't want to die from this cancer." She then switched off talk about her condition and shifted the discussion to us. She thanked Dr. Meyer for all his efforts and especially for having visited her daily at our home during January. She turned to Bill and told him how much she appreciated his efforts to come from Washington to tell her what she confronted, asked about members of his family, and then smiled at us.

All three of us had tears in our eyes and running down our cheeks. She did not. She was serene and unafraid as she contemplated what was next, and I do not mean her mortal death but, according to our faith, her eternal life. None of us could believe her courage, spirituality, generosity of spirit, and goodwill, thanking others as she always did and taking responsibility for contending with her problems.

Each daughter visited her alone the next morning. The five of us formed a continuous chain, coming from and going to her hospital room right up until the end. I, of course, was with her all day and half the night. Libby and I talked about our daughters and how proud we were of them. We reviewed our happy years and all the good things in our life. She admonished me to do nothing about my work or the house or make any other major decision for at least a year. One night as I was leaving for home about midnight, I commented that she was leaving twenty-five years too soon. "Yes," she said, "but I feel as though I have lived three lives in one."

Libby passed away peacefully in the early morning of February 8, 1991.

The funeral service was held at the LDS Stake Center, next to the Mormon Temple in Oakland overlooking the San Francisco Bay and the area where she had lived most of her life. Our daughters, my office staff, local church members, and close Bay Area friends had worked hard to make the service as memorable and suitable as possible; some 1,400 persons attended the service. Libby was interred at our family's grave site at the Sunset Lawn Cemetery in El Cerrito, just blocks from Blake House and not far from where she had grown up in Oakland.

My daughters and I were deeply touched by the outpouring of support and love from our wide circle of friends, colleagues, and well-wishers throughout the university's nine campuses and the Office of the President, and from my attentive, understanding, and very patient immediate staff: Nancy Nakayama, Janet Young, Cindy Pace, Pat Pelfrey, and Cecile Cuttitta, as well as Libby's social secretary, Pat Johnson (Libby's first social secretary, Maggie Johnston, had died some time before. Maggie and Pat were indispensable to Libby and to me in helping us meet our many social obligations; and Libby and I deeply appreciated their help and dedication to UC). Letters and expressions of sadness in many forms poured in from Utah, California, and elsewhere, from our friends and from Libby's admirers at universities across the nation including several abroad. Our family was astounded by and remains deeply appreciative of the generous outpourings of respect and affection that honor her memory and the contributions she made:

- The Hong Kong University of Science and Technology raised a substantial sum to honor her by the awarding of a scholarship each year to the university's most outstanding undergraduate woman student;
- The Elizabeth Fuhriman Gardner Prize created at the School of Dentistry, UC San Francisco, Libby's alma mater, recognizes the school's most outstanding graduating woman each year;
- The University of Utah's Center for Health Sciences awards one or two prizes in her name at its annual commencement to acknowledge the most outstanding woman graduate(s) of the School of Medicine, School of Pharmacy, College of Health, and/or School of Nursing;
- The George S. and Dolores Doré Eccles Foundation of Salt Lake City funded the construction of a 700-seat concert hall at the University of Utah (part of the David P. Gardner Hall, named in my honor when we left Utah for California in 1983) and asked that the university name the hall in her memory. This beautiful building, with the new Libby Gardner concert hall, houses the university's School of Music on historic President's Circle;
- Our family was privileged to fund the sculpting of a beautiful bronze statue of a mother reading to her young daughter. This life-size bronze accomplished by the London sculptor Nathan David was dedicated in

September 1997 to Libby's memory at Clare Hall, Cambridge. It rests in the Family Garden between two lovely facilities that house students with young families, and a fountain flows gently at its base;

– Libby and I had already established endowed alumni scholarships at Berkeley for outstanding entering undergraduate students. I fund this scholarship now; three or four Berkeley undergraduates are its recipients each year; and,

– The Graduate School of International Relations and Pacific Studies at UC San Diego most thoughtfully dedicated one of its premier classrooms in her memory.

Coping

Libby's funeral was on a Wednesday, and I was back at work the following Monday. I did not want to sit home alone. I did not want to travel. I did not want to read books or watch television. I did not want to go to the movies or the theater or to dance or musical productions. I did not, in fact, know what to do. So I went back to the office, hoping I could sort out my feelings sooner if I were obliged to be doing something familiar and useful. Besides, given the state's budget problems, UC was in a fight for its life.

As anyone else who lived through the ordeal of losing a spouse can imagine, the next several months were mostly a blur. Everyone at work was wonderful. The regents, vice presidents, chancellors, and my immediate staff all helped make my work as easy as possible. At meetings, for example, I would drift off and miss the subtleties of things. Only if engaged in solving a very difficult problem requiring a decision was I able to function effectively.

As February, March, and April came and went, I somehow and somewhat overcame the disruption in the normal workflow that had attended the three months of Libby's illness. The budget situation would not be further negotiated until June, so I decided that a change of venue and of issues would be a good thing for me, both mentally and physically.

I had declined an earlier invitation from Professor Robert Scalapino of the Berkeley campus to join him and others for a three-week trip to Asia and the Soviet Union in May 1991 under the auspices of the Asia Society of New York. Now I called Bob and asked if I could still be of help. He seemed very happy to say yes. This was a very wise decision on my part, I thought, as I made arrangements to go. I would have a new and changing environment and enjoy the company of able and congenial colleagues all engaged in an important assignment.

I returned from this trip somewhat renewed, as my sense of numbness about Libby's illness and death had suddenly left me midway through. But an unrelenting schedule, changing players, and my travels between and among North Korea, China, Japan, South Korea, and the Soviet Union had also left me drained. I returned home on a night flight from Moscow and, after saying good-bye to my new friends, was driven home, unlocked the door, and went into an empty, darkened home.

At that moment the full and terrible impact of my circumstances and the loss of Libby nearly four months earlier struck me. Exhausted and no longer numb, I had never felt so alone, so unhappy, so despondent, or so vulnerable.

When I walked into the office the next day, I faced a formidable array of work. The table in the large conference room adjoining my office seats sixteen to eighteen people, but its top was barely visible, covered by the line of folders Nancy Nakayama, my executive assistant, had laid out for my review. The folders announced "Immediate Attention," "Urgent," "Signature Required," "Memoranda and Correspondence," "Summaries—Vice Presidents and Chancellors" (matters in their respective spheres of responsibility), "Reports," "Legislation," and "Calls to Make" (in order of priority with annotations).

It was just as well to face this series of folders because by now I was able to concentrate, to analyze, and to communicate clearly. As a person I felt so low and despondent. But here I had a demanding work schedule, and as time passed, surely things would improve. They didn't.

In midsummer 1991 Nancy said it was time to review my social calendar for the upcoming academic year. There were dinners, receptions, and speeches to plan; meetings with legislators, distinguished visitors, alumni, community leaders, and others to consider—and then came functions involving students, faculty, staff, administrators, and regents. I remember saying, "But Nancy, I don't *want* a social calendar." She reminded me that much of this was obligatory, not discretionary. And she had already pruned it as best she could. She was right, of course, but for the first time I began seriously to wonder about my ability, willingness, and even desire to remain in the job.

Sadness hit me as I stood outside Blake House waiting for Chancellor and Mrs. Helmut Kohl in September 1991. He was Berkeley's Tanner lecturer, and they were my guests. This was a very happy and memorable occasion, but I remember how alone I felt at the entrance to the Blake House gardens waiting, as Libby and I had done countless times, for our guests to arrive, and then again as I showed the Kohls through Blake House, especially as Libby had completely redecorated it shortly before her illness.

Apparently some unarticulated sense of my misgivings and thoughts of resigning prompted Chancellors Krevans, Young, and Peltason to visit me in private at my office in Oakland. They urged me to "stay the course," to remain in office for at least a year, as Libby herself had advised. These were friends as well as colleagues, and I appreciated their advice and concern very much. I thanked them but made no commitment.

Some people believed my feelings were lingering beyond reason and I should pull myself together, block out the hurt, and deal with life. Well, I was dealing with life in a stark form every day, and I could no more block out the budget problems than my hurt about Libby's death. Her death was an emotional matter for me, not an intellectual one. Besides, I was who I was, and that was how I was feeling.

In November 1991 I helped inaugurate the work of the newly constructed 10-meter Keck Observatory atop Mauna Kea, on the island of Hawaii. The official party stayed at the Mauna Kea Resort on the Kona coast, and it was a great gathering, with scientists, engineers, contractors, faculty members, regents of UC and trustees of Cal Tech, and others to share in the realization of this dream, the world's largest optical telescope. Libby and I had been there at its groundbreaking ceremony and had enjoyed our visits during its extended period of construction.

So in spite of the many friends and colleagues now present, the inauguration ceremonies on site, and the dinner that night featuring remarks by Walter Cronkite, I felt very much alone the entire time. And I was up all night with food poisoning too. After a late-morning ocean swim the next day and some rest—free of visitors, phone calls, or other distractions—I felt well enough to think my situation through. My work no longer gave me energy. I was exhausted. Especially when traveling and entertaining as I did in the normal course of my duties, I felt as though half of me had been torn away with Libby's passing. Once, I recall, I picked up the phone on returning to my hotel room and started to dial Libby, as was my custom, only to remember that she wasn't there. I was facing nearly unparalleled problems at work and wondered if I was up to doing my job; I was simply unhappy.

At this point I had served UC for twenty-two years: four years with the California Alumni Association and Foundation, seven years as an assistant to the chancellor or a vice-chancellor at UCSB, nearly three years as a university vice president, and over eight years as UC's fifteenth president. Adding the last number to my ten years at the University of Utah, I had been president of a major American research university for over eighteen years. I knew what my job entailed and that, without Libby's consistent presence at my side, I really did not wish to do it any longer.

I STEP DOWN AS PRESIDENT

I sat down at a table on the balcony overlooking the Pacific Ocean and Mauna Kea's beautiful bay on November 13 and drafted a letter to Regent Meredith Khachigian, the board's chair and my friend for over twenty-five years:

> This letter is one not easily written, for it relies on mere words to convey feelings that reach far deeper than words can express, and that arise from principles of life that are more complex than I am able adequately to share or even fully to comprehend.
>
> As you know, I have been struggling since Libby's death of last February to

reconcile the reality of her passing with my ongoing life and work. Friends and colleagues, both within the University of California community and beyond, and of course members of my own family, have been constant in their support, encouragement, and love as I have tried to hold together what has been so central a fact in Libby's adult life and my own, that is, serving the University of California for over twenty years and the University of Utah for ten.

We served together because we chose to do so. It was a partnership that brought both of us immense personal pleasure, challenge, accomplishment, and satisfaction, enriched by a unique regard and respect for what each contributed.

Death has now dissolved our partnership, at least for this life, although according to our faith not forever; and it has become clearer with each passing month since Libby's death that without her I cannot remain as President of the University of California. I intend, therefore, to step down as President on October 1, 1992, a date that, among other things, will permit me to help with the 1992 legislative session and the forming and enactment of the University's 1992–93 operating and capital budgets. It will also afford the Regents ample time to seek for and find my successor and will allow that person to commence his or her duties during the University's 125th anniversary year. It should also be noted that by next October, I will be in my tenth year as President of the University of California; only Presidents Benjamin Ide Wheeler (1899–1919) and Robert Gordon Sproul (1930–58) served longer.

I have respected this institution from my earliest memories as a boy growing up in Berkeley and am proud to have earned two graduate degrees from the Berkeley campus. Libby graduated from UC San Francisco, and one of our daughters from UC Davis; another earned her master's degree at UCLA; another studied at UCLA; our youngest will complete her undergraduate studies at UC Berkeley this fall term; and a son-in-law is in graduate school at UC San Diego.

But in this respect our family is not unique. Indeed, I know of no public university in the world that has afforded its students, regardless of their race, gender, religion, or socio-economic circumstances, as excellent an education for so modest a cost while simultaneously attaining to levels of intellectual accomplishment that are world-renowned and internationally respected. . . .

I remain profoundly appreciative of the honor I have had to serve this University as its president and of the unstinting support that you and other members of the Board have accorded me these many years, the help and encouragement that I have consistently received from the University's Chancellors, Vice Presidents, its other dedicated officers and also from the gifted and committed members of the university's faculties and staff. Coming to know and work with members of the university's talented student body over the years has also been a source of great pleasure, as has been the privilege of knowing and working with the University's extended family, alumni and friends throughout the world.[3]

On my return to California the next day, and just before the board met, I handed Regent Khachigian my letter of resignation and explained why I had written it. She was shocked, disappointed, and urged me to reconsider, offering to help with my situation in any way she could. I made it clear, however, that this had been coming for some time and that the decision was irreversible. The regents were comparably surprised and saddened but accepted my resignation when the board met in Berkeley.

In the press conference after that meeting on November 14, the press had copies of my letter but pushed for other reasons to explain my decision. As there were none, the questions were easy to answer. But the *Los Angeles Times* wanted to probe the issue and sent a reporter a few days later to interview me.

I was not in an interviewing mood, but Ron Kolb, who handled the press for my office, asked me to grant the interview. I told him I would agree if the journalist were a woman, believing a man was less likely to understand my reasons and thoughts. The reporter, Laurie Becklund, then visited with me for about an hour, concluded that what I had represented in my letter was the truth, and decided that the real story was more than sufficient. She wrote a wonderful article for the *Los Angeles Times*, titled "The Gardners: An Uncommon Partnership."[4]

I had announced my intention to step down as president in November 1991, with effect from October 1, 1992, roughly a ten-month period, three or four months longer than was usual or customary. At the time I thought the extended time would be useful in negotiations on the 1992–93 budget and on a renewal of our contract with DOE to manage the national laboratories at Los Alamos, Livermore, and Berkeley (discussions on the contract were not going too well). And of course I wanted to give the regents plenty of time to find my successor. Yet if I had to do it all over again, I would have left office as soon as my successor could come but not later than July 1, 1992. Ten months was too long. As I discovered over the next several months, I had underestimated the enmity and resentment that had built up during the two years of fiscal crisis: some legislators cited my "excessive influence" over a Republican-dominated Board of Regents; some regents wanted less direction from the president; and the press, sensing my new vulnerability, went on the attack.

In retrospect, I do not know how I could have so miscalculated or misallowed for these several factors, as even under conditions of extreme pressure and stress I was not often so wide off the mark. But, given my miscalculations, the severity of their impact on UC would have been dramatically less consequential had it not also been for the six-month controversy over the terms of my retirement that ran with neither respite nor reprieve from March until October 1992.

My Retirement Imbroglio

The decision to retire as president did not affect my faculty position in Berkeley's Graduate School of Education. In the back of my mind was the thought that I might wish to teach full- or part-time. But I wasn't sure. Ten months hence I would be fifty-nine. Two of our daughters were still at the university, and there was a significant mortgage on our Orinda home. So I wanted to know sooner rather than later how the regents intended to act on my retirement and plan accordingly. I expected they would grant me a one-year administrative leave of absence when I left office and decide on treatment of deferred compensation I had earned during my service as president (I had not reached the number of years or age required to give me immediate rights to that sum).

I asked Brady to work with a committee Regent Khachigian chose to consider this matter. Not long after the committee met in fall 1991 (I never did meet with them), Brady advised me that the committee did not intend to recommend a year's administrative leave of absence but would grant three months instead. If I wished to take a more extended leave, I would have to take a sabbatical based on my faculty salary, roughly 40 percent of my salary as president.

I was stunned, not so much at the salary differential but at the reasoning behind it, since a one-year leave for senior officers was established practice at UC and elsewhere (I generally granted it to all other eligible officers). I asked Brady for additional information about the committee's views, but he said there was none. So I began to wonder if there were other surprises in the offing. I asked Brady to move the committee's work forward at a somewhat accelerated rate so that by early spring 1992 I would know of the board's pleasure on all these matters, rather then let them drag on until summer.

The special committee reported its recommendation in March 1992 to the regents' Subcommittee on Officers Salaries and Administrative Funds, which transmitted it to the Committee on Finance, which in turn reported to the full board: a three-month leave of absence and a vesting date (December 31, 1992) for my deferred and supplemental benefits. On all three occasions the regents met in closed session—consistent with university policies and with the state's "open meeting" laws—as they always did when contracts, investments, personnel, compensation, and similar matters were at stake.[5]

Brady, who had been working with the regents' committees on this matter, explained the reasoning back of the recommendation to the full board where the committee's recommendation was received and the matter was to be acted on:

- The administrative leave was routinely granted to chancellors and vice presidents and, typically to presidents who are leaving their post (actually, a one-year leave, not a three-month leave, was routine);
- The nonqualified deferred income plan and the supplemental retirement agreements were subject to forfeiture if the vesting date were later than my leaving date; and

– The deferred plans and supplemental retirement agreements were replacements for programs previously in place at UC for senior executives prior to 1986 when the U.S. Congress eliminated them as part of the mid-1980s tax reform legislation.

The regents approved the action amid a lengthy discussion on its timing and the public release about it. In consideration of what occurred later, it should be noted that Regent Hallisey voted "yes" at both committee meetings but did not vote with the full board the next morning; he had left the previous night for obligations in San Francisco.

I was at the meeting for the vote but had excused myself from the committee meetings the previous day during the discussion of my retirement benefits. I believed the regents were entitled to meet on this subject, and discuss it, without my being present. My decision, though proper, proved to have been a mistake: if I had been there, I could have taken immediate steps to deal with their expressed concerns before the next day's board meeting. These committee meetings were the last ones to be held on Thursday, and we had exceeded our time on some of the earlier ones. Thus, we were running late and pressing up against the evening's dinner schedule, to be held at the chancellor's house on the UCLA campus.

I had been waiting for the committee meetings to end sooner than later, not believing the issue would be controversial. But it lasted longer than I had expected. Thus I had little time to learn what happened at the meeting, as the regents left immediately to prepare for dinner. I was, however, able to speak with Watkins briefly. He said everything had gone well but that some regents had expressed concern about the action's timing and the language for the press advisory.

Brady confirmed Watkins's report but also said that Hallisey had not seemed very friendly to the action, though he had voted for it anyway. "Burke's concerns," he said, "were principally procedural." As to the press advisory, he reported that the regents were "all over the map" and that there had been no resolution of this question. He did not tell me, as the minutes report, that the board was to receive a draft of such a press advisory Friday morning.

With that, everyone was gone except me, pondering what I had just heard. At dinner I sought out five or six key regents to ascertain their views on the meeting. None expressed any concern about the substance of the action, only some uncertainty about how and when to report it to the press.

Having received no guidance from any of them, I then said, "That, unless instructed otherwise tomorrow morning, we should handle the press advisory on this issue just as we did any other action of the board in closed session, i.e., it would be released the following Monday or Tuesday." No one objected, nor did anyone propose an alternative.

As it was, the press advisory went out on Monday or Tuesday of the following week, reporting the action in a summary fashion, as was customary, and inviting any inquiries the press might have. Only the *San Diego Union* called for clarification and additional information, which Regent Claire W. Burgener, a former member of Congress and highly regarded member of the board who was much respected in San Diego, gave in detail. The result was a *San Diego Union* story that was complete and accurate. No other members of the press or media expressed any interest whatsoever.

After I left for a scheduled engagement in Hong Kong, this issue returned with a vengeance, prompted by Regent Jeremiah Hallisey and his friend Quentin Kopp, an independent state senator from the San Francisco peninsula. Hallisey now thought he had been wrong to support these benefits, both when the regents put the deferred compensation plans into place and when they acted to pay the benefits. He was a San Francisco lawyer, an active Democrat, and Governor Jerry Brown's appointee to the Board of Regents. Now in the latter stages of his service as a regent, Hallisey was none too happy with his treatment by other regents or by some members of my staff. He may not have liked me very much either, although I can't really say.

Once Hallisey and Kopp publicly made known their displeasure with the board and with me, a barrage of unremitting and unrestrained (mostly inaccurate) news reporting ensued, criticizing the regents for acting in "secret" and being excessively generous with my benefits and me for having accepted them. It went on for six months and came to include Regent Glenn Campbell as well (he and Hallisey were an unlikely duo: Hallisey was very much to the political left and Campbell comparably to the political right, though each was something of a maverick and a contrarian). Campbell was the senior regent and made it abundantly and frequently clear that he was not receiving the courtesies ordinarily awarded to the board's longest-serving regent. Thus both regents were very unhappy with the board's leadership, but for separate reasons. Reporters would call and tell our public relations staff that Hallisey and Campbell and perhaps others were sending document after document, "tip" after "tip" to them on an almost daily basis. This seemed not overly surprising to me, but the amount of effort it required on the part of Hallisey and Campbell to keep this going was remarkable.

Since I was in Asia during this imbroglio—first Hong Kong, for meetings of the Hong Kong University of Science and Technology's governing board, of which I was a member, then Seoul, where I delivered a paper at the third meeting of the Pacific Rim university presidents—my office informed me that my retirement benefits were developing into a controversial matter. But I had no idea of what had actually been going on. Thus, on my return home I was shocked and well back of the curve in dealing with the problem, way back. After seeking the advice of colleagues I resolved to give this issue top billing before it became resistant to any intervention.

The first thing I intended to do was to clear up the bogus issue that appeared to be causing the most fuss, the board's "secret" action on my retirement benefits. Both Hallisey and Campbell, who were seemingly making much of this, knew better because they themselves participated for years in such meetings without complaint or exception.

Chairman Khachigian and I decided to call a special "open meeting" session of the full Board of Regents, not its committees, but the full board, and to convene it as soon as practical—in fact, on April 20 at UCSF's Laurel Heights campus. The single issue on the board's agenda would be reconsideration of its March action on my retirement benefits. This meeting was to be open to the press and to the public, I explained, but I would not participate in it or call or talk with any regent except the chair, the governor, and the Speaker of the Assembly. In short, the regents could rescind the action or amend or confirm it as they wished.

I had arrived home from Hong Kong and Seoul at the end of the previous week and was still weary. I was also hard-pressed at work, catching up from my trip and helping Jack Peltason plan the transition from my administration to his (Jack had been appointed, effective October 1, while I was in Asia). I was working twelve- to fourteen-hour days plus another three or four at night, and trying to get my arms around this retirement fiasco as well.

I called Speaker Brown's and Governor Wilson's offices to clear the date and time for our open meeting; both men would be there on the 20th and would appear at a press conference afterward. Then I called a special meeting of the chancellors for my office on Friday, April 17. They were not a happy lot, as they too were now coming under criticism for having the same "excessive deferred compensation" I did. We reviewed every benefit that was implicated in this controversy: for example, the Nonqualified Deferred Income Plan replaced a qualified plan that Congress voided in 1986, when it enacted the Tax Reform Act. We reminded ourselves that even though the context of UC practices, earlier board actions, and our marketplace explained and justified each plan, the underlying concepts were hard to explain to the public and the press. Of course all of us would have been better off if the money to fund the deferred compensation had instead been part of our base salaries, thus increasing the value of our UC retirement by 10 to 20 percent.

All our comments and second-guessing amounted to nothing, because we could not turn back the clock. I expected to be at the eye of the hurricane once the regents acted on Monday, as the open debate on their March action would take the issue of "secrecy" off the deck while I remained on it.

"Have you considered resigning?" Chancellor Atkinson asked. The idea sorely tempted me, I said in effect, even though under the terms of the board's March action I would forfeit most of my deferred compensation if

I left before September 30. More important, resigning would make it appear that I had done something wrong or that the regents had erred, when I did not believe for a minute that either party had, though the issue had been handled poorly. And finally, I reminded the chancellors, if the regents dropped the deferred compensation plan without shifting that same amount into executives' base salaries—frozen since the 1989–90 fiscal year—they too would lose up to 20 percent of their retirement funds.

As the meeting ended I sensed that the chancellors were preoccupied about how best to cope with this issue for the university's sake, and for their own. Kind words and private encouragement notwithstanding, this was primarily my problem. I faced what seemed to be a scenario damaging to UC and devastating to me. In introducing my oral history Kerr referred to this time and this issue: "David took the heat and felt betrayed. . . . As Shakespeare once wrote, 'Blow, blow thou wintry winds! They are not so unkind as man's ingratitude.'"[6]

The day wore on after the chancellors left, but I kept thinking about Atkinson's question—not intended, he assured me, as a suggestion. I wondered whether this might, in fact, be a proper course of action for me to take, my arguments to the contrary aside. The news broadcasts of that Friday afternoon suggested that my resignation was imminent or would be submitted at the upcoming regents' meeting on Monday. My daughters and brother also heard this news and called Nancy, my executive assistant, asking her to tell me not to do it. I have no idea how this news item came about.

But the idea was in my mind, and around 4:00 P.M. I called in the vice presidents to discuss the matter. We went over much the same ground as the chancellors and I had that morning. I then raised the possibility of my resigning and what it would mean for UC. Their views and attitudes resembled those of the chancellors.

I found myself moving to the point of deciding to resign, and to do it that same day once I contacted the regents, Governor Wilson, and Speaker Brown. I was in the process of assigning specific tasks to each of the vice presidents. We were settling on the timing of my resignation and Nancy was typing up a draft of it, when a phone call from the governor came in about 6:00 P.M. I asked the vice presidents to remain while Wilson and I talked.

"What is this I hear about your wishing to resign?" he asked. I told him why I thought this might very well be the preferred course of action both for the university and for me—"the vice presidents and I were discussing it when you called."

He then said, "I will not support your resigning at this point. I can just imagine the scene. You are tired from your trip, harried, under attack, and feeling defeated. It's bad enough for all of us and for UC that you are leaving in October, but for you to leave now would be very hurtful to the university.

"You are fighting for your life in Sacramento. You are the president and who would take your place? You would give everyone the erroneous impression that you have breached or abused your trust and have been willing to profit from UC at its expense, when you and any informed person know that's simply not true. You are guilty of nothing, and you shouldn't act as though you were.

"Who is with you at home?" the governor asked. "My daughter Karen is here for the weekend," I said. "OK," he went on, "you need to take her and go to the Napa Valley. Get some sleep, walk, take a mineral or mud bath—cleanse your mind and body—and call me Sunday night at home. If you still wish to resign Sunday night, I will accept it without criticism, but I will not do so today."

I agreed, and our conversation ended. I told the vice presidents there would be no resignation today, but there still might be one on Sunday; if I resigned with immediate effect, the board meeting on Monday should not occur.

Karen and I took the governor's advice, and sometime on Sunday I began to get back some of my energy and mental balance. I asked myself, why am I thinking of resigning when my critics want me to resign and my friends and family do not? Good question! What was I thinking?

We stopped at a public telephone in the Napa Valley on our way home, and I called the governor, told him that his prescription had worked, that I appreciated his personal concern and professional support, and that I would see him the next morning in San Francisco at the regents' meeting.

"Good for you," he said, "UC can't have these ———— driving you out of office, now or later. Get a good sleep." I still recall with gratitude Governor Wilson's concern and sound advice at such a critical time.

The regents met in special session at 2:00 P.M. Monday, April 20 at the Laurel Heights facility of our San Francisco campus. The room was full, and the print and television media were there in large numbers. Governor Wilson and Speaker Brown were present, as were nearly all the regents who regularly attended and really made the board's decisions: twenty-one in all, a remarkable attendance on such short notice.

The meeting began with a summary of what the regents did in March (its complete text is in appendix 2). The chairman of the Finance Committee, Harold Williams, a senior regent, then spoke about the board's action on behalf of his committee and its subcommittee on officers' salaries. Williams was serving as the president of the J. Paul Getty Trust in Los Angeles. He had been president of Norton Simon, Inc., dean of the UCLA School of Business, and chairman of the U.S. Securities and Exchange Commission under President Jimmy Carter. Williams touched on the challenges in administering UC's vast enterprise and the consequent urgency of attracting the best, brightest, and most able leaders through competitive executive salaries. And he spelled out the tax code's complexities and limits on compensation that led to UC's and my retirement plan. Noting the unjustifiable cloud of controversy, Williams also observed that he and other regents on the board all knew "how fully, and even beyond our fondest expectations, [Gardner] has delivered what we needed of the next president." Even so, he asked, "What is it that the Regents 'gave' President Gardner upon his resignation? All we gave him is a three-month administrative leave with pay. Otherwise, we 'gave' him what he had earned during his years of service to the University."[7]

Interested parties who had asked to speak then did so: Assemblyman Tom Hayden, Senator Kopp, and a number of others, mostly outside the university. Their comments tied the size of the fee and tuition increases to my retirement benefits and attacked the board's misplaced priorities and inappropriate action in light of the weakening California economy.

Governor Wilson asked to speak next and restated the question before the board: whether the regents were required to honor their obligation; he believed that the answer was very clearly yes. He insisted that a refusal to update my deferred compensation

> would under these circumstances amount to a very serious breach of the Board's moral obligation. It would also destroy the Board's ability in the future to recruit or to retain top-flight administrative talent. Moreover, it would amount to a breach of the duty imposed upon the Board of Regents by the State Constitution, which protects against political interference by insulating the Board of Regents and the University of California from the legislature and from state government.[8]

Regents Hallisey, Campbell, and Burke then spoke in opposition to the motion. Hallisey argued that I had scheduled the special meeting on short notice to minimize public input (a delay would not have suited him either), that the benefits were excessive, and that I was overpaid anyway. Campbell said if he had been at the March meeting he would have voted against the recommendation (as noted earlier, both Campbell and Hallisey had participated for years in such board actions but made no objection to them and had indeed approved them). Yvonne Brathwaite Burke felt insufficiently informed about the plans' rationale over the years and would thus vote no on the motion.[9]

Regent Diana K. Darnell, the students' representative and a graduate student at UCSF, supported the motion: "because members of the executive program have not been granted salary increases since 1990, the President's retirement package is actually substantially less than he could have expected to receive."[10]

Regent Willie Brown first gave an extemporaneous lecture on free speech in America and in the university to a small band of persons in the audience who equally loudly booed the action's supporters and cheered its opponents. Then he stated that the president "has an absolute right to every dollar he had earned and that he does not deserve to have his career tainted in any fashion" by the board's actions. He would vote to confirm the arrangement.[11]

The state's lieutenant governor, Leo McCarthy, asked a few technical questions and gave his opinion that the regents' procedures for setting executive compensation should be "changed significantly." Chairman Khachigian said she agreed and was already working with Regent Burke on this matter. And finally the board's secretary, Bonnie Smotony, read letters from two other regents who favored the action and put the motion to a vote. The motion to confirm the board's earlier action passed with sixteen ayes, two no votes (Hallisey and Burke), and three abstentions (Campbell, McCarthy, and Gardner).[12]

Immediately after my brief comments that ended the meeting came a press conference. It went very well, all things considered. Senator Kopp and Regent Hallisey moved among the reporters prompting them; one question was, "Is it true that you have a maid, President Gardner, paid for by UC?" I replied, "I have a lady who spends roughly two hours a week cleaning the house and a gardener who spends roughly the same amount of time on the garden, both paid from nonstate funds, all of which is included in my housing allowance. If that means I have a maid, then I guess I do." We turned away none of their questions, but Wilson and Brown stepped up to answer any that might involve a perceived significant conflict of interest if I had answered them.

As the afternoon ended, I felt much better about my decision to remain in office through the end of September and most appreciative of the regents' action: they had made every effort to deal openly with this issue, to reconsider the entire matter, to invite public comment, and to be clear about the rationale for their actions and the facts supporting them. But as the spring gave way to summer, the media continued to grandstand the issue, in reports more and more confined to the papers in the San Francisco Bay Area, especially the *Chronicle* and the *Examiner* (and less, but persistently so, at the *Sacramento Bee*).

One example that I recall well, because it was so egregious and blatant an example of redundancy, was the July 30, 1992, edition of the *San Francisco Chronicle*, reporting on its front page the compensation package approved four months earlier for my successor, Jack Peltason, all of it fully and completely reported by the *Chronicle* at the time he was appointed. There was no "news" in this story, just a rewritten version of that April 4 article.[13]

I rehearsed the whole matter with Howard Leach, a successful San Francisco-based businessman and highly respected regent, influential in both California's and the nation's Republican Party. We had become friends over the years, and I felt altogether comfortable in calling on his responsible advice (he is now the United States ambassador to France). He agreed with my concern and arranged for a luncheon within a few days with the *Chronicle*'s senior editors and management at the Pacific Union Club in San Francisco. I brought the April and July articles that had prompted the luncheon meeting.

Much to my astonishment, one of the persons present—I believe it was the city editor—spoke up immediately and said, "We plead guilty," and apologized to Leach and to me for what had happened. Submitted for publication and turned down as old news just before the relevant editor left for vacation, the article had been resubmitted while the editor was on vacation and approved to appear as a front-page article, which it did. Changes, we were told, were being made within the *Chronicle* to make certain this would not happen again.

Louis Freedberg, the *Chronicle*'s higher education reporter and the author of both articles (April 4 and July 30), had been the most dogged reporter of all throughout this controversy. He is an intelligent and accomplished journalist (a Berkeley Ph.D. in anthropology), but he always seemed to me to be more than merely journalistically interested in this story. He was as relentless as he was insistent, with or without cause. I understood he was well acquainted with Professor Laura Nader of Berkeley's anthropology department, one of my sharpest critics about UC's management of the DOE laboratories at Los Alamos and Livermore. Ralph Nader is her brother, and, as chapter 8 made clear, he was none too pleased with me either.

Newspapers had come to be accuser, prosecutor, and judge, I felt, serving up contradictory and inconsistent "facts and figures" about my retirement benefits. One account suggested that the regents had "given me" a "golden parachute" of $2.5 million as I left office, no matter that to reach the $2.5 million figure, I would need to collect my regular UC retirement for the length of my then actuarially calculated life. The total sum I received in benefits as I left office was $737,757: approximately $432,000 from deferred-income and $300,000 from supplemental plans (and as a reading of appendix 2 makes clear, these plans had been approved in the course of my nine years as president).

But of all the sources of tribulation and grief I was enduring at this point, the worst example was the despicable, false, and contrived assertion that I had taken out a UC-sponsored insurance policy of $200,000 on Libby's life because I knew that she was terminally ill. This article appeared in the *San Francisco Examiner*, with a photograph of Libby, and cited an anonymous "tip" from some UC employee. I had never been so angry, so humiliated, or so discouraged.[14]

I promptly did what I could to set the record straight: I sent a letter to the editor, including a letter from Libby's attending physician, Dr. Morton Meyer, who rejected the article's claim to link the application's timing to my knowledge of Libby's diagnosis or prognosis, and I explained the claim's falsity to my friends and colleagues. But the article did more to harm my reputation—with the public, and especially within the university—than the entire retirement benefits controversy did.

When I asked one of my closest friends, an able and experienced San Francisco attorney, if I had grounds to sue, he said I did in theory. But I would probably not prevail against the article's use of innuendo, implied wrongdoing, suggestion, intimation, and questions without answers. "The lawyers' fingerprints are all over this article," my friend said, "and I probably shouldn't waste my time and money pursuing it." The story was out, and the damage was done.

The facts are these. A brochure went out to most UC employees citing a very favorable group rate for insurance on the life of that employee and of the employee's spouse as well. The open enrollment period to buy it was November 1990. The brochure arrived at our home in either September or early October 1990.

I had sufficient UC life insurance, but Libby had only a $10,000 policy purchased years before by her father. Over the years we had discussed the amount of insurance on my life but never on hers. So this brochure prompted a discussion on whether to avail ourselves of this offer to add coverage for her.

I was fifty-seven years old at the time, and in good health. Libby was fifty-five. Her back was giving her trouble, as it had for several years, owing, we were told, to a problem with degenerative discs in her lower back. And because of it, Libby could not return to her dental hygiene profession. We were not independently wealthy and had a consequential mortgage on our Orinda home; two of our daughters were still at university, not married, and partially reliant on us. What would happen to them and to Libby if I had a disabling accident or illness and did not die? Clearly, such a scenario was neither susceptible to a congenial outcome nor amenable to a fix with life or disability insurance for that matter, mine being quite modest.

Yet we could do something to protect our daughters and me if I were disabled but Libby died. Just as my life insurance would protect her and the girls against the loss of my income, an increased amount of insurance on her life would help protect the rest of the family if she died. Thus we took out additional insurance on Libby's life, acting as the rest of the 10,060 UC employees out of the 51,472 who were eligible for coverage also did.

I could and would have explained the circumstances to the *Examiner's* reporters, but they never asked. Indeed, the story had no input from the party under attack and no merit.

A week or two before this story broke, my public relations office and our office in Sacramento were hearing that such an article might soon appear. The rumor mill revealed the name of Senator Kopp and perhaps others, as encouraging the *Examiner* to run such a story. I asked Steve Arditti, the head of our Sacramento office, to arrange a meeting in the capitol with Senator Kopp so that I could make certain he knew the truth of the matter, whatever he may have been hearing from others.

Senator Kopp agreed to meet. I invited Senator Al Alquist of San Jose, a senior and well-respected senator, and chairman of the Appropriations

Committee, to join us; our staff had worked closely with him through the years. I liked him and trusted him. Arditti was also present. I wanted witnesses.

Kopp disclaimed any knowledge of this matter. However, he was attacking my retirement benefits publicly and frequently, and for him not to have heard through the "grapevine" (as we did) that this article was in the offing would have been unexpected. But he listened while I explained the circumstances. He asked a question or two, and that was that. I have no firm evidence of any role he might have played in the matter.

The Aftermath

In May 1992 the regents fundamentally changed their procedures for deciding on executive compensation but left intact the levels of compensation they thought necessary or appropriate for recruiting and retaining key officers. The legislature, the press, and the public reacted positively. I had recommended most of these changes, believing we had been in trouble because the form of our compensation was complex and we seemed unable to explain it clearly and straightforwardly to anyone who asked.

We were also in trouble because the backdrop of our controversy had included a divisive national political campaign, a weakened economy, and UC's grossly inadequate budgets. I recall that the *Sacramento Bee*'s Peter Schrag, an excellent and well-informed journalist, who was a less acerbic critic of the regents and me than the San Francisco journalists had been, remarked that if the issue of retirement benefits had been raised in the middle or late 1980s, when the economy was strong and UC budgets were generous, the issue would have been little noticed.

A broad unease permeated the letters I received throughout the retirement controversy from members of the public, legislators, and alumni as well as members of the university's faculty and staff. The thrust of their criticism was almost always to compare their own compensation to mine, relate the increases in student fees and tuition to my compensation and retirement benefits, and balance their "inadequate" salaries and the sparse funding for their activities (this complaint mostly from UC personnel) against the indifference I must have toward everyone else's financial plight as I sought to "enrich myself" during these troubled times. The delays UC staff and faculty had encountered before receiving their merit and cost-of-living adjustments to wages and salaries surely affected their feelings as well. During a two-year period there was no salary adjustment at all. And as earlier noted, the last adjustment in salary for the university's senior officers, including my own, was in 1989–90.

My reaction to these letters was mixed. On the one hand, I could understand the intensity of the criticism given the media's wildly erroneous and contradictory reporting of the facts each day. Certainly the nation, and California and UC in particular, had experienced hard times. And I acknowledged that the deferred compensation and supplemental retirement plans applied only to UC's senior administrative officers, and that people both within UC and out of it knew little about compensation for senior officers of American universities, especially for their presidents, or the convoluted tax code's influence on it. All this I could appreciate and, therefore, sought to be as informative and straightforward in my answers as possible, ignoring the letters' negative and often shrill tones.

On the other hand, I did not appreciate letters from faculty members and staff who attacked me for taking only what I had earned during my presidency—senior officers were not eligible for any early retirement incentive plan—but were availing themselves of the VERIPs and in doing so, taking from the university anywhere from a 10 to 20 percent lifetime increase in their annual pensions. I detected a similar hypocrisy in the letters received from some (not many) legislators who criticized me for not "giving some of it back" but retired with no hint of leaving any of their earned pensions on the table, in spite of the state's fiscal problems.

In fact I had planned to make a gift to UC of roughly half of my deferred compensation but, as the controversy intensified, recognized that no amount would be sufficient for my critics. Whatever I gave would seem to reflect guilt and ulterior motives. I decided instead to make gifts over a period of years to various campuses of UC, and to the University of Utah. I have been making such gifts regularly and will continue to do so; matching funds from the Hewlett Foundation and the J. Paul Getty Trust now multiply their value.

In any event, the criticisms I was receiving and the harm being done to the university distressed me but also disarmed me: the controversy was about my retirement benefits, which only the regents could approve and act on. Had it been someone else's compensation for which I was responsible, I could define, explain, interpret, and justify it. It was much harder for me to defend my own compensation. In a June 1992 *California Monthly* article, Russell Schoch makes the point:

> What David Gardner does best has made him a masterful tactician in guiding the University since 1983, but perhaps it has hurt him in responding to criticism over his compensation. What he does best is to separate himself from issues—for example, the issues of divestment and the weapons labs—and to argue powerfully and convincingly in favor of what he thinks is best for the University of California, despite strong opposition from other quarters. It had helped that he does not enter such frays with his own personal views; in fact, he makes a virtue of keeping his opinions out of view.
>
> When the tables are turned and people confront President Gardner directly and personally—about his part of the pie, in this case—he stops short, falls

back on the "facts," and appears aloof and uncaring. But when he separates himself from the issue and presents the context and history of the compensation he and other executives have received, he makes a strong case that the university's leaders should be good and should be well paid.

Few would dispute that David P. Gardner is, and has been, both.

Schoch quoted my argument on UC's worth: UC "did not become the world's greatest public university by paying average salaries." My management philosophy is, "we ought to give people all they can do, we should work them hard, and we should pay them well." And on my own annual salary of $243,000 I told him, "That's the market. I would insist that the president of the University be paid a competitive salary for the marketplace."[15]

On September 18, 1992, I appeared as president before the Board of Regents for the last time. I had achieved two of the three objectives I had set for October 1: Peltason had been appointed in March to succeed me and the university's 1992–93 budget had finally been approved by the legislature in early September. We had not yet concluded our negotiations with DOE to renew our management contracts with the national laboratories as I had hoped, but they were ready for signature by the November meeting. Despite the darkness that overlay the end of my presidency, I was very proud of our achievements.

My last meeting with the Board of Regents was mostly a routine one. After the regents adopted a very nice resolution of appreciation for my services, I had ample opportunity to share with the board my thoughts about UC and what had taken place during my nine plus years as president.

- Since 1983 UC had grown from 141,000 to 166,000 students, honoring its commitment to find a place for every UC-eligible high school and community college graduate wishing to enroll. Its one-millionth degree was awarded in 1990, and 312,414 students earned degrees from UC during the past nine years.
- The university made dramatic strides in increasing the racial and ethnic diversity of our student body, especially at the undergraduate level, where a 50 percent increase in minority enrollments occurred as—a source of special pride—the grade-point average for all enrolled, regularly admitted freshmen rose from 3.6 in 1983 to 3.8 in 1991.
- We put into place a variety of programs to encourage and assist exceptionally promising women and minority scholars to enter the academic profession. Since 1985 one of these, the President's Fellowship Program, has granted fellowships to 124 talented women and minority Ph.D. recipients to help them find faculty appointments at UC and other leading universities; many of them now serve on UC's faculty.
- We developed a comprehensive and strategic long-term plan for UC's further growth and development (submitted to the board in October

1988) that anticipates growth of 60,000–70,000 students to the year 2005 and the construction of three new campuses.

- UC's operating budget made dramatic improvements beginning in 1983, thanks to a supportive legislature and governor, but began to lose ground with the 1990–1991 fiscal year; its share of the total state general fund budget dropped from 5.8 percent in 1986–87 to slightly under 4.7 percent in 1992–93 (from the other side of the coin, in 1992–93 the state paid for just 26.5 percent of our total budget, excluding the three DOE laboratories, whereas in 1960 it paid for 60 percent).

- Capital funding from state sources had gone from $16.5 million in 1983 to a 1992–93 total of $240 million. Using both nonstate and state sources (less than half of the funds), between 1983 and 1991 we expended $4,308,000,000 on construction that is either completed or under way, the largest amount of construction in any comparable time in UC's history.

- Annual federal contract and grant awards to UC more than doubled over the past nine years from $500,930,000 in 1982–83 to more than a billion dollars in 1990–91, excluding the DOE labs. UC performed roughly 11 percent of the federally sponsored basic research at our nation's universities.

- Annual private support for the university increased from $157 million in 1982–83 to $433 million in 1991–92; its total was $3,109,616,845 during my tenure.

- The overall budget, including DOE labs, grew from $4.8 billion in 1983–84 to $9.6 billion in 1992–93.

- Over 45 multicampus research units, centers, and programs were established since 1983. One such research center was UCI's universitywide Humanities Research Institute, another was UCSD's Institute on Global Conflict and Cooperation. Among ones that focus on a particular region and its peoples were UCLA's Center for Pacific Rim Studies, UCR's Institute for Mexico and the United States, and UCB's Center for German and European Studies. Built in partnership with Caltech, yet another were the Keck Telescope and Observatory, the world's largest optical telescope, with a second one under way on the same site atop Mauna Kea in Hawaii.

- We increased the opportunities for our students and faculty to study abroad: in 1982–83, UC students could study in one of 46 institutions, most of them in Western Europe; they can choose from among 93 institutions in 30 countries, 12 of them in the Pacific Rim. Since 1989, when we instituted a program of faculty exchanges with our partner-universities, 358 UC and foreign faculty have participated.

- We added four new professional schools and colleges: the Graduate School of International Relations and Pacific Studies at UCSD; the College of Engineering at UCR; the School of Environmental Science and Management at UCSB; and the School of Social Ecology at UCI. A proposed college of engineering at UCSC was under active consideration [opened in 1997].

– More than a quarter of a million people attended the university as students or worked for it as faculty, administrators, and staff. We graduated about 10 percent of all Ph.D.s in the United States every year, and more women and minority Ph.D.s than any other university. Our faculty included more than 250 members of the National Academy of Sciences, about one-sixth of its membership. Through the years UC's faculty had won twenty-nine Nobel Prizes, five during my service as president; eighteen Nobel Laureates were currently active on the university's faculty.

Recognizing UC as the state's crowning jewel and as one of the world's great intellectual treasure houses, I tried to capture other facets—quiet source of much of the state's economic power and strength, repository of much of our cultural heritage, cauldron of discovery, and marketplace of ideas—before I thanked the regents for the opportunity to work with them. And, finally, "as I come to the end of my tenure as president, I am proud of my quarter-century of service to this institution, of what I have been able to contribute and of what has been accomplished on my watch. The chance to have so served this great university has been one of life's great privileges, and Libby, who until a year-and-one-half ago was in partnership with me throughout this period of service, regarded it as a privilege as well."[16]

POST-UC

This ended my work as president of the University of California. I would now be a president emeritus of the university and have the chance to look afresh and anew at my own life, where I had been, where I was, and what I would be doing.

As I left the university, I received a flood of letters and calls from friends, colleagues, and associates throughout the state, to encourage me about the future, thank me for my past contributions, and wish me well. These were highly gratifying and very welcome, given the reason for leaving my post and the battle over retirement benefits. I especially appreciated the recognition of my work by the Academic Council and the Council of Student Body Presidents, the former presenting me with a lovely late nineteenth-century photograph of the Berkeley campus and the latter a scrapbook of my work with the students.

More important than my own account of the nine plus years I served as president, however, is the judgment of my mentor these many years, Clark

Kerr, Berkeley's first chancellor from 1952 to 1958 and UC's president from 1958 to 1967, and one of the two or three leading lights in twentieth-century American higher education, worldwide for that matter. We had been friends since my days with the California Alumni Association in the early 1960s. He advised me, encouraged me, criticized me, and helped me, as needed. His tribute to my work, both in his introduction to my oral history and in his own memoir, meant more than any opinion or conclusion I could possibly offer on my presidency. I realize that it will be some time before historical distance will be achieved and a full assessment of my presidency will be accomplished; but I am extremely proud and appreciative of the assessment that such a seasoned, knowledgeable, and respected figure as Kerr has given of my work. First from his memoir,

> Under President David Gardner (1983–92), a wonderful combination of circumstances literally saved the university from decline. The economy of the state improved substantially, creating enhanced state resources. The new governor, George Deukmejian (1983–91), had campaigned for office on a program of support for education. Gardner saw the possibilities of the situation, took the risk of proposing, and then securing, the passage of an almost one-third increase in state funds for the university in a single year. His triumph equalized faculty salaries (they had fallen 18.5 percent below those of comparable institutions . . .) and made possible many other gains. That convergence of circumstances and Gardner's efforts led to the academic rankings of 1993. Gardner, as I observed the process, also restored the effectiveness of the university's presidency, which had deteriorated over the prior twenty years.[17]

And from Kerr's introduction to my oral history,

> I have known David Gardner since he was a graduate student at Berkeley working for the California Alumni Association in the early to mid-1960s. He went along with me on several tours of alumni association chapters around the state, and was always kind and helpful. Then he became vice-chancellor at Santa Barbara, and still later a vice president of the university before becoming president of the University of Utah in 1973. I kept up with him during all these years, and in his oral history he speaks of me as one of his "mentors." By 1992, when he resigned as president of the university, the University of California had been one of the great centers of his life for more than half a century. . . .
>
> David had good judgment, inventive solutions to complex problems, calmness in the midst of turmoil, a genius at persuasion, and courage bordering on daring. All of these attributes he applied to his leadership within and outside the University of California. His public triumphs brought immense benefits to many, his private tragedies mostly costs to himself.
>
> This is one oral history that justifies the reactions of great acclaim and deep sorrow.[18]

And from Glenn Seaborg's oral history, a comment I cherish from one who contributed so much to his country, to his university, and to me:

[At regents' meetings Gardner] was so articulate and quick. He dealt with the issues in a masterful way, and swiftly, so that—I don't want to put it this way, that the regents didn't have time to think . . . he did it so swiftly and so adeptly that there wasn't a great deal of time to mull things over. And in such an articulate manner. That's what I want to emphasize over and over again.

I remember I would attend yearly dinners that would be held for present and past officers of the university, which I would attend in my role as a past chancellor at Berkeley. At these dinners, David would always get up and give his remarks, and they were just spellbinding. . . .

He didn't ever need any notes. No. And he would be able to introduce all the important people there, again without any notes, just call here and here and here, past chancellors and presidents, and present chancellors, and other officers. All of them without missing a beat, and saying something relevant about them. . . .

He deserves a tremendous amount of credit for getting that report out *[A Nation at Risk]*. He had a group of members who had strong views, and many of them conflicting views, and he in his masterful style, as he did later with the Board of Regents here at the University of California, pulled them all together. He was better at that than just about anybody I know.[19]

And finally, from my friend and colleague of many years Jack Peltason, whose service to higher education at the University of Illinois and the American Council on Education (he headed both), as chancellor at UC Irvine, and as my successor and UC's sixteenth president, brings a seasoned and tested judgment to my service, in part as follows:

[I]n my judgment he will be remembered less for the dramatic moments of his presidency than for the quiet and steady building up of the university that he pursued with such remarkable success. Under his calm, strong, and determined leadership, the University of California collected on all of its nine campuses a world-class faculty. Never in all of history have so many outstanding faculty served under the aegis of one university. The quality of the faculty is the ultimate test of presidential leadership, and David passed that test brilliantly.

And—as if all of this were not enough!—David is a warm and kind person with a gift for friendship. He was never so busy nor so immersed in crisis that he did not have a moment to inquire about you and your family. He was a gracious and appreciative colleague who went out of his way to thank those who served him. . . .

From the vantage point of nearly a decade and a half later, it is clearly more accurate to describe David Gardner as an eagle among presidents.[20]

These are the opinions that count for me, not the judgments of persons who were themselves never in my arena but who shouted only from the bleachers and from whom I had heard so much toward the end of my presidency.

As for my own view of the matter—good and bad budgets, controversies over divestment, the national laboratories, my retirement benefits, CALPIRG, affirmative action, admissions, and political crisis of one kind or another aside—I regard my principal contribution to the University of California, at least as its president, as being very much as Kerr and Peltason have described it: the building of the university's academic strength *across all nine campuses,* the enhancement of its teaching programs and its overall research endeavors, the sustaining of its public service activities, and the provision of resources sufficient to keep at and to recruit to UC a disproportionate share of the world's leading scholars and scientists. This, after all, is what being president is all about, the public controversies and political machinations being mostly distractions from the university's real work and its raison d'être. Keeping such controversies at bay, of course, is crucial; otherwise, they would intrude on the university's work (in 1949–52, over the loyalty oath; in 1964–65 the FSM; in 1968–71 war in Vietnam; in 1985–86 divestment; and in 1992 my retirement benefits).

The evidence for this rests, as Kerr and Peltason have noted, with the report of the National Research Council.[21] Kerr, in vol. 1 of his memoir on the University of California, 1949–67, devotes most of his final chapter to a review and an analysis of this and related reports ranking our nation's research universities. "Only Berkeley ranks as both most distinguished and best balanced," Kerr notes and further observes, "No other American university campuses have advanced faster in the course of the entire twentieth century than Los Angeles and San Diego" (UCLA and UCSD, respectively). "Another way to view the general level of distinction among universities," he points out, "is by the percentage of programs ranked in the top ten. . . . Here Berkeley is far out in front, followed by Harvard and MIT. UCSF comes in as number seven, San Diego as number eleven, and UCLA as number fourteen." In a 1993 study looking at the quality of faculty averaged over all fields, "MIT comes in first and Berkeley second. UC-San Diego comes in as number ten with UCLA tied with Michigan at number twelve. UC-San Francisco would be tied at nine with Cornell if it were a general campus. Four of the five highest rated public institutions (including UCSF) are campuses within the University of California. Irvine (27), Davis (35), and Santa Barbara (41) are all within the top fifty."[22]

And in referring to a study covering the period 1980 to 1990, by Graham and Diamond, a study based not on reputational rankings, as was the National Research Council's Report of 1995, but on "the per capita receipt of federal R&D funds, and the per capita publication rate in leading scholarly journals," Kerr reports that nationally among "the rising public research universities, UC-Santa Barbara ranked first, UC-Riverside and UC-Santa Cruz are fourth and fifth, UC-Irvine is seventh, and UC-Davis is fifteenth."[23] Overall, Graham and Diamond conclude that "Judged by the comparative results, California designed the nation's most effective system for building research universities."[24]

And finally, in Webster's and Skinner's analysis of the National Research

Council's Report, the University of California system is described as "astonishing" in the breadth and depth of its quality all across its campuses, not just at two or three (see appendix 3).[25]

MY DEBT TO OTHERS

I am indebted beyond value for the mentoring that Kerr provided me over nearly forty years, and the many others named in these memoirs, including my colleagues on the faculty and in the administration along with members of the staff and those serving in the Office of the President who contributed so much and helped without complaint or credit.

I wish also to credit an unpayable debt to my fellow presidents at other leading universities whose experience, insight, advice, and friendship over a twenty-year period, both at Utah and California, played such a significant role in helping me both personally and professionally: Thomas Bartlett at Colgate, Alabama, and Oregon; Derek Bok at Harvard; John Brademas at New York University; William Danforth at Washington University; Joseph Duffey at Massachusetts; William Friday at North Carolina; Gordon Gee at West Virginia, Colorado, Ohio State, Brown, and Vanderbilt; Hanna Gray at Chicago; Vartan Gregorian at Brown; Father Theodore Hesburgh at Notre Dame; Stanley Ikenberry at Illinois; Donald Kennedy at Stanford; William McGill at UC San Diego and Columbia; Peter McGrath at Minnesota and Missouri; Martin Meyerson at Berkeley and Penn; Barry Munitz at Houston and CSU; John Oswald at Penn State; Wesley Posvar at Pitt; Frank Rhodes at Cornell; John Ryan at Indiana; Harold Shapiro at Michigan and Princeton; John Toll at Maryland; and Clifton Wharton at Michigan State and New York (SUNY).

My roots in the University of California grew deep and wide over my lifetime, affording me the nourishment, light, space, and cover needed for my personal maturity and professional growth. The debt cannot be repaid. I did what I could, however, in my various UC assignments, to help further the university's cause and to lift the light of learning even higher. *Fiat lux,* the university's motto, was my guide.

In this I was always keenly aware of the contributions not only of those with whom I worked, but also of those remarkable men and women who went before. Of the fifty-nine persons who served as chairman or vice chairman of the Board of Regents since 1920 to the date of my retirement in 1992, I have known fifty-three; of the university's eighteen presidents since 1869, I have known eight; of the university's forty-nine chancellors, I have known forty-five; of the twenty-nine members of the faculty who chaired the senate's Academic Council and who represented the voice of the faculty at regent meetings, I have known twenty. The students I came to work with number in the low hundreds; and 312,414 students earned their degrees at UC during my tenure as president (and another 55,000 [estimated] at Utah).

I tried as hard as I could to meet the high standards my predecessors set, and to contribute in ways that befit my responsibilities. I believe that I largely succeeded, but certainly not in every respect, as these memoirs make clear. And with the benefit of hindsight, at nearly seventy years of age I grow increasingly aware that the uncertainties and vagaries of life and work inform our biases, enliven our sensibilities, enrich our possibilities, and make our triumphs and our sorrows all the more poignant.

What a privilege it was to have served the cause of higher education, with memories and a sense of accomplishment that subordinate the bumps, barriers, and crises along the way. And thus life moves on.

EPILOGUE

YEARS OF RENEWAL AND PERSONAL REFLECTIONS

To move abruptly from the very public presidency of the University of California, with its 166,000 students, 155,000 employees, 9 campuses, 5 medical centers, 3 national laboratories, and an annual operating budget of $10 billion to the very private presidency of the William and Flora Hewlett Foundation in Menlo Park, a California-based charitable grant-making foundation with a corpus of $825 million, was at once difficult and welcome. Incomparable factors of size, scale, and reach made the shift difficult, and novelty made my endeavors welcome.

Shortly after my resignation announcement in November 1991 Roger Heyns, venerated chancellor emeritus of the Berkeley campus and long-serving director and president of the Hewlett Foundation, came to see me at my offices in Oakland. He intended to step down at the end of 1992 and asked if I would be interested in succeeding him. We discussed the matter at length, and I told him I appreciated his confidence in me. But I was receiving other invitations from within California and elsewhere and did not want to make a decision at that point. At three-week intervals thereafter he called to reassure me of his and Bill Hewlett's continuing interest. Then in mid-January 1992 I told Roger I thought the fit was not right; he very graciously wished me well.

In mid-February one of Ronald Brady's former colleagues at the University of Illinois, Chancellor Emeritus Jack Corbally, then head of the Chicago-based MacArthur Foundation, was visiting the Bay Area. I had told Brady about the Hewlett offer, and he couldn't believe I had turned it down: maybe a talk with Corbally about his work at the MacArthur Foundation would help me think things through, Brady suggested. Corbally was a longtime acquaintance of mine as well, and I agreed to join Brady and Corbally for lunch in Oakland.

Corbally was more enthusiastic about the MacArthur Foundation's work than about graduate teaching (referring to my option to teach) and urged me to pursue the offer directly with Bill Hewlett. Heyns, Hewlett, and I met at Hewlett's office in the Hewlett-Packard headquarters in Palo Alto in late February 1992.

I liked Hewlett very much, and during my years at UC we had met at Cal-Stanford Big Games: he was a Stanford graduate and Flora, his late wife, was a Berkeley graduate. It didn't take me very long to see the position's potential then and even more when Hewlett began to transfer his wealth to the foundation, as he intended to. I agreed to serve as the incoming president of the foundation, with effect from January 1, 1993, and informed the Board of Regents of my decision at our March meetings in Los Angeles.

THE HEWLETT FOUNDATION

I made few changes at the outset of my six and a half years with the Hewlett Foundation. Roger Heyns had bequeathed me an excellent but small staff of eighteen housed in leased quarters on Middlefield Road, in Menlo Park, California (including Marianne Pallotti, Heyns's equally long-serving vice president, whose previous work with the Ford Foundation and her years with Hewlett proved to be invaluable). The foundation had carved out an unusual niche in the philanthropic world of grants: it made multiyear, general operating support grants to the nonprofit sector within the United States and abroad. The foundation's endowment was $825 million and the annual grants approximated $40 million. Its areas of interest included population issues and conflict resolution worldwide; U.S.-Mexico relations; higher education issues nationally; environmental problems in the western United States; needful communities and neighborhoods in the San Francisco Bay Area; and the performing arts from Santa Cruz County in the south to Napa and Sonoma counties in the north.

The program officers, who identified the most promising nonprofits and the most recognized leaders whose focus and interests coincided with the foundation's, were experts in their respective areas. They worked closely with these groups and negotiated our grants to optimize both the use of our resources and those of the nonprofits we were supporting.

My work was to oversee the foundation's investments and to review the grant proposals, to offer my suggestions and criticisms, to monitor the work of our program officers, to look for ways of improving our efforts, and to recommend for our board's review and approval the grants that I thought best served the foundation's objectives. I was also expected to phase out support for some programs while identifying fresh opportunities for the foundation to pursue. While the program officers carried out most of the grant-making process (I handled grants that fell outside our stated purposes and was able to make grants on my own authority of $75,000 or less), I chose to participate directly in two special project grants that made a real difference here and abroad.

The School Initiative

The first was to advance the K-12 school reform effort in the San Francisco Bay Area, consistent with my continuing interest in improving the public schools. I wanted to add this component to the foundation's portfolio of interests in higher education, and to link our regional efforts with the national one being made by Walter Annenberg, one of America's major philanthropists, whose $500 million challenge grants in the mid-1990s to improve the nation's public schools were yielding encouraging results. Recipients included New York City, Philadelphia, Chicago, Los Angeles, and some other major cities. Each city was to match the grant and commit the monies to improving its public schools. But within any given state there was only one grant.

Annenberg's principal adviser in this endeavor was Vartan Gregorian, former provost of the University of Pennsylvania, former president of the New York Public Library, and then serving as president of Brown University in Rhode Island (and now as president of the Carnegie Corporation of New York). We had been friends for many years and at the time were also serving together as trustees of the J. Paul Getty Trust in Los Angeles.

I explored the possibility of mounting a K-12 improvement effort in the San Francisco Bay Area with Bill Hewlett and his son, Walter, who was also a foundation director; both supported the idea. Then I called Gregorian to see what we could do to gain an exception to Annenberg's "one grant per state" rule. Gregorian is one of the most interesting and intelligent people I have known. He is also great fun, loves a challenge, and is as creative and adaptive as circumstances require in order to make good things happen.

His initial response, however, was not encouraging, calling my attention to the fact that Annenberg had been unwilling to make any exceptions to the "one state" rule. But, I said, in making a grant to Los Angeles, "Annenberg only *thought* he was making a grant to California." Gregorian was laughing as I went on to remind him of the size of California, the regional differences within its diverse parts, the dissimilarities demographically, especially in the schools between southern and northern California—all of these characteristics unique to California.

"What do you have in mind?" he then asked. "What I have in mind is persuading you to persuade Annenberg that he should make a second grant to

California for the reform effort we wish to undertake in the several counties whose borders were contiguous with San Francisco Bay." I then described briefly what we had in mind.

It would be a five-year program (and, we hoped, renewable) and would cost $100 million. The money would come from a grant of $15 million by Bill Hewlett from his personal nonfoundation assets, $10 million by the Hewlett Foundation, plus $25 million if Annenberg wished to match the Hewlett grants. The private sector in northern California would match the $50 million one to one (up to one-third of its monies would come from the public schools in the San Francisco Bay Area).

Gregorian's reaction was very encouraging. "This would be Annenberg's long-hoped for partner," he said, "as no other major private donor in any of the other cities had stepped forward as Hewlett was now willing to do. Send me a summary of our conversation and I will discuss it with Mr. Annenberg," he concluded.

The plan worked. Annenberg's grant of $25 million was made. Hewlett grants of $25 million were also forthcoming as promised. This $50 million was matched in full as noted above, and the Bay Area School Reform Collaborative (BASRC) was launched. The program has since been renewed for a second five-year round, and the results have been encouraging. For example, BASRC sought to alter the way schools evaluate and adjust teaching methods, train teachers, share leadership, involve parents, and make decisions. In spring 2000 independent evaluations from Stanford University compared "standardized test scores of BASRC funded Leadership Schools with other non-BASRC schools serving similar student bodies and found that BASRC schools had made significantly greater gains on the SAT-9 over three years"[1]—especially in elementary and middle schools serving large numbers of students from severely disadvantaged homes.

Whereas I was instrumental in securing the funding, placing the full weight of the Hewlett resources back of it, and helping conceptualize the program, the foundation's program officer for education, Ray Bachetti, had the most important role in its early substantive success. Bachetti, a former vice president of Stanford University, was the key driver in making all this happen and in securing the support of the public schools, the teachers and their unions, the principals, superintendents, and school boards, and in obtaining the financial support of the private sector. Much credit also goes to Ms. Merrill Vargo, who headed BASRC and was responsible for the day-to-day operations of the collaborative staff.

The Universities Project in Salzburg, Austria

The second major grant in which I was directly involved came about through the common efforts of the Salzburg Seminar, an American nonprofit, and the Hewlett Foundation. This was a six-year, $5 million grant to the Salzburg Seminar to advance the cause of universities then mostly free of central control in the former republics of the Soviet Union and bordering satellite countries in Central, Eastern, and Southern Europe. It came about this way.

Olin Robison, former president of Middlebury College in Vermont but then, as now, serving as president of the Salzburg Seminar, asked to see me about projects of interest to the seminar in which he hoped Hewlett would be interested. As we talked, I found myself liking what the seminar was doing—bringing together academics and leading figures from government, business, science, the arts, and education to meet at the seminar's historic and quite magnificent Schloss Leopoldskron in Salzburg for seminars, symposia, discussions, and debate on the major issues confronting a changing Europe and an adapting America—but liking less the subjects he was hoping Hewlett would support.

Our conversation then turned to a concern I had about the long-term viability of the former Communist countries as they struggled to free their institutions and government from entrapment in their older system. I believed that the universities of these countries had a pivotal role to play in this conversion and that they would benefit from the active involvement of their Western colleagues in making the necessary transition.

"Could we consider," I asked Olin, "a partnership between our two institutions, the purpose of which would be to bring to Salzburg the rectors, vice rectors, ministers, and senior academics of the leading universities from the several former republics and satellites of the Soviet Union to meet with their counterparts from Western Europe, the United States, and Canada, along with key personnel from the United Nations and the Council of Europe? We could surely help them with this monumental transition and they could help us understand what was really going on in this rapidly changing and newly dynamic part of Europe." "Yes," said Olin, and the Universities Project was born.

By the mid-1990s these universities had been deeply affected by the socioeconomic and political transitions taking place and were looking to reinvent themselves at the local, national, regional, and international levels. Considerable outside assistance for higher education had come into the region, much of it designed to create linkages and exchanges at the student and faculty level. Yet little had been done to assist with systemic, institutional reforms in higher education—at the level of administration, governance, and finance.

It was against this backdrop that the Salzburg Seminar created the Universities Project as a forum for dialogue on issues of institutional reform. It formed networks of university leaders from the former Soviet bloc with their peers in North America and Western Europe, and over its six-year history the project garnered a reputation as a leading transatlantic center for higher education reform in these regions.

Five core subjects served as the focus of the Universities Project's work: university administration and finance; academic structure and governance within the university; students' needs and their role in institutional affairs; technology in higher education; and the university and civil society. The program has resulted in linkages and partnerships between universities in Central/Eastern/Southern Europe and the Russian federation with parallel institutions in North America and Western Europe, to promote students' leadership capacity and the transfer of knowledge and best practices on academic governance, strategic management development of human and institutional resources, and other key issues needed to renew their universities.

More than seven hundred ranking university leaders, including ministers, from forty countries participated in twenty-seven symposia at Salzburg. And the project arranged fifty team visits to individual universities in the eastern countries. It has had a remarkable and constructive effect on all involved.[2]

On a personal note, one of my most memorable visits to Salzburg had nothing to do with the Universities Project. Instead, it was to help vet the report soon to be made to President Nelson Mandela by his national commission charged with reviewing and proposing fundamental changes in the governance, management, and funding of South Africa's postapartheid universities.

Working with some ten to twelve other higher education experts from the United States and several Commonwealth countries, charged with helping Mandela's commission as best we could, was a real pleasure. To see how effectively this racially diverse commission of blacks, whites, and those of mixed ethnicity worked was not only an education but a major source of encouragement for everyone interested in South Africa's future.

But what I most recall was one of the special evenings we all had together at the schloss. After dinner on this particular night there was a piano concert in a fireplace-warmed and cozy room off the terrace fronting the lake, backdropped by a fierce thunder and lightning storm, the lightning seeming to strike within a few rods of us. The storm continued throughout the concert and during the reception that followed in the beautiful mirrored Venetian Room. The room was lit only by candles affixed to the candelabra and chandeliers, the mirrors reflecting and the walls absorbing and enlivening their flickering light. The ongoing thunder and lightning created an even more charged environment. Suddenly a courier arrived with a message from South Africa to the head of the commission: the South African Parliament had just approved their country's new constitution, thus making the work of the commission all the more significant and timely.

Members of the entire South African commission spontaneously broke into their country's national anthem, hugging and congratulating one another, all joyous with the news and happily receiving our good wishes within this quite remarkable setting and at this historic time.

Bill Hewlett

I enjoyed my time with the Hewlett Foundation because it was fundamentally dissimilar in its purposes, scale, and size from UC's. Frankly, I welcomed it after nearly twenty years of overseeing the work of two major and very public research universities. Bill Hewlett was a great man and a joy to work with. To have had this association with him was a remarkable opportunity. I met with him no less than once and sometimes twice a month, keeping him up to date, seeking his advice, and sounding him out on certain grants we were considering.

He never once asked me to make a specific grant or not to make one. He was entirely nondirective and fully supportive, although when he believed I should be more attentive to certain things and less to others, he would say so. Advancing age and ill health, however, gradually impaired his ability to remain as chairman, and in the mid-1990s he relinquished the chair to his son, Walter. Bill passed away at his home in Portola Valley on January 12, 2001. I admired him greatly.

In a biographical memoir prepared at the request of the American Philosophical Society, I wrote of Bill, in part:

> This quiet, self-effacing man, together with his longtime friend and partner David Packard, changed the world and helped usher in the modern technological age. . . . [The company they co-founded in 1939 was] the valley's first major start-up company, and one of its most successful, ranking at Hewlett's death as the nation's thirteenth largest business with annual sales of nearly $50 billion and employing some ninety thousand persons in 120 countries. . . .
>
> He was indifferent to the trappings of wealth but used his to help others and make good things happen. His wants were remarkably simple and did not seem to be in any way the object of his professional life, telling me once that he did what interested him as an engineer and "the money just happened along."[3]

The foundation, of course, grew with the bull market of the mid to late 1990s and as Bill passed more of his wealth to the foundation. This combination increased the endowment over the years of my service from $825 million in 1993 to $2.25 billion in 1999, and our annual grant making from $40 million to nearly $100 million over the same period. I knew by the mid-1990s that this growth would continue and began to plan for a foundation whose assets would eventually be closer to $9 billion than the $1.5 billion we had then.

The result of these early efforts was the building and completion of the foundation's new offices on seven acres at the corner of Sand Hill Road and Santa Cruz Avenue at the northern edge of Stanford-owned land in Menlo Park. We negotiated a lease of the land for fifty years, with an option to renew.

I was very pleased with this outcome and happy with my early involvement in obtaining the site and planning for and designing our new building. The building was constructed and occupied under the direction of my successor, Paul Brest, former dean of the Stanford University Law School. It was dedicated in October 2002.

Referring to the changes made in our programs during my service, in May 1999 Walter Hewlett touched on the projects I outlined above and among others, the regional grants program—now expanded into community reinvestment—that ensured that "David leaves an enduring mark on its programs, Board, and staff."[4]

As for my own feelings as I retired, they too were included in the foundation's annual report:

> The work has enhanced my understanding of the seemingly intractable nature of the problems our world confronts, the richness of its many religions and cultures, the interdependence of its economies, the vibrancy and courage of its peoples, and the thousands upon thousands of those in the nonprofit sector—talented, committed, and competent people—who confront these problems daily, on the ground, throughout the world. They are the ones who engage these issues where it counts; they are the ones who take the risks and live with the consequences. . . . Our grants have been quiet, steady, evolutionary, and dependable. Our interests, while periodically reshaped, rearticulated, and rearranged, have also been remarkably consistent as well as innovative, pro-active, risk-taking, and creative.[5]

In addition to making good things happen with the foundation's grants, I had a great respect for the staff with whom I was working, and affection as well. They were committed, capable, experienced people, well informed, sought after for advice by colleagues elsewhere, and fully supportive of my efforts as I was of theirs.

THE J. PAUL GETTY TRUST

No sooner had I retired as president of the Hewlett Foundation than my fellow trustees elected me as chairman of the Board of Trustees of the J. Paul Getty Trust in Los Angeles, California. I had been serving as a trustee of this remarkable institution since 1992 when Harold Williams, a UC regent, and then serving as the Getty's president, asked me to serve as one of twelve Getty trustees. So in 2000 I succeeded Robert Erburu, former chairman and CEO of the Times Mirror Corporation of Los Angeles, and also a Hewlett Foundation director.

I had known Erburu when he was active at the Times Mirror Corporation (which included in its holdings the *Los Angeles Times*) when I was at UC. I had also worked with him as vice chairman of the Getty under his excellent leadership and as a fellow director of the Hewlett Foundation. He now chairs the Board of Trustees of the National Gallery of Art in Washington, D.C.

The Getty's origins date to 1953, when J. Paul Getty, then one of the world's wealthiest individuals, created a small museum of Greek and Roman antiquities, eighteenth-century French furniture and European paintings at his ranch house near Malibu and Pacific Palisades in western Los Angeles. He later built the Roman-style villa at the same site, a near replica of one at Herculaneum, near Pompeii, covered by lava from the eruption of Mt. Vesuvius in 79 A.D. that smothered both sites. The villa housed the Getty collection from 1974 to 1997, is now under renovation, and will reopen in 2005. It will display the Getty's collection of Greek and Roman antiquities, a collection now greatly enlarged and qualitatively improved, the remainder of the Getty's collections, library, studios, galleries, and operations now located at the newly constructed Getty Center.

The Getty Center lies astride the high ridge to the west of the San Diego Freeway (405), with Brentwood to the west and UCLA, Bel Air, and Sunset Boulevard to the east. It opened in 1997. This handsome campus was designed by the renowned modernist architect Richard Meier of New York City and paid for by the trust. Approximately 1.5 million people visit it annually, and it offers special programs for schoolchildren in the Los Angeles schools and environs. Open to the public without charge, it is one of California's and the nation's most remarkable cultural centers, dramatic in its setting, stunning in architectural style and yet uncommonly functional. The Getty Center houses the Getty Museum, the Getty Research Institute, the Getty Conservation Institute, and the Getty Grant Program.

The Getty Trust that oversees the entire enterprise has a simply stated and straightforward mission: to foster and encourage a greater understanding of and appreciation for the visual arts in their many forms as an enduring expression of mankind's intellect, creativity, imagination, sensitivity, and basic humanity. Hence it constantly enlarges its library and collections of paintings, sculptures, drawings, illuminated manuscripts, photographs, Greek and Roman antiquities, decorative arts, and related historical and interpretative materials. It shares these treasures both at the Getty and through an ambitious publication effort of lectures and traveling exhibits, as well as through its Web site and other electronic means. Through the philanthropic work of its grant programs, it supports like endeavors elsewhere and arranges for Getty scholars from around the world to make use of its collections and library.

This institution is served by a professional staff and supported by an array of specialists suited to the Getty's needs. Barry Munitz, former chancellor of the CSU system, succeeded Harold Williams as president in 1997 and provides the trust with the leadership it needs to move from its present condition to its inherent potential. It is not a charitable grant-making trust, as is the Hewlett Foundation, but an operating trust. The Getty's permanent endowment is between $5 and $6 billion (excluding the value of its collections and Malibu and Brentwood sites).

Millions of people benefit from personal visits to view the Getty's collections in state-of-the-art exhibition space and special exhibits arranged by the Getty in collaboration with private collectors and with other museums within the United States and abroad. The Getty's technicians, scientists, and artists conserve, preserve, repair, clean, and authenticate works of art from throughout the world. Many of the world's cultural treasures are the beneficiary of the Getty's involvement: helping the Chinese government conserve the wall paintings and other centuries-old art at the Mogao caves on the old silk road in northwestern China, assisting in the restoration of the old colonial heart of Quito, Ecuador, helping restore the Nefetari tomb in Egypt and the great mosaic fronting St. Vitus Cathedral in Prague, by way of examples.

HIGHER EDUCATION

I also maintain a lively interest in higher education. The Tanner Lectures on Human Values form an international lectureship overseen by the presidents of the member universities, as earlier noted. Seeing these colleagues in connection with the work of the Tanner lectures, along with a handful of other old friends who help, is a source of ongoing pleasure for me.

I have been active in a group of leading university figures and scholars in America and Europe in creating and nurturing the Glion Colloquium, which every eighteen months meets alternately in Glion, Switzerland (near Geneva), and in the United States, to consider issues of common interest and concern in higher education. In a California spin-off from the Glion initiative, I join colleagues from UC—chancellors, academic senate leaders, scholars, former presidents and regents—who meet every other month to consider strategic issues of concern to UC.

I also maintain an affiliation with the Berkeley Center for Studies in Higher Education, attend seminars, see my Berkeley colleagues from time to time, and always welcome the calls from chancellors, vice presidents, and presidents as opportunities to help them deal with problems and opportunities they foresee. My equally welcome service on the President's (Clinton) Commission on the Arts and Humanities was yet another opportunity to contribute what I could to these vital areas of American life.

Finally, I am teaching one-third-time at the University of Utah in the Department of Educational Leadership and Policy, in the Graduate School of Education. I offer a course on the history of American higher education and on the management and governance of American universities to advanced graduate students, I team teach a seminar whose "students" are the chairs of academic departments and another whose students are midlevel staff (mostly women). In each instance, we take up how American universities function—their management, administration, structure, and finance—and how they relate to interested governmental entities, donors, and other external constituencies.

MARRIAGE TO SHEILA

But the most important event in my life since I left UC in 1992 is my marriage on December 27, 1995, to Sheila S. Rodgers. We met in mid-September 1991 on a flight from Dulles Airport in Washington to San Francisco. Sheila had been a senior flight attendant with United Airlines for twelve years. Her obvious professionalism and her character attracted me, and we had a lively thirty-minute conversation during the flight. I knew by the time our flight was in its final stages that I wanted to know her better and managed to obtain her home number (it wasn't easy, and completely out of character for me). Actually, if it had not been for her other flight attendant friends, I would have tried in vain to get it from Sheila.

We went out together for some four-plus years, not exclusively at first but certainly later. Sheila was living in San Mateo and was based in San Francisco. Her flights with United Airlines took her throughout our country and much of the world as well. I, of course, was still in Orinda, and working in Oakland at UC's offices in the Kaiser Center. Somehow with our respective and difficult schedules, we managed to spend time together.

Whenever possible, I would drive after work to San Mateo for dinner in a restaurant or a delicious home-cooked meal at Sheila's. These visits and our weekend trips to northern California's beautiful coastal communities, wine country, and Lake Tahoe or drives to San Francisco for a rich array of cultural events were a source of great pleasure, peace, and comfort to both of us (during my difficult and final year as UC's president, she was enormously supportive and encouraging). And it was not long before we fell in love and contemplated a future together. But it was a long time before we became engaged, waiting until it seemed right for both of us.

One evening at dusk we were swimming in the beautiful bay fronting Mauna Kea on the big island of Hawaii. The sun was setting, the ocean warm, it was her birthday, and we were relaxed—perfect circumstances for my proposal of marriage on September 17, 1995. She accepted, and we were married in our Park City, Utah, home two days following Christmas in 1995.

It was a beautiful, candlelit ceremony performed by my cousin and close friend of many years, R. J. Snow, then serving as vice president at Brigham Young University, and a stake president in the Mormon Church. Family members and close friends were with us. A reception at home followed for friends in and around Salt Lake City; and a second reception for our many friends in the San Francisco Bay Area occurred the next week at my brother Reed's home in San Mateo, California.

We honeymooned first at Sundance, our friend Robert Redford's resort thirty minutes south of Park City, and later in Hawaii, first at the Mauna Kea Resort and then at the Manele Bay Hotel on the beautiful small island of Lanai, across the channel from Molokai and Maui.

Sheila and her three siblings grew up in Elyria, Ohio, in a household with both parents. She possesses all the solid and steady values for which the nation's heartland is renowned—family-centered, dependable, hard-working, neighborly, open, and friendly. Sheila started to work part-time at fifteen and put herself through Ohio State University, graduating in 1973. She had always wanted to travel, however, and after working a few years in the travel industry, she became a flight attendant with United Airlines in 1979, working full-time in that capacity until 1997.

Marriage to Sheila in 1995 jumpstarted my life. I felt renewed, happy, content once again. We would now be sharing our lives, with our extended families, with our older as well as newer friends, and in the activities and adventures we were planning.

The first thing we did was buy a small home in San Mateo, California. Sheila was still flying full-time and needed to be close to the San Francisco International Airport. I could drive to the Hewlett Foundation offices in twenty minutes. Our small home was a source of great pleasure. We furnished it, redid the garden, remodeled the bathrooms, painted, and repaired (much of it without help).

Downtown San Mateo was within easy walking distance, and the pleasant surrounding neighborhoods were where we took our regular walks. Berkeley was not far, just across the bay to the east. San Francisco was to the north, a thirty-minute drive at nonpeak hours. Wine country was an hour past San Francisco to the north. The Pacific Ocean was twenty minutes to the west, and Santa Cruz, Monterey, and Carmel were an hour and a half to the south on California's central coast.

I have often wondered how I could have been so lucky as to have found love twice. But lucky I was and lucky I am to be sharing my life with Sheila, alive to our opportunities, appreciative of our extended families, embraced by our friends.

PARK CITY

After Sheila's retirement from United Airlines and mine from the Hewlett Foundation, in 2001 we sold our home in San Mateo and moved into our ski resort and summer mountain retreat at Park City. Twenty-five miles east of Salt Lake City, at an elevation of 7,000 feet, the town is flanked to the west by the Wasatch Range of the Rocky Mountains and to the distant east by the Uinta Range that delineates the Wyoming and Utah borders.

This nineteenth-century Wild West mining town, lovingly preserved by its now nearly 8,000 residents, nestles in a long valley at the base of the surrounding mountains and provides a rare and safe haven from the thundering character of modern American urban life while offering its own and very special summer and winter attractions in the high Rocky Mountains. For example, our family enjoyed the 2002 Winter Olympics, much of which took place within walking distance of our home.

To the west, within an easy drive, is Salt Lake City and the University of Utah, with their cultural and intellectual offerings, and to the east, within an easy fifteen-minute to an hour's drive, is some of the country's best fly fishing, the distance depending on which river or lake we pick in the east-west-running Uinta Range of the Rockies and the valley between our home and the Uintas.

We also have a small townhouse in Hawaii on the island of Lanai, near the Manele Bay Hotel and within easy walking distance of the tide pools and graceful half-moon beach at Hulopoe Bay with its resident population of spinning dolphins and reef fish, joined in the winter months by the great whales that come south from Alaska for the warm, deep blue, clear waters of Hawaii.

We move between our Park City mountain home, the San Francisco Bay Area, Lanai, and Los Angeles (for my Getty duties). In the course of these travels and others, we do our best to visit our extended family, now including fourteen grandchildren, a source of great joy and pleasure for both of us. Karen and David Dee and children live in Salt Lake City; Shari and Eric Olmstead and children live in Santa Clara, Utah; Lisa and Blair Pattenaude and children live in Snoqualmie, Washington; Marci and Patrick Dunne and children live in Orinda, California—they are all busily engaged and enjoying these special and formative years, including their own traditions and family ties. After two years of college and varsity baseball, Sheila's son, Matthew, enlisted in the U.S. Navy for air crew training.

REFLECTIONS

During the quiet moments when thinking and feeling coalesce to illuminate my deepest sense of self, the experiences I recall are remembrances more of the essence of life than of its trappings. They include more of the subtler sensibilities of private life and of family and friends than of appearances, public position, and power.

They include the simple and homey recollections of childhood in Berkeley, a loving home, grandparents and parents, siblings, aunts, uncles, and sixty-five first cousins.

They include the Berkeley public schools and lifelong friends with whom I shared the pleasures and sufferings of life in memorable abundance.

They include practicing the piano at dawn and the pipe organ in the early morning quiet and barely lit church.

They include working the fields in the western Utah desert, swimming in the irrigation ditches at midday when the desert heat is highest, and breathing in the scent of sage after a thunderous burst of summer rain.

They include driving cattle over the Milk River ridge just north of Montana where the great plains of Alberta yield to the western foothills of the Canadian Rockies and herding sheep (by the thousands) up Spanish Fork Canyon in central Utah to the lush mountain valleys and high alpine meadows blanketed with the infinite colors of their wildflowers, miles on end.

They include the high Sierra and the Rockies, with the great falls of Yosemite and Yellowstone, and their turbulent rivers and fast-moving streams and placid alpine lakes, and knowing where the trout lurk and how the line feels when they strike the fly cast at the moment and place when the taking is irresistible.

They include the early dawn and the late sunset over the Golden Gate and San Francisco Bay, the pale light reaching across the clear waters of the Flathead in northwestern Montana as the moon rises over the Mission Range, and the sparkling beauty of Echo Lake in its mountain fastness high above Lake Tahoe as the morning breeze from Desolation Valley ripples across its cold, deep blue waters.

They encompass the beauty of nature in its many forms and expressions: the interplay of sky, mountains, valleys, forests, lakes, rivers, desert, and plains and the collision of land with the earth's oceans and seas, and marine life in its infinite variety.

They include the Golden Gate Bridge, which I flew over with tears in my eyes, home from Korea safely and at last.

They include the Yellow Sea, mysterious with its dangers and luminescent beauty, entwined. They include the first snow of winter in its blanketing, and the freshness of spring's first rain, and the high country: crisp, clear, and warm, and the forest in transition from fall to winter drenched with color, at home in Park City.

They include the great sea cliffs of the island of Lanai jutting majestically from the deep blue waters of Hawaii's Pacific to form the remote and secluded Hulopoe Bay with its tide pools and teeming marine life and the elegance of its half-moon beach from which we watch the sun rise over Maui's Haleakala to the east and set in the west as the muted but ever-changing colors of the lava cliffs backdrop the melding of the vivid yellow of the sun with the brilliant blue of the ocean, and the bay is traced by Hawaiian canoes, the scene softened even more by the gentle sound of surf and the chant of the paddlers, soon followed by the unveiling of the Hawaiian night—a black velvet sky illuminated by stars sparkling and numberless.

They include the sounding bells of the Campanile at Berkeley at the close of a Saturday afternoon football game in Memorial Stadium and the lights of the great "U" on the mountain rising east of the University of Utah campus, lit for a game and then blinking in victory or steady in defeat.

They include cultures, indeed civilizations, visited but barely apprehended in Russia, Iran, India, the Holy Land, North Africa, Europe, Asia, Australia, South and West Africa, Canada, Mexico, and South America—memorable, enriching, broadening.

They include the elegance and grace of classical ballet, the majesty of the pipe organ in the great cathedrals of Europe and King's College Chapel, Cambridge, the stirring sounds of a full symphony orchestra and the intimate expressions of a chamber quartet in the quiet of home, and the Mormon Tabernacle Choir in Christmas concert at home in Salt Lake City.

They include literature, the art and architecture of Europe's great masters, the exquisite elegance of a Japanese garden and tea ceremony, Persian miniatures, African stone carvings, Japanese woodblocks, medieval European illuminated manuscripts and stained glass, the smell of old books at Oxford and Cambridge—the myriad ways people seek to comprehend themselves and the world in which we live.

They include the friends and colleagues with whom I labored in behalf of a noble cause, whose lives intersected with such force and effect as we sought to advance the cause of learning.

They include the kindnesses, unexpected but timely and telling, extended during periods of despair and illness.

They include the religion, spiritual commitments, and values that help center my life and infuse it with meaning and significance, a counterweight to the more popular, synthetic, and transitory pursuits of everyday life. And most important, they include the love of two good and wonderful women, the coming of children and grandchildren, and the meaning of family and its centrality to life in all its rich and mysterious unpredictability.

All these are what make life worthwhile and worth remembering. Here are the enduring experiences fashioned over a lifetime: valued, trusted, cherished, along with what residue of my public service yet expresses itself in the enriched lives of those my professional labors may have influenced, also warmly recalled, as the memoirs confirm.

I have been fortunate beyond telling.

APPENDIX 1

UC'S LONG-RANGE PLANNING ESTIMATES
FOR 1988–2006 BY CAMPUS

President Gardner presented the following estimated planned capacities for each campus in 2005–06.

BERKELEY

29,450 students, a reduction of 1,126 from the current enrollment of 30,576. The undergraduate enrollment would be reduced by 2,018 students while the graduate student ranks would increase by about 900, and the health sciences numbers would remain about the same. This reduction acknowledges that the Berkeley campus currently exceeds its reasonable carrying capacity in virtually all respects, including laboratory, research, and clinical space, student housing, libraries, and buildable land. Growth in recent years is also regarded by the City of Berkeley as having adversely affected the city itself. This modest reduction in size is intended to permit the campus to maintain its resource base and its programmatic capability to mount the range and quality of teaching, research, and public service for which it is internationally renowned, while easing the pressures that are taxing the campus and the community.

DAVIS

26,850, an increase of 6,059 over the current enrollment of 20,791. President Gardner commented that while this figure is higher than the administration initially thought wise, Chancellor Hullar has made a persuasive case that carefully controlled and planned growth at Davis is not only possible but highly desirable. It should permit Davis to enhance further the range and quality of its already highly regarded academic program while improving the environment for learning. The 356 students per year rate of growth, about 1.5 percent, is an acceptable annual growth rate, is compatible with the plans of the host community, and enjoys wide support on campus.

IRVINE

26,050 students, an increase of 11,125 over the planning period from current enrollments of 14,925. President Gardner observed that this translates to a growth rate of 654 students, or roughly 3.3 percent per year, which is one of the higher rates of growth projected. However, the campus is used to growth, knows how to grow, is geared for growth, and wishes to grow. Indeed, the Regents have always intended that it grow, at about this projected rate and to this projected level. This growth will permit the Irvine campus to round out existing programs, mount new ones, and enhance its research capability, while continuing to serve the needs of students from throughout the state. Mr. Gardner added that the proposed growth rate is consistent with the plans of the communities most directly affected by UCI.

LOS ANGELES

President Gardner explained that only minimal growth, 526 students over the next seventeen years, is planned for UCLA, for a total campus capacity of 34,500 students. Housing is a serious problem in the campus area, traffic is congested, and buildable land is at a premium. The campus has had a prolonged period of steady but carefully planned growth and, in recent years, has been concentrating on consolidating and strengthening its position. Significant growth is not needed to enhance UCLA's program or its well-established international reputation and would be very difficult to manage in its tightly constrained physical environment.

RIVERSIDE

15,050 students in 2005–06, an increase of 8,008 students for an annual growth rate of 471 students, or 4.6 percent per year. President Gardner noted that this is the highest rate of growth projected for any campus. The Riverside campus has grown significantly over the past few years and continues to increase in popularity. All of the campus characteristics favor growth, and land and other physical resources are available to accommodate it. Mr. Gardner commented that this projection is bullish, even though it falls short of what some people would prefer. He pointed out that, even at this projected rate of growth, the campus in the early years of the planning period will have to recruit annually between 8 and 9 percent of its current ladder rank faculty, a very ambitious project. The projected growth will permit Riverside to enlarge its graduate programs, increase the number of professional schools, and provide the means for Riverside to build further upon its reputation for excellent teaching, high quality research, and effective public service.

SAN DIEGO

26,050 students, an increase of 9,831 over the current enrollment of 16,219. This represents an annual growth rate of 578 students, or 2.8 percent per year.

President Gardner observed that this size has been anticipated by the Regents for the campus since its inception. The campus has the land and the momentum, and growth will permit the further development of the campus's already distinguished academic program while allowing for the development of new programs, professional schools, and colleges.

SAN FRANCISCO

4,000 students, an increase of 426, or 25 students per year. This figure is based on consideration of the programmatic needs of the campus, building limitations at the Parnassus site, traffic and related environmental problems which are of concern both to the campus and the surrounding neighborhoods, and it assumes the development of the Laurel Heights campus, which is crucial to UCSF's future. Mr. Gardner observed that the campus's future will in fact be influenced not so much by enrollment-related issues as by space considerations. Faculty are finding it increasingly difficult to do their teaching, their clinical work, and their research owing to an acute lack of space.

President Gardner pointed out that UCSF is indisputably the nation's leading health science campus and possesses some of the world's most distinguished clinicians and investigators. The "no" or "limited growth" attitude of the surrounding community will be an increasing problem if the campus is to sustain its present quality, continue to perform its pioneering research, offer the superb teaching and patient care for which it is renowned throughout the world, and realize its full potential. He suggested that the regents will need to pay close and careful attention to the matter of space.

SANTA BARBARA

20,000 students, an increase of 2,176 over current levels. This translates to an annual growth rate of 128 students, or 0.7 percent per year, which is below the 1 percent growth rate expected for the Santa Barbara area generally. Physical resources available to the campus for growth are limited, including water resources. Housing for students is in short supply and affordable faculty housing is limited. President Gardner observed that while there is concern within elements of the community about the university's prior growth and unconstrained growth in the future, the faculty and Chancellor Uehling welcome at least the levels of growth being planned. The figure of 20,000 students means closely limiting campus growth while allowing it to grow sufficiently to accommodate its programmatic needs and achieve its research potential. Mr. Gardner pointed out that this projection of very limited growth is being made even though UCSB's popularity continues to rise among students and its research is enjoying an ever-increasing measure of national regard and respect.

SANTA CRUZ

15,000 students in 2005–06, which represents an increase of 356 students per year, or 3.1 percent annually, and an overall increase of 6,051 over the current enrollment of 8,949. President Gardner explained that this growth rate is generally supported by the campus community and is crucial in order for the Santa Cruz campus fully and properly to develop and balance the breadth and depth of the academic program, improve the graduate/undergraduate ratio, permit the development of professional schools, enhance research, and invigorate the college system and undergraduate education. He did not believe that the campus needs to grow beyond 15,000 to accomplish these goals, even though the demand for admission indicates that the natural growth rate of the campus would easily exceed this rate and enrollment level if not otherwise constrained. He also believed that the campus will be able to accommodate the projected growth rate, and he expressed confidence in the ability of the campus and the community to work together for the benefit and common good of both.

President Gardner then presented a slide depicting the preliminary headcount enrollment feasibility to 2005–06 by campus for the entire University and a chart illustrating the preliminary planned capacity for the existing nine campuses over the planning period. He pointed out that the proposed total capacity for all campuses in 2005–06 is projected at 196,950 students, an increase of 28 percent over 1988–89, which means that the nine campuses are projected to absorb a total annual average growth of 2,534 students during the planning period. He drew the Board's attention to the data regarding the percentage of graduate students to total enrollment and the proposal that by 2005–06 the graduate student ratio be 20 percent for all campuses except Berkeley and Los Angeles, which show a percentage of 30.3 percent and 28 percent respectively. This represents an increase for all of the general education campuses.

Select quotations from David Gardner's presentation to the Board of Regents in 1988 of UC's long-range enrollment estimates, the corresponding growth estimated for the nine campuses, and the need for additional campuses 2000–2020, from minutes of the Regents of the University of California, October 20, 1988, pp. 3–6 (Office of the Secretary of the Regents, Oakland).

APPENDIX 2

TEXT OF THE REGENTS' ACTION ON THE SEPARATION OF DAVID P. GARDNER AS PRESIDENT OF THE UNIVERSITY OF CALIFORNIA, IN SPECIAL SESSION, APRIL 20, 1992

1. READING OF NOTICE OF MEETING

    For the record, it was confirmed that notice was given in compliance with the Bylaws and Standing Orders for a Special Meeting of the Regents, for this date and time, for the purpose of reviewing the actions taken March 20, 1992 with respect to separation of David P. Gardner as president of the university, and consideration of affirmance, modification, or rescission of such actions.

2. REVIEW OF ACTIONS TAKEN MARCH 20, 1992 WITH RESPECT TO SEPARATION OF DAVID P. GARDNER AS PRESIDENT OF THE UNIVERSITY AND CONSIDERATION OF AFFIRMANCE, MODIFICATION, OR RESCISSION.

    The President recommended that the regents review the actions taken on March 20, 1992 with respect to Separation of David P. Gardner as President of the University, and that, following that review, the regents consider what action the Board wishes to take in affirming, modifying, or rescinding those actions.

    It was recalled that at its March 20, 1992 meeting, the Regents took the following actions with respect to separation of David P. Gardner as President of the University:

    – Granted to President Gardner a three-month paid leave of absence, from October 1 through December 31, 1992, at his current base salary and regular benefits.

It is the practice at the University of California, as permitted in Standing Order 100.4(e), for the President to grant leaves of absence to certain senior executives at such time as they step down from their administrative appointments. This is often done in substitution for a sabbatical leave that such administrators would have earned by virtue of their professorial appointments.

Granting of a paid leave to the President requires approval of the Board of Regents. Payment of this leave will be made from nonstate funds.

- Approved a vesting date of December 31, 1992 for existing Nonqualified Deferred Income Plan (NDIP) agreements and Special Supplemental Retirement Program agreements for President Gardner.

Nonqualified Deferred Income Plan—In 1987, the Regents established a Nonqualified Deferred Income Plan for senior executives. An NDIP is a contractual arrangement between the Regents and a designated recipient, under which the regents agree to compensate the recipient in the future for services rendered currently, subject to forfeiture if the recipient does not remain in an eligible position until an agreed-upon future date. Allocations to this plan are credited annually and accrue earnings quarterly at the University-managed Short-Term Investment Pool rate. All deferred amounts are provided from nonstate funds.

Establishment of the Nonqualified Deferred Income Plan was in part to provide additional compensation as a means of responding to market-related deficiencies in officers' salaries, as described by the Towers, Perrin, Forster and Crosby study of 1987. The objective was to achieve about 20 percent of base pay in deferred income benefits. Another factor in its establishment was the need to find a replacement for certain previously approved employer contributions to the Tax Deferred (403 (b)) Plan, which contributions had to be discontinued because of the effect of the 1986 Tax Reform Act.

Under this policy, several NDIP agreements were subsequently approved for President Gardner. NDIP agreements require service for a period of five years, or to retirement if sooner. Had the President anticipated an earlier separation, that earlier date would have become the vesting date in the agreements, rather than the five-year date. The March Regents' Action provided that for purposes of these previously-approved NDIPs, the term of service in each agreement would be modified and each agreement would then vest on December 31, 1992, thereby waiving the forfeiture provisions of the agreements. As a consequence of the leave of absence and the modification to the vesting date, NDIPs will terminate and be paid out in the amounts reflected on the Attachment, NDIP Projections. Each NDIP listed was established by specific action by the Board.

Special Supplemental Retirement Program—In 1985, the regents established a University of California Special Supplemental Retirement Program (SSR I) "for the purpose of providing a supplemental benefit to selected individuals who, by virtue of their individual circumstances, find themselves at a significant financial disadvantage either as a result of accepting appointment to a University executive position in the latter stage of their career or as a result of continuing in a University executive position in the face of more lucrative employment offers, or for whom the University needs to manage the effective date of retirement." In 1988, this program was revised to implement a further SSR Program (SSR II), to mitigate the limitations imposed on the basic defined benefit retirement plan (UCRP) by the Tax Reform Act of 1986.

Each agreement approved under this program requires service for an agreed-upon period of time, with benefits to be forfeited if service is not fulfilled. Selection of individuals to participate in either SSR I or SSR II is made upon recommendation of the President, subject to approval of the Chairman of the Board, the Chairman of the Committee on Finance, and the Chairman of the Subcommittee on Officers' Salaries, acting under specific authority delegated by the Board of Regents. For any actions under SSR involving the President, the Senior Vice President—Administration serves as the recommending officer. All agreements entered into under this program received approval as required by the policy.

SSR I, dated February 21, 1986, provides for a special supplemental retirement calculated at 1/12th of 15 percent of President Gardner's highest average permissible compensation (HAPC) for a period of time equal to his service as President. The agreement as executed provided for service of fifteen years, or until July 1, 1998.

Average Base Salary	$239,200.04
Housing Allowance	40,966.72
Total HAPC	$280,166.76
	× .15
	$42,025.01 annually
or	$3,502.08 per month

If paid monthly, (i.e. $3,502.08 × 114 months), the total would be $399,237.63. If paid in a lump sum, this amount would be discounted to present value (5.8 percent) equal to $306,000. Payments would be made from nonstate funds. . . .

SSR II, executed in July 1988, provides for an indemnification from possible reductions imposed by the IRC §415 limits. Absent those limits, and based on years of service, age, and HAPC, President Gardner would upon retirement after March 1993 receive approximately $126,249 annually from UCRP. This is a more precise calculation than the estimated $130,000 used heretofore. More recent IRC §415 regulations provide that the maximum now permitted from UCRP trust funds for President Gardner would be approximately $104,771 in 1993, as contrasted to the $80,000 reported earlier. The agreement embodied in SSR II provides that if President Gardner served until June 30, 1998, he would receive an annual stipend to make up the difference between that allowed under the §415 limits and that earned as a consequence of service, an initial payment of approximately $21,478. Payment would be made from nonstate funds.

The Board's March action has the effect of modifying the term of service by establishing a vesting date of December 31, 1992 for all NDIP agreements and the two SSR agreements in effect for President Gardner, thereby waiving the forfeiture provision of the agreements. This will permit the President to receive only those funds which had accrued by virtue of previously approved actions on behalf of the regents.

– In consideration of the above actions by the Board, the President agreed to be available during the period October 1, 1992 through June 30, 1995 without further compensation for consultation with his successor as President and with the Chairman of the Board of Regents on budget and other issues of concern, as well as for participation in the University's 125th anniversary observances and ceremonial and alumni and other events in the interest of the University.

ESTIMATED VALUE OF NDIP
AND SSR AGREEMENTS

NDIP III (403(b) Substitute) Deferred Income*	$184,357
NDIP's II, IV, V, Special	$247,400
Sub Total NDIPS	$431,757
Supplemental Retirement Funds (SSR I)	$306,000
Total	$737,757

*Does not include NDIP I, which will be vested and paid on January 1, 1993, without a change in the vesting date.

The original UCRP retirement income projections were calculated in 1991, using 1991 IRC §415 limits, based upon an October 1993 retirement date. The revised estimates reflect an April 1993 retirement date utilizing recently published IRC §415 grandfather limits (applicable to governmental plans), indexed to 1993. That maximum is estimated to be $104,771, which leaves an approximate $21,478 per annum reduction to President Gardner's accrued UCRP benefits.

Minutes of the Regents of the University of California, April 20, 1992, pp. 1–5.

APPENDIX 3

DAVID S. WEBSTER AND TAD SKINNER'S "RATING PhD PROGRAMS: WHAT THE NRC REPORT SAYS . . . AND DOESN'T SAY" ON THE UC SYSTEM

Impressive as are the ratings of UC Berkeley and UC San Diego, the showing of the UC system as a whole is even more remarkable. Of its 229 programs included in the study, 119—or 52 percent—rank in the top 20 in their disciplines. The nine UC campuses represent only 3 percent of the 274 institutions included, and the eight UC campuses (all but UC San Francisco) that have 15 or more programs rated represent only 8 percent of the 104 institutions in this category.

The eight UC campuses with 15 or more programs rated, taken as a group, achieve a higher mean score than do the 11 schools in the Big Ten. They score an average of 3.55 in faculty scholarly quality, compared to the Big Ten's 3.37, and 3.38 in program effectiveness compared to the Big Ten's 3.32. This performance is astonishing, considering that the Big Ten universities, taken as a group, are much older than the UC campuses and have much larger faculties (reputational rankings of doctoral programs generally correlate quite highly with the size of program faculty). It is all the more astonishing when one considers that eight of the Big Ten universities, all except Indiana, Michigan State and Northwestern—are, according to the *Report,* the highest rated public research universities in their states.

In the past 40 years or so, many states that long had only one state university campus have established one or more other campuses, and some states are developing their new campus(es) to eventually achieve parity with the flagship campus. As of now, however, none of these non-flagship campuses has achieved anything approaching parity with any of UC's five highest non-flagship campuses. . . .

Of the 12 non-flagship campuses that have 15 or more programs rated, fully seven are UC campuses. The highest rated non-flagship campus that is *not* part of the UC system, the University of Illinois at Chicago, falls behind five non-flagship UC campuses. In addition, the other four non-flagship campuses—the SUNY campuses at Buffalo, Albany and Bridgehampton, and the University of Wisconsin-Milwaukee—score below all seven UC non-flagship campuses that had 15 or more programs rated. California, with a 1994 population of about 31 million, thus had a state university system in which five of its non-flagship campuses with 15 or more of programs included rated above any similar campuses in such populous states as Texas (18 million), New York (18 million), Florida (14 million), Pennsylvania (12 million), and Illinois (12 million).

Change *28, no. 3 (May–June 1996): 37–40.*

APPENDIX 4

UNIVERSITY HISTORY SERIES, REGIONAL ORAL HISTORY OFFICE

INTERVIEWS

Volume 1. Interviews with senior administrators in the Office of the President, as follows:

1. Stephen A. Arditti, Director of State Governmental Relations
2. William B. Baker, Vice President, Budget and University Relations
3. Ronald W. Brady, Senior Vice President, Administration
4. William R. Frazer, Senior Vice President, Academic Affairs
5. Cornelius L. Hopper, M.D., Vice President, Health Affairs

Volume 2. Interviews with chancellors, faculty members, and students, as follows:

1. Theodore L. Hullar, Chancellor at UC Riverside, 1985–87, UC Davis, 1987–93
2. Clark Kerr, President of UC, 1958–67, and Chancellor at Berkeley, 1952–58
3. Julius R. Krevans, Chancellor at UC San Francisco, 1982–93
4. Pedro Noguera, Professor of Education, student leader during the Anti-Apartheid Campaign
5. Glenn T. Seaborg, Chancellor at UC Berkeley, 1958–61
6. Neil J. Smelser, University Professor, Faculty Representative to the Board of Regents, 1986–87

7. Martin Trow, Professor of Public Policy, Faculty Representative to the Board of Regents, 1990–92

8. Charles F. Young, Chancellor at UCLA, 1969–97

Volume 3. Interviews with regents and state government officials, as follows:

1. Roy T. Brophy, Regent of the University, 1986–98

2. Robert J. Campbell, California State Assemblyman, 1981–96; member of Assembly Committees on Education, Higher Education, and Ways and Means

3. George C. Deukmejian, Governor of California, 1993–97

4. Richard G. Heggie, President of the UC Alumni Associations, Regent Ex Officio, 1988–89

5. Walter E. Hoadley, Vice President of the UC Alumni Associations, Regent Ex Officio, 1990–91

6. Meredith J. Khachigian, Regent of the University, 1987–2001

7. Howard H. Leach, Regent of the University, 1990–2001

8. Steven A. Merksamer, Chief of Staff, Governor George Deukmejian, 1983–88

9. Dean A. Watkins, Regent of the University, 1969–96

10. Harold M. Williams, Regent of the University, 1982–94

"The University of California Office of the President and its Constituencies, 1983–1995." Vols I–III. Copyright © 2002 by the Regents of the University of California, with an introduction by John Douglass and interviews by Carole Hicke, Germaine LaBerge, and Ann Lage, 1997–98 (The Regional Oral History Office, The Bancroft Library, University of California, Berkeley).

APPENDIX 5

EDUCATION, PROFESSIONAL ACTIVITIES, HONORS, AND AWARDS, WITH BIBLIOGRAPHY OF DAVID P. GARDNER

PERSONAL

- Born March 24, 1933, Berkeley, California
- Married Elizabeth Fuhriman, 1958 (deceased 1991); married Sheila S. Rodgers, 1995
- Four daughters, one stepson

EDUCATION

- University of California, Berkeley, 1962–66: Ph.D., Higher Education
- University of California, Berkeley, 1957–59: M.A., Political Science
- Brigham Young University, 1951–55: B.S., Political Science, History, and Geography

PROFESSIONAL POSITIONS

2001–	Professor of Educational Leadership and Policy, Graduate School of Education, University of Utah, Salt Lake City, Utah
1993–	President Emeritus, University of California; and, at UC Berkeley: Professor Emeritus, Graduate School of Education, and Professor Emeritus, Goldman School of Public Policy, 1999–
1993–99	President, William and Flora Hewlett Foundation, Menlo Park, California
1983–	President Emeritus and Professor of Higher Education Emeritus, University of Utah, Salt Lake City, Utah

1983–92	President, University of California, and Professor of Higher Education, Graduate School of Education, University of California, Berkeley
1973–83	President, University of Utah, and Professor of Higher Education
1971–73	Vice President, University of California, and Professor of Higher Education, University of California, Santa Barbara
1969–71	Vice Chancellor, Executive Assistant, and Associate Professor of Higher Education, University of California, Santa Barbara
1967–69	Assistant Chancellor and Assistant Professor of Higher Education, University of California, Santa Barbara
1964–67	Assistant to the Chancellor and Assistant Professor of Higher Education, University of California, Santa Barbara
1962–64	Director, California Alumni Foundation, University of California, Berkeley
1960–62	Field and Scholarship Director, California Alumni Association, University of California, Berkeley
1958–60	Administrative Assistant, Personnel Manager, and Principal Assistant to Chief Administrative Officer, California Farm Bureau Federation, Berkeley

HONORARY DEGREES

- Honorary Fellow, Clare Hall, Cambridge University, 2002

- Honorary Doctor of Laws, Pepperdine University, 1992

- Honorary Doctor of Humane Letters, International Christian University, 1990

- Honorary Doctor of Laws, Brown University, 1989

- Honorary Doctor of Laws, University of Notre Dame, 1989

- Docteur Honoris Causa de l' Université de Bordeaux II, 1988

- Honorary Doctor of Humanities, Utah State University, 1987

- Honorary Doctor of Laws, Westminster College, 1987

- Honorary Doctor of Laws, University of Nevada, 1984

- Honorary Doctor of Letters, University of Utah, 1983

- Honorary Doctor of Laws, University of the Pacific, 1983

- Honorary Doctor of Humanities, Brigham Young University, 1981

HONORS AND AWARDS

- David Pierpont Gardner Library of Main Stacks, University Library, Berkeley, 1997

- President Emeritus, University of California, 1992

- Knight Commander's Cross of the Order of Merit of the Federal Republic of Germany, 1992

- Alumnus of the Year, University of California, Berkeley, 1989

- California School Boards Research Foundation Hall of Fame Award, 1987

- Fulbright 40th Anniversary Distinguished Fellow, Japan, 1987
- James Bryant Conant Award, Education Commission of the States, 1985
- French Légion d'Honneur, 1985
- President Emeritus, University of Utah, 1985
- Benjamin P. Cheney Medal, Eastern Washington University, 1984
- David P. Gardner Hall, President's Circle, U. of Utah, 1982
- Honorary Member, Phi Kappa Phi, 1974
- Visiting Fellow, Michaelmas Term, 1979, Clare Hall, Cambridge University, England
- Selection as one of "100 young leaders of the academy" in nationwide survey conducted by *Change* magazine, October 1978
- Special August 1974 edition of *Time* magazine, named as one of the 200 men and women "destined to provide the United States with a new generation of leadership"

ACADEMIC MEMBERSHIPS

- Member, National Academy of Education, 1990
- Member, American Philosophical Society, 1989
- Fellow, American Academy of Arts and Sciences, 1986
- Fellow, National Academy of Public Administration, 1983

CURRENT MEMBERSHIPS AND PROFESSIONAL SERVICE

Board of Directors, Waddell and Reed Advisors Funds, 1998–

Board of Directors, Fluor Corporation, 1988–

PREVIOUS MEMBERSHIPS AND PROFESSIONAL SERVICE (SELECTED)

Board of Directors, the Salzburg Seminar, 2003–04

Board of Directors, Jon and Karen Huntsman Family Foundation, 1999–2002

Board of Directors, Huntsman Cancer Foundation, 1995–2003

Board of Governors, the Nature Conservancy, 1993–99

Board of Trustees, J. Paul Getty Trust, 1992–2004 (Chairman, 2000–2004)

Board of Directors, William and Flora Hewlett Foundation, 1992–99

Association of Governing Boards of Universities and Colleges Advisory Council of Presidents, 1990–92

Council on Competitiveness, Executive Committee, 1990–92

College Board, New Possibilities Commission, Co-Chair, 1989–90

Council Member, Hong Kong University of Science and Technology, 1988–96

Board of Directors, the Nature Conservancy (California), 1986–90

Chair, Southwestern District Rhodes Scholarship Selection Committee, 1986–87

Business–Higher Education Forum, 1984–92 (Chairman, 1988–90)

Board of Directors, California Chamber of Commerce, 1984–92

Board of Directors, California Economic Development Corporation, 1984–92

Regent of the University of California, 1983–92

Member, National Association of State Universities and Land Grant Colleges, Committee on Federal Legislation, 1983–92

Board of Directors (Chairman), George S. and Dolores Dore Eccles Foundation, 1982–2001

Director, the Denver and Rio Grande Western Railroad Company, 1982–85

Director, Rio Grande Industries, Inc., 1982–85

Chairman, National Collegiate Athletic Association Select Committee on Athletic Problems and Concerns in Higher Education, 1982–83

Executive Committee, National Association of State Universities and Land Grant Colleges, 1982–83

American Council on Education Member, National Commission on Student Financial Assistance, 1981–83 (Appointee of President Pro Tem, U.S. Senate)

Chairman, National Commission on Excellence in Education, 1981–83 (Appointee of the U.S. Secretary of Education)

Member, National Commission on Higher Education Issues, 1981–82

Board of Directors, America-Mideast Educational and Training Services, Washington, D.C., 1980–82

Member, Study Group for Post-Secondary Organization and Management Studies, National Institute of Education, 1980–82

Board of Trustees (Founding Trustee), Tanner Lectures on Human Values, 1978–2004 (Chairman, 1978–83)

Board of Directors, American Council on Education, 1978–81

Executive Committee, Western College Association, 1978–81

Chairman, Rhodes Scholarship Selection Committee for Utah, 1978–80

Chairman, Western Region White House Fellows Committee, 1978–80

Trustee, Herbert I. and Elsa B. Michael Foundation, 1976–83

Board of Directors, First Security Corporation, 1975–2000

Director, Prudential Federal Savings and Loan, 1975–85

Director, Utah Power and Light, 1974–83

Director, Utah Symphony, 1974–83

Chairman, National Board for Courses by Newspaper (National Endowment for Humanities), University of California, San Diego, 1974–81

BIBLIOGRAPHY

Books

W. Todd Furniss and David P. Gardner, eds. *Higher Education and Government: An Uneasy Alliance.* Washington, D.C.: American Council on Education, 1979.
The California Oath Controversy. Berkeley: University of California Press, 1967.

Other Selected Publications

"Meeting the Challenges of the New Millennium: The University's Role." In *Challenges Facing Higher Education at the Millennium,* ed. Werner Z. Hirsch and Luc E. Weber, 18–15, American Council on Education/Oryx Press Series on Higher Education. Phoenix: Oryx Press, 1999.

"Managing Transitions in a Time of Acute Modernity." *Trusteeship* (Association of Governing Boards of Universities and Colleges) 3, no. 4 (July–August 1995): 10–15.

"The Internationalization of the University." In *The Role of University Education in the Asia/Pacific Age,* ed. Ki-ouk Kwon, 19–28. Proceedings of the June 1992 Seoul International Conference. Seoul: Korean Council for University Education, 1992.

"Institutions Besieged by Invective." *Los Angeles Times,* July 30, 1991.

"Relief from Gridlock, On and Off the Road." *Los Angeles Times,* May 28, 1990.

"Internationalization: The State of the Institution." *Educational Record* 71, no. 2 (spring 1990): 8–13.

"Leadership for Excellence." A series on excellence and leadership sponsored by ITT, *Forbes,* April 16, 1990, 130–31.

Commentary on the James E. Webb Lecture delivered by Frank Press, "Science in a New Era." An occasional paper sponsored by the James E. Webb Fund for Excellence in Public Administration, National Academy for Public Administration, November 19, 1989, 19–21.

"Education and the Economy." *Stanford Law and Policy Review* 1, no. 1 (fall 1989): 75–80.

"Higher Education and the Workforce: Challenges and Opportunities." *Recruitment Times (Los Angeles Times)* 2, no. 2 (second quarter 1989).

"U.S. Human Potential Can Be Developed, If We Make Up Our Minds." *Los Angeles Times,* November 22, 1988.

"International Research: The Face of the Future?" *Western Breeze* (Hitachi Corporation) 2, no. 3 (July–August–September 1988).

Foreword to *Ideology and Power in the Middle East: Studies in Honor of George Lenczowski,* ed. Peter J. Chelkowski and Robert J. Pranger, ix–x. Durham: Duke University Press, 1988.

"Issues Confronting American Higher Education." *Higher Education Quarterly* 42, no. 3 (summer 1988): 230–37.

"On Leadership." In *Leaders on Leadership: The College Presidency,* ed. James Fisher and Martha W. Tack, 9–12. San Francisco: Jossey-Bass, 1988.

"The U.S. Business–Higher Education Forum: Reviewing the Experiment." *Industry and Higher Education* 2, no. 2 (June 1988).

"Higher Education's Future Lies on the Pacific Rim." *San Francisco Business Times*, November 23, 1987.

"Education Reform: A Continuing Agenda." *National Forum* (Phi Kappa Phi) 67, no. 4 (fall 1987): 34.

"The Pacific Century." *Science* 237, no. 4812 (July 17, 1987): 233.

"Reducing Our Nation's Risk." *Currents* 13, no. 5 (May 1987).

"The Future of University/Industry Research." *Perspectives in Computing* 7, no. 1 (spring 1987).

"The Charge of the Byte Brigade: Educators Lead the Fourth Revolution." *Educational Record* 67, no. 1 (winter 1986): 10–15.

"Geography in the School Curriculum." *Annals of the Association of American Geographers* 76, no. 1 (March 1986): 1–4.

"The Humanities and the Educational Reform Movement: What Can Be Done?" *National Forum* 66, no. 2 (spring 1986): 9–11.

"The Humanities and the Fine Arts: The Soul and Spirit of Our Universities." *Center Magazine* 17, no. 6 (November–December 1985): 5–10.

"Adding It All Up." *Los Angeles Times Magazine*, October 13, 1985.

"California and the Pacific Community." *Asian Week* 6, no. 40 (May 1, 1985).

"Managing the American University." *International Journal of Institutional Management in Higher Education* 9, no. 1 (March 1985).

"Did the Education Commissions Make a Difference?" *Shield* (Phillips Petroleum) 9, no. 3 (October 1984).

"Knowledge Is Power." *Science* 224, no. 4656 (June 29, 1984): 1384.

"Fulfilling Our Expectations." *American Education* 20, no. 2 (March 1984).

"Who's Minding the University?" *San Jose Mercury-News*, November 27, 1983.

"What Parents Must Do About Our Schools." *Ladies' Home Journal*, November 1983.

"Excellence in Education." Proceedings, Northwest Association of Schools and Colleges, 66th annual convention, Seattle,Washington, December 4–7, 1982, 65–75.

"Excellence in Education: A Brief Analysis of the Problems." *National Forum* 62, no. 4 (fall 1982): 41–42.

"A Time for Re-examination and Renewal." *American Education* 18, no. 7 (August–September 1982): 31–34.

"Forces for Change in the Governance of British and American Universities." *Policy Studies Journal* 10, no. 1 (September 1981): 123–36.

"A Living Tribute to the People of Utah." In *Remembering*, ed. Elizabeth Haglund, 213–33. Salt Lake City: University of Utah Press, 1981.

"Our Schools in the Eighties: Utah's Challenge to Honor Its Past and Ensure Its Future." In *More Students, More Quality—The Opportunity for Utah Schools*, ed. Allan Davis, 1–18. Salt Lake City: University of Utah Press, 1981.

"Campus and Government Must Reach New Understanding." *Times Higher Education Supplement* (London), January 4, 1980.

"Educational Standards: A Moving Target." In *Address and Proceedings*, Western College Association annual meeting, March 9–10, 1978, 7–11.

"What Will the Future Bring?" In *Students and Their Institutions*, ed. J. W. Peltason and Marcy V. Massengale, 100–106. Washington, D.C.: American Council on Education, 1978.

"The Honor in Honors." *Forum for Honors* (National Collegiate Honors Council) 6, no. 4 (June 1, 1976): 10–12.

"Forces for Change in American Higher Education." In *On the Meaning of the University,* ed. Sterling M. McMurrin, 103–23. Salt Lake City: University of Utah Press, 1976.

"An Analysis of Forces for Change in American Higher Education and Nontraditional Responses to Them by Colleges and Universities." In *Qualities of Life: Critical Choices for Americans,* 189–209, Commission on Critical Choices. Lexington, Mass.: Lexington Books / Heath, 1976.

"Alternatives in Higher Education—Who Wants What?" *Higher Education* 4 (1975): 317–33.

"Engaging the Future: The University's Challenge." *Forum for Honors* (December 1974): 9–15.

"A Strategy for Change in Higher Education: The Extended University of the University of California," with Joseph Zelan. Conference on future structures of postsecondary education, Organisation for Economic Co-operation and Development, Paris, 1974.

"Recurrent Education as an Alternative Educational Strategy." In *Participants and Patterns in Higher Education: Research and Reflections,* ed. Ann Heiss, Joseph Mixer, and James Paltridge, a Festschrift honoring T. R. McConnell, Professor of Higher Education Emeritus, University of California, Berkeley (winter 1973), 109–20.

"Faculty Responsibility for Professional Ethics." *Educational Record* 52, no. 4 (fall 1971): 343–47.

"The University in Disarray: Causes of Conflict and Prospects for Change." In *Cybernetics Simulation and Conflict Resolution,* ed. Douglas Knight, 13–28. New York: Spartan Books, 1970.

"Politics vs. Academic Freedom." *Los Angeles Times,* August 16, 1970.

A Convocation Anthology: Problems, Goals, and Research in Higher Education, readings compiled with Judd N. Adams for the Campus Convocation Committee on the Structure and Purpose of Higher Education in the United States, University of California, Santa Barbara (1969).

"The Power Struggle to Convert the University." *Educational Record* 50, no. 2 (spring 1969): 113–20.

"Politics and the Urban University." *Education and Urban Society* 1, no. 3 (May 1969): 337–45.

"By Oath and Association: The California Folly." *Journal of Higher Education* 40, no. 2 (February 1969): 122–34.

"Organizations and Modern Society." In *Social Studies in Mass Society,* ed. Dale L. Brubaker, 67–87. Scranton, Pa.: International Textbook, 1969.

"Some Marginal Notes on the Berkeley–Eldridge Cleaver Affair." *California Digest* 1, no. 7 (December 1968): 121–23, 142.

"The California Oath Controversy: Silence and Frustration." *California Monthly* 77, no. 7 (June–July 1967): 50–55.

APPENDIX 6

SAMPLE OF ARTICLES ABOUT OR CONVERSATIONS WITH DAVID P. GARDNER, 1983–1992

1992   *California Monthly,* "A Harsh Spotlight on UC," June 1992, 11–13.
1991   *Education,* "Looking at Issues," The Graduate School of Education,
        5, no. 3 (fall/winter 1991): 16–17.
        California Monthly, "President Gardner to Step Down," December
        1991, 8.
1990   *UCLA Magazine,* "The Noble Purpose," winter 1990, 32–35.
        Forbes, "Leadership for Excellence," April 16, 1990, 130–31.
1988   *California Journal,* "David Gardner: The Ivy-Covered Politician," August
        1988, 333–36.
        U.S. News and World Report, "The New American Establishment,"
        Special Edition, February 8, 1988, 65.
        California Monthly, "The Logical Positivist," December 1988, 6–7, 13.
1987   *California Monthly,* "California Q and A: A Conversation with David P.
        Gardner, M.A. '59, Ph.D. '66," February 1987, 8–10.
1986   *U.S. News and World Report,* "America's School System Still at Risk," May 5,
        1986, 64.
1985   *Ensign,* "David Gardner: Schooled in Mind and Spirit," June 1985, 32–36.
1984   *BYU Today,* "David P. Gardner: A Man for Education," August 1984, 20–23,
        46–47.
        Coastlines, University of California, Santa Barbara, "Ending the Decline,"
        and "Time to Rebuild One of the World's Great Universities," 14, no.
        3 (February / March 1984): 11, 30.
        California Journal, "UC Euphoria over Governor's Budget," March 1984,
        113–15.
1983   *Newsweek,* "Gardner Cultivates California," March 14, 1983, 50.
        Time, "On the Spot: Gardner Will Head Cal," March 14, 1983, 73.

NOTES

PREFACE

1. Allan M. Carter, *An Assessment of Quality in Graduate Education* (Washington, D.C.: American Council on Education, 1966), 107.

1. YOUTH AND LESSONS LEARNED

1. Founding trustees of the California Alumni Foundation—1963:

Norris Nash '21, president
   of the alumni association
Frank F. Burrows '22
Thomas G. Chamberlain '15
Fairfax M. Cone '25
Walter C. Dean '15
David P. Gardner, director
   of the foundation
Ivor de Kirby '38
Nelson C. Dezendorf '22
J. E. Drew '21
Henry O. Duque '27
Ralph L. Edwards '35, chairman
   of the board of trustees
Peter J. Haas '40

Edwin L. Harbach '25
Mrs. Parker M. Holt '33
Reuben J. Irwin '20
Daniel E. Koshland '13
William C. Meux '35
Kendric B. Morrish '28
Wayne J. Peacock '21
Rudolph A. Peterson '25
Edward J. Power '15
Robert G. Sproul '13
Connor Templeton '25
Mrs. John D. Wallace '36
Dean G. Witter '09
James D. Zellerbach '13

See California Alumni Foundation minutes of January 26, 1963. See also "Organizing for Annual Effort," *California Monthly*, January 1963, 28–29.

The Robert Gordon Sproul Associates on the Berkeley campus was formed coincident with the creation of the California Alumni Foundation in 1962. It happened this way.

As Dick Erickson and I considered how best to seek private funds for Berkeley, it occurred to us that some alumni might wish to donate $1,000 a year to Berkeley to be affiliated with an organization of like-minded alumni under a name that would resonate with Cal's history and the university's legacy of leaders.

I talked with President Emeritus Sproul about this over lunch at the Faculty Club in the fall of 1962, and we agreed to call this group the Daniel Coit Gilman Associates in honor of UC's second president, who later served as the founding president of Johns Hopkins University in 1875. Sproul and I then visited in San Francisco with Rudy Peterson, president of the Bank of America, Daniel Koshland, and Walter Haas, Sr., of the Haas family (of the famous Levi Strauss Company), Dean Witter of the brokerage firm of the same name, Herman Phleger of the law firm carrying his name as a lead partner, and Ralph Edwards, well-known Hollywood producer.

Sproul and I made our presentation and the idea was well received, but the Gilman name was not. Phleger asked Sproul to step out of the meeting so the group could discuss the idea more openly. Everyone else favored naming this new organization after Sproul, not Gilman. "After all," Haas said, "Sproul is living, Gilman is not. Sproul served as president for twenty-eight years, Gilman for only three. Besides, we are all friends of Sproul's and none of us knew Gilman."

Sproul was invited back in and after making the case once again for Gilman, finally demurred. The Robert Gordon Sproul Associates was and is a very important part of Cal's development efforts.

2. THE APPRENTICESHIP YEARS

1. See Clark Kerr, *The Gold and the Blue: A Personal Memoir of the University of California, 1949–1967*, esp. vol. 2, *Political Turmoil* (Berkeley: University of California Press, 2003); and Robert Cohen and Reginald Zelnik, eds., *The Free Speech Movement: Reflections on Berkeley in the 1960s* (Berkeley: University of California Press, 2002).

2. Memorandum from Dean of Students Lyle Reynolds to Chancellor Vernon I. Cheadle, December 2, 1968, a confidential report on the October 14 takeover of North Hall, plus comments on the black students' movement.

3. Ibid.

4. Ibid.

5. See University of California *Bulletin*, November 4, 1968, 65, for a summary of the chancellor's report on this incident.

6. This more complete account of the material mentioned in note 5 was widely available on and off campus and among the regents.

7. Speech by Governor Ronald Reagan to the Channel City Club of Santa Barbara, California, October 21, 1968 (author's files).

8. "Reagan and Cheadle on UCSB," *Santa Barbara News-Press*, October 22, 1968.

9. Cheadle's announcement of disciplinary action after the October 14 sit-in.

10. Robert Kelley, *Transformations: UC Santa Barbara, 1909–1979* (Santa Barbara: Regents of the University of California and Associated Students-UCSB, 1981), 40–41. Also see Robert A. Potter and James J. Sullivan, "The Campus by the Sea Where the Bank Burned Down: A Report on the Disturbances at UCSB and Isla Vista 1968–1970," submitted to the President's Commission on Campus Unrest, September 1, 1970, a publication of the Faculty and Clergy Observer's Program, Santa Barbara, California; and for a national perspective on student unrest at this time see *The Report of the President's Commission on Student Unrest* (Washington, D.C.: Government Printing Office, 1970), which includes my own testimony before the commission on protests within UC in general and at UCSB in particular.

11. Report of the Santa Barbara Citizens Commission on Civil Disorders, "What Occurred? Causes? What Can and Ought to be Done?" September 15, 1970, 5.

12. Kelley, *Transformations,* 49.

13. Potter and Sullivan, "Campus by the Sea," 76–96. While the conclusion noted in the text reflects the judgment of the police investigation and the coroner's inquest, the cause of Moran's death was thought by some not to have been conclusively shown.

14. Kelley, *Transformations,* 53.

15. Ibid., 54–55.

16. The best single source for information about IV at this time is the report of the commission chaired by Martin Trow, professor of sociology on the Berkeley campus, on appointment by President Charles Hitch in the late spring 1970, which met after the burning of the Bank of America in IV but before the culminating riots in May and June (the report was submitted to Hitch and the regents in October 1970). Trow and I later came to be colleagues and friends when he headed the Center for Studies in Higher Education at Berkeley and during my service first as a UC vice president and later as president. He also served as chairman of the Academic Council during my last year as UC's president, much to UC's and to my benefit.

The report made eight general recommendations and twenty-seven specific proposals. In summary, the recommendations and proposals sought to link IV and UCSB more directly and involve the campus more comprehensively in the life of the student-dominated neighborhoods in IV, restructuring UCSB's administration for this purpose to clarify the university's role and those responsible for carrying it out; to seek the cooperation and participation of all governmental and nonprofit entities with a stake in this matter as well as land developers and landlords whose interests up until then had been overridingly commercial; to improve policing in the area; and to rethink the implications for further growth at UCSB and in IV.

The commission's analysis was essentially correct and such initiatives would have gone a long way toward ameliorating the conditions that were such significant factors in the IV disturbances of 1968–70.

The Trow report can be obtained from the Office of the President of the University of California, Oakland, California, and/or the office of the Secretary of the Regents of the University of California, Oakland, California, under date of October 9, and as submitted to the regents on October 16, 1970.

17. Carnegie Commission on Higher Education, *Less Time, More Options: Education beyond the High School* (New York: McGraw Hill, 1971), 2.

18. See "A Progress Report to the Regents of the University of California on the Extended University," May 17, 1972, which included all of the information pertaining to this initiative at that time, including the operating principles and policies.

19.

A SUMMARY OF EXTENDED DEGREE PILOT PROGRAMS

Campus	Program	Enrollment (head count)	Start
1. Berkeley	Master of Business Administration	50	fall 1972
2. Davis	Experimental Group (upper-division and graduate students)	200	fall 1972
3. Irvine	(planning only in 1972–73 for programs in social ecology to begin with summer 1973)		
4. Los Angeles	Master of Business Administration	30	winter 1973 (subject to campus confirmation)
5. Riverside	Master of Administration	25	fall 1972
	Experimental Group (upper-division and graduate students)	115	fall 1972
6. San Francisco	Master of Science in Nursing	16	winter 1973
7. Santa Barbara	Bachelor of Arts in Law and Society	40	fall 1972
	Master of Science in Electrical Engineering	35	
8. Santa Cruz	Bachelor of Arts in Community Studies	40	fall 1972
9. San Diego	Experimental Group (upper-division students)	50	fall 1972
Total degree programs	7	236	
Total experimental programs	3	365	
Total enrollment (head count)		601	
Total grant for 1972–73 from president's office		$378,750	

For a detailed and comprehensive description of the extended university, see *A Strategy for Change in Higher Education: The Extended University of the University of California* (Paris: OECD, 1974); and Proceedings of the Meeting of the Association of College Registrars and Admissions Officers, Cleveland, Ohio, April 20, 1972. See also author's statement on this subject to the Joint Committee on the Master Plan for Higher Education of the California State Legislature on March 28, 1973. (All of the documents referred to in this note are available from the Office of the President of the University of California, Oakland, California, and/ or from the Office of the Secretary of the Regents of the University of California, Oakland, California.)

3. SERVING THE UNIVERSITY OF UTAH

1. See *Deseret News,* August 28, 1973, editorial page. Also for details of the reorganization and the personnel involved, see *University of Utah Review* 7, no. 1 (October 1973).

2. The University of Utah is at once the state's oldest and largest public university; graduating nearly one-half of the students receiving degrees each year from Utah's public colleges and universities, it has more alumni than any other public college or university in the state and is located in the state capital. So when I arrived in 1973 the U was the 1,000-pound "gorilla" on the block. I wanted to make common cause with the other eight colleges and universities, with the commissioner for higher education's acquiescence, so that the legislature and the governor could not play the "divide and conquer" game any longer. This plan worked, and there was very little to keep us apart and much to bring us together during my ten years at Utah. All benefited, not just the U some years and not just everyone else the other years.

3. For further information about the artificial heart implant, see Margery W. Shaw, ed., *After Barney Clark: Reflections on the Utah Artificial Heart Program* (Austin: University of Texas Press, 1984).

4. On February 7, 1982, the U's alumni association purchased a full-page ad in the Sunday edition of the *Salt Lake Tribune,* in the form of an "Open Letter to High School Students and their Parents." The letter with our enhanced requirements for freshman admissions was signed by all of the university's deans and by the university's academic vice president and me. It stated that as of 1987, entering freshman students at the U would be required to take more courses in high school in the basic academic subjects, i.e., English, science, history, the fine arts, math, and one or more foreign language (for example, at least two years of math beyond elementary algebra during grades 10–12, and at least two years of a foreign language during grades 7–12).

5. In my February 14, 1975, letter to Edward Carter, I asked the UC regents' search committee to remove my name from consideration for the presidency and explained:

> As you know, I have served as President of the University of Utah for only one year and a half and sense keenly the as yet unfulfilled obligations I assumed at the time of my appointment here. To be considered for the position of President of the University of California is an honor which I do not lightly acknowledge and for which I shall be forever appreciative; however, I must remain accountable to my own conscience and sense of duty regarding my responsibilities to the University of Utah which I gladly assumed and intend faithfully to discharge.

4. A NATION AT RISK

1. Terrel H. Bell, *The Thirteenth Man: A Reagan Cabinet Memoir* (New York: Free Press, 1988), 4–5. Reprinted with the permission of The Free Press, a division of Simon & Schuster Adult Publishing Group, from *The Thirteenth Man: A Reagan Cabinet Memoir* by Terrel H. Bell. Copyright © 1988 by Terrel H. Bell. All rights reserved.

2. Ibid., 115–17.
3. Personal letter from Ted Bell, April 10, 1981.
4. Statement of Terrel H. Bell, secretary of education, announcing the establishment of a national commission on excellence in education, August 26, 1981, contained in a Department of Education press release of the same date (author's files).
5. Bell, *Thirteenth Man*, 119.
6. Remarks of President Ronald Reagan to the members of the National Commission on Excellence in Education, October 9, 1981, the White House (author's files).
7. A portion of the author's remarks to President Reagan, October 9, 1981 (author's files).
8. See National Commission on Excellence in Education [David Pierpont Gardner, chairman], *A Nation at Risk: The Imperative for Educational Reform* (Washington, D.C.: Government Printing Office, 1983). Or see online at www.goalline.org/Goal%20Line/NatAtRisk.html.
9. Bell, *Thirteenth Man*, 120–21.
10. Ibid., 121–22.
11. Author's letter to commissioners transmitting text of the final report of *A Nation at Risk*, April 12, 1983. The report underwent modest revisions before it was submitted to Secretary Bell near midnight on April 17.
12. Recollections of Milton Goldberg, the commission's executive director, who was present when Secretary of Education Bell responded to his reading of the report.
13. See *A Nation at Risk*.
14. From verbatim transcript of White House press conference of April 26, 1983, on *A Nation at Risk* (author's files).
15. Ibid.
16. From text of President Reagan's remarks on April 26, 1983, formally receiving the report, the White House (author's files).
17. Bell, *Thirteenth* Man, 130–31.
18. Siri J. Voskuil, "A Nation at Risk: Commission Members' Perceptions and Appraisals Fifteen Years Later" (Ph.D. diss., Marquette University, 1999), 137. This work is the most complete, fair, and accurate account I have read of the commission's work, its report, and the results; chapter 5 reviews and analyzes the comments of the report's major critics and the reaction to those by some commissioners.
19. Bell, *Thirteenth Man*, 131.
20. Text of radio address to the nation by President Reagan on *A Nation at Risk*, April 30, 1983, the White House (author's files).
21. Bill Peterson, "Inside the Education Department," *Washington Post*, May 5, 1983.
22. See Albert Shanker, "A Landmark Revisited," *New York Times*, May 9, 1993.
23. Voskuil, "Nation at Risk," 42–43. Christa McAuliffe was the teacher, one of the seven who died in the explosion of the space shuttle *Challenger* just after liftoff in 1986. See also Thomas Toch, *In the Name of Excellence: The Struggle to Reform the Nation's Schools, Why It's Failing, and What Should Be Done* (New York: Oxford University Press, 1991).
24. Voskuil, "Nation at Risk," 47.

25. U.S. Department of Education, *Education Week,* June 2, 1984. Here are the major proposed state reforms that followed the issuance of our report fourteen months earlier:

MAJOR STATE REFORM INITIATIVES FOLLOWING *A NATION AT RISK*

Reform	Enacted	Under Consideration	Total
Adapt merit pay for career ladder	14	24	38
Adapt new minimum salary	18	17	35
Adapt teacher testing	29	10	39
Revise certification	28	16	44
Revise teacher training	19	10	29
Aid prospective teachers	24	13	37
Add instructional time	13	7	20
Restrict extracurricular activities	6	4	10
Reduce class size	13	7	20
Raise graduation requirements	43	5	48
Raise exit test	15	4	19
Adapt statewide assessment	37	6	43
Test for promotion	8	3	11
Increase college admission requirements	17	3	20
Adapt academic recognition programs	25	5	30
Adapt academic enrichment programs	34	8	42
Adapt state-mandated discipline policy	19	8	27
Assess teachers' professional developments	30	14	44
Assess administrators' professional developments	30	12	42

26. Edward B. Fiske, "35 Pages That Shook the U.S. Education World," *New York Times,* April 27, 1988. Entitled *American Education: Making It Work* (Washington, D.C.: U.S. Department of Education, 1988), the conference report focused on "how far we've come and what still needs to be done."

27. For Voskuil's report of the commissioners' views of my chairmanship, see "Nation at Risk," 123–24.

28. Bell, *Thirteenth* Man, 151–52.

29. Ibid., 155.

30. Ibid., 158–59.

31. Author's letter to President Reagan, June 5, 1985 (author's files).

32. Letter from Ronald Reagan to author, July 12, 1985 (author's files).

33. William J. Bennett, Willard Flair, Chester Finn, Jr., Rev. Floyd Flake, E. D. Hirsch, Will Marshal, and Diane Ravitch, "A Nation Still at Risk," *Policy Review,* no. 90 (July–August 1998): 2–9.

34. Ibid.

35. See Paul E. Peterson, ed., *Our Schools and Our Future: Are We Still at Risk?* (Stanford: Hoover Institution, 2003).

36. Bell, *Thirteenth Man,* 159.

37. For a review of the effects of *A Nation at Risk* twenty years later, see David T. Gordon, ed., *A Nation Reformed? American Education 20 Years after "A Nation at Risk"*

(Cambridge, Mass.: Harvard Education Press, 2003). See also Milton Goldberg, "Risk Chief Looks Back and Ahead," and Chester Finn, Jr., "Are We Still at Risk?" *San Francisco Chronicle*, April 25, 2003; Ben Feller, "Results Are In on 'Nation at Risk,'" *Salt Lake Tribune*, April 26, 2003; and numerous other op-ed and editorial comments in the nation's leading newspapers at about this time, the report's twentieth anniversary. See especially Gerald Holton, "An Insider's View of 'A Nation at Risk' and Why It Still Matters," *Chronicle of Higher Education*, April 25, 2003, B13.

5. BACK TO THE BLUE AND GOLD

1. "Legislator Introduces a Resolution against Gardner's California Salary," *Newsweek*, March 14, 1983, 50. See also *Deseret News*, March 17–18, 1983; "On the Spot," *Time*, March 14, 1983, 73; and Ann C. Roark, "A Quiet but Savvy Gardner Steps Up to UC," *Los Angeles Times*, March 13, 1983.
2. Utah paid for the maintenance of the home and garden, and the cost of utilities. The costs of insurance and repairs to the home were also borne by the university, and the mortgage was made by the university at a 6.1 percent interest rate. The Utah arrangement was essentially the one approved for our Orinda home. See minutes of the Regents of the University of California, Committee on Finance, closed session, July 5, 1983 (Office of the Secretary of the Regents, Oakland).
3. From the remarks I made to both the regents and the press upon my appointment as UC's president, March 2, 1983 (author's files).
4. *Sacramento Bee*, March 14, 1983, editorial.
5. *Salt Lake Tribune*, March 14, 1983.
6. See article 9, section 9, of the Constitution of the State of California. See also chapter 6 for a further explanation of this provision and its significance for UC.
7. For a comprehensive account of rankings, see Clark Kerr, *The Gold and the Blue: A Personal Memoir of the University of California, 1949–1967*, vol. 1, *Academic Triumphs* (Berkeley: University of California Press, 2001), 403–42.
8. See ibid., *Political Turmoil* (2003), 2:298.
9. See minutes of the Regents of the University of California, Committee on Finance, February 17, 1983, for a report on UC's problems with federally funded research; of May 12, 1983, for salary comparisons of UC's faculty and administration; of September 16, 1983, for a report on UC's 1983–84 operating budget; and the Committee on Educational Policy on January 19, 1984, for a report on UC's expected enrollment. See also "UC: No. 1 in the U.S., but Can It Last?" *Los Angeles Times*, April 21, 1983; "Don't Let UC System Decay," *The Tribune*, and *San Diego Union* editorial, June 7, 1983.
10. Angus E. Taylor, *The Academic Senate of the University of California: Its Role in the Shared Governance and Operation of the University of California* (Berkeley: Institute of Governmental Studies Press, University of California, Berkeley, 1998).
11. For further information on the workings of UC, see chapter 6.
12. The sources of nonstate funds were federal research grants, hospital revenues from UC's five medical centers, student fees and tuition, gifts and endowments, and auxiliary enterprises; residence halls, parking fees, intercollegiate athletics,

bookstores, student unions, and other self-supporting activities. The state's share of the $3.1 billion was approximately $1.25 billion.

13. The UC statistics included in the text and in this note come from the University of California fact sheet for 1984, published by the University Relations Office of the Office of the President.

The nine campuses of the university with the dates founded, size, and library holdings are indicated below:

Campus	Date Founded	Acreage	Library Holdings (millions of volumes)
Berkeley	1868	1,232	6.34
Davis	1905	3,600	1.83
Irvine	1965	1,510	1.07
Los Angeles	1919	411	5.74
Riverside	1907	1,200	1.12
San Diego	1912	2,040	1.57
San Francisco	1873	107	0.51
Santa Barbara	1944	815	1.53
Santa Cruz	1965	2,000	0.71
Total		12,915	20.42

Here is a head count of the university's enrollments:

Campus	Undergraduates	Graduates	Health Services	Total
Berkeley	21,132	8,090	787	30,009
Davis	13,830	3,254	1,885	18,969
Irvine	9,436	1,407	1,065	11,908
Los Angeles	23,063	7,860	3,828	34,751
Riverside	3,357	1,298	51	4,706
San Diego	11,122	1,298	1,048	13,468
San Francisco	—	—	3,644	3,644
Santa Barbara	14,744	2,008	—	16,752
Santa Cruz	6,350	542	—	6,892
Total	103,034	25,757	12,308	141,099

The university's minority enrollment looked like this:

Ethnic Category*	Undergraduates		Graduates		Total	
American Indian	498	(0.5%)	173	(0.7%)	671	(0.5%)
Asian	13,973	(14.3%)	2,437	(9.5%)	16,410	(13.3%)
Black	3,977	(4.1%)	967	(3.8%)	4,944	(4.0%)
Chicano	4,168	(4.3%)	1,025	(4.0%)	5,193	(4.2%)
Latino	2,125	(2.2%)	617	(2.4%)	2,742	(2.2%)
Filipino	2,211	(2.3%)	143	(0.6%)	2,354	(1.9%)
Total UC	26,952	(27.7%)	5,362	(21.0%)	32,314	(26.1%)

*Totals exclude foreign students and residents in teaching hospitals.

14. Minutes of the Regents of the University of California, closed session, September 16, 1983 (Office of the Secretary of the Regents, Oakland). As the minutes report, some key positions were abolished: "most notably, the positions of Vice President of the University currently held by William R. Fretter, and of Vice President–Academic and Staff Personnel Relations currently held by Archie Kleingartner. Both Dr. Fretter and Dr. Kleingartner had announced in 1982–83 their intent to resign from these positions."

15. Ibid.

6. THE WORKINGS OF THE UNIVERSITY AND THE CRUCIAL FIRST YEAR

1. For Sinsheimer's recollection, see Robert L. Sinsheimer, *The Strands of a Life* (Berkeley: University of California Press, 1994), 200.

2. Jack W. Peltason, introduction to David Pierpont Gardner, "A Life in Higher Education: Fifteenth President of the University of California, 1983–1992," Regional Oral History Office, Bancroft Library, University of California, Berkeley (1997) [hereafter Oral History, UCB], vi–vii.

3. Martin Trow, in "UC Office of the President and Its Constituencies, 1983–1995," Oral History, UCB, 2002, 2:222–24.

4. These quotations and the others to follow from speeches at the inauguration can be found in "Speeches at the Inauguration of the Fifteenth President of the University of California, David Pierpont Gardner," June 1984, a pamphlet published and distributed by the Office of University Relations, Office of the President, Berkeley, California, with a covering letter from Regent Yori Wada, chairman of the Board of Regents.

5. For a complete description of UC's budget procedures, see the minutes of the Board of Regents, January 15, 1988, as well as comments and questions of certain regents regarding this matter (Office of the Secretary of Regents, Oakland).

6. It was not long afterward that Professor Malcolm Kerr of UCLA, who was at the Bellagio meetings, was appointed president of the American University of Beirut. Within a matter of months, he was gunned down and killed in his Beirut offices on campus. The university nonetheless remained open.

7. Steven A. Merksamer, in "UC Office of the President and Its Constituencies, 1983–1995," Oral History, UCB, 2002, 3:312–13, 316.

8. George Deukmejian, in ibid., 3:115, 117.

9. For faculty response to the 1984–85 operating and capital budgets recommended for UC by Governor Deukmejian in January 1984, see minutes of the Regents of the University of California, January 20, 1984, Faculty Representative Ralph Turner's comments, p. 6.

10. At this time, Professor Neil Smelser was chairman of the Berkeley Division of the Academic Senate. His recollections of our budget success follows: "This was an absolute wonder, the fact that [Gardner] was able—he was absolutely right in his own memoirs—contrary to advice from most of the chancellors and others who thought he was going to suffer a stinging defeat by asking for too much, he went ahead more or less single-handedly and persuaded the governor to have this whopping and totally unprecedented increase of the university's budget, which included something like an 18 to 20 percent increase in faculty salaries.

It was almost a magical, triumphal entry. I can't imagine a better way ever to extend your own honeymoon in a university setting [chuckles]. . . . I had never seen the Academic Council, and I don't think my colleagues ever had seen them, spontaneously and in meeting after meeting break into applause for him. That was the kind of tone it was" (Neil Smelser, in "UC Office of the President and Its Constituencies, 1983–1995," Oral History, UCB, 2002, 2:164–65).

11. Stephen A. Arditti, in ibid., 1:14.
12. Clark Kerr, introduction to Gardner, "A Life in Higher Education: Fifteenth President of the University of California, 1863–1992," iii–iv.

7. THE UNIVERSITY ON THE MOVE

1.

- The TMT would carry the name of the Cal Tech donor, and would be built and located in such a way that a second TMT could later be built nearby
- Cal Tech would fund the construction up to an agreed upon maximum (the figures under discussion have been $75–$80 million)
- University of California would provide operating funds (from any possible source) of $X per year (the figure discussed was $2.5 million) for an agreed upon number of years (25 years discussed)
- Funds for additional programs would be a joint responsibility
- A nonprofit corporation would be formed with equal representation from the two institutions, and with a rotating chairmanship; TMT staff and director would report to the nonprofit corporation
- Cal Tech would provide contract administration and oversight of construction funds, in order to protect its donor
- The University of Hawaii would lease its property on Mauna Kea to the nonprofit corporation
- TMT time to be shared between the two institutions after the University of Hawaii, and the national astronomical community to receive their allotted time

Minutes of the Board of Regents of the University of California, closed session, November 16, 1984, p. 10 (Office of the Secretary of the Regents, Oakland). For a more complete account of this project and its fulfillment, see Robert L. Sinsheimer, *The Strands of a Life* (Berkeley: University of California Press, 1994), 257–64.

2. Minutes of the Regents of the University of California, open session, January 16, 1985, pp. 6–7 (Office of the Secretary of the Regents, Oakland).
3. By way of example, see David P. Gardner, "The Pacific Century," *Science* 237, no. 4812 (July 17, 1987): 233.
4. Personal letter from Helmut Kohl to David P. Gardner (translated from German), March 9, 1988. Kohl's concerns have been borne out.
5. David P. Gardner, "Humanities and the Fine Arts: The Soul and Spirit of Our

Universities," the David P. Gardner Lecture in the Humanities and Fine Arts, University of Utah, May 31, 1984 (published by the University of Utah, 1984) (author's files; also available from University of Utah archives). Also "The Humanities and the Fine Arts: The Soul and Spirit of Our Universities," *Center Magazine* 17, no. 6 (November–December 1985): 5–10.

6. Copies of the Smelser report, "Report on Lower Division Education," are available from the Secretary of the Regents of the University of California, Oakland. Also see Neil J. Smelser in "UC Office of the President and Its Constituencies, 1983–1995," Regional Oral History Office, Bancroft Library, University of California, Berkeley (2002), 2:193–99.

7. Minutes of the Regents of the University of California, October 16, 1986, pp. 9–10, 15 (Secretary of the Regents of the University of California, Oakland).

8. Ibid., 16–17.

9. Minutes of the Regents of the University of California, Committee on Educational Policy, July 16, 1992, pp. 7–8 (Office of the Secretary of the Regents, Oakland).

10. Memorandum from Alix Schwartz to Christina Maslach, September 26, 2002.

11. Letter from Carlton Bovell to Anne Kilmer, July 4, 1992.

12. From introductory remarks by David Gardner (Office of the President, University of California, Oakland). For a summary of the presentation, see also minutes of the Regents of the University of California, October 20, 1988, pp. 2, 3–6 (Office of the Secretary of the Regents, Oakland). See appendix 1 for details.

13. See relevant enrollment data, Office of the President of the University of California, Office of the Budget, August 2, 2002.

14. For more detailed accounts of some of the programs discussed in this chapter, see "Profile 1985," published by the Office of the President, University of California, 1985; and "Looking Forward to a New Century, The University of California, a Special Report to the People of California," published by the Office of the President, the University of California, June 1988.

8. BUMPS AND BARRIERS ALONG THE WAY

1. Letter from David Pierpont Gardner to chancellors, September 21, 1989, amending the student code and titled "Universitywide Student Conduct: Harassment Policy" (Office of the President of the University of California, Oakland).

2. Letter from Paul L. Hoffman, Edward Chen, Betty Wheeler, Ramona Ripston, Dorothy M. Ehrlich, and Linda Hills, representing California chapters of the American Civil Liberties Union to David Pierpont Gardner, August 8, 1990 (Office of the President of the University of California, Oakland).

3. Whereas the economic downturn led to slippage in the early 1990s, the later drive to reverse policies on affirmative action in part reflected the alleged subversion of UC's own policies and procedures and concealment of that subversion from the regents and the president by persons within UC responsible for admissions procedures on two or three campuses. On these campuses, critics asserted, automatic admission to UC on racial grounds alone was being substituted for UC's policy that permitted race to be considered but as only one of several other criteria for freshmen admission; by disregarding the announced criteria and allowing race to be the sole determining factor, this alleged subversion undermined the

credibility of the policy and the regents' confidence in the process. The critics also alleged that regental attitudes were negatively affected not only by the policy's subversion from within but also by Governor Wilson's strong desire that the policy be changed, some arguing that his interest in doing so was linked to his presumed interest in running for president of the United States.

In a very contentious meeting in July 1995 the Board of Regents revoked UC's procedures on behalf of affirmative action. For an account of this issue I refer the reader to President Emeritus Peltason's oral history. He was there and I was not (see Jack Peltason, "Political Scientist and Leader in Higher Education, 1947–1995: Sixteenth President of the University of California, Chancellor at UC Irvine and the University of Illinois," Regional Oral History Office, Bancroft Library, University of California, Berkeley, [2001]).

4. Minutes of the Regents of the University of California, May 20, 1988 (Office of the Secretary of the Regents, Oakland).

5. Minutes of the Regents of the University of California, November 20, 1987 (Office of the Secretary of the Regents, Oakland).

6. Minutes of the Regents of the University of California, June 15, 1990, p. 35 (Office of the Secretary of the Regents, Oakland).

7. Text of David P. Gardner's remarks to the Regents of the University of California, September 20, 1990, pp. 4–5, 6 (Office of the President of the University of California, Oakland).

8. Letter from David P. Gardner to chancellors, March 8, 1990 (Office of the President, University of California, Oakland).

9. Letter from William B. Baker, vice president for budget and university relations, to William Frazer, senior vice president for academic affairs, August 23, 1990.

10. Letter from Ralph Nader to David P. Gardner, September 19, 1990.

11. Letter from David P. Gardner to Ralph Nader, October 4, 1990.

12. Letter from David P. Gardner to Joint Legislative Conference Committee on the Budget, State Capitol, Sacramento, California, June 5, 1991, p. 4.

13. Letter from David P. Gardner to Robert J. Campbell, September 4, 1992.

14. Letter from Donald L. Reidhaar to Regent William A. Wilson, August 24, 1977.

15. Minutes of the Regents of the University of California, January 18, 1985 (Office of the Secretary of the Regents, Oakland).

16. Remarks of Chief Minister Buthelezi, chairman of the African Black Alliance, minutes of the Regents of the University of California, special meeting, June 10, 1985 (Office of the Secretary of the Regents, Oakland).

17. I did not respond to this comment by the Speaker, but I remember wondering if he really thought one's religion means nothing more than putting on or taking off a pair of shoes; I assumed any reference to this comparison would embarrass him, something I surely had no desire to do. Besides, I believed most people listening to our exchange would understand the inherent weakness of his assertion (as Pickens's comments suggest).

18. William Pickens, "The Appearance of University of California President David Gardner before the Assembly Ways and Means Subcommittee on Education Concerning the Issue of the University's Investments in Companies Doing Business in South Africa," May 14, 1985, pp. 1–4 (Pickens has the original of these recollections; copy in author's files).

19. Neil Smelser, in "UC Office of the President and Its Constituencies, 1983–1995," Oral History, UCB, 2002, 2:171–72.
20. Text of David P. Gardner's statement on university investment policy, minutes of Board of Regents meeting, San Francisco, June 21, 1985, pp. 4–5. See the same minutes for a complete account of this meeting and the particulars of the resolution I proposed as adopted by the board (Office of the Secretary of the Regents, Oakland).
21. The four newly appointed regents were Roy Brophy, Tirso del Junco, Leo J. Kolligian, and James Toledano (the alumni regent).

9. THE PUBLIC AND DIPLOMATIC LIFE

1. I was at Harvard's 350th birthday party (Foundation Day) on September 4, 1986, having been invited to represent and to bring greetings from the nation's public colleges and universities. Other speakers that morning included Paul Gray, president of MIT; Benno Schmidt, president of Yale; Lord Adrian, vice chancellor of Cambridge University; Derek Bok, president of Harvard University; and His Royal Highness the Prince of Wales.
2. David P. Gardner, "Campus and Government Must Reach New Understanding," *Times Higher Education Supplement* (London), January 4, 1980, 6.
3. For a list of Tanner lectures since 1978, see Grethe B. Peterson, ed., *The Tanner Lectures on Human Values* (Salt Lake City: University of Utah Press, 2002), 23:331–41.
4. The tour included some twenty-three rooms devoted to the exploits of the country's President Kim Il Sung during the Japanese occupation of North Korea and Manchuria before World War II.
5. In his oral history my successor, Jack Peltason, also remarked its bias: "I've been covered by the rivals of the sixties, and I've been covered by the right wing, but I've never been so unfairly covered as I was by the *San Francisco Examiner!*" (Jack W. Peltason, "Political Scientist and Leader in Higher Education, 1947–1995: Sixteenth President of the University of California, Chancellor at UC Irvine and the University of Illinois," Regional Oral History Office, Bancroft Library, University of California, Berkeley [2001], 521).

10. TRAGEDY AND TRIBULATION

1. Clark Kerr, introduction to David Pierpont Gardner, "A Life in Higher Education: Fifteenth President of the University of California, 1983–1992," Regional Oral History Office, Bancroft Library, University of California, Berkeley (1997), iv.
2. Letter from David P. Gardner to chancellors, "Policy on Associate to the President/Chancellor," November 1, 1987 (Office of the President of the University of California, Oakland). Provisions for spouses included access to UC libraries and facilities along with UC parking permits, travel expenses, automobile allowances, travel insurance for UC business, workers' compensation coverage, and business cards with "Associate" title.
3. Letter from David P. Gardner to Meredith Khachigian, chairman, Board of Regents of the University of California, dated November 13, 1991, and given to the regents on November 14, 1991.

4. Laurie Becklund, "The Gardners: An Uncommon Partnership," *Los Angeles Times,* January 1991. This article was syndicated to newspapers across the country, and I received over 2,000 letters from persons who had read it and wished to express their feelings about it.

5. According to the minutes, the only matter at issue was a technical one: setting a new date to "vest" (to give [me] a legally fixed immediate right to) the deferred compensation. As Regent Watkins explained, "the majority of the funds [in my separation package] were already in Mr. Gardner's account, having been accrued during his eight years of service as President. . . . He noted that the issue was one of paying to Mr. Gardner what had been earned but he acknowledged that the action might be difficult politically and could be misunderstood" (from the minutes of the Regents of the University of California, subcommittee on Officers' Salaries and Administrative Funds, closed session, March 19, 1992, p. 6 [Office of the Secretary of the Regents, Oakland]).

6. Kerr, introduction to Gardner, "A Life in Higher Education," iv.

7. Minutes of the Regents of the University of California, special meeting, April 20, 1992, pp. 6–9 (Office of the Secretary of the Regents, Oakland).

8. Ibid., 11–12.

9. Ibid., 14. Hallisey also objected that no such accelerated vesting had been approved for Chancellor Robert Stevens when he resigned his post at Santa Cruz. Just before the meeting I had a call from Stevens, then serving as master of Pembroke College, Oxford. Hallisey had called asking him to point out this fact in public but Stevens refused; as he saw it, his case did not warrant deferred compensation. Having advised the board I did not intend to participate in the discussion, I chose not to mention Stevens's call.

10. Ibid.

11. Ibid.

12. Ibid., 16.

13. Louis Freedberg, "Gardner Successor Gets Similar Pay Package: UC Compensation Over $400,000 a Year," *San Francisco Chronicle,* July 30, 1992. In Vice President William Baker's letter to the *Chronicle*'s assistant managing editor of news, August 4, 1992, stated:

We found the timing and the placement of your front-page story on the now University of California President's compensation to be curious, to say the least. As near as I can tell, all factual elements of the story ("Gardner successor gets similar pay package," July 30) were known to your reporter on April 3, the day that President-elect Peltason was chosen by the Board of Regents.

In fact, a review of our clipping files shows us that Mr. Freedberg included the elements of Dr. Peltason's compensation in his post-meeting story that appeared in the Chronicle on April 4. He could have made his total calculations on that day, since the university released all this information in announcing Dr. Peltason's appointment.

That brings up the question: Why now? And why on the front page, implying some new revelation emerging from or about the university?

I know you have no responsibility to broadcast journalists in town, but their behavior on this story was telling. Because of the Chronicle's influence, several radio stations and at least two TV stations did major news reports on your story, as if its subject was a new and dramatic development regarding executive compensation at UC. It certainly doesn't fit my traditional definition of what's news. We called this to the broadcast journalists' attention, too.

The effect of your story was to continue unnecessarily to stir public emotions on what has admittedly been a difficult issue for this institution, and for that reason your treatment is puzzling. Our appeal is to fairness and objectivity in your future news judgments.

14. *San Francisco Examiner,* June 7, 1992.
15. Russell Schoch, "A Harsh Spotlight on UC," *California Monthly,* June 1992, 13.
16. Drawn from my remarks at the meeting of the Board of Regents of the University of California, September 18, 1992. The board's minutes also include the text in full, pp. 3–9 (Office of the Secretary of the Regents, Oakland).
17. Clark Kerr, *The Gold and the Blue: A Personal Memoir of the University of California, 1949–1967,* vol. 1, *Academic Triumphs* (Berkeley: University of California Press, 2001), 414.
18. Kerr, introduction to Gardner, "A Life in Higher Education," iv.
19. Glenn T. Seaborg, in "UC Office of the President and Its Constituencies, 1983–1995," Oral History, UCB, 2002, 2:144–45, 143.
20. Jack W. Peltason, introduction to Gardner, "A Life in Higher Education," viii–ix.
21. Marvin L. Goldberger, Brendan A. Maher, and Pamela E. Flatteau, eds., *Research-Doctorate Programs in the United States: Continuity and Change* (Washington D.C.: National Academy Press, 1995).
22. Kerr, *The Gold and the Blue,* 1:406, 405, 407.
23. Ibid., 408. See also Hugh Davis Graham and Nancy Diamond, *The Rise of American Research Universities: Elites and Challengers in the Postwar Era* (Baltimore: Johns Hopkins University Press, 1997), 193.
24. Graham and Diamond, *Rise of American Research Universities,* 193.
25. David S. Webster and Tad Skinner, "Rating PhD Programs: What the NRC Report Says . . . and Doesn't Say," *Change* 28, no. 3 (May–June 1996): 37–40. This analysis refers to campuses with fifteen or more programs rated and hence applies to all UC campuses except UCSF.

EPILOGUE. YEARS OF RENEWAL AND PERSONAL REFLECTIONS

1. "Bay Area School Reform Consortium," a five-year summary report, Hewlett Foundation, Menlo Park, California, January 10, 2001.
2. "The Universities Project," a summary report, Hewlett Foundation, Menlo Park, California.
3. See David Pierpont Gardner, "Biographical Memoir: William Redington Hewlett," *Proceedings of the American Philosophical Society* 147, no. 2 (June 2003): 162.
4. "Chairman's Statement," in *Annual Report of the William and Flora Hewlett Foundation, 1998* (Menlo Park, Calif., May 1999), x–xi.
5. "President's Statement," in ibid., vii.

CREDITS

The following publishers and authors have generously given permission to use extended quotations from copyrighted works. FROM *Transformations: UC Santa Barbara 1909–1979* by Robert Kelley; copyright 1981 by the Regents of the University of California and the Associated Students, UCSB. FROM *The Thirteenth Man: A Reagan Cabinet Memoir* by Terrel H. Bell; copyright 1988 by Terrel H. Bell; published by the Free Press, a division of Simon and Schuster Adult Publishing Group. FROM David S. Webster and Tad Skinner, "Rating PhD Programs: What the NRC Report Says . . . And Doesn't Say," *Change* 28, no. 3 (May–June 1996): 37–40.

The Regents of the University of California have given permission to use extended quotations from minutes of their meetings, particularly those of committees, subcommittees, executive and special sessions. The Regents and the Regional Oral History Office, the Bancroft Library, University of California, Berkeley, have also given me permission to use extended quotations. FROM the oral histories of David Pierpont Gardner (1997); Jack W. Peltason (2001); and Steven A. Arditti, Glenn H. Seaborg, Neil Smelser, Martin Trow, Steven A. Merksamer, and George Deukmejian in the three-volume "UC Office of the President and Its Constituencies, 1983–1995" (2002).

Siri J. Voskuil and Williams Pickens have generously allowed extended use of their unpublished works.

INDEX

415

Morgan, Becky, 315
Morgan, Elmo, 22
Mormon Church (LDS): and alcohol at
Carnegie board visit, 298; genealogical
records, 93; and polygamous marriages,
93; University of Utah relations with,
85–86, 93, 99, 332; wedding with Libby,
28. *See also* Brigham Young University
(BYU); Mormons
Mormons: discrimination toward, 16, 75,
145–46, 150–51, 153–54, 283–84; Gardner families, 9–10, 16, 27, 29; Libby's
mother, 27; and minorities, 153–54; UC
presidency and, 145–46, 150–51, 153–
54; University of Utah founded by, 75;
Utah legislature, 78, 83, 317; Utah
population, 77; and women, 145, 154
Mormon Trail, 75
Munitz, Barry, 360, 370
music, 14–15, 309–10, 375, 376

Nader, Laura, 273–74, 350
Nader, Ralph, 269, 272–74, 350
Nahavandi, Houshang, 295–96
Nakayama, Nancy, 171, 336, 338, 346
Nash, Norris, 21, 397
National Assessment of Educational
Progress, 107
National Association of State Universities
and Land-Grant Colleges, 319
National Collegiate Athletic Association,
109, 319
National Commission on Excellence in Edu-
cation: commissioners, 112–14, 135–36,
358; Gardner as chairman, 5, 103, 108–
40, 146, 147, 227. See also *A Nation at
Risk*
National Commission on Student Financial
Assistance, 109
National Education Association (NEA), 133,
140
national government. *See* U.S. government
National Guard, 55
National Institute of Education, 110–11, 134
National Research Council (NRC), 208, 332,
359–60, 385–86
National Science Foundation, 107
A Nation at Risk (National Commission on
Excellence in Education, 1983), 118–41,
147, 152, 358; Bell and, 118–41, 147,
402n11; George H. W. Bush and, 319;

initiatives following, 133, 134–35, 136,
139, 403n25; Kohl and, 227, 309; media
and, 115, 122, 126–30, 133–34, 135;
Reagan and, 5, 111–16, 122–41, 146,
147
"A Nation Still at Risk" (Bennett), 140
Nelson, Jerry, 212–13
New Deal, 2
newspapers, 318–19; campus, 50, 53, 58, 79,
151–52; Gardner's boyhood job, 13; on
Gardner's UC appointment as president,
151–52, 153; on Gardner's UC retirement from presidency, 341, 343, 349–
52, 411–12n13; and Korea, 307; *Los
Angeles Times*, 318, 341; National Commission on Excellence in Education/*A
Nation at Risk* (1983) report, 129–30,
135; *New York Times*, 127, 129, 135, 318;
Riverside Press, 318; *Sacramento Bee*, 152,
164, 318, 349, 352; Salt Lake, 119, 401n4;
San Diego Union, 318, 344 San Francisco,
318, 349–52, 410n5, 411–12n13; *San Jose
Mercury News*, 214, 318; *Santa Barbara
News-Press*, 42, 43, 45, 61, 318; and TMT
(10-meter telescope), 214; on UC's pres-
idential search committee, 147; *Wall
Street Journal*, 307, 319; *Washington Post*,
130, 318
Newsweek, 133–34, 149
New York Times, 127, 129, 135, 318
Neylan, John Francis, 26–27
Niarakis, Ursula C., 215
Nimitz, Admiral Chester, 13
Nixon, Richard, 105, 217
Nobel Prizes, UC faculty, 356
No Child Left Behind (2001 legislation), 114
nuclear weapons, 13, 124, 211, 262–68, 265,
306

Oaks, Dallin, 79, 83
Odum, Steve, 79
oil imbroglio (1973), 107
Oppenheimer, Robert, 211, 263
Orbach, Ray, 240
Osro, Hyrum, and Maryetta Snow, 9
Oswald, John, 360
Owens, Richard, 21

Pace, Cindy, 336
Pacific Rim, 208, 226, 302–3; faculty exchanges, 355; student exchanges, 225,